forensic psychology

JOANNA POZZULO, Carleton University

CRAIG BENNELL, Carleton University

ADELLE FORTH, Carleton University

PEARSON

Prentice
Hall

Toronto

Library and Archives Canada Cataloguing in Publication

Pozzulo, Joanna, 1968–
    Forensic psychology / Joanna Pozzulo, Craig Bennell, Adelle Forth.

Includes bibliographical references and index.
ISBN 0-13-121582-5

1. Forensic psychology—Textbooks. I. Bennell, Craig II. Forth, Adelle Elizabeth, 1961– III. Title.

RA1148.P69 2006   614'.15   C2004-906818-0

ISBN 0-13-121582-5

Vice-President, Editorial Director: Michael J. Young
Acquisitions Editor: Ky Pruesse
Executive Marketing Manager: Judith Allen
Supervising Developmental Editor: Suzanne Schaan
Production Editor: Charlotte Morrison-Reed
Copy Editor: Valerie Adams
Proofreader: Dawn Hunter
Production Manager: Wendy Moran
Page Layout: Carolyn E. Sebestyen
Photo and Permissions Research: Terri Rothman
Art Director: Mary Opper
Cover Design: Michelle Bellemare
Interior Design: Gillian Tsintziras
Cover Image: Getty Images

Statistics Canada information is used with the permission of the Minister of Industry, as Minister responsible for Statistics Canada. Information on the availability of the wide range of data from Statistics Canada can be obtained from Statistics Canada's Regional Offices, its World Wide Web site at http://www.statcan.ca, and its toll-free access number 1-800-263-1136.

    5   10 09 08 07 06

Printed and bound in the United States of America.

CONTENTS

2   Research Methods and Clinical Research Assessment Techniques   32

12 Violent Offenders: Classification and Treatment   352

Preface

We remember the day that the three of us gathered in Adelle's office to lament our teaching assignment: an introductory course in forensic psychology. Not that we weren't interested in teaching the course, but we worried about not having an undergraduate Canadian textbook on the subject. Given the need to discuss the law when discussing forensic psychology, a text based on American or British law would not do. We decided to write a Canadian forensic psychology textbook that was directed at Canadian undergraduates, a comprehensive book with as much Canadian content as possible.

This is an exciting time in the field of forensic psychology, with many new developments by theorists and researchers. For example, new insights into the biological underpinnings of antisocial behaviour, innovative methods of interviewing child witnesses, and novel methods of profiling serial offenders have been developed. *Forensic Psychology* is designed primarily for use in undergraduate courses, although graduate students and practitioners may find the comprehensive and up-to-date summary of key areas a useful resource.

We have taken a broad-based perspective that incorporates both experimental and clinical topics. The text covers topics that might otherwise be discussed in traditional social and cognitive psychology courses—including eyewitness testimony, jury decision-making, and police procedures—as well as topics that are clinical in nature and might otherwise be discussed in traditional personality or abnormal psychology courses—such as the meaning of being unfit to stand trial, mentally disordered offenders, and psychopathy. We wanted to present the important ideas, issues, and research in a way that students will understand and enjoy, and in some cases find useful in their professional careers. We hope that the academic community will find this textbook a valuable teaching tool that provides a comprehensive and current coverage of forensic psychology.

DISTINGUISHING FEATURES

The pedagogical aids are designed to promote student learning and assist instructors in presenting key material. Key features include the following:

- **Learning Objectives and End-of-Chapter Summaries.** Each chapter starts with a list of learning objectives to guide students' learning of the material and closes with a summary linked to the learning objectives.

- **Vignettes.** Chapter-opening vignettes provide students with a context for the key concepts they will encounter in each chapter. These engaging vignettes present real-world scenarios in which students, or people they know, could potentially find themselves.

- **Boxes.** Boxed features within the chapters provide interesting asides to the main text. Some detail current Canadian cases and legal rulings, while others highlight "hot" topics in the news that have not yet been the subject of much psychological research. These boxes will develop students' consciousness of current issues and perhaps spark some research ideas.

- **Profiles of Canadian Researchers.** To expose students to the varied and excellent research in forensic psychology being conducted by Canadians, each chapter includes a profile of a key Canadian researcher whose work is relevant to the chapter topic. These profiles highlight educational background, current position, and research interests, along with a little about the researcher's personal life, so students realize they are people too.

- **Research Methodology.** Chapter 2 is dedicated to common research constructs and methodology. This chapter is not meant as a substitute for students who have not studied research design; rather, it is intended to remind them of basic concepts that will help them understand the research studies described throughout the textbook. Research methodology specific to forensic topics is also described in the relevant chapters, with the goal of helping students understand how studies in forensic psychology are conducted.

- **Research Studies.** Data reported in original studies is cited throughout the textbook, often in graph or table form for easy interpretation. Diagrams of psychological models and flowcharts demonstrate key processes that occur through the criminal justice system.

- **Theoretical Perspectives.** Chapter 1 describes some general theories of criminal behaviour. More focused theories that provide accounts for specific topic areas are discussed in each of the chapters. The discussion of the various theories emphasizes a multidisciplinary approach, showing the interplay between cognitive, biological, and social factors in understanding the different forensic psychology areas.

- **Law.** This textbook provides the student with current Canadian law relevant to the psychological issues discussed. At times, Canadian law is contrasted with American and/or British law; however, it is important to remember that the emphasis is on Canadian case law, statutes, regulations, and so on. We do not provide full coverage of law that is not Canadian, so students who are interested in the laws of other countries should refer to other resources.

- **Discussion Questions.** Several discussion questions are offered at the end of each chapter. Instructors can assign these questions for group discussion, or students can use the questions to examine their comprehension and retention of the chapter material. We hope these questions will inspire critical thought in students.

- **Key Terms and Glossary.** Throughout the chapters, key words with which students in forensic psychology should be familiar appear in bold type. These key words and their definitions are provided in a glossary at the end of the text for easy reference.

SUPPLEMENTS

The following supplements specific to this text can be downloaded by instructors from a password-protected location on Pearson Education Canada's online catalogue (vig.pearsoned.ca). Contact your local sales representative for further information.

- **Instructor's Manual.** The instructor's manual is a comprehensive resource that provides chapter outlines, class activities, and summaries of select cases cited. We hope our colleagues will use the textbook and instructor's manual as a foundation that they can build on in the classroom lecture.
- **Test Item File.** This test bank, offered in Microsoft Word format, contains multiple choice and short answer questions. Each question is classified according to difficulty level and is keyed to the appropriate page number in the textbook.
- **PowerPoint Presentations.** PowerPoint slides highlight the key concepts in each chapter of the text.

Students can visit Pearson Education Canada's Criminology Resource Site at www.pearsoned.ca/criminology for information about the study of criminology and careers in criminology, supplementary information, and links to other resources.

ACKNOWLEDGMENTS

This book would never have come to fruition had we not been mentored by outstanding forensic researchers. Joanna Pozzulo is indebted to Rod Lindsay at Queen's University for his unfailing support, his rich insights, and his commitment to academic excellence that she aspires to achieve. Craig Bennell is grateful to David Canter at the University of Liverpool for providing a stimulating intellectual environment in which to study and for teaching him how to think critically. Adelle Forth wishes to express her admiration, respect, and gratitude to Robert Hare at the University of British Columbia, who nurtured her interest in the area of psychopathy and who has provided consistent support and guidance. These researchers continue to be a source of inspiration to us.

We would like to acknowledge that the forensic program at Carleton University, of which we are part, would not exist without Don Andrews. He has been instrumental in guiding the forensic field both locally and internationally. Also, our colleagues Robert Hoge and Ralph Serin have contributed to our program and our thinking of forensic issues.

We are thankful to the exceptional researchers we profiled in this textbook for giving us their time and insight into their life. Specifically, Don Andrews, Nick Bala, Bob Hare, Rod Lindsay, Robert Loo, Jim Ogloff, Christopher Patrick, Julian Roberts, Ron Roesch, Kim Rossmo, Regina Schuller, Richard Tremblay, and Christopher Webster. All have made signficant contributions to the field of forensic psychology.

We would like to thank the reviewers who provided us with exceptional feedback that allowed us to make the textbook stronger. Reviewers of the manuscript and/or the original project proposal include the following:

David Baxter, University of Ottawa
J. Thomas Dalby, University of Calgary
Roy Frenzel, University of Alberta

Connie Korpan, Grande Prairie Regional College
Kristine A. Peace, Dalhousie University
Stephen Porter, Dalhousie University
Vern Quinsey, Queen's University
Joti Samra, University of British Columbia
Paul Valliant, Laurentian University
Margo Watt, St. Francis Xavier University
J. Stephen Wormith, University of Saskatchewan
A. Daniel Yarmey, University of Guelph

We have tried to incorporate as many of the suggestions as possible, but of course we were restricted in terms of page length. In the end, we feel the textbook provides excellent breadth and good depth.

We thank our many undergraduate and graduate students who over the years challenged our thinking and who influenced the ideas expressed in this book. A number of students have provided countless hours of editorial support: Carolyn Barnes, Heather Clark, Shevaun Corey, Julie Dempsey, Jillian Flight, Alberta Girardi, Natalie Jones, Bonny-Jean Klemm and Erin Robertson. Their help with tracking down references and legal cases was greatly appreciated, and their insights and suggestions were invaluable.

We would like to thank the family at Pearson Education Canada. Ky Pruesse (Acquisitions Editor), Jessica Mosher (Executive Acquisitions Editor), and Suzanne Schaan (Developmental Editor) deserve special mention, for this book would not exist without their enthusiasm, expertise, and dedication. Valerie Adams (Copy Editor), Charlotte Morrison-Reed (Production Editor), and Terri Rothman (Photo Researcher) also played an important role in making this book become a reality.

Finally, Joanna Pozzulo would like to thank her family for their unending love and support through the hardest of times. She also would like to thank Craig and Adelle for being great collaborators and dear friends. Craig Bennell would like to thank his wife Cindy for her love, patience, and support during the long hours of writing, and his son Noah for making him always remember what is most important. Adelle Forth would like to thank her partner, colleague, and friend, John Logan, for his insights, suggestions, and feedback that improved the book, as well as his understanding and support while preparing the book.

CHAPTER 1

An Introduction to Forensic Psychology

LEARNING OBJECTIVES

■ Provide a narrow and broad definition of forensic psychology.

■ Describe the differences between clinical and experimental forensic psychology.

■ List the three ways in which psychology and the law can interact.

■ Describe three major psychological theories of crime.

■ List the criteria used in Canada to decide when expert testimony is admissible.

Jennifer Harris is an undergraduate university student who wants to become a forensic psychologist. She has just finished watching her favourite movie, The Silence of the Lambs. *In fact, Jennifer always seems to be watching movies like this. If she's not watching movies, Jennifer's watching television shows like CSI or reading the latest true crime book. Fortunately, Jennifer's neighbour works as a probation officer and she has come into regular contact with forensic psychologists. This neighbour has repeatedly told Jennifer that forensic psychology isn't what you see in the movies. Jennifer finally decides to find out for herself what forensic psychology is all about and enrols in a course, much like the one you are currently taking. Throughout the course, Jennifer learns more about the field of forensic psychology. It turns out that her neighbour was correct, but what Jennifer learns in the course makes her even more confident that she has chosen the right career path.*

Although you may not appreciate it yet, **forensic psychology** is all around us. Every time you turn on the television or pick up the paper, there are news stories that relate directly to the field of forensic psychology. Hollywood has also gotten in on the act. More and more often, blockbuster movies focus on issues that are also related directly to the field of forensic psychology—whether it is profiling serial killers, selecting jury members, or determining someone's sanity. Unfortunately, the way in which the popular media portrays forensic psychology is usually inaccurate. Although forensic psychologists often carry out the sorts of tasks you see depicted in the movies, the way in which they carry them out is very different from (and certainly less glamorous than) the typical Hollywood image. One of our primary goals throughout this book is to provide you with a more accurate picture of what forensic psychology is and to encourage you to think more critically about the things you see and hear in the media.

WHAT IS FORENSIC PSYCHOLOGY?

So, if Hollywood hasn't gotten it right, what exactly is forensic psychology? On the surface, this seems like a relatively simple question to answer, and it is undoubtedly an important question to ask. When being introduced to a new field of psychology, as you are now, one of the first things you probably ask yourself is, "What am I going to be studying?" Although providing a clear and comprehensive definition of the discipline is obviously a logical way to begin a textbook on forensic psychology, this task is far more difficult than it seems, because there is no generally accepted definition of the field (Brigham, 1999). Indeed, experts in this area don't even agree on what the field should be called, let alone how the field should be defined (Ogloff, 2002). For example, you will often see forensic psychology being referred to as legal psychology or criminological psychology.

Much of the ongoing debate about how forensic psychology should be defined centres on whether the definition should be narrow or broad (Brigham, 1999). A narrow definition of forensic psychology would focus on certain aspects of the field while ignoring other, potentially important, aspects. For example, a narrow definition of forensic psychology might focus on applied aspects while ignoring the experimental research many psychologists (who refer to themselves as forensic psychologists) conduct. This appears to be how many leading psychologists prefer to define the discipline (e.g., Otto & Heilbrun, 2002). Indeed, even the major professional associations in this area, such as the American Board of Forensic Psychology (ABFP) and the American Psychology-Law Society (AP-LS), define the field in a narrow fashion. Recently, these associations have defined forensic psychology as "the professional practice by psychologists within the areas of *clinical psychology, counseling psychology, neuropsychology, and school psychology,* when they are *engaged regularly as experts* and represent themselves as such, in an activity *primarily intended to provide professional psychological expertise to the judicial system*" (emphasis added; ABFP & AP-LS, 1995, p. 6).

Thus, according to the ABFP and AP-LS definition, any psychologist who provides expertise to the judicial system but happens to *work in an area of psychology outside the scope of their definition,* such as social psychology, would not technically be doing work in the area of forensic psychology. In addition, any psychologist who spends all of his or her time conducting what appears to be forensic-related research—for example, studying whether brain damage leads to criminal behaviour—in one of the prescribed areas of psychology (in this case, neuropsychology), but *does not provide professional expertise on a regular basis to the judicial system*, would not be considered a forensic psychologist. For reasons such as these, many psychologists have problems with using narrow definitions to define the field of forensic psychology.

In contrast to narrow definitions, broad definitions of forensic psychology are not so restrictive. One of the most commonly cited examples of a broad definition of forensic psychology is the one proposed by Bartol and Bartol (1987). They define the discipline as "(a) the research endeavour that examines aspects of human behaviour directly related to the legal process ... and (b) the professional practice of psychology within, or in consultation with, a legal system that embraces both civil and criminal law" (p. 3). Thus, unlike the narrow definition of forensic psychology provided above, which focuses solely on the *application* of psychology to the legal system, this definition does not restrict forensic psychology to applied issues. It also focuses on the *research* that is required to inform applied practice in the field of forensic psychology.

Throughout this textbook, we adopt a broad definition of forensic psychology. Although we will often focus on the application of psychological knowledge to various aspects of the Canadian legal system, our primary goal is to demonstrate that this application of knowledge must always be based on a solid grounding of psychological research. In line with a broad definition of forensic psychology, this research frequently originates in areas of psychology that are often not obviously connected with the forensic area, such as social, cognitive, and developmental psychology. The fact that forensic psychology is such an eclectic field is just one of the reasons why it is such an exciting area of study.

THE ROLES OF A FORENSIC PSYCHOLOGIST

What is consistent across the various definitions of forensic psychology is that individuals who call themselves forensic psychologists are always interested in issues that arise at the intersection between psychology and the law. What typically differs across the definitions is the particular focus the forensic psychologist takes. For example, by looking at the definitions provided above, it is clear that forensic psychologists can take on the role of clinician or researcher. In reality, however, these roles are not mutually exclusive and one individual can take on more than one role. Indeed, some of the best-known forensic psychologists, many of whom will be profiled in this book, are both clinicians *and* researchers, while others are clinicians, researchers, *and* legal scholars. Since we will continually touch upon these various roles throughout the upcoming chapters, we will briefly clarify what each role entails.

The Forensic Psychologist as Clinician

Clinical forensic psychologists are broadly concerned with mental health issues as they pertain to the legal system (Otto & Heilbrun, 2002). This can include both research and practice in a wide variety of settings, such as schools, prisons, hospitals, and so forth. For example, clinical forensic psychologists are often concerned with the assessment and treatment of persons with mental disorders within the context of the law. On the research side, a frequent task for the clinical forensic psychologist might involve the validation of an assessment tool that has been developed to predict the risk of an offender being violent (e.g., Kropp & Hart, 2000). On the practical side, a frequent task might involve the assessment of an offender to assist the parole board in making an accurate determination of whether that offender is likely to pose a risk to the community. Other issues that clinical forensic psychologists are interested in may include, but are certainly not limited to, the following:

- Divorce and child custody mediation
- Determinations of criminal responsibility (insanity) and competency to stand trial
- Providing expert testimony on questions of a psychological nature
- Personnel selection (e.g., for law enforcement agencies)
- Conducting critical incident stress debriefings
- Designing and conducting treatment programs for offenders
- Preparing criminal profiles of serial offenders

As in the United States, a clinical forensic psychologist in Canada must be a licensed clinical psychologist who has specialized in the forensic area. The educational requirements to obtain a licence vary across provinces and territories, but some form of graduate-level training is always required. In Alberta, Saskatchewan, Quebec, Newfoundland and Labrador, New Brunswick, and Nova Scotia, the requirement is a master's degree in psychology, while in British Columbia, Manitoba, Ontario, and Prince Edward Island, a doctoral degree in psychology is required. The forensic specialization typically takes the form of an intense period of supervised practice after the completion of the required degree, in an applied forensic setting of some kind under the watchful eye of an experienced clinical supervisor. The last step of the licensing process is a comprehensive exam, which often involves an oral component (a score of at least 70% is typically required).

One of the most common questions that undergraduate students ask is, "What is the difference between forensic psychology and **forensic psychiatry**?" In fact, many people, including the media, confuse these two fields. To some extent, clinical forensic psychology and forensic psychiatry are more similar than they are different and, as a result, it is often difficult to clearly separate them. For example, both clinical forensic psychologists and forensic psychiatrists are trained to assess and treat individuals experiencing mental health problems who come into contact with the law, and you will see psychologists and psychiatrists involved in every component of the criminal justice system. In addition, clinical forensic psychologists and forensic psychiatrists often engage in similar sorts of research (e.g., developing causal models of violent behaviour), but, in general, psychologists tend to be involved in research more often than psychiatrists.

However, there are also important differences between the two fields. Probably the most obvious difference is that psychiatrists, including forensic psychiatrists, are medical doctors. Therefore, forensic psychiatrists undergo training that is quite different from the training clinical forensic psychologists receive, which leads to several other distinctions between the fields. For example, clinical forensic psychologists and forensic psychiatrists tend to view mental illness differently (Grisso, 1993). Clinical forensic psychologists rely on a psychological model of mental illness, in which mental illness is viewed as a product of an individual's physiology, personality, and environment. In contrast, the forensic psychiatrist's medical model views mental illness in the same way that most physical diseases are viewed. The fact that these two disciplines view mental health differently also leads to differences in the way mental illness is treated. For example, as medical doctors, forensic psychiatrists often treat mental illness in the same way physical disease is treated—by prescribing the appropriate medication. For forensic psychologists, conversely, medication is typically viewed as but one aspect of an appropriate treatment program, if it is used at all (Litman, 2004). See Box 1.1, which looks at some other important forensic-related disciplines that are often confused with the field of forensic psychology.

BOX 1.1 DIFFERENCES AMONG OTHER FORENSIC DISCIPLINES

Nowadays, people are being bombarded by media portrayals of various forensic disciplines, beyond just forensic psychology and forensic psychiatry. Although this does much to promote the respective specialities, it can also be the source of a lot of confusion. Listed below are brief descriptions of just a few forensic speciality areas. Each of these disciplines is sometimes confused with forensic psychology.

■ *Forensic anthropology*. Forensic anthropologists examine the remains of deceased victims to determine key facts about them such as their gender, age, appearance, and so forth.

■ *Forensic linguistics*. Forensic linguists examine the spoken and written word in an attempt to assist criminal investigators. For example, they can assess the language in suicide notes to determine whether the notes are fake or genuine.

■ *Forensic chemistry*. Forensic chemists study the chemical aspects of crime scenes, which can include an analysis of paint particles, dyes, fibres, and other materials.

■ *Forensic ondontology*. Forensic ondontologists study the dental aspects of criminal activity, which can include identifying deceased victims through dental records and determining whether bite marks were made by an adult or child.

■ *Forensic pathology*. Forensic pathologists examine the remains of dead bodies in an attempt to determine the time and cause of death through physical autopsy.

■ *Forensic entomology*. Forensic entomologists are concerned with how insects can assist with criminal investigations. For example, they can help determine when someone died based on the rate of body decay by way of insects.

Source: Decaire, 2004.

The Forensic Psychologist as Researcher

A second role for the forensic psychologist is that of experimenter, or researcher. As we have indicated above, although this role does not necessarily have to be separate from the clinical role, it often is. As with clinical forensic psychologists, **experimental forensic psychologists** are concerned with mental health issues as they pertain to the legal system, and they can be found in a variety of criminal justice settings. However, researchers in the forensic area are usually concerned with much more than just mental health issues. Indeed, they can be interested in any research issue that relates to the law or legal system. The list of research issues that are of interest to this type of forensic psychologist is far too long to present here, but they include the following:

- Examining the effectiveness of risk assessment strategies
- Determining what factors influence jury decision making
- Developing and testing better ways to conduct eyewitness lineups
- Evaluating offender and victim treatment programs
- Studying the impact of questioning style on memory recall
- Developing and testing strategies for assessing mental illness
- Examining the effect of stress management interventions on police officers

Not only do clinical forensic psychologists differ from experimental forensic psychologists in terms of what they do, but they also differ in terms of their training. The forensic psychologist who is interested primarily in research will have undergone graduate training in one of many different types of experimental graduate programs (and no internship is required). Only some of these graduate programs will be devoted solely to the study of forensic psychology. Many will be programs in social psychology, cognitive psychology, or developmental psychology, although the program will usually have a faculty member associated with it who is conducting research in a forensic area. Regardless of the type of graduate program chosen, the individual's graduate research will be focused primarily on a topic related to forensic psychology. For example, a student might enrol in a developmental graduate program to conduct research on the malleability of child eyewitness memory. As can be seen in the short list of topics provided above, research in forensic psychology is eclectic and requires expertise in areas such as memory processing, decision making, organizational issues, and so on. This is one of the reasons why training for experimental forensic psychology is more varied than the training for clinical forensic psychology.

The Forensic Psychologist as Legal Scholar

A third role for the forensic psychologist, which is far less common than the previous two but no less important, is that of legal scholar. Because this role is less common, we will not deal with it as much throughout this textbook, but it is important to discuss it briefly, especially considering the recent focus on this role in Canada. Much of this focus resulted from the formation of two initiatives at Simon Fraser University (SFU) in Burnaby, B.C. The first of these was SFU's Psychology and Law Program, originally established in 1991. More recently, this program has partnered with the University of British Columbia to allow students to obtain both their Ph.D. in psychology as well as their L.L.B. in law. This program is now producing a new breed of forensic psychologists in North America who are much more informed about the legal process and the legal system than was the case previously. The second initiative was the formation, in 1992, of the Mental Health, Law, and Policy Institute (MHLPI) at SFU. The purpose of the MHLPI is to "promote interdisciplinary collaboration in research and training in areas related to mental health law and policy" (Mental Health, Law, and Policy Institute, 2004).

According to Brigham (1999), forensic psychologists in their role as legal scholars, "would most likely engage in scholarly analyses of mental health law and psychologically oriented legal movements," whereas their applied work "would most likely center around policy analyses and legislative consultation" (p. 281). Other matters this group might be involved in can be seen in lists of current activities provided by institutes like the MHLPI. For example, faculty members in a similar institute in the United States are currently involved in the following projects:

- Improving the assessment of competence to stand trial and to plead guilty
- Exploring the prevalence of child sexual abuse among African-American adults
- Developing practical guidelines for criminal justice programs treating persons with a dual diagnosis of mental illness and substance abuse disorders
- Evaluating the effectiveness of managed care approaches in Florida for mental health services
- Evaluating the role of juvenile detoxification programs in substance abuse and juvenile justice systems
- Examining how the informed consent process can be improved for persons with mental illness through enhancements to consent forms and procedures
- Evaluating the feasibility of using mail survey methods to obtain and monitor outcomes for vulnerable populations (Louis de la Parte Florida Mental Health Institute, 2002)

THE RELATIONSHIP BETWEEN PSYCHOLOGY AND LAW

Not only is the field of forensic psychology a challenging field to be in because of the diversity of roles that a forensic psychologist can play, but it is also challenging because forensic psychology can be approached from many different angles. One of the most interesting ways of thinking about these various angles has been proposed by Craig Haney, a professor of psychology at the University of California, Santa Cruz. Haney (1980) suggests there are three primary ways in which psychology and the law can relate to each other. He calls these relationships **psychology** *and* the law, **psychology** *in* the law, and **psychology** *of* the law. Throughout this textbook, we will focus on the first two relationships, psychology and the law and psychology in the law. Clinical and experimental forensic psychologists are typically involved in these areas much more often than in the third. Psychology of the law is largely the domain of the legal scholar role and, therefore, we will only touch on it very briefly.

Psychology and the Law

In this relationship, "psychology is viewed as a separate discipline [to the law] examining and analysing various components of the law [and the legal system] from a psychological perspective" (Bartol & Bartol, 1994, p. 2). Research that falls under the category of psychology and the law may include, but is not limited to, the examination of eyewitness accuracy, the determination of factors in police interrogations that might cause people to falsely confess, the exploration of how judges make sentencing decisions, and the validation of tools for predicting risk of violence. When working within the area of psychology and the law, forensic psychologists attempt to answer these sorts of questions and communicate their findings to the legal community. Much of forensic psychology deals with this particular relationship. Therefore, research issues that fall under the general heading of "psychology and the law" will be thoroughly discussed throughout this textbook.

Psychology in the Law

Once a body of psychological knowledge exists in any of the above-mentioned areas of study, that knowledge can then be used in the legal system by psychologists, lawyers, judges, and others. As the label indicates, psychology *in* the law involves the use of psychological knowledge in the legal system (Haney, 1980). As with psychology and the law, psychology in the law can take many different forms. It might consist of a legal professional using his or her knowledge of psychology in the courtroom. For example, lawyers may base their questioning strategy on their knowledge of various psychological principles. Alternatively, psychology in the law might consist of a psychologist being brought into court to provide expert testimony concerning some psychological issue of relevance to a particular case. For example, the psychologist might testify that, based on his or her understanding of the psychological research, the eyewitness on the stand may have incorrectly identified the defendant from a police lineup. Many of the research applications that we focus on in this textbook fit nicely with the label "psychology in the law."

Psychology of the Law

Psychology of the law involves the use of psychology to study the law itself (Haney, 1980), and it addresses questions such as these:

- What role should the police play in domestic disputes?

■ Does the law reduce the amount of crime in our society?

■ Why is it important to allow for discretionary decision making in the Canadian criminal justice system?

Although often not considered a core topic in forensic psychology, there does appear to be a growing interest in the area of psychology of the law. The challenge in this case is that, to address the sorts of questions posed above, a set of skills from multiple disciplines (e.g., criminology, sociology, law) is often important and sometimes crucial. The new focus in North America and elsewhere on the role of forensic psychologist as legal scholar will no doubt do much to assist in this endeavour, and we are confident that in the future more research in the area of forensic psychology will focus on issues surrounding psychology of the law.

THE HISTORY OF FORENSIC PSYCHOLOGY

Now that we have defined the field of forensic psychology and discussed the various roles that forensic psychologists can play, we will turn to a discussion of where the field came from and where it is currently heading. Forensic psychology, when it is broadly defined, has a relatively short history, roughly dating back to the late nineteenth century. In the early days, forensic psychology was actually not referred to as forensic psychology and most of the psychologists conducting research in the area did not identify themselves as forensic psychologists. However, their research formed the building blocks of an emerging field of psychology that continues to be strong today. See Figure 1.1 on page 10 for a timeline of some significant dates in the history of forensic psychology.

Early Research: Eyewitness Testimony and Suggestibility

In the late nineteenth century, research in the area of forensic psychology was taking place in both North America and Europe, though as indicated above, it wasn't being referred to as forensic psychology at the time. Some of the first experiments were those of James McKeen Cattell (who is perhaps better known for his research in the area of intelligence testing) at Columbia University in New York. Cattell, a previous student of Wilhelm Wundt, who developed the first psychology laboratory in Leipzig, Germany, was one of the major powerhouses of psychology in North America. After developing an expertise in the use of quantitative methods to study human cognitive processes while in Leipzig, Cattell conducted some of the first North American experiments looking at what would later be called the psychology of eyewitness testimony (e.g., Cattell, 1895). Cattell would ask people to recall things they had witnessed in their everyday life (e.g., "In which direction do apple seeds point?"), and he found that their answers were often inaccurate.

FIGURE 1.1

SOME IMPORTANT EUROPEAN AND NORTH AMERICAN DEVELOPMENTS IN THE HISTORY OF FORENSIC PSYCHOLOGY

1843	Daniel M'Naughten is found not guilty by reason of insanity in the assassination attempt on the British prime minister. Leads to the development of the "M'Naughten rule" for determining insanity.
1893	James McKeen Cattell of Columbia University conducts the first experiment in North America on the psychology of testimony.
1906	Sigmund Freud gives a speech to a group of Austrian judges in which he suggests that psychology can be applied to the field of law.
1908	Hugo Munsterberg's *On the Witness Stand* is published. A year later, John H. Wigmore's famous critique of Munsterberg's work appears.
1909–1913	In a series of classic articles, Guy Whipple introduces North American psychologists to the classic European experiments on eyewitness testimony.
1911	One of the earliest examples of a forensic psychologist, Julian Varendonck, testifies in a criminal trial. His testimony deals with the reliability of child witnesses.
1917	William Marston develops the first modern polygraph. In the same year, Louis Terman pioneers the use of psychological testing for personnel selection in law enforcement.
1921	A North American psychologist testifies in court as an expert witness for the first time (*State v. Driver, 1921*). However, the testimony is rejected.
1954	A brief written by social psychologists is cited in a footnote of the famous *Brown v. Board of Education* decision outlawing school segregation.
1964	Hans J. Eysenck publishes *Crime and Personality*, representing the first testable theory of criminal behaviour proposed by a psychologist.
1965	Canadian psychologist Robert Hare begins studying psychopathy.
1968–1969	The American Psychology-Law Society (AP-LS) is founded.
1976	"Psychology and the Law" is reviewed by June Louin Tapp in the *Annual Review of Psychology*.
1977	*Law and Human Behavior* begins publication as the AP-LS journal.
1980-1981	The American Psychological Association's (APA) Division 41, Psychology and Law, is established. Four years later, AP-LS merges with Division 41.
1985	The Criminal Justice Section of the Canadian Psychological Association (CPA) is founded.
2001	APA recognizes forensic psychology as a speciality discipline.

Sources: Brigham, 1999; Bartol and Bartol, 2004.

At around the same time, a number of other psychologists began studying eyewitness testimony and suggestibility (see Ceci & Bruck, 1993, for a review). For example, the famous French psychologist Alfred Binet conducted numerous studies in which he showed that the testimony provided by children was highly susceptible to suggestive questioning techniques. In a study discussed by Ceci and Bruck (1993), Binet (1900), presented children with a series of objects for a short period of time (e.g., a button glued to poster board). After viewing an object, some of the children were told to write down everything that they saw while others were asked questions. Some of these questions were direct questions (e.g., "How was the button attached to the board?"), others were mildly leading questions (e.g., "Wasn't the button attached by a thread?"), and still others were highly misleading questions (e.g., "What was the colour of the thread that attached the button to the board?"). As found in numerous studies since this experiment, Binet demonstrated that asking children to report everything they saw (i.e., free recall) resulted in the most accurate answers and that highly misleading questions resulted in the least accurate answers.

Shortly after Binet's study, a German psychologist named William Stern also began conducting studies examining the suggestibility of witnesses (Ceci & Bruck, 1993). The "reality experiment" that is now commonly used by eyewitness researchers to study eyewitness recall and recognition can, in fact, be attributed to Stern. Using this research paradigm, participants are exposed to staged events and are then asked to recall information about the event. In one of Stern's experiments, participants were exposed to a scenario that involved two students arguing in a classroom setting until one of the students drew a revolver (Stern, 1910). As was the case with Binet, Stern also found that eyewitness testimony can often be incorrect, and he was perhaps the first researcher to demonstrate that a person's level of emotional arousal can have an impact on the accuracy of that person's testimony.

Because much of the original research on the psychology of eyewitness testimony and suggestibility was not written in English, North American psychologists who were becoming interested in forensic psychology did not have easy access to these studies (Ceci & Bruck, 1993). This all changed when a psychologist, Guy Whipple, published a series of influential articles in the journal *Psychological Bulletin* (Whipple, 1909, 1911, 1912, 1913). These articles summarized the studies being done by European researchers in the area of child suggestibility and they are still often cited by researchers in the area today.

Early Court Cases in Europe

Around the time this research was being conducted, psychologists in Europe also started to appear as expert witnesses in court. Unsurprisingly, much of the testimony that they were providing dealt with issues surrounding the accuracy of eyewitness testimony. For example, in 1896, Albert von Schrenck-Notzing was probably the first expert witness to provide testimony in court on the effect of pretrial publicity on memory. The case took place in Munich, Germany, and involved a series of three sexual murders. The court case attracted a great deal of attention from the press of the time, and Schrenck-Notzing testified that this extensive pretrial press coverage could influence the testimony of witnesses by causing what he called "retroactive memory falsification" (Bartol & Bartol, 1987). This referred to a process whereby witnesses confuse actual memories of events with the events described by the media. Schrenck-Notzing supported his expert testimony with laboratory research, and this research is very much in line with what we know about the effects of pretrial publicity from more recent studies (e.g., Ogloff & Vidmar, 1994).

Following this case, Julian Varendonck, a Belgian psychologist, was called on to be an expert witness in a 1911 case involving the murder of a young girl, Cecile. Ceci and Bruck (1993, p. 406) describe the case:

> Two of Cecile's friends who had played with her on the day of her murder were awakened that night by Cecile's mother to ask of her whereabouts. One of the children replied that she did not know. Later that night, she led the police to the spot where the children had played, not far from where Cecile's body was found. In the next month, the two children were repeatedly interviewed by authorities who asked many suggestive questions. The children quickly changed their original testimony of not knowing about Cecile's actions on the day of her murder. They provided details of the appearance of the murderer as well as his name. Because of an anonymous letter, the police arrested the father of one of the playmates for the murder of Cecile. On the basis of the details of the case, Varendonck was convinced of the defendant's innocence. He quickly conducted a series of studies with the specific intent of demonstrating the unreliability of children's testimony.

According to Ceci and Bruck (1993), in one of his studies, Varendonck (1911) asked a group of children to describe a person who had supposedly approached him in front of the children earlier that morning. Although this person did not exist, Varendonck was able to demonstrate, in line with previous studies, that many of the children were easily led by suggestive questioning. Based on these findings, Varendonck concluded to the court that the testimony provided by the children in this case (and in every other case) was likely to be inaccurate and that, as a group, children are very prone to suggestion.

Advocates of Forensic Psychology in North America

Although it was not until much later that psychologists began testifying on similar issues in North America, psychology in North America was making great strides in other areas of the criminal justice system. Perhaps one of the most important landmarks was the publication in 1908 of Hugo Munsterberg's *On the Witness Stand* (Munsterberg, 1908). Another student of Wilhelm Wundt, Munsterberg is considered by many to be the father of forensic psychology. Coming from Germany to Harvard University in 1892, he quickly established a name for himself because of his arrogant personality and sensationalistic writing (Brigham, 1999). In his book, Munsterberg argued that psychology had much to offer the legal system. Through a collection of his essays, he discussed how psychology could assist with issues involving eyewitness testimony, crime detection, false confessions, suggestibility, hypnotism, and even crime prevention.

Unfortunately, he presented his ideas in a way that led to heavy criticism from the legal profession. This is unsurprising when we consider the way in which he wrote. Consider the following quotation from the introduction to his book:

> The lawyer and the judge and the juryman are sure that they do not need the experimental psychologist. They do not wish to see that in this field pre-eminently applied experimental psychology has made strong strides. . . . They go on thinking that their legal instinct and their common sense supplies them with all that is needed and somewhat more . . . if the time is ever to come when even the jurist is to show some concession to the spirit of modern psychology, public opinion will have to exert some pressure. (Munsterberg, 1908, pp. 10–11)

Munsterberg's biggest critic was John Henry Wigmore, a well-respected law professor at Northwestern University in Chicago. Wigmore is known for many things, most notably his *Treatise on Evidence*, which is a critical examination of the laws of evidence. In the field of forensic psychology, however, what Wigmore is most commonly known for is his ruthless critique of Munsterberg's book. Through a series of fabricated "transcripts," Wigmore (1909) put Munsterberg on "trial," where he was sued, and found guilty, of "claiming more than he could offer" (Brigham, 1999, p. 276). Wigmore criticized Munsterberg for the lack of relevant research publications to back up his claims and, more generally, for the lack of applied research in the field of forensic psychology as a whole. Due perhaps in large part to Wigmore's comprehensive attack on Munsterberg's work, North American psychologists working in areas that we would now define as forensic psychology were largely ignored by the legal profession for a long period of time. However, according to some, Munsterberg was still instrumental in pushing North American psychologists into the legal arena (Bartol & Bartol, 1987).

The father of forensic psychology, Hugo Munsterberg, is best known for his controversial book On the Witness Stand, *which many people believe pushed North American psychologists into the legal arena.*

Forensic Psychology in Other Areas of the Criminal Justice System

After the publication of Munsterberg's controversial book, forensic psychology in North America gradually caught up to what was happening in Europe. Not only was more research being conducted in the area by psychologists, but this research was also being practically applied in a wide range of criminal justice settings. For example, as Bartol and Bartol (2004) highlight, forensic psychologists were instrumental in establishing the first clinic for juvenile delinquents in 1909, psychologists began using psychological testing for law enforcement selection purposes in 1917, and 1919 saw the first forensic assessment laboratory (to conduct pretrial assessments) set up in a U.S. police agency. After these events, psychologists in the United States began to be more heavily involved in the judicial system as well, starting with the case of *State v. Driver* in 1921.

Landmark Court Cases in the United States

Unlike their European counterparts who had provided expert testimony in courts as early as the late nineteenth century, the first time this happened in the United States was 1921 (*State v. Driver*, 1921). However, according to Bartol and Bartol (1987), the *Driver* case was only a partial victory for forensic psychology. This West Virginia case involved the attempted rape of a young girl and the court accepted expert evidence from a psychologist in the area of juvenile delinquency. However, the court rejected the psychologist's testimony that the young girl was a "moron" and, therefore, could not be believed. Again, quoting from Bartol and Bartol (1987), in its ruling the court stated, "It is yet to be determined that psychological and medical tests are practical, and will detect the lie on the witness stand" (pp. 11–12).

A number of more recent U.S. court cases are also enormously important in the history of forensic psychology. Perhaps the best-known case is that of *Brown v. Board of Education* (1954). This case challenged the constitutionality of segregated public schools (Benjamin & Crouse, 2002). Opponents of school segregation argued that separating children based on their race creates feelings of inferiority, especially among African-American children. On May 17, 1954, the U.S. Supreme Court agreed. In their ruling, Chief Justice Earl Warren stated:

> Segregation of White and colored children in public school has a detrimental effect upon the colored children. The impact is greater when it has the sanction of the law, for the policy of separating the races is usually interpreted as denoting the inferiority of the Negro group. A sense of inferiority affects the motivation of the child to learn. Segregation with the sanction of law, therefore, has a tendency to retard the educational and mental development of Negro children and to deprive them of some of the benefits they would receive in a racially integrated school system. Whatever may have been the extent of psychological knowledge [in previous court cases] this finding is amply supported by modern authority. (Benjamin & Crouse, 2002, p. 39)

Beyond the obvious importance of this ruling, it is important in the field of forensic psychology because of a footnote that was attached to the last sentence of the ruling, the famous footnote 11. The modern authority that the U.S. Supreme Court was referring to in this ruling was research in the social sciences demonstrating the detrimental effect of segregation. On the top of the list of seven references included in footnote 11 was the work of Kenneth Clark, an African-American psychologist who taught psychology at City College in New York City. This was the first time that psychological research was cited in a U.S. Supreme Court decision and some have argued that this validated psychology as a science (e.g., Benjamin & Crouse, 2002).

The last U.S. court case that we will discuss here is *Jenkins v. United States* (1962). The trial involved charges of breaking and entering, assault, and intent to rape, with the defendant, Jenkins, pleading not guilty by reason of insanity. Three clinical psychologists were presented by the defendant, each of them supporting an insanity defence on the basis that the defendant was suffering from schizophrenia at the time of the crimes. At the conclusion of the trial, the judge instructed the jury to disregard the testimony from the psychologists because "psychologists were not qualified to give expert testimony on the issue of mental disease" (American Psychological Association, 2004). The case was appealed. As part of the appeal, the American Psychological Association provided a report to the court stating their view that clinical psychologists are competent to provide opinions concerning the existence of mental illness. On appeal, the court reversed the conviction and ordered a new trial stating that "some psychologists are qualified to render expert testimony on mental disorders ... the determination of a psychologist's competence to render an expert opinion ... must depend upon the nature and extent of his knowledge and not simply on the claim to the title psychologist" (American Psychological Association, 2004). This decision helped increase the extent to which psychologists could contribute directly to the legal system as expert witnesses.

Although the landmark U.S. court cases we have discussed so far have been fundamental in shaping forensic psychology, there are also numerous Canadian court cases that have been influential. A brief discussion of some of these cases is provided in Box 1.2 on page 16. We will provide a more detailed discussion of some of the cases in the relevant chapters (where we focus on research relating to these rulings).

Psychological Theories of Crime

In addition to the increased use of psychologists in the criminal justice system, the mid-twentieth century saw a proliferation of psychological theories of crime, both in Europe and North America. This is not to say there weren't psychological theories of crime (or theories from other disciplines) proposed before this time, but there was a renewed interest in attempts to explain criminal behaviour during this period. We cannot adequately cover all of the psychological theories of crime in this one chapter. In fact, it would take more than this entire book to do justice to the topic. Instead, we will focus on three specific theories that can be categorized generally under the headings of **psychoanalytic theories**, **learning theories**, and **personality theories**. For a more detailed discussion of these theories, you can refer to Andrews and Bonta (2001). In addition, see Box 1.3 for a brief discussion of theories of crime from other disciplines.

PSYCHOANALYTIC THEORIES AND CRIME The development of psychoanalytic theory can be attributed to Sigmund Freud. However, although Freud had much to say about many psychological issues, it seems he had relatively little to say about crime or criminals. This is not to say that he did not have an influence on forensic psychology as a field. For example, Freud is known to have advocated the use of psychology in the legal system during a speech he gave to a group of Austrian judges in 1906. In that speech he suggested that "the task for the therapist ... is the same as that of the

BOX 1.2 INFLUENTIAL CANADIAN COURT CASES IN THE HISTORY OF FORENSIC PSYCHOLOGY

Some influential Canadian cases of particular interest to forensic psychologists include the following:

- *R. v. Hubbert (1975)*. The Ontario Court of Appeal states that jurors are presumed to be impartial (i.e., unbiased) and that numerous safeguards are in place within the Canadian judicial system to ensure this (e.g., limitations can be imposed on the press in terms of what they can report before the start of a trial).

- *R. v. Sophonow (1986)*. The Manitoba Court of Appeal overturns the murder conviction of Thomas Sophonow due to errors in law, many of which related to problems with the eyewitness evidence collected by the police as part of their investigation.

- *R. v. Lavallee (1990)*. The Supreme Court of Canada (SCC) sets guidelines for when, and how, expert testimony should be used in cases involving battered women syndrome. Since this ruling, expert testimony in cases of battered women who kill has increased.

- *Wenden v. Trikha (1991)*. The Alberta Court of Queen's Bench rules that mental health professionals have a duty to warn a third party if they have reasonable grounds to believe that their client intends to seriously harm that individual.

- *R. v. Swain (1991)*. The SCC makes a ruling that results in changes to the insanity defence standard in Canada, including the name of the defence, when the defence can be raised, and how long insanity acquittees can be detained for.

- *R. v. Levogiannis (1993)*. The SCC rules that children are allowed to testify in court behind screens that prevent them from seeing the accused.

- *R. v. Mohan (1994)*. The SCC establishes formal criteria for determining when expert testimony should be admitted into court.

- *R. v. William (1998)*. The SCC formally acknowledges that jurors can be biased by numerous sources, ranging from community sentiment on a particular issue to direct involvement with a case (e.g., being related to the accused).

- *R. v. Gladue (1999)*. The SCC rules that prison sentences are being relied on too often by judges as a way of dealing with criminal behaviour, especially for Aboriginal offenders, and that other sentencing options should be considered.

- *R. v. Oickle (2000)*. The SCC rules that police interrogation techniques, which consist of subtle forms of psychological coercion, are acceptable and that confessions extracted through their use can be admissible in court.

BOX 1.3 BIOLOGICAL AND SOCIOLOGICAL THEORIES OF CRIME

In addition to psychological theories of crime, a variety of biological and sociological theories of crime have also been proposed throughout the past century. Below are brief descriptions of some of the best-known theories.

BIOLOGICAL THEORIES OF CRIME

- *Sheldon's (1949) constitutional theory*. Sheldon proposed that crime is largely a product of an individual's body build, or somatotype, which is assumed to be linked to an individual's temperament. According to Sheldon, endomorphs (obese) are jolly, ectomorphs (thin) are introverted, and mesomorphs (muscular) are bold. Sheldon's studies indicated that, due to their aggressive nature, mesomorph's were more likely to become involved with crime.

- *Jacobs, Brunton, Melville, Brittan, and McClemont's (1965) chromosomal theory*. Jacobs and her colleagues proposed that chromosomal irregularity is linked to criminal behaviour. A normal female has two X chromosomes, whereas a normal male has one X and one Y chromosome. However, it was discovered that there were men with two Y chromosomes, which, it was proposed, made them more masculine and, therefore, more aggressive. According to Jacobs and her colleagues, this enhanced aggressiveness would result in an increased chance that these men would commit violent crimes.

- *Mark and Ervin's (1970) dyscontrol theory*. Mark and Ervin proposed that lesions in the temporal lobe and limbic system result in electrical disorganization within the brain, which can lead to a dyscontrol syndrome. According to Mark and Ervin, symptoms of this dyscontrol syndrome can include outbursts of sudden physical violence, impulsive sexual behaviour, and serious traffic violations.

SOCIOLOGICAL THEORIES OF CRIME

- *Merton's (1938) strain theory*. Merton proposed that crime is largely a product of the strain felt by certain individuals in society (typically from the lower class) who have restricted access to legitimate means, such as education, of achieving valued goals of success. Merton argued that, while some of these individuals will be happy with the lesser goals that are achievable, others will turn to illegitimate means, such as crime, in an attempt to achieve the valued goals.

- *Sutherland's (1939) differential association theory*. Sutherland proposed that criminal behaviour is learned through social interactions in which people are exposed to values that can either be favourable or unfavourable to violations of the law. More specifically, Sutherland maintained that a person is likely to become involved in criminal activity when he or she learns more values (i.e., attitudes) that are favourable to violations of the law than values that are unfavourable to it.

- *Hirschi's (1969) social control theory*. Hirschi proposed that individuals possess certain bonds with society and that the strength of these bonds control their behaviour (including the likelihood that they will exhibit criminal behaviour). Hirschi focused on four bonds in particular: attachment to others (e.g., teachers), commitment to conventional values (e.g., reputation), involvement in conventional activities (e.g., school), and belief in a societal value system (e.g., respect for the law). If these bonds weaken for some reason (e.g., children start to perform poorly in school and, as a result, begin to dislike teachers), individuals are more likely to become involved in criminal activity.

examining magistrate. We have to uncover the hidden psychical material ... to do this we have to invent a number of detective devices, some of which it seems that you gentlemen of the law are now about to copy from us" (Freud, 1906/1959, p. 108). This, it appears, is where Freud's involvement in forensic psychology ended. In terms of psychoanalytic theories of crime, these can be attributed to several of Freud's followers. Most of these theories have several things in common. They take the position that it is primarily dynamic internal forces within people that account for their criminal behaviour, and they argue that early childhood events and experiences are crucial for understanding crime (Hollin, 1989).

There are, in fact, many different psychoanalytic theories of crime—far too many to discuss here (see Feldman, 1969, for a review). Therefore, we will focus on just one, John Bowlby's **theory of maternal deprivation**. Bowlby (1944) argued that the early separation of a child from his or her mother prevents effective social development from taking place. Without effective social development, Bowlby hypothesized that children will experience long-term problems in developing positive social relationships and will instead develop antisocial behaviour patterns. In large part, Bowlby's theory is based on his study of juvenile delinquents. In support of his theory, Bowlby (1944) found that a far greater number of juvenile delinquents experienced early separation from their mothers compared with a nondelinquent control group. Researchers have criticized Bowlby's theory of maternal deprivation on multiple fronts, ranging from problems with his original control group to inadequate assessment procedures (Feldman, 1977; Morgan, 1975). However, since the time these criticisms were first levied against the theory, numerous studies have indicated that negative early childhood experiences can indeed influence the development of antisocial behaviour (e.g., Waschbusch et al., 2004).

LEARNING THEORIES AND CRIME As with psychoanalytic theories of crime, there are also many different learning theories that have been proposed to explain the development and maintenance of criminal behaviour (Hollin, 1989). However, here too there are threads that bind the various theories together. In this case, all learning theories are based upon principles of conditioning, which speculate that a person's behaviour, including criminal behaviour, is learned and maintained by its consequences (Skinner, 1974). By extension, these theorists also generally agree that criminal behaviour can be eliminated, or at least reduced, by modifying these consequences. Indeed, as you will see in Chapter 10, this principle is largely what guides our sentencing practices in North America. Many people believe that, if the negative consequences of committing crime are increased to a point at which they far outweigh the rewards, criminal activity will decrease. As above, we will focus on just one of the many learning theories that has had a significant impact on forensic psychology—**social learning theory**, as formulated by Albert Bandura.

Social learning theory extends learning theory as defined by psychologists like B.F. Skinner (1974) in that it recognizes that learning through consequences can come from many different sources. Not only can learning occur from the consequences that result from an individual's own behaviour, but it can also occur by observing the consequences experienced by others. In fact, according to social learning theorists, it is largely through our observations of others that we learn how to perform the observed behaviours (Bandura, 1977).

As it relates to criminal behaviour, observational learning can take place through three primary contexts: the family, peer groups, and cultural symbols, such as television shows (Bandura, 1973). Thus, an individual's antisocial behaviour is largely viewed as a function of his or her exposure to antisocial behaviour on the part of others, especially when the individual has observed antisocial behaviour being rewarded. In support of this theory, there is now a wealth of research to suggest that interacting with antisocial individuals can predict future antisocial behaviour (e.g., Andrews & Bonta, 2001). In addition, the most recent research looking at the effects of exposure to violence on television suggests that this exposure also predicts aggressive and violent behaviour (e.g., Paik & Comstock, 1994).

As with psychoanalytic theories of crime, social learning theories are not without their critics. One of the most commonly voiced criticisms is that social learning theory cannot explain the fact that many people are exposed to antisocial role models and yet not all of these people go on to commit crimes (Nietzel, 1979). However, others have argued that learning theories do in fact provide the means to explain such findings. Hollin (1989), for example, points out that learning theories consist of a variety of explanations, such as vicarious punishment, or seeing others suffer the negative consequences of being caught for their crimes. As you will see in upcoming chapters, there are some problems with Hollin's argument that still need to be addressed, since we now have substantial evidence that observing others getting punished (e.g., by seeing them get long-term prison sentences) does not have the deterrent effect many social learning theorists would predict.

PERSONALITY THEORIES AND CRIME Finally, according to some theorists, individuals who get involved in crime do so primarily because of their personality make-up. More specifically, personality theorists suggest that criminals have either developed, or inherited, a personality (i.e., a set of underlying stable traits) that differentiates them in some way from law-abiding citizens. There are numerous theories that attempt to explain the connection between personality and crime, but none have been as influential as the biosocial theory of crime proposed by Hans J. Eysenck, the famous personality psychologist. It is believed that Eysenck's theory represents the first testable theory of criminal behaviour proposed by a psychologist (Bartol & Bartol, 2004). As a result, this theory deserves special mention in a textbook such as this one and we will focus our discussion on it.

Eysenck's theory of crime, which is explained thoroughly in his book *Crime and Personality*, is one of the few that focuses on biological, social, and individual factors. According to Eysenck (1977), the three major dimensions that make up all of our personalities are **extroversion** (E), **neuroticism** (N), and psychoticism (P). Most of Eysenck's research dealt primarily with E and N, so we will focus on these two constructs here. Each of these personality constructs is thought to fall along a continuum. The E construct is represented by high extroversion on one end of the continuum and high introversion at the other end. The N construct is represented by high neuroticism on one end of the continuum and high stability at the other end. Eysenck assumed that everybody's personality makeup falls somewhere on the two-dimensional diagram in Figure 1.2. However, because most people will not exhibit the extremes of either continuum, it is assumed that the majority of us will be located somewhere in the shaded area.

In addition, Eysenck also believed that some individuals are born with cortical and autonomic nervous systems (ANS) that affect their ability to learn from the consequences of their behaviour. More specifically, Eysenck believed extroverts are cortically

FIGURE 1.2

EYSENCK'S MODEL OF PERSONALITY AND ITS RELATIONSHIP TO CONDITIONABILITY AND CRIME

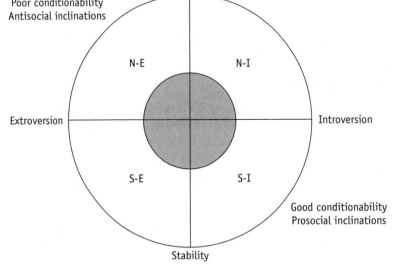

Source: Adapted from Hollin, 1989.

underaroused and therefore continually seek out stimulation. Introverts, conversely, are assumed to be cortically overaroused and therefore continually avoid stimulation. Similarly, Eysenck believed that neurotic individuals have an overreactive ANS, which causes strong reactions to unpleasant stimuli. Highly stable individuals, however, are assumed have a stable ANS.

This theory's relevance to the formation and maintenance of criminal behaviour becomes clear when we consider how Eysenck relates personality to people's ability to learn from the consequences of their behaviour, especially the negative consequences experienced in childhood as part of the socialization and conscience-building process. According to Eysenck (1977), high-E individuals condition less efficiently than high-I individuals. Compared with introverts, extroverts require more intense stimulation to achieve the same level of cortical arousal and they are, therefore, less responsive to the negative consequences of their actions and more difficult to socialize. Likewise, high-N individuals condition less effectively than high-S individuals because of the unpleasant effects of anxiety that neurotic individuals experience and, therefore, they are also more difficult to socialize. Thus, due to their poor conditionability, it is assumed that high-E/high-N individuals will have strong antisocial inclinations. Conversely, low-E/low-N individuals will have strong prosocial inclinations.

A lot of research has examined Eysenck's theory of crime, much of it using the Eysenck Personality Questionnaire to measure and contrast the various personality constructs in matched offender and nonoffender groups. Much of this research supports Eysenck's original assertions that offender samples often score higher on E and N (see Hollin, 1989, for a summary of this research). For example, in McGurk and McDougall's (1981) study of delinquents and nondelinquents, evidence emerged for high-E/low-N and low-E/high-N individuals in both groups. The supposedly antisocial high-E/high-N individual was only found in the delinquent group, and the supposedly prosocial low-E/low-N individual was only found in the nondelinquent group. However, despite some general level of support for Eysenck's theory, it is often criticized because it cannot explain how all crime emerges, the empirical evidence linking conditioning and socialization is weak, and the theory relies on a model of personality (the classic trait model, as discussed in Chapter 4) that is often challenged (Hollin, 1989).

Signs of a Legitimate Field of Psychology

Although the field of forensic psychology has perhaps not come as far as many forensic psychologists would have hoped in its relatively short history, it has now become a recognized and legitimate field of study within psychology. Indeed, forensic psychology now appears to have many of the markings of an established discipline. This is reflected in numerous ways. First, there are a growing number of high-quality textbooks in the area that provide the opportunity to teach students about forensic psychology. This is particularly so in the United States.

Second, there are now a large number of academic journals dedicated to various aspects of the field. In fact, since the establishment of *Criminal Justice and Behavior* in 1974 and *Law and Human Behavior* in 1977, new forensic psychology journals have literally popped up on almost a yearly basis. These journals provide outlets for forensic psychologists regardless of their focus (i.e., applied or experimental) or their role (i.e., clinician, researcher, or legal scholar). Some of the journals publish articles dealing with any aspect of forensic psychology, such as *Behavioral Science and the Law*, while others are more focused, such as the *Journal of Interpersonal Violence*. More mainstream journals, such as the *Journal of Applied Psychology* and *Applied Cognitive Psychology*, also regularly publish research from the forensic domain.

Third, a number of professional associations have now been developed to represent the interests of forensic psychologists and to promote research and practice in the area. The largest of these associations is the American Psychology-Law Society (AP-LS), or Division 41 of the APA. Despite being an American association, Canadian forensic psychologists have played a crucial role in the AP-LS. Many Canadian forensic psychologists are members of the AP-LS and, during the past 25 years, two Canadian forensic psychologists have served as president of the AP-LS. One of these individuals, Dr. James Ogloff, is profiled in Box 1.4. Other countries have developed similar professional associations. In Canada, for example, forensic psychologists can belong to the Criminal Justice Section of the Canadian Psychological Association (CPA).

Lastly, new training opportunities in forensic psychology are being established in North America (some in Canada) and existing training opportunities are being improved. Indeed, at the undergraduate level, a number of colleges and universities across Canada and the United States are starting to offer formal courses in the area of forensic psychology. At the graduate level, a number of high-quality forensic programs have also been developed. Currently, students in Canada who are interested in the area of experimental forensic psychology can undergo graduate training at several Canadian universities, although, as of 2004, Simon Fraser University is the only school that offers programs specifically in the areas of clinical forensic psychology and psychology and law.

MODERN-DAY DEBATES: PSYCHOLOGICAL EXPERTS IN COURT

Since the field of forensic psychology has become more widely accepted, forensic psychologists have increasingly been asked to provide expert testimony in court. The variety of topics that forensic psychologists testify about is very broad indeed, including competency to stand trial, custody issues, malingering and deception, the accuracy of eyewitness identification, the effects of crime on victims, and the assessment of dangerousness. In order for forensic psychologists to increase the extent to which they can contribute to the judicial system in this way, it is important for them to become more

BOX 1.4 CANADIAN RESEARCHER PROFILE: DR. JAMES OGLOFF

James Ogloff entered the University of Calgary intending to major in commerce and to go on to complete a law degree. His career plan was to become a corporate lawyer. While majoring in commerce, during his second year, he was required to complete an undergraduate course in social sciences. Viewing this as largely a useless requirement, he opted to complete Introduction to Psychology in an intersession course in the summer "to get it over with." Much to his surprise, he ended up being captivated with psychology, so much so that the following fall semester, he ended up dropping out of his commerce courses and transferring to psychology. At that time, his interests were in the area of child psychology. Soon, though, his longstanding interests in law re-emerged and he completed his undergraduate research on the topic of eyewitness memory and hypnosis. Dr. Ogloff entered graduate school in clinical psychology, obtaining his M.A. at the University of Saskatchewan. While there, he spent a great deal of time at the Regional Psychiatric Centre, a secure prison hospital, where he trained, conducted research, and did clinical work. Although he was working in the forensic psychology area, he still felt the need to learn more about the law.

With a desire to learn more about the law and how it relates to psychology, Dr. Ogloff went on to attend the Law/Psychology program at the University of Nebraska at Lincoln. The University of Nebraska had established the first program that offered a combined law degree and Ph.D. in psychology. He completed his Juris Doctor in Law, with distinction, and had a short stint of legal practice while still a student. He completed his Ph.D. in psychology, doing his doctoral research in the area of jury understanding of the insanity defence. His interest in this area was spawned by John Hinckley Jr.'s attempted assassination of President Ronald Reagan. John Hinckley Jr. was found "not guilty by reason of insanity" and the verdict initiated a great deal of controversy regarding the use of the insanity defence in the United States. Numerous reforms were initiated—including changing the wording of the defence in many states with the intention to limit the number of people found "not guilty by reason of insanity." Curiously, though, no one had conducted research to determine whether varying the insanity defence standards produced changes in jury verdicts. Dr. Ogloff's research showed that even fairly dramatic changes to the insanity defence standards did not produce differences in verdicts by simulated jurors.

Following graduate school, Dr. Ogloff began his academic career at Simon Fraser University, where he eventually became the University Endowed Professor of Law and Forensic Psychology. He helped develop and served as director of the Program in Law and Forensic Psychology at Simon Fraser University. He also held an appointment as Adjunct Professor of Law at the University of British Columbia, where he taught classes in mental health law and the psychology of litigation.

Dr. Ogloff has continued his research in the area of the comprehension of legal instructions, though his more recent work has focused more generally on jurors' comprehension of judges' legal instructions. In addition to his continued interest in jury research and judicial instructions, most of his research and scholarly writing has been in the areas of offenders with mental illnesses, training in law and psychology, the assessment of risk for violence, and professional ethics.

In 2001, Dr. Ogloff left Simon Fraser University to assume the position of Foundation Professor of Clinical Forensic Psychology at Monash University in Melbourne, Australia. In addition to his other work, he has shown a commitment to profes-

sional associations in psychology. He has served as the president of the Canadian Psychological Association and the president of the American Psychology-Law Society. Currently, he is the president of the Australian and New Zealand Association of Psychiatry, Psychology and Law (Victorian Branch).

Although work keeps him busy and satisfied, Dr. Ogloff's real joy in life comes from his relationship with his wife, Kathleen, to whom he has been married for more than 20 years. They have three young children who keep them very busy. Aleksandra (12 years), Andrew (9 years), and Karena (7 years) have taken to life in Australia very well. Most of their spare time is spent enjoying family activities and travelling when they have the opportunity.

knowledgeable about the law and the legal system (Ogloff & Cronshaw, 2001). This includes becoming more aware of what the role of an expert witness is, the various ways in which psychology and the law differ from one another, and the criteria courts consider when determining whether psychological testimony should be admitted.

The Functions of the Expert Witness

According to Ogloff and Cronshaw (2001), an expert witness generally serves one of two functions. One function is to provide the court with information that assists them in understanding a particular issue. The second function is to provide the court with an opinion. Understanding these functions is important because they are what separate the **expert witness** from other witnesses who regularly appear in court (e.g., eyewitnesses). To be clear on this issue, in contrast to other witnesses in court, who can only testify about what they have directly observed, expert witnesses can provide the court with their personal opinion on matters relevant to the case and they are often allowed to draw inferences based on their observations (Ogloff & Cronshaw, 2001). These opinions and inferences must always fall within the limits of expert witnesses' areas of expertise, which they typically get through specialized training and experience, and the testimony must be deemed reliable and helpful to the court. In addition, it is important to point out that, when providing testimony to the courts, the expert witness is supposed to be there as an educator to the judge and jury, not as an advocate for the defence or the prosecution.

The Challenges of Providing Expert Testimony

Providing expert testimony to the courts in an effective way is not a simple task. This probably explains why in the past few years numerous manuals have been published for the purpose of assisting expert witnesses with the task of preparing for court (e.g., Brodsky, 1991). Even judges have provided suggestions on how forensic psychologists can increase their chances of being effective witnesses in court (e.g., Saunders, 2001). In large part, these difficulties arise because of the inherent differences (often conflicts) that exist between the fields of psychology and law. Numerous individuals have discussed these differences but we will focus on one particular attempt to describe them.

According to Hess (1987, 1999), psychology and law differ along at least seven different dimensions:

1. *Knowledge.* Knowledge gain in psychology is accomplished through cumulative research. In the law, knowledge comes through legal precedent, logical thinking, and case law.

2. *Methodology.* Methodological approaches in psychology are predominantly **nomothetic**. In other words, the goal is to uncover broad patterns and general trends through the use of controlled experiments and statistical methods. In contrast, the law is **idiographic** in that it operates on a case-by-case basis.

3. *Epistemology.* Psychologists assume that it is possible to uncover hidden truths if the appropriate experiments are conducted. Truth in the law is defined subjectively and is based on who can provide the most convincing story of what really happened.

4. *Criteria.* In terms of a willingness to accept something as true, psychologists are cautious. To accept a hypothesis, results must be replicated and conservative statistical criteria are used. The law decides on what is true based on a single case and criteria that are often more lenient.

5. *Nature of law.* The goal in psychology is to describe how people behave. Law, however, is prescriptive. It tells people how they should behave.

6. *Principles.* Good psychologists always consider alternative explanations for their findings. Good lawyers always convince the judge and jury that their explanation of the findings is the only correct explanation.

7. *Latitude.* The behaviour of the psychologist when acting as an expert witness is severely limited by the court. The law imposes fewer restrictions on the behaviour of lawyers (though they are also restricted in numerous ways).

Understanding these differences is important in their own right. However, they are also important because they help us to appreciate why the courts are often so reluctant to admit testimony provided by psychological experts. For example, after considering how psychology and the law differ with respect to their methodological approach, it may not be surprising that judges often have difficulty seeing how psychologists can assist in court proceedings. Indeed, numerous legal scholars have questioned whether the general patterns and trends that result from a nomothetic psychological approach should ever be used in court. As Sheldon and Macleod (1991) state:

> The findings derived from empirical research are used by psychologists to formulate norms of human behaviour. From observations and experiments, psychologists may conclude that in circumstance X there is a likelihood that an individual … will behave in manner Y. … [N]ormative data of this sort are of little use to the courts. The courts are concerned to determine the past behaviour of accused *individuals*, and in carrying out that function, information about the past behaviour of *other individuals* is wholly irrelevant. (emphasis added, p. 815)

Currently, little attempt has been made to understand these differences between psychology and law, or their implications for the field of forensic psychology. Once we gain such an understanding, perhaps forensic psychologists will be in a better position to assist the courts with the decisions they are required to make. We believe that research conducted by forensic psychologists, particularly in their role as legal scholars, will greatly assist in this endeavour. This research will also increase our understanding of the criteria the courts use for determining the conditions under which they will accept expert testimony from psychologists.

Criteria for Accepting Expert Testimony

In order for a forensic psychologist to provide expert testimony in court, he or she must meet certain criteria. In the United States, criteria of one sort or another have been around since the early twentieth century. In fact, until quite recently, the admissibility of expert testimony in the United States was based on a decision handed down by the courts in *Frye v. United States* (1923). Frye was being tried for murder and the court rejected his request to admit the results from a polygraph exam he had passed. On appeal, the court also rejected requests to allow the polygraph expert to present evidence on Frye's behalf (Bartol & Bartol, 1994). In the ruling, the court spoke specifically to the issue of when expert testimony should be admitted into court. The court indicated that, for novel scientific evidence to be admissible in court, it must be established that the testimony (and any procedures used to arrive at this testimony) is generally accepted in the scientific community. More specifically, the court stated, "while courts will go a long way in admitting expert testimony deduced from a well-recognized scientific principle or discovery, the thing from which the deduction is made must be sufficiently established to have gained general acceptance in the particular field in which it belongs" (*Frye v. United States*, 1923, p. 1).

This criterion came to be called the "**general acceptance test,**" and although it formed the basis of admissibility decisions in the United States for a long time, it is heavily criticized. The major criticism centres on the vagueness of terms such as "general acceptance" and "the particular field in which it belongs" and whether trial judges are able to make appropriate determinations of what these terms mean. As just one example of where problems might emerge, consider a defence lawyer who would like to have a criminal profiler provide testimony in court. How should the trial judge decide whether the profiler used generally accepted profiling techniques? If the courts turned to the profiling community (typically consisting of specially trained law enforcement personnel) to make this determination, the answer would most likely be far more favourable than if they had asked forensic psychologists who conduct research in the area of criminal profiling (e.g., Alison et al., 2002). So, whom should the judge turn to and believe? In what "particular field" does criminal profiling belong?

This issue of vagueness was addressed more recently in the U.S. Supreme Court decision handed down in *Daubert v. Merrell Dow Pharmaceuticals, Inc.* (1993), when more specific admissibility criteria were set. Daubert sued Merrell Dow because he believed a morning sickness drug his mother ingested while pregnant, which was produced by the company, led to his birth defects. At trial, Merrell Dow presented experts who provided evidence that the use of the drug Bendectin does not result in birth defects. In turn, Daubert provided evidence from experts who claimed that Bendectin could lead to birth defects. The state court and the appeal court both rejected the testimony provided by Daubert's experts on the basis that the methods they used to arrive at their results were not generally accepted by the scientific community. On appeal before the U.S. Supreme Court, Daubert's lawyers challenged the state and appeal court's interpretation of "general acceptance."

In addressing this issue, the U.S. Supreme Court stated that, for scientific evidence to be admitted into court, it must (1) be provided by a qualified expert, (2) be relevant, and (3) be reliable (meaning scientifically valid). To assist judges in making the decision as to whether evidence is in fact valid, the U.S. Supreme Court laid out four specific criteria, now commonly referred to as the *Daubert* **criteria**. These criteria suggest that scientific evidence is valid if

1. The research has been peer reviewed.
2. The research is testable (i.e., falsifiable through experimentation).
3. The research has a recognized rate of error.
4. The research adheres to professional standards.

More recently, in the case of *Kumho Tire Company v. Carmichael* (1999), the U.S. Supreme Court ruled that the *Daubert* criteria apply to all expert testimony, not just scientific testimony.

Similar criteria are currently being used in Canada. The rules for admissibility in Canada were laid out in *R. v. Mohan* (1994). Mohan was a pediatrician charged with sexually assaulting several of his teenage female patients. At trial, Mohan wanted to provide expert testimony from a psychiatrist who was prepared to testify that the typical offender in such a case would be a pedophile and, in his opinion, Mohan was not a pedophile. The trial judge ruled that the testimony was inadmissible and, on appeal before the Supreme Court of Canada, the court agreed and established the standard for admitting expert testimony in Canada.

The standard is now referred to as the ***Mohan* criteria** and it includes four admissibility criteria, some of which are similar to the *Daubert* criteria:

1. The evidence must be relevant, in that it makes a fact at issue in the case more or less likely.

2. The evidence must be necessary for assisting the trier of fact (i.e., the testimony must be about something that goes beyond the common understanding of the court).

3. The evidence must not violate any rules of exclusion (e.g., the testimony must not relate to whether a witness is telling the truth).

4. The testimony must be provided by a qualified expert, which is typically determined through training, experience, and research.

Although these criteria probably make the judge's job of deciding when to admit expert testimony easier, they do not eliminate all possible problems. In large part, this is because the criteria are still highly subjective and rely heavily on the discretion of the judge. An example of one potential problem is illustrated by the case discussed in Box 1.5, in which a judge decided that testimony relating to the accuracy of eyewitness testimony was common knowledge and, as a result, inadmissible (Yarmey, 2001). Most of the research in the area of eyewitness accuracy indicates that the judge was most likely wrong in this case. This highlights the need not only to conduct high-quality research in the area of forensic psychology, but also to get that research into the hands of the legal community. As you will see as you read through this textbook, much of the high-quality research already exists but, on the whole, forensic psychologists have not done a great job at transferring this research to the legal community.

BOX 1.5 THE CASE OF *R. V. MCINTOSH AND MCCARTHY* (1997): POTENTIAL PROBLEMS WITH THE *MOHAN* CRITERIA

R. v. McIntosh and McCarthy (1997) is an important court case for forensic psychologists who want to act as expert witnesses in the area of eyewitness testimony. The case deals with the crimes of Owen McIntosh and Paul McCarthy, who were charged with attempted murder, robbery, and firearms offences (Peters, 2001). The robbery and shooting took place at a dry cleaner. During the investigation, two eyewitnesses came forward. One witness was the Chinese owner of the dry cleaner; the other was a Caucasian bystander. Both McIntosh and McCarthy are black men. At trial, the defence lawyer wanted to submit testimony provided by an expert in the area of eyewitness memory. The expert was Dr. Dan Yarmey, a professor of psychology at the University of Guelph, and his proposed testimony was going to deal with "factors present at the time of the robbery that would impair the witnesses' ability to make an accurate identification, the problem with cross-racial identification, the quality of memory recall for perceived events of different time spans, the influence of 'post event information' on memory, [and] the validity of the photographic lineup" (Peters, 2001, p. 103).

Although a large amount of research addresses each of these various points, the trial judge and the Ontario Court of Appeal judge ruled that Dr. Yarmey's testimony was inadmissible according to the *Mohan* criterion. One of the main problems raised about the testimony (there were several others) was that it did not go beyond the common understanding of the jurors and would, therefore, not assist them in their deliberations (Yarmey, 2001). The Court of Appeal judge stated, "This opinion evidence is directed to instructing the jurors that all witnesses have problems in perception and recall with respect to what occurred during any given circumstance that is brief and stressful. Accordingly, Dr. Yarmey is not testifying to matters that are outside the normal experience of the trier of fact: he is reminding the jury of the normal experience" (*R. v. McIntosh and McCarthy*, 1997, para. 20). The problem with this decision is that it was most likely wrong. As argued by Yarmey and Jones (1983), although jurors may have opinions about eyewitness testimony, "they do not necessarily have sufficient knowledge to interpret and evaluate correctly the many variables that affect its reliability" (p. 14).

When psychologists have specifically examined the issue of whether lay opinions about eyewitness testimony match the general findings from the research literature, the degree of match is often quite low, at least for certain issues. More important for *R. v. McIntosh and McCarthy* (1997) is that many of the issues that seem to be beyond the common understanding of jurors were contentious issues in that particular case. For example, research has clearly demonstrated that potential jurors have misconceptions about the effect of viewing time on eyewitness accuracy, the fairness of police lineups, the accuracy of cross-racial identifications, and the impact of violence on identification accuracy (Yarmey & Jones, 1983). Clearly, these sorts of findings need to be considered by the courts when they are deciding whether to admit expert testimony and, to a large extent, forensic psychologists can assist with this task by making it clear that such research does in fact exist.

SUMMARY

1. Forensic psychology can be defined in a narrow or broad fashion. Narrow definitions focus only on the clinical *or* experimental aspects of the field, whereas broad definitions are not so restrictive and encompass both aspects.

2. Forensic psychologists can play different roles. Clinical forensic psychologists are primarily interested in mental health issues as they pertain to law. Experimental forensic psychologists are interested in studying any aspect of human behaviour that relates to the law (e.g., eyewitness memory, jury decision-making, risk assessment).

3. Psychology can relate to the field of law in three ways. *Psychology and the law* refers to the use of psychology to study the operation of the legal system. *Psychology in the law* refers to the use of psychology within the legal system as it

operates. *Psychology of the law* refers to the use of psychology to study the legal system itself.

4. The mid-twentieth century saw a number of psychological theories of crime being proposed. Psychodynamic theories, such as Bowlby's theory of maternal deprivation, place a heavy emphasis on the internal dynamics of the offender and early childhood experiences. Learning theories, such as Bandura's social learning theory, place a heavy emphasis on how offenders learn to commit crime through a process of direct and indirect reinforcement. Personality theories, such as Eysenck's biosocial theory of crime, place a heavy emphasis on how offenders' personalities differ from those of law-abiding citizens.

5. Expert witnesses differ from regular witnesses in that expert witnesses can testify about their opinions, whereas other witnesses can only testify as to what they know to be fact. In Canada, the criteria for determining whether an expert's testimony will be admitted into court relate to whether the testimony (1) is relevant, (2) goes beyond the common understanding of the court, (3) does not violate any exclusionary rules, and (4) comes from a qualified expert.

KEY CONCEPTS

clinical forensic		forensic psychology	1	psychoanalytic theories	15
psychologists	3	general acceptance test	26	psychology and the law	8
Daubert criteria	27	idiographic	25	psychology in the law	8
experimental forensic		learning theories	15	psychology of the law	8
psychologists	6	*Mohan* criteria	28	social learning theory	18
expert witness	24	neuroticism	20	theory of maternal	
extroversion	20	nomothetic	25	deprivation	18
forensic psychiatry	4	personality theories	15		

DISCUSSION QUESTIONS

1. Forensic psychology can be defined in a narrow or broad fashion. What are some of the advantages and disadvantages of adopting a narrow definition of forensic psychology? What are some of the advantages and disadvantages of adopting a broad definition? Decide what type of definition you prefer and explain why.

2. The majority of forensic psychologists have no formal training in law. Do you think this is appropriate given the extent to which many of these psychologists are involved in the judicial system?

3. You have just been hired as a summer intern at a law office. One of your tasks is to assist in preparing for a high-profile murder case that has attracted a great deal

of media attention. One of the lawyers has found out that you've taken this course and he wants to know whether the extensive pretrial press coverage the crime has received will make it difficult to find impartial jurors. Design a study to determine whether this is likely to be the case.

4. You have just read about Bandura's social learning theory and how it relates to crime. Although you think the theory is interesting, you can't help notice that there are a lot of people who are exposed to antisocial role models, sometimes for extended periods of time, and yet not all these people go on to become criminals. What factors can you think of to explain this?

5. It took much longer for forensic psychology to become an established field of study in North America than in Europe. Why do you think this was the case?

6. Expert witnesses are supposed to act simply as educators to the judge and jury, not as advocates for the defence or for the prosecution. To what extent do you think this really happens? Do you think that it is even possible for expert witnesses to resist taking sides? Why or why not?

7. One criterion that must be met in Canada in order for expert evidence to be considered admissible is that it must go beyond the common understanding of the court. In your opinion, to what extent does forensic psychology offer something that goes beyond the common knowledge of judges and jurors? Give specific examples.

ADDITIONAL INFORMATION

Readings

Hess, A.K., & Weiner, I.B. (Eds.). (1999). *The handbook of forensic psychology* (2nd edition). New York: John Wiley and Sons.

Ogloff, J.R.P. (Ed.). (2002). *Taking psychology and law into the 21st century*. New York: Kluwer Academic.

Roesch, R., Hart, S.D., & Ogloff, J.R.P. (Eds.). (1999). *Psychology and law: The state of the discipline*. New York: Kluwer Academic.

Web Sites

APA Division 41: The American Psychology-Law Society
www.unl.edu/ap-ls/

CPA: Criminal Justice Section
www.cpa.ca/justice.html

The Ultimate Forensic Psychology Database
flash.lakeheadu.ca/~pals/forensics/

CHAPTER 2

Research Methods and Clinical Research Assessment Techniques

LEARNING OBJECTIVES

- Describe the key components to starting a research study.

- Contrast the different types of reliability and validity.

- Contrast the different types of research methodologies.

- Describe the different types of research designs.

- State the key components to informed consent.

- Identify the categories of clinical assessment techniques.

When Billy O'Neal started university, he decided to get a subscription to his local newspaper. Billy was going to study psychology at school and felt he could learn a lot about people's behaviour by reading the newspaper. In particular, stories about crime fascinated Billy. He analyzed every crime story he came across.

After about six months of reading the paper, Billy noticed that sexual assaults seemed to occur in warmer months. Billy came to believe that heat caused sexual assault. During Billy's forensic psychology course, he told his professor his explanation for why sexual assaults occur. Billy may be on his way to becoming an exceptional scientist but he made a "classic" error in his explanation. The professor explained that although two variables may appear to occur at the same time, it is not possible to conclude that one causes the other. A third variable that was not measured may be responsible for the effect. For example, testosterone levels may be higher in warmer weather and this may be what leads to sex offenders having a greater urge to commit an offence than during the colder months. But, we need to test our ideas before we can reach true or valid conclusions.

BASIC COMPONENTS TO CONDUCTING RESEARCH

Getting an Idea

Where do research ideas come from? The answer to this question is broad; questions can come from anywhere. Very generally, we can categorize ideas for research as coming from one of three areas: intuition, theory, and existing research.

In the vignette above, Billy used his intuition to explain why sexual assaults occur. We are using intuition when we look to our lives for patterns or rules to understand or explain human behaviour. We can then test our intuitive observations.

In contrast to intuition, a theory is a set of logically organized statements that describe events, describe relationships between events, and explain when these events occur (Shaughnessy, Zechmeister, & Zechmeister, 2000). Researchers can test a theory or parts of a theory to determine its accuracy. See Box 2.1 for an example of a theory used to explain criminal behaviour.

You might also turn to research that has already been conducted to get ideas. After reading some research, you might consider what questions remain to be tested and then test those. For example, a number of studies have been conducted examining interview protocols that police may use to increase their ability to collect complete and accurate information from eyewitnesses. One such protocol is the Enhanced Cognitive Interview by Fisher and Geisleman (1992). Although Fisher and Geisleman outline the necessary components to conducting a cognitive interview, it is not yet clear whether all the components, or which components, are necessary to observe the increased amount of information recalled, compared with "standard" police interviewing practices (see Chapter 6 for more on the Enhanced Cognitive Interview).

Keep in mind that, although an idea may be new, it may also be trivial. A researcher needs to consider whether the idea is worth testing and whether the information that will be gained is important. Not all ideas are worth the time, energy, and cost associated with testing them.

Translating the Idea into a Hypothesis

Regardless of where you get your research idea, your next step is to phrase it as a **hypothesis**. A hypothesis is a testable explanation for a phenomenon. For example, a hypothesis may answer the question of how or why. A hypothesis may state how variables are related or may provide a reason for why the variables are related. For example, you may hypothesize that police officers make better eyewitnesses than laypeople because of their police training. It is critical that hypotheses have clearly defined concepts in order to make testing possible.

When we define concepts, we are providing **operational definitions** of these concepts. An operational definition defines a concept in terms of the operations used to

BOX 2.1 A PERSONAL, INTERPERSONAL, AND COMMUNITY-REINFORCEMENT PERSPECTIVE ON CRIMINAL CONDUCT

Developed by Andrews and Bonta (1998), the personal, interpersonal, and community-reinforcement perspective on criminal conduct (PIC-R) considers factors that actively encourage or discourage criminal activity. The PIC-R uses knowledge from biology and the social sciences with an emphasis on behavioural and social learning principles. In particular, the PIC-R rests on the principle that changes in the immediate consequences of behaviour are responsible for the acquisition, maintenance, and modification of behaviour.

Consistent consequences account for consistent behaviour over time and across situations. For example, an individual who has a consistent positive attitude toward criminal behaviour and associates with those who in engage in criminal behaviour may maintain a relatively high likelihood of engaging in criminal behaviour across situations.

Some consequences may become relatively automatic given the nature of some acts (e.g., theft produces property), others are personally mediated (e.g. self-reward or self-gain), and others are interpersonally mediated (e.g., other people may approve or disapprove of the behaviour). In addition, the political economy and social structure of a community or society will produce and maintain certain consequences that may involve personal and interpersonal mediation. Intervention to reduce criminal behaviour is most successful at the level of personal, interpersonal, and community consequences.

The consequences of noncriminal alternative behaviour also are important in changing criminal behaviour. When noncriminal alternative behaviour is highly rewarded, the motivation for engaging in some criminal behaviour may be reduced.

Dr. Don Andrews has conducted extensive research on the PIC-R. To learn more about Dr. Andrews and his research, see Box 2.2 on page 36.

produce and measure it (Shaughnessy et al., 2000). For example, in the above hypothesis for police training, we need to operationally define police training. We may define police training as a specific six-week course all police recruits undergo before becoming an officer. In another example, we may be interested in examining the recidivism (i.e., likelihood of reoffending) rates of sex offenders who undergo treatment. Before we can undertake the study, we need to define what we mean by recidivism and how we will measure it. For example, we may define recidivism as the number of charges an offender receives once released into the community, or perhaps the number of parole violations an offender has. You can see that recidivism is a broad concept that a researcher needs to specify before testing the hypothesis. Moreover, we need to define "undergo treatment." Will we include offenders who complete only part of the treatment program? Will we include offenders who participate in the treatment but who are unmotivated or unwilling to cooperate in treatment? Before we decide on a research design to test our hypothesis, we need to provide operational definitions of the concepts in our hypothesis.

Manipulating and Measuring Variables

For any research study, there will be factors or variables that the researcher is interested in controlling or manipulating to determine their effect on behaviour. The variables that are manipulated or selected to be examined are known as **independent variables**. Returning to our sex offender treatment example, the researcher may be interested in manipulating treatment, thus treatment is the independent variable. For example, the researcher may be interested in whether treatment versus no treatment has an effect on recidivism. Another alternative would be to examine two different types of treatment programs to determine whether one reduces recidivism more so than the other. Thus, treatment is the independent variable.

Independent variables may have various **levels**. Level refers to the variations of a particular independent variable. For example, if we wanted to compare three types of treatment programs, we would say that the independent variable of treatment has three levels. We refer to conditions in which the independent variable is manipulated as *experimental conditions*. The condition in which there is an absence of the independent variable is called the *control condition*.

There are times, however, when the researcher cannot manipulate or assign participants to different independent variables. **Person characteristics**—characteristics that are part of the individual—are of great interest to psychologists, but participants cannot be assigned to them. For example, a researcher may be interested in age, such as whether children differ in their abilities to recall events they have witnessed compared with adults or the elderly. A researcher cannot manipulate age, that is, assign some participants to be children, some participants to be adults, and yet others to be elderly. Another example is of a researcher who is interested in whether shyness affects witnesses' recall ability. Although person characteristics cannot be manipulated in the true sense, the researcher can select these characteristics or variables to research.

The variables we measure to determine the effect the independent variable has on them are known as the **dependent variables**. For example, in our recidivism study, measuring the number of charges following release into the community would be the dependent variable. Dependent variables may include measures of behaviour, ratings made by the participant, and observations of naturally occurring events.

RELIABILITY AND VALIDITY OF MEASURES

In order to reach accurate conclusions about our independent variables, our dependent variables need to be both **reliable** and **valid**. A reliable measure is one that provides a consistent or similar result each time you use the measure. A valid measure is one that measures what it set out to measure. There are several different types of reliability and validity.

Reliability

When measuring variables that are stable, such as intelligence, you want to make sure that you receive the same measurement each time you assess it. If your measurement is reliable, then you can be certain your measure is free from **random error**. Random error is temporary chance fluctuations. For example, if a friend measures your intelligence on Monday and you receive a score of 100, then she measures it again on Wednesday and you receive a score of 200, and then on Friday you receive a score of 50, you know that the measure (or how it was scored) was unreliable. The differences in your intelligence scores varied far more than expected due to your own ability. If your scores were between five points and ten points of each other, we would have greater confidence in the measure (and your friend's scoring ability) being an accurate indication of your intelligence.

SOURCES OF UNRELIABILITY When you choose a measure, you want to know the degree to which it can be influenced by chance fluctuations. There are three sources of unreliability: random observer error, random changes in how the measure was administered, and changes in the participant (Mitchell & Jolley, 1988).

Random Observer Error Random observer error may result from the person scoring or recording the measure. When dependent variables require subjective judgments, random observer error can be particularly problematic. For example, the researcher might ask participants to state all that they remember about the culprit who was witnessed stealing a woman's purse. These eyewitness reports provided by the participants need to be rated for the number of descriptors provided and the accuracy of the

---

BOX 2.2 CANADIAN RESEARCHER PROFILE: DR. DON ANDREWS

As an undergraduate student at Carleton University in the early 1960s, Dr. Don Andrews recalls touring the Kingston Penitentiary and the Kingston Mental Hospital. He hated the prison and remembers saying, "I would rather be a hospital patient than a prison worker!" As fate would have it though, Dr. Andrews completed a summer internship in one of the departments of the Kingston Pen in 1963. He continued working there for two years as a B.A.-level "psychologist" gaining an appreciation for the complex histories of the offenders and the primitiveness of the psychological assessment tools. Dr. Andrews credits these experiences with fuelling his interest in the assessment and treatment of offenders.

After completing a master's degree at Carleton and a Ph.D. at Queen's University, Dr. Andrews took a full-time position as a psychologist at Rideau Correctional Centre and a part-time position at Carleton University. In 1970, Dr. Andrews switched the amount of time he spent at Rideau and Carleton, becoming a full-time faculty member at Carleton University. Dr. Andrews had started on a path of understanding criminal behaviour, how it could be predicted, and how it could be changed that is now almost 35 years old. His book *The Psychology of Criminal Conduct* (co-authored with Dr. Jim Bonta) is in its third edition and is a classic read for anyone interested in the principles of effective correctional treatment. This book has breathed new life into psychological theorizing on criminality. Dr. Andrews has argued convincingly for a paradigm shift in the field of criminology by demonstrating that trait differences among individuals do a better job of explaining criminal conduct than do the more popular theories of class differences.

Undeniably, Dr. Andrews is a pioneer in the development of assessment instruments for offenders that identify key variables that, when targeted in treatment, will lead to behavioural change. Two of Dr. Andrews's instruments that are widely in use are the Level of Service Inventory family of instruments (developed with Drs. Jim Bonta, Robert Hoge, and Stephen Wormith) and the Correctional Program Assessment Inventory (developed with Dr. Paul Gendreau). These instruments facilitate applying the principles of effective treatment that reflects the knowledge base of prediction and treatment.

Dr. Andrews gets excited about the idea of systematic research that approximates true experimental designs. He believes that the results that emerge from these studies can be used for real-world advancements. He also particularly enjoys meta-analysis and its power to reach valid conclusions over individual studies.

Dr. Andrews's research and contribution to the forensic psychology field has been recognized by numerous awards and distinctions. To name just a couple, Dr. Andrews was awarded the Margaret Mead award for Humanitarian Contributions from the International Community Corrections Association and also he holds the Career Contributions award from the Criminal Justice Section of the Canadian Psychological Association.

Dr. Andrews's love for research gets translated into his teaching. He wants students to experience the excitement of serious thought and systematic research. He states that the greatest moments at the university are when students defend their thesis. He is thrilled to see students become active members of the community of researchers, practitioners, and scholars.

Dr. Andrews is an avid filmgoer and a big fan of Brian DePalma films. He also loves music, particularly blues and rockabilly, and travelling. Don't get him on the treadmill though, because he hates it. He prefers to walk outside for exercise.

descriptors. Discrepancies may occur between the people who are asked to rate the reports. These discrepancies are random observer error.

Inter-rater reliability refers to the degree to which different raters give similar ratings to each report. To determine inter-rater reliability, researchers have two or more raters independently (i.e., not knowing how the other rater rated each report) rate the same reports. Researchers then can compare how the different raters rated each report. Each report should be rated similarly by the raters. Discrepancies between the raters would lead to low inter-rater reliability. A correlation coefficient would be calculated to determine the degree of agreement between the ratings (correlation coefficients are discussed later in this chapter).

Random Error in Test Administration Conditions Random changes in the way a measure is administered may also contribute to measurement error. You can reduce error due to test administration by ensuring that the measure is administered the same way every time, a process known as **standardization**. To standardize administration of a measure, you would give each participant the same instructions, use the same testing room, and essentially ensure that all details are the same in the administration for all the participants.

Changes in the Participant There are two types of changes a participant may experience: temporary and permanent. Temporary changes are the changes that threaten a measure's reliability. For example, a participant may be tired on testing day and, as a result, may exert less effort in responding accurately. As such, the measure's reliability is threatened. If the participant undergoes a permanent change, such as maturation, changes observed in the measure are true and do not affect a measure's reliability. Keeping a test short and making sure there are no distractions in the testing room may increase a measure's reliability.

TYPES OF RELIABILITY COEFFICIENTS You can get a sense of a measure's reliability by using a formal technique of calculating a reliability coefficient. The **test-retest coefficient** is one for which you give your participants your measure on two different occasions and calculate the degree to which each participant receives the same score from the two different testing sessions. You would expect that a participant's score would be the same on the same test that was done on different occasions. This type of reliability coefficient may not be ideal if you suspect participants may remember the questions and their answers.

Another option would be to create a parallel or alternative form of the measure so that the questions differ the second time but the construct stays the same. This type of reliability is known as **alternate forms reliability**. The same participants complete both forms and a coefficient is calculated between the two forms. The difficulty with this type of reliability is trying to establish an alternative form that is equivalent to the first one.

Another method for determining a measure's reliability and a technique that does not have the above difficulties is known as **split-half reliability**. Consider a researcher who develops a measure to assess the likelihood that someone will be abusive in an intimate relationship. The researcher comes up with a 20-item measure. To calculate split-half reliability, the items are split in half (e.g., odd-numbered questions versus even-numbered questions). The responses for the two halves are then correlated. The difficulty with this procedure is that the correlation can vary depending on how you decide to split the questionnaire.

The preferred measure of reliability is known as **Cronbach's alpha** (Cronbach, 1951). Reliability of a measure is assessed by correlating the response for each item with each other item. This strategy eliminates the need to decide how to split the test.

Validity

A measure must be reliable if it is to be valid. However, a measure may be reliable but invalid. For example, if we wanted to measure stress and had a reliable measure but that measure was examining depression, our measure would be invalid. How do you demonstrate that your measure is measuring the construct you are interested in?

One method to demonstrate that your measure is assessing what you intend it to assess is by correlating it with other measures that are supposed to measure your intended construct. A high correlation between similar measures suggests that you are tapping into the same construct. More specifically, **convergent validity** refers to the degree that different measures that are intended to measure the same construct produce similar results. The degree of agreement between the two measures tells us the degree to which we are measuring the same construct. The higher the agreement, the greater the convergent validity.

Some might argue that, even though you have demonstrated that your measure correlates with other measures supposedly measuring the same construct, perhaps all the measures are measuring a related but different construct than the one you are interested in. Demonstrating that your measure does not correlate with measures for different but related constructs would strengthen your position. **Divergent validity** refers to the degree that measures purported to assess different constructs do not agree with each other. Measures that tap into different constructs should not be related or correlated with each other.

There are two other types of validity that are particularly relevant to forensic psychology given its applied nature: internal validity and external validity.

Internal validity refers to the degree to which differences in the dependent variable can be attributed to the effect of the independent variable rather than to some other, ambiguous variable. Using our recidivism example, if we find that our treated sex offenders are less likely to reoffend than are the untreated sex offenders, we may not be able to conclude that the treatment program *caused* the decrease in recidivism. It may be that sex offenders in the treatment program are more motivated to comply with social conventions than are sex offenders who do not enter treatment. Or there may be an alternative explanation to why the treated sex offenders had a lower recidivism rate than did the untreated sex offenders. In some forensic psychology studies it is difficult to control variables that may influence the dependent variable but are not the independent variables in the research.

External validity refers to the degree to which we can generalize our results to different populations, settings, and conditions. Often with forensic psychology research, we want to apply our results to the real world. For example, we may be interested in testing a new police interview procedure for witnesses. Rather than use real police officers and witnesses, we use university students. Our goal would be to apply our results to actual police officers who interview actual witnesses. The degree to which we can successfully apply our results represents the degree to which our study has external validity.

BALANCING INTERNAL AND EXTERNAL VALIDITY Typically a trade-off occurs between internal and external validity. High internal validity suggests a great deal of control over the variables of interest. That is, the researcher manipulates the independent variables and controls extraneous variables, possibly through randomizing research participants to conditions (we'll discuss randomization later in the chapter). This control often occurs in the laboratory and allows for cause-and-effect conclusions. Unfortunately, rarely does the researcher want to draw conclusions restricted to a laboratory environment. Rather, the researcher's aim is to generalize the results to the real world. The real world, however, can be quite chaotic and the control exercised in the laboratory does not represent the context in which the conclusions will be applied. Thus, high internal validity reduces external validity or generalizability to the real world. Conversely, studying phenomena in the real world as they occur limits our ability to manipulate variables and exert control over extraneous variables. Although we may be studying the population in the setting in which we want to generalize to, we do not have the control or systematic rigour to establish cause-and-effect relations. Thus, high external validity can reduce internal validity.

CONFOUNDS

A **confound** in a research study occurs when a variable co-varies with an independent variable that the researcher is unaware of. When a study is confounded, it is not possible to determine what caused any observed differences in the dependent variable. If we return to our recidivism example, we can imagine that the sex offenders in our treatment group may be different (e.g., they may have a desire to get better) from the sex offenders who did not receive treatment. So not only does treatment vary between these two groups but so too may other variables. Any differences in our dependent variable of recidivism may be due to treatment or due to some other variable that the groups differed on to start with. We may not be able to reach a valid conclusion regarding the effect of treatment on recidivism.

Random Assignment

Perhaps the strongest method for reducing differences between groups before the independent variable is manipulated is **random assignment** (also known as randomization). With random assignment, each participant starts off with an equal chance of being assigned to any one of the groups or conditions. The researcher uses a random procedure to assign group membership, such as flipping a coin, drawing names out of a hat, or using a random numbers table. If we consider the treatment example above, the researcher could have flipped a coin for each sex offender. If the coin flipped was tails, the offender would be in the treatment group; if the coin flipped was heads, the offender would receive no treatment or would be assigned to an alternative treatment program. Random assignment ensures that any differences between the participants are varied randomly across the groups or conditions before the independent variable is introduced. With random assignment, the researcher is able to reach more definitive conclusions regarding cause-and-effect relationships generally and the effect of treatment on recidivism specifically.

Other Confounds

There are a number of other confounds that also may lead a researcher to erroneous conclusions and that random assignment may not be able to overcome. These include experimenter bias, demand characteristics, and socially desirable responding.

EXPERIMENTER BIAS It is possible for a researcher to influence a participant through subtle cues, thus influencing the outcome of the study. For example, the researcher may be friendlier to one group of participants than to participants in the other group. Participants who interact with a friendlier experimenter may be more inclined to follow instructions or to try to pick up cues that suggest the response the experimenter wants such that the hypothesis is confirmed. The subtle cues that are displayed by the researcher suggesting how a participant should respond lead to **experimenter bias**. To reduce the likelihood of experimenter bias, the researcher can use computers to automate the task, use paper-and-pencil instructions, or make the person administering the treatment blind (i.e., not aware) to the condition the participant is in.

DEMAND CHARACTERISTICS A closely related phenomenon to experimenter bias is known as **demand characteristics**. Demand characteristics are any factors (including experimenter bias) present in the study, other than the independent variables, that suggest to the participant how to respond. For example, a researcher nodding her head for every response made that is consistent with her hypothesis may influence future responding by the participant.

SOCIALLY DESIRABLE RESPONDING Like many people, research participants may be sensitive to how they appear to the researcher, wanting to present themselves in the most positive light possible. When participants are asked embarrassing or sensitive questions, they may respond less than truthfully. For example, asking a participant if he or she ever stole something from a friend is a question that may not receive a truthful response, because if the participant responds "yes," he or she may be viewed as a "bad friend." **Socially desirable responding** occurs when a participant provides responses that make him or her look good rather than providing truthful responses.

TYPES OF RESEARCH METHODOLOGIES

There are a variety of research methods a researcher may employ to test or investigate a hypothesis. These include archival, laboratory, and field research.

Archival Research

Researchers may choose to examine existing records (such as court transcripts or police records) or public archives (such as newspaper articles for the past 20 years) to test a particular hypothesis. Using existing records, databases, or public archives is known as archival research. By using archival data you may access a large amount of data that you would not otherwise be able to collect on your own or in a reasonable time period.

There are, however, a number of disadvantages to using data that have already been collected. Researchers will not know how accurately the information was collected. The information may be unreliable or inconsistent across individuals or groups. Also, the research is limited by the available information. Some information you require to answer your research hypothesis may not be available. Lastly, the information that is collected may be done using measures you would not have chosen. Although archival data provides the researcher with a large quantity of data, the reliability and validity of these data may be in question, which, in turn, limits the researcher's ability to draw cause-and-effect relationships. Although archival research has low internal validity, it may have high external validity and may be used to supplement other more stringent research methods to demonstrate its generalizabilty.

Laboratory Research

One of the most common types of research methods in psychology is laboratory research—research that is conducted in the laboratory, where the researcher has control over the independent variables and extraneous variables. In many laboratory studies the researcher will use random assignment to equate groups before introducing the independent variable, thereby resulting in high internal validity. With this type of methodology, the researcher can make cause-and-effect conclusions. As we discussed earlier in this chapter, high internal validity may result in low external validity. Because the research conducted is very controlled, it can be very artificial and not resemble the real-world conditions the researcher wants to generalize to. Moreover, the typical participants in laboratory research are university undergraduates. Results from university students may differ greatly from the population the researcher hopes to generalize to. For example, compared with a forensic population, university students may be more educated and come from a higher socioeconomic background. These variables may influence the dependent variable.

Field Research

An alternative to studying phenomena in the laboratory is for the researcher to go into the world where the phenomenon actually occurs, known as field research. A study conducted in the field has greater external validity than research conducted in the laboratory. The degree of internal validity present in the field varies with the degree of control the researcher has over random assignment and extraneous variables or influences on participants' behaviour. With a field study, the researcher may or may not be able to introduce independent variables or manipulate variables. The researcher may observe how variables of interest occur naturally and their effect on the dependent variable. In field experiments, researchers may make use of at least one **confederate**. A confederate is someone who is hired by the researcher and is informed to act in a certain way to produce an experimental condition. In eyewitness research, for example, a confederate may pose as a thief. When doing research in the field, the researcher must carefully consider whether those who will act as participants will need to provide informed consent (this issue will be discussed later in the chapter). Moreover, depending on the "field" in which the study will occur, permission may need to be sought in order to conduct the study.

RESEARCH DESIGNS

There are a number of research designs a researcher can choose from. Certain research designs may be more appropriate with certain research methodologies. However, there are no prescribed rules that state which methodology should be used with which research design.

Case Studies

The case study is an in-depth investigation of one participant. This participant is typically followed over a substantial period of time, such as a year. Very detailed notes are kept on the participant's behaviour, experiences, thoughts, and so forth. The case study is typically conducted with clinical research questions. Formal statistics are not applied to the information collected. This design has very low internal and external validity. However, rare phenomena may be studied in depth. This can then provide researchers with direction for specific hypotheses that can be tested with a design having greater internal or external validity.

Correlational Studies

A correlational design involves the investigation of how two or more variables relate to each other in terms of valence (i.e., positive or negative) and strength. For example, we might be interested on how shyness is related to suggestibility. We could give participants a shyness questionnaire to assess their degree of shyness, and we could give them a suggestibility questionnaire to assess their degree to which they acquiesce or agree to various demands by authority figures. We can determine whether high scores on shyness are related to high scores on suggestibility, whether low scores on shyness are related to low scores on suggestibility, or whether information about shyness does not provide us with any information on suggestibility.

The **correlation coefficient** is the statistic used to describe the relation between variables and is a number that can vary from –1.00 to +1.00. A +1.00 correlation coefficient indicates a perfect positive correlation—that is, a high score on one measure is related to a high score on a second measure. A –1.00 correlation coefficient is a perfect negative correlation—that is, a high score on one measure is related to a low score on a second measure. A coefficient of 0 indicates no relation between variables. For example, knowing how a participant scores on the shyness questionnaire provides us with no information on how he or she will score on the suggestibility questionnaire.

Although it is interesting to know how variables relate or co-vary, correlational designs do not allow us to infer cause-and-effect relationships. That is, we cannot say that one variable caused changes in another variable. It is important to note that some other variable not measured may be responsible for the change in both variables.

Experimental Studies

Experimental studies examine the relationship between independent and dependent variables. The distinguishing feature of an experiment is random assignment. Participants are randomly assigned to the various experimental and control conditions. Due to random assignment, an experimental study has high internal validity and may allow us to infer cause-and-effect relationships.

There are a number of variations to the experimental design. For example, a researcher may choose to examine more than one independent or dependent variable. Also, experimental designs can use individuals or groups. Below, we provide examples of experimental designs.

SINGLE-CASE EXPERIMENTAL DESIGN The single-case design has the researcher study one participant. This is similar to the case study; however, that is where the similarity ends. With the single-case design, the researcher first must establish the participant's responding pattern on the dependent variable prior to introducing the independent variable(s). This normal pattern of responding is known as a **baseline** from which responding will be compared following the introduction of the independent variable. The researcher using this design needs to worry about a participant's behaviour changing due to maturation rather than the independent variable(s). That is, the participant may experience a change in behaviour because of development or getting older.

There are variations to this design that help rule out maturation as a confounding variable. One such design is called the reversal design or A-B-A design. The researcher measures the participant's responding at three intervals: before the introduction of the independent variable, after introducing the independent variable, and then once again when the independent variable is removed. Of course, the researcher can add more measurements to this design to produce the A-B-A-B-A-B design, the A-B-A-B-A-B-A-B-A-B-A-B design, and so on.

GROUP DESIGNS The random groups design has the same number of participants in the different levels of the independent variable. Each participant experiences only one level of the independent variable. Participants are randomly assigned to conditions. The logic behind this design is that if the groups are equal (i.e., variation is randomly distributed across conditions) prior to the introduction of the independent variable, any differences observed on the dependent variable must be a result of the independent variable.

Quasi-experimental designs occur when random assignment is not possible. A quasi-experiment typically is conducted when a researcher is interested in person characteristics. Recall that random assignment is not possible with person characteristics, such as age, gender, race, and so on. With quasi-experimental designs, the researcher should make every effort to exert as much control as possible, as with the random groups design. For example, if a person characteristic and a true independent variable are being examined, the researcher can randomly assign participants with the person characteristic to the true independent variable.

The nonequivalent control group design occurs when a comparison is made between treatment and control groups that have been determined on some basis other than random assignment. For example, individuals may be given a set of measures prior to the start of the study targeting the variables the researcher is interested in. If the individuals do not differ on these pretest measures, then differences observed on the dependent variable (i.e., post-test measures) after the introduction of the independent variables may be attributed to the independent variable.

A repeated measures design occurs when participants are repeatedly tested over time to determine the effects of the independent variables. Each participant receives each level of independent variable. This design also is known as a within-subjects design.

Studying Behaviour over Time

There are some specific research designs for the researcher interested in studying developmental issues or how behaviour changes over time.

LONGITUDINAL DESIGN The longitudinal design involves multiple measurements of each participant over time. The time period can be many years. Researchers use the same measures at each time of assessment and examine how the measurements change as the participants age. Using this procedure, researchers can assess how participants change over time. One of the difficulties with employing this design is being able to rule out effects as a result of practice or testing. Also, because the studies continue for several years, participants may drop out, resulting in a small sample that may no longer be representative of the group the researcher hopes to generalize to. Also, this type of research can be extremely time consuming and expensive. However, this design can be very good at understanding developmental issues.

CROSS-SECTIONAL DESIGN An alternative method to longitudinal designs is studying the effects of age with the cross-sectional design. With this design, researchers compare children of different ages at the same point in time. For example, five-year-olds are compared with ten-year-olds. All the participants complete the same measures. The difference between groups is their age. A difficulty with this design is that groups may vary on more than age, such as education level. Another difficulty with this design when it comes to generalizing the results to other groups is known as the **cohort effect**. That is, the effect of belonging to a given generation may be responsible for differences on the dependent variable. It is possible for researchers to assume that differences between age groups is due to aging when, in fact, the difference is due to the groups growing up in different eras and having different backgrounds. However, this design is quite popular for developmental research questions because it is less time consuming and expensive to complete than a longitudinal design.

CROSS-SEQUENTIAL DESIGN The cross-sequential design involves testing two or more age groups at two or more time periods. This design combines aspects of the longitudinal and cross-sectional designs. The cross-sequential design can be cumbersome to conduct and is rarely used.

Meta-Analysis

A meta-analysis is a statistical technique used to combine the results of several studies that use the same independent or dependent variables. The first step to conducting a meta-analysis is to obtain all the studies that will be included in the analysis. The quality of the meta-analysis will depend on the quality (i.e., reliability and validity) of the studies to be combined. For each study, an **effect size** is calculated. An effect size is a measure of the strength of the relation between the independent and dependent variable (Shaughnessy et al., 2000). Effect sizes are combined to reach an overall conclusion about the relationship between the independent and dependent variables.

RESEARCH ETHICS

Once you have decided on your research question and the design you are going to use to test it, you must submit your project to an independent review board to ensure your project meets ethical standards. Researchers must conduct research that is consistent with legislation, regulations, and professional standards. Ethical review boards try to protect the rights and welfare of the individuals who will participate in your study by conducting a risk/benefits analysis. That is, review boards must consider how much risk is posed to participants by taking part in the study versus the benefits to participants and society after the study is completed.

Generally, a risk/benefit ratio considers whether the research is worthy of being conducted. Potential risks are subjectively weighed against potential benefits. In psychological studies, risks include emotional stress, psychological trauma, and social injury (e.g., embarrassment). Minimal risk constitutes a risk level that anyone would encounter in everyday life. More specifically, if participating in the research would likely not cause any greater harm and discomfort than someone would encounter going about his or her daily life, the research is said to have minimal risk. In terms of benefits, the review board (and researcher) must consider what is to be gained for the participant and society in doing the research. Studies involving minimal risk may be approved. However, it is possible to have a study that poses minimal risk but does not have any benefit. Such research probably is not worth doing. Studies that pose greater than minimal risk need to be evaluated carefully to ensure the benefits resulting from the study would outweigh the risks posed.

Informed Consent

Informed consent "is an explicitly expressed willingness to participate in a research project based on clear understanding of the nature of the research, of the consequences of participating (or not participating), and of all factors that might be expected to influence willingness to participate" (Shaughnessy et al., 2000, p. 531). Individuals who participate in research must do so fully aware of what will be required of them and the potential risks (and benefits) they may incur as a result of their participation. Moreover, individuals must be competent to understand the risks (and benefits) of their participation. Furthermore, individuals must not be coerced to participate. Although an individual may agree to participate, at any point, the participant has the right to discontinue his or her participation without penalty. Also, any questions a participant may have should be answered by the researcher. Thus, informed consent requires disclosure and competency, and it must be voluntary.

Individuals must have the study explained to them in a language and at a level they understand. Individuals who are not competent (i.e., cannot understand the nature of the research and the risks and benefits) to make informed decisions may have a substitute decision maker make the decision on their behalf. For example, such would be the case when conducting research with children or people with developmental delays. The parent or guardian must provide consent for the child to participate. When an individual is incapacitated, the legal decision maker must provide consent. It is important to keep in mind that although individuals may not be able to provide informed consent, they may be able to provide **assent** (i.e., agreeableness) to participate. A researcher should seek assent from individuals who are not capable of providing informed consent prior to undertaking the research with them. The researcher should explain to these people as much as possible about what will be asked of them and what will occur.

At times, it may be difficult to determine what might constitute coercion to participate. For example, much research is conducted with university students as participants. Often, a program is in place in which students participate in psychology experiments in exchange for course credit. It is important that students have an alternative to participating in order to receive course credit. The alternative must be of equivalent time and effort as participating in research experiments. Some universities offer students the option of reading a research article and writing a brief summary of it. Offering payment in exchange for participation may or may not be coercive, depending on the amount of payment and the financial circumstances of the participant. For example, offering middle-class adults $10 for their participation may not be coercive. However, offering homeless people $10 may be coercive. If an incentive is offered in exchange for participation, it must not be sufficient to lead to participation when in the absence of such an incentive individuals would not agree to participate.

In a forensic setting, informed consent can be complicated by other relationships potential participants may be engaged in with the researcher. For example, a large portion of clinical forensic research is conducted using an offender population. In these situations, the researcher also may be the offender's clinician who provides therapy to the offender. Furthermore, the clinician may be responsible for assessing the offender, and on that assessment decisions will be made about the offender (e.g., whether the offender should be paroled). These multiple relationships bring into question whether these offenders are truly free to decline participation. For example, the offender may feel he or she will not receive adequate therapy or that therapy will end if he or she does not agree to be a research participant. Also, the offender may feel that the researcher/clinician will provide negative assessments and recommendations if the offender does not participate. When multiple roles exist, the researcher has an additional requirement to eliminate or decrease the possible perceived coercion. For example, the researcher may not ask individuals already involved in one type of relationship with him or her to participate in the research, or the researcher may have an independent person seek informed consent and conduct the research (e.g., a research collaborator).

For some types of research questions, the researcher may want to observe individuals in a public setting. The need for informed consent in these situations is less clear. Regardless, great consideration must be given to an individual's right to privacy. **Privacy** is the notion of an individual's right to decide how information about him or her is communicated to others, if at all (Shaughnessy et al., 2000).

Researchers must keep all data confidential such that a link cannot be made between the data and the person whom the data refers to by outside individuals (i.e., individuals other than the researchers).

Use of Deception

For some types of research, it is not possible to fully disclose to the participant the nature of the research because this knowledge would invalidate the results. In other situations, the researchers may use a cover story to conceal the true nature of the research. Both of these circumstances are deceptive and violate a participant's right to disclosure and can be deemed unethical.

The use of deception to persuade individuals to participate is always unethical and should never be used. In addition, not informing participants of known potential risks is unethical and never permitted. In rare instances, a case can be made to use deception in research when the deception is deemed to pose no more than minimal risk. For example, in eyewitness research, if participants knew they were about to view a crime they may pay special attention to the culprit and details of the environment. This additional attention would limit the generalizability of the results to real witnesses, because real witnesses do not know when crime is about to occur. Thus, a researcher may ask individuals to participate in a mock experiment examining word recognition. When the participant shows up for the experiment, he or she meets a confederate who steal's the experimenter's purse. The participant is never in danger nor is something belonging to the participant stolen. Once participants have witnessed the staged crime, they are informed of the cover story and told the true nature of the experiment. Informed consent can be established at this time. Participants may choose not to participate. It is important to note that the deception used must be explained to participants at the end of the study and any harmful effects of the deception must be eliminated.

CLINICAL ASSESSMENT TECHNIQUES FOR RESEARCH PURPOSES

A variety of instruments exist for conducting clinical assessments of participants' behaviour, thoughts, attitudes, and so on. At times the results of these assessments can provide a diagnosis regarding the psychopathology of the respondent. Diagnoses are determined based on criteria delineated in the *Diagnostic and Statistical Manual of Mental Disorders* (*DSM-IV*; American Psychiatric Association, 1994). The *DSM-IV* provides a classification system for mental disorders. Mental disorders are divided into types based on criteria and distinguishing features.

The results from clinical assessments can be used for research purposes. Below we list some of the most common categories of instruments used by clinical researchers.

Self-Report

When researchers are interested in what participants are feeling or how they behave, researchers may turn to the participants themselves for answers. Participants may be in the best position to tell researchers how they have been feeling, what they think, or how they behave. Researchers may ask participants to complete self-report scales or checklists.

Researchers may provide a list of symptoms, behaviours, or characteristics to the participant, who must check the items that apply. An alternative to using a dichotomous approach (i.e., an item is either true or false for the participant) is to use a continuous approach in which participants rate how much an item or statement applies to him or her. For example, participants may be asked to rate how often they get angry using a scale from (1) rarely to (5) all the time. See Box 2.3 for an example of a commonly used self-report clinical instrument.

Interview

Interviewing is an assessment strategy whereby the researcher talks to participants to gain information about the nature of the problem, conditions under which it occurs, and possible causes. Interviews may be of either a free-format nature or structured.

FREE-FORMAT INTERVIEWS Researchers may choose to collect data by interviewing participants with a free-format interview. That is, the researcher may have a list of general questions, but the flow of the interview is directed by the participant's

---

BOX 2.3 THE MINNESOTA MULTIPHASIC PERSONALITY INVENTORY-2 (MMPI-2)

The Minnesota Multiphasic Personality Inventory (MMPI) is one of the most often used tests in clinical assessment, particularly when conducting clinical forensic assessments. It provides a profile of people's problems, symptoms, and characteristics (Graham, 1999), and it can be used to screen for personality and psychosocial disorders.

The MMPI was developed by a psychologist and a psychiatrist at the University of Minnesota in 1942. A revised MMPI, the MMPI-2, was released in 1989. There was a subsequent revision of some test items in 2001. The MMPI-2 contains 567 statements. For each statement the respondent indicates whether it is true (i.e., applies to him or her) or false (i.e., does not apply to him or her). The instrument provides information on ten basic personality scales:

1. Hypochondriasis
2. Depression
3. Hysteria
4. Psychopathic Deviate
5. Masculinity–Femininity
6. Paranoia
7. Psychasthenia
8. Schizophrenia
9. Mania
10. Social Introversion–Extroversion

There also are six validity scales that the evaluator/researcher can use to determine whether the respondent's answers are valid. For example, there is a Lie (L) scale that assesses whether the respondent is trying to provide an overly favourable impression of himself or herself. There is also an Infrequency (F) scale that assesses the degree of psychopathology the respondent has.

Once a respondent's answers are analyzed, a profile of that person is generated.

There is also a shortened version of the MMPI-2 test with only 379 items and a version for adolescents.

responses. Questions across participants may vary. Although information collected may contain rich detail, comparisons across participants are difficult to make. Moreover, general conclusions about human behaviour and cause-and-effect relations are not possible with free-format interviews. These types of interviews may be useful to generate hypotheses that can later be tested more systematically.

STRUCTURED INTERVIEWS With a structured interview, the questions are decided before the interview starts and all participants receive the same questions. It also is likely that the structured interview has a branching format whereby follow-up questions are only asked when the participant responds affirmatively (i.e., positively) to a previous question. For example, the researcher may ask if the participant has ever been in a physical fight with a partner. If the participant says yes, then the researcher will inquire further to obtain more information or details (e.g., how frequently such fights occurred). Once again, these follow-up questions are decided upon before the interview starts and everyone who responds affirmatively receives them.

Administering a structured interview typically requires training. Some interviews may require specific educational attainment (e.g., a master's degree or doctorate) before someone can administer them. Responses are scored according to detailed instructions by the researchers who constructed the interview. Structured interviews tend to have higher reliability than free-format interviews because there is less variation in the questioning and there is a coding scheme. Moreover, structured interviews may elicit more information than free-format interviews. Unfortunately, some structured interviews can be very time consuming to administer. Also, the branching system may lead to some missed information because the participant responded negatively to a previous question.

Standardized Tests

A standardized test may be employed by the researcher to assess or measure psychological characteristics of the participants. The critical feature to a standardized test is that the test has been used on a larger number of participants to establish the "average" or **norm** performance. The researcher then can compare the performance of the participants with the performance of this larger normed pool. It is important to ensure that the participants are similar to the participants used to establish the norms. Factors such as gender, ethnicity, and age may all invalidate comparisons.

Projective Tests

Projective tests contain ambiguous pictures for participants to reveal aspects about themselves to the researcher. The assumption underlying projective tests is that participants may be reluctant or unable to express their true thoughts and feelings possibly because of the nature of these thoughts and feelings. The Rorschach test is perhaps the most popular projective test. It consists of ten inkblots that the participant has to interpret. Responses are scored based on such factors as the content (nature of what was seen) and location (portion of the blot participant is responding to). Another popular projective test is the Thematic Appreciation Test (TAT). Here the participant is presented with a series of drawings and is asked to make up a story about what is happening in the drawings.

Observational Assessment

One of the oldest methods to study human behaviour is to simply observe and record what is observed. Observations may be made in the participant's natural environment or situations can be created in the laboratory to simulate real-life environments in which interactions can then occur. Observations can consist of discrete behaviours or interactions between individuals in which a sequence of behaviours are coded. **Reactivity** may occur with this technique that influences validity. Reactivity occurs when an individual changes his or her behaviour because that person is aware of being observed. To reduce reactivity, some researchers choose to have people who are already in the environment record whether certain behaviours have occurred. For example, teachers might be asked to rate children's behaviour (e.g., number of physical assaults) on the playground. An alternative to reducing reactivity is to have the participants become accustomed (habituate) to being observed before starting to code their behaviour.

Inter-rater reliability is very important to establish with this technique, given the difficulty of determining whether a particular behaviour occurred and what behaviours may have preceded or followed that particular behaviour. One factor that has been found to influence reliability is **observer drift** (Hops, Davis, & Longoria, 1995). That is, an observer may change how he or she is coding behaviours over time due to fatigue or boredom, for example.

Psychophysiological Tests

Measures of physiology (i.e., internal body responses) may be of interest to some researchers who are examining anxiety or arousal. Heart rate, blood pressure, and galvanic skin conductance (i.e., perspiration) are physiological measures of the central nervous system. Great advances have been made in regard to psychophysiological measures.

NEUROLOGICAL TESTS Computers provide a variety of sophisticated and tailored techniques to examine the functioning of the nervous system. The electroencephalograph (EEG) and the event-related potential (ERP) are procedures that require placing electrodes on a participant's scalp to record activity of the brain cortex while the participant is processing information. For example, a participant may be presented with a series of emotionally laden slides such as a growling dog or a crying baby. While the participant watches these slides, the researcher records the participant's brain activity.

Brain imaging techniques also allow researchers to examine brain structure and function. For example, computerized tomography (CT scan; also referred to as computerized axial tomography, CAT scan) can make thousands of recordings of slight variations in the density of brain tissue. These recordings are computer processed to produce a photographic image that will reveal structural abnormalities in the brain.

If a researcher is interested in the degree of activity in a certain part of the brain, positron emission tomography (PET) scans can be conducted. With this technique, a small amount of a radioactive substance is injected into the participant's bloodstream. While the participant is engaging in an information-processing task, the amounts of radiation appearing in different parts of the brain are measured. Multiple pictures of the brain are taken and a computer-produced colour picture is created that demonstrates the various levels of activity in the different parts of the brain.

Magnetic resonance imaging (MRI) is a procedure to examine the brain through the use of a large magnet and radio waves to create a magnetic field around the brain. The cells in the brain respond to the radio waves and a three-dimensional image of the brain is created. Functional magnetic resonance imaging (fMRI) uses the same technology as MRI, but it tracks changes in oxygen levels in different parts of the brain. The particular parts of the brain that are required to perform certain tasks receive greater blood flow and thus increased oxygen.

As you can see, the clinical researcher has a number of instruments to choose from when assessing participants. Often several instruments are used in combination for a research protocol.

SUMMARY

1. Someone interested in conducting a research study must first come up with a research question. This question then is phrased into a hypothesis. The concepts in the hypothesis are given operational definitions. A research methodology and design are then chosen and the research is conducted.

2. A reliable measure is one that provides the same result each time the measure is used. There are several types of reliability coefficients to assess a measure's reliability— test-retest, alternate forms, split-half, and Cronbach's alpha. Two key types of validity that are relevant to forensic research are internal and external validity. Internal validity refers to the degree to which differences in the dependent variable can be attributed to the effect of the independent variable rather than to some other ambiguous variable. External validity refers to the degree to which we can generalize research results to different populations, settings, and conditions.

3. Archival research uses existing records, databases, or public archives to investigate research questions. Laboratory research allows the researcher a great deal of

control over independent and extraneous variables, resulting in the ability to determine cause-and-effect relations. Field studies allow the researcher to study phenomena in the natural environment in which they occur.

4. There are several research designs a researcher has to choose from: case studies, correlational studies, and experimental studies. For developmental issues, the researcher may choose from longitudinal, cross-sectional, and cross-sequential studies. The meta-analysis combines several studies using similar independent and dependent variables to reach a conclusion.

5. For informed consent to occur, participants must be made fully aware of what will be required of them and the potential risks and benefits they may incur as a result of their participation. In addition, potential participants must be competent to understand the risks and benefits of their participation. Furthermore, participants must not be coerced to participate.

6. A variety of instruments are available for conducting clinical assessments. They can be categorized into self-report measures, interviews, standardized tests, projective tests, observational/behavioural assessment, and psychophysiological tests.

KEY CONCEPTS

alternate forms reliability	38	effect size	46	person characteristics	35
assent	47	experimenter bias	41	privacy	48
baseline	44	external validity	40	random assignment	40
cohort effect	46	hypothesis	33	random error	36
confederate	43	independent variables	35	reactivity	52
confound	40	informed consent	47	reliable	35
convergent validity	39	internal validity	39	socially desirable	
correlation coefficient	44	inter-rater reliability	38	responding	42
Cronbach's alpha	39	levels	35	split-half reliability	38
demand characteristics	41	norm	51	standardization	38
dependent variables	35	observer drift	52	test-retest coefficient	38
divergent validity	39	operational definition	33	valid	35

DISCUSSION QUESTIONS

1. Your university's Ethics Review Board has decided that deception of any kind will no longer be granted approval. You are interested in studying eyewitness memory. Design a study without the use of deception.

2. Much research is conducted using university students. Can research conducted with this population be used to generalize to an offender population? What types of research questions do you think may be generalizable and what types may not be generalizable to an offender population? Why or why not?

3. Walking by an elementary school playground, you notice a number of children fighting. You wonder where most fights tend to break out on the playground. Describe how you would go about testing this hypothesis. What are the strengths and weaknesses of your chosen methodology?

4. You have been curious about how stress is related to engaging in criminal acts. Not happy with any of the stress scales you found in the library, you decide to develop your own self-report measure. How would you determine the reliability and validity of your new measure? Design a study addressing a forensic issue using your new stress measure.

5. Having listened to music for many years now, you notice that there are a lot of testable questions in the lyrics of the songs you listen to. Identify a testable lyric from one of your favourite songs. What type of methodology and design would you use to test it?

6. You are interested in clinical forensic assessment. Select the types of measures you would use to determine the factors that influence sex offenders to reoffend.

7. You are interested in studying the interactions between prisoners in a federal prison. What type of research method would you use to conduct this study? What sorts of issues would you have to take into account to make sure that what you're observing is how prisoners really interact with one another?

ADDITIONAL INFORMATION

Readings

Aiken, L.R. (2003). *Psychological testing and assessment* (11th edition). Boston, MA: Pearson Education Group.

Andrews, D.A., & Bonta, J. (2003). *The psychology of criminal conduct* (3rd edition). Cincinnati, OH: Anderson Publishing Co.

CHAPTER 3

Police Psychology

- Outline the major steps in developing a valid police selection procedure.

- Describe the various instruments that are used to select police officers.

- Define what is meant by the term *police discretion*.

- List some key decisions in policing that require the use of discretion.

- Outline some of the major sources and consequences of stress in policing.

- Describe various strategies for dealing with police stress.

Officer James Leyton receives a call over his patrol car radio indicating that a domestic dispute has just been reported. According to the report, neighbours heard screaming and what sounded like a gunshot coming from a house. Officer Leyton and his partner arrive at the location and approach the front door of the residence, where they can hear arguing. They knock on the door, which is opened by a young girl. The girl is crying as she tells the officers that her mom and dad are in the kitchen fighting. As Officer Leyton approaches the kitchen, he sees a man and a woman. The man is obviously upset. Based on what Officer Leyton overhears, it appears as though the woman has caught the husband cheating on her and is threatening to divorce him and move away with their child. At this point, the man reaches for a gun on the kitchen counter and tells his wife he will kill her if she ever leaves. The husband points the gun at the wife, but before any shots are fired, Officer Leyton shoots the husband in the chest. Officer Leyton radios for an ambulance and the husband is taken to the hospital where he dies from his injuries.

The scenario described above raises many questions about police officers and the nature of the work they do. For example, we might ask whether Officer Leyton is well suited to deal with this sort of situation (e.g., is he the type of person who can think clearly under pressure?). If he is not, why was he able to successfully graduate from the police academy? Alternatively, we might question whether Officer Leyton made an appropriate choice when he decided to shoot the husband. More specifically, was there anything else he could have done (e.g., use pepper spray on the husband) to de-escalate the situation before he had to use lethal force? Finally, we might be interested in how Officer Leyton will deal with the death of the husband. Will he be able to shrug off the incident and return to his duties or will he require support (e.g., in the form of psychological counselling)? This chapter will provide some of the answers to these questions by examining a number of issues in the area of police psychology, including police selection, police discretion, and police stress.

POLICE SELECTION

Consider the following excerpt from the City of Vancouver Police Department's recruitment Web page:

> The vast majority of police work consists of common tasks…. Duties may entail attending calls to homes where the resident has discovered a break and enter…. As the primary investigator, you will determine whether or not there is sufficient evidence to continue the investigation…. There are many other logs, forms, and reports you will complete after you attend calls … the content must include the relevant facts and be presented in a concise and legible manner…. You will need to exercise strong interpersonal skills to obtain information from suspects, victims and witnesses…. You will learn and memorize portions of the Criminal Code…. You will recognize that maintaining a high fitness level will keep you ready for situations requiring physical force…. You must maintain a clear head, a positive attitude, and a willingness to work hard…. You must be prepared for the unexpected…. You will see persons who have suffered a violent death, or bodies that are decomposed…. You must conduct yourself ethically on and off the job…. If you have a family, they must understand that you will work shifts…. Learning is perpetual, and you will make independent decisions and exercise creativity in many cases. (City of Vancouver Police Department, 2003)

As this excerpt clearly indicates, police work is a complex, demanding, stressful, and potentially dangerous occupation. It requires intelligent, creative, patient, ethical, and hard-working individuals. The job may not be for everyone and, therefore, it is important for all those involved to ensure that the individuals who are accepted for the job have the highest potential for success. The purpose of police selection is to ensure this happens (Ash, Slora, & Britton, 1990). This requires the use of valid **police selection procedures** that allow police agencies to effectively screen out applicants who possess undesirable characteristics or select applicants who possess desirable characteristics (Fabricatore, 1979). These characteristics may relate to a variety of personal features, including (but not limited to) an applicant's physical fitness, cognitive abilities, personality, and performance on various job-related tasks.

A police recruit undergoing physical training

A Brief History of Police Selection

The task of selecting appropriate police officers is not a new one for police agencies, nor is it a new phenomenon in the world of psychology. Indeed, psychologists have been involved in police selection since the early twentieth century. In what is considered one of the earliest examples of police selection, Lewis Terman, in 1917, used the Stanford-Binet intelligence test to assist with police selection in California (Terman, 1917). Terman tested the intelligence of 30 police and firefighter applicants, which led him to recommend a minimum IQ score of 80 for future applicants. Following this, attempts were made to use personality tests to predict police performance in the mid-twentieth century. For example, in the 1940s, police recruits in the Los Angeles Police Department (LAPD) were tested using the Humm-Wadsworth Temperament Scale, which was found to predict job success with a reasonably high level of accuracy (Humm & Humm, 1950). By the mid-1950s, psychological and psychiatric screening procedures of police applicants became a standard part of the selection procedure in several major police forces (Reiser, 1982).

In the 1960s and 1970s, major changes to police selection procedures took place in the United States, primarily as a result of two major events. In 1967, the U.S. president's Commission on Law Enforcement and Administration of Justice recommended that police forces adopt a higher educational requirement for police officers, obviously implying that intelligence is a core characteristic of successful police officers. In 1973, the National Advisory Commission on Criminal Justice Standards and Goals in the United States recommended that police agencies establish formal selection processes, which would include the use of tests to measure the cognitive abilities and personality features of applicants (Ho, 1999). Since that time, police selection has indeed become more formalized, with police forces using a wide range of selection procedures, as indicated in Table 3.1 (Cochrane, Tett, & Vandecreek, 2003).

Although police selection research is not as common in Canada as it is in the United States, many of the same selection procedures are used in both countries. For example, all Canadian police agencies currently conduct background checks of their applicants and require medical exams (Forcese, 1999). In addition, most Canadian police agencies use a range of cognitive ability and personality tests in their selection process, such as the RCMP's Police Aptitude Test or the Alberta Police Cognitive Abilities Test. In general, the same selection procedures are used by police agencies across Canada, although there are some slight differences across provincial and territorial boundaries. For example, while some police agencies, such as the Edmonton Police Service, use polygraph tests for selection purposes, they have been banned by other jusisdictions, including Ontario (Forcese, 1999).

TABLE 3.1 U.S. POLICE AGENCY SELECTION PROCEDURES

Selection Procedure	Percentage of Police Agencies*
Background checks	99.4
Medical exams	98.7
Selection interviews	98.1
Personality tests	91.6
Drug testing	88.4
Physical agility tests	80.0
Polygraph tests	65.8
Recommendation letters	46.5
Cognitive ability tests	46.5

Source: Adapted from Cochrane et al., 2003.

*These data represent responses from 155 U.S. police agencies that responded to a survey sent out by Cochrane et al., 2003.

The Police Selection Process

Regardless of whether a police agency decides to adopt a screening-out approach or a selecting-in approach, the general stages a force must go through to develop a valid selection process are the same (Gowan & Gatewood, 1995). In general terms, there are two separate stages to this process. Stage one is referred to as the job analysis stage. Here, the agency must define the knowledge, skills, and abilities (KSAs) of a "good" police officer. Stage two is referred to as the construction and validation stage. In this stage, the agency must develop an instrument for measuring the extent to which police applicants possess these KSAs. A crucial part of this stage also requires that the agency determine the instrument's validity, or the extent to which the scores on the instrument actually relate to measures of police performance.

CONDUCTING A JOB ANALYSIS As indicated above, a job analysis involves a procedure to identify and define the KSAs that make a good police officer. An organizational psychologist, working in conjunction with a police agency, frequently conducts the job analysis. These psychologists can use a range of techniques for identifying relevant KSAs, including survey methods and observational techniques. At other times, a job analysis can be conducted more informally, simply by asking members of a police agency to list the range of qualities they feel are essential for their job. Each of these approaches has certain advantages and disadvantages. However, for the moment, we will focus on some common problems that emerge when conducting any sort of job analysis in the policing context.

One of the major problems that can be encountered is that the KSAs of a good police officer may not be stable over time, making it difficult to determine what the selection procedures should actually be testing for. For example, Pugh (1985a, 1985b) found that, at two years of service, police officers who were enthusiastic and fit in well were rated as the best officers, while at four years of service, officers who were stable and responsible were given the highest performance ratings. A potential explanation for this problem, and a problem in its own right, is the fact that different types of police officers, or different policing jobs, will be characterized by different KSAs. For example, Ainsworth (1993) draws attention to the fact that the KSAs that describe the ideal street-level police officer will not be the same KSAs that describe the ideal police administrator. Thus, as police officers move up through the ranks into supervisory or administrative positions, it should not be surprising to see relevant KSAs changing along the way.

Another problem with conducting a job analysis is that different individuals may disagree over what KSAs are important. For example, if you were to ask a group of street-level police officers and a group of senior police administrators to define the characteristics of a good police officer, the answers could be quite different (though some similarities might also be expected). To illustrate this point, consider a survey in which Ainsworth (1993) asked police officers to list the qualities they thought were essential for effective policing. Topping their list was a sense of humour. In contrast, this personal quality is rarely, if ever, found to be important when police administrators are asked to list the essential qualities for effective policing. When this is done, the most important KSAs typically relate to cognitive skills (Sanders, 2003).

Despite these problems, there does appear to be some agreement, even across police officers of varying ranks, on what type of person is "right for the job" (Sanders, 2003). For example, regardless of how the job analysis is conducted, the following KSAs are typically viewed as essential: honesty, reliability, sensitivity to others, good communication skills, high motivation, problem-solving skills, and being a team player.

CONSTRUCTING AND VALIDATING SELECTION INSTRUMENTS Before we move on to some specific police selection instruments used by police agencies in Canada and elsewhere, let's briefly review some of the concepts introduced in Chapter 2. Recall that the goals in stage two of the police selection process are (1) to develop a selection instrument for measuring the extent to which police applicants possess relevant KSAs (construction) and (2) to ensure that this instrument relates to measures of police performance (validation). The measure of validation that we are most interested in is referred to as predictive validity, which is our ability to use a selection instrument to predict how applicants will perform in the future. Box 3.1 presents a more thorough discussion of predictive validity.

Researchers have identified a number of major problems with validation research in the area of police selection, the most serious one relating to how we measure the

BOX 3.1 VALIDATION AND POLICE SELECTION

As you saw in Chapter 2, there are many different types of validation measures and each refers to something slightly different. The most common validation measure used in police selection focuses on predictive validity, in which the goal is to determine if there is a relationship between scores obtained from a selection instrument and measures of job performance (Gowan & Gatewood, 1995). In the policing context, predictive validity involves collecting data from police applicants using a selection instrument, such as scores on a test of decision making under stress. Then, the results are compared with a measure of job performance, such as the performance scores provided by supervisors. If the selection data accurately predict job performance, then the selection instrument is said to have predictive validity.

A selection instrument's predictive validity can be determined by calculating validity coefficients, which range from +1.00 to –1.00. These coefficients indicate the strength of the relationship between the scores from a selection instrument and ratings of job performance. If a selection instrument is shown to have a validity coefficient near +1.00, then a very strong positive relationship exists, indicating that, as performance on the selection instrument increases, ratings of job performance also increase (see Figure 3.1). Conversely, if a selection instrument is shown to have a validity coefficient near –1.00, a very strong negative relationship exists: as performance on the selection instrument increases, ratings of job performance decrease (see Figure 3.2). Any value between these two extreme values represents an intermediate level of predictive validity.

FIGURE 3.1

A POSITIVE RELATIONSHIP BETWEEN SCORES ON A SELECTION INSTRUMENT AND JOB PERFORMANCE RATINGS

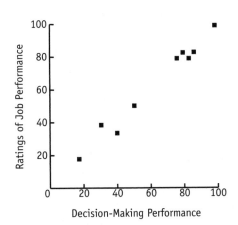

FIGURE 3.2

A NEGATIVE RELATIONSHIP BETWEEN SCORES ON A SELECTION INSTRUMENT AND JOB PERFORMANCE RATINGS

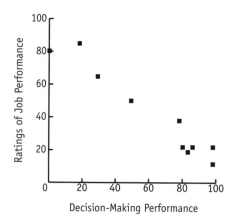

Note that validity coefficients of +1.00 and −1.00 both represent high levels of predictive validity, even if the values are not what we would expect. For example, it seems unlikely that measures of decision-making performance under stress would relate negatively to the job performance of police officers, but if they did, we could still use those measures to predict job performance. We would simply predict that people who make poor decisions under stress make great police officers!

performance of police officers (Hargrave & Hiatt, 1987). This is a crucial issue to address, since it will have a direct impact on the validity of any selection instrument. Unfortunately, no answer currently exists. This is not to say that a variety of performance measures do not exist. Indeed, researchers have used several measures as indicators of job performance, including the number of times an officer is tardy, the number of complaints against an officer, the number of commendations received by an officer, graduation from training academy, academy exam scores, performance ratings by supervisors, performance ratings by peers, and so forth. The problem is that there is no evidence to suggest that one of these measures is any better than another, and even police agencies do not agree on how to define good performance (Falkenberg et al., 1991). Furthermore, research suggests that a different picture of performance can emerge depending on what measure is used. For example, measures of performance during training often do not generalize to on-the-job performance (Kleinman & Gordon, 1986).

The Validity of Police Selection Instruments

Now that we have discussed some of the problems with constructing and validating police selection instruments, we will describe some of the instruments that are currently in use and present some research on their validity. Although some of these instruments might be new to you, there are many others, such as the job application form, that you will be familiar with. We will focus our attention here on three specific selection instruments, including the selection interview, psychological tests, and the assessment centre.

THE SELECTION INTERVIEW The **selection interview** is one of the most common selection instruments used by the police. Typically, selection interviews take the form of a semi-structured interview. In a semi-structured interview, the interviewer has a preset list of questions that are asked of each applicant, thus ensuring a more objective basis for comparing applicants (Gowan & Gatewood, 1995). One of the main goals of the selection interview is to determine the extent to which the applicant possesses the KSAs that have been deemed important in a job analysis. These qualities may differ from agency to agency and, as indicated above, they may depend on the job being applied for. The criteria evaluated by the RCMP's Regular Member Selection Interview include integrity, honesty, interpersonal skills, personal flexibility, thinking skills, leadership, and oral communication (RCMP, 2003).

Surprisingly, given its frequent use as a selection instrument, the results from research that has examined the validity of the interview for police selection are somewhat mixed. Although some research does indicate that selection interviews can be used in a relatively accurate fashion to predict job performance (e.g., Hargrave & Hiatt, 1987), the majority of research suggests that basing police selection decisions on interviews can be potentially problematic (e.g., Doerner, 1997). This finding accords well with general research findings from the field of organizational psychology, in which the selection interview is also found to be a relatively poor predictor of job performance (Ulrich & Trumbo, 1965).

To understand why many police researchers are cautious about using selection interviews, one need only look at the degree to which different interviewers disagree on their ratings of various attributes when interviewing the same applicant. For example, in a recent study Doerner (1997) examined the level of inter-rater reliability between interviewers who were interviewing the same applicant (where a score of +1.00 indicates total agreement between interviewers and a score of −1.00 indicates total disagreement). As illustrated in Table 3.2 on the next page, Doerner found that the majority of inter-rater reliability measures were relatively low. This was the case across a number of different interviewer pairs, who were assessing a range of personal attributes. Indeed, of the 42 comparisons Doerner made, only 14 were found to be statistically significant, and most of these came from only one pair of interviewers. Given such findings, the validity of the interview technique as a method for selecting police officers must be called into question, and it should continue to be used with caution.

TABLE 3.2 MEASURES OF INTER-RATER RELIABILITY

Attribute of Interviewee	Interviewers					
	1 and 2	1 and 3	1 and 4	1 and 5	1 and 6	1 and 7
Appearance	0.55*	0.14	0.58*	−0.25	0.50*	0.18
Self-confidence	0.06	0.30	0.43*	0.55	0.45*	0.63
Self-expression	0.27	0.42	0.27	0.26	0.15	0.69*
Understanding	0.85*	0.03	0.67*	0.46	0.35*	0.47
Comprehension	0.47	0.56	0.24	0.14	0.42*	0.59
Background	0.38	0.72*	0.38*	−0.28	0.26	0.70*
Overall impression	0.45	0.38	0.37*	0.00	0.30	0.52
N (number of interviews)	15	10	22	10	28	10

Source: Adapted from Doerner, 1997.
*Denotes a significant finding.

PSYCHOLOGICAL TESTS In addition to the selection interview, psychological tests are also commonly used by police agencies to select suitable officers (Cochrane et al., 2003). Some of these tests have been developed to measure cognitive abilities, whereas others have been designed to assess an applicant's personality. In addition, some of these tests have been developed with police selection in mind, whereas others have been developed in other contexts, such as the mental health field. As with other selection instruments, there are still many unanswered questions when it comes to the use of psychological tests. However, there seems to be general agreement among police researchers that psychological tests are useful in deciding whether a person possesses certain attributes, and it is believed that this knowledge can be helpful in selecting applicants to become police officers.

Cognitive Ability Tests A wide variety of **cognitive ability tests** are available for police use. Although each test may emphasize something slightly different, they are typically used to measure verbal, mathematical, memory, and reasoning abilities. Such tests are used regularly when selecting police officers in Canada. Indeed, if you were to apply to the RCMP today, part of the selection procedure would require you to take the RCMP Police Aptitude Test (RPAT). The RPAT consists of 114 multiple-choice questions designed to evaluate an applicant's potential aptitude for police work. More specifically, the test measures seven core skills that are considered essential in performing the duties of a police officer: written composition, comprehension, memory, judgment, observation, logic, and computation.

In general, the reliance on cognitive ability tests for police selection purposes is supported by empirical research. However, these tests tend to be better at predicting performance during police academy training compared with future on-the-job performance (Gowan & Gatewood, 1995). For example, Hirsh, Northrop, and Schmidt (1986) conducted a meta-analysis of 40 validation studies involving cognitive ability tests. They found average validity coefficients of 0.36 and 0.13 for predicting training success and on-the-job performance, respectively. One reason why Hirsh and his colleagues suggest they did not get higher scores for on-the-job performance is that personality variables may play a role in determining job success. Thus, it is worthwhile describing some of the personality tests used for police selection and the degree of validity associated with each.

Personality Tests   There are a number of different personality tests used for police selection, but only two of the most commonly used tests will be discussed here. Perhaps the most common test is an assessment instrument known as the **Minnesota Multiphasic Personality Inventory** (MMPI), now in its second version. According to Cochrane and his colleagues (2003), of the 155 U.S. police agencies that responded to their survey, 71.9% of them indicated that the MMPI-2 was the personality test they used most often for selection purposes. Interestingly, the MMPI, originally designed in the 1940s, was not developed for selecting police officers. Neither was the MMPI-2. Rather, this assessment instrument was developed as a general inventory for identifying people with psychopathological problems. Currently, the MMPI-2 consists of 567 true-false questions (17 more than the original version) that attempt to identify psychopathological problems including depression, paranoia, schizophrenia, and others.

The validity of the original MMPI for selection purposes in the policing context has been reviewed extensively. However, there is still little in the way of research on the MMPI-2. Given that the MMPI-2 is generally considered a valid revision of the original MMPI, it seems probable that existing research should be relevant to the MMPI-2 as well. The majority of findings indicate that the MMPI is associated with significant, but moderate, levels of predictive accuracy (Sanders, 2003). For example, studies have reported positive validity coefficients between MMPI scores and several job performance indicators, including performance at the police academy, supervisor ratings of job performance, and the number of disciplinary actions taken against an officer. In part, the moderate levels of predictive validity associated with the MMPI may be due to the fact that it was never developed as a selection instrument. If this is true, it may be that personality tests developed for police selection purposes will be associated with higher levels of predictive validity. In fact, this does appear to be the case, as indicated by studies examining the **Inwald Personality Inventory** (IPI).

Unlike the MMPI, the IPI was developed specifically for the law enforcement community. According to Inwald (1992), the creator of the IPI, the purpose of this selection instrument is to identify police applicants who are most suitable for police work by measuring their personality attributes and behaviour patterns. The instrument consists of 310 true-false questions that measure factors such as stress reactions, interpersonal difficulties, and alcohol and other drug use. According to several researchers, the IPI appears to be more predictive of police officer performance than the MMPI. For example, in one study, Scogin, Schumacher, Gardner, and Chaplin (1995) compared the MMPI, the IPI, and the Shipley Institute of Living Scale (SILS), a brief intellectual screening device, on their ability to predict seven different job performance indicators—supervisor ratings, verbal reprimands, written reprimands, vehicular reprimands, citizen complaints, an overall composite of negative indicators, and an overall composite of positive recognitions.

The participants in the study were 82 trainees at the University of Alabama Law Enforcement Academy. Each participant completed the three selection instruments during the first week of academy training. One year following their graduation from the academy, each participant's police agency was contacted to obtain job performance indicators. The results found that the IPI was a slightly better predictor of on-the-job performance in the one-year follow-up period than both the MMPI and SILS. More specifically, the MMPI and the SILS could accurately predict only one of the seven performance indicators (supervisor ratings). The IPI, on the other hand, was able to predict three of the seven indicators (supervisor ratings, citizen complaints, and the overall composite of negative indicators). In addition, combining the MMPI and IPI scores did not appreciably improve predictive power over that observed with the IPI alone. As the authors of this study indicate, the one-year follow-up used in this study might not have been long enough for sufficient positive and negative on-the-job behaviour to occur. However, the results of this study do provide some preliminary evidence that the IPI performs slightly better than the MMPI under certain conditions.

ASSESSMENT CENTRES The last selection procedure we will discuss is the **assessment centre**, a procedure that is growing in popularity in Europe and North America (Lowry, 1996). An assessment centre is a facility at which the behaviour of police applicants can be observed in a number of different ways by multiple observers (Pynes & Bernardin, 1992). The primary selection instrument used within an assessment centre is the **situational test**, which involves simulations of real-world policing tasks. Trained observers evaluate how applicants perform during these tasks, and the performance appraisals are used for the purpose of selection.

The situational tests used in assessment centres attempt to tap into the KSAs identified as part of a job analysis. For example, the assessment centre evaluated by Pynes and Bernardin (1992) was based on a job analysis that identified eight core skill sets deemed crucial for effective policing: directing others, interpersonal skills, perception, decision making, decisiveness, adaptability, oral communication, and written communication. Based on these skill sets, four assessment exercises were developed, which allowed the applicants to be evaluated across the range of relevant KSAs (see Box 3.2). For example, as is probably clear from the description in Box 3.2, the domestic disturbance exercise requires excellent interpersonal skills in order to excel.

BOX 3.2 SITUATIONAL TESTS USED IN ASSESSMENT CENTRES

◾ *Work simulation exercise*. For the first five minutes of this 60-minute exercise, applicants view videotaped instructions that explain the content of the videos and the procedures they are to follow. The exercise comprises ten video units. Each unit consists of a one-minute animation depicting illegal activity in progress that a police officer might come across while on routine patrol. After each unit is shown, the applicants are given three minutes to answer multiple-choice and true-false questions. Each questionnaire is designed to evaluate the applicant's ability to identify possible law violations, as well as his or her ability to recommend appropriate courses of action consistent with policy.

◾ *Domestic disturbance exercise*. Each applicant is given 15 minutes of this 35-minute exercise to meet with two people involved in a domestic dispute. The applicant is expected to intervene in the dispute as a police officer and resolve it. At the end of the 15 minutes, the applicant is given 20 minutes to complete an incident report.

◾ *Homeowner complaint*. Each applicant is given 15 minutes of this 35-minute exercise to speak to a homeowner who reported an incident of vandalism. At the 10-minute mark, the assessment centre administrator hands the applicant a dispatch bulletin directing the applicant to respond to a high-priority call. The applicant is required to terminate the interaction with the homeowner as quickly as possible to respond to the next call. Responding to this call constitutes the end of the homeowner exercise. The applicant is given 20 minutes to complete an incident report.

◾ *Witness probing exercise*. Each applicant has 20 minutes to interview two people who witnessed an armed robbery in a liquor store. The applicant is then given 20 more minutes to complete an incident report.

Source: Pynes and Bernardin, 1992.

Although there is not a great deal of research examining the validity of assessment centres for police selection, some research does suggest that situational tests have moderate levels of predictive validity. For example, Pynes and Bernardin (1992) examined the scores given to each applicant across the four simulation exercises. These scores were then compared with training academy performance and future on-the-job performance. Training academy performance included scores on written exams as well as on simulation tasks. On-the-job performance was based on rating scales provided by supervisors for judgment, dependability, work initiative, quality of work, appearance, cooperation, knowledge of work, and public contacts. Overall assessment centre performance correlation coefficients were 0.14 and 0.20 for training academy performance and future on-the-job performance, respectively. Each of these validity coefficients was statistically significant.

POLICE DISCRETION

As indicated by job analyses, many of the qualities deemed necessary for success as a police officer have to do with the applicant being adaptable, having common sense, possessing effective decision-making skills, and being a good problem solver (Sanders, 2003). In large part, these qualities are necessary because police officers are required to use discretion in much of their daily work (Walma & West, 2002). **Police discretion** can be defined in numerous ways, but McKenna (2002) has perhaps stated it best:

> Police discretion is the term that represents the critical faculty that individual officers must possess that will allow them to differentiate and discriminate between those circumstances that require absolute adherence to the letter of the law and those occasions when a degree of latitude is justified, based on the officer's knowledge, experience, or instinct. (p. 118)

To appreciate the extent to which the police use discretion, consider the following decisions that need to be made routinely by police officers:

- What street should I patrol tonight?
- Should I stop that vehicle for a traffic violation?
- What level of force is required to achieve my objective?
- Should I run after that suspect or wait for backup?
- Should I call an end to this investigation?
- Should I take this person to a psychiatric hospital or the police station?

The list of scenarios requiring some degree of police discretion is endless and, therefore, police discretion is a topic of major concern to researchers. More specifically, researchers are interested in whether police discretion is really necessary, the sorts of situations in which discretion is used, the factors that influence police decision making in these situations, and ways of controlling the inappropriate use of police discretion. Each of these issues will be examined in this section.

Why Is Police Discretion Necessary?

Although some individuals and interest groups believe that police officers should always enforce the law, police officers clearly do not (and perhaps cannot) do this all the time. Indeed, police officers have great latitude in how they apply the law (McKenna, 2002). But is this discretion necessary? What good are laws if they are only applied under certain conditions? The typical answers that researchers offer for such questions are based on the fact that it is impossible to establish laws that adequately encompass all the possible situations an officer can encounter and, therefore, a degree of discretion is inevitable. For example, Walma and West (2002) argue that:

> No manual or rule book can take into consideration every possible situation a police officer may face in doing his or her daily duties. No supervisor can follow a police officer

around to monitor every decision he or she makes. As a result, police officers are entrusted with the discretion to apply their training and fulfill their duties in the manner they think is best. (p. 165)

In addition to this explanation, there are many other arguments for why police discretion is a necessary part of modern-day policing. For example, Sheehan and Cordner (1989) have provided the following important reasons for police discretion:

- A police officer who attempts to enforce all the laws all the time would be in the police station and in court all the time and, thus, of little use when serious problems arise in the community.
- Legislatures pass some laws that they clearly do not intend to have strictly enforced all the time.
- Legislatures pass some laws that are vague, making it necessary for the police to interpret them and decide when to apply them.
- Most law violations are minor in nature, such as driving slightly over the posted speed limit, and do not require full enforcement of the law.
- Full enforcement of all the laws all the time would alienate the public and undermine support for the police.
- Full enforcement of all the laws all the time would overwhelm the criminal justice system, including the prisons.
- The police have many duties to perform with limited resources. Good judgment must, therefore, be used in establishing enforcement priorities.

However, it should be stressed that by accepting police discretion as an inevitable part of policing, we as a society must be prepared to deal with the consequences. Although the arguments put forward by researchers like Sheehan and Cordner (1989) highlight some obvious advantages of police discretion, there are also potential disadvantages. For police discretion to be advantageous, officers must exercise discretion in a nondiscriminatory manner (Walma & West, 2002), and unfortunately, this does not always happen (see Chapter 4 for a discussion of racial profiling). Despite the fact that all members of Canadian society have their rights protected under the Charter of Rights and Freedoms, the police do, on occasion, use their discretion inappropriately.

Areas Where Police Discretion Is Used

Having now established that there are a variety of reasons for police discretion, it is important that we consider some of the situations in which it is used. As indicated above, there are relatively few decisions that a police officer has to make that do not require at least some degree of discretion. However, there are several domains that are worthy of a more in-depth discussion, including encounters with youths, offenders with mental illnesses, domestic violence, and use-of-force situations.

YOUTH CRIME According to Siegal and Senna (1994), as the "initial gatekeepers" to the juvenile justice system, police officers have a great deal of discretion when dealing with young offenders. Common police responses to youth crime include formal arrests, police cautions, community referrals, and family conferences. Indeed, one study suggests that approximately 30% to 40% of youth crime is handled informally by police officers or through referrals to community services (Office of Juvenile Studies and Delinquency Prevention, 1992).

In Canada, police officers are actively encouraged to use discretion when dealing with youth crime (Department of Justice Canada, 2003). This encouragement appears to be the result of a growing belief that formal sentences are not the most effective response for dealing with many young offenders. Indeed, one common view is that custodial sentences make matters worse, by putting young offenders into a situation in which they are forced to interact and associate with other, often more serious, offenders. Instead, community-based intervention strategies that involve family members, teachers, social workers, and the police are thought to be more useful (Department of Justice Canada, 2003). In addition, to instill values of responsibility and accountability in young offenders, greater attention is now being paid to restorative justice options, in which the youth is made to repay the victim.

A movement toward informal processing of youths is evident in some recent programs established in Canada. For example, the Sparwood Youth Assistance Program, which began in 1995, provides young offenders in Sparwood, B.C., an opportunity to be dealt with outside the formal court system. This intervention program is based in the community and involves the young person's family and the community as a whole. An integral part of the program is the **resolution conference**, in which the offender and his or her family are brought together with the victim and the police in an attempt to come up with a plan to (1) compensate the victim, (2) penalize the youth, (3) provide support to the youth's family, and (4) establish a monitoring scheme to ensure the youth complies with the program (Sparwood Youth Assistance Program, 2004). For our purposes here, one of the most important aspects of the program is that it relies almost entirely on the discretion of the police. Not only is it up to the police to decide whether the program is suitable for the offender, it is also up to them to determine whether the program is working. If, in their view, the program is not having the intended effect, they can use their discretion to pursue a more serious course of action.

OFFENDERS WITH MENTAL ILLNESSES As is the case with young offenders, police officers frequently come into contact with offenders with mental illnesses. According to Teplin (2000), several factors have increased the likelihood of these encounters. Primary among these factors is the recent movement toward de-institutionalizing individuals who have a mental illness. In an attempt to ensure these encounters are dealt with effectively, formal policies are often put in place that specify how police officers should deal with offenders who have mental illnesses. These policies typically instruct police officers to apprehend the individual whenever he or she is a danger to the self or others or is causing some other kind of serious disturbance (Teplin, 2000). However, although these policies provide the police with the legal power to intervene, police officers must still rely on their discretion to choose the most appropriate action.

When police officers encounter a individual with a mental illness who is creating a disturbance, there are three options available to them: (1) they can transport that person to a psychiatric institution of some kind, (2) they can arrest the person and take him or her to jail, or (3) they can resolve the matter informally (Teplin, 2000). Although this decision may not seem difficult, in practice it is. In fact, when faced with such an encounter, police officers have to consider numerous issues beyond these three options. For example, as Teplin (2000, p. 9) states, "emergency hospitalization often is fraught with bureaucratic obstacles and the legal difficulties of obtaining commitment for treatment ... many psychiatric programs will not accept everyone, particularly those considered dangerous, those who also have substance abuse disorders, or those with numerous previous hospitalizations." As a result, police officers may be forced to take actions that are not in the best interest of the offender, such as taking the individual to jail.

Unfortunately, research indicates that this is often what happens. For example, Bittner (1967) found that, when police officers encounter offenders with mental illnesses, psychiatric referrals are made only in the absence of other alternatives. More recently, Teplin (1986) reported a similar finding. In her study, police officers typically resolved encounters with offenders who had a mental illness in an informal fashion (72% of cases), with arrests and emergency hospitalization occurring much less frequently (16% and 12% of cases, respectively).

The fact that police officers respond in this way to offenders with mental illnesses can result in these offenders and their behaviour becoming criminalized (Teplin, 1984). In other words, individuals who would have typically been treated within the mental health system are now dealt with by the criminal justice system. This criminalization process appears to be at work in a study reported by Teplin (2000), which involved 506 police–offender encounters, 147 of which resulted in an arrest. As you can see from Table 3.3, the probability of being arrested if you are an offender in

TABLE 3.3 MENTAL ILLNESS AND THE LIKELIHOOD OF BEING ARRESTED

| | | Presence of a Mental Illness | | |
		No	Yes	Total
	No	343 (72%)	16 (53%)	359 (71%)
Arrest	**Yes**	133 (28%)	14 (47%)	147 (29%)
	Total	476 (94%)	30 (6%)	506 (100%)

Source: Adapted from Teplin, 2000.

Teplin's study is much greater for suspects exhibiting signs of mental illness compared with other individuals. More specifically, 14 of the 30 suspects with a mental illness (47%) in this study were arrested, compared with only 133 of the 476 other suspects (28%). These figures raise many difficult questions. For example, do these figures reflect the discriminatory use of discretion on the part of the police or do they reflect the fact that mentally ill offenders commit more serious crimes? Alternatively, could it be that these figures simply reflect the fact that the hands of the police are often tied, with arrests being one of the few options available to ensure that individuals with mental illnesses remain free from harm? To know what these figures actually mean, more systematic research clearly needs to be conducted.

DOMESTIC VIOLENCE Another area in which police officers have a great deal of discretion is in their response to domestic disputes. Historically, domestic violence by a man against his wife was often ignored by the police. However, in the 1960s and 1970s people became more aware of victim needs in domestic violence situations, and numerous individuals and interest groups began pushing for a more aggressive policy of arrest (Melton, 1999).

According to Melton (1999), this push was helped along by a number of factors. First, several lawsuits were successfully brought against U.S. police departments that had failed to arrest offenders of domestic violence. Second, domestic violence research began being conducted, with some of this research suggesting that arrests had a deterrent effect on offenders of domestic violence. Eventually, pro-arrest policies were put in place in many police agencies, both in Canada and in the United States, and new government legislation was enacted. An example of such legislation in Canada is B.C.'s Violence Against Women in Relationships Policy (British Columbia Ministry of Attorney General, 2000), which attempts to ensure a strong criminal justice response to domestic violence.

However, even with new policies and legislation in place, there are still a range of responses available to police officers when faced with domestic disputes. As a result, the police must still use their discretion to decide on the best course of action. For example, Melton (1999) indicates that arrest rates range from 12% to 40% of all cases of domestic violence seen by the police, with other responses being used in the remainder of cases. These other options regularly include mediation (e.g., talking to the victim), community referrals (e.g., recommending the couple seek professional help), and separation (e.g., asking one of the participants to leave). Indeed, some studies indicate that separation is used as an intervention strategy as often as arrests are used, if not more often. In addition, Melton (1999) argues that, in many domestic violence cases, the police still decide to do nothing at all.

USE-OF-FORCE SITUATIONS Perhaps the topic that has received the most attention when it comes to police discretion is the use of force, particularly lethal force, by the police. Highly publicized cases of police use of force, such as the 1991 Rodney King incident in the United States, have done much to fuel this debate. Police officers are granted the right to use force—in fact, they are required to use force—to protect the general public and themselves (Walma & West, 2002). However, police officers can only use force that is necessary to suppress a situation, and only to the extent that is necessary to accomplish this goal. When a police officer uses force for any other purpose, or in excess of what is needed, that officer has made inappropriate use of his or her discretionary power. When this happens, the result can be deadly. It can also be very costly for the police, who may have to deal with potential lawsuits.

In Canada, the authority to use force is laid out in our Criminal Code (Walma & West, 2002). For example, Section 25 of the Criminal Code states that "Every one who is required by law to do anything in the administration of enforcement of the law ... is, if he acts on reasonable grounds, justified in doing what he is required or authorized to do and in using as much force as is necessary for that purpose." However, problems arise in use-of-force situations due to the ambiguity of terms such as "reasonable grounds" and "as is necessary." Indeed, there are many examples in which people disagree on these terms, which is what often leads to lawsuits. When this happens, we must turn to our judicial system to resolve the problem. In many cases, the court will decide that the force used by the police was inappropriate (as in the case described in Box 3.3 on the next page). This could be because the use of force was viewed as unnecessary, in excess of what was needed, or based on factors that should not have been taken into account, such as the race of the suspect. In other cases, the courts find police use of force appropriate and justifiable.

Fortunately, police use of force is a relatively rare phenomenon. As MacDonald, Manz, Alpert, and Dunham (2003) state, "Whether measured by use-of-force reports, citizen complaints, victim surveys, or observational methods, the data consistently indicate that only a small percentage of police–public interactions involve use of force" (p. 120). For example, the Police Public Contact Survey developed by the U.S. Bureau of Justice Statistics found that only 1% of people who come into contact with the police either experience force first-hand or are threatened by the use of force (U.S. Bureau of Justice Statistics, 2001). Furthermore, when the police do decide to use force, it is often the minimal amount of force necessary (Adams, 1999), and it is typically in response to a resistant suspect (Alpert & Dunham, 1999).

Factors That Influence Police Discretion

Much research in the area of police discretion has focused on identifying factors that influence police decision making, particularly the decision to make arrests. A number of factors have now been identified as having a reasonably consistent impact. For example, according to Walker and Katz (2001), a police officer is more likely to make an arrest in the following situations:

- The crime is more serious, such as an indictable offence rather than a summary offence.
- The evidence is strong, as when eyewitnesses are available.

BOX 3.3 THE CASE OF *ERNST V. QUINONEZ*

In *Ernst v. Quinonez et al.* (2003) the court examined the methods used by the defendants to arrest the plaintiff, Edward Ernst. The plaintiff and his friend, Jason Steves, drove up to Niagara Falls, Ontario, from their home in Buffalo, New York. After leaving a nightclub, the pair decided to drive Steves's vehicle up and down a street that was known to be a popular tourist area. While stopped at a red light, Steves proceeded to squeal his tires. A nearby police officer observed the incident, approached the vehicle, and asked Steves for his licence and registration. Steves retrieved some papers from his vehicle but could not locate the requested documentation. Noticing that the appropriate documentation was in Steves's hand, the police officer reached into the vehicle to take it. At this time, Steves put his car into gear and began to drive away with the police officer still halfway in his car. The officer yelled for Steves to stop the vehicle, as did the plaintiff. The plaintiff also attempted to reach the brake pedal of the car but was unable to do so. Eventually, the vehicle stopped and the police officer pulled Steves out of his car.

At this time, an unidentified uniformed officer approached the plaintiff, ordered him out of the vehicle, handcuffed him, and informed him he was under arrest. While the plaintiff was handcuffed, the unidentified officer knelt on the plaintiff's shoulder and neck to prevent him from moving. At this time, one of the defendants pulled the plaintiff from the ground and wrapped his arm around the plaintiff's neck to drag him to the hood of the vehicle. While the plaintiff was being dragged, another of the defendants punched Ernst in the stomach numerous times. According to videotape of the incident captured by an onlooker, the plaintiff did not show any sign of resisting the police officers.

Among the plaintiff's allegations was that the defendants assaulted him. All of the defendants were required to describe and justify the actions they took in dealing with the situation. Throughout the hearing, the defendants explained it was their belief they acted reasonably in response to the situation. For example, in responding to why he put his arm around the plaintiff's neck, the defendant who was responsible claimed that, when he lifted the plaintiff off the ground, the plaintiff stiffened his back and was thus being uncooperative. In order to get control of Ernst, the defendant testified that he "grabbed Ernst by the front of the shirt ... he had to reach over Ernst's shoulder in order to do this as [he] was standing slightly behind Ernst" (*Ernst v. Quinonez*, 2003, para. 26). Likewise, another defendant claimed the plaintiff attempted to kick and spit at him and, as a result, he "punched Ernst with a closed fist in the upper chest area once" (para. 31).

Largely by analyzing the videotape of the incident, the judge found that the amount of force used by the defendants on the plaintiff was far more than was necessary. The defendants were convicted for assault and false arrest and imprisonment. The plaintiff was awarded a total of $38 300 in damages.

- The victim asks for an arrest to be made.
- The victim and offender are strangers to each other.
- The suspect is resistant or disrespectful to the officer.

Other factors, such as the race of the victim and offender, and the neighbourhood environment in which the offence took place, are also known to have an impact on arrest decisions (Fyfe, 1981; Smith, Visher, & Davidson, 1984).

Controlling Police Discretion

In an attempt to ensure that police officers exercise their discretion appropriately, a number of organizations have established guidelines that allow police discretion to be controlled. As indicated by Walma and West (2002), the Charter of Rights and Freedoms can, in a sense, be seen as a guideline to control police discretion because it makes clear that all people should be treated fairly and equally. In addition, specific codes of conduct for police officers have been developed that also help control the use of discretion (Walma & West, 2002). For example, in Canada, one section of the Police Services Act states that police officers commit misconduct if they fail to treat or protect a person without discrimination. Another method for controlling police discretion is the enactment of government legislation to deal with a particular problem. As indicated previously, B.C.'s Violence Against Women in Relationships Policy is an example of such legislation.

In this section, we will deal specifically with methods for controlling inappropriate police discretion in use-of-force situations. One reason for focusing on such situations is the public's widespread interest in this area. The other reason is that numerous attempts have been made, in Canada particularly, to develop innovative approaches for controlling the abuse of force by the police. One approach is the development of administrative policies within police agencies, which are specifically meant to control the use of force by police officers. A related approach is the development of models (the most common being the **use-of-force continuum**) to help guide a police officer's decision-making process in use-of-force situations.

DEPARTMENTAL POLICIES Departmental policies for restricting use of force by police officers are not new. Research on the effectiveness of these policies is also not new. For example, Fyfe (1979) examined the impact of use-of-force policies put in place by the New York Police Department (NYPD) in 1972. These policies were meant to decrease the use of lethal force by NYPD officers and Fyfe's study indicated just that. Not only did the frequency of police shooting decrease in New York from 1971 to 1975, but the numbers of officers injured and killed during the same period also decreased. Similar findings have been reported in several other U.S. cities, indicating that departmental policies can effectively restrict the use of inappropriate force (e.g., Geller & Scott, 1992). However, White (2001) draws attention to the fact that restrictive use-of-force policies do not always have the desired impact, and that other factors can minimize their effect. For instance, he has argued that the philosophies of senior police officers can often outweigh departmental polices. As White put it, if the police leadership has a "bust their heads" philosophy, departmental policies will likely not have their intended effect (p. 135).

THE USE-OF-FORCE CONTINUUM Although use-of-force continuums may not be as direct as restrictive departmental policies, they may indirectly control force by ensuring that police officers carefully assess and evaluate potential use-of-force situations when deciding what course of action to take. In the words of Walma and West (2002, p. 67):

> The theory behind the continuum is that, in order to subdue a suspect, the officer must be prepared to use a level of force that is one step higher than that used by the suspect in resisting the officer. There is no need for the officer to move up the continuum of force step by step since it is certainly unlikely that the suspect will do so. Once the suspect displays his or her level of resistance, the officer must react with subduing force. If, however, the officer moves to a level of force that is disproportionate to the force offered by the suspect, the officer is open to the accusation of using excessive force.

Thus, use-of-force continuums control police officer actions in the sense that they encourage them to use only what force is necessary to deal adequately with a situation.

In Canada, a lot of time and energy has been put into developing a national use-of-force model. Recently, the Canadian Association of Chiefs of Police (CACP) has approved such a model, which is described more fully in Box 3.4 (CACP, 2000). It is hoped that this model will have its intended effect of assisting Canadian police officers with their decision making in use-of-force situations and in educating others on the subject.

POLICE STRESS

Many police psychologists, as well as police officers and their families, consider policing to be one of the most stressful occupations (Anshel, 2000). After our discussion of some of the dangerous situations police officers encounter, you will likely come to a similar conclusion yourself. Even if policing is not considered one of the most stressful occupations, we can all probably agree that police officers are exposed to many stressful events. Not only has research demonstrated that this is the case, but research has also indicated that these stressful events can have a negative impact on police officers and their families, as well as the organizations they work for (Brown & Campbell, 1994). In this section, we will discuss some of the sources of police stress and examine the potential consequences. In addition, we will focus on what can be done to prevent and manage police stress.

Sources of Police Stress

As Finn and Tomz (1996) make clear, "different officers are likely to perceive different events as stressful, depending on their individual background, personalities, expectations,

BOX 3.4 THE NATIONAL USE-OF-FORCE MODEL IN CANADA

In order to provide guidelines to police officers with regard to what level of force is reasonable under various circumstances, Canadian police agencies have developed a National Use-of-Force Model (see Figure 3.3). The model represents the process by which a police officer assesses, plans, and responds to use-of-force situations (CACP, 2000, p. 11):

> The assessment process begins in the center of the graphic [in Figure 3.3] with the situation confronting the officer. From there, the assessment process

moves outward and addresses the subject's behaviour and the officer's perception and tactical considerations. Based on the officer's assessment of the conditions represented by these inner circles, the officer selects from the use of force options contained within the model's outer circle. After the officer chooses a response option, the officer must continue to assess, plan and act to determine if his or her actions are appropriate and/or effective or if a new

FIGURE 3.3

THE NATIONAL USE-OF-FORCE MODEL

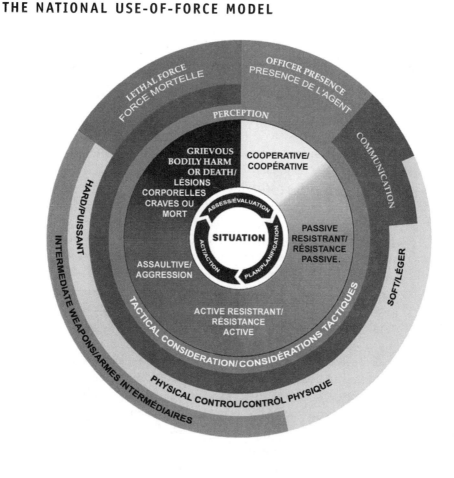

strategy should be selected. The whole process should be seen as dynamic and constantly evolving until the situation is brought under control.

Even with this model, the decisions a police officer has to make when deciding whether to use force are not easy. For example, according to the CACP (2000), a police officer will have to consider, among many other factors, whether the incident is occurring in a public place, whether there is enough light to assess the situation properly, whether the location poses a risk to him or her or the subject, whether the subject is alone, whether the subject is intoxicated, and so on. This must occur at the same time the officer is considering the subject's behav-

iour and the officer's own ability to deal with the situation. Based on this assessment, the police officer must then develop a plan that involves selecting what he or she feels to be an appropriate response. As indicated in the outermost ring of the diagram, there are five basic options. Officer presence is the least forceful option, followed by verbal and non-verbal communication, physical control, intermediate weapons, and, finally, use of lethal force. As the CACP (2000) notes, there is an approximate correspondence between the graphic's depiction of a subject's behaviour and the options available to the officer. For example, if a suspect is exhibiting potentially lethal behaviour, it may be necessary for the police officer to use lethal force.

law enforcement experience, years on the job, type of law enforcement work they perform, and access to coping resources" (p. 6). However, research suggests that there are a number of common sources of police stress (Abdollahi, 2002). Although the labelling of these categories may differ depending on what article or book you read, the major sources of police stress tend to include (1) organizational stressors, (2) occupational stressors, (3) criminal justice stressors, and (4) public stressors. Finn and Tomz (1996) have provided a reasonably comprehensive list of specific stressors that fall into each of these categories, a partial listing of which is presented in Table 3.4.

Although the majority of people assume that **occupational stressors** are the most stressful for police officers, officers indicate that they experience a degree of stress for each of the stressors described in Table 3.4. In fact, many police researchers believe they have evidence to show that **organizational stressors** more strongly affect officers than occupational stressors (Finn & Tomz, 1996). Such claims are backed up by anecdotal evidence. For example, according to the wife of an officer who ended up resigning due to stress, "My husband came home more screwed up with department problems than with anything he ever encountered on the streets" (Finn & Tomz, 1996, p. 7).

Surveys of police officers also indicate that, while occupational stressors are clearly some of the most stressful events that an officer will ever experience, organizational stressors can also be stressful, as can stressors related to responses from the criminal justice system and the general public. For example, Violanti and Aron (1994) got 103 full-time police officers to fill out the 60-item Police Stress Survey developed by Spielberger, Westberry, Grier, and Greenfield (1981). More specifically, police officers

TABLE 3.4 SOURCES OF POLICE STRESS

1. **Organizational Stressors**

   ■ *Lack of career development*. In most police agencies, there is little room for advancement, regardless of the performance of the officer.

   ■ *Excessive paperwork*. The need for duplicate forms of every police transaction is often questioned.

2. **Occupational Stressors**

   ■ *Irregular work schedule*. Shift work is disruptive to the personal lives of most police officers.

   ■ *Human suffering*. Officers are constantly exposed to the inequities and brutalities of life.

3. **Criminal Justice Stressors**

   ■ *Ineffectiveness of the corrections system*. Officers are alarmed by the recidivism rate of criminals who seem to be perpetually "on the street" rather than incarcerated.

   ■ *Unfavourable court decisions*. Many court decisions are viewed by officers as unfairly increasing the difficulty of police work.

4. **Public Stressors**

   ■ *Distorted press accounts*. Reports of incidents are often inaccurate and perceived as derogatory by officers, whether or not the inaccuracy is intentional.

   ■ *Ineffectiveness of referral agencies*. The ineffectiveness of social service agencies frustrates officers who views these agencies as their only source of assistance.

Source: Adapted from Finn and Tomz, 1996.

ranked each of the 60 stressors on a scale from 1 to 100, with a score of 1 indicating that the event never caused them stress and a score of 100 indicating that the event caused them very serious stress. For illustrative purposes, the ten highest- and lowest-ranked stressors are provided in Table 3.5 on page 80. As you can see, while the highest-ranked events are occupational stressors (e.g., killing someone in the line of duty), a number of organizational stressors (e.g., inadequate department support) also rank very high.

In addition to the categories of stressors presented in Table 3.4, a number of researchers have proposed that there are certain personality features that police officers can possess that may contribute to their experience of stress. For example, in Abdollahi's (2002) recent review of police stress research, she indicates that there is now enough evidence to suggest that low levels of self-confidence and low levels of optimism are associated with increased stress levels among police officers. Furthermore, she suggests that high levels of cynicism, authoritarianism, and type-A personality features are also associated with increased stress.

TABLE 3.5 THE TEN HIGHEST- AND LOWEST-RANKED POLICE STRESSORS

Highest-Ranked Police Stressors	Lowest-Ranked Police Stressors
Killing someone in the line of duty (79.4)*	Racial conflicts (22.5)
Fellow officer killed (76.7)	Minor physical injuries (23.2)
Physical attack (71.0)	Boredom (23.3)
Battered child (69.2)	Strained nonpolice relations (23.6)
High-speed chases (63.7)	Politics outside department (25.5)
Shift work (61.2)	Demands for high morality (26.1)
Use of force (61.0)	Nonpolice tasks (27.9)
Inadequate department support (60.9)	Promotion or commendation (28.8)
Incompatible partner (60.4)	Promotion competition (29.5)
Accident in patrol car (59.9)	Public apathy (29.5)

Source: Adapted from Violanti and Aron, 1994.
*Numbers in brackets are means out of 100.

Consequences of Police Stress

When a police officer experiences a potentially life-threatening situation, the acute stress reactions that the officer experiences can have serious repercussions that last long after the actual event. Likewise, constant exposure to other police stressors, particularly organizational stressors, can affect police officers on a more chronic basis (McCraty et al., 1999). Without an effective prevention or management strategy (at both the individual and the organizational level) to deal with police stressors, police officers, their families, and the organizations they work for will suffer in numerous ways. The consequences of police stress have been categorized by Brown and Campbell (1994) into physical health problems, psychological and personal problems, and job performance problems. See Table 3.6 for a summary of possible consequences of police stress that fall into each of these categories.

PHYSICAL HEALTH PROBLEMS One of the major consequences of police stress is the impact it can have on an officer's physical health. As McCraty et al. (1999) explain, constant exposure to acutely stressful events can result in the chronic activation of the body's stress response systems to a point where physiological breakdown occurs. The result of such a breakdown can take many different forms. For example, research by Franke, Collins, and Hinz (1998) has suggested that police officers are more than twice

TABLE 3.6 POSSIBLE CONSEQUENCES OF POLICE STRESS

Physical Health Problems	Psychological and Personal Problems	Job Performance Problems
High blood pressure	Depression and anxiety	Low morale
Cardiovascular disease	Aggression	Tardiness
High cholesterol	Post-traumatic stress disorder	Absenteeism
Stomach ulcers	Drug and alcohol abuse	Early retirement
Respiratory problems	Suicide	Reduced productivity
Skin problems	Domestic violence	Reduced efficiency
Weight gain	Separation and divorce	Citizen complaints
Diabetes	Extramarital affairs	Turnover
Death	Burnout	Hostile interactions

Source: Adapted from Brown and Campbell, 1994.

as likely as people in other occupations to develop cardiovascular disease. In addition, Kroes, Margolis, and Hurrell (1974) reported that more than 32% of the police officers they examined experienced digestive disorders, which is significantly higher than the prevalence rate in the civilian population. Finally, in a large-scale study of 2376 police officers, Violanti, Vena, and Marshall (1986) found that rates of death due to cancer were significantly higher among police officers than among the general population. However, the limited amount of research in the area makes it difficult to determine how many of these health problems are due the stressful events police officers are exposed to and how many of them are due to the lifestyle habits adopted by police officers (Abdollahi, 2002).

PSYCHOLOGICAL AND PERSONAL PROBLEMS Psychological and personal problems, including depression, post-traumatic stress disorder, drug and alcohol abuse, marital problems, and suicide, can also emerge when police officers are exposed to stressful situations. It should be noted, however, that, as in the case of physical health problems, the research in this area can often be contradictory and, therefore, caution must be used when interpreting the results of any single study. For example, although numerous studies have suggested that alcohol use may be particularly problematic among police officers (e.g., Violanti, Marshall, & Howe, 1985), Alexander, Innes, Irving, Sinclair, and Walker (1991) found that alcohol consumption by police officers was not statistically greater than consumption rates found for firefighters, prison officers, or nurses. Similarly, although some researchers have found indications of burnout among police officers (e.g., Anson & Bloom, 1988), other researchers have failed to find significant levels of burnout. Of particular interest is the work of Dr. Robert Loo, who has failed to find indications of serious police burnout among Canadian police managers (Loo, 1994). See Box 3.5 for a profile of Dr. Loo.

BOX 3.5 CANADIAN RESEARCHER PROFILE: DR. ROBERT LOO

Dr. Robert (Bob) Loo is a professor of human resource management and organizational studies at the University of Lethbridge in Alberta. Before joining the University of Lethbridge in 1989, Dr. Loo had an active managerial career dating back to the 1960s. For example, Dr. Loo has acted as program evaluation manager in the Public Service Commission of Canada, he was the manager of the Officer Selection Research Program in the Canadian Forces, and he was a project manager and research scientist in the Systems Division at Bell-Northern Research. Of particular interest here is the fact that Dr. Loo served as the first manager of Psychological Services in the RCMP from 1982 to 1987. Dr. Loo's roles in this position were many and varied. For example, he was responsible for staffing the psychology positions being used to deliver psychological services to RCMP officers, for evaluating these psychological services, and for coordinating psychological services within special duty areas, such as the undercover drug program.

Although many of Dr. Loo's current research interests focus more generally on management issues (e.g., health-care management), he still actively conducts research on various topics related to police psychology. His research interests in this area include post-shooting police stress, police suicide, the use of drugs by the police, women in policing, and psychological aspects of police selection. One of Dr. Loo's most recent studies is an impressive meta-analysis of police suicide rates (Loo, 2003). By summarizing suicide data from many different countries over an extended period of time, he was able to show a variety of interesting patterns in the data that had remained largely hidden until his study. For example, in contrast to popular thinking, the results from his meta-analysis indicate that suicide rates for police in North America are not significantly different from the suicide rates found in comparable male populations.

For the past three years, *Maclean's* magazine has identified Dr. Loo as one of the most popular professors at the University of Lethbridge. Unfortunately for his students, Dr. Loo will soon be retiring from teaching and research to pursue his other interests, such as hiking and snowshoeing in the Rockies. His retirement will also allow Dr. Loo to be more active in human rights through his involvement with Amnesty International and Anti-Slavery International.

JOB PERFORMANCE PROBLEMS Job performance problems are the third major category of stress consequences. Often as a direct result of the physical and psychological problems discussed above, the way a police officer performs on the job can suffer greatly. As with other stress reactions, impaired job performance can take many forms, including a decrease in work efficiency and productivity, increased absenteeism and tardiness, and early retirement. Although these consequences may not seem as serious as the physical and psychological problems caused by police stress, from an organizational perspective they certainly are significant. For example, consider the problem of absenteeism due to illness. According to one newspaper article from the late 1980s, it was estimated that each year in England and Wales, the police service lost approximately 1.6 million working days through sickness, some of which can undoubtedly be attributed to stress (*The Guardian*, October 28, 1988). Similar statistics are unavailable in Canada, but if they come even close to this figure, job performance problems due to stress certainly require attention.

Preventing and Managing Police Stress

Most police officers and police agencies have now recognized the need to prevent and manage negative reactions to stressful events. Indeed, over the last 10 or 20 years, formal stress programs have been set up in most agencies to combat the effects of police stress. A variety of strategies are included in these programs, including informal support networks, physical fitness programs, professional counselling services, family assistance programs, and special assessments following exposure to critical events such as shootings or accidents (Brown & Campbell, 1994). A thorough discussion of each of these strategies is beyond the scope of this chapter, but such a discussion can be found in Brown and Campbell (1994). Here, we will simply focus on one particular strategy—training police officers to use effective coping strategies.

THE IMPACT OF EFFECTIVE COPING STRATEGIES Police stress is not only a result of being exposed to stressful events. It is also a result of the poor coping skills that some police officers use when faced with these events (Anshel, 2000). Many coping strategies are maladaptive and can lead to further, more serious problems for the police officer. For example, in a study of Canadian police officers, Burke (1993) found that officers who coped with stress by using alcohol, other drugs, anger, or withdrawal were more likely to suffer from health problems and further stress than were officers who used more adaptive coping strategies. Thus, one potential method for preventing and managing stress at the level of the individual police officer is to teach officers how to use adaptive coping strategies. As Anshel (2000) points out, this may be a particularly useful approach, because "although police officers often cannot control the sources of job-related stress, their effective use of coping strategies following unpleasant events is controllable" (p. 377). Furthermore, this intervention has been shown to have a significant and positive impact, not only on the health and general well-being of police officers, but also on how they deal with stressful events in the future (McCraty et al., 1999).

To appreciate the kind of impact that such an intervention program can have, we will focus on a study by McCraty and his colleagues (1999). This study was designed to examine the potential impact of teaching police officers **adaptive coping skills**. To carry out their study, McCraty and his colleagues recruited 65 participants from seven police agencies in California, and these participants were randomly split into two groups—an experimental (i.e., trained) group and a control (i.e., untrained) group. The entire

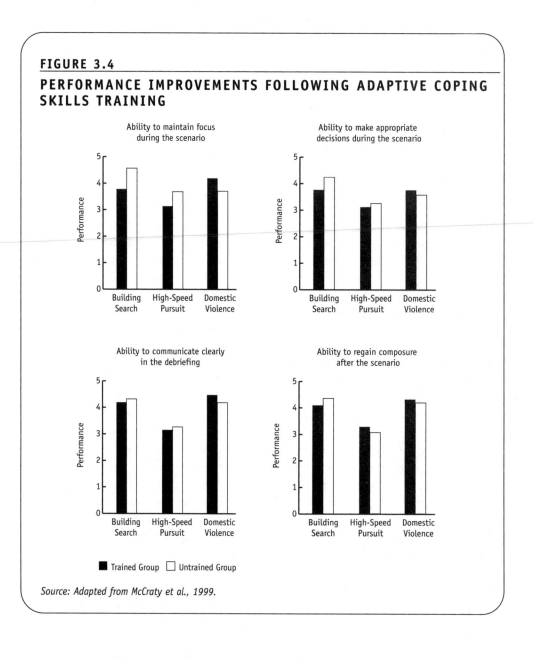

FIGURE 3.4

PERFORMANCE IMPROVEMENTS FOLLOWING ADAPTIVE COPING SKILLS TRAINING

Source: Adapted from McCraty et al., 1999.

study took place over a 16-week period. Various measures of stress were collected at the start of the study, at the five-week point during a set of simulated scenarios (including a building search scenario and a high-speed pursuit scenario), and at the 16-week point during another simulated scenario (a domestic dispute scenario). Measures of performance were also collected for every participant during each of the scenarios. The experimental group received training between week 5 and week 16 on how to use adaptive coping skills, while the control group received no such training.

The training provided to the experimental group between week 5 and week 16 was part of the HeartMath stress management program (McCraty et al., 1999). This program includes numerous techniques for recognizing and reducing stress. Some of the training teaches police officers how to use general stress-relieving techniques. For example, they are taught how to communicate with others more effectively, because ineffective communication is a primary cause of stress. Other techniques are more specific, such as Freeze-Frame[®], which is a technique in which officers are taught to "consciously disengage from negative mental and emotional reactions as they occur by shifting their attention to the area of the heart, then self-generating a positive or neutral feeling" (p. 6).

The results from this study indicate that teaching police officers how to use adaptive coping skills improves their performance on job-related tasks. For example, with regard to post-training performance during the 16th week domestic violence scenario, Figure 3.4 indicates that participants in the trained group scored higher than the untrained group on all performance measures (McCraty et al., 1999). The results also indicate that the use of adaptive coping skills has a more general impact on the well-being of officers. For example, participants in the trained group exhibited considerable reduction over time across a range of stress symptoms, including anger, distress, depression, sadness, and fatigue, while showing significant improvements in peacefulness and vitality. Likewise, the trained group reported fewer problems over time with sleeplessness, anxiety, and indigestion. Findings such as these strongly support the use of training programs like this one for reducing general stress reactions in police officers and for increasing their ability to perform well under pressure.

SUMMARY

1. The development of a useful police selection process requires two major steps: (1) an analysis of the knowledge, skills, and abilities that are required for the job and (2) the construction and validation of selection instruments that measure these qualities and compare them with job performance.

2. Some of the most common police selection procedures are semi-structured interviews, psychological tests, and the use of assessment centres.

3. Police discretion refers to the power that police officers have to decide which laws apply to a given situation and whether or not to apply them. Many view police discretion as an inevitable part of police work and, so long as it is used in an unbiased manner, police discretion can be very useful.

4. Nearly every decision that a police officer has to make requires some degree of discretion. However, four of the most commonly studied areas of police discretion deal with youth crime, offenders with mental illnesses, domestic violence, and use-of-force situations. A major effort has been made in Canada to develop policies to guide police decision making in each of these areas. One example is the National Use-of-Force Model, which provides guidelines to police officers with regard to what level of force is reasonable under various circumstances.

5. Policing is considered by many to be one of the most stressful occupations. Sources of stress include organizational stressors, occupational stressors, criminal justice stressors, and public stressors. These stressors can lead to serious physical health problems, psychological and personal problems, and job performance problems if they are not dealt with appropriately.

6. In order to combat the negative effects of stress, police forces are developing and using a variety of prevention and management strategies. One strategy that looks particularly promising involves teaching police officers how to use adaptive coping skills when faced with stressful events.

Key Concepts

Discussion Questions

1. What qualities do you, as a community citizen, feel are the most important characteristics of a good police officer? Do you think these qualities should be considered when police forces select police officers? Why or why not?

2. Given the problems with interviews for selecting good employees, do you think they should be used for police officer selection? Why or why not?

3. Police officers have rated sense of humour as an important characteristic of an effective police officer. What problems might you encounter when developing a situational test to determine whether police applicants have a good sense of humour?

4. If you were a police officer who encountered a well-dressed woman walking down the street who was obviously intoxicated, what would you do? Would you arrest her and take her to jail, or would you drive her home? What factors would you consider when making your decision? Would your decision have been different if you encountered an older man who was dressed in dirty and ripped clothes? Why or why not?

5. You are a police officer who has just received a call over your radio about a domestic violence situation. You arrive at the scene to find a woman and a man arguing. The woman has a bloody nose and it is clear the man is the one that hit her. The woman pleads with you not to arrest the man, stating that it was her fault she got hit. What would you do?

6. Why do you think organizational stressors are so stressful for police officers?

7. What sorts of things could a police force do, as an organization, to prevent and manage police stress?

ADDITIONAL INFORMATION

Readings

Blau, T.H. (1994). *Psychological services for law enforcement.* New York: John Wiley and Sons.

Brown, J.M., & Campbell, E.A. (1994). *Stress and policing: Sources and strategies.* New York: John Wiley and Sons.

Walma, M.W., & West. L. (2002). *Police powers and procedures.* Toronto, ON: Emond Montgomery Publications Limited.

Web Sites

The RCMP Recruitment Web page
www.rcmp-grc.gc.ca/recruiting/index_e.htm

Police Stress Site
police-stress.com/index.htm

The Psychology of Police Investigations

Mark Jackson was arrested for shooting a man inside a convenience store. Upon his arrest, he was taken to the police station for questioning. Over the course of a 24-hour period, Mark was interrogated on five separate occasions. The last interrogation took place at 2:00 A.M. Although Mark stated he was exhausted, he was told the interrogation would not take long and that it was best to get things over with. In reality, the interrogation lasted for more than three hours.

Initially, Mark maintained that, although he was at the store on the day of the shooting, he had nothing to do with the crime. However, throughout his interrogations the police challenged him, stating they had hard evidence proving he was the killer. This evidence not only included a security video but several eyewitnesses. None of this evidence actually existed. In addition, the police minimized the seriousness of the crime stating that the victim was a known drug dealer who "had it coming" and that Mark "did everyone a favour."

> *Over the course of his interrogations, the police continually pressured Mark to stop denying his involvement in the crime and said that if he told the truth "all of this would end." Finally, during his last interrogation, Mark admitted to the shooting. The case went to court and Mark was convicted, largely on the basis of his confession. Months later it was discovered that he had not committed the crime. Mark Jackson had confessed to a crime he had nothing to do with.*

PSYCHOLOGY AND THE INVESTIGATIVE PROCESS

As seen in Chapter 3, forensic psychology plays an important role in many aspects of police work. One aspect we have yet to discuss, however, is psychology's role in criminal investigations, such as the investigation described above. Many people are aware that psychology is used in criminal investigations and recent movies have done much to promote this fact. However, as you will see throughout this chapter, psychology played an important role in the investigative process long before Hollywood became interested in the topic, and it continues to do so today.

Psychologists have identified a number of key investigative tasks where psychology is particularly relevant. One of these tasks relates to the collection and evaluation of investigative information—information that is often obtained from suspects. Another relates to investigative decision making, especially decisions that require an in-depth understanding of criminal behaviour. This chapter will focus on how psychology contributes to these tasks by looking first at how the police interrogate suspects, and some possible consequences of their interrogation practices, and then by examining the practice of profiling the characteristics of criminals based on the way they commit their crimes.

POLICE INTERROGATIONS

Confession evidence is often viewed as "a prosecutor's most potent weapon" (Kassin, 1997, p. 221). In some countries, people may be convicted solely on the basis of their confession, although in Canada and the United States, a confession usually has to be backed up by some other form of evidence (Gudjonsson, 1992a). Regardless of whether corroborative evidence is required, it is a well-established fact that people who confess to a crime are more likely to be prosecuted and convicted than those who do not. Indeed, some legal scholars have gone so far as to claim that a confession makes other aspects of a trial unnecessary, because "the real trial, for all practical purposes, occurs when the confession is obtained" (McCormick, 1972, p. 316). Given the importance of confession evidence, it should come as no surprise that, although one of the goals of a **police interrogation** is to gain information that furthers the investigation, such as the location of important evidence, the other goal is to obtain a confession from the suspect (Kassin, 1997).

Being interrogated by the police for the purpose of extracting a confession is often considered to be inherently coercive. Imagine yourself being interrogated for the very first time. You would probably be in an environment that is foreign to you, faced with one, possibly two, police officers whom you have never met. You would know little of what the police officers are going to do to you and would have no one to turn to for support. Even if you were innocent of the crime in question, the situation would no doubt be an extremely intimidating one. In large part, this is due to the fact that police interrogators are part of a system that gives them certain powers over the suspect (Gudjonsson, 1992a).

There is no question that police interrogations were coercive in the past. Consider police tactics in the mid-twentieth century, for example, when whipping suspects was a common method used to obtain confessions (e.g., *Brown v. Mississippi*, 1936). Or consider a more recent episode occurring in the 1980s, where New York City police officers jolted a suspect with a stun gun in order to extract a confession (Huff, Rattner, & Sagarin, 1996). Although these overt acts of physical coercion have become much less frequent with time, they have been replaced with more subtle psychologically based interrogation techniques (Leo, 1992), such as lying about evidence, promising lenient treatment, and implying threats to loved ones. Although not all interrogators use these strategies, police officers often view these techniques as a necessary evil in order to obtain confessions from guilty persons. Indeed, leading authorities in the field of interrogation training openly state that, because offenders are so reluctant to confess, they must often be tricked into doing so (Inbau et al., 2001).

The extent to which some police officers use trickery and deceit in their interrogations has recently been made clear by Wakefield and Underwager (1998, p. 428):

> Police freely admit deceiving suspects and lying to induce confessions. Police have fabricated evidence, made false claims about witnesses to a crime, and falsely told suspects whatever they thought would succeed in obtaining a confession. They have lied about the suspect's culpability, assuring him that his behaviour was understandable and not really blameworthy, or telling him that if he described what happened, the victim could be helped. They have falsely told suspects that they had physical evidence such as footprints, fingerprints, or semen, that a co-defendant had confessed, that the weapon used in the crime had been found, that the suspect failed a lie detector, and that there was medical proof of sexual molestation.

Police officers around the world now receive specialized training in exactly how to extract confessions from suspects. Depending on where this training is provided, different approaches are taught. For example, as discussed later in this chapter, police officers in England are trained to use interrogation techniques that are far less coercive than those used in North America (Sear & Williamson, 1999). This is primarily because courts in England have begun to recognize some of the potential problems associated with coercive interrogation practices, such as increasing the likelihood of false confessions (Meissner & Russano, 2003).

Before moving on to discuss these potential problems and exploring some possible ways they can be prevented, let us look closely at the format of police interrogations as they typically take place across North America.

The Reid Model of Interrogation

A police officer interrogating a suspect

The most common interrogation training program offered to U.S. and Canadian police officers is based on a book written by Inbau, Reid, Buckley, and Jayne (2001) called *Criminal Interrogation and Confessions*. Within this manual, the authors describe the now-famous **Reid model** of interrogation, a technique originally developed by John E. Reid, a polygrapher from Chicago, that has been taught to more than 300 000 police investigators since 1974 (Meissner & Russano, 2003).

At a general level, the Reid model consists of a three-part process. The first stage is to gather evidence related to the crime and to interview witnesses and victims. The second stage is to conduct a nonaccusatorial interview of the suspect to assess any evidence of deception (i.e., to determine whether the suspect is guilty or not). The third stage is to conduct an accusatorial interrogation of the suspect (if he or she is perceived to be guilty) in which a nine-step procedure is implemented, with the primary objective being to secure a confession (Inbau et al., 2001).

This nine-step procedure in stage three consists of the following steps:

1. The suspect is immediately confronted with his or her guilt. If the police do not have any evidence against the suspect at this time, this fact can be hidden and, if necessary, the interrogator can pretend that such evidence exists.

2. Psychological themes are then developed that allow the suspect to justify, rationalize, or excuse the crime. For example, a suspected rapist may be told that the victim must have been asking for it.

3. Any statements of denial by the suspect are interrupted by the interrogator to ensure the suspect does not get the upper hand in the interrogation.

4. The interrogator overcomes the suspect's objections to the charges to a point at which the suspect becomes quiet and withdrawn.

5. Once the suspect has become withdrawn, the interrogator ensures that the suspect does not tune out of the interrogation by reducing the psychological distance between the interrogator and the suspect, such as by physically moving closer to the suspect.

6. Sympathy and understanding are then exhibited by the interrogator and the suspect is urged to come clean. For example, the interrogator might try to appeal to the suspect's sense of decency.

7. The suspect is offered face-saving explanations for the crime, which makes self-incrimination easier to achieve.

8. Once the suspect accepts responsibility for the crime (typically by agreeing with one of the face-saving explanations), the interrogator develops this admission into a full confession.

9. Finally, the interrogator gets the suspect to write and sign a full confession.

The Reid model of interrogation is based on the idea that suspects do not confess to crimes they have committed because they fear the potential consequences that await them if they do (Inbau et al., 2001). In addition, their fear of the potential consequences is not sufficiently outweighed by their internal feelings of anxiety associated with remaining deceptive (i.e., by maintaining they did not commit the crime in question). The goal of the Reid model, therefore, is to reverse this state of affairs, by making the "perceived consequences of a confession ... more desirable than the anxiety generated by the deception" (Gudjonsson, 1992a, p. 62). It is assumed that the consequences of confessing and the anxiety of remaining deceptive can be manipulated by the interrogator through the use of psychologically based techniques, such as the ones described above (Jayne, 1986). For example, many believe that providing the suspect with a way to rationalize his or her behaviour can reduce the perceived consequences of confessing. Conversely, focusing on feelings of guilt can increase the anxiety associated with deception.

Police Interrogation Techniques

Techniques used in the Reid model of interrogation can be broken down into two general categories. These categories are often referred to by different names, including friendly and unfriendly techniques, Mutt and Jeff techniques, and minimization and maximization techniques. You will probably know them as good cop/bad cop techniques. Throughout this chapter, the labels minimization and maximization will be used to refer to the categories, since these terms are the most commonly accepted.

Minimization techniques refer to "soft sell" tactics used by police interrogators that are designed to "lull the suspect into a false sense of security" (Kassin, 1997, p. 223). These tactics include the use of sympathy, excuses, and justifications. For example, when the interrogator in the opening scenario suggested to Mark Jackson that the victim "had it coming" because he was a drug dealer, and that Mark "did everyone a favour" by shooting the victim, that interrogator was using minimization techniques. In contrast to minimization techniques, **maximization techniques** refer to "scare tactics" that interrogators often use "to intimidate a suspect believed to be guilty" (Kassin, 1997, p. 223). This intimidation is typically achieved by exaggerating the seriousness of the offence and by making false claims about evidence the police supposedly have.

The use of the nonexistent eyewitnesses in the opening scenario is an example of such a scare tactic.

Kassin and McNall (1991) showed that the use of these techniques might send a message to the suspect that he or she will be treated in a particular way. Specifically, they found that the use of minimization techniques "implies an offer of leniency," while the use of maximization techniques "communicates an implicit threat of punishment" (Kassin, 1997, p. 224). This is an extremely important finding because the courts regularly disregard confession evidence if the confession is obtained using explicit threats (i.e., maximization tactics), but they often accept confession evidence if it is obtained through more implicit means (i.e., minimization tactics) (Kassin, 1997). This happens even though the message being sent by a police officer using minimization tactics might not be so implicit to the suspect.

Potential Problems with the Reid Model of Interrogation

Because the Reid model of interrogation is used so extensively in North America, it has been the subject of much research. This research indicates that a number of potential problems are associated with the technique. Three problems in particular deserve our attention. The first two relate to the ability of investigators to detect deception (Ekman & O'Sullivan, 1991) and to biases that may result when an interrogator believes a suspect is guilty (Kassin, Goldstein, & Savitsky, 2003). The third problem, which has received much more attention from researchers, has to do with the coercive nature of certain interrogation practices and the possibility that these practices will result in false confessions (Ofshe & Leo, 1997). We will discuss the first two problems here and reserve our discussion of false confessions for the next section of this chapter.

DETECTING DECEPTION A more thorough discussion of **deception detection** will be provided in Chapter 5, so our discussion here will be limited to how deception detection relates to police interrogations. The issue of whether investigators are effective deception detectors is an important one, especially when using the Reid model of interrogation, because the actual interrogation of a suspect begins only after an initial interview has allowed the interrogator to determine whether the suspect is guilty (Inbau et al., 2001). The decision to commence a full-blown police interrogation, therefore, relies on an accurate assessment of whether the suspect is being deceptive when he or she claims to be innocent.

As you will see in Chapter 5, there is currently very little research available to suggest that police officers can detect deception with any degree of accuracy (e.g., Ekman & O'Sullivan, 1991). This often appears to be true even after police officers receive specialized training (Köhnken, 1987), but there have been some recent exceptions in Canada (e.g., Porter, Woodworth, & Birt, 2000). As a result, it seems likely that the decision to interrogate a suspect when using the Reid model of interrogation will often be based on an incorrect determination that the suspect is guilty (Kassin et al., 2003).

INVESTIGATOR BIAS The second related problem with the Reid model of interrogation is that the police begin their interrogation believing that the suspect is guilty. The problem here is that when people form a belief about something before they enter a situation, they often unknowingly seek out and interpret information in that situation in a way that verifies their initial belief (Kassin et al., 2003). A recent study by Kassin and his colleagues (2003) demonstrates some of the potential dangers that can result from this particular form of **investigator bias**.

In a mock interrogation study, the researchers had students act as interrogators or suspects. Some of the interrogators were led to believe the suspect was guilty of a mock crime (finding a hidden key and stealing $100 from a locked cabinet), while others were led to believe the suspect was innocent. In reality, some of the suspects were guilty of the mock crime whereas others were innocent. Interrogators were instructed to devise an interrogation strategy to use on the suspects, and the suspects were told to deny any involvement in the crime and to convince the interrogator of their innocence. The interrogation was taped and a group of neutral observers then listened to the tape and were asked questions about the interrogator and the suspect.

A number of important results emerged from this study:

1. Interrogators with guilty expectations asked more questions that indicated their belief in the suspect's guilt. For example, they would ask, "How did you find the key that was hidden behind the VCR?" instead of "Do you know anything about the key that was hidden behind the VCR?"

2. Interrogators with guilty expectations used a higher frequency of interrogation techniques compared with interrogators with innocent expectations, especially at the outset of the interrogation.

3. Interrogators with guilty expectations judged more suspects to be guilty, regardless of whether the suspect was actually guilty.

4. Interrogators indicated that they exerted more pressure on suspects to confess when, unbeknownst to them, the suspect was innocent.

5. Suspects had fairly accurate perceptions of interrogator behaviour (i.e., innocent suspects believed their interrogators were exerting more pressure).

6. Neutral observers viewed interrogators with guilty expectations as more coercive, especially against innocent suspects, and they viewed suspects in the guilty expectation condition as more defensive.

In sum, these findings indicate that "investigative biases led to coercive and pressure-filled interrogations that, in turn, caused suspects to appear more 'defensive' and 'guilty' even when they were not guilty of the crime being investigated" (Meissner & Russano, 2003, p. 57).

Interrogation Practices and the Courts

The decision to admit confession evidence into court rests on the shoulders of the trial judge. Within North America, the key issues a judge must consider when faced with a questionable confession are whether the confession was made voluntarily and whether the defendant was competent when he or she provided the confession (Wakefield & Underwager, 1998). The reason for using these criteria is that involuntary confessions and confessions provided when a person's mind is unstable are more likely to be unreliable.

What is meant by "voluntary" and "competent" is not always clear, which is why debate continues over the issue. What does seem clear, however, is that confessions resulting from overt forms of coercion will not be admitted in court. As Kassin (1997) states, "A confession is typically excluded if it was elicited by brute force; prolonged isolation; deprivation of food or sleep; threats of harm or punishment; promises of immunity or leniency; or, barring exceptional circumstances, without notifying the suspect of his or her constitutional rights" (p. 221).

Conversely, confessions that result from more subtle forms of psychological coercion are regularly admitted into court, both in Canada and the United States. For example, in the recent Canadian case of *R. v. Oickle* (2000), Richard Oickle confessed to seven counts of arson occurring in and around Waterville, Nova Scotia, between 1994 and 1995. On appeal, the Supreme Court of Canada ruled that his confession was properly admitted by the trial judge, and therefore his conviction should stand, despite the use of some questionable interrogation techniques. These interrogation tactics included exaggerating the infallibility of a polygraph exam, implying that psychiatric help would be provided if the defendant confessed, minimizing the seriousness of the crimes, and suggesting that a confession would spare Oickle's girlfriend from having to undergo a stressful interrogation.

So, if these sorts of interrogation practices are condoned by the court, what sorts of practices are not? Box 4.1 on the next page provides a brief account of another recent Canadian case, *R. v. Hoilett* (1999), in which the Ontario Court of Appeals did rule that the defendant's confession was involuntary and therefore should not have been admitted at his trial. This ruling gives some indication as to how far Canadian police officers can go with their coercive interrogation tactics before it is considered too far by the courts.

Recent Changes to Interrogation Procedures

Due to the potential problems that can result from using coercive interrogation tactics, police agencies in several countries have recently introduced changes to their procedures. Perhaps more than anywhere else, these changes have been most obvious in England, where courts have restricted the use of many techniques found in the Reid model of interrogation (Gudjonsson, 1992a).

Over the last 20 years, police agencies in England have gone through several phases of change in an attempt to reduce oppressive interrogation practices. Currently, these agencies use the so-called PEACE model to guide their interrogations (PEACE is an acronym for *planning* and *preparation, engage* and *explain, account, closure, and evaluation*). According to Meissner and Russano (2003), this model provides an inquisitorial framework within which to conduct police interrogations (compared

BOX 4.1 WHEN THE POLICE GO TOO FAR: THE CASE OF *R. V. HOILETT*

Hoilett was arrested for sexual assault in Toronto at 11:25 P.M. on November 28, 1997. At the time of his arrest, Hoilett was under the influence of alcohol and crack cocaine. He was taken to the police station and placed in a cell. At 1:24 A.M. on November 29, police officers came to Hoilett's cell to remove his clothing in order for them to be forensically examined. All of his clothing was taken, including his underwear, shoes, and socks, and he was left naked in his cell with only a metal bed to sit on for one-and-a-half hours.

Shortly before 3:06 A.M., Hoilett was awakened and given some light clothes, but no underwear, and shoes that did not fit. When he asked for a tissue to wipe his nose, the police officers did not provide him with one. Hoilett was then taken from his cell to be interrogated. The interviewing officer was aware that Hoilett had consumed alcohol and crack cocaine that evening but believed the suspect was not impaired during the interrogation, only tired, which was why he kept nodding off. Although Hoilett was detained and under arrest, the interviewing officer testified that "the reason he proceeded with the interview at that hour . . . was because he was not sure he would have another opportunity to do so" (*R. v. Hoilett*, 1999, para. 5).

Hoilett made an incriminating statement to the police at this time, and the trial judge ruled that the statement was made voluntarily and knowingly and therefore it was admis-sible. In his ruling, the trial judge recognized and openly disapproved of the inhumane conduct of the police in this case. However, the judge concluded that the free will of the defendant was not affected by this treatment, and Hoilett was convicted on one count of sexual assault.

On appeal before the Ontario Court of Appeals, the court pointed out that, in reaching his conclusion that Hoilett's confession was voluntary, "the trial judge made no reference to . . . the accused's testimony where he said that his decision to speak was influenced by how cold he was and that he needed a tissue, and that the officers suggested these things could be made available to him after the interrogation" (para. 23). The Court of Appeals went on to state that "virtually everyone would have their . . . will to say no to the police significantly influenced by . . . receiving inhumane treatment . . . " (para. 25).

Referring to whether Hoilett was competent at the time he made his statement, the Court of Appeals added that there was substantial evidence he was not (e.g., Hoilett was awakened and interviewed at 3:00 A.M., he stated he was tired, and on several occasions the interrogators had to ask him whether he was awake).

As a result of their findings, the Ontario Court of Appeals reversed the decision of the trial judge, ruled that the statement of the accused was involuntary, and ordered that a new trial be held.

with the accusatorial framework used in the Reid model) and is based on an interview method known as conversation management that encourages information gathering more so than securing a confession. Although little research has been conducted to examine the impact of this new model, some research indicates that a decrease in the use of coercive interrogation tactics does not necessarily result in a substantial reduction in the number of confessions that can be obtained (Meissner & Russano, 2003).

Although North American police agencies appear more hesitant to modify their interrogation techniques, videotaping interrogations is a growing practice (Kassin, 1997). Indeed, according to Kassin (1997), approximately one third of all large police agencies in the United States videotape at least some interrogations, and 97% of police agencies that have videotaped confessions have found the videotapes useful. In addition, since various court rulings in the mid-1990s (e.g., *R. v. Barrett*, 1993), the videotaping of interrogations by the police has become common practice in Canada. Videotaping police interrogations seems a wise move for a variety of reasons. For example, White (1997) suggests that, by videotaping an interrogation, the police can protect themselves against false allegations of coercive practices, suspects can be assured they will not be subjected to interrogation methods that potentially lead to false confessions, and the courts can make more informed judgments about the appropriateness of police tactics.

FALSE CONFESSIONS

Perhaps the biggest problem that people have with the use of coercive interrogation tactics is that these techniques can contribute to the likelihood of suspects making **false confessions** (Gudjonsson, 1992a). False confessions can be defined in a number of ways. However, Ofshe (1989) provides a definition that appears to be well accepted. He suggests that a confession should be considered false "if it is elicited in response to a demand for a confession and is either intentionally fabricated or is not based on actual knowledge of the facts that form its content" (p. 13). When false confessions do occur, they should be taken seriously, especially considering the weight that juries put on confessions when determining the guilt or innocence of a defendant (Kassin & Sukel, 1997). Research indicates that when people have been wrongfully convicted of a crime, a false confession is often to blame. For example, Scheck, Neufeld, and Dwyer (2000) discovered that, in the 70 cases of wrongful convictions they examined, 21% included confession evidence that was later found to be false.

Before moving on to examine the extent of this problem, it is important to define two additional terms that are often confused with false confessions: **retracted confessions** and **disputed confessions**. As defined by Gudjonsson (1992a), "A retracted confession consists of a suspect or defendant declaring that the self-incriminating admission or confession he made is false . . . . This does not necessarily mean that the confession that the suspect made is false, because guilty people as well as innocent people may retract their confession" (p. 220). Disputed confessions, however, are confessions that are disputed at trial. This does not necessarily mean the confession is false or that it was retracted. Instead, disputed confessions may arise due to legal technicalities, or because the suspect disputes the confession was ever made (Gudjonsson, 1992a).

The Frequency of False Confessions

Most researchers readily admit that no one knows how frequently false confessions are made (e.g., Kassin, 1997). The major problem is that in most cases it is almost impossible to determine whether a confession is actually false. The fact that a confession is coerced does not mean the confession is false, just as a conviction based on confession evidence does not mean the confession is true (Kassin, 1997). As a result of this problem, researchers come up with drastically different estimates of how frequently false confessions occur. Regardless of the exact number, most researchers believe there are enough cases to treat the issue very seriously.

Different Types of False Confessions

One thing researchers do agree on is that there are different types of false confessions. According to Kassin and Wrightsman (1985), these consist of voluntary false confessions, coerced-compliant false confessions, and coerced-internalized false confessions.

VOLUNTARY FALSE CONFESSIONS Voluntary false confessions occur when someone voluntarily confesses to a crime he or she did not commit without any elicitation from the police. Research has indicated that people voluntarily false confess for a variety of reasons. For example, Gudjonsson (1992b) suggests that such confessions may arise out of (1) a morbid desire for notoriety, (2) the person being unable to distinguish fact from fantasy, (3) the need to make up for feelings of guilt by receiving punishment, or (4) a desire to protect somebody else from harm (which may be particularly prevalent among juveniles).

Although it may seem surprising, many highly publicized cases do result in voluntary false confessions. Perhaps the most famous case was the kidnapping and murder of Charles Lindbergh's baby son. (Charles Lindbergh was famous for being the first pilot to fly solo across the Atlantic Ocean in 1927.) On March 1, 1932, Charles Lindbergh Jr., at the age of 20 months, was kidnapped. Two-and-a-half months later, the decomposed body of the baby was found with a fractured skull. It is estimated that some 200 people falsely confessed to the kidnapping and murder (Note, 1953). In the end, only one man was convicted for the crime, a German immigrant named Bruno Richard Hauptman, who was executed for the crime in 1936. However, to this day, questions are still raised about Hauptman's guilt (e.g., Jones, 1997).

COERCED-COMPLIANT FALSE CONFESSIONS Coerced-compliant false confessions are those in which the suspect confesses to a crime, even though the suspect is fully aware he or she did not commit it. This type of false confession is perhaps the most common (Gudjonsson & MacKeith, 1988). Unlike voluntary false confessions, these confessions are caused by the use of coercive interrogation tactics on the part of the police, such as the maximization techniques described earlier. Specifically, coerced-compliant confessions may be given so the suspect can (1) escape further interrogation, (2) gain a promised benefit, or (3) avoid a threatened punishment (Gudjonsson, 1992b).

As with voluntary false confessions, there are a number of reported cases of coerced-compliant false confessions. For example, the 1993 movie *In the Name of the Father* starring Daniel Day Lewis is based on such a case. Gerry Conlon, along with three other Irishmen, falsely confessed to bombing two pubs in Surrey, England, as a result of coercive police interrogations. The coercive tactics included making up false evidence and threatening to harm members of Conlon's family unless he confessed. Conlon and his acquaintances were subsequently convicted and sent to prison but were later released (Gudjonsson, 1992a). Box 4.2 on page 100 provides an example of a recent coerced-compliant false confession that occurred in Canada.

COERCED-INTERNALIZED FALSE CONFESSIONS The third, and perhaps the most bizarre, type of false confession proposed by Kassin and Wrightsman (1985) is the **coerced-internalized false confession.** Here, individuals recall and confess to a crime they did not commit, usually after they are exposed to highly suggestible questions, such as the minimization techniques described earlier in the chapter (Gudjonsson, 1992a). In contrast to the coerced-compliant false confessor, however, these individuals actually end up believing they are responsible for the crime. According to Gudjonsson (1992b), there are several vulnerability factors associated with this type of false confession, including (1) a history of substance abuse or some other interference with brain function, (2) the inability of people to detect discrepancies between what they observed and what has been erroneously suggested to them, and (3) factors associated with mental state, such as severe anxiety, confusion, or feelings of guilt.

Perhaps the most frequently cited case of a false confession falls under the heading of a coerced-internalized false confession (Ofshe & Watters, 1994). The case involves Paul Ingram, who, in 1988, was accused by his two adult daughters of committing crimes against them, crimes that included sexual assault, rape, and satanic ritual abuse that involved slaughtering newborn babies. As if some of these allegations were not strange enough, Ingram confessed to the crimes after initially being adamant he had never committed them. In addition, he was eventually able to recall the crimes in vivid detail despite originally claiming he could not remember ever abusing his daughters. Ingram ended up pleading guilty to six counts of rape and was sentenced to 20 years in prison. In prison, Ingram came to believe he was not guilty of the crimes he confessed to. After having initial appeals rejected, Ingram was released from prison on April 8, 2003.

Many people feel that Ingram falsely confessed to the crimes he was sentenced for. Supporters of this position typically draw on two related pieces of evidence (see Olio & Cornell, 1998, for evidence to the contrary). First, it is known that Ingram was exposed to highly suggestive interrogation techniques that have been shown to adversely influence people's memory of events. For example, over the course of five

BOX 4.2 FALSE CONFESSION IN A CHILD-ABUSE CASE

In the case *R. v. M.J.S.* (2000), M.J.S. was accused of aggravated assault on his baby son (J.S.) and, after supplying the police with a written confession, was charged with the crime. But was M.J.S. responsible for the crime, or was this a case of a coerced-compliant false confession?

J.S. was one to three months old at the time the abuse was supposed to have happened. The boy had been admitted to the hospital for a suspected chest infection and vomiting problems. While in the hospital, X-rays were taken, and it was later discovered that the baby had several rib fractures. The injuries were unusual for a baby so young, leading the baby's pediatrician to notify Child Welfare. The testimony of an expert suggested that the most likely cause of the fractures was that the baby was shaken.

A police investigation was begun. Both M.J.S and his wife cooperated with the police throughout the investigation. On four occasions, the police interrogated the accused. During these interrogations, the police used techniques similar to those used in the Reid model of interrogation, which eventually led the accused to confess. Fortunately, all of the interrogations were videotaped, which provided the courts with a means to determine whether the confession was coerced.

Much of the interrogation consisted of developing various psychological themes to justify the crime. For example, one of the interrogating officers stated that "No doubt it was probably accidental on your part. . . . I don't believe it was intentional. . . . Children's bones are so fragile. . . . You made a mistake" (*R. v. M.J.S.*, para. 16). In addition, every time the accused denied his involvement in the crime, the officers interrupted with statements such as, "We are beyond that point—we know you did it" (para. 19).

The officers also lied to the accused, stating they had talked to everyone else who may have been involved with the incident and they were all cleared. This had not happened. Furthermore, the interviewing officers appealed to the accused's sense of honour and decency, and stressed how much better he would feel if he confessed. For example, one officer stated, "You'll be able to say to yourself ... I'm going to sleep tonight, knowing that I told the truth" (para. 20). Still denying his involvement in any wrongdoing, the accused was presented with threatening statements. One interrogator stated, "If you run from this mistake, your family disintegrates, your family falls apart.... If you want your kids to be raised in a foster home, or adopted somewhere, that is a decision that you have to make" (para 25).

In ruling on the confession evidence, the judge stated that the alleged confession in this case was extracted by threats and implied promises. The judge decided that the techniques employed by the investigators were coercive and that the accused confessed to the crime in order to escape the oppressive atmosphere created by the interrogations. The judge concluded by stating, "This case is a classic illustration of how slavish adherence to a technique can produce a coerced-compliant false 'apology' [confession] even from an accused who has denied 34 times that he did anything wrong when caring for his child" (para. 45). As a result of these findings, the confession evidence was deemed inadmissible.

months, Ingram took part in 23 interrogations in which he was instructed (on some of these occasions) to visualize scenes of satanic cult activity that he could not remember (Wrightsman, 2001). Second, a psychologist hired to evaluate the case, Dr. Richard Ofshe from the University of California, concluded that Ingram had been brainwashed into believing he was responsible for the crimes (Ofshe & Watters, 1994). To demonstrate this belief, Ofshe conducted an experiment where he presented Ingram with a fabricated scenario, that Ingram had forced his son and daughter to have sex together while he watched (Olio & Cornell, 1998). According to Olio and Cornell (1998), phase 1 of the experiment consisted of Ofshe asking Ingram if he could remember the incident (Ingram indicated he could not). Ofshe then instructed Ingram to use the same techniques he had used during his previous interview sessions. The next day, Ingram informed Ofshe he could now remember the incident and he produced a written confession providing details of his involvement. In phase 2 of the experiment, Ofshe pressured Ingram to retract his confession, but Ingram was not willing to do so.

Interrogative Suggestibility and Compliance

As we have already mentioned, the major difference between coerced-compliant and coerced-internalized false confessions is that coerced-compliant false confessors are fully aware they are not responsible for the crimes they are confessing to. Research indicates that two psychological characteristics play a key role in these two types of confessions—compliance and suggestibility. **Compliance** refers to a tendency to go along with demands made by people perceived to be in authority, even though the person may not agree with them (Gudjonsson, 1989). **Suggestibility** refers to the tendency to accept (i.e., internalize) information communicated during questioning (Gudjonsson, 1984). Dr. Gisli Gudjonsson, from the Institute of Psychiatry in London, has developed standardized scales for measuring both compliance and suggestibility.

THE GUDJONSSON COMPLIANCE SCALE The **Gudjonsson Compliance Scale** (GCS) is a self-report questionnaire consisting of 20 true-false questions that tap into two aspects of compliance: a person's eagerness to please others and a person's desire to avoid conflict and confrontation with people (Gudjonsson, 1989). For example, the section measuring a person's eagerness to please others includes questions such as "I try hard to do what is expected of me" and "I generally believe in doing as I am told." In contrast, the section measuring a person's desire to avoid conflict and confrontation includes questions such as "I give in easily to people when I am pressured" and "I tend to give in to people who insist that they are right" (Gudjonsson, 1992a).

Although the GCS has not been the subject of much research, there is some evidence that it is useful for identifying suspects who can be characterized as compliant. For example, Gudjonsson (1989) compared the GCS scores for "resisters" (suspects who did not confess even though there was evidence they were guilty) with "false confessors" (suspects who retracted confessions they had previously made). The results suggested that the former group had significantly lower GCS scores than the latter group, providing one possible reason that these individuals performed the way they did during their police interrogations (a practical example of this scale in use is presented in Box 4.3).

THE GUDJONSSON SUGGESTIBILITY SCALE The **Gudjonsson Suggestibility Scale** (GSS1) measures two distinct types of interrogative suggestibility (Gudjonsson, 1984). First, it measures susceptibility to give in to leading questions, which is known as **yield**. It also measures the tendency to alter answers after being put under pressure by an interviewer, which is known as **shift.** This scale is based on a short story, which is read to a subject. The subject is then asked to recall details from the story. The subject is asked 20 questions, 15 of which are misleading (trial 1). Next, the subject is told that he or she has made a number of errors in answering the questions (even if no errors have been made), that it is necessary to ask all the questions again, and that the subject should try to be more accurate (trial 2). The extent to which the subject gives in to the misleading questions on the first trial is scored as *yield.* Any change in answers between the first and second trial is scored as *shift.* Yield and shift are added together to make up the total suggestibility score.

Research has indicated that the GSS1 is a potentially important diagnostic tool for assessing the degree to which a suspect can be characterized as suggestible. In a study similar to what was done with the GCS, Gudjonsson (1984) compared the GSS1 scores for resisters and false confessors and, as hypothesized, found that resisters had significantly lower GSS1 scores than did false confessors. Research has also been conducted to examine the various correlates of interrogative suggestibility. Many of these correlations are consistent with what would be expected. For example, certain forms of anxiety correlate positively with suggestibility (as anxiety increases, suggestibility increases), while intelligence correlates negatively (as intelligence increases, suggestibility decreases) (Gudjonsson, 1992a).

Studying False Confessions in the Lab

It is obviously difficult to study if, and how, false confessions occur. Even in the research laboratory it is not an easy task because of obvious ethical constraints (Kassin & Kiechel, 1996). Nowadays, no university ethics committee would allow research participants to be led to believe they had committed crimes of the sort that Paul Ingram was accused of. As a result, researchers have attempted to develop innovative laboratory paradigms that allow them to study the processes that may cause false confessions to occur without putting their participants at risk. One such paradigm was proposed by Dr. Saul Kassin and his student.

In their study, Kassin and Kiechel (1996) tested whether individuals would confess to a "crime" they did not commit. They had participants take part in what they thought was a reaction time study. A co-conspirator read a list of letters out loud to a participant who had to type these letters into a computer. However, before each

BOX 4.3 USING THE GUDJONSSON COMPLIANCE AND SUGGESTIBILITY SCALES

Gudjonsson (1992a) describes the following case of the Birmingham Six. In November 1974, two pubs in Birmingham, England, were bombed by the Irish Republican Army (IRA) killing 21 people. Six Irishmen were arrested for the bombings and interrogated. Two of the suspects did not sign any confession, and the other four did sign a confession. Although the defendants argued that the police had beaten their confessions out of them, their confessions were admitted as evidence in court and the six men were convicted. They were imprisoned until 1990 at which time they were released based on new evidence.

Thirteen years after their interrogation, Gudjonsson was asked to assess all six defen-

dants. Part of the assessment protocol included the GCS and GSS1. Figure 4.1 indicates that the six men differed dramatically in their level of compliance and suggestibility. Two of the defendants scored very high on both scales, two scored very low, and two scored in the middle. Interestingly, the two defendants who scored lowest on the scales were the same two men who did not sign a written confession in 1974. Gudjonsson (1992a) is careful to point out that there is no way to know what the defendants' compliance and suggestibility scores were in 1974. Nevertheless, it is intriguing that these scores correspond so well with the behaviour exhibited by the Birmingham Six in their original police interrogations.

FIGURE 4.1

THE COMPLIANCE (GCS) AND SUGGESTIBILITY (GSS1) SCORES OF THE BIRMINGHAM SIX

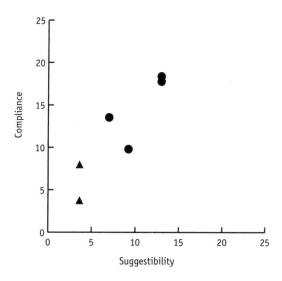

The two defendants who did not sign written confessions are indicated by triangles.

Source: Adapted from Gudjonsson, 1992a.

session began, the participant was warned that, if he or she hit the ALT key on the keyboard while typing in the letters, all the data would be lost. Sixty seconds after beginning the task, the computer automatically crashed, which brought the head researcher into the lab with accusations that the participant had hit the key.

Kassin and Kiechel were specifically interested in how two factors would affect participant reactions to the allegations. Participant vulnerability (defined as the participant's certainty concerning his or her own innocence) was manipulated by varying the speed that participants had to type. In the "not vulnerable" condition, letters were read at a rate of 43 letters per minute; in the "vulnerable" condition, letters were read at a rate of 67 letters per minute. The researchers also varied whether false evidence was presented. In the "no false evidence" condition, the co-conspirator stated she did not see what happened; in the "false evidence" condition, she stated she saw the participant hit the ALT key. The results from the study are presented in Table 4.1.

To measure the degree to which participants complied with the allegations, the researchers presented each participant with a written confession and recorded how many participants signed it. As indicated in Table 4.1, many participants accepted responsibility for the crime despite the fact they were innocent, particularly the vulnerable participants presented with false evidence. To measure the degree to which participants internalized their confession, the researchers recorded comments made by participants to another co-conspirator outside the lab who asked them what had happened. If the participant accepted blame for the crime, he or she was recorded as exhibiting **internalization**. As indicated in Table 4.1, many participants also internalized their confession. Again, this was especially true for vulnerable participants presented with false evidence. Finally, to measure the degree to which participants made up details to fit with their confession, known as **confabulation**, the researchers brought the participant back into the lab, read the list of letters again, and asked the participant to try to reconstruct where things had gone wrong. As indicated in Table 4.1,

TABLE 4.1 COMPLIANCE, INTERNALIZATION, AND CONFABULATION IN KASSIN AND KIECHEL'S STUDY

	No False Evidence (No Witness)		False Evidence (Witness)	
	Not Vulnerable (Slow Pace)	*Vulnerable (Fast Pace)*	*Not Vulnerable (Slow Pace)*	*Vulnerable (Fast Pace)*
Compliance	35%	65%	89%	100%
Internalization	0%	12%	44%	65%
Confabulation	0%	0%	6%	35%

Source: Adapted from Kassin and Kiechel, 1996.

vulnerable participants presented with false evidence were once again found to be particularly susceptible to confabulation.

In sum, these findings suggest that it is possible to demonstrate, under laboratory conditions, that people can admit to acts they are not responsible for and come to believe in their guilt to such a point that they can reconstruct details of an act that never occurred (Kassin & Kiechel, 1996). However, whether these findings can be generalized to actual police interrogations, in which people are falsely confessing to much more serious crimes, is clearly open to debate. Indeed, given the triviality of their mock crime, even Kassin and Kiechel raise this issue about their findings. Perhaps in the future, forensic psychologists will find a way to conduct laboratory studies of false confessions that are not so problematic in this regard.

The Consequences of Falsely Confessing

There are at least two major consequences of a false confession. The most obvious consequence is the impact on the individual making the confession, in particular if the confession is admitted as evidence in court. As mentioned previously, research indicates that false confessions do sometimes lead people to be convicted for crimes they did not commit (Leo & Ofshe, 1998). This finding has led some researchers to examine the impact that coerced confessions have on jurors.

In one study, Kassin and Sukel (1997) presented participants with transcripts of a mock murder trial. One group of participants received a transcript in which the defendant immediately confessed to the police during questioning (the low-pressure condition). A second group of participants received a transcript in which the defendant was coerced into confessing by having his hands cuffed behind his back and being threatened by the interrogator (the high-pressure condition). A third group of participants received a transcript in which the defendant never confessed to the murder (the control condition). The results of the study indicate that those participants presented with a confession obtained in the high-pressure condition recognized the confession was involuntary and said it would not affect their decisions. However, when actual verdicts were examined across the three groups, the presence of a confession was found to significantly increase the conviction rate, even for those participants in the high-pressure condition. Thus, not only can people be convicted of crimes they did not commit based on their false confession, but this can happen even when the confession appears to have been obtained through coercive interrogation tactics.

A second consequence of false confessions that is not as commonly recognized usually comes from people voluntarily confessing to crimes they did not commit. Although such a confession no doubt has consequences for the false confessor, it also has unappreciated consequences for the police and, therefore, the public. When somebody volunteers a false confession, the police are diverted down a false trail that may waste valuable time, time that could be used to identify and apprehend the real offender. Howitt (2002) provides an example of this happening in the Yorkshire Ripper serial murder investigation that took place in England during the 1970s. At one point in the investigation, the police were sent several tape recordings supposedly from the Ripper himself. Howitt states that senior police officers on the case, believing the tapes to be genuine, used up valuable resources investigating the tapes. However, the tapes were not genuine and these actions probably delayed the eventual arrest of Peter Sutcliffe and allowed further murders to take place.

CRIMINAL PROFILING

In order for the police to be able to conduct their interrogations, they need to have a viable suspect in custody. In some instances, the identification of probable suspects is relatively straightforward, because in many crimes the victim and the offender know each other and there is often a clear motivation for the crime, such as passion, greed, or revenge. But what about those crimes in which it is more difficult to identify a suspect, crimes in which the victim and offender are strangers and there is no clear motive? In these cases, the police often rely on unconventional investigative techniques, such as **criminal profiling**.

WHAT IS A CRIMINAL PROFILE?

There is no single definition of criminal profiling (Alison et al., 2002). Indeed, there is still little agreement as to what the technique should even be called. Numerous terms are used to describe the technique, including criminal profiling, psychological profiling, offender profiling, and investigative profiling (Wilson, Lincoln, & Kocsis, 1997). However, the definition proposed by John Douglas and his former colleagues from the Federal Bureau of Investigation (FBI) fairly accurately describes them all: profiling is "a technique for identifying the major personality and behavioural characteristics of an individual based upon an analysis of the crimes he or she has committed" (Douglas et al., 1986, p. 405).

Although criminal profiling is now used in a range of contexts, it is most commonly used in cases of serial homicide and rape (Holmes & Holmes, 2002). In particular, profiling is thought to be most applicable in cases in which extreme forms of psychopathology are exhibited by the offender, including sadistic torture and ritualistic behaviour (Geberth, 1990). Criminal profiling was originally intended to help the police identify the criminal in these sorts of cases, either by narrowing down a list of suspects or by providing new lines of inquiry. However, criminal profiling is now used for a number of purposes including the following (Homant & Kennedy, 1998):

- To help set traps to flush out an offender
- To determine whether a threatening note should be taken seriously
- To give advice on how best to interrogate a suspect
- To tell prosecutors how to break down defendants in cross-examination

Although every criminal profile will undoubtedly be different in terms of the information it contains, some of the most common personality and behavioural characteristics that profilers try to predict include the offender's age, sex, race, level of intelligence, educational history, hobbies, family background, residential location, criminal history, employment status, psychosexual development, and post-offence behaviour (Holmes & Holmes, 2002). Often these predictions are made by forensic psychologists and psychiatrists who have either clinical or research experience with offenders (Wilson et al., 1997). In North America, however, the majority of profilers are experienced and specially trained law enforcement officers (Rossmo, 2000).

The Origins of Criminal Profiling

Criminal profiling is usually thought to have been developed by agents from the FBI in the 1970s. However, there are numerous examples of profiling techniques being used long before that time (Canter, 2000). Woodsworth and Porter (1999), for example, suggest that the documented history of profiling can be traced back at least to the publication of the *Malleus Maleficarum*, "a text from the late 1400s written by contractors to the Catholic Church for the purpose of accurately identifying and eradicating witches" (p. 243). According to these researchers, this was one of the first systematic approaches for identifying and making inferences about the characteristics of supposedly guilty individuals. Beyond this example, there are other early instances of profiling techniques, which were often used for the specific purpose of inferring the background characteristics of an unknown offender from the behaviours he or she exhibited at the crime scene. The investigation that you may be most familiar with is the famous case of Jack the Ripper (Harrison, 1993).

EARLY ATTEMPTS AT CRIMINAL PROFILING In 1888, a series of murders were committed in the east end of London, around an area known as Whitechapel. The victims were all women, and all were mutilated by the offender. At one point, the unknown offender sent a letter to the newspapers, and at the end of it he signed his name, Jack the Ripper (Holmes & Holmes, 2002). A police surgeon involved with the investigation of the murders engaged in a form of criminal profiling. As Woodworth and Porter (1999, p. 244) reveal:

> Dr. George Phillips attempted to create a reconstruction of various crime scenes and describe the wounds of the victims for the purpose of gaining a greater insight into the offender's psychological make-up. In particular, Phillips believed that a circumspect examination of the wound patterns of murder victims could provide clues about both the behaviour and personality of the offender who committed the crimes.

This is probably one of the first times that criminal profiling was used in a criminal investigation. Unfortunately, it assisted little, evidenced by the fact that we still have no idea who Jack the Ripper actually was.

Another well-known case, often cited as an example of how accurate some profilers can be, is the case of New York City's Mad Bomber. Starting in 1940, an unknown offender began detonating bombs in public places around New York (Wrightsman, 2001). Stumped, the New York City Police Department turned to a local forensic psychiatrist, Dr. James Brussel, to assist with the case. By examining the actions of the bomber, Brussel began to develop a profile of the unknown offender. Dr. Brussel's profile included characteristics such as the following: the offender would be a middle-aged male, he would suffer from paranoia, he would be pathologically self-centred, he would be reasonably educated, he would be unmarried and possibly a virgin, he would be Roman Catholic, and he would wear buttoned-up double-breasted suits (Turvey, 2002). In 1957, almost 17 years after the bombings started, the police finally arrested George Metesky. Metesky fit most of the characteristics that Dr. Brussel had profiled, even down to the double-breasted suit he wore to the police station (Holmes & Holmes, 2002). Metesky was subsequently sent to a mental institution for the criminally insane. He was released in 1973 and died in 1994.

THE FBI AND BEYOND The next big milestone in the history of criminal profiling was the development of a criminal profiling program at the FBI in the 1970s (Turvey, 2002). Not only was this the first time that profiles were produced in a systematic way by a law enforcement agency, but it was also the first time that training was provided in how to construct criminal profiles. Subsequent to the development of the FBI's Behavioral Sciences Unit in 1972, the National Center for the Analysis of Violent Crime (NCAVC) was opened for the purpose of conducting research in the area of criminal profiling and providing formal guidance to police agencies around the United States that were investigating serial crimes, in particular serial murder. Similar units have now sprung up in police agencies around the world, including Canada, Germany, and England. These units typically provide operational support to police agencies in cases in which profiling may be useful, and many conduct their own research into criminal profiling. See Box 4.4 for an example of how the RCMP is moving the criminal profiling field forward.

How Is a Criminal Profile Constructed?

Once a crime series has been detected that warrants a criminal profile, profilers must go through a process of profile construction. Despite the fact that profiling has been regularly used by the police since the 1980s, very little is actually known about this process. Indeed, the descriptions of the profiling process provided by researchers and profilers are incredibly vague. For example, in a now-classic study of criminal profiling, Pinizzotto and Finkel (1990) describe the process of profiling as an equation in the form: WHAT + WHY = WHO. The WHAT of the crime refers to the material that profilers collect at the start of an investigation, such as crime scene photos, autopsy reports, and descriptions of victims. The WHY of the crime refers to the motivation for the crime and each crime scene behaviour. The WHO of the crime refers to the actual profile that is eventually constructed once the WHAT and the WHY components have been determined.

Obviously, although this conceptual model may make sense at a general level, it is much too vague to be useful. As Pinizzotto and Finkel (1990) themselves point out,

BOX 4.4 THE RCMP'S VIOLENT CRIME LINKAGE ANALYSIS SYSTEM (VICLAS)

In recent years, the RCMP has played a pivotal role in developing the field of criminal profiling. In large part, they have been able to do this by drawing on the best of modern computer technology. One of the RCMP's most significant advances has been the development in the mid-1990s of an automated system for linking serial crimes, the Violent Crime Linkage Analysis System, or **VICLAS**. One of the biggest problems the police encounter when they are faced with a possible crime series is **linkage blindness**, which refers to an inability on the part of the police to link geographically dispersed serial crimes committed by the same offender because of a lack of communication among police agencies (Egger, 2002). VICLAS was developed, in part, to prevent such linkage blindness.

The backbone of VICLAS is a booklet that police officers fill out. The questions in this booklet are supposed to capture crucial behavioural information on crimes of a serious nature. These crimes include motiveless homicides, sexual assaults, missing persons, and nonparental abductions (Collins et al., 1998). The booklet contains more than 200 questions about the offender's behaviour, the victim, and any forensic information that is available. This information is then entered into a computer and downloaded into a centralized database where it is carefully compared with other crimes. Specially trained VICLAS analysts determine if there are any possible crime linkages. If any potential links are identified, the crimes are highlighted as a series and the relevant police agencies are notified and encouraged to share information (Collins et al., 1998).

According to Woodsworth and Porter (1999), as of the year 2000, "there were more than 30 000 cases in the system, and although there are no official statistics on its success rate, there were 3200 known linkages" (p. 253). These encouraging results, in addition to anecdotal evidence that suggests the system holds promise, have earned VICLAS a reputation as one of the best crime linkage analysis systems in existence (Collins et al., 1998). Police from around the world, including agencies in England, Australia, and Germany, are currently using VICLAS to help solve their serial crimes. Following the conviction of Paul Bernardo in 1995 for the brutal murders he committed, VICLAS reporting was made mandatory for police agencies in Ontario, and it may soon be mandatory in other provinces.

the model "does not tell us precisely how … the profiler gets from the WHAT to the WHY, or from the WHY to the WHO" (p. 217). Other conceptual models have also been produced, particularly by profilers from the FBI, but these models also lack the degree of specificity required to truly understand the process by which a criminal profile is constructed (e.g., Douglas & Burgess, 1986). Undoubtedly, part of the problem with providing such detail is that profiling is still viewed primarily as an art, not a science (Homant & Kennedy, 1998). Although some are making an effort to change this (e.g., Canter, 2000), profiling is currently based to a large extent on the profiler's experience and intuition (Douglas & Olshaker, 1995). As a result, asking a profiler to provide specific details of how he or she constructs a criminal profile may be similar to asking Picasso to explain how he paints.

Different Types of Profiling Methods

Although it is not clear how criminal profilers construct their profiles, it is clear that they can draw on different types of profiling methods. Specifically, two approaches can be used by profilers—the deductive profiling method and the inductive profiling method. **Deductive criminal profiling** involves the prediction of an offender's background characteristics generated from a thorough analysis of the evidence left at the crime scenes by that particular offender (Holmes & Holmes, 2002). This deductive method of profiling largely relies on logical reasoning. This is indicated in an example provided by Canter (2000), in which the victim of an unidentified assailant noticed that the offender had short fingernails on his right hand and long fingernails on his left hand. According to Canter, "Somebody with specialist knowledge suggested that this was a characteristic of people who are serious guitar players. It was therefore a reasonable deduction that the assailant was somebody who played the guitar" (p. 24). The primary disadvantage of this profiling method is that the underlying logic of the argument can sometimes be faulty. Take the prediction we just described. Although the argument appears to be logical, it is in fact wrong. The offender in this case did not play the guitar at all. Instead, the reason he had short fingernails on his right hand was that he had a job repairing old tires.

In contrast to deductive profiling, **inductive criminal profiling** involves the prediction of an offender's background characteristics generated from a comparison of that particular offender's crimes with similar crimes committed by other, known offenders. This method is based on the premise that "if certain crimes committed by different people are similar, then the offenders must also share some common personality traits" (Holmes & Holmes, 2002, p. 5). The inductive method of profiling relies largely on a determination of how likely it is an offender will possess certain background characteristics given the prevalence of these characteristics among known offenders who have committed similar crimes. An example of the inductive profiling method is provided by Aitken et al. (1996), who developed a statistical profile of a child sex murderer. Based on their analysis of similar crimes committed by known offenders, they predicted that there was a probability of .96 that the offender would know the victim, a probability of .92 that the offender would have a previous criminal conviction, a probability of .91 that the offender would be single, a probability of .79 that the offender would live within five miles (eight kilometres) of the crime scene, and a probability of .65 that the offender would be under the age of 20. In this case, the profile turned out to be very accurate.

In contrast to deductive profiling, the major problem with the inductive method of profiling is with sampling issues (Turvey, 2002). The key problem is that it will never be possible to have a representative sample of serial offenders from which to draw profiling conclusions from. That is, if we encounter a serial crime with behaviours A, B, and C, but no crimes in our database have behaviours A, B, and C, how do we construct an accurate profile? One reason for this problem is that many offenders are never caught for their crimes and, therefore, these offenders can never be included in a database of solved offences.

THE ORGANIZED-DISORGANIZED MODEL Many profilers today use an inductive profiling approach developed by the FBI in the 1980s. This model was largely developed through interviews with incarcerated serial murderers and has come to be called the **organized-disorganized model** (Hazelwood & Douglas, 1980). The model suggests that an offender's crime scene can be classified as either organized or disorganized (see Table 4.2). Organized crime scene behaviours reflect a well-planned and controlled crime, while disorganized behaviours reflect an impulsive crime, which is chaotic in nature. Similarly, an offender's background can be classified as either organized or disorganized (see Table 4.3 on page 112). Organized background characteristics reflect a methodical individual, while disorganized characteristics reflect a disturbed individual, who is usually suffering from some form of psychopathology. The basic idea is that, when encountering a disorganized crime scene, the investigator should profile the background characteristics of a disorganized offender, and likewise for organized crime scenes and organized background characteristics. Although little research has examined whether the organized-disorganized model actually works, the research that does exist raises serious doubts (e.g., Canter et al., 2004). Indeed, even the FBI has refined this model to account for the many offenders who display mixtures of organized and disorganized features (Douglas et al., 1992).

TABLE 4.2 ORGANIZED AND DISORGANIZED CRIME SCENE BEHAVIOURS

Organized Behaviours	Disorganized Behaviours
Planned offence	Spontaneous offence
Use of restraints on the victim	No restraints used on the victim
Ante-mortem sexual acts committed	Post-mortem sexual acts committed
Use of a vehicle in the crime	No use of a vehicle in the crime
No post-mortem mutilation	Post-mortem mutilation
Corpse not taken	Corpse (or body parts) taken
Little evidence left at the scene	Evidence left at the scene

Source: Adapted from Ressler et al., 1986.

TABLE 4.3 ORGANIZED AND DISORGANIZED BACKGROUND CHARACTERISTICS

Organized Characteristics	Disorganized Characteristics
High intelligence	Low intelligence
Skilled occupation	Unskilled occupation
Sexually adequate	Sexually inadequate
Lives with a partner	Lives alone
Geographically mobile	Geographically stable
Lives and works far away from crimes	Lives and works close to crimes
Follows crimes in media	Little interest in media
Maintains residence and vehicle	Does not maintain residence or vehicle

Source: Adapted from Ressler et al., 1986.

The Validity of Criminal Profiling

Because the police frequently use profiling, it is important to consider whether the technique is actually reliable and valid. The view of some researchers is that profiling is generally accepted as a useful investigative technique (e.g., Homant & Kennedy, 1998), but others are more cautious (e.g., Alison et al., 2002). Many profilers claim they have experienced much success with their profiles, but these claims are typically based on personal observations, not empirical research (Woodsworth & Porter, 1999). The few empirical studies that do exist suggest that profiling may be beneficial, but not necessarily for the reasons we might expect. For example, in one of the most recent evaluation studies, Copson (1995) found that profiles were viewed as operationally useful by 82.6% of the police officers he surveyed, but only 2.7% of that sample said that this was because the profile led to the identification of the offender. Most of the police officers indicated that profiling was useful because it either furthered their understanding of the case (60.9%) or it reassured them of their own judgments about the offender (51.6%).

Despite the relatively high figures indicating that criminal profiling may be useful, the practice is still often criticized. Three criticisms in particular have received attention from researchers:

1. Many forms of profiling are based on a theoretical model of personality that lacks strong empirical support.

2. Many profiles contain information that is so vague and ambiguous they can potentially fit many suspects.

3. Professional profilers may be no better than untrained individuals at constructing accurate criminal profiles.

Let's now look at each of these criticisms in turn.

DOES PROFILING HAVE A STRONG THEORETICAL BASE? There seems to be general agreement that most forms of profiling, including the FBI's organized-disorganized approach, rely on a **classic trait model** of personality that was popular in psychology before the 1970s (Alison et al., 2002). In this model, the primary determinants of behaviour are stable, internal traits (Mischel, 1968). These traits are assumed to result in the expression of consistent patterns of behaviour over time and across situations. In the criminal context, this consistency is thought to persist across an offender's crimes and into the offender's noncriminal lifestyle, thus allowing him or her to be accurately profiled (Homant & Kennedy, 1998). Thus, an offender characterized by a trait of "organization" is expected to exhibit organized behaviours across his or her crimes (e.g., the offender will consistently plan the crimes, use restraints, and use weapons), as well as in his or her noncriminal life (e.g., the offender will be highly intelligent, sexually adequate, and geographically mobile) (Alison et al., 2002).

Although some researchers believe this classic trait model provides a solid basis for criminal profiling (e.g., Homant & Kennedy, 1998), other researchers disagree (e.g., Alison et al., 2002). Those who disagree draw on research from the field of personality psychology, which demonstrates that traits are not the only (or even primary) determinant of behaviour (Cervone & Shoda, 1999). Rather, situational influences are also known to be very important in shaping our behaviour, and some researchers argue that there is no reason to suspect that serial offenders will be any different (Bennell & Canter, 2002). From a profiling perspective, the impact of various situational factors (e.g., an extremely resistant victim, being interrupted during a crime, or having a bad day at work) may create behavioural inconsistencies across an offender's crimes, and between different aspects of his or her life, making it very difficult to create an accurate profile.

Those who believe the classic trait model forms a strong basis for criminal profiling also acknowledge the "checkered past" that this model has experienced (e.g., Homant & Kennedy, 1998). However, these individuals refer to instances in which behavioural consistency has been found in the noncriminal context and highlight the fact that higher levels of behavioural consistency typically emerge when we examine pathological populations (Pinizzotto & Finkel, 1990). Assuming that most serial offenders do in fact fall into this pathological population, these supporters argue that the level of behavioural consistency that they express may be adequate to develop accurate criminal profiles. Clearly, more empirical research dealing with this issue is required before any firm conclusions can be made. Until then, the debate over the validity of criminal profiling will continue.

WHAT IS THE IMPACT OF AMBIGUOUS PROFILES? Another common criticism of criminal profiling is that many profiles are so ambiguous that they can fit many suspects. If one of the goals of profiling is to help prioritize potential suspects, this concern clearly needs to be addressed. To examine this issue, Alison, Smith, Eastman, and Rainbow (2003) examined the content of 21 profiling reports and found that almost one-quarter (24%) of all the profiling opinions provided in these reports could be considered ambiguous (i.e., the opinion could be interpreted differently by different people). Of more direct relevance to the ambiguity criticism, however, is an interesting follow-up study conducted by Alison, Smith, and Morgan (2003), where they examined whether ambiguous profiles could in fact be interpreted to fit more than one suspect.

Alison and his colleagues provided details of a genuine crime to two groups of forensic professionals, including senior police detectives. The crime involved the murder of a young woman. Each group of participants was then provided with a criminal profile constructed for this case by the FBI. They were asked to read the profile and compare it to the description of a suspect. Unbeknownst to the participants, each group was provided with a different suspect description. One group was provided with the description of the genuine offender, while the other group was provided with a suspect constructed by the researchers, who was different from the genuine offender on a number of key points. For example, the genuine offender had no previous criminal convictions whereas the bogus offender had several previous convictions for assault and burglary. After comparing the profile with their suspect, each participant was asked to rate the accuracy of the profile and to state if (and why) he or she thought the profile would be operationally useful.

Despite the fact that each group received different suspect descriptions, both groups of participants rated the profile as fairly accurate, with no significant difference between the groups. In addition, both groups viewed the profile as generally useful and indicated they thought it would allow the police to narrow down the list of potential suspects and develop new lines of inquiry. This study, therefore, provides preliminary support for the criticism that ambiguous profiles can in fact be interpreted to fit more than one suspect, even when those suspects are quite different from one another. However, although such a finding could have serious implications, we must be careful in interpreting these results. For example, it would be important to know how closely the profile used in this study matches the typical criminal profile provided in the field. In addition, it should be emphasized that this study is far from realistic. For example, the crime scene details and suspect descriptions provided to the participants in this study contained much less information than would be the case in an actual police investigation. Until a more realistic study is conducted, it is difficult to know what the practical implications of the study are, but it does raise some very interesting and potentially important questions.

HOW ACCURATE ARE PROFESSIONAL PROFILERS? The last criticism that we will deal with here is the possibility that professional profilers may be no more accurate in their profiling predictions than are individuals who have received no specialized training. In early writings on criminal profiling, claims were even made that profilers may be no better than bartenders at predicting the characteristics of unknown offenders (Campbell, 1976). If this is in fact the case, the police must consider how much weight they will put on statements made by professional profilers. Unlike the previous two criticisms, this issue has been examined on numerous occasions and the results have been mixed (Kocsis et al., 2000). In other words, profilers are sometimes found to be more accurate than other groups when asked to construct profiles under laboratory conditions but, at other times, they are found to be no more accurate.

In a fairly representative study, Kocsis and his colleagues (2000) compared profile accuracy across five groups of individuals—profilers, psychologists, police officers, students, and psychics. All participants were provided with the details of a genuine crime, which they were asked to review. The participants were then given a series of questionnaires that dealt with various aspects of the offender's background, including his or her physical characteristics, cognitions related to the offence, pre- and post-offence behaviours, social history, and personality characteristics. The participants' task with these questionnaires was to select the alternatives that best described the unknown offender. Accuracy was determined for each group by comparing the responses from the participants with the correct answers. The results from this study are presented in Table 4.4, which indicates the mean number of questions that each group got correct for each subset of characteristics.

As you can see from this table, professional profilers were the most accurate when it came to profiling cognitive processes (e.g., degree of planning) and social history (e.g., marital status). Therefore, they have received the highest total accuracy score,

TABLE 4.4 COMPARING PROFILERS, PSYCHOLOGISTS, POLICE OFFICERS, STUDENTS, AND PSYCHICS*

Measure	Profilers	Psychologists	Police	Students	Psychics
Cognitions	3.20	2.27	2.49	2.03	2.60
Physical	3.60	3.63	3.43	3.42	2.80
Offence	4.00	4.03	3.09	3.64	3.65
Social	3.00	2.63	2.60	2.94	2.25
Total	13.80	12.57	11.60	12.03	11.30
Personality	24.60	34.03	22.03	26.84	27.70

Source: Adapted from Kocsis et al., 2000.

*Numbers refer to the mean number of correct questions. The number of correct questions that participants could have predicted was 7 for cognitions, 6 for physical characteristics, 7 for offence behaviours, and 10 for social history (total accuracy is, therefore, out of 30). Kocsis and his colleagues did not provide information relating to the total number of correct predictions for personality characteristics.

which is an aggregate score for all subsets of characteristics, excluding personality predictions. On the other hand, psychologists were the most accurate when it came to profiling physical characteristics (e.g., offender age), offence behaviours (e.g., degree of control), and personality features (e.g., temperament). When the results of the four non-profiler groups were combined, Kocsis and his colleagues found that the combined score of the nonprofiler groups was lower than the profilers, leading them to conclude that "the collective skills of profilers are superior to the individual skills represented by each of the comparison groups" (p. 325). However, given the preliminary nature of this study, the marginal accuracy differences between groups, and the fact that other researchers have sometimes found little support for the accuracy of professional profilers (e.g., Pinizzotto & Finkel, 1990), it seems likely that the debate over whether professional profilers can provide more accurate profiles than untrained individuals will continue.

OTHER TYPES OF PROFILING

In addition to criminal profiling, two other forms of profiling are commonly used by the police—geographic profiling and racial profiling—though the widespread use of racial profiling has just recently been uncovered.

Geographic Profiling

Geographic profiling is used frequently by the police to help them investigate serial crimes more efficiently. In simple terms, geographic profiling uses crime scene locations to predict the most likely area where the offender resides (Rossmo, 2000). As is the case with criminal profiling, geographic profiling is used most often in cases of serial homicide and rape, though it has also been used in cases of serial robbery, arson, and burglary. Geographic profiling is used primarily for prioritizing potential suspects. This is accomplished by rank ordering the suspects based on how close they live to the predicted home location, so the suspect who lives closest to the predicted home location would be focused on first (Rossmo, 2000). This is an important task considering the number of suspects who can enter a serial crime investigation. For example, in the recently solved Green River serial murder case in Washington state, the police collected more than 18 000 suspect names (Rossmo, 1995).

The basic assumption behind geographic profiling is that most serial offenders do not travel far from home to commit their crimes and, therefore, it should be possible to make a reasonably accurate prediction about where an offender lives. Fortunately for the geographic profiler, research supports this assumption. Perhaps surprisingly, it turns out that serial offenders tend to be consistent in their crime site selection choices, often committing their crimes very close to where they reside (Rossmo, 2000). Indeed, even many of the most bizarre serial killers commit their crimes close to home, but there are certainly some high-profile offenders, such as Ted Bundy and Henry Lee Lucas, who travel long distances (Canter et al., 2000). For travelling offenders, geographic profiling is typically not a useful investigative strategy but, for the majority of serial offenders who do commit their crimes locally, a number of profiling strategies can be used (Snook et al., in press).

One of the first cases in which geographic profiling techniques were used was the case of the Yorkshire Ripper in England. After five years of unsolved murders, an advisory team was set up to review the investigation. Although some on the investigative team felt the offender lived in a different part of the country from where the crimes were happening (due largely to one of the voluntary false confessions discussed earlier), the advisory team believed the offender was a local man. To provide support for this claim, the advisory team constructed a type of geographic profile (Kind, 1987). They plotted the 17 Ripper murders onto a map and calculated the centre of gravity for the points. That is, by adding up the x-y coordinates for each crime and dividing by the 17 crimes, they could calculate the x-y coordinate for the centre of gravity. In this case, the centre of gravity was near Bradford, a city close to where the majority of the murders had taken place. When Peter Sutcliffe was eventually arrested for the crimes, he was found to reside in a district of Bradford.

During the 1990s, a number of individuals built computerized **geographic profiling systems** that could assist with the profiling task. One of these individuals was Dr. Kim Rossmo, who is profiled in Box 4.5 on page 118. The locations of linked crime sites are input into these systems represented as points on a map. The systems then perform calculations using mathematical models of offender spatial behaviour, which reflect the probability that the offender lives at particular points in the area where the offences have taken place. Every single location on the map is assigned an overall probability and these probabilities are designated a colour. For example, the top 10% of probabilities might be assigned the colour red, and so on. The eventual output is a coloured map, in which each colour band corresponds to the probability that the offender lives in the area (see Figure 4.2 on page 119). The police use this map to prioritize their investigative activities. Geographic profilers also consider other factors that may affect an offender's spatial behaviour, such as the density of suitable victims in an area, but this probability map forms the basis of their prediction.

Racial Profiling

Recently, it has also become clear that the police engage in another form of profiling—**racial profiling**. Unlike criminal profiling or geographic profiling, racial profiling refers to any police-initiated action that relies on the race or ethnicity of an individual, rather than that individual's criminal behaviour (Ramirez, McDevitt, & Farrell, 2000). According to Harris (1999a), one of the most common forms of racial profiling is the police practice of stopping and searching vehicles (for drugs and weapons usually) because the driver does not "match" the vehicle he or she is driving (see Box 4.6 on page 120 for a Canadian example).

BOX 4.5 CANADIAN RESEARCHER PROFILE: DR. KIM ROSSMO

Dr. Kim Rossmo had been a police officer with the Vancouver Police Department for 16 years when he became the first Canadian police officer to get his Ph.D. in criminology. At Simon Fraser University in Burnaby, B.C., Dr. Rossmo began his doctoral studies with Paul Brantingham, a well-known environmental criminologist. Drawing on his background in mathematics and his experience as a street-wise police officer, Dr. Rossmo decided to take what was known about offender spatial behaviour from fields like environmental criminology and put them to practical use by developing an investigative tool for predicting where unknown serial offenders are likely to live.

After years of research, Dr. Rossmo developed an approach he called criminal geographic targeting and designed a geographic-profiling system called Rigel, which is now one of the most sought-after investigative tools by police agencies around the world. Dr. Rossmo is regularly called in to assist with serial crime investigations by the RCMP, the FBI, and Scotland Yard. Based on his most recent estimation, he has consulted on about 200 cases, ranging from murders to bombings to robberies. One of his most recent cases was the high-profile Washington sniper case, which proved to be a particularly difficult case for geographic profiling because of the transient nature of the suspects.

After working as a detective inspector in charge of the Geographic Profiling Section of the Vancouver Police Department for a number of years, Dr. Rossmo moved on to serve a two-year term as the director of research for the prestigious Police Foundation in Washington, D.C. Dr. Rossmo now calls Texas State University home, where he directs the newly established Advanced Criminal Investigative Research Center in the Department of Criminal Justice.

In addition to his ongoing consultancy work, Dr. Rossmo continues to conduct research on geographic profiling and is expanding his focus to deal with other issues of importance. For example, he is currently engaged in research on the geographic patterns of illegal land border crossing, and he is getting involved in studies related to his long-term interest in criminal investigative failures and the factors that lead to these failures. When asked where he sees the field going in the future, he indicates that research in his area will have to start relating to more immediate, practical concerns, such as counterterrorism issues.

Dr. Rossmo has been the recipient of many awards for his achievements as a police officer and an academic, and he recently made a guest appearance as a character in the crime novel *Burnt Bones* by Michael Slade. He is the author of numerous articles and has recently published *Geographic Profiling,* the first book on the subject. This book provides an excellent example of how academic research can successfully be applied to help with real-world policing problems.

FIGURE 4.2

A COMPUTERIZED GEOGRAPHIC PROFILE

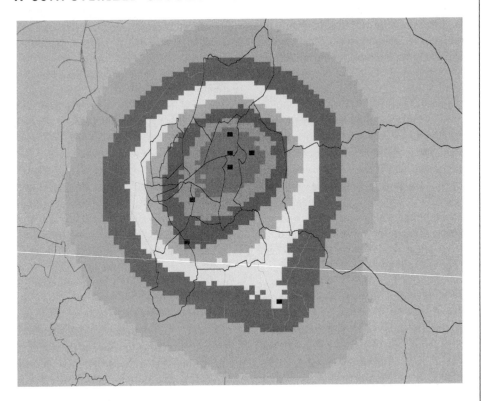

The black dots represent the crime locations and the different coloured bands (represented here by different shades of grey) correspond to the probability that the offender resides in that particular geographic area. The high priority search area in this case centres on the four crimes in the upper half of the map.

Due to some high-profile cases in the United States (e.g., *Wilkins v. Maryland State Police*, 1999), racial profiling is beginning to get more attention from researchers, the police, and the media. This attention appears to be warranted, given the results of recent public surveys. These surveys confirm that the majority of U.S. citizens believe the police actively engage in racial profiling. This seems to be the case regardless of the respondent's race. For example, a recent Gallup Poll indicated that 56% of whites and 77% of blacks believe that racial profiling is pervasive (Gallup Poll, 1999). What appears to differ by race, however, is the percentage of people who believe they have been the target of racial profiling. For example, results from the same Gallup Poll

BOX 4.6 A CANADIAN EXAMPLE OF RACIAL PROFILING

On November 1, 1999, Decovan Brown, a former Toronto Raptors basketball player, was arrested in Toronto for driving a motor vehicle while under the influence of alcohol (*R. v. Brown*, 2002). Before he was stopped, Brown was speeding slightly in his Ford Expedition. Brown is a young black man. At trial, Brown's lawyer alleged that "Mr. Brown was arbitrarily stopped by the investigating officer because of racial profiling rather than for driving at a speed slightly in excess of the posted speed limit" (*R. v. Brown*, 2002, para. 2). According to Brown's lawyer, "the arrest ... was based on the stereotypical assumption that young black men who are driving expensive motor vehicles obtained them by crime or are implicated in recent criminal activity" (para. 2).

Despite the fact that the defence had evidence to support their allegation that the police officer in this case had used racial profiling, the trial judge dismissed it, indicating that he found the allegations "nasty" and "malicious" (*R. v. Brown*, 2002, para. 2). In addition, the judge's remarks made during sentencing referred to his "distaste for the matters that were raised during the course of the trial" (para. 20), and he suggested that the defendant "might extend an apology to the officer because [the judge was] satisfied the allegations [were] completely unwarranted" (para. 20).

On appeal, the Ontario Supreme Court stressed that judges "must be particularly vigilant in their efforts to impartially determine applications like this one" (*R. v. Brown*, 2002, para. 18). The court also indicated that "judges must be particularly sensitive to the need to ... be fair to all Canadians of every race, religion, nationality and ethnic origin" (para. 19). On Brown's appeal, the Ontario Supreme Court ruled that many of the trial judge's comments to Brown and his lawyer during the trial were completely inappropriate and that the trial judge did not appear to understand the importance of some of the evidence. For example, the Court stated that for a judge to regard an application as distasteful "is materially inconsistent with the duty of a judge to hear and determine the application with an open mind" (para. 20). Ultimately, the Ontario Supreme Court ruled that the appeal by Brown should be allowed and a new trial was ordered.

indicate that only 6% of white men believe they have been stopped by the police based on their race alone, versus 42% of black men, and this percentage increases further for black men between the ages of 18 and 34.

Anecdotal accounts and empirical research also confirm that racial profiling is practised by some police agencies (Ramirez et al., 2000). For example, Lamberth (1999) conducted an analysis of police stop and searches in Maryland. Using data from the Maryland State Police, he compared the drivers who were stopped and searched along a major highway in Maryland with those who were actually violating traffic laws. According to Harris (1999b), who discussed Lamberth's study in some detail, approximately 74% of Lamberth's "law violator" sample consisted of white individuals while only 17.5% were black individuals. More important, a staggering

79.2% of the drivers who were stopped and searched were black. Studies in other countries provide similar findings (Home Office, 1998).

Of course, the possibility exists that such behaviour simply reflects an accurate perception on the part of the police that members of some minority groups are more likely to carry drugs and weapons. Existing research, however, does not support this assumption. In Lamberth's (1999) study, for example, he found that a similar percentage of black and white drivers who were stopped and searched were actually found with drugs in their possession (28.4% and 28.8%, respectively) (cited by Harris, 1999b). Other research also supports these findings (Fitzgerald, 1999). It appears, therefore, that racial profiling is not a valid police procedure, and some police forces have started to implement policies in an attempt to reduce the use of this sort of profiling.

SUMMARY

1. The police attempt to achieve two things when conducting interrogations—to gain information that furthers the investigation and to obtain a confession from the suspect. Police officers in North America use the Reid model of interrogation to interrogate suspects. This model advocates the use of psychologically based interrogation tactics to break down a suspect's resistance to telling the truth. The tactics used in the Reid model of interrogation can be broken down into minimization and maximization techniques.

2. The three potential problems with the Reid model of interrogation are (1) the inability of police officers to accurately detect deception, (2) biases that result from presuming a suspect is guilty, and (3) an increased likelihood that suspects will make false confessions.

3. False confessions must be differentiated from retracted confessions and disputed confessions. A false confession is one that is either intentionally fabricated or is not based on actual knowledge of the facts in a case. A retracted confession is simply someone declaring that his or her confession is false. A disputed confession is one that is disputed at trial, often because of a legal technicality or because the suspect disputes the confession was ever made.

4. There are three types of false confessions, each having its own set of vulnerability factors. Voluntary false confessions occur when someone voluntarily confesses to a crime he or she did not commit without any elicitation from the police. Coerced-compliant false confessions are those in which the suspect confesses to a crime, even though the suspect is fully aware that he or she did not commit it. Coerced-internalized false confessions consist of individuals confessing to a crime they did not commit—and subsequently coming to the belief they committed the crime—usually after they are exposed to highly suggestive questions.

5. Criminal profiling is used frequently by the police in serial crime investigations. They use it for prioritizing suspects, developing new lines of inquiry, setting traps to flush out offenders, determining whether an offender's actions should be taken seriously, giving advice on how to interrogate suspects, and developing courtroom strategies.

    Despite its widespread use, criminal profiling is often criticized. One major criticism centres on the lack of a strong theoretical base underlying the approach. A second criticism relates to the fact that many profiles contain ambiguous information and this may cause problems when police officers are asked to interpret the profile. A third criticism is that professionally trained profilers may be no better than other individuals at constructing accurate profiles.

6. The police also use two other types of profiling. Geographic profiling is defined as any technique that uses crime scene locations to predict the most likely area where the offender resides. Racial profiling refers to any police-initiated action that relies on the race or ethnicity of an individual, rather than that individual's criminal behaviour.

KEY CONCEPTS

DISCUSSION QUESTIONS

1. You have been called in by the police to give them advice on how to conduct a police interrogation. In particular, they want to know how far they can go to get a confession from a suspect, while at the same time making sure the confession will be admissible in court. What advice would you give to them?

2. Many police agencies now videotape their police interrogations, presenting potential advantages for the police, suspects, and the courts. Do you see any potential problems with using this procedure? What are some other possible ways to minimize the problems that result from modern-day interrogation practices?

3. Because the Reid model of interrogation can increase the degree to which people falsely confess to crimes, people seem to agree that it should not be used with particular individuals (e.g., those who have a severe learning disability). However, few police agencies have policies in place to indicate when it is not appropriate to use the Reid model. Develop a set of recommendations for when the technique should and shouldn't be used.

4. Researchers are now using laboratory-based studies in an attempt to understand the processes involved when people confess to crimes they did not commit. Do you think this is problematic? Why or why not?

5. You are a criminal profiler who uses the inductive approach to profiling. You encounter a series of crimes in which the offender consistently attacks elderly women in their apartments at night. How would you go about constructing a profile in this case? What sorts of problems would a deductive profiler have with your profile? How could you attempt to counter some of the arguments?

6. A number of studies have found that people view ambiguous criminal profiles as accurate even when they are asked to rate their accuracy against different suspects. Researchers have claimed that this occurs because people are able to creatively re-interpret ambiguous profiles to make them fit any number of potential suspects. What other factors could contribute to this finding?

7. Geographic profiling works in large part because offenders commit most of their crimes close to home. Why do you think offenders do this?

ADDITIONAL INFORMATION

Readings

Gudjonsson, G.H. (2003). *The psychology of interrogations and confessions: A handbook.* West Sussex, UK: John Wiley & Sons.

Holmes, R.M., & Holmes, S.T. (2002). *Profiling violent crimes: An investigative tool* (3rd edition). Thousand Oaks, CA: Sage.

Kassin, S.M. (1997). The psychology of confession evidence. *American Psychologist, 52*, 221–233.

Web Sites

The Homepage of the Reid Model of Interrogation
www.reid.com/index.html

Police Interrogations and Confessions
www.williams.edu/Psychology/Faculty/Kassin/research/confessions.htm

Criminal Profiling Site
www.corpus-delicti.com/

CHAPTER 5

Assessments of Credibility and Malingering

LEARNING OBJECTIVES

- Describe the different types of polygraph tests.

- List the three types of studies used to examine the accuracy of the polygraph.

- Describe the most common types of errors made by the Control Question Test (CQT) and the Guilty Knowledge Test (GKT).

- Outline the vocal and nonvocal characteristics of deception.

- Define malingering and list the three explanatory models of malingering.

- Differentiate among the types of studies used to examine malingering.

- Indicate how you might detect that someone has malingering psychosis and amnesia.

Justin Moore is in trouble. He is a suspect in a vicious attack that occurred outside a popular nightclub. He was seen driving away from the scene of the attack. He has been asked by the police to take a polygraph exam. On the date of the first scheduled test, he tells the polygraph examiner that he has a bad cold. The police examiner asks him to come back the following week to take the exam. At the next exam his numerical score on the exam is −10. The police examiner informs him of his deceptive scoring and attempts to obtain a confession from him about his role in the attack. Justin maintains that he is innocent and the polygraph must be wrong.

DETECTING DECEPTION

How do we know whether someone is telling the truth or lying? A person may lie to the police about his or her involvement in a crime, lie to a psychologist about psychological symptoms, or lie to a probation officer by claiming to be following conditional release requirements. Several techniques have been developed to try to answer this question. As seen in Chapter 4, police attempt to detect whether or not someone is telling them the truth during an interrogation. Psychologists have participated in the development and testing of a variety of techniques to detect deception. This chapter focuses on several issues associated with deception, including use of the polygraph, the relationship between verbal and nonverbal cues to deception, the use of deception by children, and methods for detecting the malingering of mental disorders.

THE POLYGRAPH TECHNIQUE

Physiological measures have long been used in an attempt to detect deception. For example, at one time the Chinese forced suspects to chew on dry rice powder and then to spit it out. If the powder was dry, the suspect was judged to be lying (Kleinmuntz & Szucko, 1984). The rationale for this technique was that anxiety causes a person's mouth to be dry. A person telling the truth would not be anxious and, therefore, would not have a dry mouth. In contrast, a person lying would be anxious and would have a dry mouth. Polygraphy relies on the same underlying principle: deception is associated with physiological change. The origins of modern polygraphy date from 1917 when Marston, a Harvard psychologist also trained as a lawyer, developed a systolic blood pressure test (Iacono & Patrick, 1999) and attempted to use this physiological response as evidence for a person's innocence (see Lykken, 1998). Marston's testimony was rejected by the courts in *Frye v. United States* (1923) because they felt the test had not gained acceptance by the scientific community, foreshadowing the debate associated with physiological measures that continues to the present day.

A **polygraph** (the word is a combination of two Greek words, "poly" = many, and "grapho" = write) is a device for recording an individual's autonomic nervous system responses. Measurement devices are attached to the upper chest and abdomen to measure breathing. The amount of sweat on the skin is measured by attaching electrodes to the fingertips. Sweat changes the conductance of the skin, which is known as the galvanic skin response. Finally, heart rate is measured by a partially inflated blood pressure cuff attached to an arm. Each of these measures is amplified and can be printed out on paper or stored in a computer to be analyzed. In a forensic context, a polygraph is used to measure a person's physiological responses to questions asked by an examiner.

In Canada, polygraph training is provided by the Canadian Police College. In the United States, there are freestanding poly-

Suspect being given a polygraph test

graph schools that can be accredited by the American Polygraph Association. The polygraph course at the Canadian Police College is restricted to police officers. The college offers a 12-week intensive course that covers the various techniques, interviewing practices, and scoring.

Applications of the Polygraph Test

Polygraph tests are used for a range of purposes. In Canada, they are often used by the police to help in their criminal investigations. The police may ask a suspect to take a polygraph test as a means to resolve the case. If the suspect fails the polygraph test, that person may be pressured to confess, thereby giving the police incriminating evidence. Although not common, police may ask alleged victims of crimes to take a polygraph test to help verify whether a crime has occurred. Insurance companies may request a polygraph test to verify the claims of the insured. More recently, the polygraph has been used in the United States to assess and monitor sexual offenders on probation. **Polygraph disclosure tests** are used to uncover information about an offender's past behaviour. Polygraph tests are also used to determine whether the offender is violating the conditions of probation or used to test for evidence of risky behaviour, such as sexual fantasies about children.

The most widespread applications of polygraph testing in the United States were for the periodic testing of employees to identify those engaged in theft or using drugs at work and for screening of prospective employees to weed out those with criminal tendencies or substance abuse problems. However, the Employee Polygraph Protection Act of 1988 restricted private companies from using the polygraph for these purposes and limited the use of the polygraph to specific investigations of job-related wrongdoing. However, governmental agencies in the United States and Canada still use the polygraph as a screening tool. For example, some police departments require applicants to take a polygraph test, and the Canadian Security Intelligence Service also requires their potential employees to take a polygraph test in order to assess "the candidate's reliability and loyalty."

Types of Polygraph Tests

The polygraph does not detect lies per se, since the physiological states associated with lying share much in common with many other states including anxiety, anger, embarrassment, and fear. Instead, polygraph tests rely on measuring physiological responses to different types of questions. Some questions are designed to elicit a larger physiological response in guilty individuals than in those who are innocent. The three main types of polygraph tests are reviewed below.

THE RELEVANT/IRRELEVANT TEST First developed in 1917 by William Marston and later refined by John Larson (1921) for use in criminal investigations, the **Relevant/Irrelevant Test** includes only two types of questions: relevant questions concerning the crime in question (e.g., Did you steal the rare gold coin?) and irrelevant questions that are unrelated to the crime (e.g., Is today Monday?). If an individual's physiological responses were larger to relevant questions than to irrelevant questions, this would be interpreted as a pattern consistent with deceptiveness. The major problem with this test is that nearly everyone responds more to the relevant questions than to the irrelevant question. This test is no longer used in law enforcement. However, for employee screening a version of this test called the Relevant/Irrelevant technique is used. In these tests, potential and current employees are asked about such areas as drug use, antisocial acts, rule breaking, and honesty.

THE CONTROL QUESTION TEST The **Control Question Test** (CQT) is the most commonly used test to investigate criminal acts. The CQT includes ten questions answered either "yes" or "no." Table 5.1 provides an example of a typical question series used in a CQT. Three types of questions are asked. Irrelevant questions, referring to the respondent's identity or personal background (e.g., Is your first name Beatrice?) are included as a baseline but are not scored. Relevant and control questions establish guilt or innocence. Relevant questions deal with the crime being investigated (e.g., On June 12, did you stab your ex-wife?). Control questions are designed to be emotionally arousing for all respondents and typically focus on the person's honesty and past history prior to the event being investigated (e.g., Before the age of 45, did you ever try to seriously hurt someone?). Polygraph examiners assume they can detect

TABLE 5.1 TYPICAL QUESTION SERIES USED IN A CONTROL QUESTION TEST

Type of Question	Questions
Irrelevant	Do you understand that I will only be asking questions we have discussed before?
Irrelevant	Do you live in Canada?
Control	Between the ages of 18 and 28, did you ever deliberately plan to physically hurt someone?
Relevant	Did you stab Petunia Bottoms on the night of March 10?
Irrelevant	Is your first name Craig?
Control	Prior to 2003, did you ever verbally threaten to hurt anyone?
Relevant	Did you use a knife to stab Petunia Bottoms?
Irrelevant	Were you born in November?
Control	During the first 28 years of your life, did you ever do anything illegal?
Relevant	On March 10 did you participate, in any way, in the stabbing of Petunia Bottoms?

deception by comparing reactions to the relevant and control questions. Guilty suspects are assumed to react more to relevant questions than control questions. In contrast, innocent suspects are assumed to react more to control questions than relevant questions. The reasoning behind these assumptions is that innocent people know they are telling the truth about the relevant question so they will react more strongly to general questions about their honesty and past history.

The typical CQT includes a pretest interview, followed by a series of questions administered while the suspect's physiological responses are measured (usually three separate question sequences are asked). The polygraph examiner then scores the charts and ends the CQT with a post-test interview in which the test results are discussed.

A critical component of this technique is the pretest interview. During the pretest interview, the polygraph examiner develops the control questions, learns about the background of the suspect, and attempts to convince the suspect of the accuracy of the polygraph test. The examiner will do this by quoting very high accuracy rates and conducting a stimulation test. For example, the suspect will pick a card with a number on it from a deck of cards, and the examiner will determine the number by examining the polygraph chart. The deck of cards is rigged so the examiner knows which card the suspect picked.

Examiners in the past used global scoring, incorporating all available information, including physiological responses, the suspect's demeanour during the examination, and information in the case file to make a decision about the guilt or innocence of the suspect. Most examiners now numerically score the charts to ensure decisions are based solely on the physiological responses. For each control/relevant pair a score is assigned for each separate physiological measure. A +1 to +3 is assigned if the response to the control question is larger (the larger the difference, the higher the score). If the response for the relevant question is larger than that for the control question, a score between −1 and −3 is assigned. A 0 is assigned if the responses to the questions are identical. A total score is obtained by summing these scores across the physiological measures and the tests, with a positive score of +5 or greater indicating a truthful outcome, a negative score of more than −5 indicating a deceptive outcome, and scores between +5 and −5 considered inconclusive. During the post-test interview the examiner tells the suspect the outcome, and if the outcome is deceptive the examiner attempts to elicit a confession.

Several psychologists have questioned the underlying rationale of the CQT (Cross & Saxe, 2001; Furedy, 1996; Iacono & Patrick, in press). Imagine yourself being falsely accused of a serious crime and taking a polygraph exam. Being innocent you might react more strongly to questions about a crime that you could get punished for (i.e., relevant questions) than about vague questions concerning your past behaviour (i.e., control questions). In contrast, guilty suspects might actually respond more to control questions because they are novel or because they believe they have other crimes to hide. In addition, the guilty suspect may no longer react to the crime-relevant questions because he or she may have been asked repeatedly about it. The validity of the CQT is discussed later in the chapter.

THE GUILTY KNOWLEDGE TEST Developed by Lykken (1960), the **Guilty Knowledge Test** (GKT) does not assess deception but instead seeks to determine whether the suspect knows details about a crime that only the person who committed the crime would know. The general form of the GKT is a series of questions in multiple-choice format. Each question has one correct option (often called the critical option) and four options that are foils—alternatives that could fit the crime but that are incorrect. A GKT question in the context of a homicide might take the following form: "If you were the one who robbed the bank, then you will know what was used as a weapon. Was with the weapon: (a) a knife, (b) an axe, (c) a shotgun, (d) a revolver, or (e) a rifle?" The guilty suspect is assumed to display a larger physiological response to the correct option than to the incorrect options. An innocent person, conversely, who does not know the details of the crime, will not have a larger physiological response to the correct option than to any of the other options.

Underlying the GKT is the principle that people will react more strongly to information they recognize as distinctive or important than to unimportant information. Suspects who consistently respond to critical items are assumed to have knowledge of the crime. The likelihood that an innocent person with no knowledge of the crime would react most strongly to the critical alternative is one in five for each question. If ten questions are asked, the odds that an innocent person will consistently react to the critical alternative are exceedingly small (less than one in 10 000 000).

The most common physiological response measured when administering the GKT is palmar sweating (i.e., galvanic skin response measured in the palm of the hand). Recently, two other responses have been studied in the lab. Preliminary research suggests that response times to questions can accurately identify participants with guilty knowledge (Seymour et al., 2000). Some researchers have also investigated using eye blinks as an index of guilty knowledge (Fukuda, 2001).

Although the GKT is not used routinely by law enforcement in Canada or United States, it is used regularly in a limited number of other jurisdictions, such as Israel and Japan (Ben-Shakhar & Furedy, 1990). Iacono and Patrick (1999) suggest two reasons for the lack of widespread acceptance of the GKT. First, since polygraph examiners believe in the accuracy of the CQT, they are not motivated to use the more difficult-to-construct GKT. Second, in order to use the GKT, there must be salient features of the crime only known to the perpetrator. If details of a crime appear in the media, the crime-related details given cannot be used to construct a GKT.

Validity of Polygraph Techniques

TYPES OF STUDIES How is the accuracy of polygraph tests assessed? Accuracy is determined under ideal circumstances by presenting information known to be true and false to an individual and measuring his or her corresponding physiological responses. In practice, studies assessing the validity of polygraph techniques vary in how closely they are able to achieve this ideal. Studies of the validity of polygraph techniques can be classified into three types: laboratory, field, and field-analogue studies.

In laboratory studies, volunteers (often university students) simulate criminal behaviour by committing a mock crime. Volunteers come to a laboratory and are randomly assigned to one of two conditions: committing a mock crime or not committing a mock crime. The main advantage of these studies is that the experimenter knows **ground truth** (who is truly guilty or innocent). In addition, laboratory studies can also compare the relative merits of different types of polygraph tests and control for such variables as the time between crime and polygraph exam. However, because of the large motivational and emotional differences between volunteers in laboratory studies and actual suspects in real-life situations, the results of laboratory studies may have limited application to real-life situations. In laboratory studies, guilty participants cannot ethically be given strong incentives to "beat" the polygraph, and both guilty and innocent participants have little to fear if they "fail" the polygraph exam.

Field studies involve real-life situations and actual criminal suspects, together with actual polygraph examinations. Field studies often compare the accuracy of "original" examiners to "blind" evaluators. Original examiners conduct the actual evaluation of the suspect. Blind evaluators are provided only with the original examiner's charts and given no information about the suspect or case. Original examiners are exposed to extra-polygraph cues—information about the case in addition to that obtained via the polygraph—such as the case facts and the behaviour of the suspect during the examination. Although polygraph examiners are taught to ignore these cues, Patrick and Iacono (1991) found that examiners are nonetheless significantly influenced by these cues.

The largest problem with field studies is establishing ground truth. Indicators of guilt, such as physical evidence, eyewitness testimony, or DNA evidence, may not always be available. In such situations, truth is more difficult to establish. To deal with this problem, two additional ways of establishing ground truth have been developed: judicial outcomes and confessions. Judicial outcomes are problematic because some people are falsely convicted and some guilty people are not convicted. Confessions are also problematic. Although rare, some people may falsely confess. More significant, however, is the problem that confessions are often not independent from the polygraph examiner's decisions. Confessions are often elicited because a person fails a polygraph exam. Moreover, cases in which a guilty suspect beats the polygraph are not included in research studies. Thus, reliance on confessions to establish ground truth likely inflates polygraph accuracy rates (Iacono & Patrick, in press). Most field studies have used confessions to establish ground truth.

The last type of study is the field-analogue study. In this type of study the act of deception is freely committed by an individual, it is independently known which individuals committed the act, the individuals are concerned about the outcome of the polygraph test, and the polygrapher does not know the proportion of guilty and innocent individuals in the sample. One concern that is raised when conducting such studies is the ethical issue. Is it fair to use such extreme deception? An example of a field analogue polygraph study by Ginton, Daie, Elaad, and Ben-Shakhar (1982) is described next.

POLYGRAPH TESTS: ACCURATE OR NOT? The accuracy of the polygraph for detecting lies is controversial. Numerous laboratory studies have assessed the accuracy of the CQT and GKT (see Iacono & Patrick, 1999, for review). However, as pointed out above, there are problems when relying on typical mock crime scenarios to estimate real-life accuracy. As a consequence, only field and field-analogue assessments of the CQT will be described. The situation concerning the GKT is different. Since the GKT is almost never used in Canada or United States, no relevant North American data are available. Thus, we will describe assessments of the GKT based on laboratory and field studies done in Israel.

Although the CQT has been investigated for more than 30 years, its ability to accurately measure deception remains controversial (Furedy, 1996; National Research Council, 2003). Most of the studies have used confessions to classify suspects as guilty or innocent, and as noted above, there are problems with using this as the criterion. The majority of guilty suspects (84% to 92%) are correctly classified as guilty (Patrick & Iacono, 1991; Raskin, Honts, & Kricher, 1997). However, the picture for innocent suspects is less optimistic, with accuracy rates ranging from 55% to 78% (Honts & Raskin, 1988; Patrick & Iacono, 1991). Many of the innocent suspects were classified as inconclusive. Between 9% and 24% of innocent suspects were falsely identified as guilty. Such a high false-positive rate indicates that innocent people respond more to relevant than control questions, suggesting that the premise underlying the CQT does not apply to all suspects.

Table 5.2 presents data from several field studies comparing the accuracy of the original examiner with the blind evaluators. The accuracy rates of the original examiner are higher than the accuracy of the blind evaluator, especially for innocent suspects. For example, Patrick and Iacono (1991) examined the accuracy of original examiner opinions to blind scoring for 37 innocent verified cases. The hit rate (excluding inconclusives) for original examiners was 90%, compared with 55% for blind scorers. The main reason original examiners are more accurate than blind examiners is

TABLE 5.2 FIELD STUDIES OF THE CONTROL QUESTION TEST*

Study	Guilty Condition			Innocent Condition		
	Guilty	Innocent	Inconclusive	Guilty	Innocent	Inconclusive
Honts & Raskin (1988)	92% (92%)	8% (8%)	0% (0%)	0% (15%)	91% (62%)	9% (23%)
Patrick & Iacono (1991)	98% (92%)	0% (2%)	2% (6%)	8% (24%)	73% (30%)	19% (46%)

*Blind examiners' results appear in parentheses.

that the original examiners appear to be using extra-polygraph cues (such as attitude of the suspect, other evidence about the case, and verbal cues), whereas blind chart evaluators have access only to polygraph information. Additional research is needed to confirm the source of these extra-polygraphic cues used by examiners.

Ginton et al. (1982) evaluated the CQT in a field-analogue study in which 21 police officers attending a police course served as participants. Given the opportunity to cheat on an aptitude test, seven officers cheated while scoring their tests. After several days had elapsed, the officers were told some of them were suspected of cheating on the test. All 21 officers were asked to take a polygraph test to prove they had not cheated. Two guilty and one innocent officer refused. In addition, three of the other guilty officers confessed to cheating prior to the polygraph test. The 15 remaining officers—two who had cheated and 13 who had not—were administered a polygraph test. The rate of correct identifications using blind evaluators was quite low—only one of the two guilty officers and 7 out of the 13 innocent officers were correctly identified. After the polygraph exam, all the officers were told they had participated in a study and that the results would be used only for research purposes. Two important issues are raised by this type of research. First, to surmount the limited emotional impact typical of laboratory studies, Ginton and colleagues used a realistic event to create a meaningful and high-impact emotional effect in their participants. Second, deception is typically required in order to produce the required emotional effect. The researchers argued they needed to use deception in order to provide a more real-life test of the polygraph.

Mock-crime laboratory studies evaluating the GKT indicate that it is very effective at identifying innocent participants (hit rate of around 95%) and slightly less effective at identifying guilty participants (hit rate of around 85%; Iacono & Patrick, 1988; Lykken, 1998). A meta-analysis of 80 GKT studies examined what factors are associated with higher accuracies (Ben-Shakhar & Elaad, 2003). Correct outcomes were better in studies that included motives to succeed, verbal response to alternatives, five or more questions, and in laboratory mock-crime studies. Two published field studies, both done in Israel, have assessed the accuracy of the GKT. Elaad (1990) found that 98% of innocent suspects were correctly classified, but only 42% of guilty suspects were correctly classified. Elaad, Ginton, and Jungman (1992) measured both respiration and skin conductance and found that 94% of innocent and 76% of guilty suspects were correctly classified.

Based on the research described above, the GKT appears to be vulnerable to false-negative errors (falsely classifying guilty suspects as innocent), whereas the CQT is vulnerable to false-positive errors (falsely classifying innocent suspects as guilty). See Box 5.1 on the next page for a new way of measuring deception.

Can the Guilty Learn to Beat the Polygraph?

Is it possible to use **countermeasures** to beat the polygraph? There are Web sites that describe the best ways to beat the polygraph. Honts, Raskin, and Kircher (1994) showed

BOX 5.1 SEEING THROUGH THE FACE OF DECEPTION

If you travel by air, you will be asked questions such as the following:

■ "Did you pack your bags?"

■ "Did you ever leave your bags unattended?"

■ "Has anyone you don't know asked you to carry something on board?"

Technologies that can provide a rapid, accurate assessment of deceit are becoming more and more important.

Pavlidis, Eberhardt, and Levine (2002) examined whether high-definition thermal imaging of the face could be used to detect deceit. Thermal imaging measures the amount of facial warming, which is linked to regional blood flow. Imaging can be done quickly without the individual even knowing his or her facial temperature is being meas-

ured. Pavlidis and colleagues wanted to know whether facial warming was associated with deception. Individuals were randomly assigned to commit a mock crime (stab a mannequin and rob it of $20) or to a control condition in which they had no knowledge of the crime. Use of thermal imaging (in particular around the eyes) correctly classified six of the eight guilty participants and 11 of the 12 of the innocent participants. This accuracy rate was similar to a polygraph exam administered to participants that correctly classified six of eight guilty, and 8 of 12 innocent participants. In the future, when ticket agents or customs officers ask you questions, they may be paying more attention to your facial temperature than to your answers.

---

that 30 minutes of instruction on the rationale underlying the CQT was sufficient for community volunteers to learn how to escape detection in a mock-crime study. Participants were told to use either physical countermeasures (e.g., biting their tongue or pressing their toes on floor) or mental countermeasures (e.g., counting backward by 7 from a number greater than 200) when asked a control question during the polygraph exam. Both countermeasures worked, with 50% of the guilty suspects beating the polygraph test. In addition, the polygraph examiners were not able to accurately detect which participants had used the countermeasures.

Iacono, Cerri, Patrick, and Fleming (1992) investigated whether anti-anxiety drugs would allow guilty subjects to appear innocent on the GKT. Undergraduate students were divided into one innocent group (who watched a noncrime videotape) and four guilty groups. Participants in the guilty groups watched a videotaped crime and then were given one of three drugs (Diazepam, meprobamate, or propranolol) or a placebo prior to being administered a GKT. None of the drugs had an effect on the accuracy of the GKT. In addition, the polygraph examiner was able to identify 90% of the participants receiving drugs.

Can psychopaths beat the polygraph? Psychopaths pose a potential challenge to polygraphy as they are described as being skilled at lying and have a limited capacity for anxiety or guilt (Cleckley, 1976). In addition, research has found that psychopaths do not display anticipatory anxiety to threatening events (Hare, 2003). Two laboratory mock crime studies have assessed psychopathic and nonpsychopathic offenders using the CQT (Patrick & Iacono, 1989; Raskin & Hare, 1978). Patrick and Iacono (1989) attempted to ensure an incentive for taking the task seriously by using a "group contingency threat." Specifically, offenders were told that if they failed the polygraph, none of the participants would obtain a bonus for participating and that their names would be made available to the other offenders. (In fact, all participants received their bonus and the names of those who failed were not told to the other offenders). Blind scoring of the charts obtained correct classification for 87% of the guilty and 57% for the innocent participants (excluding inconclusives). Both psychopaths and nonpsychopaths were detected at the same rate. Whether or not psychopaths would be able to beat the polygraph during an actual field examination has never been investigated. Christopher Patrick, the researcher who conducted this research, is profiled in Box 5.2 on the next page.

Scientific Opinion: What Do the Experts Say?

Most knowledgeable scientists are sceptical about the rationale underlying the CQT and its accuracy. Iacono and Lykken (1997) conducted a survey of 195 members of the Society for Psychophysiological Research and 168 elected Fellows of the General Psychology Divisions of the American Psychological Association. Table 5.3 presents the results from selected questions. Across both organizations, members considered the CQT neither scientifically sound nor suitable for evidence in court. In contrast, the GKT was viewed as being based on sound scientific principles. Survey respondents also believed that the CQT can be circumvented by easily learned countermeasures.

TABLE 5.3 SCIENTIFIC OPINION ABOUT THE POLYGRAPH

Question	Percent Who Agree	
	SPR	APA
CQT is based on scientifically sound theory	36	30
GKT is based on scientifically sound theory	77	72
Would advocate admitting a failed CQT as evidence in court	24	20
Would advocate admitting a passed CQT as evidence in court	27	24
Reasonable to conclude that an individual who fails 8 out of 10 GKT items has guilty knowledge	72	75
CQT can be beaten by increased response to control questions	99	—
Criminals and spies likely to beat a CQT	—	92

Source: Iacono and Lykken, 1997.

BOX 5.2 CANADIAN RESEARCHER PROFILE: CHRISTOPHER PATRICK

Dr. Christopher Patrick is a Starke R. Hathaway Distinguished Professor in the Department of Psychology at the University of Minnesota. Dr. Patrick has conducted research in numerous areas relevant to forensic psychology, including affective and temperamental bases of psychopathy and criminality, effects of alcohol and other drugs on emotional processing, and psychophysiological methods of deception detection.

Dr. Patrick first became interested in forensic issues as an undergraduate at the University of Calgary, where he majored in psychology and minored in criminology. As a graduate student at the University of British Columbia, he was strongly influenced by two faculty members doing forensic research: Dr. Robert Hare, whose research focused on criminal psychopaths, and Dr. William Iacono, who was doing work on the detection of deception. Dr. Patrick was able to merge these two areas of interest in his doctoral research, which investigated lie detection in psychopathic and nonpsychopathic incarcerated offenders.

What maintains his interest in conducting research is the opportunity to do something really new and the associated process of discovery. For example, as a young researcher conducting his dissertation research, he found interviewing real-life offenders and investigating whether actual polygraph examiners could detect which offenders had committed a staged crime unique and fascinating.

His favourite study is one in which he applied a new paradigm for the study of human emotion—the affect modulated startle paradigm—to a sample of incarcerated psychopaths (Patrick, Bradley, & Lang, 1993). This study sparked renewed interest among psychopathy researchers in the study of emotional processes, and its basic finding has been replicated by several researchers around the world. The study also served as a foundation for much of Dr. Patrick's subsequent research investigating the underlying facets of psychopathy. The two samples he has most often studied are incarcerated offenders and university students. However, recently he has begun to work with community samples of adolescent and adult twins.

Dr. Patrick believes future forensic psychology researchers should have a strong foundation in basic scientific principles along with methodological expertise in specific domains such as psychometrics, multivariate analysis, psychophysiology, brain imaging, or behavioural/molecular genetics. The course he most enjoys teaching at the undergraduate level is "Psychopaths and Serial Killers." Dr. Patrick plays guitar in two blues/rock bands, and he is an avid surfer (although his surfing activities have declined since moving to Minnesota) and reader of literary fiction (favourite novels include *Underworld* by Don DeLillo and *Continental Drift* by Russell Banks). He has been married for 23 years and is the proud father of one daughter, Sarah Kathryn.

More recently, the United States National Research Council (NRC) established a panel of 14 scientists and four staff to review the validity of the polygraph. In a comprehensive report, the committee concluded the following:

■ "The theoretical rationale for the polygraph is quite weak, especially in terms of differential fear, arousal, or other emotional states that are triggered in response to relevant and comparison questions" (NRC, 2003, p. 213).

■ "The existing validation studies have serious limitations. Laboratory test findings on polygraph validity are not a good guide to accuracy in field settings. They are likely to overestimate accuracy in field practice, but by an unknown amount" (p. 210).

■ "In summary, we were unable to find any field experiments, field quasi-experiments, or prospective research-oriented data collection specifically designed to assess polygraph validity and satisfying minimal standards of research quality" (p. 115).

■ "What is remarkable, given the large body of relevant research, is that claims about the accuracy of the polygraph made today parallel those made throughout the history of the polygraph: practitioners have always claimed extremely high levels of accuracy, and these claims have rarely been reflected in empirical research" (p. 107).

Despite scientists' negative view of it, the CQT is still used by law enforcement as an investigative tool. To understand why, we only have to know that whatever its actual validity, the polygraph will cause many suspects to confess, thereby providing resolution of the criminal investigation.

Admissibility of Polygraph Evidence

Polygraph results were first submitted as evidence in court in the United States in *Frye v. United States* (1923). James Frye was denied the opportunity to have the results of a polygraph test conducted by William Marston admitted as evidence. This ruling led to the requirement that a technique must obtain "general acceptance" by the relevant scientific community before it can be admitted as evidence. Some states permit the admission of polygraph evidence if there is a prior agreement between prosecuting and defence lawyers. In a recent decision, the United States Supreme Court (*U.S. v. Scheffer, 1998*) rejected the admissibility of the polygraph because of the belief that polygraph evidence will usurp the role of the jury as determinant of the credibility of a witness. Justice Thomas ruled: "Jurisdictions, in promulgating rules of evidence, may legitimately be concerned about the risk that juries will give excessive weight to the opinions of the polygrapher, clothed as they are in scientific expertise and at times offering, as in respondent's case, a conclusion about the ultimate issue in the trial" (p. 422).

Polygraph evidence is not admissible in Canadian courts of law. The same concerns that have been raised by United States courts have been a focus of concern in Canadian courts. In *R. v. Beland* (1987), the Supreme Court of Canada ruled that polygraph evidence should not be admitted to help determine whether or not a person is telling the truth. They referred to the polygraph as being falsely imbued with the "mystique of science," thus causing jurors to weight polygraph evidence more than it deserves when determining the verdict.

Impact of Polygraph Evidence on Jurors

Do jurors regard polygraph evidence with an aura of infallibility? Recent studies have shown that polygraph evidence has a limited effect on jurors and their verdicts (Myers, Rosol, & Boelter, 2003; Spanos et al., 1992–1993). For example, Myers and colleagues (2003) presented college students with a mock transcript of a sexual assault trial. Participants were randomly assigned to polygraph expert testimony (defendant was deceptive) or no polygraph expert testimony groups, and to whether there was corroborating evidence (medical testimony and eyewitness evidence) or no corroborating evidence. Presence of polygraph evidence did not influence verdicts, whereas the presence of corroborating evidence did influence verdicts. Although polygraph evidence may not affect a jury's decision in a laboratory study, we must be careful before generalizing these findings to real-life criminal cases. Consider a rape case in which the outcome depends on the credibility of the victim versus the suspect. In many such cases, the crux of the case is whether or not the victim consented. If both parties appear to be credible, but one enhances his or her claim by passing a polygraph test, the jury might be swayed by this information. Future research is needed to investigate the effect of polygraph testimony as a function of the extent and quality of other evidence.

BRAIN-BASED POLYGRAPH TECHNIQUES

In the past decade, researchers have attempted to use brain-based responses to detect deception. **Event-related brain potentials** (ERPs) are a type of brain-based response that have been investigated for detecting deception. ERPs are measured by placing electrodes on the scalp and noting changes in electrical patterns related to presentation of a stimulus. ERPs reflect underlying electrical activity in the cerebral cortex. One type of ERP that has shown promise is known as the P300. This ERP occurs in response to significant stimuli that occur infrequently. When using GKT procedures, guilty suspects should respond to such crime-relevant events with a large P300 response, compared to non-crime-relevant events. No difference in P300 responses to crime-relevant and irrelevant events should be observed in innocent suspects. One of the advantages of ERPs is that they have been proposed as a measure resistant to manipulation. (However, Rosenfeld, Soskins, Bosh, & Ryan, 2004, have obtained results that suggest participants who are knowledgeable about ERPs can evade detection.)

Several studies have been conducted to assess the validity of the P300 as a guilt detector (e.g., Allen & Iacono, 1997; Farwell & Donchin, 1991; Rosenfeld et al., 1991; Rosenfeld et al., 1987) and as a detector of feigned memory loss (Allen, 2002; Allen, Iacono, & Danielson, 1992; Rosenfeld et al., 1996).

Farwell and Donchin (1991) conducted one of the first studies on the use of the P300 to detect the presence of guilty knowledge. The study consisted of two experiments. In the first experiment, participants role-played one of two espionage scenarios, which involved the exchange of information with a foreign agent, during which they were exposed to six critical details (e.g., the colour of the agent's hat). In the second experiment, participants were asked about details of minor offences they had committed in their day-to-day lives. In the first experiment, using P300 as the measure, 18 of 20 participants were correctly classified in the guilty condition, and 17 of 20 were correctly classified in the innocent condition. In experiment two, all four of the guilty participants were correctly classified, and three of the four innocent participants were correctly classified. Although the results look impressive, there are several limitations to this study. First, guilty participants reviewed the crime-relevant details just prior to taking the GKT. In addition, there was no punishment linked to performance in this study. Finally, the sample size, especially in experiment two, was very small. Rosenfeld et al. (1991) also examined the accuracy of the P300 as an index of deception in a GKT procedure. Correct classification rates were 92% and 87% for guilty and innocent participants, respectively.

Other brain responses have also been tested with some success in the laboratory, including the N400 response (Boaz et al., 1991) and the contingent negative variation (Fang, Liu, & Shen, 2003).

More recently, the researchers have begun to investigate the cognitive processes used when people are deceptive. Johnson, Bernhardt, and Zhu (2004) recorded ERPs while participants made truthful and deceptive responses about words they had been told to memorize. The results revealed different patterns of brain activity when a person was being truthful versus deceptive. When participants made deceptive responses, they showed activity in the medial frontal cortex (more specifically the anterior cingulate cortex). This area of the brain plays an important role when the person is deciding between conflicting responses.

Investigators have also begun to use functional magnetic resonance imaging (fMRI) to determine which areas of the brain are associated with deception (Ganis et al., 2003; Langleben et al., 2002). For example, Ganis and colleagues (2003) examined which brain areas were activated when someone told a spontaneous or rehearsed lie. Lies that were part of a story and that had been rehearsed repeatedly produced a higher level of activation in the right anterior frontal cortex than did spontaneous isolated lies. In contrast, spontaneous isolated lies produced a higher level of activation in the anterior cingulate and posterior visual cortices. These findings and others indicate that brain-imaging techniques can differentiate which parts of the brain are involved in lying and can even indicate which areas are associated with different types of lying.

Iacono and Patrick (in press) provide a comprehensive review of these brain-based methods for detecting deception. Box 5.3 (on page 140) describes the case of Terry Harrington, a man convicted of murder who attempted to use the results of brain-based deception testing to prove his innocence.

BOX 5.3 BRAIN FINGERPRINTING: EVIDENCE FOR A NEW DECEPTION DETECTION TECHNOLOGY?

The case that put brain fingerprinting in the news was *State v. Harrington*. On July 22, 1977, retired police officer John Schweer was shot and killed while working as a security guard for a car dealership in Iowa. Seventeen-year-old Terry Harrington and Curtis McGhee were arrested for the murder. At his trial Terry Harrington claimed he was not at the crime scene and several witnesses testified that Harrington had been at a concert on the night of the murder. The prosecution's key witness was another teenager, Kevin Hughes, who testified that he was with Harrington and McGhee the night of the murder. According to Hughes, the three teenagers decided to steal a car. They went to the car dealership. Hughes testified that he waited in the car while Harrington, who first removed a shotgun from the trunk, and McGhee went around a building at the car dealership. Hughes claims he heard a gunshot and Harrington and McGhee came running back to the car. Hughes testified that Harrington had stated he had just shot a cop. Both Terry Harrington and Curtis McGhee were convicted of first-degree murder and sentenced to life without the possibility of parole.

Throughout his 25 years of imprisonment, Terry Harrington has maintained his innocence. All his attempts to appeal his conviction were unsuccessful. From his prison cell, Harrington heard about a new technology that might help his case. He contacted Lawrence Farwell, a cognitive psychophysiologist and head of Brain Fingerprinting Laboratories. On April 18 and 25, 2000, Farwell came to the Iowa State Penitentiary to test Harrington to determine if he had knowledge of the crime scene and of details about his alibi (the concert he claims he attended). Farwell measured the amplitude of Harrington's P300 brain potential to irrelevant and relevant crime scene and concert details. According to Farwell, Harrington's lack of P300 response to crime-relevant details indicated that Harrington had not participated in the murder. In contrast, Harrington showed a prominent P300 to alibi-relevant information.

Harrington's case received national attention in December 2001 when the CBS show *60 Minutes* featured Farwell's research and his testing of Harrington. In March of 2002, Harrington's lawyer submitted a report to the Supreme Court of Iowa describing the results of Farwell's testing.

Although the results of the "brain fingerprinting" were entered as evidence, the judges relied on other evidence to overturn the murder conviction. During the hearing, three of the prosecution witnesses recanted their testimony. Kevin Hughes stated that he had made up the story about what happened the night of the murder. Hughes claimed that he lied to obtain the $5000 reward being offered about the murder and to avoid being charged with the crime. In addition, the police failed to turn over all the police reports to Harrington's defence lawyer. These police reports documented the police investigation of an alternative suspect. On February 26, 2003, the Supreme Court of Iowa overturned the murder conviction of Terry Harrington and the case was remanded for a new trial. On October 24, 2003, the Pottawattamie County Attorney announced that he was dropping the murder charges against Terry Harrington.

VOCAL AND NONVERBAL BEHAVIOUR CUES TO LYING

Another method of deception detection is through the analysis of vocal characteristics and nonverbal behaviours. The underlying assumption is the same as that for polygraphy: The act of deception produces a physiological change compared with telling the truth. The argument here is that it is more difficult for people to control aspects of their nonverbal behaviour than their verbal behaviour (DePaulo & Kirkendol, 1989). The typical experiment involves one group of participants (called the "message source") who are told to provide either true or deceptive messages. For example, DePaulo, Lassiter, and Stone (1982) asked participants to honestly describe people they like and dislike. They also asked participants to describe the same people dishonestly (i.e., to pretend to like the person they disliked and vice versa). Another group of participants was asked to detect when the message source participants were truthful or deceptive.

Researchers have also assessed facial cues and vocal cues to deception. For example, Ekman and Friesen (1974) showed student nurses a film of an ocean scene and videotaped them describing what they were seeing and how they felt while watching the film. They also watched a gruesome medical training film (e.g., amputation of hand or severe industrial burn) and were videotaped while pretending to watch a pleasant film. In order to motivate the nurses, the researchers told them that in order to be successful in nursing, they would have to be able to mask feelings when dealing with unpleasant events. Other studies have motivated participants by offering incentives, such as money, if they successfully get away with their lies.

Across studies, the ability to distinguish lies tends to be only slightly better than chance. For example, a meta-analysis by Kraut (1980) indicated the average accuracy rate was 57%. This poor performance in deception detection has been explained in two ways. First, people tend to rely on behaviours that lack predictive validity (Fiedler & Walka, 1993). Second, most people have a **truth-bias**. Truth-bias refers to the tendency of people to judge more messages as truthful than deceptive (Anderson, Ansfield, & DePaulo, 1999).

Table 5.4 on the next page describes the types of vocal and nonvocal indicators used to detect deception. The vocal indicator that has been most strongly associated with deception is voice pitch. Liars tend to speak in a higher-pitched voice than those telling the truth. Most studies have found increased use of speech disturbances (ah, umm) and a slower rate of speech during deception (DePaulo et al., 1982; Fiedler & Walka, 1993). However, if you ask participants only to conceal information or instruct them on what they should lie about, deception is associated with fewer speech disturbances and a faster speech rate (Vrij, 1995). In summary, it appears that cognitively more difficult lies (lies in which you have to fabricate an answer) may be associated with one pattern of speech disturbances, whereas cognitively simpler lies (lies in which you must conceal something) may be associated with a different pattern of speech disturbances.

TABLE 5.4 VOCAL AND NONVOCAL CHARACTERISTICS OF DECEPTION

Vocal Characteristics

- Speech fillers (frequency of saying "ah" or "mmm")
- Speech errors (word or sentence repetition, sentence change, sentence incompletion, or slips of the tongue)
- Pitch of voice (changes in pitch)
- Rate of speech (number of words spoken in a specific time period)
- Speech pauses (length of silence between question asked and answer given; number of noticeable pauses in speech)

Nonvocal Characteristics

- Gaze aversion (avoiding looking at the face of conversation partner or interviewer)
- Smiling (frequency of smiles or laughs)
- Blinking (frequency of eye blinks)
- Fidgeting (scratching head, playing with jewellery)
- Illustrators (gestures to modify or supplement what is being said)
- Hand/finger movement
- Leg or foot movements
- Body movements
- Shrugs (frequency of shoulders raised in an "I-don't-know"–type gesture)
- Head movements (nods or shakes head)
- Shifting positions

Source: Adapted from Vrij, 1998.

When someone is lying to you, does that person look you straight in the eye or avert his or her gaze? The research on whether nonverbal behaviours can be used to identify liars is mixed. However, two nonvocal indicators of deception have been found across studies. Liars tend to move their hands or arms and feet or legs less than truth tellers. Nonverbal behaviours such as gaze aversion, smiling, and self-manipulations have not been found to be reliable indicators of deception (Vrij, 1998).

If the liar is not feeling excited, scared, or guilty, or when the lie is easy to fabricate, behavioural cues to deception will likely not be present. In a study of everyday lying, DePaulo, Kashy, Kirkendol, Wyer, and Epstein (1996) found that both college students and community members practised deception daily. Most of the deception was not considered serious and the participants reported they were not concerned or worried about being caught. Participants lied about their opinions, feelings, achievements, reasons for doing things, and possessions. Most of the lies were told for psychological reasons, such as protecting the liar from embarrassment. For example, "I told her Ted and I still liked each other when really I don't know if he likes me at all." The reason this person lied was "Because I'm ashamed of the fact that he doesn't like me anymore."

If people are under stress it is possible to detect deceit by paying attention to signs of emotions, which are seen as micro facial expressions (Ekman, 1992; Frank & Ekman, 1997). In addition, DePaulo and her colleagues (DePaulo, LeMay, & Epstein, 1991; Forrest & Feldman, 2000; Vrij, 2000) have found that high-stakes lies are easier to detect than low-stakes lies. Recently, Vrij, Edward, Roberts, and Bull (2000) found that in cases where participants were given little time to prepare their deception, 71% of truths and 85% of lies could be detected if several nonverbal and verbal indicators were measured.

In a comprehensive meta-analysis, DePaulo and her colleagues (2003) coded 158 cues to deception from 120 samples of adults. Most of the verbal and nonverbal behaviours coded did not discriminate between liars and truth tellers. One of the most reliable indicators was that liars provide fewer details than do truth tellers. Liars also told less compelling accounts as compared with truth tellers. For example, liars' stories are less likely to make sense (be less plausible, lack logical structure, have discrepancies), be less engaging, and be less fluent than were truth tellers' stories. Liars were also rated as less cooperative and more nervous and tense than truth tellers. Finally, truth tellers were more likely to spontaneously correct their stories and more likely to admit to a lack of memory than liars were. Deception cues were easier to detect when the liar was motivated to lie or when he or she was attempting to cover up a personal failing or a transgression.

Can You Detect Deception through Voice Stress Analysis?

You can purchase a voice stress analysis system, which its sellers claim can be used to detect inaudible "microtremors of the vocal muscle" that are associated with heightened stress. Companies advertise them as "hand-held lie detectors" to be used to see whether your partner, boss, friends, or mechanic is lying to you. According to a review conducted by the U.S. National Research Council, current voice stress analysis technology is of little or no use (NRC, 2003).

Are Some People Better at Detecting Deception?

Several studies by Ekman and his colleagues have investigated the abilities of diverse professional groups to detect deception. In the 1991 study by Ekman and O'Sullivan, forensic psychiatrists, custom agents, Federal Bureau of Investigation agents, and judges all performed around chance levels in detecting deception. The only group that performed better than chance (64% correct) were Secret Service agents. About a third of Secret Service agents were 80% accurate or better. The most accurate participants were those who relied on multiple cues to assess credibility rather than on any one cue.

More recently, Ekman, O'Sullivan, and Frank (1999) showed professional groups videotaped speakers describing a true or false opinion. Both federal law enforcement and clinical psychologists were able to detect deceit at above chance levels (around 70% correct). In a Canadian study, Porter, Woodworth, and Birt (2000) found that parole officers performed below chance levels (40% correct) at distinguishing videotaped speakers describing a truthful or fictitious stressful personal experience, such as an animal attack or a serious car accident. However, after attending a deception detection workshop, they were significantly more accurate (77% correct). Thus, although detecting deception is difficult, it is possible to improve judgment accuracy through training.

In a recent review of 40 studies, Vrij (2000) found a 67% accuracy rate for detecting truths and a 44% accuracy rate for detecting lies. Table 5.5 presents the accuracy rates of "professional lie catchers." In most of the studies, the professional lie catchers were not very accurate at detecting deception. The results also showed that in most studies, truthful messages were identified with more accuracy than deceptive ones. Thus, even professional lie catchers have a truthfulness bias. One reason even professionals are not good at detecting lies is that they rely on the wrong cues. For example, Vrij and Semin (1996) found that 75% of police and custom officers believe that gaze aversion is a reliable indicator of deception, but empirical research has not found it to be a reliable indicator of deception (Vrij, 1998). The Mann, Vrij, and Bull (2004) study

TABLE 5.5 ACCURACY RATES OF PROFESSIONAL LIE CATCHERS

Study	Accuracy Rates		
	Truth	Lie	Total
DePaulo & Pfeifer, 1996 (Experienced police)*	64%	42%	52%
DePaulo & Pfeifer, 1996 (New police recruits)*	64%	42%	53%
Ekman & O'Sullivan, 1991 (Federal polygraphers)			56%
Ekman & O'Sullivan, 1991 (Police officers)			56%
Ekman & O'Sullivan, 1991 (Secret Service)			64%
Köhnken, 1987 (Police officers)	58%	31%	45%
Vrij, 1994 (Police detectives)	51%	46%	49%
Ekman et al., 1999 (Federal law enforcement officers)	66%	89%	73%
Ekman et al., 1999 (Sheriffs)	56%	78%	67%
Porter, Woodworth, and Birt, 2000 (Parole officers)	41%	47%	52%
Mann et al., 2004 (Police officers)	64%	66%	65%

*Accuracy rates for experienced police and new recruits were collapsed together.

examined police officers' ability to detect lies and truths told by suspects during police interrogations. These police officers were able to reach accuracy rates similar to more specialized law-enforcement groups, such as Secret Service agents (Ekman et al., 1999). There are two potential explanations for the higher-than-usual accuracy. First, the suspects were highly motivated to lie and research has shown that high-stakes lies are easier to detect than low-stakes lies. Second, the police are more familiar with the setting and type of individual they were judging, namely suspects. Box 5.4 looks at police detection of high-stakes lies.

Two factors one might think would be related to deception detection ability are level of job experience and confidence in judgment. DePaulo and Pfeifer (1996) compared the proficiency of detection deception of university students, new police recruits, and experienced police officers. None of the groups were better than others at detecting deception; however, the experienced police officers reported being more

---

BOX 5.4 DETECTING HIGH-STAKES LIES

You are watching the news, and a mother is being interviewed outside her home, begging for the return of her two sons. She says that while stopped at a stop sign, a black man approached her car with a gun and demanded she get out of the car. Her two young sons were in the backseat. Frightened for her life, she got out of the car and the carjacker jumped into the car and drove off with the children in the back. Over the next nine days, she is often on the news pleading with the carjacker to return her sons. Your initial reaction is concern for the mother and hope that the children will be found unharmed. On the ninth day, the mother confesses to police that there was no carjacker, that she had driven her car to a local lake, left the car on the boat ramp in neutral, got out, and watched as the car slowly rolled into the lake and sank. The two children's bodies were found in the car, still in their car seats.

This is the true case of 23-year-old Susan Smith. Smith was convicted of first-degree murder of three-year-old Michael and 14-month-old Alex. During the penalty phase of

the trial, the assistant prosecutor, Keith Giese, stated, "We're going to go back over the nine days of lies, the nine days of deceit, the nine days of trickery, the nine days of begging this country to help her find her children, while the whole time they lay dead at the bottom of that lake" (Reuter, 1995).

Would you have been able to detect if Susan Smith was lying by what she said or by her behaviour during her numerous press conferences? Vrij and Mann (2001) asked a similar question. They asked 52 police officers to view videotaped press conferences of people who were asking the public's help in locating their missing relatives or the murderers of their relatives. Vrij and Mann asked the officers to determine who was lying and who was telling the truth. What they didn't tell the officers was that every video showed people who had actually been found guilty of killing their own relatives. The officers were not very accurate at detecting the deception. Moreover, accuracy was not related to age, years of police work, level of experience interviewing suspects, or confidence.

confident in their decisions. This finding is consistent with more recent research (Ekman & O'Sullivan, 1991; Porter, Woodworth, & Birt, 2000) indicating that neither level of experience nor confidence in deception detection ability are associated with accuracy rates. For example, in a meta-analysis examining the relation between judges' accuracy at detecting deception and confidence in their judgments, DePaulo, Charlton, Cooper, Lindsay, and Muhlenbruck (1997) found the average correlation was 0.04. Men were more confident than women were (even though men are not more accurate detectors) and as the relation between sender and judge was closer (e.g., dating partner, friend versus stranger), the higher the confidence (but again, not the accuracy). The reason that confidence is unrelated to accuracy may be that people rely on cues they believe are related to deception and when they see these cues, their confidence increases. However, since the cues people believe are related to deception are often not valid, their accuracy tends to be poor.

Porter, Campbell, Stapleton, and Birt (2002) investigated several factors related to the ability to detect deceit, including characteristics of the judge (e.g., handedness, type of cues used, personality), characteristics of the target (e.g., attractiveness, gender), and modality of reports (e.g., audiovisual or audio only). The findings were intriguing. In university students, detection accuracy was highest when the judge was left-handed, the target was unattractive, the target and judge were of opposite genders, and if facial cues were relied on. Porter and colleagues interpreted the left-handed advantage as being due to left-handers relying more on right-hemisphere processes, which in turn may be associated with greater emphasis on processing facial cues rather than relying on other, less informative, cues. Attractive liars are assumed to be more readily believed due to the activation of stereotypes (i.e., attractive people are more likely to tell the truth). Gender differences may also arise via the activation of stereotypes.

DECEPTION IN WITNESSES

Not all eyewitnesses are honest. Some may be deceitful for a variety of reasons. For example, imagine you are at the front of a line to get into a popular bar. A tough-looking biker pushes his way to the front of the line. The doorman refuses to allow the man to enter. The biker pulls out a knife, stabs the doorman, and flees. You are worried about the potential consequences to you and your family if you identify the biker to the police. When the police ask you to identify the biker from a photo array that includes the perpetrator, you quickly state the person is not present. Research on deception by eyewitnesses is more limited compared with research on other types of deception. Recently, however, researchers have begun to study the types of choices and decision times associated with eyewitness deception.

Parliament and Yarmey (2002) showed 128 university students a videotaped crime of a man abducting a child. The students were randomly assigned to tell the truth and to accurately identify the perpetrator or to lie to protect the perpetrator. Participants were shown a photo lineup and asked to identify the perpetrator. Participants in the lie-to-protect group more often stated that the perpetrator was not present (in the target-present condition) and made their decision faster compared with the truthful group.

Judges in court are faced with the challenging task of assessing the credibility of witness testimony. In some cases, two witnesses will totally contradict each other. Judges rely on common sense, personal experience, and the demeanour of the witness to determine the credibility of a witness. Some judges have based their assessments of credibility on generalizations rather than on specific demonstrations of deception from the specific witness. For example, in the case *Foto v. Jones* (1974), the judge stated that the plaintiff was not a credible witness, giving the reason as "I regret to have to say that too many newcomers to our country have as yet not learned the necessity of speaking the whole truth.... They have not learned that frankness is essential to our system of law and justice." The Court of Appeal concluded that judges should not use this type of information when determining credibility.

Judges often need to decide on the credibility of only two witnesses. In a case in Nova Scotia, a youth court judge needed to determine the credibility of a white police officer and a 15-year-old black defendant. During the youth court trial, the judge made a statement to the Crown attorney that "police officers were known to mislead the court in the past, that they had been known to overreact particularly to non-white groups." The trial judge placed more credibility on the youth's testimony and the youth was acquitted on the charge of unlawfully assaulting a police officer. The Crown attorney appealed to the Nova Scotia Court of Appeal, claiming that the trial judge was biased against the police officer and this influenced her assessment of his credibility. The appeal was successful and a new trial was ordered. The defence appealed to the Supreme Court of Canada (*R. v. S. [R. D.]*, 1997) and the Supreme Court set aside the Court of Appeal decision and upheld the youth court judges' acquittal.

DECEPTION IN CHILDREN

Even young children engage in deception. Several studies indicate that children will deny engaging in a prohibited behaviour. Like deception in adults, deception in children varies along several dimensions, including the likelihood of engaging in deception and the rationale for lying, such as to protect themselves or another person. However, striking differences also exist when deception is compared in children and adults. For example, children may lack the cognitive sophistication to understand how one lie may require additional lies in order to achieve a coherent story.

Polak and Harris (1999) provide a representative example of a study designed to assess deception in young children. They assigned three- and five-year-olds to two conditions. In the permission condition, children were told they were allowed to touch a toy guitar when the experimenter was absent. In the prohibition condition, they were told not to touch the toy guitar in the experimenter's absence. All the children in the permission condition touched the toy and admitted touching it. However, in the prohibition condition, 54% of the children touched the toy guitar. Of these children, 86% denied when asked if they had touched the toy.

In a second study, children's ability to sustain a false claim was examined. Children were told that a toy house contained a particular animal, such as a stuffed horse. In the prohibition condition, they were told not to look inside the house when the experimenter was absent. In the permission condition, they were told they could look. In both conditions, the animal inside the toy house was different from what they had been told—not a stuffed horse but a stuffed tiger. Children were asked if they had looked inside the house and were also asked to point to the picture of the animal that was inside. Children in the prohibition condition who wanted to mislead the experimenter had to first deny looking in the house and, to sustain this deception, had to feign ignorance about the animal inside (pointing to the animal the experiment had told them was in the house—the stuffed horse). All the children in the permission condition looked inside the house and admitted doing so. However, 95% of the children in the prohibition condition peeked inside the house and of these, 84% denied having looked. Of those children denying, 75% identified the animal that was actually in the house. Thus, although denying wrongful behaviour is widespread in young children, it is difficult for them to sustain a coherent story as part of the deception.

Not all lies are considered to be negative. **White lies** are untruthful statements told with no malicious intent (Bok, 1978). For example, expressing gratitude for an unwanted gift would is usually intended to spare the gift-giver psychological duress arising from the lack of appreciation for the gift by the recipient. In other words, the intent of white lies is to avoid hurting the feelings of the listener and to avoid negative reactions from the listener if speaker told the truth. Talwar and Lee (2002) examined white-lie-telling behaviour in three- to seven-year-olds using a reverse rouge task. In this task, before children are asked to take a photo of the experimenter, they are asked, "Do I look okay for the photo?" In the experimental condition, the experimenter had a large red dot on his nose; in the control condition there was no dot. In the experimental condition, 55 of the 65 children (85%) told the experimenter that he looked okay. All the children who told a white lie to the experimenter admitted to the confederate (who looked at the photo with the children) that the experimenter did not look okay. When the confederate asked why they didn't tell him, about half of the children stated they did not know why or said that they had forgotten to tell. Another 17% said that they thought the mark was permanent, and 11% indicated they did not want to embarrass the experimenter. These results indicate that although some children have insight into their behaviour, it is not clear what motivates other children to tell a white lie.

Overall, the results from these studies and similar ones indicate that white-lie behaviours and lying to conceal a transgression emerge from age three onward. Although young children are capable of deception, they often fail to make their deception believable. Deception in young children may be "inadequate" because their cognitive system has not developed either basic memory or attentional mechanisms, or because they lack metacognitive abilities that would allow them to understand what is required to maintain a believable deception.

ASSESSMENT OF MALINGERING AND DECEPTION

Disorders of Deception

Deception may be a central component of some disorders. The disorders described below vary on two dimensions: (1) whether the person intentionally or consciously produces the symptoms, and (2) whether the motivation is internal or external.

The *Diagnostic and Statistical Manual of Mental Disorders*—Fourth Edition (*DSM-IV*; APA, 1994) diagnostic criteria for a **factitious disorder** include (1) physical or psychological symptoms that are intentionally produced, (2) internal motivation to assume the sick role, and (3) an absence of external incentives. Eisendrath (1996) has suggested that patients with factitious disorders might be aware they are intentionally producing the symptoms, but they may lack insight into the underlying psychological motivation.

There are many different subtypes of factitious disorders, with most being rare. An example of a physical factitious disorder is **Munchausen syndrome**. In this syndrome the patient intentionally produces a physical complaint, such as abdominal pain, and constantly seeks physician consultations, hospitalizations, and even surgery to treat the nonexistent illness. In some cases patients will ingest poison or purposely infect wounds in order to maintain a patient role. This disorder often emerges by age 20, is difficult to treat, and is chronic in nature (APA, 1994). Meadow (1977) coined the term "Munchausen syndrome by proxy" (MBP) to describe cases in which parents or caregivers falsified symptoms in their children. A study by Rosenberg (1987) evaluated 117 reported cases of MBP and found 98% of the individuals were the biological mother of the child; in almost 9% of the cases, the child died. In a more recent review of this syndrome, Sheridan (2003) analyzed the characteristics of 451 MBP cases. Although the most common perpetrator was the child's biological mother (77%), other perpetrators were also identified (the father in 7% of cases). Most the victims were young (age four or younger), with 6% of the victims dying and 7% suffering long-term physical injuries. Nearly one-third (29%) of the perpetrators had some symptoms of Munchausen syndrome.

The two key components of **somatoform disorders** include (1) physical symptoms that cannot be explained by an underlying organic impairment, and (2) the symptoms are not intentionally produced. In this disorder, patients truly believe they have a physical problem and often consult with their physicians for treatment of their physical problems. There are several different subtypes of somatoform disorders, including somatization disorder (patient complains of eight or more physical symptoms) and conversion disorder (patient complains of numbness in a specific area that makes no anatomical sense). Somatoform disorders are rare and often co-occur with other disorders such as depression or anxiety (Gureje et al., 1997).

The two key components to **malingering** are that (1) the psychological or physical symptoms are clearly under voluntary control and (2) there are external motivations for the production of symptoms. People typically malinger mental illness for one of the following external motivations:

- A criminal may attempt to avoid punishment by pretending to be unfit to stand trial, to have a mental illness at the time of a criminal act, or to have an acute mental illness in order to avoid being executed.
- Prisoners or patients may seek drugs, or prisoners may want to be transferred to a psychiatric facility to do easier time or to escape.
- Malingerers may seek to avoid conscription to the military or to avoid certain military duties.
- Malingerers may seek financial gain from disability claims, workers' compensation, or damages from alleged injury.
- Malingerers may seek admission to a hospital to obtain free room and board.

Any psychiatric or physical disorder may be malingered. As new syndromes are developed, such as post-traumatic stress disorder, they provide new opportunities for people to attempt to malinger them. Malingering varies in terms of severity from benign (e.g., "Not tonight, honey; I have a headache") to serious (e.g., "I heard a voice telling me to kill my neighbour so I obeyed it.").

Individuals with factitious and somatoform disorders often encourage and even insist on having physical tests and invasive procedures, whereas malingerers will often refuse to cooperate with invasive procedures to determine the veracity of their symptoms. The incidence of malingering in the general population is unknown. Patients who malinger rarely admit it. Thus, individuals who successfully malinger are never included in the statistics. Moreover, mental health professionals are often reluctant to label a patient as a malingerer.

The prevalence rate of malingering is relatively high in forensic contexts. For example, Frederick, Crosby, and Wynkoop (2000) reported that 45% of patients evaluated for competency or mental state at the time of offence produced invalid psychological test profiles. Rogers, Ustad, and Salekin (1998) reported that 20% of emergency jail referrals feigned psychological symptoms. Rogers (1986) reported that 4.5% of defendants evaluated for mental state at the time of offence were definite malingerers and another 20% were suspected. Given these large numbers, it is clear that malingering should be considered in all forensic evaluations. Estimates of malingering psychological symptoms following personal injury range widely. For example, Lees-Haley (1997) reported that about 25% of personal injury claimants were feigning post-traumatic symptoms in an attempt to receive financial compensation.

The opposite of malingering is called **defensiveness**. Defensiveness refers to the conscious denial or extreme minimization of physical or psychological symptoms. These are patients or offenders who present themselves in a favourable light. Minimization of physical and psychological symptoms varies both in degree and motivation. Some people might want to appear to be functioning well in order to meet an external need, such as being a fit parent, or an internal need, such as unwillingness to acknowledge they are a "patient." Degree of defensiveness can range from mild, such as downplaying a minor symptom, to outright denial of a more serious psychological impairment, such as denying hearing command hallucinations. Defensiveness is commonplace in evaluations of sex offenders. The majority of sex offenders either deny their sexual offending or greatly minimize the effect of their sexual offending (Barbaree, 1991).

Explanatory Models of Malingering

Based on the primary motives, Rogers (1990) described three explanatory models of malingering: pathogenic, criminological, and adaptational. The pathogenic model assumes that people are motivated to malinger due to an underlying mental disorder. According to this model, the patient attempts to gain control over his or her pathology by creating bogus symptoms. Over time, these patients experience more severe mental disorders and the true symptoms emerge. Little empirical support exists for this model.

The criminological model focuses on "badness"—"a bad person (Antisocial Personality Disorder), in bad circumstances (legal difficulties), who is performing badly (uncooperative)" (Rogers, 1997, p. 7). This is similar to the definition of malingering expressed in the *DSM-IV* (APA, 1994). According to this definition, malingering should be strongly suspected if two or more of the following factors are present: (1) presence of antisocial personality disorder, (2) forensic assessment, (3) lack of cooperation, and (4) marked discrepancy between subjective complaints and objective findings. Like the pathogenic model, little empirical support exists for this model. No research indicates that persons with antisocial personality disorder are any more likely to malinger than are other offenders (Rogers, 1990). In addition, many different types of patients are uncooperative with evaluations, including those with eating disorders or substance use problems. In contrast, some malingerers appear to be highly cooperative. Rogers (1990) found that *DSM-IV* indicators of malingering tended to overdiagnose malingering in a forensic sample.

According to the adaptational model, malingering is likely to occur when (1) there is a perceived adversarial context, (2) personal stakes are very high, and (3) no other viable alternatives are perceived. Research findings support this model in that there are higher rates of malingering in adversarial settings or when the personal stakes are high. This model provides the broadest and least pejorative explanation of malingering. Rogers, Sewell, and Goldstein (1994) asked 320 forensic psychologists to rate 32 items subdivided into pathogenic, criminological, and adaptational models on how important the item was to malingering. The adaptational model was rated the most important and the pathogenic model as the least important.

How to Study Malingering

Research comprises three basic designs: case study, simulation, and known groups. Each of these designs has its associated strengths and weaknesses. Although case studies are not used as often as they once were, they are useful for generating a wide variety of hypotheses that can be tested using designs with more experimental rigour. In addition, a case study is the only way to study rare syndromes, such as Munchausen-by-proxy syndrome.

Most research on malingering has used a **simulation design** (similar to polygraph laboratory studies). Participants are told to malinger a specific disorder and are typically compared with two groups: (1) a control group randomly selected from the same population as the malingerers and (2) a clinical comparison group representing the disorders or symptoms that are being feigned. These studies address whether measures can detect malingering in nonclinical samples. However, individuals with mental disorders may also malinger. Studies have begun to ask patients with mental disorders to feign a different mental disorder or to exaggerate the severity of their symptoms. These studies address how effectively participants with mental disorders can malinger. In an early study using a clinical sample, Rogers (1988) reported that nearly half of the psychiatric inpatients either did not remember or did not follow the instructions to malinger. In order to examine the relative efficacy of detection methods for disordered and nondisordered samples, the optimal simulation design would use four groups—nonclinical experimental, nonclinical-control, clinical-experimental, and clinical-control.

The primary strength of the simulation design is its experimental rigour. The main disadvantage is its limited generalizability to the real world. Simulation studies are often limited in their clinical usefulness because of the minimal levels of preparation and level of motivation by participants. Early studies used brief and nonspecific instructions, such as "Appear mentally ill"). Instructions are now becoming more specific, with some studies giving participants a scenario to follow: for example, "Imagine you have been in a car accident and you hit your head. You have decided to exaggerate the amount of memory problems you are having in order to obtain a larger monetary settlement from the car insurance company." In addition, participants may be given time to prepare.

Some studies have coached participants by providing information about genuine mental disorders or by telling them about detection strategies. Research suggests that telling participants about disorders does not help them, whereas information about detection strategies does help them avoid detection (Baer, Wetter, & Berry, 1995; Storm & Graham, 2000). In contrast, Bagby, Nicholson, Bacchiochi, Ryder, and Bury (2002) found that providing students with information about validity scales designed to detect deception did not enhance their ability to feign successfully.

Ethical concerns have been raised about whether participants should be taught how to become skilled malingerers. Ben-Porath (1994) has argued that such research does not "appear to have sufficient scientific justification to make up for the potential harm that might be caused by publishing such as study" (p. 150). A recent survey of lawyers and law students indicates that about 50% would provide information about psychological testing, including whether the test had any validity scales to detect deception (Wetter & Corrigan, 1995). See Box 5.5 for a discussion of the conflict between ethics and research design when doing this type of research.

BOX 5.5 ETHICS OF DECEPTION RESEARCH

Simulation laboratory studies are often used to study the accuracy of detection measures. In order to make these experiments more similar to real-world situations, rewards are given for successful deception but punishment is meted out for unsuccessful deception. In the studies described below, both positive and negative incentives were used to approximate real-life criminal investigation settings.

PSYCHOPATHY, THREAT, AND POLYGRAPH TEST ACCURACY

The participants in a laboratory polygraph study by Patrick and Iacono (1989) were incarcerated Canadian male offenders. The experimenters wanted to "create a realistic threat context for the polygraph tests.... A failure to live up to group expectations can provoke responses much stronger than mere disapproval: Peer labeling in the prison environment frequently leads to ostracism, persecution, and physical brutality" (p. 348). Offenders were offered $10 for participating in the experiment and the potential of a $20 bonus. Offenders were told that if more than ten offenders were judged by the polygraph examiner as deceptive, no one would receive the $20 bonus. In order to increase the offenders' motivation, they were told that a list of the names of participants who failed would be made public.

Offenders were randomly assigned to commit or not commit a mock crime. The mock crime consisted of sneaking into the doctor's office and removing $20 from the pocket of the doctor's jacket. Each participant was given a polygraph test. It was clear that some of the participants were concerned about their test outcomes. For example, one offender stated, "I hope they [the other inmates] don't beat my head if I fail" (Patrick and Iacono, 1989, p. 353).

At the end of the study all participants were given the $20 bonus and participants' polygraph test outcomes were not made public.

DETECTING DECEIT AND DIFFERENT TYPES OF HIGH-STAKES LIES

In a study of observers' ability to detect deception, Frank and Ekman (1997) used both positive and negative incentives to motivate their participants. Participants engaged in a mock crime, which involved stealing $50 from a briefcase. They were told they could keep this money if they were able to convince an interviewer they had not taken the money (positive incentive). However, they were also warned that if the interviewer judged them as lying they would have to give back the $50 and would not get the $10 for participating in the study (negative incentive). Some participants were also told that if they were unsuccessful liars they would have to sit in a cold, small, darkened room, on a metal chair, and listen to repeated blasts of 110 dB white noise for an hour (even more negative incentive). At the end of the experiment, all participants received their $10 and were told they did not need to face the additional punishment.

Researchers often have to balance ethical concerns with attempts to increase the validity of their research. In the two studies just described, deception was used to motivate the participants. Some researchers might consider that the level of deception borders on unethical, whereas others would argue that this level of deception is necessary to make the research meaningful. Researchers submit their research protocols to ethical committees for review to ensure the rights of participants are protected. Thus, although you may have some concerns about the level of deception, both of these studies were approved by ethical review.

When individuals engage in malingering in applied settings, the stakes are often high. For example, they may obtain funding for a disability or avoid a harsher sentence. Both the type and magnitude of incentives are typically limited in simulation studies. Studies that use incentives often offer monetary rewards to malingerers for being successful. The magnitude of the incentive ranges from very modest (e.g., $5) to more substantial (e.g., having their name in a lottery with the chance of getting $100). Simulation studies have rarely used negative incentives. For example, the researcher could offer money for participating in a malingering study but take some of the money away if the participant was detected.

Studies investigating malingering in applied settings would ideally use the known-groups design. The **known-groups design** involves two stages: (1) the establishment of the criterion groups (e.g., genuine patients and malingerers), and (2) an analysis of the similarities and differences between these criterion groups. The main strength of the known-groups design is its generalizability to real-world settings. Its chief limitation is the establishment of the criterion groups. Samples of the genuine patients likely include errors, and some of the classified malingerers may be genuine patients. Because of the difficulty with the reliable and accurate classification of criterion groups, this design is rarely used in malingering research.

Malingered Psychosis

How often people attempt to feign psychosis is unknown. Pope, Jonas, and Jones (1982) found nine patients with factitious psychosis in a sample of 219 consecutive admissions to a forensic psychiatric hospital. They followed these patients for seven years, and none went on to develop a psychotic disorder, although all were diagnosed with either borderline personality disorder (a personality disorder defined by instability in mood, self-image, and interpersonal relationships) or histrionic personality disorder (a personality disorder defined by excessive emotionality and attention-seeking behaviours). Cornell and Hawk (1989) reported that 8% of 314 consecutive admissions were diagnosed as malingering psychotic symptoms by experienced forensic psychologists. Box 5.6 describes one of the first studies of malingered psychosis.

WHAT ARE THE INDICATORS OF MALINGERED PSYCHOSIS? Table 5.6 on page 156 provides a list of the potential indicators of malingered psychosis. Resnick (1997) provides a comprehensive description of these indicators. Malingerers often tend to overact, believing the more bizarre they are, the more psychotic they will appear. Early observers have also reported this. For example, Jones and Llewellyn (1917) stated the malingerer "sees less than the blind, he hears less than the deaf, and is more lame than the paralysed ... he ... piles symptom upon symptom and so outstrips madness itself" (p. 17). Malingerers are often willing to discuss their symptoms when asked, whereas actual patients with schizophrenia are often reluctant to discuss their symptoms. Some malingerers may attempt to control the assessment by behaving in an intimidating manner or accusing the clinician of not believing them. In an interview, a malingerer may be evasive when asked to provide details, take a long time

BOX 5.6 BEING SANE IN INSANE PLACES

Imagine you are one of the pseudo-patients taking part in Rosenhan's (1973) study. You go to your local hospital complaining that you have been hearing voices. When asked what the voices are saying, you reply it is sometimes unclear but you think they are saying "empty," "hollow," and "thud." You state that you do not recognize the voice. Other than falsifying your name and occupation, everything else about your personal history is true. Like the actual eight pseudo-patients in the study, you also have no history of any serious pathology. To your surprise you are immediately admitted to the psychiatric inpatient ward with a diagnosis of schizophrenia. Once you are admitted, you tell the staff that your auditory hallucinations have disappeared. Like the real pseudo-patients, you are feeling somewhat apprehensive about what might happen to you. You are cooperative and friendly toward staff and patients. When the staff member asks you how you are feeling, you answer, "I am fine." You follow the rules in the hospital and pretend to take the medication given to you. You have been told that you have to get out of the hospital on your own accord. So you try to convince the staff you are "sane." To deal with the boredom you pace up and down the hall, engage staff and patients in conversation, and write extensive notes about your daily activities. The staff members do not question you about this behaviour, although the other patients on the ward comment on your note-taking and accuse you of being "a journalist or a professor."

In the actual experiment pseudo-patients were hospitalized from 7 to 52 days. Staff failed to recognize the lack of symptoms in the pseudo-patients. Not one of the pseudo-patients was identified as "normal" by staff. As noted by Rosenhan (1973, p. 253), "Once a person is designated abnormal, all of his other behaviors are colored by that label." For example, the nurses interpret your pacing behaviour as a manifestation of anxiety and your note-taking as a behavioural manifestation of your pathology. Pseudo-patients' attempts to initiate conversations with staff were not very successful, since the staff would "give a brief response while they were on the move and with head averted, or no response at all" (Rosenhan, 1973, p. 255). An example of one conversation was:

[Pseudo-patient]: "Pardon me, Dr. X. Could you tell me when I am eligible for grounds privileges?"
[Physician]: "Good morning, Dave. How are you today?" (moves off without waiting for a reply).

This study raises concerns about the use of labels and how such labels can influence the meaning of behaviours. What are the consequences of psychiatric diagnoses? As stated by Rosenhan (1973, p. 257), "A diagnosis of cancer that has been found to be in error is cause for celebration. But psychiatric diagnoses are rarely found to be in error. The label sticks, a mark of inadequacy forever."

to answer, or answer "I don't know." Malingerers often report rare or atypical symptoms, blatant symptoms, or absurd symptoms that are rarely endorsed by genuine patients. For example, a person attempting to malinger psychosis may claim have seen "a large 60-foot Christ who told me to kill my mother."

TABLE 5.6 CUES TO MALINGERED PSYCHOSIS IN CRIMINAL DEFENDANTS

- Understandable motive for committing crime
- Presence of a partner in the crime
- Current crime fits pattern of previous criminal history
- Suspicious hallucinations
    - Continuous rather than intermittent
    - Vague or inaudible hallucinations
    - Hallucinations with no delusions
    - Inability to describe strategies to diminish voices
    - Claiming all command hallucinations are obeyed
    - Visual hallucinations in black and white
- Suspicious delusions
    - Abrupt onset or termination
    - Eagerness to discuss delusions
    - Conduct markedly inconsistent with delusions
    - Elaborate delusions that lack paranoid, grandiose, or religious themes
- Marked discrepancies in interview versus noninterview behaviour
- Sudden emergence of psychotic symptoms to explain criminal act
- Absence of any subtle signs of psychosis

Source: Adapted from Resnick, 1997.

Malingerers are more likely to report positive symptoms of schizophrenia such as delusions (a false belief that is persistently held) or hallucinations (a perceptual experience in absence of external stimulation), as compared with negative or subtle symptoms of schizophrenia, such as blunted affect, concreteness, or peculiar thinking. Both auditory and visual hallucinations are common in psychotic patients. When a person is suspected of malingering auditory hallucinations, he or she should be asked the vocal characteristics (e.g., clarity, loudness, duration), source (inside or outside of the head), characteristics (e.g., gender, familiar or unfamiliar voice, command), and response (insight into unreality, coping strategies, obeying them). Comparing genuine and feigned auditory hallucinations is one way to detect a malingerer. For example, actual patients often report coping strategies to make the "voices go away," such as watching TV, seeking out interpersonal contact, or taking medications (Kanas & Barr, 1984). The malingerer may report there is nothing that will make the "voices go away."

In other cases, malingerers may report atypical auditory command hallucinations (hallucinations telling people to act in a certain way), such as "Go commit a sex offence" or "Rob, rob, rob."

Genuine visual hallucinations are usually of normal-sized people seen in colour, and remain the same if eyes are open or closed. Atypical visual hallucinations such as seeing "a green devil in the corner laughing" or "a dog that would change in size when giving messages" or seeing hallucinations in only black and white are indicative of malingering.

ASSESSMENT METHODS TO DETECT MALINGERED PSYCHOSIS

Interview-Based Methods The *Structured Interview of Reported Symptoms* (SIRS; Rogers, Bagby, & Dickens, 1992) was initially developed in 1985, and in the most recent version consists of 172 items that are scored from a structured interview. The items are organized into the following eight scales that represent different strategies that a person may employ when malingering:

- Rare symptoms (RS)—symptoms very infrequently endorsed by true patients
- Symptom combinations (SC)—pairings of symptoms that are uncommon
- Improbable or absurd symptoms (IA)—symptoms unlikely to be true since they are rarely endorsed by true patients
- Blatant symptoms (BL)—items that are obvious signs of mental disorder
- Subtle symptoms (SU)—items that contain what most people consider everyday problems
- Selectivity of symptoms (SEL)—ratio of symptoms endorsed versus those not endorsed
- Severity of symptoms (SEV)—number of severe symptoms reported
- Reported versus observed symptoms (RO)—discrepancy between self-report and observable symptoms

The SIRS has been extensively validated using both simulation and known-groups designs, and research has consistently demonstrated differences in SIRS scores between honest and simulating samples, and between clinical samples and suspected malingerers (Rogers, 1997).

Self-Report Questionnaires The first attempt to develop a self-report test of malingering was the M test (Baeber, Marston, Michelli, & Mills, 1985). The M test is a 33-item true-false test designed to screen for malingering schizophrenia. Items include genuine schizophrenic symptoms and bogus symptoms, such as atypical hallucinations and extremely severe symptoms. Simulation studies have found that students feigning schizophrenia consistently score higher than control students and psychiatric inpatients on the M test (see Smith, 1997, for review). However, using the known-group design has produced variable results. In some studies, suspected malingerers have been detected at moderate levels (70%; Smith & Borum, 1992), whereas Hankins,

Barnard, and Robbins (1993) found that only 31% of the malingerer group was correctly classified.

The most widely used personality inventory to assess nonoffenders and offenders is the Minnesota Multiphasic Personality Inventory (Hathaway & McKinley, 1942) or the MMPI-2 (Butcher et al., 1989). The MMPI includes several clinical scales to assess psychopathology but also includes several scales specifically designed to test "faking-bad" or malingering. For example, the items on the infrequency (F) scale from the MMPI and the Back F (F_B) scale from the MMPI-2 were selected to detect unusual or atypical symptoms and consist of items endorsed by less than 10% of a normative sample. Another scale often used to detect malingering is the Gough Dissimulation Scale (Ds; Gough, 1950). This scale consists of 74 items and was developed to differentiate a group of truly neurotic patients from a sample of college students told to simulate neuroses.

A comprehensive meta-analyses of the MMPI/MMPI-2 and malingering found that the F and F_B scales were the most useful at detecting malingerers (Rogers et al., 2003). However, the optimal cut-off score to use varies across the samples studied. Across studies, the Ds scale was also considered effective at detecting malingerers. A study by Storm and Graham (2000) examined whether the MMPI-2 validity scales would be able to correctly classify college students who have been coached on malingering strategies, students told to malinger but given no coaching, and psychiatric inpatients. Some validity indicators were more susceptible to coaching whereas others, such as the Infrequency Psychopathology scale, could still discriminate coached malingerers from psychiatric inpatients.

Malingered Amnesia

Memory problems are a common symptom in both forensic and clinical practice. Memory deficits may consist of an inability to recall specific, highly salient incidents from the past (i.e., **retrograde amnesia**) or an impaired ability to establish new memories (i.e., **anterograde amnesia**). For example, the murderer who claims to have no memory for what happened before or during the homicidal event would be suffering from retrograde amnesia. In contrast, the patient who has been injured in a car accident who claims not to "remember anything" may be suffering from anterograde amnesia. Offenders may claim amnesia for their criminal behaviour in order to avoid or reduce the punishment (Parwatikar, Holcomb, & Menninger, 1985).

ASSESSMENT METHODS TO DETECT MALINGERED AMNESIA Several measures have been developed to catch the potential malingerer. Often these tests appear to be difficult, but they are actually simple enough that even brain-damaged individuals perform adequately. The assumption underlying these tests is that the person attempting to fake will "overplay" the role and fail on even simple tasks. Many of the tasks available examine the effects of feigned impairments of anterograde amnesia or the acquisition of new information. A number of different versions of the Symptom Validity Test (SVT;

Pankratz, 1988) have been developed to assess malingered amnesia. In these tests, patients are typically presented with 20 to 100 stimuli, such as words or shapes, and following the presentation, they are asked which of two choices they saw previously. Chance responding would result in 50% correct. Individuals who demonstrate below chance responding are presumed to be feigning amnesia, because in order to systematically select the incorrect answer, memory for the correct alternative must be retained.

The Test of Memory Malingering (TOMM; Tombaugh, 1996) is a 50-item recognition test designed to identify true memory-impaired patients from malingerers. In this test, the person is shown 50 drawings for three seconds each, and then is given a forced-choice recognition task in which he or she must choose the drawing he or she just saw from two drawings. People are given feedback about their correct and incorrect choices. Trial 2 repeats the recognition task and, after a delay of ten minutes, a retention trial is administered (same recognition test but no feedback). Five or more errors on Trial 2 or the retention trial indicate the person might be malingering a memory deficit. Using the cut-off of five on Trial 2, Rees, Tombaugh, Gansler, and Moczynski (1998) correctly classified 95% of the brain-injured patients and 100% of controls attempting to malinger memory deficits. In a review of the validity of the TOMM to detect feigned memory impairment, Tombaugh (2002) concludes that the TOMM does meet the required standards for court admissibility.

Recently, attempts have been made to develop tests of retrograde memory based on information from police reports about a crime or from family members. A set of yes/no questions is then developed. If the person is genuinely amnesic, he or she should respond at chance levels to these questions. However, the person whose performance falls below chance is suspected of malingering. This task has been used in several case studies in which malingering was suspected (Frederick, Carter, & Powel, 1995).

SUMMARY

1. The Relevant/Irrelevant Test includes only two tests of questions: relevant questions concerning the crime in question and irrelevant questions that are unrelated to the crime. The Control Question Test (CQT) is the most commonly used polygraph exam in North America. It consists of three types of questions: neutral, control (questions relating to past behaviours that are suppose to generate emotion), and relevant (questions relating to the crime being investigated). The Guilty Knowledge Test (GKT) probes for whether the suspect has knowledge about the details of a crime that only the guilty person would have. This test is rarely used in North America but is used in Israel and Japan.

2. Three types of designs have been used to assess the accuracy of polygraph tests: laboratory, field, and field-analogue studies. In laboratory studies, volunteers (often university students) simulate criminal behaviour by committing a mock

crime. Field studies involve real-life situations and actual criminal suspects, together with actual polygraph examinations. In field-analogue studies the act of deception is freely committed by an individual, it is independently known which individuals committed the act, the individuals are concerned about the outcome of the polygraph test, and the polygrapher does not know the proportion of guilty and innocent individuals in the sample.

3. The CQT is quite accurate at detecting guilt but is not very good at determining a suspect's innocence (i.e., it has a high false-positive rate). Original examiners' accuracy is higher than blind chart examiners' scores, suggesting the original examiners are using extra-polygraphic cues to aid in their decisions. The GKT is quite accurate in detecting innocence but is not very good at determining a suspect's guilt (i.e., it has a high false-negative rate).

4. Another method of attempting to detect whether someone is lying is through the analysis of vocal characteristics and nonverbal behaviours. The vocal indicator most strongly associated with deception is voice pitch. A nonverbal indicator of deception that has been found consistently across studies is that liars tend to move their hands, arms, feet, and legs less than truth tellers.

5. The two key components to malingering are that the psychological or physical symptoms are clearly under voluntary control and that there are external motivations for the production of symptoms. Malingering should be considered in any forensic evaluation. Three explanatory models of malingering have been proposed: pathogenic, criminological, and adaptational. Only the adaptational model has received empirical support.

6. Malingering research utilizes three basic designs: case study, simulation, and known groups. Each of these designs has its associated strengths and weaknesses. The most common is the simulation design.

7. Both interview-based methods and self-report questionnaires have been developed in order to detect whether someone is malingering a mental disorder or memory deficit.

Key Concepts

DISCUSSION QUESTIONS

1. You have been called in by the police to give them advice on how to conduct a study to assess the accuracy of their polygraph examiners. In particular, they want to know whether or not their examiners are using any extra-polygraphic cues in making their decisions about guilt or innocence. What advice would you give to the police?

2. You are a conducting a study on deception in children. You want to know the role of age and why children lie. How would you elicit lying behaviour in the children and what variables would you measure?

3. You are a forensic psychologist hired to determine if a defendant is truly psychotic. What sorts of information would you base your assessment on? What clinical indicators would you look for?

4. Many of the studies designed to detect deception involve deceiving research participants. What ethical concerns have been raised? What types of studies should be allowed?

5. The Control Question Test is the polygraph test commonly used by police in North America. Do you think this test has sufficient validity for use by the police? Should it be admissible in court?

6. You recently got hired as a customs agent. Knowing what you do about nonvocal and vocal cues to deception, what cues would you be watching out for?

7. List the advantages and disadvantages to using simulation studies to study malingering of mental disorders.

ADDITIONAL INFORMATION

Readings

DePaulo, B.M., Lindsay, J.J., Malone, B.E., Muhlenbruck, L., Charlton, K., & Cooper, H. (2003). Cues to deception. *Psychological Bulletin, 129,* 74–118.

Lykken, D.T. (1998). *A tremor in the blood: Uses and abuses of the lie detector.* New York: Plenum.

Rogers, R. (1997). *Clinical assessment of malingering and deception.* New York: Guilford Press.

Web Sites

American Polygraph Association
www.polygraph.org

Criticism of the Polygraph
www.antipolygraph.org

CHAPTER 6

Eyewitness Testimony

LEARNING OBJECTIVES

- Describe two categories of independent variables and three general dependent variables found in eyewitness research.

- Describe and explain the misinformation effect.

- Outline the components of the cognitive interview.

- Describe lineup procedures and how they may be biased.

- Summarize the debate surrounding expert testimony on eyewitness issues.

- Outline the recommendations for collecting eyewitness identification evidence.

Carol Swanson went to the bank on her lunch hour. As she approached the teller, a man pushed her out of the way so that he could quickly exit the bank. Seconds later, Carol found out that the man had robbed the teller. Carol was an eyewitness. The police interviewed her along with the others in the bank. The witnesses were able to hear each other describe what they saw. Six months after the robbery, Carol was asked to go to the police station to view a series of photographs. When she was asked whether the man who robbed the bank was pictured, Carol very quickly pointed and said, "That's him, I am certain."

EYEWITNESS TESTIMONY: THE ROLE OF MEMORY

Eyewitness evidence is one of the earliest and most widely studied topics in forensic psychology. As you read in Chapter 1, the German psychologist Albert von Schrenck-Notzing testified during a serial killer trial about the influence of pretrial media exposure on witnesses' memory. Today both the police and the courts rely on eyewitness evidence. Eyewitness testimony is one of the most compelling types of evidence presented in criminal trials. Thus, information about the likelihood and types of mistakes made by eyewitnesses is vitally important in terms of justice. This issue will be highlighted later in the chapter when we discuss research on wrongful convictions.

A large part of eyewitness testimony rests on memory. The concept of memory can be viewed as a process involving several stages. The encoding stage occurs first, when you perceive and pay attention to details in your environment. For example, you are perceiving and paying attention when you look at a stranger's face and notice his big, bushy eyebrows. To some extent, the stranger's face and eyebrows have been encoded. The encoded information then passes into your short-term holding facility, known as your short-term memory. Your short-term memory has a limited capacity. Consequently, in order to make room for other, new information, information in your short-term memory passes into your longer-term holding facility, known as your long-term memory. Information from long-term memory can be accessed or retrieved as needed. For example, if you are asked to describe the stranger you saw, you will retrieve the information you stored in your long-term memory and report that the stranger had bushy eyebrows. It is important to remember that not all information will go through all the memory stages and also that there are factors that can affect each stage. For example, not all details from an event will be encoded, nor will all information in short-term memory move to long-term memory. Using our example of Carol Swanson witnessing a bank robbery, consider the factors that are occurring to affect memory and retrieval.

Carol is filling out a deposit slip so she will be ready for the bank teller. She is not paying attention to her environment (factor: inattention). Unexpectedly, there is a brief interaction between her and an unfamiliar male (factors: unexpectedness, amount of time to view environmental details). Carol is now a witness and she is interviewed with several other people in the bank by police (factor: hearing others describe the same environmental details she saw). The police officer asks Carol a few, brief questions (factor: the wording of the questions). Carol is called six months after the crime, to examine a lineup (factors: the amount of time elapsed between having witnessed the event and having to retrieve the information, type of lineup procedure used). Carol is confident when she identifies the culprit (factor: relation between confidence and accuracy). Figure 6.1 on the next page delineates the stages of memory.

Look at this scene for five seconds

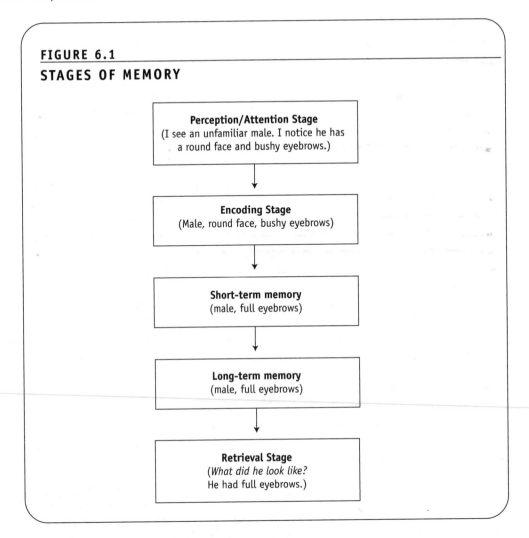

FIGURE 6.1

STAGES OF MEMORY

Perception/Attention Stage
(I see an unfamiliar male. I notice he has
a round face and bushy eyebrows.)

Encoding Stage
(Male, round face, bushy eyebrows)

Short-term memory
(male, full eyebrows)

Long-term memory
(male, full eyebrows)

Retrieval Stage
(*What did he look like?*
He had full eyebrows.)

As you may have figured out by now, memory is not like a videotaped recording in which an identical representation of the event is stored and then can be played on request (Loftus, 1979b). Our memory can change each time we retrieve the event; some parts of the event may be embellished or guessed at because we cannot remember all the details. Often in our everyday life, our memory fallibilities are insignificant. For example, remembering that you bought a coffee at Second Cup when you actually bought it at Tim Hortons is harmless, most likely. In contrast, remembering whether the culprit was right- or left-handed may be critical if police are going to arrest the guilty suspect.

Eyewitness memory retrieval can be broadly partitioned into either recall or recognition memory. **Recall memory** refers to reporting details of a previously witnessed event or person. For example, describing what the culprit did and what the culprit looked like are both recall tasks. In contrast, **recognition memory** refers to determining whether a previously seen item or person is the same as what is currently being viewed. For example, hearing a set of voices and identifying the culprit's voice or identifying clothing worn by the culprit during the crime are both recognition tasks.

HOW DO WE STUDY EYEWITNESS ISSUES?

Researchers interested in studying eyewitness issues can examine data from actual crimes. For example, they can use archival data such as police reports, or they can examine witnesses in naturalistic environments by accompanying police to crime scenes and interviewing witnesses after the police have done their job. Alternatively, they can conduct laboratory simulations. The laboratory simulation study is the most common paradigm used to study eyewitness issues.

The Laboratory Simulation

To study eyewitness memory using a laboratory simulation, an unknowing participant views a critical event, such as a crime, either through a slide sequence, videotaped recording, or live. The participant is unaware that he or she will be questioned about the event until after the event is witnessed. The participant, now witness, is asked to describe what happened and the target/culprit involved. Following the descriptions of what was witnessed, the witness may be asked to examine a lineup. There can be many independent variables that are manipulated or examined; however, there are only three general dependent variables in eyewitness studies.

INDEPENDENT VARIABLES Numerous independent variables can be manipulated or examined within the laboratory simulation. Wells (1978) has coined the terms *estimator variable* and *system variable* to help classify them. **Estimator variables** are those variables or factors that are present at the time of the crime and that cannot be changed. These can include the age of the witness, the amount of lighting, the presence of a weapon, and whether the witness was intoxicated. These are variables over which the criminal justice system *cannot* exert control. Thus, their effect on eyewitness accuracy can only be estimated after the crime. **System variables** are those variables or factors that can be manipulated to increase (or decrease) eyewitness accuracy, such as the type of procedure used by police to interview the witness or the type of lineup procedure used to present the suspect to the witness. These variables are under the control of the justice system. Both estimator and system variables can be manipulated in eyewitness laboratory studies.

DEPENDENT VARIABLES The three general dependent variables in eyewitness studies are (1) recall of the event/crime, (2) recall of the culprit, and (3) recognition of the culprit.

Recall of the crime or culprit can take two formats. With **open-ended recall**, also known as a **free narrative**, witnesses are asked to either write or orally state all they remember about the event without the officer (or experimenter) asking questions. With this type of recall, the witness also may be asked to describe the culprit. With **direct question recall**, witnesses are asked a series of specific questions about the crime or the culprit. For example, the witness may be asked the colour of the getaway car or the length of the culprit's hair.

A witness's *recall* of the crime or culprit can be examined for the following:

- *The amount of information reported.* How many descriptors of the crime do witnesses report? How many descriptors of the culprit do witnesses report?
- *The type of information reported.* What is the proportion of peripheral details versus central details? What is the proportion of culprit details versus environment details?
- *The accuracy of information reported.* What is the proportion of correct descriptors reported? What is the proportion of omission errors (information the witness failed to report)? What is the proportion of commission errors (details falsely reported to be present)?

As for the recognition of the culprit, the typical recognition task is a lineup. A culprit **lineup** is a set of people presented to the witness, who in turn must identify the culprit if he or she is present. Another type of lineup takes the form of a set of voices, and the witness is asked to identify the culprit's voice. Clothing lineups, in which the witness examines clothing that may have been worn by the culprit, sometimes are also used.

A witness's *recognition* response can be examined for the following:

- *Accuracy of decision.* What is the rate of correctly identifying the culprit in the lineup? What is the rate of correctly stating that the culprit is not present in the lineup?
- *Types of errors made.* What is the rate of identifying an innocent person? What is the rate of stating that the culprit is not present when he or she is actually in the lineup?

RECALL MEMORY

The primary goal for an officer interviewing an eyewitness is to extract from the witness a complete and accurate report of what happened (Fisher, Geiselman, & Raymond, 1987). Insufficient information may provide the officer with few leads to pursue, resulting in a case that will not be solved. In this situation, the culprit will remain free to commit further crimes. If inaccurate information is supplied, an officer may pursue innocent suspects, thus reducing the likelihood that the guilty person will be caught.

Now test your own recall. Without looking back at the crime scene photo on page 163, how many details can you remember?

Interviewing Eyewitnesses

Fisher, Geiselman, and Raymond (1987) were curious about the techniques police were using to interview eyewitnesses. They analyzed 11 tape-recorded interviews from a police department in Florida. Eight different detectives, who averaged 10.5 years of experience each, conducted these interviews. The researchers found that there was a lot of variation in how the interviews were conducted. In general, however, the researchers found that the officers would introduce themselves, ask the eyewitnesses to report what they remembered using an open-ended format, and then ask the witnesses a series of direct questions to determine specific information, such as the age or height of the culprit. The officers usually ended the interview by asking the eyewitnesses if there was any additional information that they could remember.

Fisher and colleagues (1987) found that the police officers' approach limited their ability to collect complete and accurate information in a number of ways. First, the researchers found that police often interrupted eyewitnesses when they were providing an open-ended recall report. The police may limit the amount of information eyewitnesses have in their conscious memory by preventing them from speaking or distracting them with questions.

Second, police questioned eyewitnesses with very short, specific questions. This type of question format uses a more superficial level of concentration than open-ended questions and tends to result in very short answers. The other problem with short, specific questions is that a police officer may not ask a relevant question that would provide critical information. For example, the culprit may have a tattoo, but if the officer does not ask about tattoos, the eyewitness may not report this feature. Thus, the police officer may miss a descriptor that could help in narrowing the suspect pool and arresting the culprit.

Third, police officers tended to ask questions in a predetermined or random order that was inconsistent with the information that witnesses were providing at the time. For example, a police officer may have asked a question about the culprit's voice while the witness was describing the culprit's clothing. Mixing visual and auditory questions has been found to decrease recall by approximately 19% (Fisher & Price-Roush, as cited in Fisher et al., 1987). Lastly, officers tended to ask questions that are "leading" or suggestive, which can be very dangerous when trying to collect accurate information.

The Leading Question—The Misinformation Effect

Elizabeth Loftus, one of the most prominent researchers in the area of leading questions, has conducted many experiments that have demonstrated that a witness's recall report can be altered by the phrasing of a question. In one study, Loftus and Palmer (1974) had university students watch a videotape of a car accident. After viewing the accident, the participants were asked the identical question with a variation in one critical word, *hit*: "About how fast were the cars going when they *hit* each other?" *Hit* was replaced with either *smashed, collided, bumped,* or *contacted*. Even though all participants saw the same videotape, the speed reported by the participants varied depending on which critical word was used. Participants reported the highest rate of speed when the word *smashed* was used and lowest rates of speed when the words *bumped* and *contacted* were used.

The experiment did not end there. The researchers called participants back a week later and asked whether they had seen any broken glass. Participants who were questioned with the word *smashed* were more likely to recall seeing broken glass than were the other participants. However, there was no broken glass in the videotape. This study illustrates how the wording of a question can influence memory for the incident.

Loftus went on to demonstrate that simply introducing an inaccurate detail to witnesses could lead them to report that inaccurate detail when questioned later (Loftus, Altman, & Geballe, 1975). The **misinformation effect**, also called the **post-event information effect**, is a phenomenon in which a witness who is presented with inaccurate information after an event will incorporate that misinformation in a subsequent recall task (Loftus, 1975).

In one classic study, Loftus conducted four experiments demonstrating that how a question is worded can influence an eyewitness's recall at a later date. We'll discuss two of these experiments below.

These studies used a common method or paradigm to investigate the misinformation effect. Participants were exposed to an event via slides, videotape, or live action. They were then given a series of questions about the event, some of which contained misinformation. Later, the participants were asked a series of questions about the event, probing their response to the misinformation introduced. They were asked to respond from a forced-choice/multiple-choice set. That is, they were given a set of responses to choose from, with one response being correct, one response containing the misinformation, and one or two incorrect responses.

EXPERIMENT 1 Forty university students watched a three-minute film clip of a class being interrupted by eight demonstrators. Following the clip, participants were given 20 questions. Half of the participants were asked, "Was the leader of the four demonstrators who entered the classroom a male? The remaining participants were asked, "Was the leader of the 12 demonstrators who entered the classroom a male?" All other questions were the same for the two groups. After a one-week delay, the participants were asked 20 new questions about the film. The critical question in this new set was, "How many demonstrators did you see entering the classroom?" The participants that were asked a question about 12 demonstrators reported seeing an average of almost 9 demonstrators (8.85). Those who were asked about four demonstrators reported seeing an average of 6.40 demonstrators. Thus, incorporating the number of demonstrators into the question posed to witnesses affected the number of demonstrators witnesses recalled seeing later.

EXPERIMENT 2 One hundred and fifty university students watched a brief videotape of a car accident involving a white sports car. Participants then answered ten questions about the car accident. Half of the participants were asked, "How fast was the white sports car going when it passed the barn while travelling along the country road?" The remaining participants were asked, "How fast was the white sports car going while travelling along the country road?" A week later, all participants were asked ten new questions. The critical question was, "Did you see a barn?" No barn was shown in the videotape. For the first group who had the word barn embedded in the first set of questions, 17.3% stated they saw a barn. In contrast, 2.7% of participants in the no-barn group reported seeing a barn.

As you can see, the misinformation effect occurs using a number of different types of questions and methodology. But why does it occur?

EXPLAINING THE MISINFORMATION EFFECT Many studies have demonstrated that a witness's report can include misinformation that was previously supplied (Cole & Loftus, 1979; Loftus, 1979a), and these have fuelled debates on how and why this phenomenon occurs (Loftus, Miller, & Burns, 1978; McCloskey & Zaragoza, 1985). Were witnesses' memories changed? Were the participants just going along with the experimenter (or guessing) and providing the answer they thought was wanted. Or maybe the witness had two memories, a correct one and an incorrect one, and could not remember where each memory came from. These are the three general positions that researchers have tried to advance or argue against, with each position having different implications for memory:

1. With changes in the methodology, some studies have found support for guessing or experimenter pleasing. Some witnesses will guess at the answer they think the experimenter wants, resulting in the misinformation effect. This explanation is known as the **misinformation acceptance hypothesis** (McCloskey & Zaragoza, 1985).

2. Some studies have found that witnesses can recall both memories—the original, accurate one and the inaccurate one. However, witnesses cannot remember where each memory came from. When asked to recall what was seen, the witness chooses the incorrect memory. This explanation is called the **source misattribution hypothesis** (Lindsay, 1994).

3. Loftus is perhaps the biggest proponent of the **memory impairment hypothesis**. This hypothesis refers to the original memory being replaced with the new, incorrect memory (Loftus, 1979b). The original memory is no longer accessible.

The debate on which explanation is responsible for the misinformation effect is far from over. Researchers continue to come up with different methodologies that point to alternative explanations. One issue that has been put to rest, though, is that the misinformation effect happens. The misinformation effect is a real phenomenon.

How can the misinformation effect happen in real life? A witness can be exposed to inaccurate information in a number of ways:

1. An officer may make assumptions about what occurred or what was witnessed and then inadvertently phrase a question consistent with his or her assumption. For example, the officer may ask the witness, "Did you see the gun?" rather than ask the more neutral question, "Did you see a gun?"

2. There may be more than one witness, and the witnesses overhear each other's statements. If there are discrepancies between the witnesses, a witness may change his or her report to make it consistent.

3. A police officer may incorporate an erroneous detail from a previous witness's interview. For example, the officer may ask the witness, "What was the culprit with the scar wearing?" The witness may subsequently report that the culprit had a scar when in fact there was none.

PROCEDURES THAT HELP POLICE INTERVIEW EYEWITNESSES

Psychologists have been instrumental in developing procedures that can be beneficial at eliciting accurate information from witnesses.

Hypnosis

In some cases, eyewitnesses may be unable to recall very much that was witnessed, possibly because they were traumatized. With the help of hypnosis, they may be able to recall a greater amount of information. It is assumed that a person under hypnosis is able to retrieve memories that are otherwise inaccessible. A hypnotized witness may be able to produce a greater number of details than a nonhypnotized witness; this phenomenon is termed **hypnotically refreshed memory** (Steblay & Bothwell, 1994). Although most people can experience some effect of hypnosis, approximately 10% of the population cannot be hypnotized, and about 5% to 10% are highly suggestible (Hilgard, 1965). The ability to be hypnotized peaks in late childhood (Spiegel & Spiegel, 1987). A variety of factors can influence whether hypnosis can be induced:

- The degree of trust the witness places in the hypnotist
- The witness's willingness to be hypnotized
- The witness's belief in hypnosis
- The seriousness of the context for being hypnotized

However, police are not just interested in collecting more information—they are interested in collecting accurate information. For hypnosis to be useful in a forensic context, we need to know about the accuracy of the information recalled while under hypnosis.

Several reviews have examined the effectiveness of hypnosis in enhancing memory recall (e.g., Brown, Scheflin, & Hammond, 1998; Reiser, 1989; Steblay & Bothwell, 1994). These reviews find that individuals under hypnosis will provide more details, but those details are just as likely to be inaccurate as accurate (see also Fisher, 1995). The hypnotized individual seems to be more suggestible to subtle cues by the interviewer than under normal conditions. The difficulty with using hypnosis is not being able to differentiate between the accurate and inaccurate details. Witnesses recall both accurate and inaccurate details with the same degree of confidence (Sheehan & Tilden, 1984), and as we will see later, this confidence may be misleading.

The Canadian courts are aware of the difficulties with hypnotically induced recall and typically do not permit the use of information gained that way.

The Cognitive Interview

Given the limitations of hypnosis, researchers have developed an interview procedure based on principles of memory storage and retrieval called the cognitive interview (Geiselman et al., 1984). The cognitive interview can be used with eyewitnesses, but it is not a procedure recommended for use with unwilling participants such as suspects (see Chapter 3).

The cognitive interview is based on four memory retrieval techniques (see Box 6.1) to increase recall: (1) reinstating the context, (2) reporting everything, (3) reversing order, and (4) changing perspective.

BOX 6.1 HOW THE COGNITIVE INTERVIEW COMPONENTS ARE IMPLEMENTED WITH WITNESSES

Below are sample statements that correspond to the cognitive interview memory retrieval techniques:

1. *Reinstate the context:* "Try to reinstate in your mind the context surrounding the incident. Think about what the surrounding environment looked like at the scene, such as the room, the weather, and any nearby people or objects. Also think about how you were feeling at the time and think about your reactions to the incident" (Geiselman et al., 1986, p. 390).

2. *Report everything:* "Some people hold back information because they are not quite sure that the information is important. Please do not edit anything out of your report, report even things you think may not be important" (pp. 391–392).

3. *Recall the event in different orders:* "It is natural to go through the incident from beginning to end. However, you also should try to go through the events in reverse order. Or, try starting with the thing that impressed you the most in the incident and then go from there, going both forward in time and backward" (p. 391).

4. *Change perspectives:* "Try to recall the incident from different perspectives that you may have had or adopt the perspectives of others that were present during the incident. For example, try to place yourself in the role of a prominent character in the incident and think about what he or she must have seen" (p. 391).

It should be noted that changing perspectives has been criticized for eliciting erroneous information. If a witness is asked to imagine what he or she saw from a different perspective, the witness might report details that are made up or inaccurate.

Source: Geiselman et al., 1986.

In an initial study, Geiselman and colleagues (1985) compared the "standard" police interview, hypnosis, and the cognitive interview to determine differences in the amount and accuracy of information recalled by witnesses. Participants watched a police training film of a crime. Forty-six hours after viewing the film, each participant was interviewed with one of the procedures by experienced law enforcement professionals. Compared with the "standard" police interview and hypnosis, the cognitive interview produced the greatest amount of accurate information without an increase in inaccurate details.

Bekerian and Dennett (1993) reviewed 27 studies that tested the cognitive interview. Across the studies, the cognitive interview produced more accurate information than the alternatives, such as the "standard" police interview. Approximately a 30% increase in accurate information was obtained with the cognitive interview over other procedures, and there was an insignificant decrease in errors for the cognitive interview compared with other methods.

Over the years, Fisher and Geiselman (1992) expanded the cognitive interview into the **enhanced cognitive interview,** including various principles of social dynamics in addition to the memory retrieval principles used in the original cognitive interview. The additional components include the following:

1. *Rapport building.* An officer should spend time building rapport with the witness and make him or her feel comfortable and supported.

2. *Supportive interviewer behaviour.* A witness's free recall should not be interrupted; pauses should be waited out by the officer, who should express attention to what the witness is saying.

3. *Transfer of control.* The witness, not the officer, should control the flow of the interview; the witness is the expert—that is, the witness, not the officer, was the person who saw the crime.

4. *Focused retrieval.* Questions should be open-ended and not leading or suggestive; after free recall, the officer should use focused memory techniques to facilitate retrieval.

5. *Witness-compatible questioning.* An officer's questions should match the witness's thinking; if the witness is talking about clothing, the officer should be asking about clothing.

The enhanced cognitive interview, the original cognitive interview, and the standard police interview have been compared (Memon & Bull, 1991). Both cognitive interviews produced more accurate information, without an increase in inaccurate information, than standard interviews. Significant differences between the two cognitive interviews have not been found (Köehnken, 1995). The question remains as to which components are responsible for the increase in accurate information (Kebbell & Wagstaff, 1998).

Although some officers in Canada have been trained to use the cognitive interview, some are reluctant to use it, stating that it requires too much time to conduct and that the appropriate environment is not always available. However, trained officers report that they use some of the cognitive interview components on a regular basis when interviewing witnesses.

RECALL MEMORY FOLLOWING A LONG DELAY

Is it possible to forget a traumatic event such as abuse, only to recall it many years later? This question is at the centre of a heated debate about memory repression. Some argue that childhood sexual abuse memories are so traumatic for some individuals that they repress them in their unconscious. It is only as adults, and through the help of therapy, that they come to recall the abuse, through what are known as recovered memories. Others argue that it is only through therapy and the use of suggestive techniques that clients come to believe that they were sexually abused as children when in fact they were not; such recollections are known as false memories. Loftus is among the proponents of this second group. **False memory syndrome** was a term coined to describe a client's false belief that he or she was sexually abused as a child. Clients may have no memories of this abuse until they enter therapy to deal with some other psychological problem such as depression or substance abuse (Read, 1999). See Box 6.2 on the next page for a case involving "delayed" memory.

Can Traumatic Memories Be Forgotten?

Perhaps the greatest point of contention regarding false memory syndrome is whether traumatic memories can be completely forgotten only to be remembered many years later.

In a study by Porter and Birt (2001), university students were asked to describe their most traumatic experience and their most positive experience. A number of different experiences were reported in each condition. Approximately 5% of their sample of 306 participants reported sexual assault or abuse as their most traumatic experience. The majority of these participants stated that they had consciously forced the memory out of their minds rather than never having a memory of it. Proponents of the false memory argument contend that not having any memory of abuse is different from preferring not to think about it. When there is absolutely no memory of abuse, and it is only through the use of suggestive techniques that the abuse is remembered, many argue that these memories should be interpreted cautiously.

Lindsay and Read (1995) suggest five criteria to consider when trying to determine the veracity of a recovered memory:

1. *Age of complainant at the time of the alleged abuse.* It is unlikely that anyone would have a memory (of abuse or otherwise) prior to age two.

2. *Techniques used to recover memory.* Techniques such as hypnosis and guided imagery heighten suggestibility and encourage fantasy.

3. *Similarity of reports across interview sessions.* Do the reports become increasingly more fantastic, or are they similar?

BOX 6.2 DELAYED MEMORY GOES TO COURT

On October 2, 1992, a 48-year-old teacher, Michael Kliman, from Richmond, B.C., was arrested and charged with the sexual abuse of two female students. The complainants ("A" and "B") were in their late 20s when they made the allegations, but the abuse allegedly occurred in 1975, when the complainants were in Grade 6.

The complaints alleged that Kliman would take each of them out of class three or four times a week for up to 20 minutes at a time. It was alleged that Kliman would bring them to a small room in the school where he would sexually fondle them or they would fondle him. In addition, one of the complainants claimed that when she was on a class camping trip in Grade 7, Kliman took her to his tent and raped her. Both complainants alleged that they suffered from dissociative amnesia—that is, memory loss of an event because of the trauma of the event.

Both "A" and "B" testified that they had no memory of the abuse until many years later. "A" stated that she recovered the repressed memory after she was admitted to a hospital psychiatric ward for an eating disorder when she was 19. "B" stated that she recalled the past events after she was questioned by police following "A"'s claim.

In "A"'s hospital record for anorexia, Mr. Kliman's name was not mentioned. "A" testified that while she worked at an insurance company she was sexually abused/harassed by a superior. She also testified that she was repeatedly abused and stalked by a man between October 1990 and December 1991. She consulted a therapist as a result of this abuse in February 1991. The therapist specialized in adult survivorship of childhood sexual abuse, post-trauma reactions, dissoci-

ation, and memory. At the time "A" sought therapy, she had no memory of abuse at her elementary school. It was during the course of this therapy that "A" first identified Mr. Kliman as an abuser.

"B" was sexually abused by a foster brother and neighbour when she was 11 years old. She has a continuous memory of this abuse. "B" had no memory of abuse by Mr. Kliman until interviewed by the police officer following up "A"'s allegation of abuse.

Dr. John Yuille and Dr. Elizabeth Loftus were called in to discuss memory and dissociative amnesia. The experts reached somewhat differing conclusions. Dr. Loftus noted that at present there is no scientific evidence to support the notion that several incidents of traumatic sexual abuse could cause memory of the events to be lost. She also testified that the use of leading questions and suggestive interviewing techniques could contaminate memory. Dr. Yuille testified that there is literature, including some of his work, that supports the notion of dissociative amnesia.

Mr. Kliman was tried three times. In the first trial, the jury convicted him. The decision was appealed and the Court of Appeal set aside the conviction because of inadequate disclosure. In the second trial, the jury was unable to reach a unanimous verdict. In the third trial, Mr. Kliman was acquitted on all counts. The trial judge noted that there were many improbabilities about the details of the complainants' testimony that made it difficult to believe, aside from the memory issues. For example, it is hard to imagine how Mr. Kliman could excuse himself from class several times a week for 15 to 20 minutes at a time.

Source: R. v. Kliman, 1998.

4. *Motivation for recall.* Is the client experiencing other psychological distress and wanting an answer to explain such feelings?

5. *Time elapsed since the alleged abuse.* It may be more difficult to recall abuse that occurred 25 years ago than two years ago.

RECALL OF THE CULPRIT

Along with a description of what happened, the witness will be asked to describe the culprit's appearance. Perusal of newspapers and news broadcasts find that descriptions are vague and apply to many. For example, a culprit may be described as white, male, between five-foot-nine and six feet tall, with short, brown hair. Think of how many people you know who fit this description.

Quantity and Accuracy of Descriptions

Research examining culprit descriptions provided by witnesses finds that descriptions are limited in detail and accuracy (Sporer, 1996). Lindsay, Martin, and Webber (1994) examined descriptions provided by adults in real and staged crimes. Witnesses to staged crimes reported an average of 7.35 descriptors. In contrast, witnesses to real crimes reported significantly fewer descriptors—3.94 on average. Hair and clothing items were commonly reported descriptors.

In a study examining real-life descriptions, Van Koppen and Lochun (1997) conducted an archival review of official court records examining descriptions of culprits from 400 robberies. Data were coded from 1300 witnesses and 1650 descriptions of culprits were analyzed. Consistent with anecdotal evidence, witnesses provided few descriptors. On average, witnesses reported eight descriptors. The researchers found that sex and height were the items most often reported. Witnesses were correct 100% of the time when identifying the sex of the culprit. Unfortunately, sex is not a great discriminator! Only 52% of witnesses were accurate when identifying the height of the culprit.

Yarmey and Yarmey (1997) examined person and clothing descriptors provided by a sample of 603 participants. Accuracy ranged dramatically across the various descriptors (see Figure 6.2 on the next page).

Accuracy was highest for hair colour and the type of clothing worn below the waist. Wagstafff, MacVeigh, Boston, Scott, Brunas-Wagstaff, and Cole (2003) also found that hair colour and hairstyle were reported most accurately. Yarmey, Jacob, and Porter (2002) found that witnesses had difficulty correctly reporting weight (27% accuracy), eye colour, (24% accuracy), and type of footwear (13% accuracy).

As you can see, culprit descriptions are limited in quantity and accuracy, which, in turn, limits their usefulness to the police in their investigation. Given the strides psychologists have made in other areas of police procedure, such as interviewing techniques, it would be worthwhile for psychologists to develop a technique or procedure that could be used to increase the amount and accuracy of witnesses' descriptions of culprits.

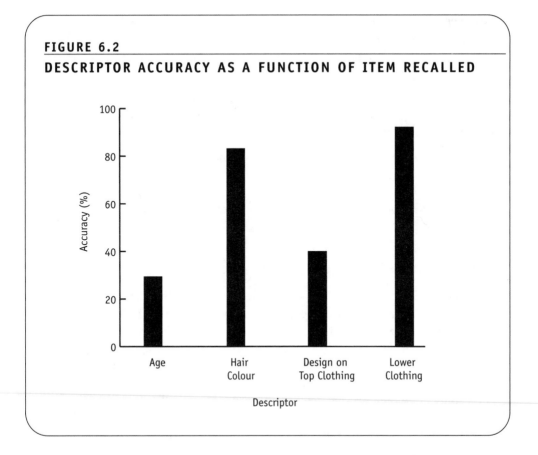

FIGURE 6.2

DESCRIPTOR ACCURACY AS A FUNCTION OF ITEM RECALLED

RECOGNITION MEMORY

As defined at the beginning of the chapter, recognition memory involves determining whether a previously seen item or person is the one that is currently being viewed. A witness's recognition memory can be tested in a number of ways:

- live lineups or photo arrays
- video surveillance records
- voice identification

Lineup Identification

"It's number 5, I'll never forget that face!" The typical method used to gain proof about the identity of the culprit is to conduct a lineup identification, in which a witness views a group of possible suspects and determines whether one is the culprit.

Why Conduct a Lineup?

A critical distinction needs to be made between the terms *suspect* and *culprit*. A suspect is a person the police "suspect" committed the crime. However, a suspect may be guilty or innocent of the crime in question. In contrast, a **culprit** is the guilty person who committed the crime.

A lineup identification reduces the uncertainty of whether a suspect is the culprit beyond the verbal description provided (Wells, 1993). A witness identifying the suspect increases the likelihood that the suspect is the culprit. In contrast, not identifying the suspect decreases the likelihood that the suspect is the culprit.

An alternative view of a lineup identification is that it provides police with information about the physical similarity between the lineup member chosen and the culprit (Navon, 1990). Police will have some notion of what the culprit looks like based on the person selected from the lineup.

Lineup Distractors

In addition to placing a suspect in a lineup, other lineup members may be included. These members are called **foils** or **distractors** and they are known to be innocent for the crime in question. Police can use two types of strategies to decide on the physical appearance of the lineup distractors. A similarity-to-suspect strategy matches lineup members to the suspect's appearance. For example, if the suspect had brown hair, blue eyes, and a moustache, then each lineup member would have these characteristics. A difficulty with this strategy, however, is that there are many physical features you could match such as width of eyebrows, length of nose, thickness of lips, and so on. If taken to the extreme, this strategy would produce a lineup of clones—everyone would look exactly like the suspect, making it virtually impossible to identify the culprit. In contrast, a match-to-description strategy sets limits on the number of features that need to be matched. With this strategy, distractors are matched only on the items that the witness provided in his or her description. For example, if a witness stated the criminal had brown hair, blue eyes, a round face, and no facial hair, then those would be the features on which each lineup member is matched.

Lindsay, Martin, and Webber (1994) noted that some general characteristics that might not be mentioned would need to be included to produce a "fair" lineup. A **fair lineup** is one in which the suspect does not stand out from the other lineup members. For example, if skin colour was not mentioned, then a lineup could be constructed with one white face (the suspect) and five black faces. Thus, the lineup would be unfair or biased. Some characteristics, such as sex and race, are known as default values and should be matched even if not mentioned in the witness's description.

Also in order to avoid a biased lineup, Luus and Wells (1991; Wells, Rydell, & Seelau, 1993) suggest that if a feature is provided in the witness's description but does not match the suspect's appearance, then the distractors should match the suspect's appearance on that feature. For example, if the culprit is described as having brown hair but the suspect has blond hair, then the distractors should have blond hair.

Estimating Identification Accuracy

When we are interested in finding out how often witnesses will make an accurate (or inaccurate) identification decision, we need to create the condition when police have arrested the right person, the guilty suspect. We also need to create the condition when police have arrested the wrong person, an innocent suspect. Thus, we create two lineups in our research. One lineup—the **target-present lineup**—contains a picture of the culprit. In the other lineup—the **target-absent lineup**—we substitute the culprit's picture with another photo. Identification decisions are different with each type of lineup. See Table 6.1 for the types of identification decisions possible as a function of type of lineup.

Three types of identification decisions can occur with a target-present lineup. The witness can identify the guilty suspect, which is a correct identification. If the witness identifies a foil, that is a foil identification. In addition, the witness may state that the culprit is not present, which is a false rejection.

Three types of identification decisions can occur with a target-absent lineup. The witness can state that the culprit is not present, which is a correct rejection. The witness can identify a foil, which is a foil identification. The witness can also identify an innocent suspect, in which case the witness makes a false identification. Sometimes, researchers will not make a distinction between false identifications and foil identifications from a target-absent lineup and will refer to these two errors simply as false positives.

Identification Decision Implications

The only correct decision with a target-present lineup is to make a correct identification. The only correct decision with a target-absent lineup is to make a correct rejection. The other decisions with each type of lineup are errors and have different implications for the witness and the justice system (Wells & Turtle, 1986):

TABLE 6.1 POSSIBLE IDENTIFICATION DECISIONS AS A FUNCTION OF LINEUP TYPE

Type of Lineup	Identification Decision				
	Correct Identification	False Rejection	Foil Identification	Correct Rejection	False Identification
Target-present	X	X	X	Not possible	Not possible
Target-absent	Not possible	Not possible	X	X	X

Source: Wells, 1993.

- A foil identification (with either a target-present lineup or a target-absent lineup) is a known error to the police, so the person identified will not be prosecuted. The witness, however, may be perceived as having a faulty memory. Moreover, the other details provided by this witness may be viewed with some skepticism because a known recognition error was made.

- A false rejection is an unknown error and may result in the guilty suspect going free and possibly committing further crimes.

- A false identification also is an unknown error in real life and may result in the innocent suspect being prosecuted and convicted for a crime he or she did not commit. Moreover, with a false identification, the real criminal remains free to commit further crimes. False identifications may be the most serious type of identification error a witness can make.

Live Lineups or Photo Arrays?

Most often, police will use a set of photographs rather than live persons to assemble a lineup (Turtle, Lindsay, & Wells, 2003). Photo array is the term used for photographic lineups. Photo arrays are more common than lineups for a number of reasons:

- They are less time consuming to construct. The police can choose foils from their mug shot (pictures of people who have been charged with crimes in the past) files rather than find live persons.

- They are portable. The police are able to bring the photo array to the witness rather than have the witness go to the police department.

- The suspect does not have the right to counsel being present when a witness looks at a photo array. This right is present with live lineups.

- Because photos are static, the police need not worry that the suspect's behaviour may draw attention to himself or herself, thus invalidating the photo array.

- A witness may be less anxious examining a photo array than a live lineup.

An alternative to photographs or live lineups is to use videotaped lineups. Advantages to videotaped lineups include the ability to enlarge faces or focus on particular features. Also, lineup members can be paused to demonstrate a specific body position. In a study by Cutler, Fisher, and Chicvara (1989), they found that correct identification and correct rejection rates did not differ across live and videotaped lineups. However, this conclusion needs to be tempered given the limited research on the topic and the small number participants in the study.

Lineup Presentation Procedures

Lineups can be presented in different formats or with different procedures to the witness. Perhaps most common is the procedure known as the **simultaneous lineup** (Wells, 1993). The simultaneous procedure presents all lineup members at one time to the witness. Wells (1993) suggested that this procedure encourages the witness to make a **relative judgment,** whereby lineup members are compared with each other and the person who looks most like the culprit is identified.

An alternative lineup procedure is the **sequential lineup.** This lineup procedure involves presenting the lineup members serially to the witness. The witness must make a decision as to whether the lineup member is the culprit before seeing the next lineup member (Lindsay & Wells, 1985). Also, with the sequential procedure, a witness cannot ask to see previously seen photos and the witness is unaware of the number of photos to be shown. Wells (1993) suggested that the sequential procedure reduces the likelihood that the witness *can* make a relative judgment. Instead, witnesses may be more likely to make an **absolute judgment,** whereby each lineup member is compared with the witness's memory of the culprit and the witness decides whether it is the culprit.

Lindsay and Wells (1985) compared the identification accuracy rate achieved with the simultaneous and sequential lineup procedures. University students witnessed a videotaped theft and were asked to identify the culprit from six photographs. Half the students saw a target-present lineup and the other half of students saw a target-absent lineup. Across target-present and -absent conditions, the lineups were either presented using a simultaneous procedure or a sequential procedure. See Figure 6.3 for identification rates according to lineup procedure.

Correct identification (target-present lineups) rates did not differ across lineup procedures. However, correct rejection rates were significantly different across lineup procedures. Only 42% of the participants made a correct rejection with a simultaneous lineup, whereas, 65% of the participants made a correct rejection with a sequential lineup. In other words, if the culprit was not included in the lineup, witnesses were more likely to correctly indicate that he or she was not present if they were shown a sequential lineup than a simultaneous lineup. The higher correct rejection rate with the sequential procedure compared with the simultaneous procedure has been replicated numerous times (Steblay et al., 2001). In real life, the sequential lineup could decrease false identifications. The sequential lineup is the procedure used in some Canadian jurisdictions, such as Ontario, and some U.S. states, such as New Jersey.

Dr. Rod Lindsay has been a key researcher in the area of lineup identification. See Box 6.3 on page 182 to read about him and his research.

An alternative identification procedure to the lineup is a **showup.** This procedure shows one person to the witness: the suspect. The witness is asked whether the person is the culprit. Although an absolute judgment is likely with a showup, it has a number of other difficulties, making it a less than ideal procedure. Both courts and researchers have argued (*Stovall v. Denno*, 1967; Wells, Leippe, & Ostrom, 1979) that because there are no other lineup members shown, the witness is aware of who the police suspect and this knowledge may increase a witness's likelihood of making an identification, that may be false.

Not everyone agrees with this view, however. In the mid-1990s, a series of studies were conducted by Gonzalez and his colleagues (Gonzalez, Ellsworth, & Pembroke, 1993). They did not find false identifications to be higher with a showup than with a

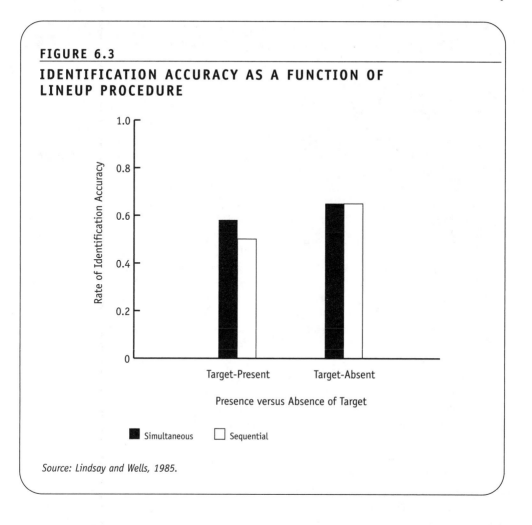

FIGURE 6.3

IDENTIFICATION ACCURACY AS A FUNCTION OF LINEUP PROCEDURE

Source: Lindsay and Wells, 1985.

lineup. In fact, they found witnesses were more likely to reject a showup than a line-up. Gonzalez concluded that witnesses are more cautious with their decision making when presented with a showup rather than a lineup, and as a result will err on making a rejection rather than an identification. Yarmey, Yarmey, and Yarmey (1996), however, reached a different conclusion. They found that lineups produced lower false-identification rates than showups. Also, in an analysis of 271 actual police cases, the suspect was more likely to be identified in a field showup (76%) than in a photographic lineup (48%; Behrman & Davey, 2001). These results are consistent with the notion that showups are suggestive. Further research is needed to understand the discrepancy in identification rates for showups across studies.

For now, there are only two acceptable uses of a showup. It may be used for deathbed identifications, when there is a fear that the witness will not be alive by the time a lineup is assembled (Wells et al., 2000). Also, police may use a showup if a suspect is apprehended immediately at or near the crime scene.

BOX 6.3 CANADIAN RESEARCHER PROFILE: DR. R.C.L. LINDSAY

Dr. Rod Lindsay recalls the fortuitous meeting that started his more than 25-year career researching eyewitness issues. As a graduate student at the University of Alberta, while working in his office one day, a new faculty member walked in and introduced himself as Gary Wells. It was January 1978 and Dr. Wells was looking for graduate students who would be interested in working on a research project he was planning. The project was examining jurors' perceptions of eyewitness identification. In 1979, this project was published in the *Journal of Applied Psychology*, and it would be one of the first in a long list of articles that would follow for Dr. Lindsay.

More than two decades ago, Dr. Lindsay joined the faculty at Queen's University, where he has continued conducting his eyewitness research. Dr. Lindsay describes his favourite research questions as those that can lead to real-world applications. He prefers to use experimental methodology to investigate the research questions that intrigue him. Although he respects surveys, case studies, and many other forms of methodology, he likes how a good experiment can answer a very specific and narrowly defined question such as, "Which of two lineup procedures will generate more accurate identifications?"

Dr. Lindsay's extensive eyewitness expertise has led him to the courts as an expert witness in a number of cases. Perhaps one of the most emotionally difficult cases for him was a Rwandan war crime trial. The defendants were charged with 20 000 counts of murder in one afternoon.

There have been two recent Canadian cases that Dr. Lindsay consulted on that he found professionally interesting and very frustrating. In one of the cases, a First Nations suspect was placed in a 12-person lineup where no other lineup member was First Nations. In the other case, a Filipino suspect also was placed in a 12-person lineup, this time, all the other lineup members were First Nations! In each case, the court decided there was nothing wrong with the lineup, decisions that Dr. Lindsay did not agree with.

To deal with eyewitness issues on a practical level, Dr. Lindsay would like to see the Canadian government create something like the British "Home Office." Such an organization could take responsibility for researching police procedures, then decide on the best practices, and write and distribute this information through directives for law enforcement. Moreover, the courts would have the clout to back up this "Home Office" by throwing out any evidence that resulted from procedures that did not meet the standards outlined.

In addition to informing the justice system on how to improve eyewitness evidence, Dr. Lindsay is committed to teaching and training future eyewitness researchers. He enjoys getting students excited about the eyewitness world: "If you love it, they will."

Eyewitness research is not the only thing Dr. Lindsay is passionate about. Often, he will escape the lab on a Friday afternoon and only re-emerge Monday morning, having spent the time in between playing duplicate bridge and lots of it.

Dr. Lindsay has received numerous distinctions for his work. Most recently, in 2002,

Dr. Lindsay's contribution to the eyewitness field was recognized by the Canadian Psychological Association, with the career award for Distinguished Contributions to the Application of Psychology.

One other identification procedure that may precede a lineup identification is known as a **walk-by**. This identification occurs in a naturalistic environment. The police take the witness to a public location where the suspect is likely to be. Once the suspect is in view, the witness is asked whether he or she sees the culprit.

Lineup Biases

Constructing a fair lineup is a challenging task. **Biased lineups** suggest who the police suspect and thereby who the witness should identify. In some way, the suspect stands out from the other lineup members in a biased lineup. The following biases have been investigated and found to increase false positives:

1. *Foil bias.* The suspect is the only lineup member who matches the description of the culprit. For example, the suspect has a beard and moustache while the other lineup members are clean-shaven (Lindsay, Lea, & Fulford, 1991).

2. *Clothing bias.* The suspect is the only lineup member wearing similar clothing to that worn by the culprit. For example, the culprit was described as wearing a blue baseball cap. The suspect is wearing a blue baseball cap while the foils are not (Lindsay et al., 1991; Lindsay, Wallbridge, & Drennan, 1987).

3. *Instruction bias.* The police fail to mention to the witness that the culprit may not be present; rather, the police imply that the culprit is present and that the witness should pick him or her out (Malpass & Devine, 1981; Steblay 1997).

Use of Surveillance Recordings for Identification

When you walk into a bank or convenience store, for example, you may notice a video recorder in the top corner of the wall. In the event that a

What is wrong with this lineup?

crime occurs, the culprit is caught on tape for a permanent record. Surely it would be easier to identify the culprit in this situation than if no recording existed.

In a related study, Kemp, Towell, and Pike (1997) had supermarket cashiers match credit card photos to the shopper. For half of the transactions, the shoppers presented a credit card that included their picture, while for the other transactions, they used cards that included someone else's picture. Overall, approximately 67% of the cashiers' decisions to accept or reject a card were correct. Errors were common though. The researchers found that the cashiers falsely accepted more than 50% of the fraudulent cards. Thus, the ability to match a surveillance tape to a culprit may be challenging. A number of factors may be critical for accurate identification decisions from surveillance tapes, such as lighting, view, and disguise.

Voice Identification

Perhaps one of the first and most prominent cases involving voice identification (or "ear-witness" identification) occurred in the United States in 1937. The infant son of Charles Lindbergh, a well-known doctor and aviator, was kidnapped and murdered (see Chapter 3). Lindberg identified Bruno Hauptmann's voice as the one he heard three years earlier when he paid the ransom. The kidnapper had said, "Hey, doctor, over here, over here." Hauptmann was convicted of kidnapping and murder. At the time, no studies on voice identification existed. Unfortunately, little has changed over the past 65 years, as very few studies have been conducted in this area.

In one study examining many key voice variables, Orchard and Yarmey (1995) had 156 university students listen to a taped voice of a mock kidnapper that varied in length—either 30 seconds or eight minutes. The voice was varied such that the kidnapper either had a distinctive or nondistinctive voice. The researchers also varied whether the speaker spoke in a whisper or a normal tone. Voice identification accuracy was tested using six-person voice lineups two days after the participants heard the taped voice. Here are some of the results:

- Identification accuracy was higher with longer voice samples.
- Whispering significantly decreased identification accuracy.
- Distinctiveness interacted with whispering, influencing identification accuracy.

FACTORS THAT DECREASE VOICE IDENTIFICATION Other studies have found that the likelihood of a correct identification is reduced if a voice is changed by whispering or muffling, or through emotion (Bull & Clifford, 1984; Saslove & Yarmey, 1980). Orchard and Yarmey (1995) have stated that "when voices are disguised as whispers, or changed in tone between first hearing the perpetrator and the conduction of the voice lineup, identification evidence should be accepted with critical caution" (p. 259).

In terms of target voice position in a lineup, if the target voice occurs later in the lineup, correct identification decreases compared with an earlier presentation (Doehring & Ross, 1972). Cook and Wilding (1997) reported that when the target's face was visible when participants originally heard the voice at encoding, correct identification decreased greatly. Also, as the number of foils increased from four to eight voices, correct identification decreased (Clifford, 1980).

Are Several Identifications Better than One?

If identification decisions for different pieces of evidence were combined, would the decision regarding the suspect's guilt be more accurate? Pryke, Lindsay, Dysart, and Dupuis (2004) conducted two experiments examining the usefulness of multiple independent lineups to identify a culprit: for example, having the participants identify the clothing worn by the culprit in one lineup and identify the culprit's face in another lineup. If both of these identification decisions are of the suspect, then the likelihood that the suspect is the culprit should be greater than if just one identification decision implicates the suspect. In the first experiment, following exposure to a live target, participants were shown a face lineup, then a voice lineup, and lastly a body lineup (Pryke et al., 2004). In the second experiment, a clothing lineup was added to the other three lineups. The researchers found that exposing witnesses to more than one lineup, each consisting of a different aspect of the suspect, increased the ability to determine the reliability of an eyewitness's identification of the suspect. Thus, the likelihood of the suspect's guilt increased as the number of independent identifications of the suspect increased by any one witness. This research presents an interesting avenue for future research, with many questions still unanswered. For example, are certain types of lineups more diagnostic of a suspect's guilt than others?

Are Confident Witnesses Accurate?

In a landmark U.S. Supreme Court Case in 1972 (*Neil v. Biggers*), the Court stated that the confidence of a witness should be taken as an indicator of accuracy. This assertion implies that witnesses who are certain in their identification of the culprit are likely to be accurate. Many studies, however, have investigated this relationship and found a different result (Cutler & Penrod, 1989a, 1989b; Penrod & Cutler, 1995; Sporer et al., 1995). Overall, there appears to be a small positive correlation between accuracy and confidence. There also are a number of moderator variables that can increase or decrease this relation.

Recently, Wells and his colleagues have investigated post-lineup identification feedback and its effect on the confidence–accuracy relationship (Bradfield, Wells, & Olson, 2002; Luus & Wells, 1994; Wells & Bradfield, 1998). In one study (Wells & Bradfield, 1998), after the witness made a lineup identification decision, the experimenter provided one of the following:

1. Confirming feedback: "Good, you identified the actual suspect."
2. Disconfirming feedback: "Actually, the suspect is number ___."
3. No feedback.

Participants were asked to make a number of judgments following the feedback or lack thereof. Of key interest were the ratings the participants made regarding how confident they were that they identified the correct person on a 1-to-7-point scale in which 1 means not at all certain, and 7 means totally certain. See Figure 6.4 for the confidence ratings as a function of feedback condition.

Participants who were informed that they had identified the culprit reported significantly higher confidence ratings than did participants who received disconfirming feedback or no feedback. Thus, confidence can be manipulated and inflated, thereby affecting the confidence–accuracy relation.

Research also indicates that the more often you express a decision, the greater your confidence in subsequent reports (Shaw, 1996; Shaw & McClure, 1996). You can imagine that by the time a witness testifies in court, he or she has been interviewed many times. Consequently, the confidence the witness expresses in the courtroom may be inflated. Inflated confidence may be problematic given that it is an indicator used by fact finders (judges and juries) to assess accuracy. Wells and colleagues (1998) have

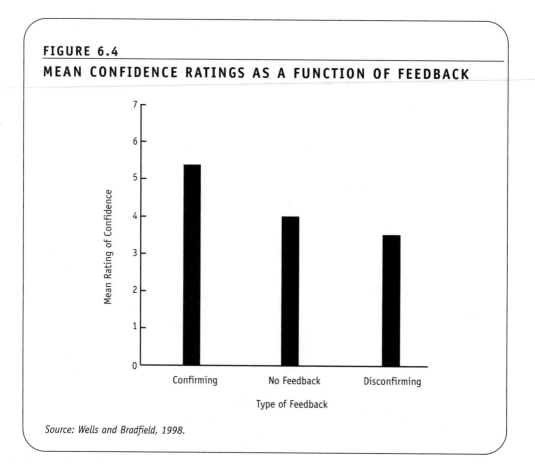

FIGURE 6.4

MEAN CONFIDENCE RATINGS AS A FUNCTION OF FEEDBACK

Source: Wells and Bradfield, 1998.

recommended that police ask witnesses for their confidence rating immediately following their identification decision prior to any feedback and that this rating be used in court. This rating may be more informative with regard to accuracy.

Estimator Variable Research in Recognition Memory

Three estimator variables have received much attention in eyewitness research: age, race, and weapon focus.

AGE Differences in the ability to make correct identifications have *not* been found between younger and older adults. Although older adults (over age 60) are just as likely as younger adults to correctly identify the culprit from a target-present lineup, older adults are more likely to make an incorrect decision from a target-absent lineup than are younger adults (Wells & Olson, 2003). In other words, older adults make similar correct identifications but fewer correct rejections than do younger adults. This pattern of responding can also be found between children and young adults (see Chapter 7 for more on this topic).

Memon and Gabbert (2003) tested younger (age 18 to 30) and older (age 60 to 80) witnesses' identification abilities. A crime video was shown, and target-present and target-absent lineups were presented using either a simultaneous or sequential lineup. Younger and older witnesses did not differ in their correct identification rate with the simultaneous lineup or the sequential lineup. Greater correct identifications were obtained with the simultaneous lineup compared with the sequential lineup for both groups. Older witnesses made fewer correct rejections with the simultaneous and the sequential lineup than did younger witnesses. Thus, older witnesses were more likely to make a false positive than were younger witnesses when shown a target-absent lineup, regardless of the procedure used. However, older witnesses made more correct rejections with a sequential lineup than with the simultaneous lineup (as did younger adults). This result replicates the superiority of the sequential lineup over the simultaneous lineup to reduce false positive responding found with younger adults in other studies. Overall, though, older adult witnesses may have more difficulty than younger adult witnesses do in making correct rejection decisions.

RACE The cross-race effect, also known as the **other-race effect**, is the phenomenon of witnesses remembering faces of people of their own race with greater accuracy than they remember faces of people of other races. In a meta-analysis, Meissner and Brigham (2001) examined 30 years of research, including almost 5000 participants, on the topic of cross-race identification. They found that own-race faces produced higher correct identifications and lower false positives than other-race faces. A number of explanations for this phenomenon have been suggested. Below are three of the more common explanations.

Attitudes One hypothesis to explain the other-race effect is based on attitudes. More specifically, people with less prejudicial attitudes may be more inclined to distinguish among members of other races. However, research to date does not support this explanation (Platz & Hosch, 1988; Slone, Brigham, & Meissner, 2000). Having said that, Meissner and Brigham (2001) do note that prejudicial attitudes may be related to the amount of contact a person has with other-race members, which, in turn, may help explain the other-race effect (see below).

Physiognomic Homogeneity An alternative hypothesis to explain the other-race effect suggests that some races have less variability in their faces—"they all look alike." This hypothesis has not received much empirical support either. Goldstein (1979) for example, examined Japanese, black, and white faces and did not find that one group was more similar across members than the others were. Although physical similarity may not explain the other-race effect, there are some features that may be more appropriate for discriminating among faces of certain races, such as hair colour (Ellis, Deregowski, & Shepherd, 1975; Shepherd, 1981; Shepherd & Deregowski, 1981). Thus, persons from other races may not pay attention or encode relevant features that distinguish between members of a particular race. For example, paying attention to hair colour for Asian faces may be less discriminating than hair colour for Caucasian faces. This explanation, however, does not seem adequate at explaining the cross-race phenomenon.

Interracial Contact Perhaps the hypothesis receiving the most attention examines the amount or type of contact people have had with other races. This hypothesis states that the more contact you have with other races, the better you will be able to identify them. In the 1970s, some researchers examined children and adolescents living in integrated neighbourhoods versus those living in segregated neighbourhoods. It was predicted that participants from integrated neighbourhoods would be better at recognizing other-race faces than would those living in segregated neighbourhoods. Some support for this prediction was found Cross, Cross, & Daly, 1971; Feinman & Entwisle, 1976).

In another test of this hypothesis, Li, Dunning, and Malpass (as cited in Meissner & Brigham, 2001) examined white basketball "experts" (dedicated fans) and white basketball novices in their ability to recognize black faces. Given that the majority of professional basketball players are black, it was thought that the experts would have more experience distinguishing black faces because of their experience watching basketball. Indeed, the experts were better at identifying black faces than were the novices.

It is important to note that not all studies that have investigated interracial contact have found the predicted effect. For example, Ng and Lindsay (1994) examined university students from Canada and Singapore and the other-race effect was not completely supported.

A definitive conclusion on the contact hypothesis and how it factors into the other-race effect remains unclear. Further work in this area is needed.

WEAPON FOCUS Weapon focus is the term used to describe the phenomenon of a witness's attention being focused on the culprit's weapon rather than on the culprit (Steblay, 1992). The witness will remember less about the crime and culprit when a weapon is present than when no weapon is present. It is clear that this phenomenon occurs, but why it occurs is less clear. There have been two primary explanations for the weapon focus effect, namely arousal and unusualness.

Arousal The **cue-utilization hypothesis** was proposed by Easterbrook (1959) to explain why a witness may focus on the weapon rather than other details. The hypothesis suggests that when emotional arousal increases, attentional capacity decreases. With limited attentional capacity, central details, such as the weapon, are more likely to be encoded than are peripheral details, such as the colour of the culprit's hair. There is some support for this hypothesis.

Unusualness An alternative explanation for the weapon focus phenomenon has to do with unusualness, in that weapons are unusual and thus attract a witness's attention. Because a witness is not paying attention to and encoding other details, these other details are not remembered (Mitchell, Livosky, & Mather, 1998; Pickel, 1998). To follow this line of thinking, you would predict that not only weapons but also other objects might produce a "weapon focus" effect, if they were unusual for the situation.

Pickel (1999) conducted two experiments to investigate the unusualness explanation. In the first experiment, university students watched one of four videotapes in which a woman was approached by a man with a handgun. The scenarios differed in their location and the degree of threat posed to the witness. In one video, the interaction occurred at a baseball game in the parking lot. In the other video, the interaction occurred at a shooting range. In the low-threat condition, the man kept the gun pointed to the ground. In the high-threat condition, the man pointed the gun at the woman. Participants provided less accurate descriptions of the man if he was carrying a gun in the parking lot rather than at the shooting range. The degree of threat did not influence the descriptions of the man. These data suggest that unusualness can produce the weapon focus phenomenon. However, it should be noted that identification of the target was not affected.

In the second experiment, a man was dressed as a police officer or a priest and was carrying a gun or cell phone. A gun would be usual for a police officer but unusual for a priest. However, neither the gun nor cell phone would be unusual for the officer. Witnesses should remember less about the priest if he was carrying a gun compared to a phone. Witnesses should remember about the same amount of information about the officer whether he carried a gun or phone. Indeed, Pickel found that witnesses reported a similar number of descriptors for the police officer regardless of what he was carrying. Furthermore, witnesses were more likely to describe the priest when he was carrying a phone than when he was carrying a gun. Once again, identification of the target was not affected.

Thus, there is some support for the unusualness explanation for the weapon focus effect. More research, however, is needed to definitively conclude why the weapon focus effect occurs.

EXPERT TESTIMONY ON EYEWITNESS ISSUES

Eyewitness testimony is an area for which experts may be able to provide the courts with data that can help the fact finders with their decision making. However, not all eyewitness experts agree as to whether there is sufficient reliability across eyewitness studies and whether it is appropriate to apply the results of laboratory simulations to the real world. An additional criticism lodged against the testimony of eyewitness experts is that the information provided is common sense and therefore, not necessary for the fact finder.

Kassin, Tubb, Hosch, and Memon (2001; Kassin, Ellsworth, & Smith, 1989) surveyed researchers to determine which eyewitness issues they felt were reliable enough to provide expert testimony in court. Issues that were deemed sufficiently reliable included lineup procedures, interview procedures, and the confidence–accuracy relationship.

There are, however, some dissenters (e.g., Egeth, 1993; McCloskey & Egeth, 1983). In one critique, Ebbesen and Konecni (1997) argue that eyewitness experts are over-confident in their conclusions and have thus misled the courts about the validity, consistency, and generalizability of the data. The researchers take issue with the lack of theory in the eyewitness area, and argue that the studies are too far removed from real-world eyewitness situations to be useful in predicting how "actual" witnesses would behave. They outline a number of weaknesses in eyewitness research that should limit its usefulness to real-world application and experts testifying:

1. Studies examining the same issue produce different results.

2. Most of the studies use university students; real-life witnesses vary in age and other demographic variables.

3. Most studies allow a witness to view the culprit for approximately six seconds; in reality witnesses may view the culprit for five or more minutes.

In defence of eyewitness research, Leippe (1995) noted that eyewitness research uses a number of methodologies and types of participants (see also Loftus, 1983). In addition, a number of studies are highly reliable. In support of the laboratory simulation using staged crimes, Wells (1993) asks, "If subjects believe that they are witnessing real crime, for instance, in what important way are they different from people who witness a real crime?" (p. 555). Perhaps the eyewitness field will always have critics on each side.

Currently, the Canadian justice system tends to limit and may not allow eyewitness experts to testify on these issues in court. For example, the Ontario Court of Appeal in *R. v. McIntosh and McCarthy* (1997) ruled not to permit expert testimony on eyewitness identification issues. Other Canadian jurisdictions may feel bound to this decision and follow suit. It is unclear how the Canadian courts will respond to eyewitness experts providing testimony on the topic in the future.

PUBLIC POLICY ISSUES AND GUIDELINES

In a survey of commonly held beliefs by the public about eyewitness testimony, Leippe (1995; see also Brewer et al., 1999) found that the public makes several fundamental errors:

■ Overestimating identification accuracy

■ Not understanding the influence of situational factors on identification accuracy

■ Not being aware of system variables that may lead to increases (or decreases) in identification accuracy

Furthermore, Yarmey (2001) has concluded that many results found with eyewitness studies are counterintuitive and contradict the common-sense beliefs of those in the community. A number of criminal cases involving eyewitness identification may have reached erroneous conclusions based on what we know about eyewitness identification. Examples include *R. v. Sophonow* (1986) in Canada, *Neil v. Biggers* (1972) in the United States, and *R. v. Turnball et al.* (1976) in the United Kingdom. Several reports dealing with eyewitness testimony have been commissioned in these three countries, including Brooks (1983), the Technical Working Group for Eyewitness Evidence (1999), and the *Devlin Report* (1976).

In the mid-1990s, then-U.S. Attorney General Janet Reno commissioned a set of guidelines for the collection and preservation of eyewitness evidence. She was prompted by the large body of empirical literature on eyewitness issues. In addition, the more sensational factor that caught her attention involved a review of DNA exoneration cases (Wells et al., 2000). According to Turtle, Lindsay, and Wells (2003), in more than 75% of DNA exoneration cases, the primary evidence used to convict was eyewitness identification. See Table 6.2 for some of the cases that involved mistaken identification.

TABLE 6.2 DNA EXONERATION CASES

Name	Crime	Years in Prison	Evidence
Adams, Kenneth	Murder, rape	16	Witness I.D.*
Bloodsworth, Kirk	Murder, rape	9	Five witness I.D.s; Self-incriminating statements
Chalmers, Terry	Rape	8	Victim I.D.; Weak alibi
Cotton, Ronald	Rape	10.5	Victim I.D.; Similarity of shoes, flashlight
Jimmerson, Verneal	Murder	11	Witness I.D.
Rainge, Willie	Murder	18	Witness I.D.
Scruggs, Dwayne	Rape	7.5	Victim I.D.; similarity of boots
Smith, Walter	Rape	11	Victim I.D.
Toney, Steven	Rape	14	Victim I.D.; Witness I.D.
Web, Thomas	Rape	13	Victim I.D.
Williams, Dennis	Murder	18	Witness I.D.

I.D. = identification.
Source: Wells et al., 1998.

Eyewitness researchers along with police officers and lawyers constituted the Technical Working Group for Eyewitness Evidence (1999) in the United States to respond to Janet Reno's request. They developed a national set of guidelines known as *Eyewitness Evidence: A Guide for Law Enforcement*. The guide is divided into five stages of criminal investigation concerning eyewitness evidence:

1. Managing witnesses at the crime scene
2. Mug books and composites
3. Follow-up investigative interviews
4. Field identification
5. Lineup identifications

In terms of lineup identification, Wells et al. (1998) proposed that the guidelines be limited to four recommendations:

1. The person who conducts the lineup or photo array should not know which person is the suspect.
2. Eyewitnesses should be told explicitly that the criminal may not be present in the lineup and, therefore, witnesses should not feel that they must make an identification.
3. The suspect should not stand out in the lineup as being different from the foils based on the eyewitness' previous description of the criminal or based on other factors that would draw extra attention to the suspect.
4. A clear statement should be taken from the eyewitness at the time of the identification and prior to any feedback as to his or her confidence that the identified person is the actual criminal.

Kassin (1998) added one more rule for lineup identification. He stated that the entire lineup procedure should be videotaped to ensure accuracy in recording. In particular, the lineup and the interaction between the officer and the witness should be videotaped so that lawyers, the judge, and the jurors can later assess for themselves whether the reports of the procedure made by police are accurate.

Parallel guidelines have also been developed in Canada. In the early 1980s, law professor Neil Brooks (1983) prepared Canadian guidelines, entitled *Police Guidelines: Pretrial Eyewitness Identification Procedures*. In addition, psychologists (eyewitness researchers) were asked to consult in the preparation of these guidelines. Thirty-eight recommendations were made with the goal of increasing the reliability of eyewitness identification. These recommendations, however, have not always been followed.

One Canadian case involving poor police techniques in collecting eyewitness identification was that of Thomas Sophonow (*R. v. Sophonow*, 1986). Sophonow was convicted of murdering Barbara Stoppel in Winnipeg, Manitoba. Sophonow spent four years in prison for a murder that he did not commit. DNA evidence exonerated him 15 years later. Supreme Court Justice Peter Cory (2001) requested a public inquiry into the case. Forty-three recommendations were made, including these:

■ The photo lineup procedure with the witness should be videotaped or audiotaped from the point the officer greets the witness to the completion of the interview.

■ Officers should inform witnesses that it is just as important to clear innocent suspects as it is to identify guilty suspects.

■ The photo lineup should be presented sequentially.

■ Officers should not discuss a witness's identification decision with him or her.

See Box 6.4 to read more about the Sophonow case. It will be interesting to examine future cases to determine whether the recommendations from the inquiry are met.

BOX 6.4 A CASE OF WRONGFUL CONVICTION

On the evening of December 23, 1981, Barbara Stoppel was working as a waitress at the Ideal Donut Shop in Winnipeg, Manitoba. At about 8:45 P.M., several patrons found her in the women's washroom of the donut shop, where she had been strangled and was close to death. Barbara later died in hospital.

A number of eyewitnesses were available in this case. For example, Mrs. Janower worked at a drugstore in the same plaza as the donut shop. She went to the donut shop at about 8:20. She saw a man standing inside who had locked the door and headed toward the washroom. Mr. Doerksen was selling Christmas trees near the donut shop. He chased a man who walked out of the donut shop when Barbara's body was found. Mr. McDonald sat in his parked truck as he waited for his wife to finish her shopping in the plaza. He could see into the donut shop and noticed a man talking to the waitress. He saw the man walk with the waitress to the back of the shop. He then came out to lock the front door of the donut shop. In addition to eyewitness accounts, police accumulated much physical evidence.

Police discovered that Thomas Sophonow was in Winnipeg visiting his daughter on the night Barbara was murdered. Sophonow was forthcoming with hair samples and so on. The police interview notes suggested that Sophonow might have been at the donut shop between 8:00 and 9:00 P.M. A few days later, Sophonow was interrogated for more than four hours. He was arrested in Vancouver and charged with Barbara's murder on March 12, 1982.

Sophonow's first trial was a mistrial, but he was convicted in the second trial. The verdict was appealed, and the Court of Appeal overturned the guilty verdict from the second trial and ordered a new trial. After the third trial, the Court of Appeal overturned the guilty verdict and acquitted Sophonow. For 15 years that followed, he sought exoneration of the crime.

In 1998, the Winnipeg Police Service reopened the investigation of the murder of Stoppel. On June 8, 2000, it was announced that Sophonow was not responsible for the murder and that another suspect had been identified. The Manitoba government issued a news release stating that the attorney general had made an apology to Sophonow, as he had endured three trials and two appeals, and spent 45 months in jail for an offence he did not commit. An inquiry was ordered into the police investigation and court proceedings to determine if mistakes were made and to whether compensation should be provided.

On the next page are some of the issues that may have contributed to Sophonow's wrongful conviction.

- Detective notes when interviewing Sophonow were not verbatim and a misquote was recorded. For example, Sophonow stated, "I could not have been in Ideal Donut Shop," but the statement recorded was "I could have been in Ideal Donut Shop."

- Winnipeg police did not inform Sophonow that he could call a lawyer at any time or inform him that the statements he made could be used against him. Sophonow stated that he asked for a lawyer on several occasions during interrogation but the officers did not allow him to call one.

- Sophonow was strip-searched and a search of his anal cavity was done to determine if he was carrying any drugs, even though there was no reason to believe this was the case. Sophonow felt that there was nothing he could say that the police would believe and felt it best to keep quiet.

- Mr. Doerksen was hypnotized and asked to describe the assailant. Mr. Doerksen called the police when he thought he saw the culprit at a hotel. This man was quickly exonerated. Mr. Doerksen also identified a reporter as the culprit, who was also quickly exonerated. Mr. Doerksen failed to identify Sophonow from a lineup that the police assembled. The sergeant conducting the lineup told Mr. Doerksen to consider number 7—Sophonow was number 7.

- Sophonow had an alibi that was not considered seriously. He had stopped at the Canadian Tire the night of the 23rd, spoke to a woman and her daughter waiting for their car repairs, went to a Safeway store, bought some red mesh stockings, and went to hospitals to deliver the stockings for Christmas. These events occurred around 8:00 and, given the timeline of the killing, could not allow Sophonow to be the murderer.

- Terry Arnold lived near the donut shop and reportedly had a crush on Barbara. He fit the description and did not have an alibi. He was not fully investigated.

Dr. Elizabeth Loftus testified in the inquiry and noted a number of problems with the eyewitness evidence:

- When there is more than one witness, they can inadvertently influence each other.

- People under hypnosis are suggestible and often assume that what they retrieve under hypnosis is accurate, even though it may not be.

- The photo arrays shown to the Janower had Sophonow's picture stand out—his picture had a yellow background and his hat was off to the side, as was the suspect's hat in the composite drawing initially issued to the public. There also was a live lineup in which Sophonow stood out in terms of his height.

Source: R. v. Sophonow, 1986.

SUMMARY

1. Independent variables in the eyewitness area can be categorized as estimator or system variables. The effect of estimator variables on eyewitness accuracy can only be estimated after the crime. In contrast, system variables can be manipulated

by the criminal justice system to increase (or decrease) eyewitness accuracy. The three dependent variables in the eyewitness area are recall of the event, recall of the culprit, and recognition of the culprit.

2. The misinformation effect is a phenomenon in which a witness who is presented with inaccurate information after an event will incorporate that misinformation into a subsequent recall task. This effect can occur as a result of a witness guessing what the officer wants the response to be. Alternatively, this effect can occur because a witness has two memories, one for the correct information and one for the incorrect information, but cannot accurately remember how he or she acquired each piece of information. The misinformation effect can also occur because the inaccurate information replaces the accurate information in memory.

3. The cognitive interview is based on four memory-retrieval techniques to increase recall: reinstating the context, reporting everything that comes to mind, recalling the event in different orders, and changing the perspective from which the information is recalled. In addition to these techniques, the enhanced cognitive interview includes five more techniques: building rapport, exhibiting supportive interviewer behaviour, transferring the control of the interview to the witness, asking for focused recall with open-ended questions, and asking the witness questions that match what the witness is recalling.

4. The simultaneous lineup, sequential lineup, showup, and walk-by are lineup procedures used by police to determine whether the suspect is the culprit. Biased lineups suggest who the police suspect and thereby who the witness should identify. In some way, the suspect stands out from the other lineup members in a biased lineup. Foil bias, instruction bias, and clothing bias have been investigated and shown to increase false-positive responding.

5. Not all eyewitness experts agree on the reliability of research findings and whether we can apply the results of laboratory simulations to the real world. An additional criticism lodged against the eyewitness expert testifying is whether the information provided is common sense and therefore not necessary for the fact finder.

6. Four rules were outlined to reduce the likelihood of false identification. First, the person who conducts the lineup should not know which member of the lineup is the suspect. Second, eyewitnesses should be told explicitly that the criminal may not be present in the lineup and, therefore, witnesses should not feel that they must make an identification. Third, the suspect should not stand out in the lineup as being different from the foils based on the eyewitness's previous description of the criminal or based on other factors that would draw extra attention to the suspect. Fourth, a clear statement should be taken from the eyewitness at the time of the identification (and prior to any feedback) as to his or her confidence that the identified person is the actual criminal.

KEY CONCEPTS

DISCUSSION QUESTIONS

1. Imagine you are a judge and are allowing an eyewitness psychological expert to testify. What factors would you consider appropriate for the expert to testify about? What factors would you disallow testimony on?

2. A neighbour informs you that she has just entered therapy to help understand why she is no longer happy in her marriage. She says the therapist feels she may have been abused as a child, even though she has no memory of it. She is uncertain whether to continue with the therapy and wonders whether, in fact, she could have been abused. What advice do you give her?

3. One of your friends is training to be a police officer. His training is almost complete but he is worried that he has not received sufficient training on how to interview eyewitnesses. He asks you whether you can describe some of the techniques you learned in your "forensic" class. Explain interview strategies to elicit complete and accurate recall, as well as the techniques that may hinder the process.

4. There has been a considerable amount of research on the misinformation effect. Design an experiment to test whether the misinformation effect also occurs if participants witness a violent crime.

5. Different types of lineup procedures are used by police. Describe these different types of procedures and distinguish among the types of identification decisions that can occur in both target-present and target-absent lineups.

6. A number of explanations have been proposed to account for the finding that witnesses remember the faces of people of their own race better than faces of people of other races. Which of these explanations do you think best accounts for this cross-race effect? Why?

7. You friend works as a cashier at the 7-11. She was robbed while at work by someone who was armed with a sawed-off shotgun. She is upset because she could not provide the police with many details of the robber. How would you explain her lack of memory?

ADDITIONAL INFORMATION

Readings

Scheck, B., Neufeld, P., & Dwyer, J. (2000). *Actual innocence: Five days to execution and other dispatches from the wrongly convicted.* New York: Doubleday.

Loftus, E.F., & Ketchum, K. (1991). *Witness for the defense.* New York: St. Martin's Press.

Web Sites

The Association in Defence of the Wrongfully Convicted
www.aidwyc.org

Dr. Gary Wells's Eyewitness Page
www.psychology.iastate.edu/faculty/gwells/homepage.htm

CHAPTER 7

Child Victims and Witnesses

LEARNING OBJECTIVES

■ Differentiate between techniques that decrease versus increase the likelihood of accurate recall in child witnesses.

■ Summarize children's ability to recall/describe people's appearances.

■ Describe a lineup technique designed for children's identification.

■ Outline the competency inquiry and courtroom accommodations available for child witnesses.

■ Explain child maltreatment categories and related consequences.

■ List the negative outcomes that are related to divorce for children.

Six-year-old Carrie Webber was attending the Nature Adventures Day Camp during her summer vacation. For some activities, children were able to scavenge in the small, wooded grounds on their own while supervisors walked around observing.

One day when Mrs. Webber picked up her daughter, she noticed some scrapes on Carrie's knees. When Mrs. Webber asked what happened, Carrie said, "I fell when the man helper touched my bum." When they arrived home, Mrs. Webber questioned Carrie further, examined her, and noticed that Carrie's inner thighs were irritated. Immediately, Mrs. Webber took Carrie to the hospital, where police were called.

Following an examination, the cause of the irritation could not be determined. Carrie was questioned by a police officer and a social worker about the events occurring at the camp. Fairly certain abuse had occurred, they launched a full investigation.

> The "man helper" was identified as 25-year-old Jason Smith, one of the
> three male supervisors at the camp, who had been at the camp for two years.
> All children (ages six to eight) who had ever taken part in the camp's programs
> under Mr. Smith's supervision were interviewed. Social workers used anatomically
> detailed dolls with the reluctant children to help them to describe what Mr.
> Smith did to them. Many times, social workers had to describe what they
> thought happened and children were asked whether they agreed or disagreed.
> Some children were interviewed for six hours or more. Mr. Smith was charged
> with the sexual assault of seven children.

HISTORY

The way in which child victims and witnesses have been viewed by the justice system
has changed dramatically over the years. Some early views can be traced back to the
Salem witch trials in 1692, when children claimed to have witnessed the defendants
perform supernatural feats and other falsehoods (Ceci & Bruck, 1993). Several years
following the execution of the defendants for witchcraft, some of the children recanted their testimonies. For the most part, the prevailing legal attitude toward child witnesses for the following 300 years was that of skepticism.

Research testing the validity of these negative attitudes toward child witnesses
started in Europe in the early twentieth century. Reviews from this time seemed to
conclude that young children were highly suggestible and had difficulty separating fact
from fantasy, and thus, were capable of providing inaccurate testimony, even if the testimony was of personal significance (Whipple, 1909, 1910, 1911, 1912). Unfortunately,
little is known about the details of the research on which these conclusions were
based. Also, the criminal justice system was not very interested in these reviews. As a
result, few studies were conducted on children's competencies during the early and
mid-twentieth century.

A flurry of research on children's witness abilities started in the 1970s and continues to this day. Ceci and Bruck (1993) outlined four factors that led to the renewed
interest in child witnesses:

1. Expert psychological testimony was becoming more acceptable in the courtroom.
2. Social scientists were interested in research that could be applied to real-world
   problems.
3. Studies on *adult* eyewitness testimony were increasing.
4. The legal community became interested in behavioural science research regarding child witnesses.

This last point was in response to the increasing number of reported sexual and physical abuse cases where a child was a victim or witness. These cases, arising in both the United States and Canada, often involved numerous children and numerous defendants. Box 7.1 describes a Canadian case in which children were the primary victims and witnesses.

RECALL FOR EVENTS

Are children able to recall events accurately? How does their performance compare with adults'? The Martensville case and others similar to it may suggest that children do not make very reliable witnesses, even about events they supposedly experienced. However, studies have found that children *are* capable of accurately recalling forensically relevant details of events (e.g., Ceci & Bruck, 1993). Moreover, children are capable of recalling much that is accurate. The challenge, of course, is determining when children are recalling accurately and when they are fabricating—making false claims.

BOX 7.1 THE MARTENSVILLE BABY-SITTING CASE

In the fall of 1991, Ms. L. noticed a rash on her two-and-half-year-old daughter's bottom. Ms. L. suspected that child abuse had occurred at the baby-sitting service run by Linda Sterling. Following a medical examination of the child, a doctor concluded that the rash was not indicative of abuse.

The investigation continued, however, and several claims were made against Linda Sterling, her husband, Ronald, and her son Travis. The child in question was interviewed intensely and eventually stated that a man had touched her. Many more children were subsequently interviewed, some claiming that they had been confined in cages, penetrated with axe handles, forced to drink blood, whipped, and thrown naked into freezers. The children also claimed to have witnessed a ritual murder, a child's nipple being bitten off, a body dumped into an acid bath, and a dog stabbed to death.

Linda, Ronald, and Travis Sterling, along with one other woman and five other men,

were arrested and charged. More than 40 charges, including sexual assault, sexual assault with a weapon, unlawful confinement, and intercourse with a minor, were laid against the Sterlings.

Dr. John Yuille from the University of British Columbia was an expert witness in the case. He noted that the interviews with the children were fraught with leading questions and that rewards were offered to children for giving the "right answer." Moreover, there was a lack of physical evidence consistent with the claims being made.

The investigation and trial spanned over two and a half years. Linda and Ronald Sterling were found not guilty, while Travis was found guilty on several of the charges. Eventually, this verdict was overturned due to the inappropriate interview techniques that were used with the children.

Source: R. v. Sterling, 1995.

Research suggests that the accuracy of children's reporting is highly dependent on *how* they are asked to report.

Free Recall versus Directed Questioning

When children are asked to report all they can remember, using a free narrative approach, their accuracy in reporting is comparable with adults' (Ceci & Bruck, 1993). Unfortunately, children report very little information using a free narrative. Direct questions or probes, such as "What else do you remember?" or "Tell me more about what you remember," are often necessary to elicit the required information. The dilemma arises when we consider the accuracy of direct questioning.

As we have seen with adult eyewitnesses in Chapter 6, when children are asked leading, direct questions, they are more likely to produce an erroneous response than when they are asked nonleading, direct questions (Roebers et al., 2002). Generally, older children are more resistant to leading questions than are younger children, and adults are even more resistant to leading questions (Ceci & Bruck, 1993).

Direct questions that require a yes/no response or use a forced-choice format are particularly problematic for preschoolers (Peterson & Biggs, 1997). For example, Peterson and Grant (2001) examined preschoolers' responses to yes/no and multiple-choice questions. In the first of two sessions, the experimenter interacted with the children for a few minutes. During this session, a second experimenter entered and the two had a disagreement over a crayon. In the second session that took place a week later, an experimenter whom the children had never met asked them questions about the appearance, actions, speech, and emotions of the two experimenters from the first session. Children were asked yes/no questions such as "Did the woman knock over the crayons?" and multiple-choice questions with two options such as "Did the woman wear a flowered hat or a straw hat?" The preschoolers demonstrated a bias toward saying yes to yes/no questions. They did not demonstrate a bias for multiple-choice questions; that is, children were just as likely to choose either of the two options. If neither of the options in the multiple-choice question were correct, children tended to respond with "I don't know." Thus, both yes/no questions and multiple-choice questions are not ideal for preschoolers if we are interested in accuracy.

The content and format of questions posed to child witnesses should be considered carefully. Interviewers need to balance asking direct questions with the risk of obtaining false information. Many would recommend relying on free recall as much as possible to obtain accurate information.

Anatomically Detailed Dolls

If children have difficulty providing a verbal account of what they witnessed or experienced, props may be useful. When interviewing children suspected of being sexually abused, some mental health professionals may introduce **anatomically detailed dolls.** Just as the name implies, anatomically detailed dolls, sometimes like a "rag doll," are consistent with the male or female anatomy. Dolls may be of an adult male or female or a young male or female. The assumption underlying the use of these dolls is that children may have difficulty verbalizing what occurred, and in their play with the dolls they will demonstrate the events they experienced. Is this assumption correct though? The research provides some contradictory results.

In one study, suspected victims of child sexual abuse between the ages of 4 and 12 were interviewed either with or without detailed dolls (Lamb et al., 1996). Children's responses to open-ended questions and prompts were longer and more detailed when questioned *without* the dolls than when questioned with the dolls.

In another study, DeLoache and Marzolf (1995) asked children aged three to five to describe an upsetting event that had occurred in their classroom. Some of the children were asked to re-enact the event with the use of anatomically detailed dolls and the others were asked to orally describe the event. Both groups of children provided a similar number of details. However, a greater proportion of inaccurate details were provided when children used the dolls than when they provided an oral description.

Contrary to the above results, Goodman, Quas, Batterman-Faunce, Riddlesberger, and Kuhn (1997) found that three- to ten-year-olds who had been touched during an examination were more likely to report such touching with dolls than when questioned orally. In another study, Saywitz, Goodman, Nicholas, and Moan (1991) interviewed five- and seven-year-old girls who had received a physical examination. For half the girls, a genital examination was included. In this study, many of the children failed to report genital touching when they were asked for a verbal report of their examination, or they failed to show on the dolls what had actually happened. However, when asked a direct question—such as "Did the doctor touch you here?"— many of the children correctly agreed. Children who had not received the genital examination never made false reports of genital touching in either the oral free recall or the doll enactment conditions. For this group, very few errors were made when the experimenter pointed to the genital area of the doll and asked, "Did the doctor touch you here?"

SHOULD ANATOMICALLY DETAILED DOLLS BE USED?

The use of anatomically detailed dolls in the assessment of abuse is a controversial and hotly debated topic, and a number of difficulties have been identified (Koocher et al., 1995). For example, no specifications or guidelines are available for

Anatomically detailed dolls being used in a therapy session

manufacturers of these dolls. Consequently, wide variation exists and some mental health professionals even make their own dolls. Not only is there no standardization for what the dolls should look like, there also are no standard procedures for scoring the behaviours children exhibit when interacting with the dolls. Research is not available to answer how nonabused versus abused children play with the dolls. Moreover, it is not clear whether abused versus nonabused children play with the dolls differently. Thus, the use of anatomically detailed dolls for diagnosing sexual abuse should be undertaken cautiously.

Other Techniques for Interviewing Children

Although we can see that numerous challenges face the evaluator when trying to get at the truth during interviews with children, psychologists have developed techniques and protocols that may be useful.

CRITERION-BASED CONTENT ANALYSIS Criterion-based content analysis (CBCA) was developed in Germany by Udo Undeutsch to facilitate distinguishing truthful from false statements made by children (Stellar, 1989). It is part of a more comprehensive protocol called **statement validity analysis** (SVA). SVA consists of three parts: (1) a structured interview of the child witness; (2) a systematic analysis of the verbal content of the child's statements (CBCA), and (3) the application of the statement validity checklist.

For the first part of SVA, the child is interviewed without the use of leading questions. In the second part, the CBCA criteria are applied to the child's report to determine its truthfulness. The underlying assumption is that descriptions of memories of real events differ in quality and content from memories that are fabricated. The child's interview is scored on 18 items. For example, the evaluator will examine the logical structure of the account. Is it coherent? Do the different segments fit together? When a criterion is present in the report, it suggests truthfulness. In the last part of SVA, the statement validity checklist is applied. The statement validity checklist contains 13 criteria for other characteristics that might be indicative of truthfulness. For example, the evaluator will examine the language the child used and whether the depth of knowledge displayed is appropriate given the age of the child. Lastly, an overall evaluation decision is reached regarding the truthfulness of the report.

To evaluate the accuracy of CBCA, two types of studies have been used: simulations and field studies (see Chapter 2 for a description of these types of studies). Stellar (1989) described a simulation study John Yuille conducted in 1988 with children aged six to nine. In the study, a research assistant told each child participant that he or she would be asked to tell two stories—one that had happened to him or her and one that was made up but could have happened. After a couple of days, the children were interviewed. An SVA procedure was used when interviewing the child. Two blind evaluators then scored the children's interviews using the CBCA criteria. Table 7.1 illustrates the evaluators' classification decisions for children telling true and false stories. These data indicate that the majority of the children's stories were accurately classified; most of the true stories were classified as true and most of the false stories were classified as false.

However, as you may recall from Chapter 2, simulation studies have been criticized for lacking ecological validity in that they are different from the phenomena they are meant to generalize to in the real world. For example, the topics children discussed in Yuille's study are not comparable with accounts of child sexual abuse. At times, field studies are conducted because they have greater ecological validity than the simulation (but may fall short in other areas, such as truly knowing whether an event occurred as reported or not).

Stellar (1989) described a field study conducted by Esplin, Boychuk, and Raskin in 1988 to evaluate the accuracy of the CBCA. Children aged three-and-a-half to 17 were interviewed using the SVA procedure. The criteria used to categorize alleged abuse cases as confirmed was whether there was a confession by the alleged offender and/or there was medical evidence clearly substantiating the allegation. In total there were 20 cases of confirmed sexual abuse. The criteria used to categorize alleged abuse cases as unconfirmed were whether there was persistent denial by the alleged perpetrator, absence of medial evidence, dismissal of the case by the justice system, or other corroborating evidence, and a psychologist concluding sexual abuse was unlikely. In total there were 20 cases of unconfirmed allegations of sexual abuse. Each case was subjected to CBCA scoring by a professional who had been trained to use the criteria and was blind to the initial categorization. Each interview received a total score for the CBCA criteria. The mean score for confirmed cases of sexual abuse was 24.8, and the mean score for unconfirmed sexual abuse cases was 3.6 (Stellar, 1989), indicating that the criteria were successful at distinguishing between true and false reports.

CBCA is not without its critics, however. For example, Ruby and Brigham (1997) suggest that the technique needs further research before it should be used in forensic cases. They note a number of difficulties with CBCA, such as inconsistencies with the

TABLE 7.1 CLASSIFICATION DECISIONS AS A FUNCTION OF CHILDREN'S STORY

Child's Story	Classification Decision		
	True	False	Unclassified*
True	29	3	3
False	6	21	9

Source: Stellar, 1989.

*Story did not contain enough information to be scored.

number of criteria that need to be present to conclude truthfulness and the different decision rules for reaching a conclusion.

Nonetheless, SVA is being used in parts of Europe to distinguish between children's truthful and false reports. Recently, SVA has also been applied to adult statements to distinguish between truthful and false reports, and studies report great success (Parker & Brown, 2000).

STEP-WISE INTERVIEW An alternative procedure for interviewing children that aims to keep false claims at a minimum is the **step-wise interview** developed by Yuille and his colleagues (e.g., Yuille et al., 1993). This interview protocol consists of a series of "steps" designed to start the interview with the least leading and directive type of questioning, and then proceeding to more specific forms of questioning as necessary (see Table 7.2 on the next page). The objective with this protocol is to provide the child with lots of opportunity to report using a free narrative before other types of questioning is used.

Lindberg, Chapman, Samsock, Thomas, and Lindberg (2003) have tested the step-wise procedure, along with a procedure they developed, the modified structured interview, and a procedure developed by the Action for Child Protection in West Virginia that uses doll play. The three procedures are similar in terms of rapport building and the general question phases. The major difference is in terms of specific questioning. With the step-wise procedure, specific questioning occurs through progressively more focused questions and probes information obtained from the more general questions. With the modified structured interview, specific questioning occurs through the use of who, what, where, and when questions. With the Action for Child Protection procedure, specific questioning occurs through doll play.

To test these three procedures, children in Grades 1 and 2 watched a video of a mother hitting her son. The children were then randomly assigned to be interviewed using one of the three procedures. The interviewers were blind to what the children witnessed on the videotape. Interviews were transcribed and then coded for correct and incorrect statements. The results indicated that the procedure developed by the Action for Child Protection group was less effective than the other two, and the step-wise and modified interviews produced a comparable amount of information during the free narrative portions. The modified procedure was superior to the step-wise or the Action for Child Protection procedure for "where" questions.

Overall, the step-wise procedure is consistent with what we know about children's recall abilities and how to elicit accurate information. The step-wise interview is the procedure most commonly used in Canada.

NARRATIVE ELABORATION In the United States, Saywitz and Snyder (1996) developed an interview procedure called **narrative elaboration**. With this procedure, children learn to organize stories into relevant categories:

- participants
- settings
- actions
- conversation/affective states
- consequences

TABLE 7.2 THE STEP-WISE INTERVIEW

Step	Goal	How
1	Rapport building	Talk to the child about neutral topics, trying to make him or her feel comfortable.
2	Recall of two nonabuse events	Have the child describe two experienced events such as a birthday party and going to the zoo.
3	Explanation of truth	Explain truth in general and have the child agree to tell the truth.
4	Introduction of critical topic	Start with open-ended questions, such as "Do you know why you are talking with me today?" Proceed to more specific questions if disclosure does not occur, such as "Who are the people you like/don't like to be with?"
5	Free narrative	Ask the child to describe what happened using a free narrative approach.
6	General questions	Ask questions based on what the child said, in a manner the child understands.
7	Specific questions (if necessary)	Follow up and clarify inconsistencies with more specific questions.
8	Interview aids (if necessary)	Have the child draw if he or she is not responding. Dolls may be introduced only after disclosure has occurred.
9	Conclude	Thank the child for helping and explain what will happen next.

Source: Yuille et al., 1993.

A card containing a line drawing is available for each category (see Figure 7.1 for four of them). These visual cues help children remember to state all that they can. Children practise telling stories with each card before being questioned about the critical event. Then, they are asked for a free narrative about the critical event—for example, "What happened?" Lastly, children are presented with each card and asked, "Does this card remind you to tell something else?"

To test the narrative elaboration procedure, children in Grades 1 and 2 and children in Grades 4, 5, and 6 witnessed a staged event (Saywitz & Synder, 1996). The children then were interviewed with either the narrative elaboration procedure (involving training in the use of reminder cue cards), exposure to the cue cards without training, or a "standard" interview without training or cue cards. Children interviewed with the narrative elaboration procedure reported more accurate information but not more

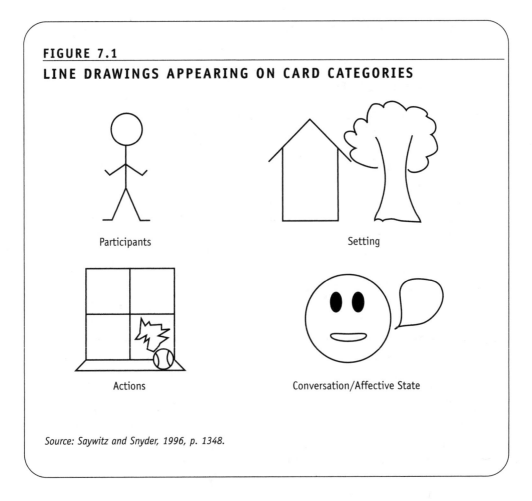

FIGURE 7.1

LINE DRAWINGS APPEARING ON CARD CATEGORIES

Participants

Setting

Actions

Conversation/Affective State

Source: Saywitz and Snyder, 1996, p. 1348.

inaccurate information for the staged event compared with when just the cue cards were presented without training or the standard interview. Also, children did not fabricate more information with the narrative elaboration procedure.

As you can see, there are a number of techniques available to those who interview children. These techniques limit the use of direct questions and attempt to have the child provide as much information as possible using a free recall format. The interview protocols being used by police vary by jurisdiction. For example, the SVA is popular in parts of Europe, while the step-wise procedure is common in parts of Canada.

RECALL FOR PEOPLE

Not only must children report the events that happened, it is likely they will have to describe the culprit, especially if he or she is a stranger. Culprit descriptions, also known as recall for people, by child witnesses have been examined in only a few studies relative to the number of studies that have examined recall for an event.

Describing the Culprit

In one study, Davies, Tarrant, and Flin (1989) asked for descriptions of a stranger from younger (age six to seven) and older (age 10 to 11) children. The younger children recalled fewer items ($M = 1$ descriptor) than the older children ($M = 2.21$ descriptors). The researchers also found that older children recalled more interior facial features, such as freckles and nose, than younger children. Hair was the most frequently mentioned feature by both younger and older children.

The exterior feature of hair seems to be a dominant descriptor focused on by both children and adults (Ellis, Shepherd, & Davies, 1980; Sporer, 1996). Pozzulo and Warren (2003) found that exterior facial descriptors such as hair colour and style were predominant and accurately reported by 10- to 14-year-olds and adults. Moreover, interior facial features were problematic for *both* youth and adults.

Height, weight, and age are descriptors commonly reported, and if they are not reported, police may ask about them directly. Unfortunately, children and youth may have considerable difficulty with their estimates of such characteristics. Davies, Stephenson-Robb, and Flin (1988) found that children/youths (age 7 to 12 years) were inaccurate when asked to report the height, weight, and age of an unfamiliar visitor. Pozzulo and Warren (2003) found that accuracy for body descriptors such as height and weight were consistently problematic for youth. One possible explanation for this result is that children and youth may not understand the relation between height and weight—that is, taller people are heavier than shorter people of similar girth. Alternatively, children and youth simply may lack experience with height and weight. It is only in later adolescence that people become body conscious and more familiar with weight (and height proportions).

Factors Affecting Children's Person Descriptions

Leichtman and Ceci (1995) examined the effect of stereotypes and suggestions on preschoolers' reports. Children between the ages of three and six years were assigned to one of four groups:

1. Control—no interviews contained suggestive questions.
2. Stereotype—children were given expectations about a stranger who visited the class.
3. Suggestion—children were given misinformation about acts committed by the stranger.
4. Stereotype and suggestion—children were given expectations plus misinformation about the stranger.

Children witnessed a stranger by the name of Sam Stone visit their classroom. Sam was present for a story that was read by the teacher. All children were interviewed repeatedly after the event in one of the four conditions described above. For example, in the stereotype condition children were told that Sam was kind and well meaning but very clumsy and bumbling. In the suggestion condition, children were misled that Sam ripped a book and soiled a teddy bear during his classroom visit. So which group was most accurate?

Using open-ended interviews, children were most accurate in the control condition and least accurate in the stereotype plus suggestion condition. Children in the stereotype condition produced a fair number of false reports. Children in the suggestion condition produced a great number of false reports. Overall, the older children were more accurate than the younger children.

As this study illustrates, it is important for interviewers not to introduce their own biases or inaccurate information when interviewing children. Once again, the argument can be made that children should be asked to describe the culprit in terms of what he or she did and looked like using a free narrative. Given the few descriptors children provide, it may be important to probe this information for detail. Some of the techniques described above for event recall may be helpful with person recall. More research is needed on how to elicit person descriptions from children, as well as adults!

RECOGNITION

One other task a child victim or witness may be called upon to perform is an identification of the culprit from a lineup. In a meta-analysis comparing children's identification abilities to adults', Pozzulo and Lindsay (1998) found that children over age five produced comparable correct identification rates to adults, provided the culprit was present in the lineup (target-present lineup). However, when the culprit was not in the lineup (target-absent lineup), children as old as 14 produced greater false positives than adults. That is, children were more likely to select an innocent person from a lineup than adults were (see Chapter 6 for a review of general lineup identification issues).

Lineup Procedure and Identification Rates

Pozzulo and Lindsay (1998) examined whether identification rates differed between children and adults as a function of the lineup procedure used. As you may recall from Chapter 6, the sequential lineup has been demonstrated to decrease false-positive responding compared with simultaneous presentation for adults (Lindsay & Wells, 1985). Would the use of the sequential lineup with children decrease their false-positive responding? Pozzulo and Lindsay (1998) found that with sequential lineup presentation, the gap for false-positive responding between children and adults *increased*. Thus, the sequential lineup increased false-positive responding with child witnesses, whereas for adults the sequential lineup decreased false-positive responding.

AN IDENTIFICATION PROCEDURE FOR CHILDREN In an attempt to develop an identification procedure that decreases children's false-positive responding, Pozzulo and Lindsay (1999) proposed a two-judgment theory of identification accuracy. The researchers postulated that to reach an accurate identification decision, witnesses conduct two judgments: relative and absolute. First, witnesses compare across lineup members and choose the most similar-looking lineup member to the culprit, a relative judgment. Second, witnesses compare the most-similar lineup member to their memory of the culprit and decide if it is in fact the culprit, an absolute judgment. Pozzulo and Lindsay (1999) speculated that children often fail to make an absolute judgment and thereby produce greater false positives than adults.

The researchers explain how a failure of making an absolute judgment would result in greater false positives. They argue that with target-present lineups, a relative judgment is *sufficient* to lead to a correct identification because it is likely that the culprit looks most like himself or herself compared with the other lineup members. Thus, the culprit is selected. In contrast, with target-absent lineups, solely relying on a relative judgment may lead to an identification of an innocent person because the most similar-looking lineup member is *not* the culprit—recall that with a target-absent lineup the culprit is not there. An absolute judgment is necessary with target-absent lineups. If children fail to conduct an absolute judgment, a greater false-positive rate may result.

Based on these notions, Pozzulo and Lindsay (1999) developed an identification procedure known as the **elimination lineup** for children that is consistent with the two-judgment theory of identification accuracy. The elimination lineup procedure requests two judgments from the child:

1. All lineup photos are presented to the child and the child is asked to select the lineup member who looks most like the culprit (relative judgment). Once this decision is made, the remaining photos are removed.

2. The child is asked to compare his or her memory of the culprit with the most-similar photo selected in the first stage and decide if the photo is of the culprit (absolute judgment).

Pozzulo and Lindsay (1999) tested variations of this procedure and the "standard" simultaneous procedure with children and adults. The elimination procedure was found to significantly decrease children's false-positive responding with target-absent lineups compared with the simultaneous procedure. In other words, children's correct rejection rate increased using the elimination procedure compared with the simultaneous procedure. Moreover, children's false positive rate (or correct rejection rate) with the elimination procedure was similar to that of adults when the simultaneous procedure was used. Figure 7.2 illustrates the correct rejection rates for target-absent lineups for children and adults as a function of lineup procedure.

The elimination procedure has captured the attention of the criminal justice system in Ontario. Currently, more research is being conducted on this procedure to determine its effectiveness at reducing false positives (and maintaining correct identifications) in different situations. For example, the elimination procedure is being tested when the culprit undergoes a change of appearance (Pozzulo & Balfour, 2004). The procedure is also being further tested with adults (Pozzulo & Lawandi, 2004).

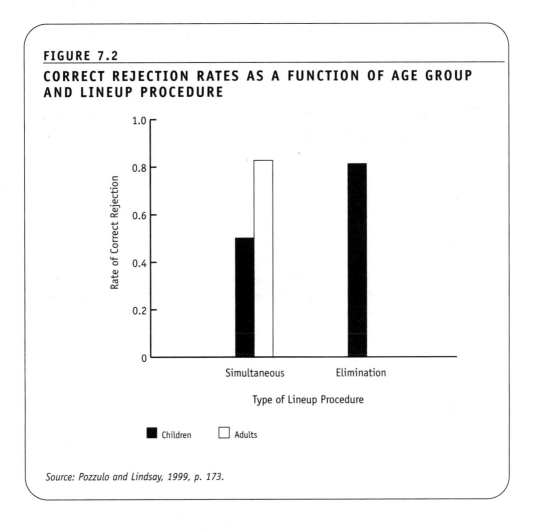

FIGURE 7.2

CORRECT REJECTION RATES AS A FUNCTION OF AGE GROUP AND LINEUP PROCEDURE

Source: Pozzulo and Lindsay, 1999, p. 173.

TESTIFYING IN COURT

In Canada (as well as the United States and some European countries), children under 14 must pass a **competency inquiry** before testifying. The notion behind the competency inquiry is that children must demonstrate that they can communicate what they witnessed or experienced. Also, it is critical that they understand the difference between being truthful and lying and that they feel compelled to tell the truth. It can be argued that the competency inquiry is historically entrenched in the negative views of child witnesses discussed earlier in this chapter.

Competency Inquiry

The legislation for competency inquiries can be found in section 16 of the Canada Evidence Act. It states that witnesses under 14 must (1) be able to communicate the evidence, and (2) understand the difference between the truth and a lie, and in the circumstances of testifying feel compelled to tell the truth. Judges typically conduct the inquiry, although the lawyer for whom the child is testifying (typically the Crown/prosecutor) may ask the questions because rapport may be easier to establish. Hence, the child may be more forthcoming and provide more accurate responses.

In the first part of the inquiry, children need only demonstrate a general ability to perceive, recall, and communicate rather than demonstrate specific abilities for describing the event/crime in question. Common questions may include

- What grade are you in?
- What is your teacher's name?
- How many siblings do you have?

Children as young as two or three may be able to demonstrate a general ability to communicate.

For the second part of the exam, children are questioned regarding their ability to distinguish between the truth and a lie, and must demonstrate an understanding of the meaning of *oath*. Common themes for questioning in this section include

- defining terms
- religion and church
- consequences of lying

The second part of the inquiry seems particularly difficult for young children. See Box 7.2 for excerpts from Canadian competency inquiries.

If the judge determines that the child has met the competency requirements, the child presents his or her testimony under oath. If a child does not understand the nature of an oath, and if the judge determines that the child's conscience will compel him or her to tell the truth by making a promise to God, the child may provide testimony through a solemn affirmation. The last option for a child who does not understand the nature of an oath or affirmation but who can communicate the evidence is to testify under a promise to tell the truth. In such an instance, the child needs to demonstrate a moral responsibility to tell the truth. This responsibility can be accomplished if the child states it is bad or not good to lie. If the child is deemed not competent to testify, his or her out-of-court statements may be allowed into evidence as **hearsay**—that is, a second-party reports of what another (the child in this case) said.

Preparing Children to Testify

The Centre for Children and Families in the Justice System is a nonprofit agency that is part of the London Family Court Clinic based in London, Ontario. The agency advocates for the special needs of children and families involved in the justice system. A key service provided by the centre is known as the Child Witness Project.

The Child Witness Project consists of a multidisciplinary team that helps children and adolescents who have to give evidence in criminal court. Usually the children

BOX 7.2 QUESTIONS FOR A COMPETENCY INQUIRY

In *R. v. Marquard* (1993), the judge posed the competency inquiry questions to a five-year-old girl. The questions below were posed during the first portion of the competency inquiry that addresses the child's ability to communicate the evidence.

Judge: Do you know what a memory is? Do you remember things that happened?

Child: No.

Judge: You don't? What did you do yesterday?

Child: I went down to the donut shop, and I got a drink and bubble gum.

Judge: Okay. That's what I am saying is remembering, okay, so when I ask you do you remember what you did yesterday, that was your answer. You went to the donut shop and got a drink and some bubble gum, okay.

Child: I mean gum.

Judge: Plain gum, okay. Well that's good. It's important to be pretty exact. All right, now, Miss A. is going to ask you some questions, and I know you know the difference between the truth and a lie, and you answer her questions as truthfully and as best as you can remember, okay?

Below are a judge's questions posed during the second portion of a competency inquiry addressing the child's ability to distinguish between truth and lie. The child is a six-year-old boy.

Q. Okay. Can you tell me whether you know the difference between the truth and a lie?

A. The truth, you tell somebody what the matter and a lie is you don't tell nobody, so it is not a lie.

Q. Yes. If I were to tell you that it was snowing outside right now, would that be a lie?

A. Yeah.

Q. Okay. If I were to tell you that it is raining outside now, would that be a lie.

A. No.

Q. It would be what?

A. Right.

Q. The truth?

A. Yeah, truth.

. . .

Q. Why is it wrong to tell a lie?

A. Because everybody want to know, or maybe.

. . .

Q. Yeah. What happens if you tell a lie?

A. You tell a lie and then you . . . everybody want . . . to know, because you asked what is the matter and then they say they tell a lie.

Q. Oh, do you think it is wrong to tell a lie?

A. Yeah, it is wrong.

Q. Well if you were allowed to tell something today, would you promise me to tell the truth?

A. Yes.

Source: Bala et al., 2002.

and adolescents are witnesses or victims of alleged physical or sexual abuse. A preparation program exists for the child (and family) to make the process of testifying easier. For example, the child undergoes an individual assessment to determine his or her special needs and to identify the child's salient fears about testifying. There is court preparation for the child during which he or she learns court procedures and etiquette, oath taking, and legal terminology. A mock courtroom, puppets, a judge's gown, and so forth, are also used. Children are also taught stress reduction techniques. Support for parents is available through the project so that they too understand the process. But does such a program work?

A prospective follow-up study of 126 child victims of sexual assault who had been referred to the Child Witness Project for court preparation in 1988 and 1989 was conducted (London Family Court Clinic, 1993). Pre- and post-court data were available for each child, including

- psychological testing
- clinical interview
- court observation
- file data

For the post-court data, 61 children were re-interviewed, in addition to the parents of 73 children. Children were interviewed on average three years following the verdict. A number of key findings emerged:

- Children regretted testifying if the defendant was found not guilty.
- Some children experienced mental health problems.
- Children were better adjusted when a guilty verdict was rendered.
- A mother's support was a critical mediator for children's adjustment.

Children identified a number of fears, including facing the accused, having to describe the details of the abuse, having strangers hear the testimony, and being worried about not understanding the questions posed by lawyers. Children made a variety of suggestions that they felt would improve the criminal justice system for other children testifying. These changes included the following:

1. Not having to see the accused while testifying
2. Receiving preparation for the experience
3. Closing the courtroom to the public
4. Using simpler language
5. Having support people in the courtroom

Courtroom Accommodations

Child witnesses may experience extreme stress and trauma by having to testify in court while facing the defendant (Goodman et al., 1992). The Canadian justice system has responded to child victims and witnesses by providing a set of alternatives to testifying in court in the presence of the defendant. For example, in 1988 legislation was enacted that allowed children to testify from behind a screen or from another room by way of closed-circuit television (Bala, 1999a). These provisions applied to children under 18 years who were the complainants in sexual offence cases. Further amendments in 1997 extended these provisions to any child witness for any sexual offence or assault.

Professor Nicholas Bala has conducted extensive work in the area of child witness testimony. Bala (1999a) identifies a number of alternatives to in-court testimony that have been used in the Canadian system, including the following:

1. A shield/screen to separate the child and defendant so that the child does not see the defendant's face. However, the child is visible to the defendant and the rest of the courtroom and may be able to see the defendant's feet.

2. The child may be allowed to provide testimony via a closed-circuit television monitor. The child and lawyers are in a separate room from the courtroom and the child's testimony is televised to the courtroom where the defendant, judge, and jury are present. The defendant can be in touch with his or her lawyer by telephone. The onus is on the Crown attorney/prosecutor to request this accommodation; however, when requested it typically is granted.

3. Some Canadian courts allow the child to have a support person with him or her while providing testimony. The child can decide whom he or she wants, although a person who is a witness in the same case cannot be a support person unless he or she has already provided testimony.

4. A child may be videotaped while being interviewed about the details of the crime. The videotape may be admitted into evidence, so that the child does not have to repeat the details in court. In this instance, the child would be cross-examined on the stand.

5. Generally, previous statements made by a witness are considered hearsay and not admissible. However, in sexual abuse cases, judges can apply the rules liberally, and statements made by the child during the initial disclosure of the abuse may be allowed as evidence. For example, a mother may testify about what her child said when disclosing the abuse.

6. The judge may close the courtroom to the public and/or media to protect the privacy of the child. A publication ban prohibiting any information that would identify the complainant or any witness also may be granted to protect the child's identity.

These alternatives also are available in the United States. To learn more about Professor Bala and his work, see Box 7.3.

CHILD MALTREATMENT

So far we have highlighted sexual abuse against children; however, there are other forms of maltreatment that a child may experience. Other forms of maltreatment

BOX 7.3 CANADIAN RESEARCHER PROFILE: PROFESSOR NICHOLAS BALA

Professor Nicholas Bala completed his undergraduate degree at the University of Toronto. With an interest in law, he went on to complete his law degree at Queen's University. Professor Bala's interest in the intersection between law and children's issues started when he articled for a law firm working with the Children's Aid Society. Following his articling, Professor Bala continued his education and he completed a Masters of Law degree at Harvard Law School. In 1980, he joined the Faculty of Law at Queen's University. His legal scholarship spans many areas of child law.

In terms of child witnesses and victims, Professor Bala recalls his work in the early 1980s when children's reports of being sexually abused were often dismissed by a number of agencies, including the justice system. The work of community advocates, clinicians, and researchers clearly established that child sexual abuse was a widely underreported phenomenon and that the justice system would need to deal with it more effectively.

Professor Bala was concerned that children undergoing the competency inquiry were being asked questions that had no bearing on their ability and willingness to accurately and honestly report what they witnessed or experienced. One example of a case that caused him concern involved a five-year-old girl alleging sexual assault perpetrated by an older cousin. After extensive questioning, the judge was satisfied that the girl understood what it meant to "promise to tell the truth" and found the girl competent to testify. The accused was convicted at trial, based primarily on her testimony. However, the defendant appealed the verdict claiming that the child should not have been allowed to testify given her poor response about the meaning of the concept of "promising" during the competency inquiry. The British Columbia Court of Appeal overturned the verdict and ordered a new trial. The Crown's office tried to appeal to the Supreme Court of Canada. Professor Bala was helping the Crown's office to prepare this case, but when the Supreme Court refused to hear the case, it became clear to him that legislative reform would be needed.

Professor Bala believes that effective advocacy for law reform needs to be supported with strong empirical research. Indeed, he and his colleagues have demonstrated that a child's ability to "correctly" answer the questions commonly asked in the competency inquiry about the meaning of such abstract concepts as "promise," "truth," and "lie" is unrelated to whether they will be honest witnesses. Professor Bala would like to see more education from interdisciplinary perspectives, such as psychology and criminology, in law schools and for judges and lawyers. He also would like to see support services enhanced for children and other vulnerable witnesses.

Professor Bala lives with his wife and four children in Kingston, Ontario.

require the same considerations as sexual abuse. The Child Maltreatment Section (CMS) of Health Canada distinguishes among four categories of child maltreatment:

1. **Physical abuse** is defined as the deliberate application of force to any part of a child's body that results or may result in a nonaccidental injury. Examples include shaking, choking, biting, kicking, burning, and poisoning. See Box 7.4 for a debate on whether corporal punishment is physical abuse.

BOX 7.4 CORPORAL PUNISHMENT: DISCIPLINE OR PHYSICAL ABUSE?

Seventy-eight-year-old Lucille Poulin was a religious leader in a commune on Prince Edward Island. Poulin was given the responsibility of looking after the children while their parents worked. She believed children needed discipline to prevent them from engaging in evil acts. Poulin used a wooden paddle when disciplining the children, resulting in assault charges in 2002.

At Poulin's trial, several children testified that she often beat them, at times causing them to pass out. Poulin was found guilty of assaulting five children. The court ruled that Poulin went beyond discipline. She was sentenced to eight months in jail and ordered not to live with or care for children younger than age 14 for three years following her release.

Corporal punishment has been put to the Supreme Court of Canada in a challenge by the Canadian Foundation for Children, Youth, and the Law (*Canadian Foundation for Children, Youth, and the Law v. The Attorney General in Right of Canada*, 2004). The legislation under scrutiny was section 43 of the Canadian Criminal Code that states: "Every schoolteacher, parent, or person standing in the place of a parent is justified in using force by way of correction toward a pupil or child, as the case may be, who is under his or her care, if the force does not exceed what is reasonable under the circumstances."

The Canadian Foundation for Children, Youth, and the Law argued that section 43 of

the Criminal Code violates sections 7 (security of the person), 12 (cruel and unusual punishment), and 15 (equality) of the Canadian Charter of Rights and Freedoms and that it conflicts with Canada's obligations under the United Nations' Convention of the Rights of the Child.

In July 2000, the Ontario Superior Court of Justice upheld the constitutionality of section 43. In January 2002, the decision went to the Ontario Court of Appeal, who upheld the lower court's decision and dismissed the appeal. The appeal then went to the Supreme Court of Canada. In January 2004, the Supreme Court of Canada held that section 43 was constitutional. The Supreme Court also ruled that

- Corporal punishment is prohibited in schools. Teachers in Canada will still be able to use physical force to remove a student or prevent immediate threats of harm to person or property, but a student can no longer be physically punished.
- Parents are not permitted to spank, slap, or otherwise use any corporal punishment on children younger than 2 or older than 12.
- Parents may use physical force on children between the ages of 3 and 12 but may not use an object to hit them.
- Parents are not permitted to strike children between the ages of 3 and 12 on the head or face, under any circumstances.

Source: R. v. Poulin, 2002.

2. **Sexual abuse** occurs when an adult or youth uses a child for sexual purposes. Examples include fondling, intercourse, incest, sodomy, exhibitionism, and exploitation through prostitution or the production of pornographic materials.

3. **Neglect/failure to provide** occurs when a child's caregivers do not provide the requisite attention to the child's emotional, psychological, or physical development. Examples include failure to supervise or protect leading to physical harm (such as drunk driving with a child), failure to provide adequate nutrition or clothing, failure to provide medical treatment, and exposing the child to unhygienic or dangerous living conditions. See Box 7.5 for a case of a father forgetting his child in a hot car and whether the court found it to be a case of neglect.

4. **Emotional maltreatment** is defined as acts or omissions by caregivers that cause or could cause serious behavioural, cognitive, emotional, or mental disorders. Examples include verbal threats, socially isolating a child, intimidation, exploitation, terrorizing, or routinely making unreasonable demands on a child.

It is likely that children experience multiple forms of maltreatment simultaneously. For example, it is hard to imagine that a child who is neglected is not also emotionally abused.

Government agencies have the authority and responsibility to remove children from their caregiver when the child is maltreated or at risk for maltreatment. Also, a child may be removed if a caregiver is unwilling or unable to prevent abuse by a third

---

BOX 7.5 A CASE OF NEGLECT OR FORGETFULNESS?

For Dominic Martin and Sylvie Dubé of Montreal, a weekday's typical morning routine involved dropping off their daughter, Audrey, at day care, then Martin would drop his wife off at work, and head to work himself. Martin would park his car in the subway parking lot and take the subway to work. On Thursday, July 17, 2003, Martin was running late so he dropped his wife off first. He then headed to the subway parking lot, as he did so many times before, while Audrey lay asleep in the backseat of the car. Martin got on the subway and went to work, forgetting to drop off his 23-month-old daughter.

After approximately eight hours, Martin returned to his car and found Audrey unconscious. It was estimated that the temperature in the car was hotter than 60°C. Audrey later died in the hospital and Martin was charged with manslaughter.

Martin argued that with the change in his morning routine, he had forgotten to drop off his daughter. Audrey was asleep so he did not hear her in the back seat. Although initially Martin was charged with manslaughter, the charges against Martin were dropped (Hanes, 2004).

General Motors commissioned a study in 2001 to determine the number of children who had died of hyperthermia, that is, severe heatstroke or heat exhaustion (as cited in Picard, 2003). One hundred and twenty children were reported to have died from being left in hot, parked cars since 1996. Of course, not all cases are a result of forgetfulness.

Source: Picard, 2003.

party. For example, children may be removed from their caregivers' custody because of neglect, physical and sexual abuse, alcohol or other drug use, and mental illness. It is important to recognize that for children to be apprehended, these factors must have negative effects on parenting to the extent that the caregiver cannot adequately parent. The term "in need of protection" is used to describe a child's need to be separated from his or his caregiver due to maltreatment.

With the exception of the Yukon, Canadian jurisdictions require the reporting of children suspected to be in need of protection. Legislation across Canada varies the age below which an individual is considered a child. Generally, an individual is no longer considered a child between the ages of 16 and 19 years. In Ontario, for example, the Child and Family Services Act (i.e., legislation pertaining to children) denotes children as under 18 years of age. See Box 7.6 on page 220 for a case of physical abuse in which the child was in need of protection but did not receive it.

Beck and Ogloff (1995) surveyed Canadian psychologists and found that more than 98% of the respondents were aware of mandatory reporting laws in their jurisdiction. Although psychologists may be aware of reporting laws, they do not necessarily comply. According to the survey results, psychologists may not report child maltreatment because of insufficient evidence or a belief that child protection agencies cannot help.

When trying to understand how often maltreatment occurs, it is important to clarify the distinction between incidence and prevalence. The CMS defines **incidence** as the "number of new cases in a specific population occurring in a given time period, usually a year." In contrast, the **prevalence** of maltreatment is defined as "the proportion of a population at a specific point in time that was maltreated during childhood."

The first Canadian Incidence Study of Reported Child Abuse and Neglect provided a national estimate of the number of instances of child maltreatment reported to and investigated by child welfare services in Canada in 1998. According to the final report by Trocme et al. (2001), 135 573 reported cases of child maltreatment were investigated in Canada in 1998. The annual incidence rate was 21.52 investigations per 1000 children. Approximately 45% (61 201) of child maltreatment cases investigated were substantiated (i.e., the balance of evidence indicates that the maltreatment occurred), 22% (29 668) remained suspected (i.e., not enough evidence to substantiate maltreatment but there remains a suspicion that maltreatment has occurred), and 33% (44 704) were found to be unsubstantiated (i.e., sufficient evidence to conclude that the child has not been maltreated).

Of the child maltreatment cases reported and investigated by child welfare services in Canada in 1998, 31% involved alleged physical abuse as the primary category of abuse, 10% involved sexual abuse, 40% involved neglect, and 19% involved emotional maltreatment. Figure 7.3 on page 221 illustrates the percentage of cases per category that were found substantiated, suspected, and unsubstantiated. In the United States, more than 2.8 million cases of maltreatment were reported in 1998. Approximately 903 000 cases either were substantiated or were consistent with some evidence of maltreatment (Golden, 2000). More than 50% of the cases pertained to neglect, 25% to physical abuse, and nearly 12% to sexual abuse.

BOX 7.6 ONE OF THE WORST CASES OF PHYSICAL ABUSE IN CANADA'S HISTORY

Until Randal Dooley was six, he lived in Jamaica with his older brother, Teego, and a number of relatives. Randal's biological father, Tony Dooley, left when Randal was one year old, moving to Canada with his new wife, Marcia. The couple sent for the boys in the fall of 1997.

Shortly after Randal started school in Toronto, Randal's Grade 1 teacher wondered if Randal was maltreated. The first incident that caused her concern was when Randal lost a mitten. He was frantic about finding it. Randal mentioned that he would get a "licking from his mother." By the end of the same month, Randal had a badly broken elbow. The second incident that led his teacher to notify officials occurred when she noticed Randal had welts on his arm. She took Randal to the vice principal's office where they looked at his back and saw more than 25 welts. They called the Toronto police. No charges were laid at the time, however.

In April 1998, the Dooley family moved to the east end of Toronto. Mr. Dooley registered Teego at a new school but not Randal. There was no mention of another school-aged child.

Randal was found dead on the lower bunk bed that he shared with Teego on September 25, 1998. Mr. Dooley called 911 to report that his son had committed suicide. Randal's autopsy, however, raised doubts about a suicidal cause. His autopsy described Randal as a gaunt boy, his entire body almost completely covered with welts, bruises, scratches and U-shaped marks, and with extreme internal damage, usually seen when someone has been hit by a car. Randal had four separate brain injuries, 14 fractured ribs, and a lacerated liver. His elbow had been broken in three places and his own tooth was in his stomach.

Mr. Dooley explained that in late August he had "flogged' Randal with a belt and was concerned that the Children's Aid Society would be called. It also was reported that Mrs. Dooley made Randal eat his vomit and would not let him use the bathroom. She was reported to have punched him in the head, kicked him, broken his arm by putting her foot in his back and twisting it, and to have thrown Randal against a door where his eye was struck by the doorknob and swollen shut for three days. Moreover, it was reported that Mr. Dooley beat Randal on various occasions.

Tony and Marcia Dooley were charged with second-degree murder in Randal's death. At the trial, medical experts suggested that Randal's vomiting and incontinence were likely a result of a brain injury. Moreover, a pediatric neurosurgeon who testified at the trial noted that in his opinion Randal's death came from a fatal brain injury that caused a seizure.

After three days of deliberation, on April 18, 2002, Tony and Marcia Dooley were convicted of second-degree murder. Superior Court Justice Eugene Ewaschuk who presided over the case stated that Randal "may very well be the worst victim of child abuse in Canadian penal history." Marcia received a life sentence without eligibility for parole for 18 years. Tony also received a life sentence without eligibility for parole for 13 years.

Source: Blatchford, 2002.

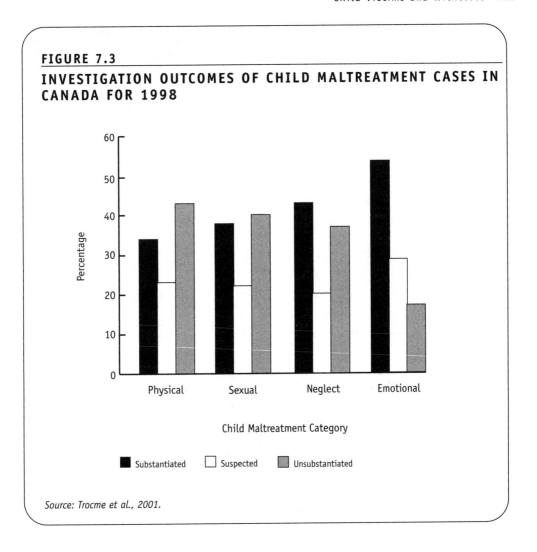

FIGURE 7.3

INVESTIGATION OUTCOMES OF CHILD MALTREATMENT CASES IN CANADA FOR 1998

Source: Trocme et al., 2001.

Risk Factors Associated with Child Maltreatment

A number of risk factors—factors that are associated with an increased likelihood of abuse—have been identified for physical and sexual abuse. These can be categorized as child factors, parental factors, and social factors (see Table 7.3 on page 222).

The risk factors for physical and sexual abuse differ. Physical abuse risk factors are varied and include a parent's past childhood physical abuse as well as the parent's attitude toward the pregnancy. In contrast, sexual abuse risk factors tend to revolve around family composition.

TABLE 7.3 RISK FACTORS FOR ABUSE

Type of Abuse

	Physical Abuse	*Sexual Abuse*
Child Factors		
	Male sex	Female sex
Parental Factors		
	Young maternal age	Living in a family without a biological parent
	Single-parent status	Poor relationship between parents
	History of childhood physical abuse	Presence of a stepfather
	Spousal assault	Poor child–parent relations
	Unplanned pregnancy or negative attitude toward pregnancy	
	History of substance abuse	
	Social isolation or lack of social support	
Social Factors		
	Low socioeconomic status	
	Large family size	

Source: MacMillan, 2000, p. 704.

Short-Term and Long-Term Effects of Physical Abuse

A number of short-term effects of physical abuse have been determined. These include greater perceptual-motor deficits, lower measured intellectual functioning, lower academic achievement, externalizing behaviour such as aggression, and internalizing mental health difficulties such as hopelessness and depression (Ammerman et al., 1986; Conaway & Hansen, 1989; Lamphear, 1985).

In a review of studies examining the long-term effects of physical abuse, Malinosky-Rummell and Hansen (1993) report strong relations between physical abuse and nonfamilial and familial violence. Physically abused persons, especially males, engage in more nonfamilial violence than nonabused persons. In terms of familial violence, about 30% of physically abused or neglected persons abuse their own children (Kaufman & Zigler, 1987; Widom, 1989a). Moreover, being abused as a child predicted inflicting and receiving dating violence in a sample of university students. Also, spouses who were abusive reported higher rates of physical abuse than nonabusive spouses. Thus, experiencing physical abuse appears to increase the likelihood of perpetrating physical abuse.

Short-Term and Long-Term Effects of Sexual Abuse

Kendall-Tackett, Williams, and Finkelhor (1993) examined 45 studies that considered the short-term effects of childhood sexual abuse. Common effects across the studies were behaviour problems, lowered self-esteem, inappropriate sexuality, and symptoms consistent with post-traumatic stress disorder. Research has found that within two years of being abused, children report a number of physical difficulties such as sleep disturbance, eating disorders, stomach problems, and headaches (Adams-Tucker, 1982).

Putnam (2003) identified three categories of outcomes in adults with a history of childhood sexual abuse: (1) psychiatric disorders, (2) dysfunctional behaviours, and (3) neurobiological dysregulation.

Under psychiatric disorders, major depression in adulthood has been found to be strongly related to sexual abuse in childhood (Paolucci, Genuis, & Violato, 2001). Sexualized behaviour is one of the most closely related dysfunctional behaviours with those who have a history of childhood sexual abuse (Widom & Ames, 1994). In terms of neurobiological dysregulation, magnetic resonance imaging (MRI) studies have found reduced hippocampal volume in adults who experienced sexual abuse as children, similar to that found in war veterans experiencing post-traumatic stress disorder (Stein et al., 1997).

Browne and Finkelhor (1986) also found that women who were sexually abused as children have somatic (physical) problems along with lowered self-esteem. Messman-Moore and Long (2003) reported that adults who were sexually abused as children have an increased risk of being sexually abused as adults. Other long-term risks for sexually abused children include depression, self-injurious behaviours, anxiety, and interpersonal distrust (Browne & Finkelhor, 1986).

A recent survey in the United States found that about one in five young people is solicited for sex over the Internet each year (Mitchell, Finkelhor, & Wolak, 2001; see also Box 7.7 on the next page). Canadian law is catching up to computer technology with the enactment of Bill C-15A in 2002. Now, it is a criminal offence to use the Internet to communicate with a child for the purpose of committing a sexual act (s. 172.1 of the Canadian Criminal Code). This offence carries a maximum five-year prison sentence. This legislation in part satisfies Canada's commitment to a United Nations protocol on the rights of the child that was signed by 105 countries in 2002. An advantage of this protocol is that it sets out consistent law to deal with child issues across countries. Given that the Internet does not have borders, this type of consistency is critical.

BOX 7.7 LURING CHILDREN OVER THE INTERNET

Advances in computer technology provide a host of benefits to its users. Unfortunately, however, this technology can be abused. With the Internet, sexual predators have access to countless children while remaining anonymous, until they decide to meet the child. The child often assumes he or she is meeting another child; however, the Internet stranger may be a sexual predator.

One international Internet-luring case involved a 33-year-old former U.S. marine named Toby Studabaker. He met a 12-year-old girl in an Internet chat room aimed at children. Studabaker sent the girl numerous sexually explicit e-mail messages. After communicating with her online for about a year,

in July 2003, Studabaker arranged to meet the girl at Manchester Airport in the United Kingdom. The girl told her parents she was going into town with friends. When the girl did not return, her parents reported her missing, and an international manhunt was underway.

From Manchester, Studabaker and the girl flew to Paris, then to Strasbourg, and then on to Stuttgart, Germany. In Stuttgart, the girl called her parents to let them know she was fine. She flew back to the U.K. the following day, and Studabaker went to Frankfurt where he confessed to German police.

Sources: Boyd, 2003; Ex-Marine jailed for abduction, 2004; Ex-Marine: No sex with girl, 2003.

Behaviours that might predispose a young person to being lured over the Internet (Mitchell et al., 2001) include revealing emotional problems, admitting to being in need of help or having low self-esteem, and expressing agreement in chat rooms.

Protective strategies against sexual luring over the Internet include

- Avoiding sexually provocative screen names. Sexual predators are more likely to target youth with screen names of a sexual nature (U.S. Department of Justice, 2001).
- Not providing any personal information over the Internet.
- Contacting police when sexual solicitation of children and youth has occurred.

CHILD CUSTODY AND ACCESS

Children also may come into contact with the justice system as a result of parents separating or divorcing. The divorce rate in Canada is approximately 31% and appears to be relatively stable (Gentleman & Park, 1997). Approximately 50% of all divorces involve children under the age of 18 (Amato, 2000). Custody and **access** (the noncustodial parent's right to see the child) issues need to be decided when couples with children dissolve their union. For the most part, parents come to mutually satisfactory agreements about custody and access without the involvement of the legal system. It is only in about 10% of cases, in which there is high conflict or parents cannot agree, that courts become involved (Melton et al., 1987). In these instances, courts are faced with the responsibility of determining custody and access.

Legal History of Custody and Access

In the eighteenth century, the rights of children were disregarded when a couple decided to divorce. The courts viewed only the father as having legal status and children were treated as property, their father's property. In 1855, the Custody of Infants Act was enacted in Upper Canada giving mothers the right to seek custody or access to children under 12 years (Bala, 1999b).

In the early twentieth century, mothers were perceived as better caregivers, particularly for young children (Bala, 1999b). Typically, mothers were granted custody, all other things being equal. One exception to maternal custody was mothers who were judged "morally unfit," such as women who committed adultery.

Another change in legal perspective came in the 1970s when the "best interests of the child" became the guiding principle for custody and access decisions. By 1973, Canadian courts were starting to accept that the "welfare of the child" should be used to decide on custody issues. Although there are wording variations between provincial or territorial and federal legislation, the meaning does not change. Canadian courts made decisions in accordance with the best interests of the child (Bala, 1999b). However, there could be differences in how courts determined the best interest of the child.

Currently, courts tend to grant divorcing parents joint custody of the children (Rohman, Sales, & Lou, 1990), a move generally seen as being in the children's best interests. Exceptions include situations involving domestic abuse. The term *joint custody* may be a little deceiving, however, because it does not necessarily mean equal physical custody (Maccoby & Mnookin, 1992). Rather, the child may live with one parent but both parents have legal decision making regarding the child's health and welfare (Felner & Terre, 1987). Of course, joint custody may include joint physical custody in which the child alternates living with each parent on a weekly or biweekly basis. In Canada, approximately 25% of divorced families have a joint custody arrangement (Statistics Canada, as cited in Bala, 1999b).

Canadian judges recently have started to rule for **parallel parenting** (Tibbetts, 2003), which divides decision-making power between the parents. Courts may choose this option when parents are hostile and cooperative parenting does not seem possible. For example, one parent may make decisions regarding medical care and the other parent makes decisions regarding education.

When the courts are faced with challenging custody and access decisions, psychologists or other mental health professionals may be consulted for assistance.

Factors Related to Divorce

Many studies have examined the relation between parental divorce and children's academic achievement, behaviour, psychological adjustment, self-esteem, social competence, and relationships with parents. Although the results are far from consistent, children from divorced families generally tend to score lower than children from intact families in these areas (Demo & Acock, 1988; Krantz, 1988; Kurdek, 1981).

Amato and Keith (1991) conducted a meta-analysis to examine the well-being of children following divorce. They used data from 92 studies that compared children living in single-parent families with children living in intact families. Amato and Keith (1991) reported that children from divorced families tended to show a lower level of well-being than children from intact families. For example, compared with children and adolescents from intact two-parent families, those from divorced families had higher rates of behavioural problems, emotional difficulties, and substance use, and lower levels of self-esteem, social competence, and achievement. However, the differences tended to be small.

A few studies have found a positive outcome for children from divorced families. For example, Arditti (1999) found that children from divorced families, especially females, reported developing a close relationship with their mothers. Children also may be better off if parents in high-conflict relationships divorce rather than remain together (Hanson, 1999).

Zill, Morrison, and Coiro (1993) examined longitudinal data from the National Survey of Children, a representative sample of youth in the United States, to determine whether divorce presents long-term difficulties for the children involved. The first part of the survey was conducted in 1976–77 and was based on children aged 7 to 11 years; the second part was conducted in 1981, when the children were aged 12 to 16 years; and the third part was conducted in 1987, when the children, now young adults, were 18 to 22 years. The children's ages at the time of their parents' divorce varied. Overall, the average age at disruption was six years. For the early-disruption group, the average age was three years. For the later-disruption group the average age was 10 years. The analyses showed some negative effects of divorce present 12 to 22 years following the disruption. Such effects included poor relationships with parents, problem behaviours, an increased probability of dropping out of high school, and the receiving of psychological treatment. It should be noted, however, that many of the children who were in the study scored within the "normal range" on many of the well-being indicators examined. The authors argued that the fact that "a young person comes from a divorced family does not, in itself, tell us a great deal about how he or she is faring on embarking into adulthood" (p. 100).

Summary

1. The accuracy of children's reporting is highly dependent on how they are asked to report. When describing what was witnessed using a free narrative, children are as accurate as adults. As with adults, leading questions are likely to produce erroneous responses in children. Yes/no questions are particularly problematic for very young children. The use of anatomically detailed dolls for interviewing children is controversial and should be used with caution. A number of procedures and pro-

tocols to increase children's accurate responding have been investigated, including, statement validity analysis, the step-wise interview, and narrative elaboration.

2. Children report few person descriptors when asked to describe a stranger or culprit. Interior facial items such as freckles and nose shape are more likely to be reported by older children than younger children. However, accurately reporting these features is difficult. The exterior feature of hair is frequently mentioned by both children and adults. Height, weight, and age are unlikely to be reported accurately by children and youth.

3. Children produce comparable correct identification rates with adults' when presented with a target-present lineup. However, children are more likely than are adults to select an innocent person with a target-absent lineup. A procedure called the elimination lineup asks children first to pick out the person who looks most like the culprit from the pictures displayed. Then the children are asked if that most-similar person is in fact the culprit. This procedure decreases children's false positive responding compared with a simultaneous lineup procedure.

4. In Canada, children under 14 years must pass a competency inquiry before being allowed to testify. Children need to demonstrate an ability to communicate the evidence, distinguish between the truth and a lie, and feel compelled to tell the truth in a court of law. Canadian courts provide alternatives to in-court testimony for child witnesses. These accommodations include screens separating the child from the defendant, providing testimony via closed-circuit television, allowing the child to have a support person, admitting into evidence a videotaped interview of the child detailing the events, allowing hearsay evidence, and banning the public and media from the courtroom.

5. Maltreatment can be categorized into sexual abuse, physical abuse, neglect/failure to provide, and emotional abuse. Short-term effects of physical abuse include perceptual-motor deficits, lower measured intellectual functioning, lower academic achievement, externalizing behaviour, and internalizing mental health difficulties such as hopelessness and depression. Long-term effects of physical abuse include nonfamilial and familial violence. Short-term effects of sexual abuse include behaviour problems, lowered self-esteem, inappropriate sexuality, and physical symptoms consistent with post-traumatic stress disorder. Long-term effects of sexual abuse include physical problems, lowered self-esteem, and being abused as an adult. Other long-term risks include depression, self-injurious behaviours, anxiety, and interpersonal distrust.

6. Compared with children from intact homes, children from divorced homes tend to score lower on measures of academic achievement, behaviour, psychological adjustment, self-esteem, social competence, and relationships with parents. Also, children from divorced families tend to show a lower level of well-being than children from intact families.

Key Concepts

Discussion Questions

1. In your local community newspaper you read of a seven-year-old boy who has been physically abused and then left abandoned. You wonder what difficulties this boy may experience in the next couple of years and when he becomes an adult. Describe the short-term and long-term effects of maltreatment.

2. Why is the use of anatomically correct dolls a controversial tool when assessing child sexual abuse?

3. After completing an undergraduate course in forensic psychology, you are interested in telling your colleagues in the police department the best interview techniques to use with child witnesses. You decide to develop a mini-workshop on good and bad interview techniques. Put together a curriculum for your workshop.

4. An eight-year-old girl has witnessed the abduction of her best friend by an adult male. What factors will likely influence this child's ability to describe the kidnapper and what procedures should the police use when conducting a lineup with this child witness?

5. Children are sometimes needed to testify in court. What type of help can we provide children who testify in court?

6. Your best friend tells you that her parents are getting divorced. She confides in you that she worries her parents' divorce will have negative consequences on her future well-being. Discuss the possible long-term psychological problems of children whose parents get divorced.

7. You have been hired by the Children's Aid Society to help them design a study to identify the risk factors for sexual and physical abuse. Describe the study you would propose, focusing on the methodology and what risk factors you would measure.

ADDITIONAL INFORMATION

Readings

Ceci, S.J., & Hembrooke, H. (1998). *Expert witnesses in child abuse cases: What can and should be said in court.* Washington, DC: American Psychological Association.

Sattler, J.M. (1998). *Clinical and forensic interviewing of children and families: Guidelines for the mental health, education, pediatric, and child maltreatment fields.* La Mesa, CA: Jerome M. Sattler Publishers, Inc.

Web Sites

Centre for Children and Families in the Justice System, London Family Court Clinic
www.lfcc.on.ca

CHAPTER 8

Juries: Fact Finders

LEARNING OBJECTIVES

■ Describe how jurors are selected in Canada.

■ Distinguish between representativeness and impartiality.

■ Describe the effects of pretrial publicity and the available options for dealing with it.

■ Outline the stages to reaching a jury verdict.

■ Describe the categories of variables that have been examined to predict the verdict.

Harry Glick was excited to be part of the jury to hear a first-degree murder case involving an organized crime leader, Jackie "Benny" Benitto. The case had made headlines the previous summer when the head of a local steel union in Hamilton was found floating in Lake Ontario. News about the case and Benny's lengthy involvement with organized crime was reported on a daily basis for almost the entire summer. Benny's lawyer argued fiercely that it would be impossible for his client to receive a fair trial in Hamilton, given all the pretrial publicity. The judge agreed to move the trial to Toronto, where a larger pool of potential jurors existed and where there had been less media coverage about the case.

Before Harry was accepted to sit on the jury, Benny's lawyer had asked him a few questions. Harry wondered if there was something he said that made him sound sympathetic to the defendant. Maybe it was the way he looked. Or maybe it was because he was an engineer. For the next four weeks, Harry sat with 11 others listening to the evidence. Following closing arguments, the jury was required to deliberate and reach a unanimous decision regarding Benny's innocence or guilt. The deliberations took place in a private room with only the jurors present. They reached a verdict in four days, finding Benny "not guilty."

JURY SELECTION IN CANADA

Before a jury trial can begin, a jury needs to be selected or seated. The process of jury selection differs by province, territory, and country, although there are a number of commonalities across jurisdictions. Before we discuss jury selection, it is important to consider the types of cases juries will hear.

The Cases Heard by Juries

Television has bombarded us with crime shows such as *Law and Order* and *The Practice*. We can even view real-life trials, such as the O.J. Simpson case, from the comfort of our own home. All this media coverage may distort perceptions of the frequency of trials heard by juries. Only some types of offences can proceed with jury trials. Moreover, in some instances defendants are given an option of a jury trial; however, they may opt to be tried by judge alone. Thus, in Canada, relative to the total number of trials that take place, only a few are tried by jury. The remainder of trials are heard and ruled on by judges alone.

There are three types of offences in Canada: (1) summary offences, (2) indictable offences, and (3) hybrid offences.

Summary offences involve a sentence of less than six months in prison and a fine of less than $2000 (section 787 [1] of the Criminal Code). However, for some offences, the maximum sentence is 18 months (R.S.C. 1985, C-46, s. 787[1]). These offences are tried by judge alone. Moreover, the defendant charged with a summary offence does not have a right to a trial by jury.

There are three categories of indictable offences:

1. Less serious indictable offences are heard by a judge sitting alone. These are found in section 553 of the Criminal Code and include theft (other than theft of cattle), obtaining money or property by false pretences, and failure to comply with a probation order.

2. Highly serious indictable offences must be tried by judge and jury. These offences include treason, murder, and piracy. However, an exception under section 473 of the Criminal Code indicates that if the attorney general and the accused agree, the trial can proceed without a jury, and the case is tried by judge alone.

3 There are the indictable offences for which the accused can choose whether the trial proceeds by judge and jury or judge alone. These are the indictable offences not listed in either section 553 or 469 of the Criminal Code, such as robbery (R.S.C. 1985, C-46, s. 343; 1995, C-34, s. 302), arson (R.S.C. 1985, C-46, s. 433; 1990, C-15, s.1), and sexual assault with a weapon (R.S.C. 1985, C-46, s. 272;

1995, C-39, s. 145). The defendant has the option to choose (1) to be tried by a provincial or territorial court judge without a jury and without having had a preliminary inquiry, (2) to have a preliminary inquiry and to be tried by a judge without a jury, or (3) to have a preliminary inquiry and to be tried by a judge and jury. If a defendant does not make a selection, he or she will have a preliminary inquiry and be tried by a judge and jury.

Hybrid offences are a cross between indictable offences and summary offences. These are offences for which the maximum sentence is five or more years in prison if they proceed by indictment. If the Crown proceeds summarily, the maximum penalty is six months, or 18 months in some cases, such as sexual assault. It is up to the Crown attorney to decide whether to proceed with the case as an indictable offence or a summary offence. If the Crown opts for a summary offence, the case is tried by judge alone and the defendant does not have the right to a jury trial.

As you can see, these criteria greatly reduce the number of cases that are tried by jury. Also, it is important to keep in mind that jury trial options vary somewhat across provinces and territories.

Jury Selection

The **Jury Act** is provincial and territorial legislation that outlines the eligibility criteria for jury service and how prospective jurors must be selected. Although legislation varies across jurisdictions, there are a number of commonalities. Box 8.1 outlines the criteria for jurors in Ontario. Differences in eligibility criteria include the minimum age to be a juror and the professions that keep individuals exempt from jury duty.

Juror selection is governed by federal law. A set of random names from a community are determined, often by telephone directories or voters' lists. Prospective jurors receive a **jury summons**—that is, a court order that states a time and place for jury duty. Receiving a jury summons does not guarantee that you will be a juror, though. It simply means that you are expected to show up prepared to be a juror. If you ignore a summons and do not show up, you may incur a severe legal penalty such as a fine or jail time.

When you arrive at the designated location, typically the courthouse, you are given a number and escorted to a room with other potential jurors. You are not allowed to talk, eat, or drink while in this room. Once everyone has arrived—usually there are about 100 people—a judge explains the jury selection process and how many will be chosen that day. In Canada, criminal trials have 12-person juries, whereas civil trials have six-person juries.

If you are selected from the juror pool, you will be a juror unless one of the lawyers presents a challenge. Generally, there are two types of challenges lawyers can use to reject a potential juror: (1) peremptory challenge and (2) challenge for cause.

Both the Crown and defence have a limited number of peremptory challenges. In murder trials, each side has 20 peremptory challenges, whereas for most other crimes

BOX 8.1 ONTARIO'S CRITERIA FOR SERVING ON A JURY

Below are Ontario's criteria for serving on a jury. The criteria are fairly similar in other provinces and territories.

ELIGIBILITY CRITERIA

To serve on a jury in Ontario, a person must

- be a Canadian citizen;
- live in Ontario; and
- be at least 18 years of age.

INELIGIBILITY CRITERIA

A person may not serve on a jury in Ontario if he or she

- is a member of the Privy Council of Canada or the Executive Council of Ontario,

Senate, House of Commons of Canada, or Legislative Assembly;

- is a judge, justice of the peace, barrister, solicitor, or law student;
- is a medical doctor, veterinary surgeon, or coroner;
- works in law enforcement;
- has a physical or mental disability that would prevent him or her of performing the required duties; or
- has been convicted of an indictable offence (unless pardoned).

Sources: R.S.O. 1990, J.3; S.O. 1994, c. 27, s. 48; S.O. 1997, c. 4, s. 82.

each side has 12 peremptory challenges. The Crown or defence can use a peremptory challenge to reject jurors who they believe are unlikely to reach a verdict in their favour. When using a peremptory challenge, the lawyer does not need to provide a reason for rejecting the prospective juror.

In contrast, when using a challenge for cause, the lawyer must give a reason for rejecting the prospective juror. We will discuss challenge for cause later in this chapter. Keep in mind that Canadian lawyers have very limited information about prospective jurors. This information includes name, address, occupation, and physical demeanour. Also, in many Canadian cases the lawyers are not allowed to ask prospective jurors questions to gain more information about them. Consequently, lawyers have very little information on which to decide whether a juror will reach a verdict in their favour. If a prospective juror is successfully challenged, he or she will go back to the room with the others who have not yet been selected. Although a prospective juror may be challenged and not able to sit for one trial, he or she may be selected for another trial.

Once the jurors are selected they are told when the trial will start and where to show up.

Are Lawyers Able to Select Favourable Jurors?

In a study examining lawyers' ability to select jurors favourable to their position, Olczak, Kaplan, and Penrod (1991) provided lawyers with the facts of a case and the demographic information for 36 potential jurors. The lawyers were asked to assume the role of the defence attorney in the case and to select 12 jurors that they would want on the jury and 12 jurors that they would want to reject. The results indicated that the lawyers were *not* very good at selecting favourable jurors. The lawyers were more likely to make erroneous decisions than accurate decisions; that is, they discarded jurors who found the defendant not guilty and selected jurors who found the defendant guilty. Thus, demographic information and lawyer judgment may be insufficient for identifying favourable jurors.

Scientific Jury Selection

The idea behind **scientific jury selection** is that prospective jurors are evaluated based on predetermined characteristics to identify those who would be sympathetic or unsympathetic to the case. Many consulting firms in the U.S. are in the business of identifying these characteristics, which include demographic variables, personality traits, and attitudes, in order to determine whether potential jurors are likely to side with the prosecution or the defence. There are two approaches to scientific jury selection—broad based and case specific.

BROAD-BASED APPROACH The **broad-based approach** to scientific jury selection starts with the presumption that there are certain traits or attitudes that make people more likely to be pro-prosecution versus pro-defence. Two traits that are commonly measured using a broad-based approach are authoritarianism and dogmatism. Individuals high on authoritarianism or dogmatism may be more likely to side with the prosecution. Thus, without knowing any of the evidence of a particular case, some individuals with these traits will be more inclined to favour the prosecution. Prospective jurors may be given questionnaires assessing these traits/attitudes so that lawyers will know who they should and should not challenge. Alternatively, lawyers can ask prospective jurors questions to assess these traits directly during the **voir dire**, the question period when selecting people to serve on the jury.

CASE-SPECIFIC APPROACH In contrast to a broad-based approach, the **case-specific approach** to scientific jury selection starts with the issues and facts of the case. A specific questionnaire is developed to assess a number of characteristics that may influence the verdict. Individuals in the community from which the jury pool will be drawn are asked to complete the questionnaire. By analyzing the responses to the questionnaire items, profiles of the ideal juror for the prosecution and the ideal juror for the defence are developed. The trial lawyers can then ask each prospective juror relevant questions to decide whether he or she should be challenged. Some jurisdictions in the United States allow lawyers to distribute questionnaires to the actual jury pool prior to jury selection. The answers to the questionnaires are made available to the lawyers on both sides, who then can "prescreen" the prospective jurors prior to the voir dire.

The broad-based and case-specific approaches provide lawyers with information that they may use in an attempt to "stack the jury" in their favour. Recall that in Canada lawyers do not have the privilege of asking prospective jurors questions in most cases. Consequently, scientific jury selection is not possible in Canada.

CHARACTERISTICS AND RESPONSIBILITIES OF JURIES IN CANADA

The Supreme Court of Canada indicated two fundamental characteristics of juries (*R. v. Sherratt*, 1991):

1. A composition that represents the community in which the crime occurred. This is known as **representativeness.**
2. Jurors who are unbiased, known as **impartiality.**

Representativeness

In order for a jury to be considered "representative," it must allow any possible eligible person from the community the opportunity to be part of the jury. Representativeness is achieved through randomness. For example, a community's telephone directory or voter registration is used as a pool from which to randomly draw 100 or so names for potential jury duty. Of course, one could argue that neither of these "pools" is truly representative of the community because there may be people who can serve on a jury but whose names do not appear on these lists. For example, a homeless person may not have a phone but may be eligible to serve on a jury. Also, the Jury Act lists "exemptions" for those who cannot serve on a jury, thus limiting the true representativeness of the jury pool.

In some cases, the Crown or the defence may challenge the composition of the jury, arguing that it does not represent the community on some characteristic. For example in *R. v. Nepoose* (1991) the defendant was an Aboriginal woman. The jury composition for her trial was successfully challenged for having too few women. See Box 8.2 on page 236 for a jury composition challenge of representativeness on the basis of race.

Impartiality

The juror characteristic of impartiality centres on three issues:

1. For a juror to be impartial, he or she must set aside any pre-existing biases, prejudices, or attitudes and judge the case based solely on the admissible evidence. For example, a juror must ignore that the defendant belongs to an ethnic group against which he or she holds a bias. An impartial juror will not let his or her prejudice cloud the evaluation of the evidence.

BOX 8.2 BALANCING A JURY BY RACE

In 2001, two Caucasian men, Jeffrey Brown and Jeffrey Kindrat, were charged with sexually assaulting a 12-year-old Aboriginal girl. Of approximately 100 potential jurors who showed up for jury duty in Melfort, Saskatchewan, only one was visibly Aboriginal. Not surprisingly, once the jury was composed, all those sitting on the jury were Caucasian.

During the trial, the defendants admitted to picking the girl up, giving her five beers to drink, and then engaging in sexual activity with her outside a truck belonging to a third man, Dean Edmonson. The jury heard the evidence and then deliberated to reach verdicts of not guilty for both Mr. Brown and Mr. Kindrat.

Were these verdicts a product of a racist jury? The case raised concern about the jury selection process. The Saskatchewan Justice Department stated that it would contact officials across Canada to determine whether changes to the selection process could be made to make juries more racially balanced. The effect of this case on jury selection has yet to be determined.

Interestingly, in the trial of Mr. Edmonson, he was found *guilty*, also with an all-Caucasian jury. One main difference between the cases was the testimony of the victim. The victim testified more fully against Mr. Edmonson; however, she was reluctant to testify against Mr. Brown and Mr. Kindrat, providing far less information.

Source: Warick, 2003.

2. To be impartial also means that the juror must ignore any information that is not part of the admissible evidence. For example, prior to the start of a trial, a case may have received media attention highlighting facts about the defendant that are biased, irrelevant, or inadmissible.

3. It also is important that the juror have no connection to the defendant so that the juror does not view the evidence subjectively and does not unduly influence the other jurors. See Box 8.3 for a Canadian case dealing with juror partiality.

THREATS TO IMPARTIALITY   A number of threats to impartiality exist. For example, is it possible to forget the emotionally charged headlines that we read before going to jury duty? Typically, the media attention is negative for the defendant, and that could mean that the defendant does not receive a fair trial. Thus, the concern is that verdicts will be based on emotion and biased media coverage rather than on admissible evidence. Recently, Steblay, Besirevic, Fulero, and Jimenez-Lorente (1999) conducted a meta-analysis of 44 studies examining the effects of pretrial publicity. They found a modest, positive relationship between exposure to negative pretrial publicity and judgments of guilt. This relation means that as exposure to negative pretrial publicity increases, so do the number of guilty verdicts.

BOX 8.3 CANADA'S MOST FAMOUS PARTIAL JUROR

Peter Gill and five others were tried in Vancouver for two gang-style murders in 1995. Gillian Guess was one of the 12 jurors hearing Peter Gill's case. During the trial, Guess and Gill ran into each other outside the courtroom; thereafter, they began to flirt in the courtroom. This flirtation led to a meeting outside the courtroom and escalated into a sexual relationship. Their relationship was ongoing as Guess continued to serve on the jury hearing Gill's case.

The jury, including Guess, found Peter Gill and the other defendants not guilty. When the court became aware of the relationship, both Guess and Gill were charged with obstruction of justice. Guess was found guilty and sentenced to 18 months in jail. She was the first *juror* in North America convicted of attempting to obstruct justice and

ended up serving three months in prison. Peter Gill had been convicted of obstruction of justice in the past and was sentenced to five years and ten months in prison. Justice Barry Davies of the Supreme Court of British Columbia noted, "Mr. Gill pursued a deliberate and persistent attack upon one of society's most fundamental democratic institutions" (*R. v. Gill*, 2002, para. 29) by getting involved with Guess.

The B.C. Court of Appeal ordered a new murder trial for Peter Gill and two other men who were acquitted on the murder charges in 1995. The Appeal Court noted that Guess's impartiality was compromised and that it was hard to imagine a more remarkable violation of a juror's duty.

Sources: *R. v. Budai, Gill, and Kim*, 2001; *R. v. Gill*, 2002; *R. v. Guess*, 1998.

In one study examining pretrial publicity, Kramer, Kerr, and Carroll (1990) manipulated emotional and factual components of pretrial publicity, as well as the time between the pretrial information and hearing the trial. A number of key results were obtained:

- Juries exposed to pretrial publicity were more likely to render a guilty verdict than juries without exposure to the publicity.
- Juries exposed to publicity with high factual content were more likely to render a guilty verdict when there was no trial delay.
- Juries exposed to publicity with low factual content were more likely to render a guilty verdict when there was a delay.

These results imply that people tend to forget the factual details of the information they heard or read, but they remember the emotions that it raised. These emotions can then have a biasing effect when it comes to rendering a verdict. In particular, if the emotion was negative, the jurors are more likely to render guilty verdicts.

KEEPING POTENTIAL JURORS IMPARTIAL Before a case goes to trial, a preliminary hearing occurs in which the Crown presents the evidence against the defendant.

The judge then determines whether there is sufficient evidence for the case to proceed to trial. In Canada, at the preliminary hearing the judge typically places a ban on the media to not report the evidence until the end of the trial process. If the details of the case can be kept from the public, then the likelihood of potential jurors being exposed to information that may compromise their ability to remain impartial is decreased. Moreover, the likelihood of jurors using only the evidence presented during the trial to reach their verdict is increased.

Unfortunately, details do get leaked, especially in high-profile cases involving child victims or violent offences. For example, details about numerous missing women from Vancouver found buried on Robert Pickton's farm in Port Coquitlam made headlines across Canada before Pickton's case was heard (e.g., Saunders & Thompson, 2002). What are the legal options when the defence or Crown fears a partial or biased jury pool?

Some methods for increasing the likelihood of an impartial jury are as follows:

1. The Crown or defence may argue that the trial should be moved to another community because it would be very difficult to obtain an impartial jury from the local community. This option is called a **change of venue** and is found in section 599(1) of the Criminal Code (R.S.C., 1985, C-46, s.599). The party raising the issue must demonstrate that there is a reasonable likelihood that the local community is biased or prejudiced against the defendant. Factors that may lead to a biased community include extensive pretrial publicity, a heinous crime, and a small community in which many people know the victim and/or the defendant (Granger, 1996).

   A change of venue is not granted very often, but when it is, the trial typically stays within the province or territory in which the crime occurred. An example was the trial of Kelly Ellard, a teen charged with the murder of 14-year-old Reena Virk in a suburb of Victoria, British Columbia. Adrian Brooks, the defence lawyer, successfully argued to move the trial from Victoria to Vancouver. Brooks claimed that the media attention the case received would prohibit Ellard from getting a fair trial in Victoria (Meissner, 2000).

2. An alternative to moving a trial to a new community is to allow sufficient time to pass so that the biasing effect of any pretrial prejudicial information has dissipated by the time the trial takes place. Thus, the judge may call for an **adjournment**, delaying the trial to sometime in the future. A major limitation to adjourning cases is that not only may prospective jurors' memories fade, so may those of the witnesses. Witnesses may forget critical details that they are to testify about. Also, witnesses may move or die. Consequently, courts infrequently call for an adjournment.

3. Another option that may be granted in cases for which bias is suspected among the prospective jury pool is known as a **challenge for cause.** The Crown or defence may argue that, although the prospective jury pool may be partial, if questioned, these prospective jurors could be identified and rejected from serving on the jury. As with the change of venue, the side desiring the judge to allow a challenge for cause must demonstrate that there is reasonable partiality in the community

from which the jury pool will be drawn. If the judge grants a challenge for cause, both the Crown and defence will be allowed to question prospective jurors. However, the questions must be kept to a minimum (perhaps five or so) and only the prospective jurors' state of mind or thinking can be probed. Lawyers are not allowed to ask prospective jurors about their background or personality. See Box 8.4 for sample questions a lawyer may (and may not) ask a prospective juror.

A challenge for cause changes how the jury is selected. This process is unique to Canada (Granger, 1996). First, two individuals are selected from the jury pool and are sworn to act as "triers." A third person is selected as a prospective juror. The lawyers question the prospective juror, while the two triers listen to the answers provided. The triers then discuss the answers with each other to reach a unanimous decision as to whether the prospective juror is impartial. If the triers decide that the prospective

---

BOX 8.4 THE PASCOE CASE

In *R. v. Pascoe* (1994), the defendant was facing charges of sexual assault and sexual touching of two young boys aged 8 and 12 years.

The following questions were allowed during jury selection for the Pascoe trial by Judge McIsaac:

1. Have you read newspaper articles or listened to any radio or TV broadcasts on the subject of the psychosexual disorder known as homosexual pedophilia?

2. Have you ever discussed with friends, associates, or family how the police or the courts should deal with persons suffering from this form of psychosexual disorder?

3. Do you hold any personal opinion as to how persons suffering from this form of psychosexual disorder should be dealt with by the police or the courts?

4. Are you or any of your close friends or relatives associated with any professional or volunteer agency which deals with child victims of sexual assault?

5. Do you have such strong feelings about the issue of sexual abuse of young children that it would prevent you from giving Mr. Pascoe a fair trial based only on the evidence given at trial?

6. Would the evidence that Mr. Pascoe suffers from this psychosexual disorder cause you as a juror to lessen the burden on the prosecution to prove these allegations beyond a reasonable doubt?

7. Expert evidence will be used in this trial relating to Mr. Pascoe's psychosexual disorder. This will include psychiatric and psychological testimony. Do you feel that you can assess this form of evidence and not give it undue weight because of the fact that it will be given by so-called experts?

The following question was not allowed by Judge McIsaac:

1. Have you or any of your close friends or relatives been the victim of sexual assault such that it would prevent you from giving Mr. Pascoe a fair trial based only on the evidence given at trial?

Source: R. v. Pascoe, 1994.

juror is not impartial, another person is selected and the process begins again. If the triers decide that the prospective juror is impartial, then that person becomes the first member of the jury (unless the Crown or defence uses a peremptory challenges) and replaces one of the triers. This first juror acts as a trier for a second juror. Thus, jurors one and two will act as triers for juror three, jurors two and three will act as triers for juror four, and so on, until 12 jurors are selected.

When trying to evaluate whether a challenge for cause is useful for identifying biased individuals, a number of issues need to be considered:

1. The process may be conducted in open court, where the jury pool can hear the questions the lawyers ask and the responses provided. Moreover, they can hear the answers that lead to a positive or negative decision from the triers. Thus, it is possible for prospective jurors to alter their answers according to whether they want to serve on the jury.

2. Prospective jurors may find it difficult to be honest when answering questions about bias that may put them in an unflattering light, especially if the questioning is conducted in open court.

3. Prospective jurors must be aware of their biases and how their biases may influence their behaviour. Some classic work by Nisbett and Wilson (1977) suggests that individuals are unaware of their biases and how their biases affect their behaviour.

Jury Functions

The main legal function of a jury is to apply the law, as provided by the judge, to the admissible evidence in the case and render a verdict of guilt or innocence. As we will discuss, there are cases in which the jury will ignore the law and apply some other criteria to reach a verdict. In addition to the main legal function of juries, four other jury functions have been identified:

1. To use the wisdom of 12 (rather than the wisdom of one) to reach a verdict
2. To act as the conscience of the community
3. To protect against out-of-date laws
4. To increase knowledge about the justice system

IGNORING THE LAW The jury has a responsibility to apply the law as defined by the judge to the admissible evidence and to render a verdict. Ignoring that law and the evidence, and rendering a verdict based on some other criteria is known as **jury nullification.** Juries may choose to ignore the law for a number of reasons. For example, they may believe the law is unfair given the circumstances of the case or the punishment accompanying a conviction is too harsh for the crime. In both these instances, jury nullification may result.

Jury nullification typically can occur when the case involves controversial issues such as abortion and euthanasia (see Box 8.5).

BOX 8.5 TWO CASES OF JURY NULLIFICATION

DR. HENRY MORGENTALER: BABY KILLER OR CHAMPION OF WOMEN'S RIGHTS?

Dr. Henry Morgentaler conducted his first abortion, secretly, in 1968. He began performing illegal abortions openly in Montreal in 1969, and in 1970 he was arrested for conducting an abortion. The arrest occurred three years before the U.S. Supreme Court landmark case of *Roe v. Wade* (1973) that made abortion a constitutional right for American women.

A Quebec jury of 11 men and one woman found Dr. Morgentaler not guilty. The verdict was appealed and overturned in 1974. Dr. Morgentaler was sentenced to prison. When he was released, he continued conducting illegal abortions. In two more trials, juries returned not guilty verdicts. In 1975, a significant change to Quebec law occurred in which a jury verdict could no longer be overturned on appeal, known as the Morgentaler Amendment. Furthermore, in 1976, the Quebec government announced it would no longer prosecute abortion cases.

In 1983, while conducting abortions in Ontario, Dr. Morgentaler and two colleagues were charged with conducting illegal miscarriages. The jury found them not guilty. The Ontario Court of Appeal then reversed this verdict.

Clearly, the voice of the community, via the jury, was incongruent with the law. Change in legislation occurred in 1988 when the Supreme Court of Canada ruled that Canadian women have the right to a safe abortion. More than 105 000 abortions were conducted in Canada in 2000.

ROBERT LATIMER: A LOVING FATHER?

Tracy Latimer lived with her family in Wilkie, Saskatchewan. She had severe cerebral palsy, was quadriplegic, and could only communicate by means of facial expression, laughter, and crying. It was estimated that she had the mental capacity of a four-month-old baby. Tracy had five to six seizures a day and it was believed that she was in constant pain. She also underwent several surgeries. Another surgery was scheduled for Tracy when she was 12 years old.

Robert Latimer, Tracy's father, felt that it would be a mutilation and could no longer live with seeing his daughter suffer. He decided that he would end his daughter's life. He connected a hose from his pick-up truck's exhaust pipe into the cab and seated Tracy in the cab. Tracy died from carbon monoxide inhalation. At first, Latimer claimed that Tracy had passed away in her sleep, but he later confessed to taking Tracy's life. The jury found Robert Latimer guilty of second-degree murder.

Second-degree murder carries a life sentence without eligibility for parole for a minimum of 10 years and up to 25 years. Juries are allowed to make sentencing recommendations in this situation. The jury sent the judge a note asking if they could recommend less than ten years. The judge explained the mandatory minimum recommendation as outlined in the Criminal Code; however, they could make any recommendation they liked. The jury recommended one year before parole eligibility.

The judge granted a constitutional exemption from the mandatory minimum and sentenced Robert Latimer to one year in prison and one year of probation. In keeping with the law, however, the Court of Appeal upheld the conviction but changed the sentence to life imprisonment with eligibility for parole in ten years. Once again, the law was inconsistent with the community's sentiment that was expressed by the jury.

Sources: R. v. Morgentaler, 1988; Mallick, 2003; R. v. Latimer, 2001.

If juries are allowed to ignore the law and vote with their conscience, won't we end up with a biased or random system? Niedermeier, Horowitz, and Kerr (1999) examined whether telling jurors of their option to nullify the law would lead to biased verdicts. In one of their experiments, university students in groups of four were randomly assigned to consider one of four versions of a criminal trial. The trial involved a male victim of an HIV-infected blood transfusion who later died of AIDS. The blood was not screened for HIV prior to the transfusion.

The researchers manipulated the status of the defendant who decided to give the blood transfusion, knowing the blood was not screened: high status (medical director) versus low status (medical resident). The researchers also manipulated the defendant's remorsefulness on the outcome of the victim: presence of remorse versus absence of remorse.

These independent variables were examined to determine whether they were affected by nullification instructions. The four-person juries received either standard or nullification instructions after hearing the trial evidence. The juries were asked to reach a unanimous verdict. See Figure 8.1 for percentage of guilty verdicts as a function of nullification instructions, status of defendant, and remorse of defendant.

Overall, juries who received nullification instructions were less likely to render guilty verdicts than juries receiving standard instructions. The high-status defendant who was not remorseful was given fewer convictions than when he did express remorse. In contrast, the low-status defendant received fewer convictions when he expressed remorse than when he did not. Thus, in general, informing juries of their power to disregard the law may lead to more *not* guilty verdicts, but there are factors that will interact with these instructions, including the defendant's status and level of remorse.

HOW DO WE STUDY JUROR AND JURY BEHAVIOUR?

Now that we know how juries are selected and their characteristics and responsibilities, we can start understanding and predicting their behaviour. Many researchers in the forensic area have focused their careers on trying to predict verdicts and the variables that affect verdicts. We will now discuss four methodologies that have been used to gain understanding of juror and jury behaviour.

Post-Trial Interviews

In trying to understand why juries reached particular verdicts, perhaps it seems most logical and simple to ask the jurors themselves why they reached the verdicts they did. In Canada, however, actual jurors are not allowed to discuss what occurred in deliberations. All discourse that occurs during the deliberations is confidential. Breaking this confidentiality is a violation of section 649 of the Criminal Code (R.S.C., 1985, C-46, s. 649). A juror who discusses any part of the deliberation process would be committing a summary offence that carries a fine of up to $2000 and/or imprisonment for up to six

FIGURE 8.1

GUILTY VERDICTS BASED ON NULLIFICATION INSTRUCTIONS, STATUS OF DEFENDANT, AND REMORSE OF DEFENDANT

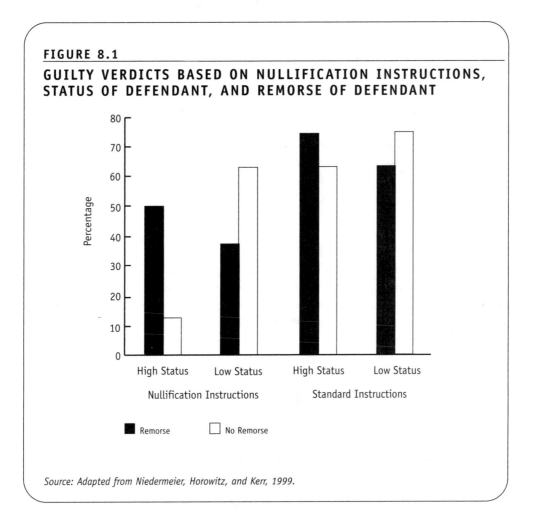

Source: Adapted from Niedermeier, Horowitz, and Kerr, 1999.

months. Although researchers cannot talk to Canadian jurors regarding their deliberations, they can turn to the United States or other countries that do not have this rule.

The main strength of post-trial interviews is high external validity; that is, results come from using real cases and the actual jurors that deliberated. Consequently, results may be more likely to generalize to the real world. This methodology, however, also has a number of weaknesses. For one, jurors' accounts may not be reliable. For example, jurors may recall details inaccurately, they may forget critical aspects of the deliberation, they may embellish or downplay elements to present themselves more favourably, or they may be unaware of the reasons for their decisions and behaviour. Thus, conclusions may be based on data that are unreliable. Moreover, a cause-and-effect relationship cannot be established with this type of methodology. At best, researchers can talk about variables that occur together. Alternative hypotheses cannot be ruled out with this methodology.

Archives

Records of trials such as transcripts and police interviews of witnesses can be reviewed to uncover relationships between variables. The strength of this methodology is similar to post-trial interviews in that external validity is high. A similar weakness, however, is the inability to establish cause-and-effect relationships. Also, the researcher is restricted to the data available in that the types of questions that can be posed are limited by the information that can be accessed. The researcher is unable to go back and collect more information. Furthermore, the researcher is unaware of how the information was collected and the reliability of that information. For example, police interviews may have been conducted using biased procedures.

Simulation

One of the most common methodologies used to investigate jury issues is the simulation. Researchers simulate a trial, or aspects of it, using a written, audio, or video format. Participants are presented with the trial information. The information that the participants receive about the trial can be varied and manipulated by the researcher. Examples of possible independent variables of interest include the age of the witness or the race of the defendant. Following the presentation of the trial, participants are asked to respond individually (juror research) or in groups (jury research). Typically, jurors and juries will be asked to render a verdict or make other judgments. Verdicts and other participants' responses can be compared to determine whether the independent variable(s) had an effect.

One of the major strengths of this methodology is its high internal validity; that is, the researcher can reveal cause-and-effect relationships because he or she systematically manipulated the independent variables. However, the control the researcher has over the independent variables limits the external validity of this methodology. For example, in simulations, cases are not real and there are no consequences to the verdicts or decisions the jurors render. Furthermore, the participants typically are university students, who may not be representative of real jury pools. These factors limit the generalizability of the results obtained with simulations.

Field Studies

This methodology involves using actual jurors while they are serving on jury duty, so cooperation from the courts and the jurors is required. Researchers are able to observe variables of interest as they are occurring. For example, they may be interested in how prospective jurors respond to questions posed during the voir dire. Alternatively, researchers may be able to introduce variables that they want to examine. The court may agree to let jurors take notes while the evidence is being presented, for example. Trials in which jurors were allowed to take notes can be compared with trials in which jurors were not allowed to take notes. A comparison of the verdicts can be undertaken across these cases.

The strength of field studies is high external validity. A number of limitations, however, are also present. For example, receiving approval from the courts for conducting the research may be difficult. Even when approval is granted, it is likely that only a small sample of participants will be available, and appropriate comparison groups may be to difficult to identify. Additionally, there are a host of confounding variables that the researcher may not be able to control, such as the gender of lawyers and witnesses.

As you can see, the researcher interested in juror/jury issues has a variety of methodologies to choose from. Each methodology has some strengths and weaknesses. By using all of these methodologies, we may be able to gain a more accurate understanding of juror and jury behaviour.

REACHING A VERDICT

Once a jury has been selected, their work begins. Jurors must listen to the admissible evidence and disregard any evidence that the judge does not allow. Once the lawyers deliver their closing arguments, the judge provides the jury with the law that they must apply to the evidence in order to reach a verdict. The jury then makes its **deliberation**—that is, they discuss the evidence privately among themselves to reach a verdict, which is then provided to the court. We will discuss each stage involved in reaching a jury verdict and the factors that may affect each stage.

Listening to the Evidence

Two innovations have been proposed as aids for jurors while listening to the evidence: (1) note taking and (2) asking questions. Advantages and disadvantages have been identified for each aid. We will discuss each aid in turn and the Canadian justice system's position on each.

NOTE TAKING Trials can be lengthy and complex, leading to missed or forgotten evidence by the time the jury is asked to deliberate. Some have suggested that allowing jurors to take notes may facilitate memory and understanding of the evidence (e.g., Heuer & Penrod, 1994). Moreover, note takers may be more attentive during the trial than those who do not take notes. Not everyone is in agreement, however, that allowing jurors to take notes is advantageous or even preferable. For example, in the Canadian case of *R. v. Andrade* (1985), a number of disadvantages to juror note taking were identified:

- Jurors who take notes may exert influence while in deliberation over those who do not.
- If disagreements occur about the evidence, jurors will rely on those who took notes to clarify the issue.

In one study examining juror note taking, Horowitz and ForsterLee (2001) had community citizens watch a videotape of a complex civil trial involving multiple plaintiffs. Mock jurors were either allowed to take notes or not allowed to take notes. Also, juries were either allowed to view trial transcripts during deliberations or not. The researchers found that, compared with those who did not take notes, the note takers were better able to differentiate among multiple plaintiffs and were better able to assign monetary awards accordingly. Also, having notes was more helpful for increasing juror knowledge about the evidence than having access to trial transcripts was.

In another study, Rosenhan, Eisner, and Robinson (1994) examined jurors' recall and comprehension of trial evidence from a group who took notes versus a group who did not. Note takers recalled more information than those who did not take notes. Also, the note takers scored higher on comprehension than those who did not take notes.

A recent review of the research examining juror note taking was conducted by Penrod and Heuer (1997). They reached the following conclusions regarding juror note taking:

- Jurors' notes serve as a memory aid.
- Jurors do not overemphasize the evidence that they have noted at the expense of evidence they have not recorded.
- Notes do not produce a distorted view of the case.
- Note takers can keep up with the evidence as it is being presented.
- Note takers do not distract jurors who do not take notes.
- Note takers do not have an undue influence over those who do not take notes.
- Jurors' notes are an accurate record of the trial.
- Juror note taking does not favour either the prosecution/Crown or the defence.

As you can see, allowing jurors to take notes does not appear to pose major difficulties. At present in Canada, it is up to the trial judge in each case to decide whether jurors will be allowed to take notes (Granger, 1996).

ASKING QUESTIONS When watching trials on television, or if you have ever had the opportunity to listen to a trial in court, you may have found yourself wondering about a detail that was mentioned. Would it not help if you could stop the trial and ask a question? The courts have considered the issue of jurors being allowed to ask questions. As with note taking, a number of advantages and disadvantages have been identified with regards to this innovation (Heuer & Penrod, 1994).

Some advantages of allowing jurors to ask questions include the following:

- It promotes greater understanding of the evidence.
- It can help reveal the truth.
- It can identify for lawyers issues that are unclear.
- It increases satisfaction with the judicial process.

Some disadvantages include the following:

- Jurors might ask unallowable questions.
- Lawyers might be reluctant to object to jurors' questions.

- Jurors could misunderstand lawyers' objections to their question.
- Jurors could confuse their role in the judicial process and take on an advocate role.

Heurer and Penrod (1994) report that typically juries have few questions (usually not more than three) and they tend to be concerned with the meaning of key legal terms such as reasonable doubt. In a review of the research examining juror questions, Penrod and Heuer (1997) reached the following conclusions:

- Jury questioning promotes juror understanding of the facts and issues.
- Juror questions do not clearly help get to the truth.
- Juror questions do not increase the jurors', judges', or lawyers' satisfaction with the trial and verdict.
- Jurors ask legally appropriate questions.
- If counsel objects, and the objection is sustained, the jury does not draw inappropriate inferences from unanswered questions.
- Jurors do not become advocates.

Thus, the research on allowing jurors to ask questions does not appear to be particularly harmful or helpful. At present in Canada, jurors may submit their questions in writing to the judge after the lawyers have completed their questioning of the witness. The judge then determines whether the question is permissible. Questions that are permissible then are posed by the judge. Ultimately, allowing jurors to ask questions is up to the judge presiding over the trial.

Disregarding Inadmissible Evidence

Are jurors able to "forget" what they heard? This question is not only relevant when we consider pretrial publicity but also when judges request that jurors disregard inadmissible evidence. Often juries will hear inadmissible evidence when lawyers or witnesses make statements that are not allowable according to legal procedure. Following an inadmissible statement or inadmissible evidence, the judge will instruct the jury to disregard it. The critical component to a fair trial and a just verdict is that only admissible statements and evidence are used by the jury. The question is, are jurors able to disregard evidence they have heard?

In one study by Hans and Doob (1976), participants were given a summary of a hypothetical burglary. Some of the participants were made aware of evidence about the defendant's prior convictions that they were asked to disregard. The remaining participants were not given this inadmissible evidence. Participants who were given the inadmissible evidence were more likely to reach a guilty verdict (40%) than participants who did not receive this evidence (0%). It seems that jurors are not very good at ignoring evidence once they have heard it, even if it is inadmissible.

FACTORS THAT AFFECT INSTRUCTIONS TO "DISREGARD" One factor that seems to influence a jury's ability to disregard inadmissible evidence is the *strength* of the evidence. Sue, Smith, and Caldwell (1973) discovered that when evidence against the defendant was weak, jurors were more likely to consider the inadmissible evidence and render more guilty verdicts than when the inadmissible evidence was not presented at all. In contrast, when evidence against the defendant was strong, jurors were more likely to disregard the inadmissible evidence. Inadmissible evidence also seems to have a greater influence when a crime is of a less serious nature, such as vandalism, compared with a more serious crime such as homicide or arson (Rind, Jaeger, & Strohmetz, 1995).

Kassin and Sommers (1997) argued that whether jurors will follow a judge's instruction to disregard inadmissible evidence is related to the reason for the instruction rather than to the instruction itself. In their study, mock jurors were presented with a murder trial, and a piece of evidence was manipulated. Jurors in the control condition only received circumstantial and ambiguous evidence. In the experimental conditions, an audiotaped telephone conversation in which the defendant confessed to the murder was included. When this audiotape was admitted into evidence, the defence lawyer objected. The judge either overruled the objection, allowing it into evidence, or sustained the objection and asked jurors to disregard it because it was either illegally obtained or difficult to comprehend. When jurors were asked to disregard the evidence because it was illegally collected, their verdicts were similar to the jurors who received the ruling that the tape was admissible. In contrast, when jurors were instructed to disregard the tape because of comprehension difficulty, they rendered verdicts similar to the control jurors who had not heard about the inadmissible evidence. Thus, Kassin and Sommers concluded that jurors who are provided with a logical and legitimate reason for the judge's decision to disregard evidence do disregard it.

One other interesting result has been found with the disregard instruction. Some researchers have found that a judge's instruction to disregard evidence simply makes the evidence more memorable than if no instruction were given. This is known as the backfire effect (Paglia & Schuller, 1998). Thus, jurors are more likely to pay attention to inadmissible evidence following a disregard instruction than if no instruction was provided.

Overall, the influence of the disregard instruction is not straightforward. There are other factors that come into play and interact with the effect of the instruction.

Judge's Instructions

A number of studies have examined jurors' abilities to understand the legally dense instructions that the judge charges the jury with prior to their deliberation. The results of these studies generally are not positive. Lieberman and Sales (1997) have concluded that jurors do not remember, understand, or accurately apply judge's instructions. Reifman, Gusick, and Ellsworth (1992) surveyed 224 citizens from Michigan who were called for jury duty. The goal was to assess jurors' comprehension of judge's instructions. These prospective jurors understood less than 50% of the instructions they received.

Four reforms for judges' instructions have been proposed: (1) rewriting instructions, (2) providing a written copy of the instructions to jurors, (3) pre- and post-evidence instructions, and (4) having lawyers clarify legal instruction during their presentation to the jury.

REWRITING INSTRUCTIONS Judges' instructions often contain several legal terms and complex sentence structure. These instructions could be simplified by relying on psycholinguistic and cognitive research. However, there is some disagreement as to whether rewriting instructions aids comprehension (Kagehiro, 1990). In a review of the research, Tanford (1992) reported that errors in comprehension remain fairly high, at about 75%, even with rewritten instructions.

PROVIDING WRITTEN INSTRUCTIONS The notion behind providing jurors with written instructions is that jurors have the judge's instructions in a supplemental form that they can access as they deliberate. In a review of studies examining this supplement to judges' oral instructions, Lieberman and Sales (1997) found that written instructions can aid juror understanding of the judge's oral instructions. However, some studies have not found a difference in comprehension as a function of supplemental written instructions (e.g., Heuer & Penrod, 1989). It seems that the jury is still out on whether written instructions are a helpful supplement to a judge's oral instructions to the jury.

PRE- AND POST-EVIDENCE INSTRUCTIONS Some researchers have argued that providing jurors with instructions both before and after they hear the evidence may help in their comprehension of the instructions. For example, Smith (1991) found that when mock jurors were given instructions both before and after they heard the evidence, they were correct on 70% of the questions probing their comprehension of the instructions. When mock jurors only heard the instructions after the evidence was presented, they were correct on 68% of the questions. This difference between groups is not significant. However, with different dependent measures, it is possible to demonstrate that pre- and post-evidence instructions are more beneficial than only post-evidence instructions (Smith, 1991).

LAWYER CLARIFICATION Ellsworth and Reifman (2000) have suggested that lawyers could clarify complex legal terms during their closing arguments to aid juror comprehension of judges' instructions. Little direct research exists on this topic to determine whether this technique would increase juror comprehension. Thus, it is not clear whether lawyer clarification will be beneficial to jurors trying to comprehend judges' instructions.

These four proposed reforms have not been implemented with any consistency within the Canadian justice system.

Jury Decision-Making Models

How do jurors combine the trial evidence to reach a verdict? Moreover, what is the process by which verdicts are reached? Although a number of models of juror/jury

A jury listens to evidence

decision making have been proposed, they may be categorized as either using a mathematical or explanation-based approach.

MATHEMATICAL MODELS The common theme with mathematical models is that they view jurors as conducting a set of mental calculations regarding the importance and strength of each piece of evidence (Hastie, 1993). A guilty or not guilty verdict is determined by the outcome of the calculations for all the relevant evidence. For example, an eyewitness who identified the defendant may be perceived as strong evidence and be weighed heavily toward a guilty verdict; however, learning that the DNA found at the crime scene does not match the defendant's decreases the likelihood of a guilty verdict. The verdict is a function of the calculation of all the relevant evidence.

Ellsworth and Mauro (1998) examined the congruency of mental calculations and how jurors perceive their process of reaching a verdict. They found that a mathematical approach was inconsistent with how jurors' report that they reach verdicts. Jurors do not appear to provide a value for each piece of evidence presented. Moreover, it may be difficult to partition evidence into discrete pieces of evidence that can then be assigned a value. Perhaps an explanation-based approach is more consistent with how jurors process the trial evidence.

EXPLANATION MODELS In contrast to mathematical models, explanation models suggest that evidence is organized into a coherent whole. Pennington and Hastie's (1986) explanation approach is called the story model. They proposed that jurors are active at understanding and processing the evidence. Jurors interpret and elaborate on the evidence and make causal connections, and in doing so, they create a story structure. These "stories" are then compared with each verdict option presented by the judge. The verdict option most consistent with the story is the verdict reached.

Of course, jurors listening to the same evidence may construct different stories that are consistent with alternative verdicts. That is to say that individual differences can influence the story construction process. Jurors bring in their personal experiences, knowledge, beliefs, and attitudes when constructing their story. Thus, jurors may reach different decisions after hearing the same evidence.

To test the story model, Pennington and Hastie (1986) had 26 participants watch a simulated murder trial and then make individual verdicts at the end of the trial. Following their verdicts, participants were interviewed to determine how they thought about the evidence. The researchers found that participants put the evidence into a story format and different stories were related to different verdicts.

In a follow-up study, Pennington and Hastie (1988) varied how easily a particular story could be constructed by altering the order in which the evidence was presented. They found that when the evidence was presented in a chronological order, it was more likely that the verdict reached was consistent with that story order. This information could be useful to lawyers who may choose to present evidence in a story format that is consistent with the verdict they want. The story model seems to be consistent with how jurors process trial evidence and reach a verdict.

Deliberations

As you may recall, a 12-person jury is necessary for criminal cases in Canada. However, cases can continue as long as no more than two members are excused, possibly for illness or other reasons, during the trial (Granger, 1996). For example, in the 2003 murder trial of Matti Baranovski in Toronto, an 11-person jury convicted Lee Cochrane and Meir Mariani of manslaughter.

Once all the evidence has been heard and the judge has delivered his or her instructions to the jurors, the jury retires to a secluded room to deliberate. In Canada, the jury is sequestered until the final verdict is reached and the jury is dismissed by the judge (Granger, 1996). This means that the jury is not allowed to talk to anyone outside their 12-person panel, with the exception of the court-appointed officer in the event that they have a request or question.

The expectation from the justice system is that the jury reviews the evidence and determines the most consistent match between the verdict options that were provided by the judge and the admissible evidence. A number of factors can influence a juror's position on the case. A phenomenon known as **polarization** occurs when individuals tend to become more extreme in their initial position following a group discussion (Baron & Bryne, 1991). In contrast, a **leniency bias** also has been found whereby jurors move toward greater leniency following deliberations (MacCoun & Kerr, 1988).

The Final Verdict

The Canadian jury must reach a unanimous verdict. If not, the jury is said to be a **hung jury** or deadlocked and a mistrial is declared. Following a hung jury, the Crown must decide whether it will retry the case.

In contrast to required unanimous verdicts in Canada, the United States has permitted majority votes of eleven to one, ten to two, and nine to three. Similarly, the United Kingdom has allowed juries to render eleven-to-one or ten-to-two majority votes provided that the jury has deliberated for a minimum of two hours. In a meta-analysis examining the effects of jury size, Saks and Marti (1997) found that six-person juries are less representative of the community, they remember less of the evidence, they return quicker verdicts, and they are more likely to reach a unanimous verdict than 12-person juries. Hastie, Penrod, and Pennington (1983) found that when a jury could retire with a majority vote, they tended to reach a decision faster and did not fully discuss both the evidence and law, compared with when the jury was required to reach a unanimous verdict.

In general, when a first verdict poll is taken, the final verdict tends to be consistent with the first poll in about 90% of cases (Kalvern & Zeisel, 1966; Sandys & Dillehay, 1995). MacCoun and Kerr (1988) conducted a meta-analysis of 12 studies examining juror preferences at the beginning of deliberation as well as final verdicts. They found that a pro-defence faction was more persuasive than a pro-prosecution faction. More specifically, if seven or fewer jurors vote guilty at the beginning of deliberation, the jury will tend to render a not guilty verdict. If ten or more jurors initially vote guilty, the final verdict will likely be guilty. If eight or nine jurors initially vote guilty, the final verdict is unpredictable.

Hastie, Penrod, and Pennington (1983) identified two broad styles that juries tend to adopt when trying to reach a verdict: verdict driven and evidence driven. Verdict-driven juries tend to start the deliberation process by taking an initial verdict poll. In contrast, evidence-driven juries tend to start the deliberation process by discussing the evidence. A verdict poll is not taken until much later during the deliberation. These two styles can influence the outcome of the initial verdict poll (Sandys & Dillehay, 1995).

PREDICTING VERDICTS

A great deal of research has been conducted examining juror characteristics to determine whether verdicts can be predicted based on these characteristics. We will examine the following six types of variables that have been studied and their relation to the verdict: (1) demographic variables, (2) personality variables, (3) attitudes, (4) defendant characteristics, (5) victim characteristics, and (6) expert testimony.

Demographic Variables

Variables such as the gender, race, socioeconomic status, and education of jurors are demographic variables that have been examined, in part because they are readily available to lawyers and also because they can be used to challenge witnesses. For example, are female jurors more lenient? Are Caucasians more likely to render guilty verdicts? Unfortunately, when using juror demographic variables to predict verdicts, results are less than reliable. Overall, only a small and inconsistent relation exists between juror demographic variables and jury verdicts (e.g., Bonazzoli, 1998).

Some researchers highlight a more intriguing finding that there is an interaction between juror demographic variables and defendant demographic variables (Devine et al., 2001). For example, the defendant's race has been found to interact with the race of the juror. In a study examining race, Perez, Hosch, Ponder, and Trejo (1993) found that juries that were predominately white were more likely to render guilty verdicts for

Hispanic defendants versus white defendants. However, the relationship was not straightforward. Results were influenced by the strength of the evidence. When the evidence was weak or ambiguous (not clearly favouring one side), similarity between defendant and jury led to leniency. When evidence was strong, similarity between defendant and jury led to punitiveness. This is known as the **black sheep effect** (Chadee, 1996).

Personality Traits

The two personality traits that have been commonly measured in connection to jurors are **authoritarianism and dogmatism**. Individuals high in authoritarianism tend to have right-wing political views and are conservative and rigid thinkers who acquiesce to authority. Similarly, individuals high in dogmatism also tend to be rigid and closed-minded but without the political overtones found with the authoritarianism construct. Are personality traits better at predicting verdicts than are demographic variables?

Given the underlying traits associated with dogmatism and authoritarianism, anyone would predict that jurors who score high on these constructs would be more likely to align themselves with the prosecution and, thus, render more guilty verdicts than jurors who score low on these constructs. In a meta-analysis that examined authoritarianism and juror verdicts across 20 studies, Narby, Cutler, and Moran (1993) found a moderate, positive relationship between authoritarianism and verdict such that those who score high on these traits tend to be more inclined to render guilty verdicts. That is, they have a pro-prosecution bias. Jurors' personality traits seem to be more effective at predicting verdicts than do demographic variables.

Attitudes

Researchers have examined a variety of attitudes linked to specific topics or issues that may be present in cases, such as drunk driving, rape, child sexual abuse, and capital punishment. For example, Spanos, Dubreuil, and Gwynn (1991–1992) examined rape myths (e.g., a woman who wears provocative clothing is interested in having sex) in connection to a date rape case. University students heard a version of a date rape case involving expert testimony about rape myths and cross-examination of such, and then deliberated in small groups to reach a verdict. A gender split was observed in which females did not believe the defendant and voted him guilty more often than male mock jurors. However, regardless of the gender of the mock jurors, those with feminist attitudes were more likely not to believe the defendant's testimony.

Devine et al. (2001) reported that no group of attitudes or values has received sufficient investigation to reach a definitive conclusion at this point. The one notable exception is attitudes toward capital punishment. For example, Horowitz and Seguin (1986) reported that juries comprising death-qualified jurors (i.e., jurors who are willing to impose the death sentence) had a 19% higher conviction rate than non-death-qualified jurors. In general, death-qualified jurors are more likely than non-death-qualified jurors to vote for conviction at the end of a trial (Ellsworth & Mauro, 1998).

Overall, attitudes that are case specific seem to have some predictive power over verdict than do more general attitudes.

Defendant Characteristics

A number of studies have examined characteristics relevant to the defendant and the influence on verdicts. For example, if jurors hear about a defendant's prior criminal record that contains one or more convictions, they are more likely to find the defendant guilty than if the jurors did not have this knowledge (Hans & Doob, 1976).

There also seems to be a small relation between the attractiveness of the defendant and jury verdict. Izzett and Leginski (1974) provided mock jurors with a picture of an unattractive or attractive defendant and found verdict preferences to be more lenient for the attractive defendant and more severe for the unattractive defendant.

Victim Characteristics

Characteristics of the victim may become particularly relevant in cases of sexual assault in which a guilty verdict may hinge on the testimony of the alleged victim. In Canada, before the mid-1980s, a woman's prior sexual history was admissible and could be used to infer her credibility and the likelihood that she consented to sexual relations with the defendant. Rape shield provisions were legislated in 1985 that prevented lawyers from introducing a woman's prior sexual history (R.S.C. 1985, c. C-46, s. 276).

In the early 1990s, however, some began to challenge these provisions in that they prevented defendants from receiving a fair trial (*R. v. Seaboyer*, 1991; *R. v. Gayme*, 1991). Defence lawyers argued that it was necessary to admit the accuser's prior sexual history because it would support defendants' claims of an honest but mistaken belief in consent. The rape shield provisions were amended in 1992, allowing inquiry into a woman's sexual history at the judge's discretion (R.S.C. 1985, C-46, s. 276; 1992, c. 38, s.2). Only if a woman's sexual history was deemed relevant would the judge allow it to be heard by the jury. Further, the Supreme Court of Canada (*R. v. Seaboyer*, 1991) recommended that the trial judge provide the jury with cautionary instructions on how this evidence should be used. More specifically, the jurors must be cautioned that a woman's sexual history should only be used in determining a defendant's claim of an "honest but mistaken belief in consent." A woman's sexual history must not be used to demonstrate that the woman is less trustworthy or that she is likely to consent to sexual intercourse. Some have argued that such a distinction is too fine to be made by jurors.

Schuller and Hastings (2002) conducted a study in which the victim's sexual history was varied to include either sexual intercourse, kissing and touching, or no history information in a sexual assault trial. In addition, a judge's instructions limiting the use of the sexual history information was examined. Compared with the participants who heard no sexual history information, those who heard that the victim and defendant had sexual intercourse in the past were less likely to find the alleged victim credible, more likely to find her blameworthy, and more likely to believe she consented to sexual intercourse. Thus, they were more likely to find the defendant innocent. The sexual history information did not influence participants' judgments about the defendant's belief in consent, which is contrary to the goal of judge's instructions as intended by the Supreme Court of Canada. It would appear that a judge's instruction to limit the use of the sexual history information is not effective. If a woman's sexual history is admitted into evidence, it is used to assess her credibility.

Cases have continued to challenge the 1992 rape shield provisions. In *R. v. Darrach* (2000), the defendant, Andrew Darrach was found guilty of sexually assaulting his former girlfriend. Mr. Darrach appealed his conviction arguing that he did not receive a fair trial because he was unable to present information about his prior sexual history with the accuser. Mr. Darrach stated that, given his past relationship with the accused, he thought that the sexual encounter was consensual. During the trial, the judge heard the defence's arguments and ruled that the evidence was inadmissible when Mr. Darrach refused to testify or be cross-examined on the claims he was making. In Mr. Darrach's appeal, he claimed that the law unfairly required him to testify and denied him access to a full defence. In October 2000, the Supreme Court of Canada upheld Mr. Darrach's conviction and upheld the country's rape shield provisions. The Supreme Court noted that the onus is on the defendant to demonstrate that the accuser's sexual history is relevant before it will be allowed (*R. v. Darrach*, 2000).

Expert Testimony

How well do jurors understand the evidence presented? Sometimes jurors don't have the background knowledge to understand certain types of evidence, such as DNA. Lawyers may ask that an expert be allowed to testify to explain the evidence. What influence does expert evidence have on jurors' decisions?

A number of findings about expert testimony are available, but no simple conclusion has emerged. For example, the influence of expert testimony may vary depending on the race and gender of the expert. Memon and Shuman (1998) presented participants with one of four experts: a black female, a black male, a white female, or a white male. The experts testified as to whether a doctor was negligent in a civil case regarding a birth defect. The black female expert was rated as most persuasive and she garnered the most support from the white jurors. It was speculated that the content of the testimony may interact with the gender of the expert. For example, if the subject of the testimony is a women's issue, it may be more effective to have a female expert. The race of the expert may interact with the race of the juror and may be complicated by the content of the testimony. It is not clear how these factors work together.

In addition, the expert's credentials and the complexity of the testimony may be critical. Cooper, Bennett, and Sukel (1996) had participants watch a videotaped civil trial during which two experts provided evidence regarding the cause of a plaintiff's illness. The complexity (easy versus difficult) of the testimony as well as the expert's credentials (strong versus weak) were varied. Participants were more convinced by a strong expert witness than by a weak expert witness but only when the testimony was complex. When the testimony was easier to follow, expert credentials had little impact on the persuasiveness of the testimony; rather, participants relied on the content of the testimony.

Expert testimony need not produce a positive effect, however, and jurors may disregard it completely. For example, Sundby (1997) examined the transcripts of 152 jurors who participated in 36 first-degree murder cases in California. Jurors were asked about their perceptions and reactions to three types of witnesses: professional experts, lay experts, and families/friends of the defendant. Professional experts were most likely to be viewed negatively and with little credibility along with hurting the side they were testifying for. Overall, expert testimony may be carefully considered by jurors.

A SPECIAL CASE OF EXPERT TESTIMONY ON BATTERED WOMEN'S SYNDROME Dr. Regina Schuller and her colleagues have conducted a number of studies examining battered women who kill their abusers and the influence of expert testimony (Schuller, 1992, 1995; Schuller & Hastings, 1996; Schuller & Rzepa, 2002; Schuller, Smith, & Olson, 1994). See Box 8.6 to learn more about Dr. Schuller and her research.

BOX 8.6 CANADIAN RESEARCHER PROFILE: DR. REGINA SCHULLER

Dr. Regina Schuller mentions how she was bitten by the jury bug as a graduate student at the University of Western Ontario. Her supervisor, Neil Vidmar, was just finishing up his classic book *Judging the Jury* and had asked her to read a preliminary copy. Dr.

Schuller has never looked back. She immersed herself in the psychology-law area, completing her Ph.D. at Western and also spending two years at Northwestern University in the United States, where she was part of an interdisciplinary program focused on the law and social science.

While in the United States she also spent a significant amount of time working with Tom Tyler at the American Bar Foundation. Dr. Schuller joined the faculty in the department of psychology at York University in Toronto in 1990. She has been there ever since, receiving numerous awards and grants. For example, in 1995, she received the York's President Prize for Promising Scholars. Her research is funded by the Social Science and Humanities Research Council of Canada.

Dr. Schuller describes her program of research as centring on issues of gender in the legal system. For example, she has investigated violence against women in the form of expert testimony pertaining to battered women in the trials of women who killed their abusers. She also has an interest in investigating the impact of legislative changes that allow for greater information about a claimant's (typically a woman) sexual and medical history into the court. Dr. Schuller notes that one of her favourite pieces of research was a study conducted with Patricia Hastings examining alternative ways to introduce expert testimony on battered women and its influence on juror verdicts and ratings of the defendant (i.e., the woman who killed her abuser). She states that it was important to consider empirically whether there might be some negative effects associated with battered woman syndrome testimony. For instance, might it pathologize battered women, as some critics were suggesting? This research study was published in the journal *Law and Human Behavior*.

Dr. Schuller primarily uses laboratory simulations to conduct her research. She says that the reason for this methodology is twofold. First, in Canada you are restricted from talking to actual jurors so fieldwork is virtually impossible, and second, simulation provides a strong methodology when you are trying to uncover cause-and-effect relationships.

When asked what keeps her going in the field of jury research, she emphatically says, "It's fun." The entire process is fun, from creating mock trials to collecting the data and writing it up for others to read. She also states how jury research is an application of the broader area of social psychology and it is fascinating to see how social psychological phenomena occur in the microcosm of the jury, such as how group processes can affect jury verdicts.

Her philosophy for training future leaders in the field includes a strong suggestion for psychologists to immerse themselves in reading case law. Dr. Schuller stresses that we need to keep in mind that if we want lawyers, judges, and the justice system to listen to what we have to say, we need to understand the context in which the research will be applied.

Dr. Schuller uses an apprenticeship model with the students she trains. She works closely with them, from conceptualizing research ideas to designing studies and manuscript writing. It is clear that Dr. Schuller is a great role model and mentor for future researchers in the psychology-law area.

Dr. Schuller lives with her partner, Richard, two children, René and Andrée, and their newest addition, a dog, in the Toronto area.

In one study, Schuller, Smith, and Olson (1994) examined the impact of four variables including jurors' pre-existing beliefs about wife abuse, jurors' beliefs in a "just world" (believing that you receive what you deserve), the presence or absence of expert testimony on battered women's syndrome, and sex of the juror (male versus female). Mock jurors listened to a homicide trial involving a woman who killed her abusive husband. They then made various judgments about the case. The mock jurors who heard the expert testimony were more likely to believe the woman's account of what happened than were those who did not hear expert testimony. Those who had a weak belief in a "just world" were more lenient in their judgments and felt that the expert testimony was more relevant to the battered woman than did those who had a strong belief in a "just world." Female mock jurors who had a weak belief in a "just world" were more likely to find the defendant not guilty.

In another study involving a trial of a homicide in which a battered woman killed her abuser, Schuller and Cripps (1998) varied the gender of the expert providing testimony. They also varied the timing of that testimony. The expert testimony was either heard early, before the defendant's testimony, or it was heard late, after the defendant's testimony. University students acted as jurors and listened to a version of the trial. See Table 8.1 for percentages of guilty verdicts as a function of the gender of the expert and the timing of the testimony.

These results suggest that the gender of an expert witness may interact with the content of testimony. That is, expert testimony about female issues may be viewed as more credible when the expert is female and vice versa for males. When the expert witness in this study was female, jurors tended to evaluate the expert evidence more favourably and were more lenient in sentencing the defendant. Moreover, in keeping with the story model of jury decision making, expert testimony that occurs early may be helpful in setting up a particular structure of the evidence that will be heard later on. Indeed, it was found that when the expert testimony was presented before the

TABLE 8.1 GUILTY VERDICTS AS A FUNCTION OF EXPERT'S GENDER AND TIMING OF TESTIMONY

Timing of Testimony		Male	Female	No Expert
			Gender of Expert	
Early				
	Murder	22.9%	2.8%	
	Manslaughter	54.3%	52.8%	
	Self-defence	22.9%	44.4%	
Late				
	Murder	13.5%	22.2%	
	Manslaughter	54.1%	27.8%	
	Self-defence	32.4%	50.0%	
Murder				20.0%
Manslaughter				48.6%
Self-defence				31.4%

Source: Schuller and Cripps, 1998.

defendant's testimony, jurors were more likely to believe the defendant and to place more responsibility on the husband.

SUMMARY

1. In Canada, prospective jurors are selected from a set of random names from the community. These prospective jurors receive a jury summons stating the time and place to go for jury duty. When they arrive to the designated location, typically the courthouse, they are given a number and escorted to a room with others who also are potential jurors. Once everyone has arrived a judge will explain the jury selection process and how many juries will be chosen that day. If you are selected from the juror pool, you will be a juror unless one of the lawyers presents a challenge.

2. In order for a jury to be considered representative, it must allow any possible eligible juror from the community the opportunity to be part of the jury. Representativeness is achieved through randomness. Juror impartiality centres on three issues: (1) being able to set aside any pre-existing biases, prejudices, or attitudes to solely judge the case based on admissible evidence; (2) ignoring any information that is not part of the admissible evidence; and (3) not being connected to the defendant in any way.

3. Pretrial publicity threatens juror impartiality. Typically, the media attention is negative for the defendant, which could mean that the defendant does not receive a fair trial. Thus, the concern is that verdicts will be based on emotion and biased media coverage rather than admissible evidence. In order to reduce or limit the negative effects of pretrial publicity, the judge can order a publication ban until the end of the trial. Other options for dealing with pretrial publicity are for the Crown or defence to request a change of venue, an adjournment, or a challenge for cause.

4. Once a jury has been selected, their work begins by listening to the admissible evidence and disregarding any evidence that the judge does not allow. Once the lawyers deliver their closing arguments, the judge provides the jury with the law that they must apply to the evidence to reach a verdict. The jury then deliberates to reach a verdict.

5. Categories that have been examined in terms of predicting verdicts include demographic variables, personality variables, attitudes, defendant characteristics, victim characteristics, and expert testimony.

KEY CONCEPTS

DISCUSSION QUESTIONS

1. You have recently graduated with a degree in psychology. Given your interest in forensic psychology, you decide to move to the United States and become a jury consultant. Describe the approach you would take to scientific jury selection. What variables would you consider critical to evaluate when giving advice to lawyers?

2. You have decided to take a summer job with a criminal defence lawyer. After working there for a few weeks, you realize that the lawyer does not "win" very many cases. What advice would you give to your boss to help with his track record?

3. Design a study to evaluate jury aids (e.g., note taking, asking questions) to ensure that they do not negatively alter the judicial process.

4. Your neighbour drops by for coffee. She has received a summons for jury duty and asks you about the jury selection process. Describe the jury selection process and fundamental qualities of a "good juror."

5. A battered woman who shot and killed her sleeping abusive husband is standing trial for murder. The defence has retained a prominent forensic psychologist to give expert testimony. What impact do you think this expert will have on the jury?

6. Should juries be permitted to ignore the law? Discuss the issues surrounding jury nullification.

7. To study juror decision making, researchers have used four different methodologies. Describe the advantages and disadvantages of each method.

ADDITIONAL INFORMATION

Readings

Tanovich, D.M., Paciocco, D.M., & Skurka, S. (1997). *Jury selection in criminal trials: Skills, science, and the law.* Toronto, ON: Irwin Law.

Wrightsman, L.S. (1999). *Judicial decision making: Is psychology relevant?* New York: Plenum.

CHAPTER 9

Fitness and Mental State at Time of Offence

LEARNING OBJECTIVES

■ Outline the fitness standard and the changes made to legislation.

■ Contrast unfit and fit offenders.

■ Explain Canada's insanity standard.

■ Describe automatism and examples of cases in which it was used as a defence.

■ State the explanations for high rates of mental illness in offender populations.

■ Explain the various treatment goals and options for offenders with mental disorders.

Janis Baum was a 52-year-old single female. She had not been able to keep a job for more than six months. Her employers would often comment on her strange behaviour. For example, Janis would talk to herself and often said that TV cooking shows were directed at her, mocking her cooking skills. Janis had received a diagnosis of schizophrenia when she was in university and was given anti-psychotic medication that she would need to take for the rest of her life. Janis rarely took her medication, though, because she disliked the side effects. When she did not take her medication, Janis would often shoplift, mostly food items.

Thanksgiving was a week away and Janis decided that she wanted a turkey. She walked to the local grocery store and put a frozen turkey under her coat. The store manager, familiar with Janis's behaviours, called the police and Janis was arrested and charged with shoplifting.

At the police station Janis was incoherent, and when the officer started asking her questions, she started to talk in a language she had made up as a

> teenager. The officer called a lawyer from the legal aid office for Janis, given that she was not in a state where she could do it herself. When the lawyer arrived to meet with Janis, he quickly became concerned that Janis would not be able to assist in her own defence. The lawyer requested that the court order an assessment for Janis's fitness to stand trial.

PRESUMPTIONS IN CANADA'S LEGAL SYSTEM

The cornerstone of English-Canadian law identifies two elements that must be present for criminal guilt: (1) a wrongful deed, also known as **actus reus**, and (2) criminal intent, also known as **mens rea**. Both of these elements (and the elements of the specific case) must be found beyond a reasonable doubt for a guilty verdict to be reached. Issues of fitness, insanity, automatism, and mental disorders all call into question these two basic elements of criminal law.

FITNESS TO STAND TRIAL

It is reasonable to expect that individuals who are charged with the commission of a crime, in order to be tried fairly, have some understanding of the charges and proceedings, and be able to help in preparing their defence. A defendant who is deficient in these domains, possibly because of a mental disorder, may be considered unfit to stand trial. Thus, **unfit to stand trial** refers to an inability to conduct a defence at any stage of the proceedings on account of a mental disorder. For example, a defendant may be found unfit to stand trial if he or she is experiencing an episode of schizophrenia and lacks the ability to understand the situation and tell the lawyer the facts of the case. The degree of impairment necessary for an unfit determination has been difficult to pinpoint, however.

Historically, little direction was provided by means of legislation for a finding of unfitness; rather, case law was used to determine the criteria that should be met. Specifically, the case of *R. v. Prichard* (1836) has been considered the key case for the fitness standard (Lindsay, 1977). Three points were delineated in the Prichard case:

- Whether the defendant is mute of malice
- Whether the defendant can plead to the indictment
- Whether the defendant has sufficient cognitive capacity to understand the trial proceedings

With the enactment of Bill C-30 in 1992, the Canadian Criminal Code stated a fitness standard. The fitness standard can be found in section 2 of the Code: A defendant is unfit to stand trial if he or she is

> unable on account of mental disorder to conduct a defence at any stage of the proceedings before a verdict is rendered or to instruct counsel to do so, and, in particular, unable on

account of mental disorder to a) understand the nature or object of the proceedings b) understand the possible consequences of the proceedings, or c) communicate with counsel. (R.S.C., 1985, c. C-46, s. 2; 1992, c. 20, s. 216, c. 51, s. 32)

This last point about communicating with counsel has been further specified in case law in *R. v. Taylor* (1992). In this case, the Ontario Court of Appeal stated that the test to be applied in terms of "communication with counsel" is with regard to limited cognitive capacity. The Court ruled that a defendant need only be able to state the facts relating to the offence that would allow an appropriate defence. Moreover, the defendant need not be able to communicate facts that are in his or her best interests. The Court decided that applying the "best interest rule" was too strict of a criterion.

One other issue that was altered with Bill C-30 was the length of time a defendant could be held in custody for a fitness evaluation. A five-day limit on court-ordered assessments was legislated with provisions for extensions, if necessary, to complete the evaluation. The extension, however, is not to exceed 30 days, and the entire length of detention should not exceed 60 days (R.S.C., 1985, C-46, s. 672.15). The evaluation can occur while the defendant is in a detention, outpatient, or inpatient facility. Roesch, Ogloff, Hart, Dempster, Zapf, and Whittemore (1997) found that the average length of time for evaluation was approximately three weeks and that 88% occurred in inpatient facilities (also Zapf & Roesch, 1998).

Raising the Issue of Fitness

The issue of a defendant's fitness may be raised at various points from the time of arrest to the defendant's sentence determination. Examples of instances in which fitness may be raised include entering a plea, when a defendant chooses not to be represented by counsel, and during sentencing (Ogloff, Wallace, & Otto, 1991). The Canadian Criminal Code states that a defendant is assumed to be fit to stand trial unless the court is satisfied on the balance of probabilities that he or she is unfit (R.S.C., 1985, C-46, s. 672.22). Also noted in the Code is that the burden of proving unfitness is on the party who raises the issue (R.S.C., 1985, C-46, s. 672.23(2)).

How Many Defendants Are Referred for Fitness Evaluations?

Webster, Menzies, Butler, and Turner (1982) estimated that approximately 5000 fitness evaluations were conducted annually in Canada. In a more recent investigation, Roesch et al. (1997) found that 61% of a sample from a remand facility in British Columbia underwent fitness evaluations. Moreover, 24% were held for assessments of both fitness and criminal responsibility (we will discuss criminal responsibility in more detail later in the chapter). In the United States, Bonnie and Grisso (2000) estimated that somewhere between 2% and 8% of all felony defendants are referred for fitness evaluations—that is, about 25 000 to 38 000 defendants (Hoge et al., 1997). See Table 9.1 for a distribution of unfit cases in Canada.

Who Can Assess Fitness?

Traditionally, only medical practitioners have been allowed to conduct court-ordered assessments such as fitness to stand trial and criminal responsibility (Viljoen et al., 2003). Unlike in the United States and Australia, the Canadian Criminal Justice system continues to take this position. In fact, the Canadian Criminal Code excludes psychologists from conducting court-ordered assessments. The Code specifies that these assessments must be carried out by medical practitioners (R.S.C., 1985, C- 46, s. 672.1). It is important to note that the medical practitioners need not have any background in psychiatry or experience with forensic populations. In contrast, Farkas, DeLeon, and Newman (1997) reported that 47 U.S. states allow psychologists to conduct fitness and criminal responsibility evaluations.

TABLE 9.1 UNFIT CASES HEARD BY REVIEW BOARDS ACROSS CANADA

Jurisdiction	New Unfit Cases		Total Active Cases*	
	2000	*2001**	*2000*	*2001**
Newfoundland and Labrador	4	3	26	28
Prince Edward Island	0	0	4	3
Nova Scotia	2	2	83	98
New Brunswick	3	11	62	78
Quebec	40	41	912	906
Ontario	91	66	952	966
Manitoba	3	—	70	75
Saskatchewan	1	4	30	34
Alberta	13	11	111	113
British Columbia	11	—	411	411
Yukon	2	1	2	3
Northwest Territories	0	0	0	0
Nunavut	1	0	2	2
TOTAL	171	139	2 665	2 717

Source: Justice Canada, 2002.

*Total active cases includes cases where defendant was found not criminally responsible on account of mental disorder.

** Preliminary figure.

Canadian psychologists can, however, be involved in court-ordered assessments in a variety of ways. For example, psychologists may be asked to conduct psychological testing and to *assist* with the assessment of defendants who are referred for evaluation. Psychologists submit their results to psychiatrists or other medical practitioners, who then incorporate the results into a report to the court.

Fitness Instruments

A number of screening instruments have been developed to help evaluators quickly screen out defendants who are competent to stand trial. Comprehensive fitness assessments can then be reserved for those defendants who are "screened in." Zapf and Roesch (1998) examined the fitness decisions that were made using a screening instrument versus those decisions made following a stay in a psychiatric facility. The researchers found that the two sets of decisions were consistent with each other. They concluded that long stays in mental facilities were unnecessary for most of the fitness decisions. Rather, many fitness decisions could be made quickly using a screening instrument and would result in a more cost-effective system.

One screening instrument that has particular relevance for Canadians is the Fitness Interview Test Revised (FIT-R; Roesch, Zapf, Eaves, & Webster, 1998), which was developed to meet the fitness criteria outlined in the Canadian Criminal Code. The FIT-R is in the form of a semi-structured interview and assesses the three psychological abilities stated in the Code's fitness standard. Each section contains several items that the evaluator probes with the defendant. For example:

- Understand the nature or object of the proceedings (six items in total)
  - Factual knowledge of criminal procedure
    - i defendant's understanding of the arrest process
    - ii the nature and severity of the current charges
    - iii the role of key participants
- Understand the possible consequences of the proceedings (three items in total)
  - Appreciation of personal involvement in and importance of the proceedings
    - i appreciation of range and nature of possible penalties and defences
- Communicate with counsel (seven items in total)
  - Ability to participate in defence
    - i defendant's ability to *communicate* facts
    - ii relate to his or her attorney
    - iii plan legal strategy

Each response is rated on a three-point scale ranging from 0 (indicates no to little impairment) to 2 (indicates severe impairment). Once the interview is complete, the evaluator must make a decision regarding overall fitness. The final decision involves three stages: (1) determining the existence of a mental disorder, (2) determining the defendant's capacity regarding each of the three psychological abilities stated above, and (3) examining the previous information. Although performance on the items contained in each section is considered in determining the section rating, decisions are not made based on a specific cut-off score. Instead, these section ratings constitute a separate judgment based on the severity of impairment and its perceived importance. See Box 9.1 for a look at some other fitness instruments.

BOX 9.1 FITNESS INSTRUMENTS

COMPETENCY SCREENING TEST (CST)

The CST (Lipsitt, Lelos, & McGarry, 1971) has 22 uncompleted sentences that the respondent must finish. For example:

- The lawyer told Bill that ...
- When I go to court the lawyer will ...
- Jack felt that the judge ...

The items measure three constructs: the potential for a constructive relationship between the defendant and his lawyer, the defendant's understanding of the court process, and the ability of the defendant to emotionally cope with the criminal process. Responses are scored using a three-point scale (0, 1, 2) depending on the relation between the defendant's response and example responses provided in the scoring manual. A score of 0 would be assigned if the response demonstrated a low level of legal understanding. For example, "The lawyer told Bill that he is guilty" would receive 0 points (Ackerman, 1999). A score of 2 would be assigned if the response demonstrated a high level of legal understanding. For example, "The lawyer told Bill that he should plead guilty" would receive 2 points (Ackerman, 1999). Scores for each of the items are summed to produce a total CST score. The CST score, in addition to a brief psychiatric interview, is aimed at distinguishing between competent defendants who could proceed to trial and those defendants who should undergo a more complete competency assessment. A score of 20 or below suggests that the

defendant should undergo a more comprehensive evaluation.

COMPETENCY TO STAND TRIAL ASSESSMENT INSTRUMENT (CAI)

The CAI (Laboratory of Community Psychiatry, Harvard Medical School, 1973) was designed to accompany the CST in that the CAI is a semi-structured interview and constitutes a comprehensive competency evaluation. The CAI assesses 13 functions corresponding to a defendant's ability to participate in the criminal process on behalf of his or her best interests. Each function is represented in a statement with two or three sample questions that the evaluator may pose to the defendant. For example (Ackerman, 1999):

Function: Appraisal of available legal defences

Statement: The defendant's awareness of possible legal defences and how consistent they are with the reality of his or her particular circumstances

Question: How do you think you can be defended against these charges?

Following a response, the evaluator can ask follow-up questions to further probe the defendant's response if it is unclear or ambiguous. For each function, responses are rated on a scale from 1 (reflecting a total lack of capacity for function) to 5 (reflecting no impairment, defendant can function adequately). A score of 6 can be given when there is insufficient information to rate the function. The evaluator examines the scores for each function and then makes an overall determination.

INTERDISCIPLINARY FITNESS INTERVIEW (IFI)

The IFI (Golding, Roesch, & Schreiber, 1984) was developed following an analysis of the CAI. As with the CAI, the IFI is a semi-structured interview measuring three areas of competency: functional memory, appropriate relationship with lawyer, and understanding of the justice system. There are four main sections to the IFI:

Section A: Legal items

Section B: Psychopathological items

Section C: Overall evaluation

Section D: Consensual judgment

Each section has a number of subsections and areas within each subsection that can be assessed. The revision of the IFI (IFI-R; Golding, 1993) retains the semi-structured interview protocol; however, there are only two sections: Current Clinical Condition and Psycho-Legal Abilities. Each section has a number of subsections. For example, under the heading current clinical condition are the following categories:

- Attention/consciousness
- Delusions
- Hallucinations
- Impaired reasoning and judgment
- Impaired memory
- Mood and affect

The evaluator assesses these major areas of clinical dysfunction. Responses are rated with a scale ranging from 0 (absent or does not bear on defendant's fitness) to 2 (symptom is likely to significantly impair the defendant's fitness).

Under the Psycho-Legal Abilities section there are four subsections:

- Capacity to appreciate charges and to disclose pertinent facts, events, and motives
- Courtroom demeanour and capacity to understand the adversarial nature of proceedings
- Quality of relationship with attorney
- Appreciation of and reasoned choice with respect to legal option and consequences

Responses are rated on a scale ranging from 0 (no or minimal capacity) to 2 (substantial capacity). It also has been recommended that when conducting a competency assessment, the defendant's lawyer, previous mental health contacts, and jail personnel be interviewed. In addition, mental health reports, police reports, and prior arrest history should be reviewed (Golding, as cited in Ackerman, 1999).

MACARTHUR COMPETENCE ASSESSMENT TOOL—CRIMINAL ADJUDICATION (MACCAT-CA)

The MacCAT-CA (Hoge, Bonnie, Poythress, & Monahan, 1992) is a structured interview containing 22 items that assess competencies in three areas:

- Factual understanding of the legal system and the adjudication process
- Reasoning ability
- Understanding of own legal situation and circumstances

These areas are assessed via hypothetical scenarios. Following the presentation of the scenario, the defendant is asked a series of specific questions. The evaluator assigns a score of 0, 1, or 2 based on the scoring criteria. For each area, score ranges are provided for three levels of impairment: none to minimal, mild, or clinically significant.

Distinguishing between Fit and Unfit Defendants

Zapf and Roesch (1998) examined the demographic, mental health, and criminal characteristics that differentiate fit from unfit defendants using a sample of 180 males undergoing evaluation in a facility in British Columbia. Using the fit/unfit decision offered to the court by the psychiatrist, the data were divided into these two categories and then compared across criteria.

In examining the demographic variables, only marital status was significant. Collapsing across marital categories to identify those who were never married versus those who were married at some time, fit defendants were significantly more likely to have been married (married, divorced, separated, common law) than were unfit defendants. Previous studies have found defendants who are referred for fitness evaluations to be primarily single, unemployed, and living alone (Roesch et al., 1981; Webster et al., 1982). In a meta-analysis of 30 studies conducted in both Canada and the United States, Nicholson and Kugler (1991) found that fit and unfit defendants differed on age, gender, race, and marital resources. Unfit defendants were more likely to be older females belonging to a minority group and to have fewer marital resources. See Table 9.2 for a distribution of the demographic variables as a function of fitness categorization for the Zapf and Roesch (1998) study.

Zapf and Roesch (1998) also found that defendants who were unfit were four times more likely to have met criteria for a psychotic disorder, whereas defendants who were fit were about as likely to have been diagnosed with a psychotic disorder as not. It is important to note that not all psychotic defendants are unfit, and the presence of psychosis is not sufficient or equivalent to unfitness (Golding, Roesch, & Schreiber, 1984). Substance abuse disorders were significantly less likely to be found in unfit defendants than in the fit defendants.

In examining criminological variables, Zapf and Roesch (1998) found that there were no significant differences between fit and unfit defendants. The two groups were similar in the frequency with which they had committed violent, property, and miscellaneous crimes. Moreover, both groups had a similar criminal history and were just as likely to have previously been in prison.

As you can see, Dr. Ron Roesch has worked extensively in the area of fitness to stand trial. To learn more about Dr. Roesch and his research, see Box 9.2 on page 270.

How Is Fitness Restored?

When a defendant is found unfit to stand trial, the goal of the criminal justice system is to get the defendant fit. The most common form of treatment for fitness is medication. A question facing the justice system concerning this form of treatment is whether a defendant has the right to refuse medication. Under the Health Care Consent Act and the Mental Health Act, an individual can refuse medication; however, if that person is incapable of making decisions concerning his or her medical treatment, a decision may be imposed by the law (R.S.O., 1996, s. 25). The courts will take into account

TABLE 9.2 DEMOGRAPHIC VARIABLES AS A FUNCTION OF FITNESS DECISION

Demographic Variable	Found Fit	Fount Unfit
Age (average)	35.2 years	35.1 years
Marital status		
Single	57.6% (91)*	85.0% (17)
Married	12.7% (20)	10.0% (2)
Divorced	13.9% (22)	5.0% (1)
Separated	10.1% (16)	0.0% (0)
Common-law	5.7% (9)	0.0% (0)
Ethnic group		
White	69.6% (110)	63.1% (12)
Aboriginal	10.8% (17)	5.3% (1)
Asian	2.5% (4)	10.5% (2)
Other	17.1% (27)	21.1% (4)
Education		
Elementary	8.9% (14)	10.0% (2)
Junior high (Grades 8–10)	31.0% (49)	20.0% (4)
Senior high (Grades 11–12)	32.9% (52)	40.0% (8)
Postsecondary	9.5% (15)	15.0% (3)
University	13.9% (22)	5.0% (1)
Unknown	3.8% (6)	10.0% (2)
Employment (at admission)		
Full-time	8.9% (14)	5.0% (1)
Part-time/occasional	5.7% (9)	0.0% (0)
Unemployed	70.9% (112)	75.0% (15)
Retired or other	14.6% (23)	20.0% (4)
Living status		
Alone	45.9% (72)	52.6% (10)
With family	33.1% (52)	21.1% (4)
Other	21.0% (33)	26.3% (5)
Dwelling (prior to admission)		
House or apartment	74.7% (118)	73.3% (14)
Hotel	7.6% (12)	0.0% (0)
No fixed address	10.7% (17)	10.5% (2)
Other	7.0% (11)	15.8% (3)

Source: Zapf and Roesch, 1998.

*The percentage refers to the proportion of the group in the particular category. The number in parentheses represents the number of participants.

BOX 9.2 CANADIAN RESEARCHER PROFILE: DR. RON ROESCH

Early in Dr. Ron Roesch's career, his research on fitness to stand trial won awards and gained substantial recognition. His Ph.D. dissertation on fitness was awarded the best psychological dissertation concerned with social issues by the Society for the Psychological Studies of Social Issues. It also won the Consulting Psychology Research Award for being the most fruitful research of the year related to consultation. Dr. Roesch used his dissertation research to produce a book with Dr. Stephen Golding called *Competency to Stand Trial* in 1980. This book won a merit award in the American Bar Association Gavel Awards Competition.

Dr. Roesch followed his graduate studies from the University of Illinois with a faculty position at Simon Fraser University, where he is now the director of the Mental Health, Law, and Policy Institute.

Dr. Roesch remains interested in research focusing on fitness issues for both adult and juvenile offenders. His current focus is on competency to waive arrest rights, such as the right to a lawyer. This research considers developmental differences in a juvenile offender's capacity to understand rights as well as make decisions about the conduct of his or her defence. Dr. Roesch also has stated that he is interested in pursuing research focused on interventions to be used with youth: "So much of my research has focused on assessment that I would like to shift to examining the effectiveness of interventions with high-risk juveniles." Dr. Roesch finds that the changing nature of the law makes researching psycholegal issues an exciting endeavour.

Dr. Roesch would like to see changes in legislation concerning expert testimony. He noted that it is ironic that even though he developed the Fitness Interview Test, as a clinical psychologist he is not allowed to use it according to Canadian legislation (only medical physicians can provide court-ordered fitness assessments). Dr. Roesch would like to see the Canadian government provide psychologists with equal status as medical practitioners with respect to assessment and expert testimony.

Dr. Roesch is excited about training future forensic psychologists. He remains dedicated to teaching and graduate training. Dr. Roesch teaches a psychology and law foundation course for graduate students that provides a broad overview of the field. Preparing for this course helps to keep him well informed of the latest developments in the field and provides an excellent foundation for students in this area of research.

In his spare time Dr. Roesch and his wife, Kim, enjoy travelling. He has formed many partnerships and collaborations for research with colleagues throughout the world and makes efforts to meet with them on a regular basis. Dr. Roesch and his wife also enjoy running. They maintain a regular running schedule to keep fit for 10 km races that they enter often.

the individual's capacity to comprehend and appreciate the consequences of his or her actions and public safety. Defendants sometimes may argue for not taking medication because of the serious side effects. A treatment order may be imposed by the court (R.S.C., 1985, C-46, s. 672.58); however, the courts also must grapple with having a heavily medicated defendant and whether this serves justice. See Box 9.3 for a look at a case involving a defendant with a mental illness, who fought against medication.

What Happens after a Finding of Unfitness?

The proceedings against a defendant who is found unfit to stand trial are halted until competency is restored. In the United States, almost all jurisdictions limit the time a

---

BOX 9.3 MENTALLY ILL BUT COMPETENT TO MAKE TREATMENT DECISIONS?

Scott Starson (also known as Scott Jeffery Schutzman) has a special skill in physics. Without having formal training, he works with the top physics researchers in the world. In 1991, he co-authored an article with a physics professor from Stanford University. In addition to his physics ability, Starson also has a long history of battling a mental disorder. He has been diagnosed as having bipolar affective disorder. Starson has been admitted to several mental health facilities over the years.

In 1998, Starson was charged with uttering two death threats to tenants in his apartment complex. He was found not criminally responsible on account of mental disorder. In January 1999, the Ontario Review Board ordered that he be detained at the Centre for Addiction and Mental Health (CAMH) in Toronto. Dr. Ian Swayze and Dr. Paul Posner, both psychiatrists at CAMH, proposed to treat Starson with mood stabilizers, anti-psychotic, anti-anxiety, and anti-parkinsonian medication. Starson refused pharmaceutical intervention and appealed the Ontario Review Board's decision in provincial court. He argued that "he would not be able to do his work while on the proposed medication,

not because of the side effects, but because of the very effects that the drugs are intended to achieve.... Starson said that after periods of treatment with such medications, it would always take him some time to 'work his way up the academic ladder'" (*Starson v. Swayze*, 1999, para 55.).

In November 1999, the Ontario Superior Court of Justice overturned the Ontario Review Board's decision stating it was unreasonable. Justice Molloy stated that the Board's conclusion that Starson was in denial of his mental illness was an error and that it was wrong for the Board to accept unsubstantiated claims that Starson suffered delusions that others were out to harm him. Starson's doctors appealed the decision to the Ontario Court of Appeal. The Appeal Court ruled that Starson was capable of making treatment decisions and could appreciate the possible consequences of refusing treatment. The doctors appealed to the Supreme Court of Canada. In June 2003, the Supreme Court upheld the lower court's decision that Starson had the capacity to refuse medical treatment.

Sources: Starson v. Swayze, 1999; Starson v. Swayze, 2003.

defendant may be "held" as unfit. In the landmark case of *Jackson v. Indiana* (1972), the United States Supreme Court stated that a defendant should not be held for more than a reasonable period of time to determine whether there is a likelihood of the person gaining competency fitness. Of course, what constitutes a reasonable period of time is open to interpretation.

For unfit defendants in Canada, the judge may order that the defendant be detained in a hospital or that the defendant be conditionally discharged. The defendant is reassessed for fitness within 45 days. In the event that the defendant becomes fit, he or she returns to court and the proceedings resume (R.S.C., 1985, C-46, s. 672.28). If the defendant remains unfit after 90 days, he or she is referred to a review board for assessment and disposition (R.S.C., 1985, C-46, s. 672.47). Cases of defendants who continue to be unfit are reviewed on an annual basis by the review board. In these cases, the Crown must prove that there is sufficient evidence to bring the case to trial (referred to a making a **prima facie case**) every two years and at anytime the defendant requests the proceeding. If the Court determines that sufficient evidence is no longer available to prosecute the case, the case is dropped and the defendant is found not guilty (R.S.C., 1985, C-46, s. 672.33).

Even though a defendant may be restored to fitness, it is possible that he or she will become unfit once again during the trial proceedings. If unfitness occurs again, the proceedings stop until the defendant becomes fit. If a defendant becomes fit while in custody (e.g., detained in a mental facility) and there is reason to believe that he or she may become unfit if released, the defendant will be required to remain in the mental facility until the trial is complete (R.S.C., 1985, C-46, s. 672.29).

If a defendant is deemed unlikely to become fit (e.g., possibly due to permanent brain damage), then a civil commitment (e.g., hospitalization, institutionalization in a mental facility) proceeding can be started. A defendant may be committed indefinitely or may be discharged. See Figure 9.1 for key processes in cases involving fitness.

MENTAL STATE AT TIME OF OFFENCE

Insanity has been defined as not being of sound mind, and being mentally deranged and irrational (Sykes, 1982). In a legal context, insanity removes the responsibility of performing a particular act because of uncontrollable impulses or delusions, such as hearing voices. There have been two primary British cases that have shaped the current standard of insanity in Canada (as cited in Moran, 1985). The first was that of James Hadfield who in 1800 attempted to assassinate King George III. Hadfield had suffered a brain injury while fighting against the French. His lawyer successfully argued that he was out of touch with reality and therefore met the insanity standard of the time. Following this case, the Criminal Lunatics Act (1800) was established, and it stated the insanity standard of the day.

The second case influencing Canada's current insanity standard was that of Daniel M'Naughten in 1843 (*R. v. M'Naughten*, 1843). M'Naughten felt that the Tory political party was out to persecute him. He claimed that they followed him everywhere. He

FIGURE 9.1
KEY PROCESSES IN CASES INVOLVING FITNESS

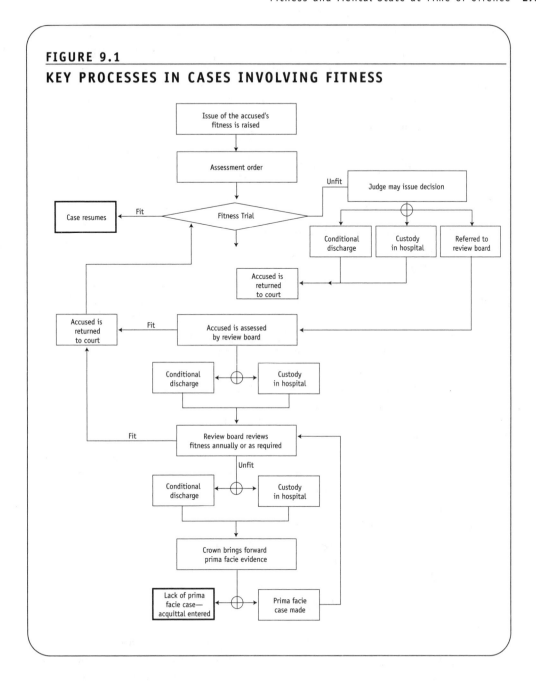

felt that he could not sleep nor get any rest from them. M'Naughten wanted to put an end to this and decided to murder the Tory leader, Prime Minister Robert Peel. M'Naughten charted Peel's travel when the prime minister was going on a speaking engagement. M'Naughten shot into the carriage he believed was transporting

Peel. M'Naughten's shot hit Edward Drummond, Peel's secretary, and killed him. When M'Naughten attempted to shoot again, he was arrested and charged with murder. M'Naughten was found not guilty because of his mental status, insanity. He would serve out his life in a mental institute.

There were three critical elements that emerged from the M'Naughten verdict:

1. A defendant must be found to be suffering from a defect of reason/disease of the mind.

2. A defendant must not know the nature and quality of the act he or she is performing.

3. A defendant must not know that what he or she is doing is wrong.

The elements in the M'Naughten standard emerged in legislation in parts of the United States, England, and Canada. Little would change for the insanity standard in Canada for many years.

In the mid-1970s, a review of the policies for offenders with mental disorders was undertaken by the Law Reform Commission of Canada. Forty-four recommendations on law and policy were provided (Law Reform Commission of Canada, 1976). In response to this review, the Department of Justice commissioned the Mental Disorder Project in the early 1980s. This review found that the mental disorder legislation in the Criminal Code was in conflict with the Charter of Rights and Freedoms. The ruling from the Supreme Court of Canada in *R. v. Swain* (1991) was consistent with the review and foreshadowed the changes to the Criminal Code. For example, in *R. v. Swain* (1991), the Supreme Court ruled that "the automatic detention of defendants found not guilty by reason of insanity without any hearing to determine the level of dangerousness or the appropriate disposition was in conflict with the Charter." The Court also stated that "the Crown could not raise the issue of the defendant's mental capacity before the Crown proved that the crime had been committed or until the accused put their mental capacity into issue. The accused however had the right to raise the issue at any point during the trial."

In 1992, Bill C-30 was enacted and the following changes were made to the justice system:

- The term "not guilty by reason of insanity" was changed to "not criminally responsible on account of mental disorder" (NCRMD).

- The wording of the standard was altered and stated in section 16 of the Canadian Criminal Code: "No person is criminally responsible for an act committed or an omission made while suffering from a mental disorder that rendered the person incapable of appreciating the nature and quality of the act or omission or of knowing that it was wrong."

- **Review boards** were created. These were legal bodies mandated to oversee the care and disposition of defendants found unfit and/or not criminally responsible on account of a mental disorder. Review boards were required to review each unfit and NCRMD case every year.

Another change occurred in 1999. In *Winko v. British Columbia*, the Supreme Court of Canada stated that a defendant who is NCRMD should only be detained if he or she poses a criminal threat to the public; otherwise, the defendant should receive an absolute discharge. Another review on justice and human rights was undertaken in 2002 concerning mental disorder provisions in the Criminal Code. A second review for 2007 has been recommended, and it will allow data to be collected on the issues that have emerged. See Box 9.4 for a description of a case in which the defendant was found NCRMD.

BOX 9.4 SPORTSCASTER SHOT DEAD BY PATIENT WITH A MENTAL ILLNESS

Brian Smith, a former hockey player, was a sportscaster for CJOH, an Ottawa television station. On August 1, 1995, after the evening newscast, Smith left the station and walked out to the parking lot, where he was shot in the head. A day later, Smith died in the hospital. In the reports of Smith's death, many questioned the reason for his murder. Why would someone kill him? Jeffrey Arenburg, the confessed killer, said that he was angry with the media and wanted to harm a media personality. Arenburg said he went to the CJOH parking lot and shot the first media personality he recognized, Brian Smith.

Before Arenburg was tried for Smith's murder, he was assessed for fitness to stand trial. The jury found Arenburg fit and he was charged with first-degree murder. The defence raised the issue of Arenburg's sanity and argued for an NCRMD verdict. Indeed, in May 1997 Arenburg was found NCRMD for first-degree murder. He was sent to a maximum-security psychiatric facility, the Ontario Mental Health Centre in Penetanguishene, for an indefinite period of time. Less than ten years following the shooting, Arenburg wanted to be released. He had a mandatory review before the Ontario Review Board in May 2004, at which time his lawyer argued for a conditional discharge. Arenburg was granted a conditional discharge and must live with his brother in Barrie. It should be noted that

since fall 2003, Arenburg has freely attended classes at Georgian College during the day and lived with his brother in the evening.

This case drew a great deal of attention to current legislation regarding the Mental Health Act. Arenburg had a history of mental illness. For example, in 1990, he went to a Nova Scotia courthouse demanding to be seen by a judge. When taken to the local hospital he said that he heard his thoughts being broadcast by television and radio. He was diagnosed with paranoid psychosis and released. In 1991, he was brought to the Royal Ottawa Hospital because he had threatened a radio station. Once again, Arenburg stated that he was hearing voices. Arenburg was committed to the hospital. However, he appealed his commitment to the psychiatric review board. The board did not find Arenburg mentally ill or at risk to hurt others. However, it did find that Arenburg was not competent to refuse treatment. Arenburg discharged himself against doctor's advice. Arenburg was able to refuse treatment for two years following Smith's shooting. In response to an inquest into Smith's death, it was recommended that there should be more public protection against people with mental illnesses. Both the Mental Health Act and the Health Care Consent Act in Ontario were reviewed, and in 2000, Bill 68, also known as Brian's Law, was passed.

Brian's Law led to the implementation of community treatment orders, which are requirements for people with mental illnesses who are living in the community to report to a mental health caregiver on a regular basis. Also, as a condition of being released from a mental health facility to the community, those who have a mental illness may be forced to take prescribed medication. If they refuse medication, they can be re-institu- tionalized. Also under the new legislation, the word "imminent" was removed from the Mental Health Act. This change means that there no longer must be an immediate danger for someone to be confined to a psychiatric facility (R.S.O., 1990, s. 33.1). Other provinces, including British Columbia, Manitoba, and Saskatchewan, have similar legislation.

Source: Campbell, 2004.

Raising the Issue of Insanity

Studies find that few defendants use the insanity defence. For example, in the United States, one study found that fewer than 1% of all felony cases will argue an insanity defence (Steadman et al., 1993). Moreover, the success rate of such a defence is variable. It has been reported that approximately 25% of defendants who argue an insanity defence succeed (Steadman et al., 1993). See Table 9.3 for a distribution of NCRMD cases in Canada.

Insanity defences typically occur when opposing sides (prosecution and defence) agree to such a verdict (Melton et al., 1997). It is not common to have opposing experts testify on this issue in jury trials. Ogloff, Schweighofer, Turnbull, and Whittemore (1992) reported that defendants found NCRMD are likely to have major psychiatric disorders, such as schizophrenia, and many past mental health problems that resulted in hospitalization or prior rulings of unfitness.

Within the Canadian criminal justice system, a defendant is considered not to suffer from a mental disorder. Of course, the defendant may raise the issue of insanity for his or her defence. In Canada, there are only two situations in which the Crown may raise the issue of insanity:

1. Following a guilty verdict, the Crown could argue that the defendant was NCRMD. This situation may occur if the Crown believes that the defendant requires psychiatric treatment and a mental facility is best suited for the defendant's needs.

2. If the defence states that the defendant has a mental illness, the Crown can then argue it.

The party that raises the issue must prove it beyond a balance of the probabilities (R.S.C., 1985, c. C-46, s. 16).

Assessing Insanity

Just as with fitness to stand trial, an insanity defence requires a psychiatric assessment. Richard Rogers developed the first standardized assessment scales for criminal responsibility, the Rogers Criminal Responsibility Assessment Scales (R-CRAS; Rogers, 1984).

TABLE 9.3 NCRMD CASES HEARD BY REVIEW BOARDS ACROSS CANADA

Jurisdiction	2000	2001*
Newfoundland and Labrador	7	3
Prince Edward Island	0	0
Nova Scotia	22	36
New Brunswick	11	24
Quebec	319	362
Ontario	126	132
Manitoba	8	—
Saskatchewan	2	2
Alberta	17	20
British Columbia	72	—
Yukon	0	2
Northwest Territories	0	0
Nunavut	1	0
TOTAL	585	581

Source: Justice Canada, 2002.
* Preliminary figure.

The R-CRAS is the only instrument of its kind. It has five scales:

- patient reliability
- organicity
- psychopathology
- cognitive control
- behavioural control

Each scale has 30 items, which are given a score from 0 to 6, with higher values representing greater severity (Rogers & Sewell, 1999). It is important to note that the R-CRAS was developed to standardize evaluations and ensure particular areas are evaluated, rather than produce a cut-off score to indicate criminal responsibility (Rogers & Ewing, 1992). The clinician is to take all the information into account and use it as the basis for a decision regarding the defendant's mental status and criminal responsibility.

What Happens to a Defendant Found NCRMD?

There are three dispositions that can be made following a finding of NCRMD. If the defendant is not a threat to society or poses low risk for reoffending, the court or review board can order an **absolute discharge.** That is, the defendant is released into the community without restrictions on his or her behaviour. A second disposition option is to order a discharge with conditions, known as a **conditional discharge.** In this case, the defendant is released but must meet certain conditions, such as not possessing firearms. Failure to meet the conditions imposed with a conditional discharge may result in the defendant being incarcerated or sent to a psychiatric facility. Lastly, the court or review board may order that the defendant be sent to a psychiatric facility (R.S.C., 1985, C-46, s. 672.54).

It is important to note that a defendant who is sent to a psychiatric facility need not comply with treatment. It is only when the defendant's mental health has deteriorated to a point that he or she is no longer competent to make treatment decisions that steps may be taken to force treatment on the defendant (R.S.C., 1985, C-46, s. 672.54). In such instances, the provincial and territorial mental health policies would be followed.

In Canada, dispositions may be made by the court or referred to a provincial or territorial review board. Dispositions that are made by the court also are reviewed by a review board within 90 days and can be changed at any point. An exception to this rule occurs if the court makes an absolute discharge (R.S.C., 1985, C-46, s. 672.81). This decision does not go before a review board. In addition, review boards review the defendant's disposition every year. There is a great deal of information that review boards will take into account, including

- charge information
- trial transcript
- criminal history
- risk assessment
- clinical history, such as previous admissions to hospital
- psychological testing
- hospital's recommendation

As you read earlier, historically, defendants who were found insane would spend the remainder of their lives in an insane asylum. More recently, it was not uncommon for "insane" defendants to be given indeterminate sentences, only to be released when they were deemed sane. Moreover, insane defendants often would serve more time in a mental institute than their prison sentence would have been following a standard guilty verdict. Bill C-30 introduced **capping,** which refers to the maximum period of time a person with a mental illness can be affected by their disposition. For example, the disposition period for a defendant with a mental illness who committed a violent offence is ten years, the same length of time as the prison term.

When deciding on a disposition, the court and review board must choose the option that is least limiting to the defendant. There are four main criteria that are considered when deciding a disposition:

- public safety
- mental state of the defendant
- reintegration of the defendant into society
- other needs of the defendant

See Figure 9.2 for key process in cases involving NCRMD defences.

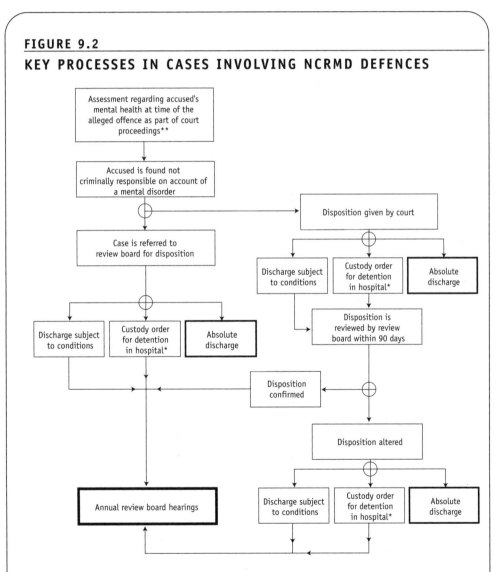

FIGURE 9.2
KEY PROCESSES IN CASES INVOLVING NCRMD DEFENCES

*Although both the court and review board have the authority to detain a person found NCRMD in hospital, the accused may refuse treatment while detained.
**In accordance with the decision of the Supreme Court of Canada in R. v. Swain in 1991, the Crown may not raise the issue of the accused's mental state before the Crown proved that the crime had been committed or where the accused had put their mental capacity into issue.

AUTOMATISM

If you don't have control over your behaviour, should you be held responsible for your actions? Consider the case of Kenneth Parks (*R. v. Parks*, 1992). He got up in the middle of the night, got dressed, got into his car, and drove to where his parents-in-law lived. He went into their home, got a kitchen knife, stabbed his mother-in-law to death and almost killed his father-in-law. He then drove to the police station and turned himself in. He was charged and tried for murder and attempted murder. Parks's defence was that he was sleepwalking, a form of automatism. **Automatism** refers to unconscious, involuntary behaviour; that is, the person committing the act is not aware of what he or she is doing. Parks was acquitted on both charges.

The Canadian Criminal Code does not specifically address automatism as a defence; rather, judges have had to rely on their own judgment and case law when such defences are raised. Recently in *R. v. Stone* (1999; see Box 9.5), the Supreme Court of Canada stated that there were two forms of automatism, noninsane and insane. Noninsane automatism refers to involuntary behaviour that occurs because of an external factor. The verdict in such cases is "not guilty." Insane automatism refers to an involuntary action that occurs because of a mental disorder. In these cases, a finding of NCRMD would be entered and the legislation for NCRMD would be applied.

In *R. v. Stone* (1999) the Supreme Court outlined a two-stage process for addressing defences of automatism. First, the trial judge must decide whether there is sufficient evidence that a jury could find that the defendant's behaviour was involuntary. The following factors are considered:

- psychiatric assessments
- severity of triggering event
- history of automatic behaviour

BOX 9.5 CAN INSULTS LEAD TO AUTOMATISM?

There was no question that Bert Stone stabbed his wife 47 times (*R. v. Stone*, 1999). He was holding a hunting knife and his wife was dead in her seat. His defence was that his behaviour was not under his control. Stone argued that he was in an automatistic state that was triggered by his wife's insults when he stabbed her. After Stone stabbed his wife, he got rid of the body, cleaned up, left a note for his step-daughter, and then checked into a hotel. Later, he sold his car and flew to Mexico. It was here that he woke up one morning to a feeling of having his throat cut. While trying to remember this bad dream, he remembered stabbing his wife two times. After about six weeks, Stone returned to Canada and gave himself up to police. He was charged with murder. Stone was found guilty and sentenced to seven years in prison.

Second, the trial judge determines if the condition is a mental disorder (insane) or non-mental-disorder (sane) automatism.

If the judge decides that the condition is the result of an external factor, the defence can argue noninsane automatism. The judge and/or jury will need to decide whether the defendant acted involuntarily. If so, the defendant will be found not guilty. If the judge decides that the condition is the result of a mental disorder, the defence can argue insane automatism, and the case proceeds as an NCRMD case. The NCRMD standard as outlined in section 16 of the Canadian Criminal Code must be met. A successful defence in this situation would result in an NCRMD verdict.

Canadian courts have recognized defences of noninsane automatism in the following circumstances:

- a physical blow
- physical ailments such as stroke
- hypoglycemia
- carbon monoxide poisoning
- sleepwalking
- involuntary intoxication
- psychological blow from an extraordinary external event that might reasonably be expected to cause a dissociative state in an average, normal person

It is important to note that everyday life stresses that may lead to a dissociative state would not be sufficient for a defence of automatism. Dissociative states from psychological factors, such as grief and mourning or anxiety, are more consistent with diseases of the mind and may be applicable for the insanity defence.

How Do NCRMD and Automatism Differ?

The main difference between defences of NCRMD and automatism lie in their verdict outcomes. An NCRMD verdict may result in the defendant being sent to a mental health facility. In contrast, a successful (noninsane) automatism verdict means that the defendant is not guilty and is then released without conditions. Insane automatism verdicts result in an NCRMD ruling. The defendants in these cases are subject to the same dispositions as those with a successful NCRMD defence.

Intoxication as a Defence

One evening, Mr. Daviault brought a 40-ounce bottle of brandy over to Ms. X's home at her request (*R. v. Daviault*, 1994). Ms. X was 65 years old and partially paralyzed. She was confined to a wheelchair. Ms. X had a half glass of brandy and fell asleep in her wheelchair. During the middle of the night, she awoke to go to the bathroom, at which point Mr. Daviault sexually assaulted her and left the apartment. Ms. X noticed that the bottle of brandy was empty. Mr. Daviault had drunk the remainder of the bottle; he was an alcoholic. During the trial proceedings, Mr. Daviault stated that he had had seven or eight bottles of beer earlier that day. Although he remembered having a glass of brandy when he arrived at Ms. X's, he did not remember what happened afterward and that he awoke nude in Ms. X's bed. He denied sexually assaulting her.

A pharmacologist testified for the defence and stated that "an individual with this level of alcohol in his blood might suffer an episode of 'L'amnesie-automatisme,' also known as a blackout. In such a state the individual loses contact with reality and the brain is temporarily dissociated from normal functioning. The individual has no awareness of his actions when he is in such a state and will likely have no memory of them the next day" (*R. v. Daviault*, 1994, para. 73).

The judge found that the defendant committed the offence but, because of the level of intoxication, found that he did not have the intent to commit the act. Mr. Daviault was found not guilty. On appeal, the court reversed the judge's decision, entering a guilty verdict for Mr. Daviault. The Appeal Court stated that self-induced intoxication resulting in a state similar to automatism is not available as a defence for a general intent offence, that is, an offence that only requires an intention to commit the act. Moreover, in 1995 Bill-C-72 was passed, and it stated that intoxication was not recognized as a defence for violent crimes.

As you can see, automatism is not a straightforward defence. It is a challenge to prove and may result in variable verdicts. Until legislation can clarify this defence, there will remain ambiguity in the use and success of this defence.

DEFENDANTS WITH MENTAL DISORDERS

If a defendant does not receive an unfit finding or an NCRMD verdict, it does not necessarily mean that he or she does not have mental health difficulties. In a Canadian study examining males from the Edmonton Remand Centre, Bland et al. (1990) found that 92% of the sample had a lifetime prevalence of psychiatric disorders (see Table 9.4).

TABLE 9.4 PREVALENCE RATES OF PSYCHIATRIC DISORDERS IN AN EDMONTON SAMPLE OF DEFENDANTS

Type of Mental Disorder	Rate
Substance abuse	87%
Antisocial personality disorder	57%
Affective disorder	23%
Anxiety/somatoform disorders	16%
Schizophrenia	2%

Source: Bland et al., 1990.

Why Are There Such High Rates of Mental Illness in Offender Populations?

A variety of explanations have been postulated to understand the high rates of mental illness in offender populations in Canada (Bland et al., 1990):

1. Individuals with a mental illness are likely to be arrested at a disproportionately high rate compared with those who do not have a mental illness.

2. Individuals with a mental illness are less adept at committing crime and therefore more likely to get caught.

3. Individuals with a mental illness are more likely to plead guilty, possibly because of an inability to access good representation or to understand the consequences of their plea.

It is possible that all these explanations are appropriate. Moreover, there may be alternative explanations to the high rates of mental illness in offender populations that have yet to be articulated. Further research is needed to explain this phenomenon.

Dealing with Offenders Who Are Mentally Ill

Police have great latitude in how they deal with offenders who are mentally ill in the community. Provincial and territorial mental health legislation grants police two options for handling these offenders. If an individual has a mental disorder and poses a threat to him- or herself or to others, the police may bring the individual to a hospital or mental health facility for assessment and possible treatment. As an alternative, the police may charge and arrest the individual. In this scenario, mental health services may be obtained through the criminal justice system. Thus, the mental health system and the criminal justice system are both available to police, providing two alternative routes for dealing with people with a mental illness. Some have argued that people with a mental illness are more likely to be processed through the justice system because of the difficulty of obtaining services for them through the mental health system (Teplin, 1984).

Bias against Mentally Ill Offenders

As part of a Canadian national study examining mental health problems in federally incarcerated offenders, Porporino and Motiuk (1995) compared 36 male offenders meeting criteria for a mental disorder (e.g., mania or schizophrenia) with 36 male offenders not meeting this criteria. The two groups were similar on a number of variables including age, type of crime committed, and history of criminal activity. The researchers were interested in the conditional release patterns for both groups. Specifically, they wanted to know whether offenders with a mental illness were treated differently.

There are two ways in which offenders can receive a conditional release from a federal facility in Canada; parole or mandatory supervision. Parole is determined by a parole board and is dependent on eligibility criteria. Ultimately, the National Parole Board has discretionary power in whether parole is granted. In contrast, mandatory supervision occurs after serving two-thirds of a sentence.

Porporino and Mortiuk found that a similar proportion of offenders from both groups (67% of those with a mental disorder versus 75% of those without one) received conditional releases. However, the reason for granting a conditional release differed across the two groups. Offenders with mental disorders were more likely to be conditionally released as a result of mandatory supervision, whereas offenders who did not have a mental disorder were more likely to be conditionally released because of parole.

Moreover, the researchers found that the offenders with mental disorders were more likely to have their release suspended (e.g., for not abiding by their supervision order) compared with other offenders. The offenders without mental disorders were likely to be re-admitted for committing a new offence. Thus, offenders with mental disorders may be treated cautiously by the criminal justice system because of a presumption that they are a greater risk for committing more crime. Is this presumption correct?

In a six-year follow-up study, Teplin, Abram, and McClelland (1994) examined the relationship between post-release arrest rate for violent crime and mental disorders. Offenders with either schizophrenia or a major affective disorder had a 43% likelihood of re-arrest. Those with substance abuse had a similar re-arrest rate of 46%. Moreover, offenders with a prior history of violent crime were twice as likely to be re-arrested as those with no prior history. Offenders with a history of hallucinations and delusions (i.e., schizophrenia symptoms) were not more likely to be subsequently arrested. As you can see, a number of factors can be related to rates of re-arrest, not just mental illness.

Are People with Mental Illnesses Violent?

A commonly held belief is that those who have a mental illness are violent predators. Does the research support this view? Two epidemiological surveys were conducted to examine the relationship between violence and mental disorders. In a Canadian study conducted in Edmonton, violence referred to physical acts such as fist fighting and using weapons (Bland & Orn, 1986). Mental disorders included anti-social personality disorder, major depression, and alcohol/drug dependence. Approximately 55% of respondents who met criteria for a psychiatric diagnosis committed violent acts. In contrast, only about 16% of respondents who did not meet criteria for a psychiatric diagnosis engaged in violent behaviour. When respondents met criteria for two diagnoses, for example, alcoholism and antisocial personality disorder and/or depression, 80% to 93% of these respondents committed violent acts. Similar results were found in a sample from the United States (Swanson et al., 1990). Over 50% of the American respondents who met criteria for a psychiatric disorder committed violent acts. In both studies substance abuse increased the risk of engaging in violence.

Examining a European sample, Hodgins (1992, 1993) reviewed the criminal and mental health records of approximately 15 000 30-year-olds born in Stockholm,

Sweden, in 1953. Persons who had been admitted to mental health facilities were classified according to their most serious diagnosis. For example, participants were grouped according to whether they had a major mental disorder such as schizophrenia, alcohol and/or drug abuse or dependency, or another mental disorder. Hodgins found that individuals with a major mental disorder, especially those individuals with substance abuse or dependency, were significantly more likely to have committed a crime than those without a mental disorder. However, most persons with a major mental disorder who committed offences committed them before the age of 18, before the symptoms of the major mental disorder would have been present. Thus, these results cast doubt on the notion that major mental illness precipitates violence.

Cirincione, Steadman, Clark-Robbins, and Monahan (1992) examined the degree to which a diagnosis of schizophrenia was predictive of violence, after controlling for arrest history. Two cohorts, one from 1968 and one from 1978, in a New York State psychiatric facility were reviewed. Results differed across cohorts. Prior arrest was a significant predictor of violence in both cohorts. A schizophrenia diagnosis was predictive of violence in the 1968 cohort but not in the 1978 cohort. For those without a history of prior arrest, a diagnosis of schizophrenia did not predict engaging in later violence. This research indicates that prior violence and substance abuse seem to have much greater effects on the likelihood of future violence than psychiatric diagnoses such as schizophrenia. The notion that the people with mental illness are more violent may not be a completely accurate view.

Types of Offences Committed by People with Mental Illnesses

Rice and Harris (1990) compared three groups of offenders: a group of males found NCRMD, a random group of convicted offenders who were sent for pretrial psychiatric evaluations, and a group of convicted offenders who were matched on the offence committed. The researchers found that NCRMD defendants were more likely to have committed murder or attempted murder than the other groups. Overall, however, offenders with mental disorders committed a variety of crimes, such as fraud, shoplifting, and murder. In other words, mentally disordered offenders were similar to other offenders and not distinguishable based solely on offence type (Rice & Harris, 1997).

Recidivism Rates and People with Mental Illnesses

In order to determine whether offenders with mental disorders are more likely to reoffend, Rice and Harris (1992) examined 96 NCRMD defendants who were diagnosed with schizophrenia and 96 nonschizophrenic offenders. The two groups were matched on age, offence, and criminal history. The schizophrenics were less likely, although not significantly so, to violently reoffend than were the nonschizophrenics. In another study using some of the same participants as in the Rice and Harris (1992) examination,

210 NCRMD defendants were compared on post-release recidivism to a matched convicted group (Rice et al., 1990). The NCRMD defendants had lower rates of both general and violent recidivism than the convicted offenders. It appears that, compared with other offenders, those with a major mental illness are not more likely to commit future crimes, especially violent crimes.

Treatment of Offenders with Mental Disorders

The goals for treatment for offenders with mental disorders vary greatly and are somewhat dependent on whether the offender is dealt with through the mental health system or the criminal justice system. Some of the treatment goals identified for those with mental disorders include symptom reduction, decreased length of stay in the facility, and no need to be re-admitted to hospital (Test, 1992). Of course, reducing the risk of recidivism has garnered much attention as a treatment goal among those in the criminal justice system (Lipsey, 1992).

There are a number of types of facilities at which mentally disordered offenders can receive treatment: psychiatric institutions, general hospitals, and assisted housing units. There appears to be little agreement on which type of treatment is appropriate for offenders with mental disorders (Quinsey & Maguire, 1983). However, for those who experience active psychotic symptoms such as delusions, hallucinations, suspicion, and noncompliance with medication, there are two key treatment options: antipsychotic drugs and behaviour therapy (Breslin, 1992). Medication can help control psychotic symptoms, while behaviour therapy can help to ensure that patients take the medication consistently. The critical aspects of behaviour therapy appear to be in providing positive social and material reward for appropriate behaviour, while decreasing or eliminating attention for symptomatic behaviour (Paul & Lentz, 1977; Beck et al., 1991).

The availability of facilities and the treatment programs offered vary across the country. Moreover, the willingness of an offender to engage in a particular program will vary. Even if an offender is motivated to receive treatment, an appropriate program may not be available at a particular facility. Thus, there are difficulties in matching programs to offenders' needs and willingness to participate.

One overarching treatment goal of many offender programs is to reintegrate the offender into society. The mental health and criminal justice system has developed options with this goal in mind. For example, a **community treatment order** allows the offender who has a mental illness to live in the community, with the stipulation that he or she will agree to treatment or detention in the event that his or her condition deteriorates. Another option for the courts dealing with offenders with mental illnesses who are facing minor charges is **diversion**—that is, to divert them directly into a treatment program rather than have them go through the court process. Generally, only defendants who are willing to participate in treatment will be diverted.

Treatment can be critical for offenders who have certain mental disorders such as schizophrenia.

SUMMARY

1. A defendant is found to be unfit if he or she is unable, due to a mental disorder, to understand the nature of the proceedings, understand the consequences of the proceedings, or communicate with counsel. The Ontario Court of Appeal in *R. v. Taylor* (1992) ruled that a defendant need only be able to tell counsel the facts. The defendant need not be able to communicate facts that are in his or her best interests. One other change to legislation that was introduced in Bill C-30 in 1992 was with regard to the length of time a defendant could be held in custody for a fitness evaluation. A five-day limit with provisions if necessary was legislated.

2. Compared with fit defendants, unfit defendants are more likely to be unemployed and living alone, and to never have been married. Moreover, unfit defendants tend to be older females belonging to a minority group who have fewer marital resources. In terms of mental disorders, unfit defendants have been found to be four times more likely to have met criteria for a psychotic disorder, whereas defendants who were found fit were about as likely to have been diagnosed with a psychotic disorder as not. Also, unfit defendants are less likely to have problems with substance abuse than fit defendants.

3. The term used for Canada's insanity standard is "not criminally responsible on account of mental disorder (NCRMD)." The defendant is not criminally responsible for an act that was committed (or omitted) while he or she was suffering from a mental disorder to the extent that he or she could not appreciate the nature or quality of the act or of knowing that it was wrong.

4. Automatism is defined as unconscious, involuntary behaviour. Canadian courts have recognized factors such as a physical blow, carbon monoxide poisoning, and sleepwalking as defences for automatism.

5. A number of explanations have been suggested for the high rates of mental illness in offender populations. For example, individuals with a mental illness may be more likely to be arrested at a disproportionately higher rate compared with those who do not have a mental illness. Alternatively, individuals with a mental illness may be less adept at committing crime and, therefore, more likely to get caught. Lastly, people with mental illnesses may be more likely to plead guilty, possibly because they do not have access to good counsel or because they do not understand the ramifications of their plea.

6. Treatment goals for offenders with mental disorders vary greatly. Some goals are symptom reduction, decreased length of stay in the facility, no need to be readmitted to hospital, and reduced recidivism. Medication and behaviour therapy are two common types of treatment for offenders with mental disorders .

KEY CONCEPTS

DISCUSSION QUESTIONS

1. As part of your summer internship program at the courthouse, the judge has asked you to review the cases heard over the past year and identify the ones in which noninsane automatism was used as a defence. Describe some factors that may lead to automatism and that may come up in the cases you will review.

2. While having dinner with your parents, your father mentions an article that he read in the newspaper highlighting the dangerousness of offenders with mental disorders. He makes the inference that mental illness leads to violent offending. Describe the data that calls your father's conclusion into question.

3. When you show up for your social psychology class, you are informed that the professor has been arrested for voyeurism. When she was arrested she was confused and incoherent. She is scheduled to undergo a fitness to stand trial evaluation. Your friends mention that they heard a rumour that the professor has some sort of mental illness. Describe the characteristics associated with unfit defendants and the process your professor will undergo following an unfit determination.

4. You have been hired by the police department to help police quickly identify those who may need psychiatric services rather than need to be processed through the criminal justice system. Develop a brief checklist for police to use when they come in contact with disorderly individuals so that they can take the most appropriate action.

5. Legislation changes with regards to offenders with mental disorders and their dispositions. Design a study to evaluate the various dispositions and their influence on recidivism, the likelihood of reoffending.

6. The evening news reported that offenders with mental disorders are likely to engage in more violent crime. Having taken a forensic psychology course, you feel this reported result is inaccurate. Describe how a researcher might go about testing the relationship between mental status and types of offences likely to be committed.

ADDITIONAL INFORMATION

Reading

Howells, K., & Hollin, C. (1993). *Clinical approaches to the mentally disordered offender.* New York, NY: John Wiley & Sons.

Web Sites

The Schizophrenia Society of Canada
www.schizophrenia.ca

Schizophrenia: A Handbook for Families
www.mentalhealth.com/book/p40-sc01.html#Head_1

CHAPTER 10

Sentencing and Parole in Canada: Practices and Public Opinions

LEARNING OBJECTIVES

- List the primary purposes and principles of sentencing.

- Describe the various sentencing options available in Canada.

- Define the term *sentencing disparity* and explain how it can be studied.

- Discuss the arguments used to justify the abolishment of the death penalty in Canada.

- List the principles that form the basis for effective correctional interventions.

- Describe some of the myths associated with parole decision making.

Judge Harrison is sitting in his office in a Toronto courthouse reviewing a case he has recently presided over. Jeremy Patterson, a young man of 22, has pled guilty to the crime of breaking and entering. Late one night, Jeremy broke into his neighbour's house and stole thousands of dollars worth of stereo equipment. This is the first time Jeremy has ever been charged with a crime and, despite the fact he has a full-time job, Jeremy told the court he stole the equipment in order to buy food for his wife and newborn child.

Given the circumstances, Judge Harrison feels it might be counterproductive to sentence Jeremy to prison, even though Canada's Criminal Code prescribes a maximum penalty for break and enter that does involve prison time. In Judge Harrison's view, a prison term would probably cost Jeremy his job and his family would suffer greatly as a result. Not only that, but Jeremy would be placed in an environment in which he would be forced to interact with more serious criminals, and this might result in Jeremy becoming involved in more serious crime upon his release. Instead, Judge Harrison sentences Jeremy to one year of community service, hoping he will learn a good lesson from his experience in court.

In a Vancouver courthouse at about the same time, Judge Fidell is considering a similar case. In fact, this case is just one in a long list of similar cases Judge Fidell has presided over. The defendant, 24-year-old Paul Lorenzo, broke into a neighbourhood house and was charged for the first time. Like Jeremy, Paul has a full-time job and a young family, and the stolen items from the house are worth about $2000. However, unlike Judge Harrison, Judge Fidell has developed the view that the only way to teach young men they can not get away with breaking the law is to send them to prison. As a result, Paul receives a sentence of one year in prison.

Thus, two judges from Canada, who were both fully aware of Canada's Criminal Code, handed down very different sentences to very similar offenders committing very similar crimes. How could this happen in a country that is supposed to have a fair criminal justice system?

Throughout this chapter, we will discuss sentencing and parole in Canada by focusing on issues like those raised in the opening vignette. We will first discuss the sentencing process, focusing specifically on the purposes and principles of sentencing, and the various sentencing options available to Canadian judges. Our attention will then turn to one of the major problems that can result from this process and various solutions that have been proposed to solve this problem. More specifically, we will focus on sentencing disparity that can often result from the high degree of discretion Canadian judges have when deciding on appropriate sentences. We will finish our discussion of sentencing by reviewing research that examines whether the goals of sentencing are actually achieved and what we can do if they are not. We will then move on to describe in some detail the parole process as it is commonly practised by Canada's National Parole Board. We will focus on parole decision making and on research that looks at the effectiveness of these decisions. To conclude the chapter, we will present research findings that deal with Canadians' perceptions toward sentencing and parole and discuss where these perceptions come from.

SENTENCING IN CANADA

Sentencing is defined as "the judicial determination of a legal sanction upon a person convicted of an offence" (Canadian Centre for Justice Statistics, 1997). According to Roberts (1991), this process is probably the most visible and controversial phase of the criminal justice system in Canada. The sentencing process is highly visible because, unlike the majority of decisions made in the criminal justice system, sentencing decisions are made in the open and presented before the court. The sentencing process is highly controversial because of the great number of problems that can potentially result from the sentencing process, such as problems with sentencing alternatives and sentencing effectiveness (Roberts, 1991). As a result, the sentencing process in Canada has been the subject of extensive research.

The Purposes of Sentencing

In order to understand the sentencing process in Canada, we must begin by discussing the reasons that we sentence offenders. Perhaps the most obvious goal of sentencing is to change the behaviour of convicted offenders and the behaviour of potential offenders who reside in the community. More specifically, offenders are sentenced to reduce the probability that they, and the rest of the community, will violate the law (referred to as **specific deterrence** and **general deterrence**, respectively). One of the reasons that sentencing attracts so much attention from forensic psychologists is that psychologists as a group are interested in understanding human behaviour and how that behaviour can be changed (Roberts, 1991). The area of sentencing provides fertile ground for psychologists to explore many issues in this area.

As made clear in Canada's Criminal Code, there are also many other reasons that we sentence offenders. In fact, the Criminal Code lays out explicitly the various purposes of sentencing in an attempt to provide direction to judges in making sentencing decisions. For example, as stated in section 718 of the Criminal Code, the fundamental purpose of sentencing is to contribute to respect for the law and the maintenance of a just, peaceful, and safe society by imposing sanctions on individuals who commit crimes. Other objectives include

- To denounce unlawful conduct
- To separate offenders from society
- To assist in rehabilitating offenders
- To provide **reparations** for harm done to victims or the community
- To promote a sense of responsibility in offenders

At present, it is not clear if one of these sentencing goals is any more dominant than another. The following, however, are clear:

1. Judges often consider more than one goal when handing down a sentence. For example, an offender may be sentenced to prison in order to reduce the probability that he or she will commit another crime and to separate that offender from society.

2. These goals can, at times, be incompatible with one another. For example, handing down a sentence of 25 years in prison will separate an offender from society but it may not be an effective way of rehabilitating an offender.

3. Different judges across Canada often hand down sentences for different reasons, even when dealing with offenders and offences that are similar. For example, under similar circumstances, one judge may hand down a sentence that he or she feels promotes a sense of responsibility in the offender, while another judge may hand down a sentence primarily intended to deter the general public from violating the law.

The Principles of Sentencing

Just as there are numerous reasons for imposing sanctions on offenders, there are also numerous sentencing principles in Canada, which are meant to guide sentencing decisions. Again, these are laid out explicitly in the Criminal Code. The **fundamental principle of sentencing**, as defined in section 718.1 of the Criminal Code, is that a sentence must be proportionate to the gravity of the offence and the degree of responsibility of the offender. Thus, when handing down a sentence in Canada, judges should consider the seriousness of the specific offence in addition to any other factor that might relate to the offender's degree of responsibility, such as the offender's age at the time of the offence.

However, beyond this fundamental principle, the Criminal Code also consists of other sentencing principles. For example, section 718.2 indicates that, when handing down sentences, judges should take into account the following principles:

- A sentence should be adjusted to account for any relevant aggravating or mitigating circumstances relating to the offence or the offender. For example, if the offender abused a position of authority when committing their offence, this should be considered.
- A sentence should be similar for similar offenders committing similar offences under similar circumstances.
- Where consecutive sentences are imposed, the combined sentence should not be unduly harsh.
- An offender should not be deprived of liberty (i.e., imprisoned) if less restrictive sanctions are appropriate under the circumstances.
- If reasonable, sanctions other than imprisonment should be considered for all offenders.

Sentencing Options in Canada

In addition to the purposes and principles of sentencing, Canada's Criminal Code also describes the various sentencing options available for particular offences and the maximum penalties that can be handed down. However, although the Criminal Code provides a general framework for making sentencing decisions, judges still have a great deal of discretion. For example, while it is possible to sentence a petty criminal to prison for a substantial amount of time, it is highly likely that some other sentencing option will used instead, such as a fine. Indeed, Roberts and Birkenmayer (1997) found that judges in Canada rarely provide the maximum penalty that is prescribed in the Criminal Code for any offence. For example, the maximum penalty for breaking and entering in Canada is life in prison, but the median sentence length reported by Roberts and Birkenmayer for Canadian judges was just three months imprisonment. Box 10.1 on the next page provides a detailed description of some of the sentencing options available to judges in Canada.

BOX 10.1 SENTENCING OPTIONS IN CANADA

Depending on the offence being considered, judges in Canada have many sentencing options available to them, including the following:

- *Absolute or conditional discharge.* Canadian judges have the option to impose an **absolute discharge** or **conditional discharge**. When making this decision, judges will consider whether a discharge would be in the best interest of the offender and the community. If an offender is given an absolute discharge, that person is released and is free to do as he or she wishes in the community. An offender who is given a conditional discharge will have to follow certain rules in the community for a specified period of time in order for the discharge to become absolute. If the offender breaks these rules, he or she can serve time in prison.

- *Probation.* Offenders placed on **probation** are released into the community and must follow certain conditions. For example, while on probation, offenders will have to (1) be of good behaviour, (2) appear before the court when required to do so, and (3) notify their probation officer of any change of name, address, or employment status. Other conditions may also be put in place, such as abstaining from alcohol and drug use. Offenders who break the conditions of their probation order may be imprisoned for up to two years.

- *Restitution.* **Restitution** is a payment made by an offender to the victim to cover expenses resulting from a crime, such as monetary loss resulting from property damage. When someone is injured, restitution can be used to cover medical bills and lost income.

- *Fines and community service.* The most common sentencing option in Canada is the **fine**. A court that fines an offender will set the amount of the fine, the way the fine is to be paid, and the time by which the fine must be paid. In many cases, the offender will be able to pay off the fine by performing **community service**. If an offender, without a reasonable excuse, does not pay the fine, he or she can serve a term of imprisonment.

- *Conditional sentence.* A **conditional sentence** is a prison sentence served in the community. This sentencing option was only introduced to Canada in 1996 as part of Bill C-41. An offender serving a conditional sentence is released into the community and must follow a set of rules for a specific period of time. The prison sentence is suspended as long as the offender abides by these rules. If an offender breaks these rules, he or she may be required to serve the remainder of the sentence in prison.

- *Imprisonment.* **Imprisonment** is a last resort where less restrictive sanctions are inappropriate. For summary (i.e., less serious) offences, the maximum term of incarceration is six months. For indictable (i.e., more serious) offences, the term of incarceration varies by offence and can include life imprisonment. Offenders sentenced to prison terms of less than two years serve their sentences in provincial or territorial prisons. Sentences of two or more years are served in federal prisons.

Source: John Howard Society, 1999.

In addition to the options discussed in Box 10.1, Canadian judges have a number of additional options open to them when handing down sentences of imprisonment, especially for high-risk offenders. One of these options is to declare the offender a **dangerous offender**. The prosecution can submit a dangerous offender application to the court for any offender convicted of a serious personal injury offence who constitutes a danger to others (John Howard Society, 1999). According to the Criminal Code, the determination of dangerousness in these cases is based on evidence that one of the following conditions is met:

1. The offender exhibits a pattern of unrestrained behaviour that is likely to cause danger.

2. The offender exhibits a pattern of aggressive behaviour with indifference as to the consequences of this behaviour.

3. The offender exhibits behaviour that is of such a brutal nature that ordinary standards of restraint will not control it.

4. The offender shows a failure to control sexual impulses that are likely to harm others.

If someone receives the dangerous offender designation, that person can be imprisoned for an indefinite period of time. This is a very extreme measure and, therefore, it is important that the appropriate offenders are targeted. Fortunately, this does appear to be happening in Canada. For example, Bonta, Zinger, Harris, and Carriere (1998) compared a group of dangerous offenders from Canadian prisons with a group of offenders who had been released from prison only to go on to commit a violent crime. The assumption was that "similarities between the two groups would imply that [dangerous offenders] would also be at high risk to offend violently if released" (Bonta et al., 1998, p. 383). In accordance with what should happen if the appropriate offenders are being targeted for the dangerous offender designation, Bonta and his colleagues found that the two groups in their study were quite similar. Offenders in both groups had similar criminal histories and had committed offences against similar victims. The groups also had similar backgrounds with respect to education, employment, marital status, and upbringing. Objective risk assessment scales, which will be discussed in Chapter 11, did not distinguish between the two groups of offenders either.

Alternatively, prosecutors can submit an application to the court to have an offender designated as a **long-term offender**. This is a relatively new sentencing option in Canada. Based on the description provided in section 753.1 of the Criminal Code, any offender who meets the following criteria can be designated a long-term offender:

1. It would be appropriate to impose a sentence of two years or more for the offence.

2. There is a substantial risk that the offender will reoffend.

3. There is a reasonable possibility of eventual control of risk in the community.

A long-term offender will be given a sentence of imprisonment of at least two years, followed by a period of supervision in the community (John Howard Society, 1999).

Factors That Affect Sentencing Decisions

We will now briefly discuss factors affecting sentencing decisions. As indicated above, the Criminal Code highlights various factors that should be taken into account when judges decide on sentences in Canada. These include the seriousness of the offence, the offender's degree of responsibility, various aggravating and mitigating factors, the harshness of the sentence, and so forth. According to Roberts (1991), some researchers suggest that these legally relevant factors can explain most of the variation that occurs in sentencing decisions across judges (e.g., Andrews, Robblee, & Saunders, 1984). This clearly is as it should be. However, other researchers argue that many judges appear to rely on extra-legal factors (i.e., factors that have little to do with either the offender or the crime) when making their sentencing decisions, and this is cause for concern.

For example, in an important study by Hogarth (1971), he found that "only about 9% of the variation in sentencing could be explained by objectively defined facts, while more than 50% of such variation could be accounted for simply by knowing certain pieces of information about the judge himself" (p. 382). Likewise, in a more recent study from the United States, Clancy, Bartolomeo, Richardson, and Wellford (1981) found that factors that had no direct bearing on the cases they considered accounted for a large percentage (40%) of the variation in sentence length handed down by judges. Some of these factors included the political ideology of the judge and the race of the judge. Canadian studies of sentencing decisions report similar findings. For example, as you will see in Chapter 13, a number of researchers have suggested that certain groups of offenders in Canada, especially Aboriginal offenders, are more likely to be incarcerated for their crimes (e.g., LaPrairie, 1989).

A prison cell in one of Canada's maximum prisons

Sentencing Disparity

One of the reasons that it is important to appreciate the various factors that affect sentencing decisions is so that we can understand **sentencing disparity**. Sentencing disparity is defined as "any difference in severity between the sentence that an offender receives from one judge on a particular occasion and what an identical offender with the identical crime would receive from either the same judge on a different occasion or a different judge on the same or a different occasion" (McFatter, 1986, pp. 151–152). Because sentencing disparity can lead to serious injustices, it is commonly viewed as a major problem within our criminal justice system. Indeed, a number of leading Canadian researchers have proposed that sentencing disparity is the single most important problem with sentencing at the moment (e.g., Roberts, 1991). This should not, however, be taken to mean that sentencing disparity has not been viewed as a serious problem for a long time. For example, Roberts (1991) cites a study by Gaudet (1938) that dealt with this very issue.

SOURCES OF UNWARRANTED SENTENCING DISPARITY

The real problem occurs when disparities in sentencing happen because of a reliance on extra-legal factors. In this case, we can refer to the disparity as **unwarranted sentencing disparity** (Roberts, 1991). Unwarranted sentencing disparity can result from many factors and researchers have attempted to classify these factors into groups. For example, McFatter (1986) identifies two major sources of unwarranted sentencing disparity—**systematic disparity** and **unsystematic disparity**. Systematic disparity represents *consistent* disagreement among judges about sentencing, such as how lenient they feel sentences should be. As you saw in this chapter's opening vignette, sources of systematic disparity can include differences between judges in terms of their personality, philosophy, experience, and so on.

Unsystematic disparity, conversely, results from a given judge's *inconsistency* over occasions in judging the same type of offender or crime. This type of disparity can also arise from a number of sources, including fluctuations in mood, focusing on irrelevant stimuli, or the way in which the facts of the case are interpreted by the judge on any particular day (McFatter, 1986). Why is it important to understand these different sources of sentencing disparity? As McFatter (1986) suggests, only by understanding the various sources of sentencing disparity can we come up with effective strategies to combat its existence.

STUDYING SENTENCING DISPARITY

Researchers in this area typically use one of two procedures to study sentencing disparity—laboratory-based simulation studies or the use of official sentencing statistics. Of the two procedures, simulation studies are more common. Here, researchers present mock judges, or real judges, with the details of a trial, and the researcher manipulates particular variables of interest, such as the defendant's age, ethnicity, or gender. The goal is to manipulate these variables while attempting to control for as many other variables as possible, so that if evidence for sentencing disparity is found, the researcher can be fairly confident as to what caused it.

Simulation Studies

The experiment conducted by McFatter (1986) provides an excellent example of a simulation study. He provided six judges with 13 crime and offender descriptions, which included brief details of the crime and the offender's age, prior record, drug use, and employment status. The descriptions were chosen to represent a wide range of typical crime and offender descriptions. For example, the crimes ranged from a fight that broke out after a minor traffic accident to a rape and murder of an 11-year-old girl. In the first phase of the study, judges were asked to rate various aspects of the crime, such as its seriousness, and to recommend a sentence. Approximately two months later, the judges were given the same crime and offender descriptions and were asked to make ratings and recommend sentences once again. In both phases, the severity of sentences handed down by judges was transformed into numbers using the scale developed by Diamond and Zeisel (1975), which is provided in Table 10.1.

The raw severity scores for the sentences handed down by the judges in each phase of McFatter's (1986) experiment are presented in Table 10.2. A number of interesting things emerge from these data:

1. The results indicate that there is a good deal of agreement among judges about the severity of sentences appropriate for each crime. For example, all six judges consistently handed down very lenient sentences for crime 1 (the fight that resulted from a minor traffic accident), while five of the six judges consistently

TABLE 10.1 SENTENCING SEVERITY SCORES

Sentence	Severity Score
Fine or suspended sentence	1
Probation (months)	
1–12	1
13–36	2
Over 36	3
Split sentence (jail + probation)	4
Prison	
1–6 months	3
7–12 months	5
13–24 months	7
25–36 months	9
(Add 2 points for every year up to 50 years)	
50 years	103
Life imprisonment or death	103

Source: Adapted from McFatter, 1986.

handed down very serious sentences for crime 13 (the rape and murder of the 11-year-old girl).

2. However, despite these similarities, there are also many instances of unwarranted sentencing disparity. For example, the sentences handed down for crime 9 (an armed robbery that took place on the street) varied drastically across judges, with severity scores ranging from 2 to 53.

3. Most of this disparity appears to come from unsystematic sources. In a large number of cases, the same judge handed down different sentences when presented with the same crime and offender after a two-month delay. Indeed, in some cases the degree of disparity was extremely high, as in the case of crime 12 and 13, where judge 4 handed down much more lenient sentences in phase 1 compared with phase 2.

Similar findings have also been reported in simulation studies conducted in Canada (e.g., Palys & Divorski, 1986).

Studies Based on Official Statistics Studies using official sentencing statistics have come to the same conclusion—a relatively high degree of disparity does exist in judicial sentencing decisions. For example, Birkenmayer and Roberts (1997) have

TABLE 10.2 SENTENCING SEVERITY SCORES FOR THE JUDGES

						Judge (Phase)							
Crime	1(1)	1(2)	2(1)	2(2)	3(1)	3(2)	4(1)	4(2)	5(1)	5(2)	6(1)	6(2)
1	1	1	2	4	2	2	2	3	1	4	1	4
2	3	2	4	4	1	2	2	2	1	4	3	2
3	2	1	5	4	4	2	3	4	2	2	2	3
4	5	5	9	9	3	3	3	3	3	3	2	3
5	3	3	4	9	4	4	3	4	7	4	7	3
6	5	2	7	7	4	4	3	3	3	3	3	13
7	2	4	5	4	3	3	4	5	13	3	4	13
8	4	3	5	9	23	5	13	4	1	4	4	3
9	53	39	53	43	2	5	13	5	3	4	13	23
10	103	103	103	103	5	103	23	23	12	23	103	53
11	63	103	103	103	103	43	13	13	103	103	13	23
12	103	103	103	103	103	103	53	103	103	103	103	103
13	103	103	103	103	103	103	53	103	103	103	103	103

Source: McFatter, 1986.

found high levels of sentencing disparity in incarceration rates from courts across Canada. Based on their analyses, certain provincial courts appear to be much more harsh in terms of the number of prison terms they hand out. For example, in Ontario, 72% of break and enter offences resulted in incarceration, whereas only 33% of such offences in Quebec resulted in incarceration.

Reducing Sentencing Disparity Regardless of how sentencing disparity is studied, the conclusion is typically that a high degree of disparity exists across sentences handed down by different judges considering similar crimes and across sentences handed down by the same judge when considering similar crimes on different occasions. As discussed above, there are a number of sources that can account for this disparity but, ultimately, sentencing disparity exists because the law in Canada allows judges a great deal of discretion when making sentencing decisions. Although sentencing guidelines exist in Canada's Criminal Code, these guidelines are often so broad that they do little to decrease sentencing disparity. For example, as Roberts (1991) points out, "there are over 70 offences contained in the Criminal Code that can be punished by dispositions ranging from a discharge to a sentence of imprisonment of 14 years or life" (p. 471).

Although certain forms of sentencing disparity are probably inevitable (some would argue essential), there has been a move within Canada in recent years toward reducing unwarranted disparity. Just as people debate the extent to which sentencing disparity exists, debates are also ongoing as to how this disparity can best be minimized. The most common approach for reducing sentencing disparity, especially in Canada, is to implement **sentencing guidelines**. In this section, we will briefly discuss what sentencing guidelines are, what they are meant to achieve, and whether existing research suggests they work.

Sentencing Guidelines in Canada

Many different types of sentencing guidelines have been proposed but they all have one thing in common—they all attempt to provide a more consistent, structured way of arriving at sentencing decisions. The following is a partial list, provided by Roberts (1991), of various guidelines that could be used to reduce sentencing disparity:

1. *Advisory guidelines.* These guidelines are purely suggestive in nature when it comes to sentencing decisions and have no force in the law.

2. *Presumptive sentencing guidelines.* These guidelines force a judge to make specific sentencing decisions unless there are important reasons for departing from the recommendation.

3. *Mandatory sentencing laws.* Such laws require the judge to make specific sentencing decisions when confronted with particular crimes, regardless of case-specific circumstances.

By 1999, sentencing guidelines in the Criminal Code specified mandatory minimum sentences (MMS) for a total of 29 offences (Gabor & Crutcher, 2002). Table 10.3 provides the guidelines for some of these offences. One reason that these MMS were introduced was to reduce unwarranted sentencing disparity by decreasing the amount of discretion that judges have when making sentencing decisions. Unfortunately, there is little in the way of empirical research to suggest whether current sentencing guidelines in this country are effective in this regard. However, there is research from the United States that has examined the issue. This research frequently suggests that, although judicial discretion seems to be reduced by MMS, sentencing disparity often is not. The likely reason is that the discretion of judges is simply shifted to other criminal justice professionals, namely prosecutors and police officers (Wallace, 1993).

However, despite some negative findings, there are examples in which guidelines have resulted in decreased levels of sentencing disparity. For example, Roberts (1991) discusses Minnesota's sentencing guidelines, which have been in place since the early 1980s. Citing from the original report, Roberts (1991) states that "Disparity in sentencing decreased under the sentencing guidelines. The reduction in disparity is indicated by increased sentence uniformity and proportionality. Sentences were more uniform in terms of who goes to prison and in how long imprisoned offenders serve" (p. 473). Similar findings have also been reported in Pennsylvania (Kramer & Lubitz, 1985). Thus, there are certainly examples in which sentencing guidelines have been successful, just as there are examples in which they have not. What this indicates is that more research is clearly needed to understand the discrepancy in these results. Only in this way will the Canadian criminal justice system learn from these experiences.

TABLE 10.3 MANDATORY MINIMUM SENTENCES FOR SELECTED OFFENCES

Offence	Minimum	Maximum
High treason	Life	Life
First–degree murder	Life	Life
Kidnapping—firearm	4 years	Life
Robbery—firearm	4 years	Life
Sexual assault—firearm	4 years	14 years
Aggravated sexual assault—firearm	4 years	14 years
Driving while impaired	14 days	5 years
Refusing to provide breath sample	14 days	5 years

Source: Adapted from Gabor and Crutcher, 2002.

Are the Goals of Sentencing Achieved?

Recall from the beginning of this chapter that there are many different goals of sentencing. As a result, the question of whether the goals of sentencing are achieved is a difficult one to answer because, to a large extent, the answer depends on what goal we are most concerned with. For some goals, the answer to this question is often yes. For example, if we sentence an offender to a term in prison, we can be reasonably confident that the offender will be separated from society for a certain period of time. However, with respect to some other goals, the answer is less clear-cut. In particular, there is an ongoing debate as to whether current sentencing practices in Canada achieve the goals of deterring people from committing crimes and whether they assist in the rehabilitation of offenders. Canadian forensic psychologists have played, and continue to play, a crucial role in this debate. See Motiuk and Serin (2001) for an excellent overview of the contributions made by these psychologists.

A lot of recent research has focused specifically on the effectiveness of "get tough" strategies (Cullen & Gendreau, 2000), including a range of punishment-based sentencing options, some consisting of incarceration. Other strategies fall under the heading of intermediate strategies, which are less severe than incarceration but more severe then probation (Gendreau et al., 2001). These include "confining offenders to their homes, enforcing curfews, submitting offenders to random drug testing, requiring offenders to pay restitution to victims, electronically monitoring offenders, and requiring offenders to pay for the privilege of being supervised" (Gendreau et al., 2001, pp. 18–19). It has long been assumed that experiencing one of these sanctions would change the antisocial behaviour of offenders and reduce the likelihood that they will reoffend. However, as is the case with the most serious of sanctions, the death penalty, recent research does not support this hypothesis (Gendreau et al., 2001). See Box 10.2 for a discussion of this issue as it relates to the death penalty.

Recent research suggests that "get tough" strategies for offenders, such as incarceration, may not reduce the chance of reoffending

In a recent review, Gendreau and colleagues (2001) examined the rehabilitative and deterrent effect of various community-based sanctions and prison sentences. These researchers used the technique of meta-analysis to summarize findings from research studies that examined the impact of specific sanctions (see Chapter 2 for a discussion of this technique). For our purposes here, the most important measures to focus on from the study are the rate of recidivism for offenders who experienced the sanction, the rate of recidi-

BOX 10.2 THE DEATH PENALTY IN CANADA: WERE WE RIGHT TO ABOLISH IT?

At 12:02 A.M. on December 11, 1962, in Toronto, Ontario, Arthur Lucas and Robert Turpin were the last people to be executed in Canada. Although the death penalty in Canada was formally abolished in 1976 for offences under the Criminal Code, and in 1999 for military offences under the National Defence Act, there are three very good reasons that it is still important to discuss this issue. The first reason is that, since the time when the death penalty was abolished in Canada, there have been attempts to reinstate capital punishment. Indeed, as recently as 1987, Canadian MPs voted on the issue in the House of Commons, with a close vote (148 versus 127) in favour of not reinstating the death penalty. The second reason is that these attempts to reinstate the death penalty seem to reflect public opinion on the issue. Although public support for the death penalty has varied over time, recent Canadian polls indicate that the majority of Canadians are in favour of reinstating the death penalty (notably, the 1998 Gallup poll indicates that 61% of Canadians are in favour of the death penalty for murder) (Edwards & Mazzuca, 1998). The third reason, and one that we will explore here, is that most of the research examining the death penalty suggests that it should not be reinstated in Canada. Although many members of the public believe that the

death penalty acts as an effective crime deterrent, research does not support this view.

Existing research suggests there are a number of problems with the crime deterrent argument. First, this argument assumes that offenders think about the punishment before acting. This simply does not appear to be the case for the majority of offenders (Benaquisto, 2000). In fact, a very large number of murders are committed in the heat of passion, or under the influence of alcohol or other drugs, with the offenders paying very little attention to the consequences of their crimes. Second, if the death penalty did act as a crime deterrent, we would expect to see an increase in the Canadian murder rate since abolition. However, the murder rate in Canada has continually declined since 1975 (National Parole Board [NPB], 2002). Third, the argument that the death penalty ensures that the offenders will never murder again is based on the belief that a high proportion of those released will murder again. In fact, as you will see when we get to the section on parole later in this chapter, it is relatively rare for convicted murderers to commit another murder upon their release from prison (NPB, 2003).

Source: John Howard Society, 2001.

vism for offenders who experienced regular probation (this group was used as a control group), and the average effect size that resulted from a comparison of these two rates. The consideration of effect size is particularly important since this measure summarizes the impact that a particular sanction was found to have across a range of studies. In this case, effect sizes can range from +1.00 to −1.00, with positive effect sizes indicating that the sanction increased recidivism (i.e., compared with probation, those offenders who received the sanction reoffended at a higher rate) and negative effect sizes indicating that the sanction decreased recidivism (i.e., compared with probation, those offenders who received the sanction reoffended at a lower rate).

Based on the results from this study, it must be concluded that there is very little evidence that community sanctions lead to substantial decreases in recidivism rates. Indeed, most of the average effect sizes listed in Table 10.4 are positive, indicating that, on average, the sanctions resulted in increases in recidivism. There were only two sanctions (fines and restitution) that resulted in average effect sizes that were negative, and in these cases the observed decrease in recidivism rates was very small (−0.04 and −0.02, respectively). In addition, this study found that sanctions consisting of incarceration also had little impact on recidivism. In fact, longer periods of incarceration led to slightly higher rates of recidivism across the studies that were examined (+0.03). In addition, those offenders who were sent to prison for brief periods of time also exhibited higher rates of recidivism compared with offenders who received a community-based sanction (+0.07).

What Works in Offender Treatment?

So, given these results, does this mean that nothing can be done to deter or rehabilitate offenders? Historically, some researchers have taken the view that nothing will work with offenders (most notably Martinson, 1974), but new research suggests this is not the case. In fact, Canadian researchers have led the way in establishing principles of effective correctional intervention and a growing body of research is beginning to show the value of these principles (Andrews & Bonta, 2001). Although quite a large

TABLE 10.4 EFFECTS OF COMMUNITY-BASED SANCTIONS AND INCARCERATION ON RECIDIVISM

Type of Sanction	Sample Size	Average Effect Size
Supervision program	19 403	0.00
Arrest	7 779	0.01
Fine	7 162	−0.04
Restitution	8 715	−0.02
Boot camp	6 831	0.00
Scared straight	1 891	0.07
Drug testing	419	0.05
Electronic monitoring	1 414	0.05
More versus less prison	68 248	0.03
Prison versus community	267 804	0.07

Source: Adapted from Gendreau et al., 2001.

number of principles are emerging as potentially important (Andrews, 2001), we will focus on three that appear to be particularly valuable in determining which correctional interventions will be effective.

The first of these principles is known as the **need principle**. It states that effective intervention will target known criminogenic needs (factors that are known to contribute to reoffending), including (1) antisocial attitudes, beliefs, and values, (2) antisocial associates, (3) antisocial personality factors (such as impulsivity, risk taking, and low self-control), and (4) antisocial behaviours (Cullen & Gendreau, 2000).

The second principle is known as the **risk principle**. It states that effective interventions will focus on those offenders who are at high risk of reoffending (Cullen & Gendreau, 2000). Not only are low-risk offenders unlikely to reoffend, their chances of reoffending may actually increase if exposed to an intervention, due to the fact they will be brought into contact with people who hold antisocial attitudes (Andrews, 2001).

The third principle is known as the **responsivity principle**. It states that effective interventions will match the general learning styles, motivations, and abilities of the offender being targeted as well as more specific factors such as the offender's personality, gender, ethnicity, and so on (Cullen & Gendreau, 2000).

The often-cited meta-analytic study conducted by Andrews et al. (1990) was one of the first attempts to determine whether interventions consisting of these core principles do in fact lead to reductions in recidivism. These researchers examined 80 program evaluation studies and coded the interventions in each study as appropriate, inappropriate, or unspecified. Interventions were defined as appropriate if they included the three principles of effective intervention described above. Interventions were coded as inappropriate if they were inconsistent with these principles. Interventions were coded as unspecified if they could not be categorized as appropriate or inappropriate due to a lack of information. The hypothesis in this study was that offenders exposed to appropriate interventions would exhibit lower rates of recidivism compared with offenders exposed to inappropriate interventions.

This is exactly what was found. Using the same terminology we described above, the average effect size for appropriate interventions was –0.30, indicating a substantial decrease in recidivism for offenders taking part in the programs. In contrast, the average effect size for unspecified programs was –0.13, indicating a decrease in recidivism for offenders taking part in the programs, and the average effect size for inappropriate programs was +0.07, indicating an increase in recidivism for offenders taking part in the programs. Since this study, this same general pattern of results has been found on numerous occasions (e.g., Andrews, Dowden, & Gendreau, 1999; Antonowicz & Ross, 1994; Pearson, Lipton, & Cleland, 1996).

In conclusion, then, it does appear that something can be done to deter and rehabilitate offenders. By focusing on current research in the area of forensic psychology, interventions can be developed that significantly reduce the chance that offenders will go on to commit further crimes. Certainly, this does not suggest that all new sentencing options will be effective, since many of these new options will not be consistent with the principles of effective correctional programming. However, a number of options have been developed, many in Canada, that do correspond with these principles. Early indications suggest that they hold promise for achieving some of the goals of sentencing that we discussed at the beginning of this chapter (Motiuk & Serin, 2001).

PAROLE IN CANADA

Ever since August 11, 1899, when Parliament enacted the Ticket of Leave Act, **parole** has played an important part in the history of criminal justice in Canada. Sir Wilfrid Laurier, the prime minister at the time, recognized the value of actively reintegrating certain offenders into society as soon as possible in order to enhance their chances of rehabilitation (National Parole Board [NPB], 2003). Indeed, he even went so far as to describe the sort of offender that the act was meant for:

> ... a young man of good character, who may have committed a crime in a moment of passion, or perhaps, have fallen victim to bad example, or the influence of unworthy friends. There is a good report on him while in confinement and it is supposed that if he were given another chance, he would be a good citizen. (NPB, 2003)

Since the time of Laurier, many things about parole have changed, but the essence of parole remains the same. Notably, parole still involves (1) the conditional release of offenders into a community so they can serve the remainder of their sentence outside an institution, (2) an attempt to rehabilitate offenders so they can become productive contributors to society, (3) a high degree of community supervision to ensure the parolee is abiding by certain rules, and (4) a clause that, if the conditions of parole are not complied with, an offender's parole can be revoked and he or she can be sent back to prison.

Parole Decision Making

Although the essence of parole may be similar to what it was a century ago, parole decision making has changed drastically. Compared with how parole decisions were once made, the decision-making process is now far more complex and objective. The process that currently exists is more complex because of the range of information that is considered when making parole decisions and because of the way in which that information is evaluated. The process is more objective because, unlike parole decisions made in the past, where an elected member of government was responsible for the decision, parole decisions are now made by a group of experts forming Canada's **National Parole Board** (NPB). The process that the NPB goes through when making their decisions is open to scrutiny by the public because the public are allowed to attend and observe parole hearings and to request copies of written parole board decisions (NPB, 2002a). See Box 10.3 for more information about the NPB.

So, how are parole decisions made? In Canada, an offender must usually serve the first third of the sentence or the first seven years, whichever is less, before being eligible for full parole (NPB, 2002b). Most parole decisions are made after a formal hearing with the

BOX 10.3 MYTHS AND REALITIES CONCERNING PAROLE DECISION MAKING

The general public has many misconceptions when it comes to issues of parole, and the NPB continually strives to correct them. The following list provides some of the myths people adhere to, along with the correct information provided by the NPB.

Myth #1: Parole reduces the sentence imposed by the courts.

Parole does not reduce the sentence imposed by the courts; it only affects the way in which a sentence will be served. Parole allows offenders to serve their sentences in the community under strict conditions. If offenders abide by these conditions, they will remain in the community under strict conditions until their sentence is completed.

Myth #2: Parole is automatically granted when an inmate becomes eligible for parole consideration.

Parole is not automatically granted when inmates become eligible. In fact, the NPB denies full parole to approximately six out of ten offenders at their first parole review date.

Myth #3: The NPB grants parole to offenders who express remorse for the offences they have committed.

Whether offenders express remorse is only one of the factors the NPB considers. Of greater importance is whether offenders understand the factors that contributed to their criminal behaviour, the progress they made while incarcerated, and the feasibility of their plans upon release.

Myth #4: Most of the offenders released on parole are convicted of new crimes.

Most offenders released on parole successfully complete their sentences without committing new offences or breaching the conditions of their parole.

Myth #5: Victims do not have a role in the parole process and their views are not taken into account.

Victims and their families have a significant role in the parole process. They have the opportunity to present a statement directly to the NPB about any concerns they have for their safety or the safety of the community. In addition, victims may remain in contact with the NPB while the offender is under sentence. Moreover, the NPB allows victims, as well as other members of the public, to observe parole hearings and to request copies of written decisions.

Source: NPB, 2002b.

offender. When making their decisions, NPB members carefully review the risk that an offender might present to society if he or she is released. According to the NPB (2002b), this involves an initial risk assessment where the following issues are considered:

1. Information about the offender's current offence
2. The offender's criminal history
3. Social problems experienced by the offender, such as drug use and family violence

4. The offender's mental status

5. Performance on earlier releases

6. Information about the offender's relationships and employment history

7. Psychological or psychiatric reports

8. Opinions from other professionals, such as police officers

9. Information from victims

10. Any other information indicating whether release would pose a risk to society

After this initial assessment, the NPB examines specific risk factors, such as

1. The offender's institutional behaviour

2. Information that indicates evidence of change and insight into the offender's own behaviour

3. Benefits derived from treatment that may reduce the risk posed by the offender

4. The feasibility of the offender's release plans

The NPB members then decide whether to grant parole.

Types of Parole

The NPB can grant various types of parole to offenders. These include temporary absence, day parole, full parole, and statutory release.

TEMPORARY ABSENCE A temporary absence is usually the first type of release an offender will be granted (NPB, 2002b). Offenders may be granted unescorted or escorted temporary absence so that they can take part in activities such as substance abuse programs, family violence counselling, technical training courses, and so on.

DAY PAROLE Day parole allows offenders to participate in community-based activities. Offenders on day parole must typically return to their institution or halfway house at the end of the day (NPB, 2002b). Performance on day parole is considered when the NPB reviews an offender's application for full parole.

FULL PAROLE Full parole allows the offender to serve the remainder of the sentence under supervision in the community. Before an offender is granted full parole, a thorough assessment is done to predict the likelihood of reoffending (NPB, 2002b). Consideration is also given to what conditions should be implemented to address the chance of risk. In order to be granted full parole, offenders must usually have been granted (and successfully completed) unescorted temporary absences and day parole.

STATUTORY RELEASE By law, most federal inmates must be released with supervision after serving two-thirds of their sentence, which is known as **statutory release**

(NPB, 2002b). (Offenders serving life, however, are not eligible for statutory release.) As with full parole, an assessment is done to predict the likelihood of reoffending and consideration is given as to what conditions should be implemented to address the chance of risk.

In each of the above cases, Correctional Service Canada is responsible for supervising offenders on parole, usually with the assistance of community agencies such as the John Howard Society. If an offender does not abide by the parole conditions, he or she may be returned to prison. The following is a partial list of parole conditions provided by the NPB (2002b):

1. Offenders must report to their residence immediately upon release.
2. Offenders must report to their parole office on dates set by their parole officer.
3. Offenders must remain in Canada.
4. Offenders must obey the law and keep the peace.
5. Offenders must inform their parole officer if they come into contact with the police.
6. Offenders must advise their parole officer of any changes in address or employment.
7. Offenders must not own or possess any weapon.

Research on the Effectiveness of Parole

As was the case with sentencing, there has been a great deal of research examining the effectiveness of parole decision making. In fact, the NPB provides updates on the success of their parolees on an annual basis. Many of the statistics published by the NPB compare the success rates of offenders granted day and full parole to those offenders granted statutory release. Recall that, by law, most federal inmates must be released with supervision after serving two-thirds of their sentence. If the NPB is making effective decisions, we would expect to see higher rates of success for offenders on day and full parole, compared with those who have been granted statutory release. This is exactly what the statistics suggest.

For example, as indicated in the most recent *Performance Monitoring Report* published by the NPB (2003), "offenders who are granted parole, based on an assessment of their risk of re-offending, are more likely to complete their supervision period in the community and are less likely to re-offend ... than offenders released as a result of statute-based systems such as accelerated parole review or statutory release" (p. 1). Of course, this is not to say that offenders granted day or full parole never breach the conditions of their parole or commit further crimes—just that this tends to be the exception rather than the rule.

In support of these claims by the NPB, Figure 10.1 on the next page provides data relating to the rate of parole revocation for breach of conditions across different types of parole. This graph clearly indicates that, during the period 1998 to 2003, offenders

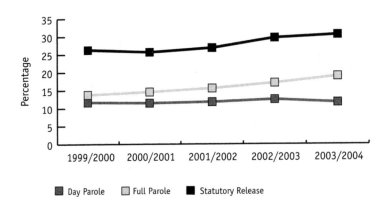

FIGURE 10.1

PAROLE REVOCATION FOR BREACH OF CONDITIONS

■ Day Parole   □ Full Parole   ■ Statutory Release

Source: Adapted from NPB, 2004.

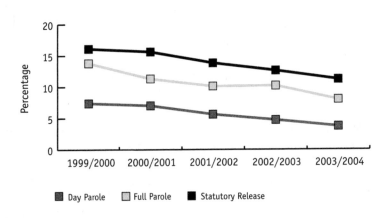

FIGURE 10.2

PAROLE REVOCATION FOR NONVIOLENT OR VIOLENT OFFENCES

■ Day Parole   □ Full Parole   ■ Statutory Release

Source: Adapted from NPB, 2004.

who were granted statutory release were far more likely to have their parole revoked due to a breach of conditions; however, even in the case of statutory release, a large majority of offenders do not breach their conditions (NPB, 2003).

A similar picture emerges when we examine the rate of revocation due to non-violent or violent offences. As indicated in Figure 10.2, offenders granted statutory release are again the most likely to have their parole revoked due to the commission of a nonviolent or violent offence; however, even these offenders are unlikely to commit further crimes.

PUBLIC ATTITUDES TOWARD SENTENCING AND PAROLE

Having examined in some detail the sentencing and parole process in Canada, let us now focus our attention on the attitudes that Canadians have about these processes. In fact, there is a great deal of research that examines public opinion of the criminal justice system in Canada. Much of this research has been conducted by Dr. Julian Roberts, who is profiled in Box 10.4. This research typically involves the use of one of the following research methods: public opinion surveys, simulation studies, or focus groups (in which a small number of people are brought together for an in-depth discussion of their views on a particular topic). For the most part, the results that emerge from these three different approaches are similar, so we will focus our discussion on the results from public opinion surveys because they are the most commonly used.

One of the major advantages of using surveys for the purpose of studying attitudes toward sentencing and parole is that they are distributed to a very large number of people. The responses, therefore, are probably quite representative of the typical Canadian. A second major advantage is that public opinion surveys often consist of a large number of scenarios, which allows researchers to examine the views that Canadians hold on a wide range of important issues. The major disadvantage of using large-scale surveys to capture peoples' attitudes is that, by necessity, the questions making up the survey have to be kept quite broad. In addition, there is obviously no opportunity to explore peoples' attitudes in any sort of detailed way, since it is not possible to follow up with the respondent.

A number of general trends can be observed from the results of public opinion surveys. We will provide details of some of the more interesting and important ones before briefly exploring where these attitudes may come from.

1. *Canadians believe that offenders are treated too leniently.* In general, the results from public opinion polls indicate that Canadians perceive that offenders are treated too leniently (Stein, 2001). For example, when respondents are asked about how particular criminal justice institutions deal with offenders, their view is that the courts and the federal government do not treat criminals harshly enough (see Table 10.5). Interestingly, as seen in Table 10.5, Canadians do not

BOX 10.4 CANADIAN RESEARCHER PROFILE: DR. JULIAN V. ROBERTS

Since being a graduate student at the University of Toronto, Dr. Julian Roberts has been interested in what the public thinks about criminal justice issues. In fact, this is what led him to the area of sentencing research in the first place. He realized this was the criminal justice topic of greatest concern to members of the public. Over the past 30 years, Dr. Roberts has built up a research program around this general issue and has conducted research that is both academically important and practically important in terms of its impact on criminal justice policy.

For example, Dr. Roberts recalls a favourite study he recently conducted with one of his graduate students. The study examined peoples' attitudes toward community-based punishments, specifically conditional sentences. Respondents to a national survey were asked to read a scenario and sentence the offender. When respondents were simply given the choice between a prison sentence and a conditional sentence, they favoured the prison sentence. However, when they were given specific details of what a conditional sentence entails, the large majority favoured that option, indicating clearly that public opposition to the conditional sentence reflects a lack of knowledge. Since this study was published in the *Canadian Journal of Behavioural Science* in 2000, it has been cited in numerous legal judgments.

After working in various government agencies, such as the Department of Justice Canada and the Canadian Sentencing Commission, Dr. Roberts is now a professor of criminology at the University of Ottawa. He is very well known for his research in the area of public attitudes toward criminal justice, especially as those attitudes relate to sentencing. Much of this research is available in the books he has written or co-written, including *Public Opinion, Crime, and Criminal Justice*, *Making Sense of Sentencing*, and *Criminal Justice in Canada: A Reader*. In addition, Dr. Roberts has been the editor of the *Canadian Journal of Criminology* for several years. Dr. Roberts has recently been appointed the University Research Chair at the University of Ottawa where he plans to continue his studies in the area of public attitudes toward criminal justice issues.

necessarily hold the same view of police agencies. This may indicate, as Stein (2001) argues, that these views are specific to agencies involved in the sentencing process.

This general finding is also supported by public views of priority areas in the criminal justice system. For example, in a 1998 public opinion poll, respondents were asked to rate how important various criminal justice issues were to them. More specifically, respondents were presented with the question, "Given that

TABLE 10.5 PERCEPTIONS OF HOW CRIMINAL JUSTICE INSTITUTIONS DEAL WITH OFFENDERS

	Not Harshly Enough	Correct Manner	Too Harshly	No Opinion
Courts	72%	19%	2%	7%
Federal government	63%	24%	2%	10%
Police agencies	27%	59%	9%	6%

Source: Adapted from Stein, 2001.

there are limited resources to spend, do you think each of the following should be a high priority, a medium priority, or a low priority in the areas of crime and justice?" (Stein, 2001). Consistent with the views expressed in Table 10.5, many of the areas given high priority consisted of getting tougher on crimes and criminals. For example, among the issues at the top of the priority list were implementing harsher sentences for violent youth (77%), deporting offenders who were not Canadian citizens (77%), and ensuring that offenders serve full sentences (65%) (Stein, 2001).

2. *Canadians do not have a lot of confidence in our criminal justice system.* A similarly negative picture emerges when the general public is asked about the level of confidence they have in the Canadian criminal justice system. For example, relatively few respondents to a 1998 public opinion poll had a lot of confidence in the criminal justice system, but the degree of confidence varied widely depending on the institution considered (Stein, 2001). The institution the public had the most confidence in was the police. The institutions responsible for sentencing and releasing offenders—courts, judges, lawyers, and parole boards—were viewed with much less confidence. To a large extent, of course, these findings of low confidence are probably related to public perceptions that these agencies treat offenders too leniently, as seen in Table 10.5.

3. *Canadians support alternatives to sentencing, but only under certain conditions.* Given the recent introduction into Canada of new sentencing options, such as the conditional sentence, it is important to consider public opinion on these alternatives. Responses to recent pubic opinion surveys indicate that a large majority of the public is supportive, in principle, of alternative sentences (Stein, 2001). However, this finding varies depending on the type of penalty and the type of crime considered. For example, the highest level of public support is found for penalties consisting of community service (85%), while the lowest level

of support is for parole (37%), but these results only hold for certain offences. For example, conditional sentences are viewed as a viable option for crimes such as fights (76% in favour of a conditional sentence versus 24% in favour of imprisonment). They are not considered viable for offenders charged with sexual assault (3% in favour of a conditional sentence versus 97% in favour of imprisonment) (Stein, 2001).

Factors That Influence Public Opinion

Many researchers have claimed that public opinion on issues of sentencing and parole does not fairly reflect the state of affairs in Canada (e.g., Sprott & Doob, 1997). It has been suggested that this discrepancy between public opinion and reality occurs because of an inadequate understanding on the part of the public of crime and our criminal justice system (Sprott & Doob, 1997). Certainly, the results of public opinion surveys support the idea that the public lacks the knowledge required to develop accurate perceptions of the criminal justice system, as do experimental studies that have looked at this issue more directly (e.g., Doob & Roberts, 1988). For example, a very common finding in public opinion surveys is that the public believe that crime in general is increasing in Canada (Stein, 2001). This perception, however, does not correspond to actual crime trends in Canada. In fact, based on recent statistics, violent crime has steadily decreased over the last five years. Likewise, as indicated above, the public clearly has views on the appropriateness of conditional sentences. Yet, responses to public opinion polls indicate that most people (57%) cannot select the correct definition of a conditional sentence from a list that includes definitions of a conditional sentence, parole, and bail (Stein, 2001).

So if public opinion is not based on the facts, where does public opinion come from? Sprott and Doob (1997) discuss the view that one important contributing factor is the media or, more specifically, the way the media portray criminal justice issues in Canada. Many studies have shown that the media provide a biased view of our criminal justice system (Doob, 1985), and many researchers hold the view that "members of the public do not adequately correct for the unrepresentative range of cases they hear about in the news media. As a result, the negative feelings and perceptions of leniency that the news media create are perpetuated" (Sprott & Doob, 1997, p. 276). The few experiments that have been done to examine media effects on public opinion in the area of sentencing and parole confirm these views (e.g., Doob & Roberts, 1988).

Another factor that may contribute to this discrepancy, particularly the discrepancy between public opinion of sentencing severity and actual sentencing severity, is the fear people have about being victimized. For example, Sprott and Doob (1997) hypothesized that, the higher the fear of victimization, the more likely a person will be to view the criminal justice system in a negative light. Their reasoning is that fear of crime may motivate an individual to do something about the source of their fear.

These individuals may look to the judicial system for safety. Since the judicial system has been unable to adequately deal with the crime problem, those with the most fear might be more likely to view the courts as being too lenient. Because many Canadians are afraid of being victims of crime (Hung & Bowles, 1995), Sprott and Doob's reasoning leads to an expectation that a large portion of the Canadian public will view the criminal justice as lenient, which is exactly what public opinion surveys indicate. By using pre-existing data, Sprott and Doob (1997) were able to examine the relationship between fear of crime and attitudes toward the criminal justice system. Their results confirm their hypotheses. Generally, they found that as "level of fear increased, so did perceptions of leniency in sentencing, dissatisfaction with the courts generally, and dissatisfaction with the police" (Sprott & Doob, 1997, pp. 285–286).

SUMMARY

1. Sentences are supposed to serve a number of different purposes in Canada. Deterring people from committing crimes and offender rehabilitation are two of the primary purposes. Sentencing in Canada is also guided by numerous principles, such as the fundamental sentencing principle, which states that a sentence must be proportionate to the gravity of the offence and the degree of responsibility of the offender. Such principles are meant to provide judges with guidance when handing down sentences.

2. Judges have many sentencing options at their disposal. The most common sentencing option in Canada is the monetary fine, and the most serious option is imprisonment. New sentencing options have also been recently proposed, such as the conditional sentence, in which an offender can serve his or her prison time in the community.

3. One of the major problems with sentencing in Canada is unwarranted sentencing disparity, which refers to differences in the severity of sentences handed down by different judges (or the same judge on different occasions) due to a reliance on extra-legal factors. These factors can include the judge's personality, philosophy, experience, and so on. One of the primary strategies for reducing sentencing disparity is to implement sentencing guidelines.

4. The death penalty was abolished in Canada in 1976. Its abolishment fits well with research about the death penalty, which indicates that offenders often do not consider the consequences of their actions before committing a crime. Furthermore, research indicates that violent crime rates decrease without having to rely on the death penalty. Moreover, the death penalty does not seem to be needed as a way of preventing murderers from killing upon their release, since most of these offenders do not go on to commit murder anyway.

5. Research examining the impact of punishment-based sentences suggests they are not effective for reducing recidivism. In contrast, correctional interventions based on core correctional principles show more promise. These principles include the need principle (effective interventions target criminogenic needs), the risk principle (effective interventions target high-risk offenders), and the responsivity principle (effective interventions match the general learning style, and the particular characteristics, of the offender).

6. The National Parole Board (NPB) makes parole decisions in Canada. Contrary to popular belief, parole is not automatically granted to offenders as soon as they become eligible, offender remorse only plays a very small part in parole decisions, most offenders let out on parole do not go on to commit more crimes, and victims do have a significant say in the parole process.

KEY CONCEPTS

absolute discharge	294	general deterrence	292	risk principle	305
community service	294	imprisonment	294	sentencing disparity	296
conditional discharge	294	long-term offender	295	sentencing guidelines	300
conditional sentence	294	National Parole Board	306	specific deterrence	292
dangerous offender	295	need principle	305	statutory release	308
day parole	308	parole	306	systematic disparity	297
fine	294	probation	294	temporary absence	308
full parole	308	reparations	292	unsystematic disparity	297
fundamental principle of sentencing	293	responsivity principle restitution	305 294	unwarranted sentencing disparity	297

DISCUSSION QUESTIONS

1. As you saw in this chapter, there are many different reasons that we sentence offenders in Canada. From the list we presented, which do you think is the most important reason, or are there many that you feel are important? Why?

2. In your opinion, should offenders who are convicted for serious crimes such as sexual assault ever be eligible for parole? Why or why not?

3. What does it mean when an offender is sentenced to life in prison?

4. You have just been hired as a research assistant by one of your professors. She is working on a government project looking at ways to deal with sentencing disparity. Together, you and your professor must propose strategies, beyond the sentencing guidelines that currently exist, that could be used to reduce unwarranted sentencing disparity in Canada. What types of strategies would you propose?

5. Your neighbour thinks Canada is getting soft on crime by providing community "rehabilitation" programs. He thinks the only way to really rehabilitate offenders is to lock them up in cells with nothing to do but think about the crimes they've committed. Do you think your neighbour is right? Explain.

6. Recent results from public opinion polls suggest that, even when the public is told that the death penalty has little impact as a crime deterrent, the majority still support the death penalty. Why do you think this happens?

7. Beyond the factors we have discussed in this chapter, what might account for the inaccurate perceptions of the public when it comes to sentencing and parole practices in Canada? What can be done to decrease these inaccurate perceptions?

ADDITIONAL INFORMATION

Readings

Andrews, D. & Bonta, J. (2001). *The psychology of criminal conduct* (3rd edition). Cincinnati: Anderson Publishing Company.

Palys, T.S., & Divorski, S. (1986). Explaining sentencing disparity. *Canadian Journal of Criminology, 28,* 347–362.

Roberts, J.V., & Cole, D. (Eds.). (1999). *Making sense of sentencing.* Toronto: University of Toronto Press.

Web Sites

Correctional Service Canada
www.csc-scc.gc.ca/

The John Howard Society
www.johnhoward.ca/

Canada's National Parole Board
www.npb-cnlc.gc.ca/about/about_e.htm

Risk Assessment and Violence Prediction

Joanne Marshall has served one year of a three-year sentence for assault causing bodily harm. The assault occurred late one evening after Joanne had returned home from drinking with her friends. She got into a heated argument with her boyfriend, grabbed a knife from the kitchen, and stabbed him in the shoulder. A prison psychologist has completed a risk assessment and her case management officer is supporting her application for parole. Joanne is going to appear tomorrow in front of three members from the National Parole Board to discuss the offence she committed, her plans if released, and what intervention programs she has participated in. The parole board members will need to consider what level of risk Joanne poses for reoffending, including whether or not she will engage in another violent act. They will also attempt to determine whether she has developed more appropriate ways of dealing with interpersonal conflict.

Every day individuals make judgments about the likelihood of events. Predictions are made about midterm exam grades, being admitted into law school, recovering from an episode of depression, or committing a criminal act after release from prison. Our legal system frequently requires decisions about the likelihood of future criminal acts that can significantly influence the lives of individuals. With the possibility that offenders could spend years or even the remainder of their lives in confinement, decisions by psychologists can have a significant impact. Predicting future violence has been described as "one of the most complex and controversial issues in behavioral science and law" (Borum, 1996, p. 945).

Although it is clear that significant advances have taken place since the 1990s, risk assessment and prediction remains imperfect. Bonta (2002) concludes that "risk assessment is a double-edged sword. It can be used to justify the application of severe sanctions or to moderate extreme penalties.... However, the identification of the violent recidivist is not infallible. We are not at the point where we can achieve a level of prediction free of error" (p. 375). However, the systematic assessment of risk provides judicial decision makers, such as judges and the National Parole Board, with much needed information to help them make challenging decisions.

The goal of this chapter is explore the major issues associated with risk prediction in a forensic context. In particular, the focus will be on understanding the task of assessing risk and predicting violence.

WHAT IS RISK ASSESSMENT?

The past decade has seen a change in the way risk is viewed. Prior to the 1990s, risk was viewed as a dichotomy—the individual is either dangerous or not dangerous. Nowadays, risk is viewed as a range—the individual can vary in the degree to which he or she is considered dangerous (Steadman, 2000). In other words, the shift has added a dimension of probability to the assessment of whether a person will commit violence. The focus on probability reflects two considerations. First, it highlights the idea that probabilities may change across time. Second, it recognizes that risk level reflects an interaction among a person's characteristics, background, and possible future situations that will affect whether or not the person engages in violent behaviour.

The process of risk assessment includes both a "prediction" and "management" component (Hart, 1998; Heilbrun, 1997). The prediction component describes the probability that an individual will commit future criminal or violent acts. The focus of this component is to identify the risk factors that are related to this likelihood of future violence. The management component describes the development of interventions to manage or reduce the likelihood of future violence. The focus of this component is to identify what treatment(s) might reduce the individual's level of risk or what conditions need to be implemented to manage the individual's risk. As described by Hart (1998), "the critical function of risk assessments is violence *prevention*, not violence *prediction*" (emphasis in the original; p. 123).

RISK ASSESSMENTS: WHEN ARE THEY CONDUCTED?

Risk assessments are routinely conducted in the civil and criminal contexts. Civil contexts refer to the private rights of individuals and the legal proceedings connected with such rights. Criminal contexts refer to situations in which an individual has been charged with a crime. Common to both contexts is a need for information that would enable legal judgments to be made concerning the probability of individuals committing some kind of act that would disrupt the peace and order of the state or individuals within the state.

Civil Setting

A number of civil contexts require risk assessment:

- *Civil commitment* requires a person to be hospitalized involuntarily if he or she has a mental illness and poses a danger to himself or herself or others. A mental health worker, usually a psychiatrist or psychologist, would need to know the probability of violence associated with various mental disorders and be able to identify whether the circumstances associated with individual patients would affect the likelihood that they would harm others or themselves.

- Assessment of risk in *child protection* contexts involve the laws that are in place to protect children from abuse. The risk of physical or sexual abuse or neglect is considered when a government protection agency, such as the Children's Aid Society, decides whether to temporarily remove a child or to terminate parental rights. In order to provide assistance to protection agencies, professionals need to be familiar with the risk factors that predict childhood maltreatment.

- *Immigration* laws prohibit the admission of individuals into Canada if there are reasonable grounds to believe they will engage in acts of violence.

- *School* and *labour regulations* also provide provisions to prevent any kind of act that would endanger others.

- Other civil contexts include *duty to warn* and *limits of confidentiality*.

The precedent-setting case of *Tarasoff v. Regents of University of California* (1976) illustrates some of the issues involved in civil contexts, especially what can happen to psychologists who fail to protect a threatened person from danger. Prosenjit Poddar was a graduate student at the University of California at Berkeley who had seen a clinical psychologist at the student health centre on campus. The psychologist became worried that Poddar might be planning to kill Tatiana Tarasoff, a young woman who Poddar felt had rejected him. When Poddar disclosed to the psychologist that he had bought a gun, the psychologist contacted the campus police, warning them that he felt Poddar was dangerous and should be hospitalized for observation. The police talked to Poddar, thought he appeared rational, and secured a promise from him to stay away from Tarasoff. Two months later, Poddar stabbed Tarasoff to death. Tatiana Tarasoff's parents sued the psychologist for failing to warn them or their daughter about the danger. The California Supreme Court ruled that the psychologist was negligent in failing to warn Tarasoff. In the ruling, the court did not impose a specific duty to warn but required that reasonable steps be taken to protect the potential victim. More recent cases have expanded the duty to protect by requiring mental health professionals to protect society from potentially dangerous clients, even if they do not know who the specific victim might be (*Currie v. United States*, 1986).

As a result of the Tarasoff case and similar cases involving disclosure of risk potential, mental health professionals are expected to consider the likelihood that their patients will act in a violent manner and to intervene to prevent such behaviour. According to Birch (1992), litigation surrounding duty to protect is only just beginning in Canada. In her review of Canadian cases, she found none in which a mental health professional had been sued by a third party for injuries their clients had committed against a third party.

Patients may decide not to disclose their deviant thoughts and fantasies to professionals for fear that their doctors will contact the police. In the United Kingdom, the precedent-setting case that balances the duty of confidentiality and the duty to disclose is *W. v. Egdell* (1990). In this case W. was a patient confined to a psychiatric facility after committing a series of murders. Dr. Egdell, a psychiatrist, was hired by W.'s lawyers to conduct mental health assessment. The psychiatrist's report concluded that W. expressed a lack of remorse and maintained an interest in making homemade bombs. Dr. Egdell asked the lawyers for their permission to send his report to the medical director of the hospital where W. was institutionalized. Dr. Edgell's request was refused, but he went ahead anyway and forwarded his report to the hospital. W. launched an injunction to stop the hospital from using the report and for damages for breaching confidentiality. W.'s suit was dismissed, showing that public safety overrides the duties of confidentiality.

Criminal Settings

The assessment of risk occurs at nearly every major decision point in the criminal justice and forensic psychiatric systems, including pretrial, sentencing, and release. A person can be denied bail if there is a substantial likelihood that he or she will commit another criminal offence. In the case of adolescent offenders, the judge can decide to apply adult criminal sanctions depending on the age, type of offence, and risk level posed by the youth. Risk also plays a role in decisions about whether a youth should be sent to secure custody or not. For example, adolescent offenders should only be committed to custody if they are considered at high risk if placed in open custody, or if they were to serve a probation term in the community.

As in civil settings, an important issue in risk assessment in criminal settings is the disclosure of information about potential risk. However, in criminal settings, this must be considered in light of the solicitor–client privilege that is fundamental to criminal proceedings. In order for lawyers to adequately represent their clients, they must be able to freely discuss the case with the clients.

This privilege is also extended to experts retained by lawyers. A recent case in Canada has clarified when solicitor–client privilege and doctor–patient confidentiality must be set aside for the protection of members of the public. *Smith v. Jones* (1999) involved a psychiatrist who was hired to aid a defence lawyer in preparing a case. The client was a man accused of aggravated sexual assault on a prostitute. The accused told the psychiatrist of his plans to kidnap, sexually assault, and kill prostitutes. The psychiatrist told the defence lawyer about his concerns that the accused was likely to commit future violent offences unless he received treatment. When the psychiatrist found out that the defence lawyer was not going to address his concerns at the sentencing hearing (the accused pled guilty to the charge of aggravated assault), he filed an affidavit providing his opinion about the level of risk posed by the accused. The trial judge ruled that due to concerns about public safety the psychiatrist was under duty to disclose the information he obtained to the police and the Crown counsel. The case was appealed to the Supreme Court, which ruled that in cases in which there is "clear, serious, and imminent danger," public safety outweighs solicitor–client privilege.

Although risk assessment is a routine component of many sentencing decisions, it is a critical component of certain kinds of sentencing decisions. For example, after 1947, when habitual criminal legislation was introduced, offenders could be sentenced to an indefinite period of incarceration. In 1977, dangerous offender legislation was enacted that requires mental health professionals to provide an assessment of risk for violence. Changes to the legislation in 1997 made indefinite incarceration the only option if an offender is found to be a dangerous offender (see Chapter 10 for more information about dangerous offenders). At the same time, a new category of dangerous persons was created, referred to as long-term offenders. To be declared a long-term offender, a person must pose a substantial risk for violently reoffending. Thus, risk assessment is also a core component of this legislation.

Risk assessment is also required for decisions concerning release from correctional and forensic psychiatric institutions, such as parole. If a person is sentenced to prison in Canada, he or she can apply to the National Parole Board to get early release. Parole Board members use a variety of sources of information (including risk assessments provided by institutional psychologists) to decide the likelihood that the offender will commit another violent offence if released. Although most offenders get released on statutory release (after serving two-thirds of their sentence), statutory release can be denied if the offender is likely to commit further violent offences. Finally, a patient who has been found not criminally responsible on account of a mental disorder (see Chapter 10) can be released from a secure forensic psychiatric facility only if a risk assessment is completed.

Clearly, risk assessment plays an integral role in legal decision making, both in civil and criminal settings, allowing informed decisions that weigh the likelihood that an individual will engage in a dangerous or criminal act in the future. In the sections that follow, we will look at the predictive accuracy of these assessments, as well as the factors that actually predict violence.

TYPES OF PREDICTION OUTCOMES

Predicting future events will result in one of four possible outcomes. Two of these outcomes are correct, and two are incorrect. The definitions provided below are stated in terms of predicting violent acts but could be used for any specific outcome (see also Table 11.1):

- A **true positive** (TP) represents a correct prediction and occurs when a person who is predicted to be violent engages in violence.

- A **true negative** (TN) is also a correct prediction and occurs when a person who is predicted not to be violent does not act violently.

- A **false positive** (FP) represents an incorrect prediction and occurs when a person is predicted to be violent but is not.

- A **false negative** (FN) is also an incorrect prediction and occurs when a person is predicted to be nonviolent but acts violently.

The two types of errors are dependent on each other. Minimizing the number of false positive errors results in an increase in the number of false negative errors. The implication of these errors varies depending on the decisions associated with them, and in many cases the stakes are high. A false positive error has implications for the individual being assessed (such as denial of freedom), whereas a false negative error has implications for society and the potential victim (such as another child victimized by a sexual offender). In some cases, it is perhaps tolerable to have a high rate of false positives if the consequences of such an error are not severe. For example, if the consequence of being falsely labelled as potentially violent is being supervised more closely while released on parole, the consequence may be acceptable. However, if the consequence of being falsely labelled as potentially violent contributes to a juror's decision to decide in favour of the death penalty, then perhaps this is too high a price to pay. As in many legal settings, the consequences for the individual must be weighed in relation to the consequences for society at large.

TABLE 11.1 PREDICTIONS: DECISIONS VERSUS OUTCOMES

Decision	Outcome	
	Reoffends	Does Not Reoffend
Predicted to reoffend	True positive (correct prediction)	False positive (incorrect prediction)
Predicted to not reoffend	False negative (incorrect prediction)	True negative (correct prediction)

The Base Rate Problem

A problem with attempting to predict violence is determining base rates. The **base rate** represents the percentage of people within a given population who commit a criminal or violent act. It is difficult to make accurate predictions when the base rates are too high or too low. A problem that emerges when attempting to predict events that have a low base rate is that many false positives will occur. For example, the past decade has seen several high-profile school shootings. However, although these events generate much media coverage, they occur infrequently. Any attempt to predict which individual youths might engage in a school shooting would result in many youths being wrongly classified as potential shooters.

The base rate can vary dramatically depending on the group being studied, what is being predicted, and the length of follow-up period over which the individual is monitored. For example, the base rate of sexual violence tends to be relatively low, even over extended follow-up periods, whereas the base rate for violating the conditions of a conditional release is very high. The base rate problem is not such a concern if predictions of violence are limited to groups with a high base rate of violence, such as incarcerated offenders. The general rule is that it is easier to predict frequent events than infrequent events.

Consider the following example. Assume you have developed a test that accurately identifies 90% of those offenders who will reoffend (recidivists). You administer this test to 1000 offenders. In sample A, assume that the base rate of reoffending is 50%. Thus 500 of your offenders will be recidivists and 500 will not reoffend. Table 11.2 presents the number of correct and incorrect predictions you will make. In this case, you will correctly identify 450 of the recidivists, with only 50 offenders being incorrectly identified as potential recidivists (i.e., false positives). In contrast, consider what happens when the base rate is changed to 10% (see Table 11.3). Your test is still 90% accurate, but now there are only 100 recidivists. You correctly identify 90 of the recidivists but you also identified 90 nonrecidivists as recidivists. This example illustrates that when the base rate for recidivism is low, even the most accurate tests will result in many mistakes.

TABLE 11.2 OUTCOME OF PREDICTIONS WHEN BASE RATE IS 50%

	Outcome	
Prediction	500 Reoffend	500 Do Not Reoffend
Predicted to reoffend	True positive ($n = 450$)	False positive ($n = 50$)
Predicted to not reoffend	False negative ($n = 50$)	True negative ($n = 450$)

TABLE 11.3 OUTCOME OF PREDICTIONS WHEN BASE RATE IS 10%		
	Outcome	
Prediction	*100 Reoffend*	*900 Do Not Reoffend*
Predicted to reoffend	True positive (*n* = 90)	False positive (*n* = 90)
Predicted to not reoffend	False negative (*n* = 10)	True negative (*n* = 810)

A HISTORY OF THE PREDICTION OF VIOLENCE

Before 1966 relatively little attention was paid to how well professionals could assess risk. In the 1960s, civil rights concerns provided the rare opportunity to study the accuracy of mental health professionals to predict violence. In the case of *Baxstrom v. Herald* (1966), the U.S. Supreme Court ruled that the plaintiff Johnnie Baxstrom had been detained beyond his sentence expiry and was ordered released into the community. More than 300 mentally ill offenders from the Dannemora State Hospital for the Criminally Insane and another state hospital were released into the community or transferred to less secure institutions. Steadman and Cocozza (1974) followed 98 of these patients who were released into the community but had been considered by mental health professionals as too dangerous to be released. Only 20 of these patients were arrested over a four-year period, and of these, only seven committed a violent offence.

In a larger study, Thornberry and Jacoby (1979) followed 400 forensic patients released into the community due to a similar civil rights case in Pennsylvania (*Dixon v. Attorney General of the Commonwealth of Pennsylvania*, 1971). During an average three-year follow-up period, 60 patients were either arrested or rehospitalized for a violent incident.

The two studies we have just described are known as the Baxstrom and Dixon studies. These cases and similar ones call into question the ability of mental health professionals to make accurate predictions of violence. Two key findings emerged from the research. First, the base rate for violence was relatively low. For example, in the Baxstrom study, seven out of 98 (roughly 7%) violently reoffended, as did 60 out of 400 (15%) in the Dixon study. Second, the false positive rate was very high. In the Baxstrom and Dixon studies, the false positive rates were 86% and 85%, respectively.

Ennis and Litwack (1974) characterized clinical expertise in violence prediction as similar to "flipping coins in the courtroom" and argued that clinical testimony be barred from the courtroom. Other researchers have gone even further, concluding that "no expertise to predict dangerous behavior exists and … the attempt to apply this supposed knowledge to predict who will be dangerous results in a complete failure" (Cocozza & Steadman, 1978, p. 274).

This pessimism continued into the 1980s. John Monahan, a leading U.S. researcher, summarized the literature in 1981 and concluded that "psychiatrists and psychologists are accurate in no more than one out of three predictions of violent behavior over a several-year period among institutionalized populations that had both committed violence in the past (and thus had a high base rate for it) and who were diagnosed as mentally ill" (Monahan, 1981, p. 47).

Notwithstanding the above conclusion, both Canadian and U.S. courts have ruled that predictions of violence do not violate the basic tenets of fundamental justice, nor are they unconstitutional. In *Barefoot v. Estelle* (1983) the Supreme Court of the United States determined the constitutionality of a Texas death penalty appeal decision. Thomas Barefoot burned down a bar and shot and killed a police officer. Barefoot was convicted of capital murder and, at the sentencing phase of the trial, testimony was presented from two psychiatrists (one being Dr. James Grigson, whom we'll discuss later in the chapter) about the threat of future dangerousness posed by Thomas Barefoot. Both psychiatrists testified, based on a hypothetical fact situation, that the individual described would be a threat to society. The judge sentenced Barefoot to death. The United States Supreme Court rejected the defendant's challenge that psychiatrists were unable to make sufficient accurate predictions of violence and ruled that the use of hypothetical questions to establish future dangerousness was admissible. The court concluded that mental health professionals' predictions were "not always wrong ... only most of the time" (p. 901).

Canadian courts have also supported the role of mental health professionals in the prediction of violent behaviour (*Moore and the Queen*, 1984). For example, in a dangerous offender case, the issue of whether psychiatric testimony should be admitted as evidence was evaluated. The court concluded, "the test for admissibility is relevance, not infallibility ... psychiatric evidence is clearly relevant to the issue whether a person is likely to behave in a certain way" (*R. v. Lyons*, 1987).

METHODOLOGICAL ISSUES

Risk assessment assumes that risk can be measured. Measurement, in turn, assumes that an instrument exists for the measurement of risk. What would be the ideal way to evaluate an instrument designed to measure risk? The way to proceed would be to assess a large number of offenders and then, regardless of their risk level, release them into the community. The offenders would then be tracked to see if they commit another criminal act. This way the risk instrument could be evaluated to determine if it could accurately predict future criminal acts. Although an ideal scenario from a research perspective, it is not ethically feasible to release high-risk individuals into the community. In reality, the sample available for evaluating a risk assessment instrument is limited to those with a relatively low risk of reoffending. This constrains the kinds of conclusions that can be drawn when risk assessment is evaluated in the real world.

Monahan and Steadman (1994) have identified three main weaknesses of research on the prediction of violence. The first issue concerns the limited number of risk factors being studied. Violent behaviour is due to a complex interaction between individual dispositions and situational factors. In other words, there are many different reasons that someone engages in violence. Thus many risk factors are likely involved, including the person's background, social situation, and biological and psychological features. Many studies have focused on only a limited number of risk factors.

The second issue concerns how the criterion variable (the variable you are trying to measure) is measured. Researchers have often used official criminal records as their criterion measure. However, many crimes, including violent crimes, may never engage the criminal justice system. Thus, many false positives may be undiscovered true positives. In short, use of official records underestimates violence. When official records are combined with interviews with patients or offenders and with collateral reports (information from people or agencies who know the patient or offender), the rate of violence increases. The MacArthur Violence Risk Assessment Study (Steadman et al., 1998) illustrates the effect of using different measures. Using official agency records, the base rate for violence was 4.5%, but, when patient and collateral reports were added, the base rate increased to 27.5%, a rate of violence six times higher than the original base rate.

Finally, how the criterion variable is defined is a concern. In some studies researchers will classify their participants as having either engaged in violence or not. Monahan and Steadman (1994) recommend that researchers expand this coding to include the severity of violence (threatened violence versus severe violence), types of violence (spousal violence versus sexual violence), targets of violence (family versus stranger-directed violence), location (institutions versus community) and motivation (reactive [violence as the outcome of or reaction to an event] versus instrumental [violence used as an instrument in the pursuit of some goal]). It is likely that some risk factors will be associated with certain forms of violence; for example, a history of sexual offences may predict future sexual offences but not future bank robberies.

Measuring Predictive Accuracy

The ability of a risk assessment instrument to accurately predict a specific outcome can be evaluated by various means. Two statistical techniques that are currently used are survival analysis and the receiver operator characteristic. Survival analysis is a technique that estimates how long it takes (i.e., survival time) to reach some event, such as to be arrested for new offence. Prior to being used to evaluate risk assessment measures, survival analysis was used to evaluate the efficacy of drugs. For example, if patient A has cancer and is given an experimental drug, whereas patient B is given a different drug, does patient A survive longer than patient B? When applied to risk assessment, survival means not being arrested for some type of offence or having the release revoked. For recidivists, survival time is the length of time between the date of release and the recidivism date. For nonrecidivists, survival time is the length of time between date of release and when the study ended (i.e., the length of the follow-up period). Survival analysis is useful because it controls for the variable follow-up times (i.e., not all offenders are released at the same time). One problem with survival analysis is that its accuracy is based on the base rate for the outcome.

The receiver operator characteristic (ROC) is a statistical technique that is not unduly influenced by the base rate (Mossman, 1994; Rice & Harris, 1995). For this reason, it has become a commonly used technique to evaluate the predictive accuracy of a risk assessment instrument. Within risk assessment, ROCs are applied to data that comprise a continuous measure (a risk assessment scale) and a dichotomous outcome measure (e.g., did the person commit another offence?). The statistic of primary interest is the area under the curve (AUC). To obtain an AUC, a curve is plotted that compares the true positive rate as a function of the false positive rate at various cut-offs on the risk-assessment measure. A perfectly accurate test would yield an AUC of 1.00, which would mean you were correct 100% of the time. An AUC of 0.50 would be equivalent to tossing a coin. You would be right 50% of the time and wrong 50% of the time.

JUDGMENT ERROR AND BIASES

How do psychologists make decisions when conducting risk assessments? Researchers have identified the typical errors and biases in clinical decision making (Elbogen, 2002). The shortcuts people use to help make decisions are called **heuristics** (Tversky & Kahneman, 1981). Some of these heuristics lead to inaccurate decisions. Clinicians may make several types of decision errors. A clinician may include intuitively important traits or traits assumed to be associated with the outcome but that actually are not. Chapman and Chapman (1967) define an **illusory correlation** as the belief that a correlation exists between two events that in reality are either not correlated or correlated to a much lesser degree. For example, a clinician might assume a strong correlation between a diagnosis of mental disorder and high risk for violent behaviour. Although some forms of mental disorder are related to an increased risk, a relationship has not been consistently found (Monahan & Steadman, 1994). Clinicians also tend to ignore base rates of violence (Monahan, 1981). Clinicians working in prisons or forensic psychiatric facilities may not be aware of how often individuals with specific characteristics act violently. For example, the base rate for recidivism in homicide offenders is extremely low. Other investigators (Borum, Otto, & Golding, 1993) have noted the tendency to rely on highly salient or unique cues, such as bizarre delusions.

In general, people tend to be overconfident in their judgments (see Kahneman & Tversky, 1982). In one of the few studies that have investigated the link between confidence and violence prediction, McNiel, Sanberg, and Binder (1998) measured the association between clinicians' ratings of the probability of inpatient violence and their confidence level in their ratings. Clinicians working in an acute psychiatric unit were asked to rate the likelihood a patient would physically attack other people within one week of arrival and to indicate their degree of confidence (low, moderate, high). The prediction of violence accuracy depended on the confidence of the clinician. The more confidence expressed by a clinician in his or her risk judgment, the more accurate that person was. Conversely, clinicians who were less confident were less accurate in their risk judgments. For example, clinicians rated eight patients with a high likelihood of committing a physical attack and expressed a high level of confidence in their ratings for these patients. Of these patients, six (75%) were later physically assaultive. In contrast, clinicians rated 11 patients as very likely to commit a physical attack but expressed a low level of confidence in their estimate. Of these patients, only four (36%) were later physically assaultive.

There is some evidence that the gender of the decision maker may be influential. Elbogen, Williams, Kim, Tomkins, and Scalora (2001) asked 81 male and female clinicians (including nurses, psychiatrists, psychologists, and social workers) to rate the dangerousness of male and female patients. Male clinicians perceived the level of dangerousness to be similar for male and female patients. However, female clinicians judged male patients to be significantly more dangerous than female patients. Other researchers have also found that both male and female clinicians tend to underpredict female violence (Lidz, Mulvey, & Gardner, 1993).

APPROACHES TO THE ASSESSMENT OF RISK

What are the existing methods of risk assessment? There are three methods of risk assessment most commonly described. **Unstructured clinical judgment** is characterized by a substantial amount of professional discretion and lack of guidelines. There are no predefined rules about what risk factors should be considered, what sources of information should be used, or how the risk factors should be combined to make a decision about risk. Thus, risk factors considered vary across clinicians and vary across cases (Bonta, 1996; Grove & Meehl, 1996; Grove, Zald, Lebow, Snitz, & Nelson, 2000). Grove and Meehl (1996) have described this type of risk assessment as relying on an "informal, 'in the head,' subjective, impressionistic, subjective conclusion, reached (somehow) by a human clinical judge" (p. 294). See Box 11.1 on the next page for an example of a professional using this type of risk assessment.

In contrast, mechanical prediction involves predefined rules about what risk factors to consider, how information should be collected, and how information should be combined to make a risk decision. Thus, risk factors do not vary as a function of the clinician and the same risk factors are considered for each case. A common type of mechanical prediction is called **actuarial prediction**. With actuarial prediction, the risk factors used have been selected and combined based on their empirical or statistical association with a specific outcome (Bonta, 1996; Gove & Meehl, 1996; Grove et al., 2000). In other words, a study has been done in which a number of risk factors have been measured, a sample of offenders have been followed for a specific time period, and only those risk factors that were actually related to reoffending in this sample are selected (for an example of an actuarial scale, see the Violence Risk Appraisal Guide described later in this chapter).

BOX 11.1 DR. DEATH: A LEGENDARY (NOTORIOUS) FORENSIC PSYCHIATRIST

Dr. James Grigson is a Dallas psychiatrist who has earned the nicknames "Dr. Death" and "the hanging shrink" because of his effectiveness at testifying for the prosecution in death-penalty cases. For nearly three decades, Dr. Grigson has been testifying in death-penalty cases in Texas.

Death-penalty trials are divided into two phases. First, whether or not the defendant is guilty is decided. Next, the same judge and jury decide whether to impose life in prison or to sentence the defendant to die. One of the issues the jurors must decide on is "whether there is a probability that the defendant would commit criminal acts of violence that would constitute a continuing threat to society." Psychiatrists and psychologists are often hired to testify about the likelihood for future violence.

Dr. Grigson's testimony is very effective. He often diagnoses defendants as being sociopaths and states with 100% certainty they will kill again. For example in *Estelle v. Smith*, Dr. Grigson testified on the basis of a brief examination that the defendant Smith was a "very severe sociopath," who, if given the opportunity, would commit another criminal act. The diagnosis of sociopath appears to have been based on the sole fact that Mr. Smith "lacked remorse."

Dr. Grigson has been proven wrong. In the case of Randall Dale Adams (a documentary about this case was made called *The Thin Blue Line*), Dr. Grigson testified that Randall Adams was a "very extreme" sociopath and would continue to be a threat to society even if kept locked in prison. Randall Adams was sentenced to death. However, after spending 12 years on death row, his conviction was overturned and he was released (another inmate confessed to the murder). It has been 13 years since Randall Adams has been released. He is now married, employed, and living a nonviolent life. Dr. Grigson was wrong in this case—and potentially how many others?

In 1995, Dr. Grigson was expelled from the American Psychiatric Association (APA) for ethical violations. He was expelled for claiming he can predict with 100% certainty that a defendant will commit another violent act (and, on at least one occasion, testifying that the defendant had a "1000%" chance of committing another violent act). The APA was also concerned that Dr. Grigson often testifies in court based on hypothetical situations and will diagnose an individual without even examining the defendant. Dr. Grigson often diagnoses defendants as sociopaths on the basis of his own clinical opinion and not on any structured assessment procedures.

Dr. Grigson was also involved the death-penalty case of Canadian Joseph Stanley Faulder, who was convicted and sentenced to death for the robbery and murder of Inez Phillips. Dr. Grigson testified that Stanley Faulder was an "extremely severe sociopath," that there was no cure, and that he would certainly kill again. We will never assess the accuracy of Dr. Grigson's predictions, since on June 17, 1999, after spending 22 years on death row, Stanley Faulder was executed.

A debate in the literature exists concerning the comparative accuracy of unstructured clinical versus actuarial prediction. The first study to compare actuarial and unstructured clinical judgment was conducted by sociologist Ann Burgess in 1928.

Burgess compared the accuracy of 21 objective risk factors (such as age, number of past offences, length of sentence) to clinical judgments of three psychiatrists in predicting parole failure in a sample of 3000 criminal offenders. The actuarial scale was markedly superior to the psychiatrists in identifying which offenders would fail on parole. In a review of 20 studies, Paul Meehl (1954) concluded that actuarial prediction was equal to or better than unstructured clinical judgment in all cases. A similar conclusion was reached almost 50 years later, when Meehl and his colleagues (Grove et al., 2000) conducted a meta-analysis of prediction studies for human health and behaviour (including criminal behaviour). In sum, the weight of the evidence clearly favours actuarial assessments of risk (Mossman, 1994), even with samples of offenders with mental disorders (Bonta, Law, & Hanson, 1998) and sex offenders (Hanson & Bussiere, 1998).

Arising from the limitations associated with unstructured clinical judgment and concern that the actuarial method did not allow for individualized risk appraisal or for consideration of the impact of situational factors to modify risk level, a new approach to risk assessment has emerged—**structured professional judgment** (SPJ; Borum, 1996; Webster et al., 1997). According to this method, the professional (the term "professional" is used to acknowledge that it is not only clinicians who make evaluations of risk but a diverse group, including law enforcement officers, probation officers, and social workers) is guided by a predetermined list of risk factors that have been selected from the research and professional literature. The professional considers the presence and severity of each risk factor, but the final judgment of risk level is based on the evaluator's professional judgment. The reliability and predictive utility of these risk summary judgments are only beginning to be assessed. Dr. Christopher Webster, the Canadian researcher profiled in Box 11.2 on the next page, has done extensive research in the use of SPJ.

Some authors have also described an anamnestic (recollection of past events) approach to risk assessment (Melton et al., 1997). According to this method, the evaluator attempts to identify the factors that explain why the individual has committed past violent acts. The evaluator interviews the individual and reviews collateral information to identify the unique and dynamic risk factors that recur across violent acts. The purpose of this approach is to target these individual risk factors for intervention in order to prevent future acts of violence. To date, the utility of this approach has not been investigated by empirical research.

Types of Predictors

There are hundreds of potential risk factors that clinicians and researchers might use to predict antisocial and violent behaviour. A **risk factor** is a measurable feature of an individual that predicts the behaviour of interest, such as violence. Traditionally, risk factors were divided into two main types: static and dynamic.

Static risk factors are factors that do not fluctuate over time and are not changed by treatment. Age at first arrest is an example of a static risk factor, since no amount of time or treatment will change this risk factor. **Dynamic risk factors** fluctuate over

BOX 11.2 CANADIAN RESEARCHER PROFILE: DR. CHRISTOPHER WEBSTER

Dr. Christopher Webster completed his undergraduate degree at the University of British Columbia, his Masters at Queen's University, and his Ph.D. at Dalhousie University. His doctoral thesis focused on avoidance conditioning in guinea pigs. Currently, Dr. Webster is a consultant to various forensic and mental health agencies in Ontario and is affiliated with the psychiatry departments of both the University of Toronto and McMaster University, and is professor emeritus in psychology at Simon Fraser University.

Dr. Webster's first position after graduating was as a research scientist at the Addiction Research Foundation in Toronto. Later he transferred to the Clarke Institute of Psychology, where he established clinical and research programs for autistic children and their families. There he conducted fitness and criminal responsibility evaluations of defendants for the court.

In the late 1970s he accepted a position as senior research scientist with a new forensic program established by the Clarke Institute. He also began collaborating with practitioners and researchers from different

disciplines and started conducting research on risk assessment and risk management. Over the past two decades, Dr. Webster has made substantial contributions to this field, and his work has provided clinicians with essential ways to structure their risk assessments.

Dr. Webster notes that one of his favourite pieces of research was a study conducted with Robert Menzies (at that time a graduate student in sociology at the University of Toronto), identifying risk factors for violence in a large sample of offenders with mental disorders. In 1993, Dr. Webster joined the Department of Psychology at Simon Fraser University. One of the many projects he worked on while there was the development of a structured professional judgment manual called the HCR-20 (this was done in collaboration with Stephen Hart, Kevin Douglas, and Derek Eaves). Research that Dr. Webster finds particularly rewarding entails working with an interdisciplinary team and collaborating with researchers and clinicians from different countries. "Manualization" of violence risk is the essential theme.

Of the many courses he has taught, his two favourites are *Psychology and the Law* and *Clinical Criminology*. He thinks one important aspect of training future forensic researchers is to have undergraduates involved in conducting research in forensic settings.

Dr. Webster recently purchased a 1957 Triumph TRW motorcycle (military model). He was glad that it came complete with its original manual. This should help with the challenge "to get it running."

time and are amenable to changing. An antisocial attitude is an example of a dynamic risk factor, since it is possible that treatment could modify this variable.

More recently, correctional researchers have begun to conceptualize risk factors as a continuous construct (Grann, Belfrage, & Tengström, 2000; Hanson & Harris, 2000; Zamble, & Quinsey, 1997). At one end of the continuum are the static risk factors described above. At the other end are acute dynamic risk factors. These risk factors change rapidly within days, hours, or minutes and often occur just prior to an offence. Factors at this end of the continuum include variables such as negative mood and level of intoxication. In the middle of the continuum are stable dynamic risk factors. These are risk factors that change but only over long periods of time such as months or years and are variables that should be targeted for treatment. These factors include criminal attitudes, coping ability, and impulse control. Some researchers also include enduring personality traits such as psychopathy as a stable dynamic risk factor (Zamble & Quinsey, 1997), although whether or not the psychopathic traits observed in some adults can be modified through appropriate treatment remains to be determined.

IMPORTANT RISK FACTORS

Since the late 1980s a great deal of research has investigated what factors are associated with future violence. These can be classified into historical, dispositional, clinical, and contextual risk factors. **Historical risk factors** are events experienced in the past and include general social history and specific criminal history variables, such as employment problems and a history of violence. **Dispositional risk factors** are those that reflect the person's traits, tendencies, or style and include demographic, attitudinal, and personality variables, such as gender, age, negative attitudes, and psychopathy. **Clinical risk factors** are the symptoms of mental disorders that can contribute to violence, such as substance abuse or major psychoses. **Contextual risk factors** are aspects of the individual's current environment that can elevate the risk, such as access to victims or weapons, lack of social supports, and perceived stress.

Some of these factors are likely relevant to risk assessment only, while others are relevant to both risk assessment and risk management. These factors vary in terms of how much they are subject to change. For example, some are fixed (e.g., gender), some cannot be undone (e.g., age of onset of criminal behaviour), and some may be resistant to change (e.g., psychopathy), whereas others (e.g., social support or negative attitudes) may be subject to intervention or may vary across time.

There have been several meta-analytic reviews examining the predictors of general and violent recidivism in adult offenders and patients with mental disorders (Bonta, Law, & Hanson, 1998; Gendreau, Little, & Goggin, 1996). Two key findings have emerged. First, factors that predict general recidivism also predict violent recidivism. Second, predictors of recidivism in offenders with mental disorders overlap considerably with predictors found among offenders who do not have a mental disorder. A recent meta-analytic study examined the predictors of general recidivism in 23 studies of adolescent offenders (Cottle, Lee, & Heilbrun, 2001). The strongest predictors were age of first police contact, nonsevere pathology (e.g., stress or anxiety), family problems, conduct problems (e.g., presence of conduct disordered symptoms), ineffective use of leisure time, and delinquent peers.

Dispositional Factors

DEMOGRAPHICS Researchers in the 1970s identified young age as a risk factor for violence (Steadman & Cocozza, 1974): the younger the person is at the time of his or her first offence, the greater the likelihood that person will engage in criminal behaviour and violence. Dozens of studies have firmly established age of first offence as a risk factor for both general and violent recidivism in both offenders with mental disorders (Bonta et al., 1998) and offenders without mental disorders (Gendreau et al., 1996). Males are at higher risk than are females for general offending (Cottle et al., 2001; Gendreau et al., 1996). Notably, males engage in more serious violent acts, such as sexual assaults, homicides, and assaults causing bodily harm (Odgers & Moretti, 2002). Some studies using self-report measures have found that females engage in similar or even higher rates of less serious violence (Lidz, Mulvey, & Gardner, 1993; O'Leary et al., 1989; Steadman et al., 1994). Newhill, Mulvey, and Lidz (1995) conducted a six-month follow-up of 495 male and 317 female civil psychiatric patients who returned to the community. Men and women did not differ in terms of subsequent violence but had different targets of their violence (family members: males 38%, females 53%) and committed the violence at different locations (home: males 57%, females 75%).

PERSONALITY CHARACTERISTICS Two personality characteristics have been extensively examined: impulsiveness and psychopathy. Not being able to regulate behaviour in response to impulses or thoughts increases the likelihood of engaging in crime and violence (Farrington, 1989; Webster & Jackson, 1997). Lifestyle impulsivity (being impulsive in most areas of life) distinguishes recidivistic rapists from non-recidivistic rapists (Prentky et al., 1995).

Psychopathy is a personality disorder defined as a callous and unemotional interpersonal style characterized by grandiosity, manipulation, lack of remorse, impulsivity, and irresponsibility (see Chapter 13 for more information on psychopaths). Given these features, it is not surprising that psychopathic individuals engage in diverse and chronic criminal behaviours. Three meta-analytic reviews have found that psychopathy is moderately (Gendreau et al., 2002; Hemphill, Hare, & Wong, 1998) to strongly (Salekin, Rogers, & Sewell, 1996) related to general and violent recidivism. For example, Serin and Amos (1995) measured general and violent recidivism rates of 300 federal male offenders followed for an average of 5.5 years. The general failure rate for psychopathic offenders was about 80%, compared with 32% for nonpsychopathic offenders. The violent failure rate was about 35% for the psychopathic offenders and only 5% for the nonpsychopathic offenders. Psychopathic offenders also reoffend sooner after release compared with other offenders (Hart, Kropp, & Hare, 1988; Porter, Birt, & Boer, 2001). For example, Porter et al. (2001) found that psychopaths spent an average of 473 days, and nonpsychopaths 797 days, on conditional release before returning to prison. Psychopathy predicts reoffending across different countries (e.g., Canada, United States, United Kingdom, Belgium, Netherlands, New Zealand, Sweden; Hare, 2003), in both male and female offenders (Richards et al., 2003), offenders with mental disorders (Steadman et al., 2000; Strand et al., 1999), adolescent offenders (Corrado et al., 2004; Forth et al., 1990; Gretton et al., 2001), and sexual offenders (Barbaree et al., 2001; Harris et al., 2003; Rice & Harris, 1997).

Several studies have found that the combination of psychopathy and deviant sexual arousal predicts sexual recidivism (Harris et al., 2003; Rice & Harris, 1997). Deviant sexual arousal is defined as evidence that the sexual offender shows a relative preference for inappropriate stimuli, such as children or violent nonconsensual sex. For example, Rice and Harris (1997) found that about 70% of sexual offenders with psychopathic features and evidence of deviant sexual arousal committed a new sexual offence, compared with about 40% of the other offender groups.

Historical Factors

PAST BEHAVIOUR The most accurate predictor of future behaviour is past behaviour. Past violent behaviour was first identified as a predictor in the 1960s and 1970s (see Cocozza, Melick, & Steadman, 1978) and has consistently been associated with future violence in diverse samples, including adolescents and adults, correctional offenders, mentally disordered offenders, and civil psychiatric patients (Farrington, 1991; Grisso, 1998; McNiel et al., 1988). Interestingly, it is not only past violent behaviour that predicts violence but also past nonviolent behaviour (Harris et al., 1993; Lipsey & Derzon, 1998). For example, offenders who have a history of break and enter offences are at an increased risk for future violence.

AGE OF ONSET As noted earlier, individuals who start their antisocial behaviour at an earlier age are more chronic and serious offenders (Farrington, 1991; Tolan & Thomas, 1995). For example, Farrington (1991) found that 50% of the boys who committed a violent offence prior to age 16 were convicted of a violent offence in early adulthood. In another longitudinal study, Elliott (1994) reported that 50% of youth who committed their first violent acts prior to age 11 continued their violent behaviour into adulthood, compared with 30% whose first violence was between the ages of 11 and 13, and only 10% of those whose first violent act occurred during adolescence.

CHILDHOOD HISTORY OF MALTREATMENT Having a history of childhood physical abuse or neglect is associated with increased risk for violence (Smith & Thornberry, 1995; Zingraff et al., 1994). In a large-scale study of childhood abuse, Widom (1989) reported that victims of sexual abuse were no more likely than those who were not sexually abused to commit delinquent or violent offences. Those who were victims of physical abuse or who were victims of neglect were much more likely to commit criminal acts as compared to those who were not abused.

PAST SUPERVISION FAILURE, ESCAPE, OR INSTITUTION MALADJUSTMENT

Offenders and patients who have failed to comply with release conditions in the past are at an increased risk for engaging in general and violent recidivism (Bonta et al., 1998; Harris et al., 1993; Simourd et al., 1994; Swanson et al., 2001). Ball and colleagues (1994) found that forensic inpatients who were judged to be an escape risk were more likely to behave violently in the institution than those who were not a risk. Poor institutional adjustment has also been linked to higher rates of general and violent recidivism in offenders with mental disorders (Bonta et al., 1998).

Clinical Factors

SUBSTANCE USE Drug and alcohol use has been associated with criminal behaviour and violence. The obvious link between drugs and crime is that the use, possession, and sale of illegal drugs are crimes. In some cases, the individual commits offences in order to support a drug habit (Klassen & O'Connor, 1994). For example, Chaiken and Chaiken (1983) found that severe drug users commit 15 times as many robberies and 20 times as many burglaries as compared with non-drug-using offenders. The drug that has been most associated with crime is heroin (Inciardi, 1986).

Dowden and Brown (2002) conducted a meta-analysis of 45 studies to examine the association between substance abuse and recidivism. Alcohol and drug use problems were moderately related to general recidivism. Zanis et al. (2003) followed a sample of 569 offenders with a prior history of substance abuse or dependence for two years after release from prison on parole. Factors relating to a new conviction included the number of prior convictions, younger age, parole without treatment, and cocaine dependence.

Drug abusers also come in contact with antisocial people, thus leading to violent confrontations. Laboratory research (Taylor & Sears, 1988) has found that aggression displayed by intoxicated individuals is a joint function of the pharmacological effects of alcohol intoxication (disinhibition effects), expectancies, and the situation (what is happening in the environment).

In one of the largest surveys done, Swanson (1994) interviewed 7000 individuals in two U.S. cities (Durham and Los Angeles), asking about the presence of substance abuse, psychiatric disorders, and violent behaviour. Based on data from the past year, less than 3% of men and women with no psychiatric diagnosis committed violence. However, for those with a diagnosis of substance abuse, the rates of violence for men and women were 22% and 17%, respectively.

MENTAL DISORDER Much controversy exists over the connection between major mental disorder and violence. Although most people with mental disorders are not violent, a diagnosis of affective disorders and schizophrenia has been linked to higher rates of violence (Swanson, 1994). Hillbrand (1995) reported that in a sample of forensic psychiatric patients, those with a history of suicide attempts and engaging in self-harm behaviours were more likely to engage in verbal and physical aggression than were other patients.

Considerable research has investigated the link between psychotic symptoms (experiencing hallucinations and delusions) and violence (Link, Andrews, & Cullen, 1992; McNiel & Binder, 1994). Link and Steuve (1994) investigated the link between violence and specific types of psychotic symptoms. They proposed that symptoms overriding a person's self-control (i.e., feeling as if your mind is being dominated by forces beyond your control) or threatening a person's safety (i.e., thinking that someone is planning to hurt him or her) increase the likelihood of violence. They have labelled these types of symptoms "threat/control override" (TCO) symptoms. They compared these psychotic symptoms with other symptoms, such as having thoughts taken away, seeing visions, or hearing voices. TCO symptoms were strongly related to violence (hitting, fighting, and use of weapons) in both patients and community controls. TCO symptoms were a significant predictor of violence even when the other psychotic symptoms were held constant. The link between TCO symptoms and violence has been reported in a large study of more than 10 000 people (Swanson, Borum, Swartz, & Monahan, 1996). People who had TCO symptoms were 2.9 times more likely to have engaged in violence since age 18 than were those with no TCO symptoms. These authors also examined whether a combination of TCO symptoms and other mental disorder diagnoses would be related to violence since age 18. Large differences were found. The highest prevalence of violence was the combination of major mental disorder, substance abuse, and TCO symptoms, with an amazing 86% of such individuals reporting violence; for individuals with major mental disorder and TCO symptoms, the rate was 63%; for individuals with major mental disorder and no TCO symptoms, the rate dropped to 39%; and for individuals with no disorder and no TCO symptoms, the rate was 17%. These results demonstrate the importance of major mental disorders, substance abuse, and TCO symptoms in explaining violence.

Research has also examined the link between command hallucinations (hearing a voice telling you to harm yourself or others) and violence. Junginger (1990) reported a weak link between command hallucinations and dangerous behaviour. In a sample of 51 patients who reported experiencing command hallucinations, 20 (39%) complied with them but only eight (17%) complied by committing acts that were a danger to themselves or others. Other studies have found no link between command hallucinations and violence (Thompson, Stuart, & Holden, 1992).

Contextual Factors

LACK OF SOCIAL SUPPORT This risk factor refers to the absence of strong support systems to help the individual in his or her day-to-day life. Hengeller, Schoenwald, Borduin, Rowland, and Cunningham (1998) describe four kinds of support: (1) *instrumental*, "to provide the necessities of life"; (2) *emotional*, "to give strength to; (3) *appraisal*, "to give aid or courage to"; and (4) *information*, "by providing new facts." Assessing the kinds and levels of support a person has and what types of support must be created will help to evaluate that person's level of risk. Klassen and

O'Connor (1989) found that the current relationship an offender with a mental disorder has with his or her parents and siblings is related to violence.

ACCESS TO WEAPONS OR VICTIMS If the offender is released into an environment that permits easy access to weapons or victims, the potential for another violent act increases. An offender who moves into a skid-row rooming house in which there are many other antisocial individuals living and there is easy access to drugs may start associating with antisocial people or using drugs (Monahan & Steadman, 1994). If the offender had engaged in violence with other associates or under the influence of substances, then releasing the offender to live in the same circumstances that led to past violence may induce future violence. In addition, if offenders who have assaulted their spouse and refused treatment for domestic violence return to live with their spouse, they have a much higher likelihood of violence than those who do not have easy access to a past victim. See Box 11.3 for a look at the risk factors associated with stalking.

BOX 11.3 RISK FACTORS RELATING TO STALKING

Interest in stalking has increased dramatically over the past decade. Often it has been the cases of celebrity stalking that have caught the attention of the media. However, not only celebrities get stalked. A national survey done in the United States found that around 1 million women are stalked annually, and 8% of women and 2% of men will be stalked at some point in their lifetime (Tjaden & Thoennes, 1998). Stalking refers to the repeated and unwanted communicating with, following, or approaching of other people. It has also been referred to as harassment or obsessional following. Most stalkers are men and most victims are women. Most victims know their stalkers. In fact, the stalker is usually a current or ex-romantic partner of the victim.

If you are a victim of harassment, one of the most important questions to ask is, "What is the likelihood of being a victim of a violent act?" A study by Rosenfeld and Harmon (2002) has attempted to discriminate between stalkers who represent a significant risk of violence from those who pose less of a risk. The researchers analyzed 204 stalking and harassment cases in which the stalkers were court-ordered to undergo a mental health evaluation. Violence occurred in 34% of the cases. (Violence was defined as unwanted physical contact or confrontation with a weapon.) The variables listed below were significantly related to violence:

- *Offender characteristics.* Youth (under age 30), lack of education (less than high school), and race (nonwhite) predicted violence.
- *Clinical variables.* Substance abuse, below-average intelligence, and absence of a psychotic disorder predicted violence.
- *Case-related variables.* A former intimate relationship between offender and victim and threats toward the victim predicted violence.

RISK ASSESSMENT INSTRUMENTS AND PREDICTIVE ACCURACY

Many of the factors affecting risk assessment discussed above serve as the basis for various kinds of risk assessment instruments. Some instruments have been developed to predict specific kinds of risk, while others utilize particular strategies outlined above, such as actuarial or structured clinical assessments. The instruments described below do not exhaust those that are available but illustrate the range of options open for the systematic evaluation of risk.

Actuarial Instruments

GENERAL STATISTICAL INFORMATION ON RECIDIVISM The one instrument that is routinely used by Correctional Service Canada and the National Parole Board is the General Statistical Information on Recidivism (GSIR; Nuffield, 1982). All of the 15 items in the scale are static risk factors that were statistically selected because they predicted general reoffending in a sample of federal male offenders during a three-year follow-up period. Twelve of the items measure the nature and extent of past criminal involvement, while the remaining three consider whether the offender was married, employed, or had dependants at the time of their most recent criminal offence. Scores are differentially weighted (based on their statistical association with recidivism) to create five risk categories ranging from very good risk (80% chance of not reoffending) to poor risk (33% chance of not reoffending).

The GSIR scale has proven to be a good predictor of criminal behaviour. In a validation study by Bonta, Harman, Hann, and Cormier (1996) involving 3267 male offenders, the GSIR was found to be a strong predictor of general recidivism. A weaker association has been reported between the GSIR and violent recidivism (Bonta et al., 1996), and the GSIR has been found to be less predictive when used with female federal offenders (Bonta, Pang, & Wallace-Capretta, 1995).

VIOLENCE RISK APPRAISAL GUIDE An actuarial risk-for-violence instrument developed in Ontario is the Violence Risk Appraisal Guide (VRAG; Harris, Rice, & Quinsey, 1993). The VRAG is an empirically derived 12-item measure designed to assess the long-term risk for violent recidivism in offenders with mental disorders. Researchers coded about 50 risk factors from institutional files in a sample of 618 male adult patients with mental disorders who had been transferred to less secure institutions or released into the community. Statistical analyses were used to select the 12 best predictors of violence from childhood history, adult adjustment, offence history, and assessment results. The 12 predictors varied in terms of how strongly they were related to violent recidivism and included the following (ordered from most to least predictive):

- Hare Psychopathy Checklist-Revised score
- elementary school maladjustment

- diagnosis of any personality disorder
- age at index offence (young age is a higher risk)
- separation from biological parents prior to age 16
- failure on prior conditional release
- prior nonviolent offences
- single marital status at time of offence
- diagnosis of schizophrenia (lower risk)
- victim injury (less injury higher risk)
- history of alcohol problems
- victim gender (female victim lower risk)

Using scores on each of these risk factors, nine risk categories or "bins" were created. Each risk bin has a probably of violent recidivism within ten years ranging from 9% (bin 1) to 35% (bin 5) to 100% (bin 9).

Subsequent research has found the VRAG predicts violence with other samples of offenders with mental disorders (Harris, Rice, & Cormier, 2002) and sexual offenders (Barbaree et al., 2001; Harris et al., 2003; Rice & Harris, 1997). There is some evidence that the relationship between the VRAG and violent recidivism is not as strong in correctional samples (Glover et al., 2002; Kroner & Mills, 2001) or with Swedish schizophrenic forensic patients (Grann et al., 2000).

ITERATIVE CLASSIFICATION TREE The Iterative Classification Tree (ICT; Steadman et al., 2000) was designed as a tool to assess the risk for violence in samples of psychiatric patients. This approach to risk assessment allows for a many different combinations of risk factors to be used to classify a person into low- and high-risk categories. A clinician scores the patient on one risk factor and, contingent on how the patient is scored, assesses the patient on another risk factor. This sequence continues until the patient is classified into a risk category.

The ICT has been validated using a large-scale study of risk factors for violence in civil psychiatric patients (MacArthur Violence Risk Assessment Study; Steadman et al., 2000). Researchers coded 134 risk factors in 939 male and female civil psychiatric patients admitted to psychiatric in-patient hospitals in the United States. Most of these patients were diagnosed with depression (42%), followed by alcohol/drug abuse (22%), schizophrenia (17%), and bipolar disorder (14%). Patients were followed up for 20 weeks following discharge from the hospital. Using arrest and rehospitalization records and patient and collateral interviews, patients were assessed for engaging in any violent behaviour toward others (physical violence resulting in injury, sexual assaults, assaults with a weapon, or threats with a weapon). The base rate for violence was 18.7% (i.e., the percentage committing one violent act during the 20-week follow-up period). Low-risk groups were those whose rate of violence was half the base rate (i.e., 9% or less) and high-risk groups were defined as those whose rate of violence was greater than twice the base rate (i.e., 37% or greater).

The ICT contains 12 risk factors that form six risk groups (four low-risk groups and two high-risk groups). The first risk factor that differentiates the risk groups is the score on the Hare Psychopathy Checklist: Screening Version (Hart, Cox, & Hare, 1995). If the patient scored high on the measure of psychopathy, the clinician would inquire about whether the patient had experienced serious childhood abuse. If the patient responded yes, the clinician would indicate whether the patient had a diagnosis of alcohol or drug abuse. If the patient did have such a diagnosis, the clinician would indicate whether the patient had been admitted to the hospital for a suicide attempt. If the patient had not been admitted for a suicide attempt, the patient would be placed in risk group C, a group of 53 patients of whom 58.5% committed a violent act. If, however, the patient scored low on the psychopathy measure, a different series of risk factors would be assessed. For example, none of the 66 patients in Risk Group A committed a violent act. Monahan et al. (2000) have developed another ICT based on 15 risk factors that are easiest to obtain and that can be administered quickly. How the ICT will work with other civil psychiatric samples remains to be tested.

Most of the items in the actuarial scales described above comprise static risk factors. Scales that rely primarily on static factors have a number of limitations. First, they provide little practical information about what risk factors need to be targeted for intervention. Second, they do not allow for the incorporation of treatment gain into the prediction, nor can they indicate when an offender might fail, or when the level of supervision should be changed (Bonta, 1996; Zamble & Quinsey, 1997). Third, they have been criticized for not being theoretically derived (Krauss, Sales, Becker, & Figueredo, 2000). From a practical standpoint, whether or not the risk factors are derived from a specific theory may not be very important as long as they accurately predict the outcome.

In response to the limitations associated with actuarial measures, risk assessment methods that include dynamic risk factors have been developed.

Structured Professional Judgment Schemes

LEVEL OF SERVICE INVENTORY-REVISED The Level of Service Inventory-Revised (LSI-R; Andrews & Bonta, 1995) consists of static and dynamic risk items that tap into the theoretical model of criminal behaviour outlined by Andrews and Bonta (1995). The 52 items are divided into ten main subscales:

- criminal history
- education/employment
- financial
- family/marital
- accommodation
- leisure recreation
- companions

- alcohol/drug problems
- emotional/personal
- attitudes/orientation

These subscales highlight the areas that should be targeted for intervention. The LSI-R total score has also been used for assigning offenders to different levels of supervision based on their likelihood for recidivism. The LSI-R has been used with a variety of offenders, including sex offenders (Simourd & Malcolm, 1998) and female and male offenders (Coulson et al., 1996), and a modified version with adolescent offenders (Ilacqua et al., 1999). A meta-analysis reported by Gendreau, Goggin, and Smith (2002) found that the LSI-R functioned effectively as a predictor of general recidivism and, to a lesser extent, of violent recidivism.

HCR-20 The HCR-20 (Webster et al., 1997) was designed to predict violent behaviour in correctional and forensic psychiatric samples. The HCR-20 uses the structured professional judgment approach to risk assessment developed by a group of researchers in British Columbia. In this approach the evaluator conducts a systematic risk assessment referring to a list of risk factors, each having specific coding criteria and a demonstrated relationship with violent recidivism based on the existing professional and empirical literature. The HCR-20 stands for the list of 20 items organized into three main scales that align risk factors into past (Historical), present (Clinical), and future (Risk Management):

Historical (primarily static in nature):

- past violence
- age at first violent offence
- relationship instability
- employment instability
- relationship problems
- substance use problems
- major mental disorder
- psychopathy
- early maladjustment
- personality disorder
- prior supervision failure

Clinical (reflect current, dynamic risk factors):

- lack of insight
- negative attitudes
- active mental disorder symptoms
- impulsivity
- treatability

Risk Management (future community or institutional adjustment of the individual):

- feasibility of plans
- exposure to destablizers
- level of personal support
- stress
- likelihood of treatment compliance

   The validity of the HCR-20 has been investigated in forensic psychiatric and correctional samples. Much of this research with forensic psychiatric patients has been done in Sweden. Research with Swedish forensic patients reported that the Historical scale of the HCR-20 was related to violent recidivism in patients with personality disorders and schizophrenia (Grann et al., 2000). In a sample of 40 Swedish forensic patients, Strand, Belfrage, Frannson, and Levander (1999) reported that the HCR-20 was strongly related to violent recidivism. In this sample, the Clinical and Risk Management scales were better than the Historical scale at differentiating the violent and nonviolent recidivists. The HCR-20 also predicted inpatient violent behaviours in a sample of 54 Swedish forensic patients (Dernevik, Grann, & Johansson, 2002). Douglas and Webster (1999) reported that the H and C scales of the HCR-20 were correlated with past violence in a sample of Canadian male offenders. However, Kroner and Mills (2001) found that H and C scales were only weakly related to future violence in a sample of Canadian male offenders.

CAN WE PREDICT SPECIFIC TYPES OF VIOLENCE?

The instruments described above were designed to predict criminal behaviour or any form of violence. Instruments also have been developed for specific populations and more narrowly defined types of violence. Two types of violence that have been a focus of much research are sexual violence and spousal assault (see also Chapter 12).

Spousal Assault

The Spousal Assault Risk Assessment (SARA; Kropp et al., 1999) consists of 20 risk factors designed to assess the risk for spousal violence. The risk factors were identified on the basis of a review of the empirical literature. The SARA consists of ten general violence risk factors (Part 1) and ten spousal violence risk factors (Part 2). Part 1 items code for past history of violence and substance use, as well as employment and relationship problems. Part 2 items code the nature and severity of violence in the most recent spousal assault incident, attitudes concerning spousal assault, and violations of "no contact" orders. Users code each of the 20 items using a three-point scale, indicate the presence of any additional case-specific risk factors, designate any "critical" risk factors (those that are particularly salient to the degree of risk), and make a summary risk judgment (low, moderate, or high) for future spousal violence.

Research by Kropp and Hart (2000) has found that offenders with a spousal assault history score higher on the SARA than do offenders with no history of spousal assault. Recidivistic spousal assaulters scored higher on Part 2 (spousal violence) of the SARA as compared with nonrecidivistic spousal assaulters. When examining the summary risk judgments, 60% of the high-risk ratings were recidivists, as compared with 33% of the moderate-risk ratings, and 8% of the low-risk ratings. The only other study evaluating the predictive utility of the SARA was done in Sweden. Grann and Wedin (2002) used files to code SARA items on a sample of 88 male spousal assaulters. During the seven-year follow-up period, 28% of the individuals in the sample were reconvicted of spousal assault. The SARA total score was moderately related to spousal assault recidivism. Three SARA items were most strongly related: past violation of conditional release, personality disorder, and extreme minimization or denial of spousal assault history.

Sexual Violence

In a meta-analysis of 61 studies, Hanson and Bussière (1998) investigated the predictors of sexual recidivism. Of the 28 972 sex offenders followed for an average of four to five years, the rate of sexual recidivism was 13.4%, 12.2% for nonsexual violent recidivism, and 35.3% for any offence. The strongest predictors of sexual recidivism included phallometric assessment of sexual preference for children, prior sexual offences, age (negatively related), any prior offences, and never having been married. Other significant predictors, although less strongly related to sexual recidivism, were having a male victim and assaulting stranger victims. Factors unrelated to sexual recidivism included experiencing childhood sexual abuse, substance abuse, and psychological problems such as depression or poor self-esteem.

RAPID RISK ASSESSMENT FOR SEX OFFENCE RECIDIVISM The simplest scale developed to predict sexual recidivism is the Rapid Risk Assessment for Sex Offence Recidivism (RRASOR; Hanson, 1997). Using the risk factors identified in the Hanson and Bussière (1998) meta-analysis, the four best predictors were selected using data from seven different follow-up studies from several countries: prior sexual offences, younger age, male victim of a sexual offence, and unrelated victim of sexual offence. Despite consisting of only four items, the RRASOR predicts sexual recidivism (Barbaree et al., 2001; Sjöstedt & Langström, 2001). However, the RRASOR does not provide (nor was it intended to provide) a comprehensive measure of all the factors relevant to the prediction of sexual recidivism. Hanson (1997) recommends that it only be used to screen offenders for more intensive assessment.

STATIC-99 In 1999, David Thornton and Karl Hanson decided to combine two measures to create a new ten-item they called the Static-99 (Hanson & Thornton, 1999). This scale includes the four items from the RRASOR plus six items focusing on prior nonsexual violent history, current nonsexual violence, prior noncontact sexual offences, marital status, number of sentences received, and stranger victim. Explicit scoring is provided and individuals are assigned to one of four risk categories: low, medium-low, medium-high, and high risk. On a combined sample of 1208 sexual offenders, the Static-99 correlated 0.33 with sexual recidivism and 0.32 with violent recidivism (Hanson & Thornton, 2000). Other researchers have also found the Static-99 predicts sexual recidivism (Barbaree et al., 2001; Harris et al., 2003; Sjöstedt & Langström, 2001).

The above two scales are actuarial and consist only of static risk factors. Recent research has attempted to identify dynamic predictors of sexual offence recidivism. Hanson and Harris (2000) explored dynamic risk factors in a sample of 200 sexual recidivists and 201 nonrecidivists using file information and interviews with community supervision officers. Dynamic factors were coded twice: one month and six months prior to the sexual offence for the recidivists and at one month and six months for the nonrecidivists (i.e., at intervals that corresponded to the periods measured for the recidivists). The following factors changed for the worse and were related to sexual recidivism: poor social supports, antisocial lifestyles, poor supervision compliance, attitudes supportive of sexual aggression, and negative mood (anger and distress).

CURRENT ISSUES

Where Is the Theory?

Much of the focus in risk assessment research has been on perfecting the prediction of violence. This is especially true for actuarial methods of risk assessment in which risk factors are selected based on their statistical relation to a specific outcome. There is less attention as to *why* these risk factors are linked to violence. Understanding the causes of violence will aid in the development of prevention and intervention programs. Box 11.4 presents one model to explain criminal recidivism.

BOX 11.4 COPING-RELAPSE MODEL OF CRIMINAL RECIDIVISM

Zamble and Quinsey (1997) have attempted to explain why an individual will commit another offence after release. Figure 11.1 on the next page illustrates the recidivism process and how each level interacts. According to the model, the first event is some type of environmental trigger. What will be considered a trigger varies across individuals and can range from stressful life events, such as losing a job, having relationship problems, and financial difficulties, to more mundane daily events, such as being stuck in a traffic jam. Once the event has occurred, the individual will invoke both an emotional and cognitive appraisal of the event. If this appraisal process results in the experience of negative emotions (e.g., anger, hostility, fear) or elevated levels of stress, the individual will attempt to deal with these unpleasant feelings. If the individual does not possess adequate coping mechanisms, a worsening cycle of negative emotions and maladaptive cognitions occur, eventually resulting in criminal behaviour. The model also posits that how an individual perceives and responds to an environmental trigger is dependent on two factors: individual and response mechanisms.

Individual influences include factors such as criminal history and enduring personality traits (e.g., psychopathy, emotional reactivity). These factors influence how an individual will perceive an event and the likelihood they will engage in criminal conduct, both of which are relatively stable. For example, research has found that psychopathic individuals are more likely to interpret ambiguous events as hostile (Serin, 1991) and are impulsive. These factors increase the likelihood of engaging in criminal behaviour.

Available response mechanisms also influence how an individual will perceive a situation, in turn mediating that person's response. These factors are considered to be more dynamic in nature and thus important targets for intervention. Examples of these factors include coping ability, substance use, criminal attitudes and associates, and social supports. Imagine an individual who loses his job. He becomes angry and upset, and reverts to drinking to deal with these negative feelings. His drinking angers his intimate partner who becomes less and less supportive of him. These factors increase the likelihood that he will resume his criminal behaviour.

FIGURE 11.1
THE RECIDIVISM PROCESS

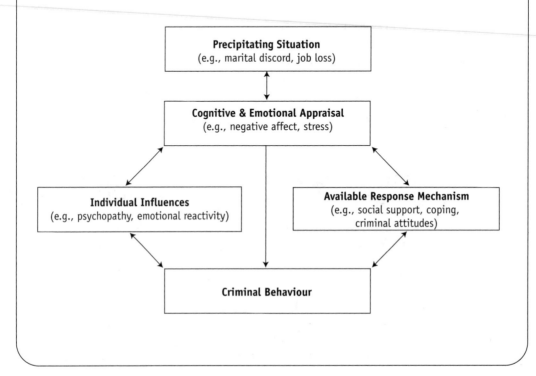

What about Protective Factors?

Various historical, dispositional, clinical, and contextual risk factors have been shown to have predictive utility. **Protective factors** are factors that mitigate or reduce the likelihood of antisocial acts or violence in high-risk offenders (Borum, 1996). Understanding the positive attributes could help explain why some individuals with many risk factors do not become violent. For example, a youth may have antisocial parents at home (a risk factor) but also be strongly attached to school (a protective factor). Like risk factors, protective factors vary across time, and the impact they have depends on the situation. Most of the research on protective factors has been conducted with children and youth. The following factors have been identified as protective factors: prosocial involvement, strong social supports, positive social orientation (school, work), strong attachments (as long as attachment is not to an antisocial other), and intelligence (Caprara, Barbaranelli, & Pastorelli, 2001; Hoge, Andrews, & Leschied, 1996; Lipsey & Derzon, 1998).

Are Decision Makers Using the Scientific Research?

Despite the considerable strides that have been made in refining methods of violence prediction, many practitioners are not using these instruments. This gap in integrating science and clinical practice represents a significant challenge to this area. A survey by Boothby and Clements (2000) asked 820 correctional psychologists what tests they used in their assessments. The most commonly used test was the Minnesota Multiphasic Personality Inventory, used by 87% of the psychologists. Only 11% of the respondents mentioned using the Hare PCL-R, and fewer than 1% mentioned using the VRAG or the LSI-R. It is not clear why so few correctional psychologists are using these instruments. Research is needed to understand the obstacles to the adoption of new risk assessment measures. One potential reason is that these newer instruments have not been part of the training programs for psychologists. Borum (1996) has recommended that clinical practice guidelines for risk assessment be developed. Development of such guidelines by professional organizations such as the American Psychological Association and Canadian Psychological Association would result in more standardized use.

What is the impact of psychologists' recommendations on forensic decision making? Past research has found that judicial decision making relies heavily on recommendations made by mental health professionals (Konecni & Ebbesen, 1984). In Canada, decisions to release forensic patients are strongly related to recommendations by clinicians (Quinsey & Ambtman, 1979), and reports by clinicians about treatment gains made by sex offenders strongly influence decisions about granting parole (Quinsey, Khanna, & Malcolm, 1998). Another related question is whether decision makers are relying on results of the newly developed actuarial risk instruments. Hilton and Simmons (2001) studied the influence of VRAG scores and clinical judgments on decisions made to transfer offenders with mental disorders in a maximum-security facility to less secure institutions. Review board decisions were not related to scores on the VRAG but were related to senior clinicians' testimony at the review board hearing. Patients who caused few institutional problems, who were compliant with medication, who were more physically attractive, and who had less serious criminal histories were more likely recommended by the clinician for transfer. Hilton and Simmons (2001) conclude that "the availability of an empirically validated actuarial risk assessment report did not substantially influence clinical opinions or tribunal decisions to release forensic patients from maximum security" (p. 406).

Why Do Some Individuals Stop Committing Crimes?

Much of the research discussed in this chapter focuses on the risk factors related to engaging in crime and violence. However, if we want to prevent or reduce crime, knowledge about the factors relating to desistance from crime is probably equally important. Laub, Nagin, and Sampson (1998) postulate that the factors that relate to the onset of a criminal career do not necessarily explain desistance from crime. Some researchers have linked the desistance process to such factors as "good" work or "good" marriages (Laub et al., 1998; Ouimet & LeBlanc, 1993; Uggen, 1999). Age is strongly related to criminal behaviour. The reason for the age-related decline in criminal

---

BOX 11.5 WHY DO HIGH-RISK VIOLENT OFFENDERS STOP OFFENDING?

In a study titled "Against All Odds: A Qualitative Follow-up of High-Risk Violent Offenders Who Were Not Reconvicted," Haggard, Gumpert, and Grann (2001) explored what factors were related to why repeat violent offenders stopped reoffending. To be eligible to participate in the study, the offender had to score high on the Historical subscale of the HCR-20, to have been convicted of at least two violent crimes, and not to been convicted for any crime for at least ten years. From a sample of 401 violent offenders, only six individuals were eligible to participate. Of these six, only four consented to be interviewed. The following factors were reported by the participants to be related to desistance. For each factor, a quotation from one of the participants is provided.

■ *Insight triggered by negative events connected to their criminal lifestyle.* "It grows within during a long time, the insight, but you have to reach a point where it feels wrong.... To me it was mostly due to the last time, when I was admitted to the forensic psychiatric hospital. The whole thing was crazy, and then I realized how off track I was—when you strike down a person with an axe because of a trivial thing ... then you start wondering. I did anyway" (p. 1055).

■ *Social avoidance.* "I have a terrible temper and I can become violent, very violent.... You have to avoid different situations, you have to think about it all the time so that you don't put yourself in situations you can't handle" (p. 1057).

■ *Orientation to the family.* "After I served my sentence, I became more committed to my children. To help them not to make the same mistake I did" (p. 1057).

offending has been related to the maturation process (Menard & Huizinga, 1989). LeBlanc (1993) defines maturation as the "development of self- and social control" (p. 65). Shover and Thompson (1992) have suggested that as people age, they become less interested in a criminal lifestyle and are more able to understand and fear the consequences of engaging in crime. A study examining why high-risk offenders stop offending is described in Box 11.5.

SUMMARY

1. An assessment of risk requires two components—an analysis of the likelihood of future criminal or violent acts and the development of strategies to manage or reduce this risk level.

2. Risk assessments are routinely conducted in the civil and criminal contexts. Risk assessments in civil contexts include civil commitments, child protection, immigration, and duty to warn. In criminal settings, the assessment of risk occurs at pretrial, sentencing, and release stages.

3. There are different types of errors when attempting to make predictions. Each of these errors has different consequences. False-positive errors affect the offender, whereas false-negative errors affect society and the victim.

4. Risk factors vary in terms of how fixed or changeable they are. Static factors either do not change or are highly resistant to change. Dynamic factors are changeable and are often targeted for intervention.

5. Various approaches have been developed to assess violent prediction. These include unstructured clinical judgment, actuarial prediction, structured professional judgment, and the anamnestic approach. There are advantages and disadvantages to each approach.

6. Major risk factors can be classified into historical, dispositional, clinical, and contextual factors. Historical risk factors include general social history and specific criminal history variables, such as employment problems and past history of violence. Dispositional factors include demographic, attitudinal, and personality variables such as gender, age, negative attitudes, and psychopathy. Clinical factors refer to those that contribute to violence, such as substance abuse or major psychoses. Contextual factors refer to aspects of the individual's situation that can elevate the risk, such as access to victims or weapons, lack of social supports, or perceived stress.

Key Concepts

actuarial prediction	329	false negative	323	static risk factor	331
base rate	324	false positive	323	structured professional	
clinical risk factors	333	heuristics	328	judgment	331
contextual risk factors	333	historical risk factors	333	true positive	323
dispositional risk		illusory correlation	328	true negative	323
factors	333	protective factors	347	unstructured clinical	
dynamic risk factor	331	risk factor	331	judgment	329

Discussion Questions

1. Do you think Canadian courts should allow expert testimony about the risk for violence? What level of predictive accuracy do you think should be required before allowing a clinician to use a newly developed risk assessment instrument?

2. You have decided to take a summer job working at Correctional Service Canada. You are asked to help design a study to evaluate the accuracy of a new instrument designed to predict hostage taking by federal offenders. How would you approach this task?

3. What factors do you think the National Parole Board should rely on when making decisions about releasing offenders?

4. Distinguish among the different types of risk assessment: unstructured clinical judgment, actuarial prediction, and structured professional judgment. Develop a study to evaluate which of these types of risk assessment is most accurate.

5. You think there should be more research on why offenders decide to stop offending. Describe a study you would conduct, focusing on the methodology and what factors you would measure that might relate to the desistance process.

6. Researchers have developed several risk assessment instruments, but not all psychologists conducting risk assessments are using these scales. Why is this? What could be done to encourage forensic psychologists to start using these instruments?

7. A school board has contacted you wanting to know how to identify the next potential school shooter. Describe what you know about threat assessment and problems with trying to identify low-base-rate violent acts.

Additional Information

Readings

Bonta, J. (2002). Offender risk assessment: Guidelines for selection and use. *Criminal Justice and Behavior, 29,* 355–379.

Zamble, E., & Quinsey, V.L. (1997). *The criminal recidivism process.* Cambridge: Cambridge University Press.

Web Sites

Correctional Service Canada
www.csc-scc.gc.ca

Public Safety and Emergency Preparedness Canada
www.psepc-sppcc.gc.ca

CHAPTER 12

Violent Offenders: Classification and Treatment

Mike Dawson is serving a federal sentence for two counts of sexual assault. He has been attending a cognitive-behavioural treatment program for sexual offenders for two months. The program consists of individual and group therapy. One therapist thinks Mike is making considerable progress in treatment, whereas the other therapist is less optimistic. In group therapy Mike is evasive when challenged, has been vindictive toward other group members, and is continually testing boundaries. The therapist that has been concerned with Mike's attitudes and behaviour thinks he is a psychopath who is not genuinely interested in changing.

PSYCHOLOGY OF VIOLENCE

Violence has a major impact on victims and society. Although the violent crime rate in Canada, the United States, and Britain has been dropping over the past decade, there is a substantial fear of violence in the community. Newspapers and television focus on violent crime, particularly homicide and sexual offences. As a consequence, violence is often in the mind of the public. Violence and its aftermath is also a major focus of forensic psychology. Psychologists are involved in developing assessment and intervention programs for violent offenders. This chapter describes several types of violent offenders, including homicidal offenders, domestic assault offenders, and sexual offenders. The chapter ends with a description of the psychopath—an individual who is particularly prone to violence.

HOMICIDAL OFFENDERS

The ultimate violent crime is homicide. Canadian criminal law recognizes four different types of homicide: first-degree murder, second-degree murder, manslaughter, and infanticide. Different penalties are imposed for each type, with a maximum of five years for infanticide to life in prison for the other three. In considering the different kinds of homicide, it should be noted that some killing is exempt from penalties, such as killing during war or killing in self-defence.

First-degree murder is usually murder that is planned and deliberate. If, however, the victim is a law enforcement officer or correctional staff member, or if the murder occurred during the commission of another violent offence (e.g., sexual assault, kidnapping), regardless of whether the murder was unplanned or deliberate, it is considered first-degree murder.

All murder that is not considered first-degree murder is classified as second-degree murder. Manslaughter is unintentional murder that occurs during the "heat of passion" or due to criminal negligence. For example, a man returns home unexpectedly from a business trip and finds his wife in bed with her lover. He grabs a rifle and shoots and kills the lover.

Infanticide occurs when a woman kills her newly born child due to a mental disorder arising from the effects of childbirth. Infanticide is a controversial legal category (Dobson & Sales, 2000). Are women in the year following childbirth at such an increased risk of a mental illness that they would not be held fully responsible if they murdered their baby? In 1984, the Law Reform Commission of Canada recommended that infanticide as a distinct legal entity be abolished. Despite this recommendation, infanticide remains in the Criminal Code.

Canada's homicide rate peaked in the 1970s and has been gradually declining since 1975 (Statistics Canada, 2003). Figure 12.1 on the next page presents the homicide rate in Canada between 1961 and 2002. In 2002, the homicide rate was 1.85 per 100 000 population, reflecting 582 homicides committed. This was a slight increase in the homicide rate from the year 2001. Contributing to this increase were the reported homicides of 15 women (previously classified as missing) in British Columbia. Although the rate of homicide is substantially higher in the United States (7.1 per 100 000 in 2001, which includes the 9/11 terrorism deaths; the rate was 6.1 in 2000), the homicide rate in the United States has also been declining (the peak rate was in 1980 with 10.2 per 100 000; Department of Justice, 2002).

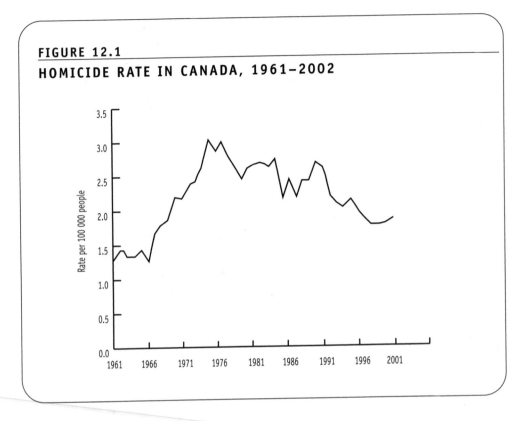

FIGURE 12.1

HOMICIDE RATE IN CANADA, 1961–2002

Characteristics of homicide in Canada include the following (Statistics Canada, 2003):

- You are most likely to be killed by someone you know. In 2002, 44% of solved homicides were committed by an acquaintance, 40% by a family member, and 15% by a stranger. Among the 200 victims killed by an acquaintance, 100 were killed by a casual acquaintance, 37 by someone known to them through a criminal relationship, such as drug dealing and prostitution, 29 by a close friend, and 34 by another type of acquaintance.

- Females are more likely to be killed by an intimate partner than are males. Forty-four percent of all female victims and 8% of all male victims in 2002 were killed by an individual with whom they had an intimate relationship at one time, either through marriage or dating.

- About two-thirds of the accused had a prior criminal history and about half of the victims had a criminal record.

- Consistent with past years, not only do men commit most murders (nine out of ten in 2002), but they are also the most likely victims (about two-thirds of the victims are men).

■ There were 45 gang-related homicides in 2002, 27 fewer than the peak of 72 in 2000. For a second consecutive year, gang-related homicides dropped substantially. The falling gang-related homicide rate was due to a dramatic decrease in these homicides in Quebec.

■ There are regional differences in homicide rates across Canada. Homicide rates have been consistently higher in the territories, followed by Western provinces, with the lowest rates in the Atlantic provinces.

Filicide: When Parents Kill

The killing of a child by a parent is difficult to understand. Fortunately, it is a rare event. The term *filicide* refers to the killing of children by their biological parents or stepparents and includes neonaticide (killing a baby within 24 hours of birth) and infanticide (killing a baby within first year of life). Attitudes toward parents killing their children vary across cultures and time. For example, in ancient Rome, a father had a right to kill his children (Finkel, Burke, & Chavez, 2000). A few cultures have sanctioned the gender-based killing of children. Notably, in China and India, female children are more likely to be killed due to the greater value these societies place on male children. In the past, certain Inuit and African societies killed infants that had birth defects or killed one infant when twins were born (Garber, 1947; Stewart, 2000).

Child murder in Canada is uncommon. In 2002, 44 children under the age of 12 were killed. Babies killed within the first 24 hours are nearly always killed by their mothers, with equal numbers of male and female infants killed. After one year of age, those who commit filicide are more likely to be male than female. Some studies have found that stepfathers are more likely to kill a child than are biological fathers (Daly & Wilson, 1996). However, a recent study in Sweden failed to replicate this finding (Temrin, Buchmayer, & Enquist, 2000).

Mothers Who Kill

Why would a mother kill her child? Several studies have classified maternal filicides (Cheung, 1986; Resnick, 1970). Stanton and Simpson (2002) reviewed these and other studies of child murder and concluded there are three broad types of maternal filicides: (1) neonaticides, (2) those committed by battering mothers, and (3) those committed by mothers with mental illnesses.

The neonaticide group, those who kill their children within 24 hours of birth, are typically young, unmarried women with no prior history of mental illness, who are not suicidal, and who have concealed their pregnancy, fearing rejection or disapproval from their family. Battering mothers have killed their children impulsively in response to the behaviour of the child. These mothers have the highest rates of social and family stress, including marital stress and financial problems. The group with mental disorders tend to be older and married. They are likely to have killed older children, to have multiple victims, and to be diagnosed with a psychosis or depression, and they are the group most likely to attempt suicide after the murder. Some researchers have used the term "altruistic filicide" (Resnick, 1969) to describe mothers who kill out of love. In these cases, the murder is in response to the mother's delusional beliefs that the child's death will somehow protect the child.

Infanticide and Mental Illness

Does childbirth trigger mental illness? The assumption underlying the offence of infanticide is that women who kill their infants are suffering from a mental illness related to childbirth. Three types of mental illness have been identified during the postpartum period (period after childbirth): postpartum blues, postpartum depression, and postpartum psychosis. The most common type of mental illness is postpartum blues (experienced by up to 85% of women), which includes crying, irritability, and anxiety beginning within a few days of childbirth and lasting from a few hours to days but rarely continuing past day 12 (Affonso & Domino, 1984; O'Hara, 1995). Given the onset and short time span of postpartum blues, it has not been considered a causal factor in either neonaticide or filicide.

Postpartum depression (experienced by 7% to 19% of women) occurs within the first few weeks or months after birth and usually lasts for several months (O'Hara, 1995). The symptoms are identical to clinical depression and include depressed mood, loss of appetite, concentration and sleep problems, and suicidal thoughts. Recent studies have found that postpartum depression is not a mental illness that occurs as a consequence of childbirth (O'Hara, 1995).

The most severe and rare type of mental illness that has been associated with childbirth is postpartum psychosis (occurring in one or two of every 1000 births). Postpartum psychosis usually involves delusions, hallucinations, and suicidal or homicidal thoughts within the first three months after childbirth (Millis & Kornblith, 1992). Research does support a link between childbirth and postpartum psychosis. For example, in a study done in Scotland, Kendell, Chalmers, and Platz (1987) tracked the number of admissions for psychosis prior to and after childbirth. In the three months following childbirth, the number of women admitted to hospital with a diagnosis of psychosis was 25 times higher than prior to childbirth. Box 12.1 describes the case of Andrea Yates, the Houston mother who killed her five children, and the case of Suzanne Killinger Johnson, who jumped in front of a Toronto subway holding her infant son. These cases illustrate the potential lethality of postpartum psychosis.

Fathers Who Kill

Fathers rarely commit neonaticide. In contrast to maternal filicides, paternal filicides are often described as fatal child abuse (Brewster, Nelson, & Hymel, 1998). Fathers have lower rates of psychotic disorder but higher rates of alcohol abuse and previous criminality.

Familicide occurs when a spouse and children are killed. It is almost always committed by a man, and is often accompanied by a history of spousal and child abuse

BOX 12.1 FROM DEVOTION TO DEPRESSION: MOTHERS WHO KILL

Postpartum depression affects about 10% of new mothers; this rate increases to about 20% to 30% for those who have had previous depressive episodes. If a mother has experienced postpartum depression with one child, she has about a 50% chance of developing postpartum depression if she has another baby.

Postpartum psychosis is the most rare but also the most severe postpartum mental illness. It afflicts about one in 1000 mothers within six months of birth. Symptoms include hearing voices, seeing things, and feeling an irrational guilt that they have somehow done something wrong. Without treatment, women may try to harm themselves or their infants. The following two cases illustrate the potential lethality of postpartum depression and psychosis.

SUZANNE KILLINGER JOHNSON

Suzanne Killinger Johnson was a physician with a psychotherapy practice in Toronto. She had a history of depression while in medical school at the University of Western Ontario. She had a successful marriage, flourishing career, and supportive family and friends. In February 2000 she gave birth to a son named Cuyler. Sometime after the birth, Killinger Johnson started to become more and more obsessive about caring for Cuyler. By the spring she started to see a therapist and was taking medication for depression. In July she stopped taking her antidepressants, worried about the effects of the medicine in her breast milk, avoided her friends, and missed her therapist appointments. Her husband, family, and friends attempted to help her. However, at 6:30 A.M. on August 11, while her father had left her alone for a few minutes, she took her son, drove to a nearby subway station, and with Cuyler in her arms jumped in front of subway train. Cuyler died instantly and his mother died eight days later on August 19, 2000.

ANDREA PIA YATES

Andrea Yates had been diagnosed with postpartum depression after the birth of her fourth son, Paul. She had attempted suicide twice, was hospitalized, and was given antidepressant medication. After the birth of her daughter, Mary, Yates also experienced severe postpartum depression, was hospitalized twice, and was given antidepressants. According to her defence lawyers and mental health experts, Andrea Yates was not only experiencing postpartum depression but also postpartum psychosis.

On June 20, 2001, after her husband had left to go to work and prior to her mother arriving to help her, Andrea Yates drowned each of her five children—Noah (age seven), John (five), Luke (three), Paul (two), and Mary (six months)—in a bathtub at their family home. According to the defence lawyers, Yates was delusional when she murdered her children, believing that she had to murder them in order to save them from Satan. The prosecution agreed that Andrea Yates had a mental illness but that she knew what she was doing and knew that killing them was wrong.

In March 2002, it took a jury four hours to reject Andrea Yates's insanity plea and find her guilty of capital murder. A week later, the same jury took 40 minutes to reject the death penalty but to sentence her to life in prison. Andrea Yates will be eligible for parole in 2041, when she is 77 years old.

Treatment of postpartum depression and postpartum psychosis is possible. However, in both of these cases, the women had sought medical intervention but the treatment had limited success. Continuing research holds the promise of improved treatment and, ultimately, the prevention of these devastating illnesses.

prior to the offence. Wilson, Daly, and Daniele (1995) examined 109 Canadian and British cases and found that in about half of the cases the killer committed suicide. They also found that those who killed their spouse and their own children (i.e., genetic offspring) had a greater likelihood of committing suicide than those who killed their spouse and their stepchildren. Wilson et al. (1995) also described two types of famili-cide murderers, the despondent nonhostile killer and the hostile accusatory killer. The despondent nonhostile killer is depressed, worried about an impending disaster for himself or his family. He kills his family and then commits suicide. Past acts of violence toward children and spouse are not characteristic of this type of killer. The hostile accusatory killer, however, expresses hostility toward his wife, often relating to alleged infidelities or her intentions to terminate the relationship. A past history of violent acts is common for this type of killer.

Youth Who Kill

Youth killed 42 people in Canada in 2002 (Statistics Canada, 2003). Researchers have searched for distinguishing characteristics among youth who commit murder. Corder, Ball, Haizlip, Rollins, and Beaumont (1976) compared ten youths charged with killing parents with ten youths charged with killing relatives or acquaintances with ten youths charged with killing strangers. Youth charged with parricide (killing parents) were more likely to have been physically abused, to have witnessed spousal abuse, and to report amnesia for the murders, compared with the other youth who committed murder. More recently, Darby, Allan, Kashani, Hartke, and Reid (1998) examined the association between family abuse and suicide attempts in a sample of 112 adolescents convicted of homicide. Abused youth were younger, more often Caucasian, and more likely to have attempted suicide prior to the homicide than nonabused youth.

Cornell, Benedek, and Benedek (1987) developed a typology of juvenile homicide offenders based on the circumstances of the offence: psychotic (youths who had symptoms of severe mental illness at time of murder); conflict (youths who were engaged in an argument or conflict with the victim when the killing occurred); and crime (youths who killed during the commission of another crime, such as robbery or sexual assault). When the classification system was applied to 72 juveniles charged with murder, 7% were assigned to the psychotic subgroup, 42% to the conflict sub-group, and 51% to the crime subgroup. Differences across these homicide subgroups in family background, criminal history, and psychopathology have been reported (Greco & Cornell, 1992).

Myers, Scott, Burgess and Burgess (1995) classified 25 juvenile homicide offenders using the *FBI Crime Classification Manual.* Offenders were classified as either as "criminal enterprise" or "personal crime." Youths in the criminal enterprise group were more likely to have been abused and to have killed an adult or elderly stranger. Personal crime group murderers tended to select child or adolescent victims whom they knew.

Spousal Killers

During the period 1974–1983 in Canada, 812 wives and 248 husbands were killed by their spouses (Daly & Wilson, 1988). As this statistic makes clear, husbands are much more likely to kill their wives than wives are to kill their husbands. **Femicide** is the general term applied to killing of women, uxoricide is the more specific term denoting the killing of a wife by her husband, and mariticide is the term denoting the killing of a husband by his wife (for more information on mariticide see Chapter 13). In 2002, 84 spousal homicides occurred in Canada (Statistics Canada, 2003). A married woman in Canada is about nine times more likely to be killed by her partner than by a stranger (Wilson & Daly, 1993). In a study of 896 femicides in Ontario between 1974 and 1990, Crawford and Gartner (1992) found that 551 (62%) of the femicides were uxoricides. A consistent finding concerning uxoricide is the high incidence of perpetrator suicide following the murder (Crawford & Gartner, 1992). Offenders rarely commit suicide after killing acquaintances or strangers (Stack, 1997). For example, Crawford and Gartner (1992) found that after the homicide, 32% of the men committed suicide and 7% attempted suicide.

Why do men kill their spouses? Crawford and Gartner (1992) found that the most common motive for uxoricide (in 43% of cases) was the perpetrators' anger over either estrangement from their partners or sexual jealously about perceived infidelity. Comparing police records in Canada, Australia, and United States, Wilson and Daly (1993) found that recent or imminent departure by the eventual victim was associated only with a husband killing his wife and not with a wife killing her husband. A study of risk factors for femicide in abusive relationships by Campbell, Webster, and Koziol-McLain (2003) found the following factors increased the risk for homicide: offender access to a gun, previous threats with a weapon, estrangement, and the victim having left for another partner.

In a study of 90 Canadian offenders convicted of spousal homicide, Dutton and Kerry (1999) reported the following: 87% of murders were reactive and unplanned, 33% of the time the offender attempted suicide, in 67% of cases there was a history of domestic assault, and in 67% there was evidence of estrangement. This study also compared Millon Clinical Multiaxial Inventory scores (Millon, 1987) from a subsample of 50 of the spousal killers with 50 men who were attending a court-mandated treatment program. The most prevalent type of personality disorder in the spousal killers were passive-aggressive, avoidant, self-defeating, and dependent. In the domestic assault group, the most common personality disorders were passive-aggressive, sadistic, and antisocial.

Bimodal Classification of Homicide

Over the past few decades a number of researchers have attempted to characterize aggression in animals and humans in a bimodal manner (Weinshenker & Siegel, 2002). In animals a distinction has been made between affective defence and predatory attack behaviours. In the former, an aggressive response occurs in the presence or perceived presence of fear or threat. For example, a mother animal attacks an animal that approaches her young. Predatory attack is aggression that occurs in response to prey. When you see your domestic cat stalk and try to catch a bird, it is an example of this type of aggression. Animal research has found that you can elicit affective defence or predatory attack behaviours by electrical stimulation of different parts of an animal's brain (Luo, Cheu, & Siegel, 1998).

Recently, Kingsbury, Lambert, and Hendrickse (1997) proposed a bimodal classification scheme for the study of aggression and homicide in humans, in which homicides are classified as **reactive (or affective) aggression** and **instrumental (predatory) aggression**. Reactive homicide is defined as impulsive, unplanned, immediate, driven by negative emotions, and occurring in response to some perceived provocation. Instrumental homicide is defined as proactive rather than reactive, and is a premeditated, calculated behaviour, motivated by some goal. This goal could be to obtain money, power, control, or even the gratification of sadistic fantasies (Meloy, 1997).

Reactive homicide occurs more often among relatives, and instrumental homicide among strangers (Daly & Wilson, 1982). The majority of homicides are reactive in nature. In a large-scale study, Miethe and Drass (1999) coded 34 329 single-victim, single-offender homicides in the United States between 1990 and 1994. Eighty percent were classified as reactive, and 20% as instrumental. In this study the victim–offender relationship was divided into three categories: strangers, acquaintances, and family members/intimates. Most of the homicides involved acquaintances (55%), with most of these being classified as reactive (80%). Family members and intimate partners account for 28% of the cases, with nearly all of these homicides being classified as reactive (93%). Finally, in 17% of the cases the victim was a stranger, with 52% being classified as reactive. This study indicates that instrumental homicides do not occur exclusively among strangers, nor are reactive homicides confined to those who are well known to each other.

In a Canadian study, Woodworth and Porter (2002) used a continuum of violence—from purely reactive, reactive-instrumental, instrumental-reactive, to purely instrumental—to code homicides committed by 125 adult male offenders. In this sample, 12.8% were coded as purely reactive, 23.2% as reactive-instrumental, 20% as instrumental-reactive, and 36% as purely instrumental (8% of the sample could not be coded).

Some homicide offenders report psychological problems as a consequence of killing. One of the necessary diagnostic criteria for post-traumatic stress disorder (PTSD) is exposure to a traumatic event. Pollock (1999) speculated that offenders who engage in reactive homicide are more likely than those committing instrumental homicide to develop PTSD symptoms. Eighty British male adult homicide offenders were classified as committing an instrumental (38%) or reactive (62%) homicide. Of these, 52% were diagnosed with PTSD and nearly all (95%) had committed a reactive homicide. Thus, reactive homicide is associated with a diagnosis of PTSD following the homicide.

DOMESTIC VIOLENCE

The term **domestic violence** refers to any violence occurring between family members. Domestic violence typically occurs in private settings. Although not necessarily condoned, historically it was tolerated and was not subject to effective legal sanctions. Reasons for this were varied, but religious and cultural attitudes generally positioned women and children in deferential roles within families. In Canada, little attention was paid to domestic violence prior to the 1980s. It was the women's liberation movement and the growth of feminism that gave women the courage to speak out against violence. Since that time, however, domestic violence has become a major focus of research and legal action. The Jane (Stafford) Hurshman-Corkum case in Nova Scotia brought to the forefront the plight of abused women (see Chapter 13).

This section will focus on violence occurring between intimate partners who are living together or separated (called spousal violence or **intimate partner violence**). Abuse and aggression within intimate relationships has a long history and is, unfortunately, still common. Violence against partners is varied in terms of types and severity and includes physical (e.g., hitting, punching, stabbing, burning), sexual, and emotional abuse (e.g., verbal attacks, degradation, threats to hurt pets or family members, isolation from family members, unwarranted accusations about infidelity).

The Conflict Tactics Scale

The most commonly used scale to measure domestic assault has been the Conflict Tactics Scale (CTS; Straus, 1979). This scale consists of 18 items intended to measure how the person and his or her partner resolve conflict. The items range from constructive problem solving (e.g., discuss the item calmly) to verbal or indirect aggression (e.g., swearing or threatening to hit) to physical aggression (e.g., slapping to using a gun). Respondents are asked how frequently they have engaged in the behaviour and how often they have experienced these acts. Researchers using the CTS have found that male and female respondents report the same frequency and severity of violent behaviour (Magdol, Moffitt, & Caspi, 1997).

Archer (2002) conducted a meta-analysis of 48 studies using the CTS and found that females are more likely to engage in minor physical aggression, such as slapping, kicking, or hitting with an object, whereas men are more likely to beat up or to choke their partner. Large differences were found when comparing community, university student, and treatment samples (couples in treatment for husband's violence). Within treatment samples, men engage in much higher rates of minor and severe physical violence compared with students and community samples. Within community and university student samples, males and females commit equal amounts of violence. Comparing self- and partner reports, respondents report fewer violent acts than their partners, and men are more likely to underreport than women.

Although commonly used, the CTS is often criticized for a number of reasons (Dobash & Dobash, 1979; Ratner, 1998):

1. The way it is introduced to respondents has been criticized. Respondents read the following: "No matter how well a couple get along, there are times when they disagree, get annoyed with the other person or just have spats or fights because they're in a bad mood or for some other reason. They also use many different ways of trying to settle their differences" (Straus, 1990, p. 33). The introduction to a questionnaire is crucial since it provides respondents with information on what to focus on. In the case of the CTS it is on how they settle disputes. However, some acts of violence are not precipitated by an argument and therefore the respondent may not report these.

2. The CTS does not include the full range of potential violent acts. For example, sexual aggression is not included.

3. It is likely that different results may be found if acts like kicking, biting, and punching were not combined into one item.

4. The CTS does not take into account the different consequences of the same act for men and women. For example, treating a punch by a woman and man as equivalent ignores the differential injury that might be inflicted (Nazroo, 1995). Surveys have consistently shown that women are more likely than men are to suffer both physical and psychological consequences from domestic violence (Saunders, 2002). Tjaden and Thoennes (2001) reported an injury rate of 42% for women versus 19% for men in the most recent violent episode. Canadian women reported that they had been physically injured in 45% of all cases of intimate violence, and in 20% of cases they sought and received medical care.

5. The CTS does not assess motive for violence and therefore offensive violence is treated as equal to a defensive response. For example, consider the case of a couple arguing. If he threatens to punch her, and she pushes him away from her, both acts would be included on the CTS.

In response to these and other criticisms, Straus, Hamby, Boney-McCoy, and Sugarman (1996) revised the CTS (CTS2), deleting some items and adding new items. For example, physically aggressive acts, such as slamming a person against a wall, burning them on purpose, and sexual aggression, have been included. Moreover, the consequence (physical injury) has also been added. To date, the CTS2 has not been widely used (Archer, 2002).

Intimate Partners: A Risky Relationship

In the 1993 Statistics Canada Violence Against Women Survey, 51% of women reported at least one incident of physical or sexual violence since the age of 16 (Johnson, 1996). Violence within dating relationships is also common in university students. DeKeseredy, and Kelly (1993) surveyed 3142 university students across Canada and reported that 35% of female students and 17% of male students had been physically abused at least once in a dating relationship.

The most recent survey in Canada to measure intimate violence was done by Statistics Canada in 1999. This survey used a modified CTS to measure psychological, physical, and sexual violence in intimate relationships. A large sample of men (11 607) and women (14 269) were asked questions about physical violence, ranging from threats to sexual assault in any relationship in the last 12 months and the past five years. In the past year, 4% of men and women reported experiencing physical violence and 18% experienced emotional abuse. Table 12.1 presents the percentage of men and women experiencing different types of physical violence in the past five years. The results indicate that both men and women experience violence, although women report experiencing more severe forms of violence (e.g., being choked, sexually assaulted, partner used or threatened to use a gun or knife). Respondents were asked about whether the violence was reported to the police. Violence against women was more likely to be reported to the police (37%) than was violence against men (15%).

Theories of Intimate Violence

Some researchers believe that a patriarchal society contributes to the domestic assault of women by men (e.g., Dobash & Dobash, 1979; Ellis, 1989; Straus, 1977). The theory of patriarchy was first described in the 1970s and is often associated with sociology and feminism. **Patriarchy** refers to a broad set of cultural beliefs and values that support the male dominance of women. As stated by Dobash and Dobash (1979), "the

TABLE 12.1 TYPES OF RELATIONSHIP VIOLENCE EXPERIENCED OVER THE PAST FIVE YEARS

Type of Violence	Men (%)	Women (%)
Threw something	56	44
Pushed, shoved	43	81
Threatened to hit	61	65
Slapped	57	40
Hit with object	26	23
Kicked, bit, hit	51	33
Beat up	10	25
Forced sex	3	20
Choked	4	20
Threat/used gun or knife	7	13

Source: Statistics Canada, 2000.

seeds of wife beating lie in the subordination of females and in their subjection to male authority and control" (p. 33). Smith (1990) has proposed a distinction between "social" patriarchy (male domination at the social level) and "familial" patriarchy (male domination within the family). To study the association between patriarchy and spousal abuse, Yllo and Straus (1990) compared the rates of spousal abuse across American states with the degree to which each state was characterized by patriarchal structure. States with male-dominant norms had much higher rates of spousal assault than states with more egalitarian norms.

Patriarchy likely influences the development of individual expectations about the appropriate level of authority within intimate relationships. One difficulty for patriarchal accounts of domestic violence is that it does not predict which individuals within a system will engage in intimate violence. Other factors operating in the community (e.g., work, peers), family (e.g., communication level between couple) and individual (e.g., coping skills, empathy) are needed to provide an explanation (Dutton, 1995). For example, consider two men who are raised to value the same cultural beliefs, who have similar social supports and identical levels of conflict in the home; one man may react with violence whereas the other does not.

Social learning theory, developed by Bandura (1973) to explain aggression, has been applied by Dutton (1995) to account for spousal assault. There are three main components to social learning theory: origins of aggression, instigators of aggression, and regulators of aggression. One way people acquire new behaviours is via **observational learning**. Bandura (1973) describes three major sources for observational learning: family of origin, the subculture the person lives in, and televised violence. Studies of the family background of male batterers have found they are much more likely to have witnessed parental violence than are nonviolent men (Kalmuss, 1984; Straus, Gelles, & Steinmetz, 1980). Not all behaviour that is observed, however, will be practised. Social learning theory posits that in order for a person to acquire a behaviour, it must have functional value for him or her. Behaviour that is rewarded increases in likelihood of occurrence and behaviour that is punished decreases in likelihood occurrence.

The next requirement is that even acquired behaviours are only manifested if there is an appropriate event in the environment to act as a stimulus for the behaviour. These are called **instigators**. Dutton (1995) describes two types of instigators in domestic assault: aversive instigators and incentive instigators. Aversive instigators produce emotional arousal and how a person labels that emotional arousal will influence how he or she responds. Studies with male batterers have found that they tend to label many different emotional states as anger (Gondolf, 1985, labels this the male-emotional funnel system). Incentive instigators are perceived rewards for engaging in aggression. When people believe they can satisfy their needs by using aggression, they may decide to be violent.

Social learning theory assumes that behaviour is regulated by its consequences. Two types of **regulators** include external punishment and self-punishment. An example of external punishment would be if the person was arrested for engaging in violence. An example of self-punishment would be if the person felt remorse for engaging in violence. If the consequences outweigh the rewards for engaging in the behaviour and if alternatives are provided to cope with instigators, the likelihood of violence should diminish.

Why Do Battered Women Stay?

One of the more perplexing questions is, "If a woman is in an abusive relationship, why doesn't she just leave?" Although intimate violence is no longer sanctioned by society, negative myths and stereotypes concerning battered woman still prevail. These myths range from a belief that a battered woman has a masochistic desire to be beaten, that she is emotionally disturbed, that the violence cannot be as bad as she claims, and that the woman is partially to blame for her victimization (Ewing & Aubrey, 1987; Harrison & Esqueda, 1999; Walker, 1979).

The extent to which people believe such myths varies (Ewing & Aubrey, 1987; Greene, Raitz, & Lindblad, 1989). To examine myths about battered women, Ewing and Aubrey (1987) gave community samples a hypothetical scenario about a couple having ongoing marital problems, including a description of an incident in which the husband assaulted his wife (the husband accused his wife of cheating on him and grabbed her and threw her to the floor). The percentage of males and females agreeing with each statement are shown in parentheses:

- The female victim "bears at least some responsibility." (Males = 47%; Females = 30%)
- The battered woman could simply leave her battering husband. (Males = 57%; Females = 71%)
- The battered woman who stays is "somewhat masochistic." (Males = 24%; Females = 50%)
- The woman can prevent battering by seeking counselling. (Males = 86%; Females 81%)
- Battering is an isolated event. (Males = 40%; Females = 27%)
- The woman can rely on upon the police to protect her. (Males = 18%; Females = 15%)

Researchers have asked victims of domestic violence why they stay in the relationship and for those who returned after separating, why they did so. The decision to stay with, to leave, or to return to an abusive partner is complex. According to the Violence Against Women Survey (Johnson, 1996), 42% of women left their abusive partners for a short while or permanently. The primary reasons given for leaving were related to the increases in the severity of the violence (e.g., if they feared for their lives or were physically injured), having children witness the violence, and reporting the abuse to the police. Seventy percent of women who left their abusive partners returned home at least once. The most common reasons for returning were:

- for the sake of the children (31%)
- to give the relationship another chance (24%)
- partner promised to change (17%)
- lack of money or place to go (9%)

Similar findings have been reported by Anderson, Gillig, Sitaker, McCloskey, Malloy, and Grigsby (2003) in a study of victims of intimate violence. In this study, 400 women who sought help from a domestic violence advocacy centre were asked, "If you never left your mate or returned to your mate after separating, check those factors that affected your decision" (p. 152). Thirty-two potential factors were listed and most women endorsed several different reasons. The reasons included:

- mate promised to change (71%)
- lack of money (46%)
- mate needed me (36%)
- nowhere to go or stay (29%)
- threats of mate to find me and kill me (22%)
- children wanted to go back (19%)
- shelter was full (5%)

This study and others point to the environmental, socialization, and psychological barriers that exist for victims. In order for a woman to leave, she needs resources such as money, a place to go, and support from the criminal justice system (examples of environmental barriers). Women are socialized to be the primary caretaker in relationships and appear to place a high value on the promises of the abuser to change. In addition, they return because they did not want their children to suffer (35%). Psychological barriers also exist. Some victims reported that they felt safer remaining in the relationship than leaving because they knew what the abuser was doing (22%).

Recently researchers have begun to study the link between family violence and animal maltreatment. Growing evidence suggests that batterers often threaten or harm their partners' pets and that one reason women delay leaving is out of concern for the welfare of their pets (Ascione, 1998; Faver & Strand, 2003; Flynn, 2000). Box 12.2 describes one such study. Although a link between maltreatment of animals and domestic violence may appear insignificant in relation to other factors, it underscores the complexity of the variables associated with remaining in a violent relationship.

Typologies of Male Batterers

Categories of male batterers have been developed in order to help understand the causes of intimate violence. Holtzworth-Munroe and Stuart (1994) divided male batterers into three types based on severity of violence, generality of violence, and personality disorder characteristics: family only, dysphoric/borderline, and generally violent/antisocial.

BOX 12.2 WOMAN'S BEST FRIEND: PET ABUSE AND INTIMATE VIOLENCE

Only recently have researchers started to investigate the link between animal maltreatment and violence against women (Ascione, 1998; Faver & Strand, 2003). In a study of women in domestic violence shelters, Ascione reported that 72% said their partners had either threatened to harm or actually had harmed their pets. Moreover, 54% reported that their pets had actually been injured or killed by their abusive partners. Faver and Strand (2003) questioned 50 abused women who owned pets and found that 49% reported their partners had threatened their pets and 46% indicated that their partner had actually harmed their pets.

Flynn (2000) asked a series of questions about the women's experiences with their pets:

1. In dealing with the abuse, how important has your pet been as a source of emotional support?

2. Has your partner ever threatened to harm your pet, actually harmed your pet, or killed your pet?

3. Where is your pet now?

4. Did concern about your pet's safety keep you from seeking shelter sooner?

Flynn divided the sample of 42 battered women into a pet-abuse group (n = 20) and the no-pet-abuse group (n = 22). Ninety percent of the women in the pet-abuse group considered their pet a source of emotional support, compared with 47% of the no-pet-abuse group. About half of the pets in both groups were left with the abusive partner. In light of the partner's history of pet abuse, it is not surprising that 65% of the women in the pet-abuse group worried about the safety of their pets, whereas only 15% of the women in the no-pet-abuse group were concerned. Eight women actually delayed leaving their abusive partner out of concern for their pets' safety, with five of these women reporting that they delayed leaving for more than two months. Flynn concluded that "efforts to prevent and end such violence must not only recognize the interconnections, but grant legitimacy to all victims, human and animal" (p. 176).

The **family-only batterer**

- engages in the least amount of violence
- is typically neither violent outside the home nor engages in other criminal behaviours
- does not show much psychopathology and if a personality disorder is present, it would most likely be passive-dependent personality
- does not report negative attitudes supportive of violence and has moderate impulse-control problems
- typically displays no disturbance in attachment to his partner

The **dysphoric/borderline batterer**

- engages in moderate to severe violence
- exhibits some extra-familial violence and criminal behaviour

- displays the most depression and borderline personality traits, and has problems with jealousy
- has moderate problems with impulsivity and alcohol and drug use
- has an attachment style that would be best described as preoccupied

The **generally violent/antisocial batterer**

- engages in moderate to severe violence
- engages in the most violence outside of the home and in criminal behaviour
- has antisocial and narcissistic personality features
- likely has drug and alcohol problems
- has high levels of impulse-control problems and many violence-supportive beliefs
- shows a dismissive attachment style

Several studies have provided support for this typology both in offender and in community samples of male batterers (Tweed & Dutton, 1998; Waltz, Babcock, Jacobson, & Gottman, 2000). Other typologies have also been proposed. For example, Gondolf (1988), using data from battered women admitted to shelters in Texas, proposed three typologies. The Type I batterer, identified as the *sociopathic* (accounting for about 5% to 8% of batterers), engaged in the most severe abuse against both women and children and was most likely to have a criminal record. The Type II batterer, labelled *antisocial* (accounting for about 30% to 40% of batterers), was similar to the sociopathic batterer but was less likely to have a criminal record. The Type III batterer, referred to as the *typical* batterer (most common type), perpetrated less severe violence, was more likely to be apologetic after abusive behaviour, and was least likely to have a criminal record.

Criminal Justice Response

For centuries, wife battering was seen as a private family matter and police were reluctant to become involved (Dobash & Dobash, 1979). When called to a domestic violence scene, police would attempt to calm the people involved and, once order was restored, they would leave (Jaffe et al., 1993). Since the 1980s, however, mandatory charging policies have been in effect in Canada and in most jurisdictions in United States. **Mandatory charging policies** give police the authority to lay charges against a suspect when there is reasonable and probable grounds to believe an assault has occurred. Prior to mandatory charging, women were required to bring charges against their husbands. Women were often too intimidated and feared further violence so often charges were not laid.

The first experimental study to examine the specific deterrence effect of arrest on spousal violence was conducted by Sherman and Berk (1984) in Minneapolis. This study involved the random assignment of 314 domestic assault calls to three police responses: separation (order for suspect to leave premises for at least eight hours), mediation (provide advice to victim), or arrest. A six-month follow-up of the men was conducted using both police reports and victim reports. Figure 12.2

presents the recidivism rates across the groups for both police and victim reports. The recidivism rates for the arrested men were much lower than those of men in the separation or mediation groups. Attempts to replicate this finding have met with mixed results. Tolman and Weisz (1995) also found a deterrent effect for arrest, whereas Hirschell, Hutchinson, and Dean (1992) did not. In an attempt to replicate their findings, Sherman, Schmidt, and Rogan (1992) randomly assigned police calls of domestic violence to nonarrest or arrest. Using police and victim reports, lower rates of recidivism were reported in the short term (30 days after police contact). However, in the long-term follow-up (seven to nine months after police contact) the arrest group had slightly higher rates of recidivism than did the nonarrest group. The authors found that arrest does not work for those offenders who were unemployed. In other words, arrest worked as a deterrent only for those men who had something to lose.

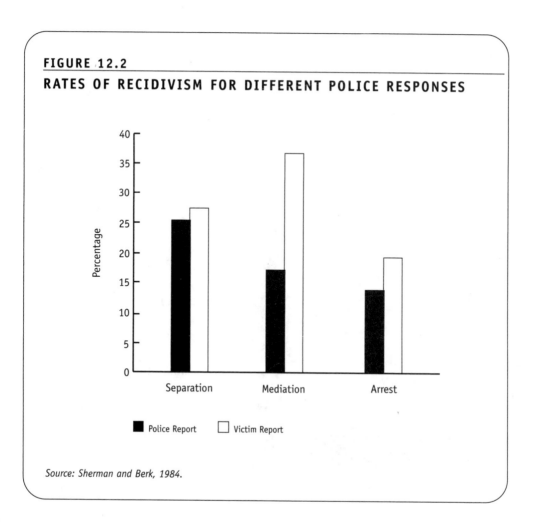

FIGURE 12.2

RATES OF RECIDIVISM FOR DIFFERENT POLICE RESPONSES

■ Police Report   □ Victim Report

Source: Sherman and Berk, 1984.

Do mandatory arrest policies increase the probability of domestic abusers being arrested? Arrest rates for intimate-partner violence have increased dramatically since mandatory arrest polices were implemented. For example, in the 1970s and 1980s, arrest rates in Canada and United States ranged from 7% to 15%, whereas more recent rates of 30% to 75% have been reported. However, one unanticipated outcome of these polices has been an increase in dual arrests (Hirschel & Buzawa, 2002). If the police are unable to determine the identity of the primary aggressor and if there are minor injuries to both parties, the police will charge both the man and woman.

Another consequence of the increase in the number of arrests for domestic assault has been the dramatic increase in the number of men who are court-mandated to attend treatment. Since most batterers are not motivated to attend treatment programs, having judges impose a treatment order forces men to obtain treatment. If the man fails to attend treatment, a prison term can be imposed. The use of court-mandated treatment is based on the belief that it is possible to treat male batterers. However, the effectiveness of treatment for batterers is still controversial.

Does Treatment of Male Batterers Work?

A number of different procedures have been developed to treat male batterers. The two most common forms of intervention are feminist psychoeducational group therapy (also referred to as the Duluth model, since the treatment was designed at the Duluth Domestic Abuse Intervention Project in Minnesota) and cognitive-behavioural group therapy. According to the Duluth model (Pence & Paymar, 1993), the primary cause of domestic violence is patriarchal ideology. Group therapy in this model focuses on challenging the man's perceived right to control his partner. In contrast, cognitive-behavioural therapy subscribes to the belief that violence is a learned behaviour and that use of violence is reinforcing for the offender by obtaining victim compliance and by reducing feelings of tension (Sonkin, Martin, & Walker, 1985). Cognitive-behavioural therapy focuses on the costs of engaging in violence. Alternatives to violence are taught, such as anger management and communication skills training. Some cognitive-behavioural treatment programs also address perpetrators' attitudes about control and dominance. The rationale for using group therapy is to help break through the barriers of denial and minimization.

Group therapy for male batterers

Babcock, Green, and Robie (2004) conducted a meta-analysis of 22 studies to evaluate the efficacy of treatment for male batterers. Studies were only included if the outcome was measured by either police reports or partner reports of violence (i.e., studies using only batterer self-report were not included). Studies were also divided into three types of treatment: Duluth model, cognitive-behavioural, and other (e.g., couples therapy). There were no differences in efficacy among the three treatment types in terms of recidivism rates. Based on partner reports, the effect size for quasi-experimental studies was $d = 0.34$ and for experimental studies it was $d = 0.09$. The authors conclude that "regardless of reporting method, study design, and type of treatment, the effect on recidivism rates remains in the small range" (p. 1044). Based on experimental studies and using partner reports, these results mean there is a 5% increase in success rate due to treatment. This small effect does not mean we should abandon attempts to treat batterers. As stated by the authors, "a 5% decrease in violence … in United States … would equate to approximately 42,000 women per year no longer being battered" (p. 1044). Although the effects appear to be small, they are similar to treatment effects for alcohol abuse if abstinence from alcohol is the outcome (Agosti, 1995). Future research should examine the treatment response of specific subsamples, such as types of batterers (e.g., family-only, borderline/dysphoric, and generally violent/antisocial), batterers with substance abuse problems, batterers at different levels of motivation, and female batterers.

SEXUAL OFFENDERS
Nature and Extent of Sexual Violence

In 2002, just over 24 000 sexual assaults were reported to the police in Canada (Statistics Canada, 2003). The rate per 100 000 population was 78 and has remained stable over the past five years. However, official statistics do not provide an accurate measure of the true incidence of this type of crime since the majority of victims do not report the crime to the police (Yurchesyn, Keith, & Renner, 1992). As indicated in the Statistics Canada 1993 survey of violence against women, only six out of every 100 sexual assaults were reported to the police (Johnson, 1996).

Sexual assault affects a large percentage of the population. High victimization rates are reported among children (about 10% of boys and 25% of girls; Finkelhor et al., 1989; Finkelhor & Dziuba-Leatherman, 1994) and adult women (10% to 20% report being raped; Johnson & Sacco, 1995; Koss, 1993). In a review of community samples, Gorey and Leslie (1997) calculated the prevalence of childhood sexual abuse as 17% for females and 8% for males. Given the large number of victims, it is not surprising that sexual offenders admit to having many victims. For example, Abel, Becker, Mittelman, and Cunningham-Rathner (1987) investigated the number of victims reported by 127 rapists, 224 female-victim child molesters, and 153 male-victim child molesters. High victim rates were reported, with rapists having on average seven victims, female-victim child molesters having 20 victims, and male-victim child molesters averaging 150 victims. In studies of community samples (university students, hospital staff), in which the respondent was assured there would be no negative consequences of reporting, 10% to 20% of men admit to sexually assaulting women or children (Hanson & Scott, 1995; Lisak & Roth, 1988). Society's recognition of the seriousness and widespread occurrence of sexual assault has been in part responsible for the substantial increase in the number of Canadian federal sexual offenders. Since the late 1970s, the number of sexual offenders incarcerated has grown rapidly. For example, in 1984 there were 870 federal sex offenders, but that number climbed to 4500 in 1996.

Sexual aggression has serious negative psychological and physical consequences. Victims of rape report high levels of stress and fear that disrupt social, sexual, and occupational functioning, while also generating high levels of anxiety and depression (Hanson, 1990). Physically, Koss (1993) reports that up to 30% of rape victims contract sexually transmitted diseases, and pregnancy results in about 5% of cases.

Child victims of sexual abuse develop a wide range of short- and long-term problems. In the year following disclosure of the abuse, up to 70% of children experience significant psychological symptoms. Longer-term problems include substance abuse, depression, eating disorders, and prostitution (Hanson, 1990).

Definition of Sexual Assault

In Canada the definition of sexual assault has undergone substantial change over the past 20 years. Prior to 1983, a number of different offences were lumped together under the label of "rape," which was defined as "a male person commits rape when he has sexual intercourse with a female person who is not his wife ... without her consent" (section 143, Canadian Criminal Code). In response to criticism and to make the definition more inclusive of diverse sexual relationships and more representative of the nature of sexual assault, rape was reclassified. Sexual assault became defined as any nonconsensual sexual act by either a male or female person to either male or female persons, regardless of the relationship between the people involved. Sexual assault, like physical assault, was divided into three levels based on severity issues and with different maximum penalties: simple sexual assault (maximum sentence ten years), sexual assault with a weapon or causing bodily harm (maximum sentence 14 years), and aggravated sexual assault (maximum sentence life imprisonment).

Rape Myths

Rape myths are stereotypic ideas people have about rape, such as the following: women falsely accuse men of rape, women want or enjoy rape, rape is not harmful, or women cause or deserve rape by the way they dress or act (Burt, 1980). According to Lonsway and Fitzgerald (1994), rape myths "are generally false but are widely and persistently held, and serve to deny and justify male aggression against woman" (p. 217). Rape myths appear to be accepted across many levels of society, including high school students (Kershner, 1996), university students (Szymanski et al., 1993), and prosecuting lawyers (Gylys & McNamara, 1996). One of the most consistent findings is that men are more accepting of rape myths than women are (Bohner et al., 1998). Box 12.3 lists some of the common rape myths.

Effects of Rape

The term **rape trauma syndrome** was first used by Burgess and Holmstrom (1974) to describe the after-effects of rape. Burgess and Holmstrom interviewed 92 women who had been raped; the interviews took place within 30 minutes of arriving at the hospital and one month later. They divided the effects of rape into two phases: an acute crisis phase and a long-term reactions phase. The acute crisis phase lasts for a few days to several weeks and the symptoms are often quite severe. Those who have been raped often report very high levels of fear, anxiety, and depression. They often ask questions

---

BOX 12.3 SEXUAL ASSAULT: DISCOUNTING RAPE MYTHS

There are many myths associated with sexual assault. Below is a list of myths followed by facts that challenge these false beliefs.

Myth 1: Sexual assault is not a common problem.

One in every four women and one in every six men has experienced some type of sexual assault. You likely know someone who has been sexually assaulted.

Myth 2: Sexual assault is most often committed by strangers.

Women face the greatest risk of sexual assault from men they know, not from strangers. About half of all rapes occur in dating relationships. In about 80% of cases, victims of sexual assault knew the attacker.

Myth 3: Women who are sexually assaulted "ask for it" by the way they dress or act.

Victims of sexual assault range across the age span (from infants to elderly) and sexual assaults can occur in almost any situation. No woman "deserves" to be sexually assaulted regardless of what she wears, where she

goes, or how she acts. Blaming sexual assault on how a victim behaves would be like blaming a mugging on a person for carrying a wallet.

Myth 4: Avoid being alone in dark, deserted places, such as parks or parking lots, and this will protect you from being sexually assaulted.

Most sexual assaults occur in a private home and many in the victim's home.

Myth 5: Women derive pleasure from being a victim.

Sexual assault is associated with both short- and long-term serious problems. High rates of anxiety, fear, depression, and post-traumatic stress disorder are seen in survivors of sexual assault. Some women are physically injured during the assault.

Myth 6: Women lie about sexual assault.

False accusations are very rare. Sexual assault is a vastly underreported crime, and most sexual assaults are not reported to the police.

about why the rape happened to them and commonly engage in self-blame (Janoff-Bulman, 1979). For example, they might say, "I should not have taken that short-cut home" or "I should have not gone back to his apartment." Heightened levels of distrust and self-doubt are also common reactions.

The second phase is more protracted, lasting anywhere from a few months to several years. One-quarter of women who have been raped do not significantly recover, even after several years (Resick, 1993). Long-term reactions include the development of phobias, such as the fear of being left alone or the fear of leaving the house. Another long-term reaction is the development of sexual problems and depression. Often victims make dramatic changes in their lifestyles.

The psychological consequences of rape victimization also include **post-traumatic stress disorder** (PTSD). The *DSM-IV* (APA, 1994) defines PTSD as an anxiety disorder that can develop in response to exposure to an extremely traumatic event. PTSD symptoms include frequent, distressing, and intrusive memories of the event, avoiding stimuli associated with the traumatic event, and persistent anxiety or increased arousal symptoms. Rothbaum, Foa, Riggs, Murdock, and Walsh (1992) assessed the PTSD symptoms in 95 female rape victims over a nine-month follow-up period. One month after the rape, 65% of victims were diagnosed with PTSD and at nine months 47% were classified as having PTSD. Some victims continue to experience PTSD symptoms years after the rape. An average of 15 years after the rape, 16.5% of rape victims had PTSD (Kilpatrick et al., 1987). Effective treatment programs have been developed to help rape victims overcome the emotional suffering caused by this trauma (Foa & Rothbaum, 1998).

Classification of Sexual Offenders

Sexual offenders are usually divided into categories based on the type of sexually deviant behaviour, the relationship between victim and offender, and the age of the victim. **Voyeurs** obtain sexual gratification by observing unsuspecting people, usually strangers, who are either naked, in process of undressing, or engaging in sexual activity. **Exhibitionists** obtain sexual gratification by exposing their genitals to strangers. These two types of sexual offenders are sometimes referred to as hands-off or no-contact sexual offenders. **Rapists** are offenders who sexually assault victims aged 16 years or older. The term pedophilia means, "love of children." Thus, **pedophile** is often used to refer to an adult whose primary sexual orientation is toward children. Other researchers use the term **child molester** to refer to individuals who have actually sexually molested a child. Child molesters are also divided into two types: intra-familial and extra-familial. **Intra-familial child molesters** (also called incest offenders) are those who sexually abuse their own biological children or children for whom they assume a parental role, such as a stepfather or live-in boyfriend. **Extra-familial child molesters** sexually abuse children outside the family. Child molesters have also been classified into groups based on whether they target male or female victims.

Perceptions of sexual offenders are uniformly negative. Studies examining perceptions of sex offenders have found that nonsexual offenders, correctional staff, treatment providers, psychologists, and students (Hogue & Peebles, 1997; Lea, Auburn, & Kibblewhite, 1999; Valliant, Furac, & Antonowicz, 1994) all judge them very negatively. Sex offenders who commit sex offences against children are judged the more harshly than sex offenders who commit offences against adult women.

Rapist Typologies

Rapists are not a homogenous group and do not all engage in sexual assault for the same reasons. Several different rapist typologies have been proposed. During the 1990s an ambitious project was undertaken at the Massachusetts Treatment Centre to develop and empirically validate a typology for rapists. The resulting classification system, *The Revised Rapist Typology, Version 3* (MTC:R3; Knight & Prentky, 1990), consists of five primary subtypes of rapists based on motivational differences:

1. The opportunistic types commit sexual assault that is generally impulsive, void of sexual fantasies, controlled primarily by situational or contextual factors, and void of gratuitous violence. These offenders often engage in other criminal behaviours. For example, a rapist who breaks into a home with the intention of stealing but who rapes the female occupant could be classified as opportunistic.

2. The pervasively angry types has a high level of anger that is directed toward both men and women. They tend to be impulsive, use unnecessary force, cause serious victim injury, and are void of sexual fantasies.

3. The sexual type is distinguished from the other types in that their crimes are primarily motivated by sexual preoccupation or sexual fantasies.

4. The sadistic type is differentiated from sexual type in that there must be a sadistic element to the offence.

5. The fifth type is labelled vindictive. In contrast to the pervasively angry type, the vindictive rapist's anger is focused solely on women. They are not impulsive nor are they preoccupied by sexual fantasies. The goal of this type of rapist is to demean and degrade the victim.

The opportunistic, sexual, and vindictive subtypes are further subdivided based on the their level of social competence. The sadistic type is also further subdivided into overt or muted sadists based on the presence or absence of gratuitous violence (Knight & Prentky, 1990). Research using the MTC:R3 has found that these types differ on prevalence of psychopathy (Barbaree et al., 1994; Brown & Forth, 1997), rates of sexual recidivism (Knight, Prentky, & Cerce, 1994), and treatment needs (Knight, 1999).

Another typology that uses motivations to classify rapists was proposed by Groth (1979). Groth proposed that rapists can be divided into three main types: anger rapists, power rapists, and sadistic rapists.

The features of the **anger rapist** include

- the use of more force than necessary to obtain compliance and engaging in a variety of sexual acts to degrade the victim
- high levels of anger directed solely towards women
- not being motivated primarily by sexual gratification

Most of these rapes are precipitated by conflict or perceived humiliation by some significant women, such as the offender's wife, mother, or boss. Approximately 50% of rapists fit this type.

The features of the **power rapist** include

- intention to assert dominance and control over victim
- variation in the amount of force used depending on the degree of submission shown by the victim
- not being motivated primarily by sexual gratification
- frequent rape fantasies

About 40% of rapists fit into this category.

The features of the **sadistic rapist** include

- obtaining sexual gratification by hurting the victim
- high levels of victim injury, including torture and sometimes death
- frequent violent sexual fantasies

Approximately 5% of rapists fit this type.

There is considerable overlap between the MTC:R3 and Groth typologies. Both typologies describe a sadistic rapist. The vindictive rapist is similar to the anger rapist and the pervasively angry rapist shares some of the features of the power rapist.

Is Resisting a Sexual Attack a Good Idea?

One question often posed by women is, "If attacked, should I fight back or not?" Based on the typologies described above, the answer will likely depend on the type of rapist attacking them. Research with incarcerated rapists indicates that they search for vulnerable victims in certain areas and attack women they believe cannot or will not resist the attack (Stevens, 1994). Studies of women who were raped or who avoided being raped have found that forceful verbal resistance, physical resistance, and fleeing are all associated with rape avoidance (Ullman & Knight, 1993; Zoucha-Jensen & Coyne, 1993), whereas nonresistance strategies (e.g., pleading with rapists, crying, reasoning) are not.

The association between victim injury and resistance is inconclusive. Zoucha-Jensen and Coyne (1993) found no association between resistance and injury. In contrast, Ullman and Knight (1993) found that if the offender had a weapon, women who resisted the rape suffered more physical injury than those who did not resist. In a review of universities' sexual assault prevention programs, Söchting, Fairbrother, and Koch (2004) conclude that the most promising prevention program is teaching self-defence skills.

Child Molester Typologies

The most widely used typology is Groth's typology of the fixated and regressed child molester (Groth, Hobson, & Gary, 1982). Groth developed his typology based on research with incarcerated child molesters.

Fixated child molesters tend to have the following features:

- Their primary sexual orientation is toward children, and they have little or no sexual contact with adults.
- Their sexual interest in children begins in adolescence and is persistent.
- Male children are their primary targets.
- Precipitating stress is not evident.
- Their offences are planned.
- They are emotionally immature, have poor social skills, and are usually single.
- They usually have no history of alcohol or drug abuse.
- They often feel no remorse or distress over their behaviour.

Regressed child molesters usually have the following characteristics:

- Their primary sexual orientation is to adults.
- Their sexual interest in children begins in adulthood and is episodic.
- Female children are their primary targets.
- Precipitating stress and feelings of inadequacy are usually present.
- Their offences are more impulsive.
- They are often married and are having marital problems.
- Many of their offences are related to alcohol use.
- They are more likely to report feeling remorse for their behaviour.

Groth also subdivided child molesters into two types based on the type of coercion they used. The sex-pressure child molesters use persuasion or entrapment to make the child feel obligated to participate in sexual acts. For example, this type of child molester may buy the child gifts or take the child on fun outings. The sex-force child molester threatens or uses physical force to overcome any resistance by the child. This latter group has been divided into the exploitative type who uses the threat of force to obtain compliance and the sadistic type who obtains gratification from hurting a child. The sadistic type of child molester is, fortunately, rare.

Models of Sexual Aggression

Finkelhor's (1984) theory of child molesting proposes that in order for the sexual abuse to occur there are four preconditions:

1. The offender must be motivated to sexually abuse. Motivation is due to three factors: (1) emotional congruence, which is the offender's desire for the child to satisfy an emotional need; (2) sexual attraction to the child; and (3) blockage of emotional outlets for the offender to meet his sexual and emotional needs.

2. The next precondition relates to the offender's lack of internal inhibitions. For example, alcohol and impulse-control problems can weaken the offender's ability to restrain the behaviours that lead to abuse.

3. The offender must overcome external inhibitors for the abuse to occur. For example, the offender might need to create opportunities to be alone with the child.

4. The offender must overcome the child's resistance. Offenders will reward the child with attention or bribes in order to encourage the child to cooperate. Alternatively, some offenders will use the threat of harm to intimidate the child.

Marshal and Barbaree (1990) have proposed an integrated model of sexual aggression that includes biological factors, childhood experiences, sociocultural influences, and situational events. They argue that males normally learn to inhibit sexually aggressive behaviour via a socialization process that promotes the development of strong, positive attachments. The authors suggest that sexual offenders fail to acquire effective inhibitory control because they experienced childhood abuse (emotional, physical, or sexual abuse) or because they were raised in extremely dysfunctional families (e.g., harsh and inconsistent punishment, lack of supervision, hostility). They also acknowledged the importance of the structure of society that reinforces the use of aggression and the acceptance of negative attitudes toward women.

Adolescent Sexual Offenders

Prior to the 1980s, sexually aggressive behaviour by adolescents was not deemed serious and was discounted by some as normal experimentation. However, crime reports and victimization surveys indicate that about 20% of rapes and between 30% and 50% of child sexual abuse is committed by adolescents (Davis & Leitenberg, 1987). In Canada, 1115 adolescents were tried in youth court for sexual assault in 2002.

Like their adult counterparts, adolescent sexual offenders consistently report having been victims of sexual abuse themselves. The prevalence rate for sexual abuse committed against adolescent sexual offenders ranges from about 40% to 80% (Friedrich & Luecke, 1988; Ryan et al., 1996). Although early sexual victimization and later sexual offending are related, the majority of sexually abused children do not go on to become adolescent or adult sexual offenders. Clearly, being the victim of sexual abuse is only one factor that affects later sexual offending. Rasmussen, Burton, and Christopherson (1992) suggest that in addition to sexual abuse, other factors such as social inadequacy, lack of intimacy, and impulsiveness also play a role.

Prior history of childhood sexual victimization is not related to sexual recidivism in samples of adult sexual offenders (Hanson & Bussiere, 1998) or samples of adolescent sexual offenders (Worling & Curwen, 2000).

In a national sample of adolescent sex offenders undergoing treatment, Ryan and colleagues (1996) investigated victim characteristics. Adolescent sexual offenders tend to sexually abuse young female victims. Notably, Ryan and colleagues found that 63% of the adolescent sexual offenders' victims were younger than age nine.

Female Sexual Offenders

Research on female sexual offenders is limited. This relative lack of attention is probably because only 2% to 5% of incarcerated sex offenders are female. However, some researchers have suggested that sexual abuse of children by women is more prevalent than previously believed.

The rates of sexual abuse by females vary dramatically depending on the definition used. For example, should a female be classified as a sexual abuser if she knew that her husband was sexually abusing their child and did nothing to stop the abuse? Does a mother sleeping with her child constitute sexual abuse in the absence of sexual touching? What if the child is a teenager who becomes sexually aroused by sleeping with his mother? Most people would agree that it is sexual abuse for a 20-year-old to have sexual contact with an eight-year-old boy, but not if the boy is 16. However, what about if the boy is 14? If the 14-year-old boy initiates the sexual act and views it positively, should this be classified as sexual abuse?

Retrospective surveys of university students have found a large percentage of perpetrators were females. For example, Fritz, Stoll, and Wagner (1981) reported that of the 5% of college men who were molested as children, 60% were molested by females, most being older female adolescents. In a large survey of 2972 university students that used broad criteria for sexual abuse, Risin and Koss (1987) reported that 7.3% were abused. They found that almost half the perpetrators were female (43%), and of these almost half were female adolescent babysitters. Similar to other studies, about half the male respondents reported they participated in the sexual acts voluntarily and did not feel victimized. Fewer female perpetrators have been reported by other researchers (Finkelhor, 1984; Reinhart, 1987). For example, Finkelhor (1984) found that only 6% of university women and 16% of university men who reported childhood sexual abuse indicated that the offender was a woman.

Some researchers have speculated that the rate of sexual abuse by females is underestimated. Some reasons include the following (Banning, 1989; Groth, 1979):

■ Women are able to mask their sexually abusive behaviours through caregiving activities and thus are more difficult to recognize.

■ Women sexual offenders are more likely to target their own children, who are less likely to disclose the abuse.

■ Boys are more frequent targets than girls, and boys are less likely to disclose abuse.

Research designed to determine the characteristics of female sexual offenders has generally been plagued with very small sample sizes. Whether the findings will generalize to larger samples of female sexual offenders remains to be investigated. Keeping this limitation in mind, Atkinson (1996) suggests there are four types of female sexual offenders:

1. *Teacher/lover.* These offenders initiate sexual abuse of a male adolescent that they relate to as a peer. The offender is often in a position of authority or power. It is unknown how common this type of female sex offender is because the victim rarely reports the abuse to authorities. This type has not likely experienced childhood sexual abuse, although substance use problems are common. These offenders often are not aware their behaviour is inappropriate. Teacher/lovers often describe themselves as being "in love" with the victim. Victims often report they participated voluntarily and do not feel victimized.

2. *Male-coerced.* These offenders are coerced or forced into sexual abuse by an abusive male. Often the victim is the female offender's own daughter. These offenders are unassertive, dependent on men, and are relatively passive partners in the abuse.

3. *Male-accompanied.* These offenders also engage in sexual abuse with a male partner. However, they are more willing participants than are the male-coerced type. Victims are both inside and outside the family.

4. *Predisposed.* This offender initiates the sexual abuse alone. She has often experienced severe and persistent childhood sexual abuse and has been a victim of intimate violence. This type often reports having deviant sexual fantasies, the offences are more violent and bizarre, and they typically involve younger children. Victims are often their own children and they also frequently physically abuse and neglect the victim.

In a study of 40 female sexual offenders, Faller (1987) reported that most had significant psychological and social functioning problems. Most of the offenders (29 out of the 40, or 73%) were classified as engaging in poly-incestuous abuse, which involved two perpetrators and generally two or more victims. The male offender usually instigated the sexual abuse, while the women played a secondary role.

In summary, female sexual offenders, although relatively rare, do exist. Most retrospective surveys of university men who reported sexual abuse by women have found that most engaged in the sexual incidents voluntarily and did not feel victimized. Finally, most of the incarcerated female sexual offenders have engaged in abuse in conjunction with a dominant male.

Assessment and Treatment of Sexual Offenders

Much of the assessment of sexual offenders is to help determine future risk for re-offending, to identify treatment needs, and to evaluate whether or not the treatment has had the desired effect. Risk factors for sexual reoffending were discussed in Chapter 11. The focus of this section will be on the assessment of treatment needs and the effectiveness of treatment programs.

Most treatment programs are designed to address the following: denial, minimizations and cognitive distortions, victim empathy, modification of deviant sexual interest, enhanced social skills, substance abuse problems, and development of relapse-prevention plans (Marshall, 1999).

DENIAL, MINIMIZATIONS, AND COGNITIVE DISTORTIONS Sex offenders often deny (i.e., they claim they didn't do what are accused of or that the victim consented) or fail to take full responsibility for their sexual offending (Barbaree, 1991). Often blame is shifted to someone else, including the victim or some external factor. For example, "The victim wanted to have sex with me" or " I was drunk and didn't know what I was doing." Assessments of denial and acceptance of responsibility are most often done through self-report questionnaires like the Clarke Sex History Questionnaire (Langevin et al., 1985) or by comparing police and victim reports with what the offenders admit in interviews.

Cognitive distortions are deviant cognitions, values, and beliefs that are used by the sexual offender to justify deviant behaviours. For example, a child molester who states, "Having sex with a child in a loving relationship is a good way to teach a child about sex" or an incest offender claiming, "It was better for her to have her first sexual experience with me since I love her, rather with some teenager who would just want to use her." Both these child molesters are reporting cognitive distortions that are self-serving and inhibit them from taking full responsibility for their offences.

Some treatment programs refuse to accept deniers into their treatment programs. The reason is that if the person refuses to admit to having committed a sexual offence, it is difficult for that person to fully participate in the treatment, since the focus is on sexual offending. In treatment, offenders are asked to disclose in detail what happened before, during, and after the sexual abuse. The therapist has access to the police and victim reports in order to challenge an offender who is denying or minimizing aspects of the event. Other group members are encouraged to also challenge what the offender discloses.

EMPATHY Although some sex offenders have a general deficit in empathy (e.g., psychopathic sex offenders), most have a specific deficit in empathy toward their victims (Marshall et al., 1995). Empathy is the ability to perceive others' perspectives and to recognize and respond in a compassionate way to the feelings of others. Empathy problems in sexual offenders arise in part due to cognitive distortions. Because they minimize the amount of harm they have done, they do not think the victim has suffered, and therefore they do not empathize with the victim. Measures of empathy have focused on self-report scales such as the Rape Empathy Scale (Deitz et al., 1982) and interviews.

Empathy training typically focuses on getting the offender to understand the impact of the abuse on the victim and the pain caused, and to develop feelings such as remorse. Offenders read survivor accounts of rape and child abuse and compare these accounts with how their victim likely felt. Videotapes of victims describing the emotional damage they have suffered and the long-term problems they experience are often used. Some therapy programs use role-playing, with the offender playing the role of the victim. Finally, although controversial, some programs may have sexual offenders meet with adult survivors of rape or child sexual abuse. Only those sexual offenders who are demonstrating empathy are permitted to take part in these meetings.

SOCIAL SKILLS Sexual offenders have been found lacking in a variety of social skills, including self-confidence in interpersonal relations, capacity for intimacy, assertiveness, and dealing with anger (Bumby & Hansen, 1997; Marshall, Anderson, & Champagne, 1997; Marshall, Barbaree, & Fernandez, 1995). Self-report questionnaires, interviews, and responses to scenarios have all been developed to assess social skill deficits (see Marshall, 1999, for review). Treatment programs for sexual offenders vary in terms of which social skill deficits are targeted. Some programs focus on anger and communication skills (Pithers, Martin, & Cumming, 1989), whereas others target relationship skills, anger control, and self-esteem (Marshall et al., 1997).

SUBSTANCE ABUSE Substance abuse problems are common in nonsexual offenders and sexual offenders (Lightfoot & Barbaree, 1993). It is likely that some sexual offenders use alcohol to facilitate offending by reducing their inhibitions. Self-report measures are often used to assess problems with alcohol and drugs.

Sexual offenders with substance abuse problems are often referred to substance abuse programs. These programs are usually based on the relapse-prevention model developed by Martlatt and his colleagues (Martlatt & Gordon, 1985).

DEVIANT SEXUAL INTERESTS Deviant sexual interests motivate some sexual offenders. However, many other salient motives also play a role, including power and control over others, anger toward others, and desire for emotional intimacy. One of the most popular methods to assess deviant sexual interests is the use of **penile phallometry**. Penile phallometry involves placing a measurement device around the penis to measure changes in sexual arousal. To measure deviant sexual interests in child molesters, photos of naked male and female children and adults are presented, as well as rapists' audiotaped descriptions of nondeviant and deviant sexual behaviour. Phallometric assessments have been used to differentiate extra-familial child molesters from nonoffenders. However, most intra-familial child molesters do not differ in their phallometric responses from nonoffenders (see Marshall, 1999, for review). Research with rapists is mixed. Some studies have found differences between rapists and nonrapists (Quinsey, Chaplin, & Upfold, 1984), whereas others have not (Marshall & Fernandez, 2003). Another problem has been the relatively high rate of nonresponders. About 20% of all sexual offenders fail to show any arousal during phallometric testing.

There are also ethical concerns with showing images of naked children or having rapists listen to graphic, violent sexual assaults. Unfortunately, simply asking offenders to indicate their sexual interests is not an option due to the tendency of all individuals, including offenders, to portray themselves in the best possible light.

Many different techniques have been developed to train offenders to eliminate deviant thoughts and interests and to increase the frequency of appropriate sexual thoughts and interests. For example, in aversion therapy the offender is given an aversive substance to smell (e.g., ammonia) whenever he has a deviant sexual fantasy. The underlying goal is to reduce the attractiveness of these deviant fantasies by pairing them with a negative event. The 1971 Stanley Kubrick film *A Clockwork Orange* provides a graphic illustration of aversion therapy.

Another approach is called masturbatory satiation. In this treatment, the offender is told to masturbate to ejaculation to a nondeviant fantasy. After ejaculation, he is told to switch to a deviant fantasy, thus pairing the inability to become aroused to this deviant fantasy. The effectiveness of these techniques to change deviant sexual interests has been questioned by several researchers (Quinsey & Earls, 1990).

Pharmacological interventions appear to be effective at suppressing deviant sexual desires (Bradford & Pawlak, 1993). Drugs used in the past acted to suppress all sexual interests and compliance was a serious problem (Langevin, 1979). Recently, the use of serotonin-reuptake inhibitors have shown to be effective at controlling deviant sexual fantasies and not eliminating all sexual functioning (Federoff & Federoff, 1992).

RELAPSE PREVENTION Sexual offenders need to identify their offence cycle (emotional states and stress factors that put them at risk, grooming strategies) and develop ways to avoid these problems or to deal with them.

Programs with a **relapse prevention** component usually consist of two main parts. First, offenders are asked to list emotional and situational risk factors that lead to either fantasizing about sexual abuse or actually committing the abuse. For example, for a rapist, perhaps feelings of anger toward women would be a risk factor; for a child molester, perhaps feeling lonely and sitting on a bench, watching children in a playground would be a risk factor. Second, offenders need to develop plans to deal more effectively with their problems (e.g., meeting their emotional needs in a prosocial way) and ways to avoid or cope with high-risk situations. Box 12.4 describes in more detail how the relapse prevention model has been applied to sexual offenders.

BOX 12.4 RELAPSE PREVENTION WITH SEXUAL OFFENDERS

Relapse prevention (RP) is a self-control program designed to teach sexual offenders to recognize risky situations that could lead to reoffending and to learn coping and avoidance strategies to deal with those situations. The RP model was initially developed for the treatment of addictive behaviours such as smoking, alcohol abuse, and overeating (Marlatt & Gordon, 1985). Sexual offenders are asked to develop a personalized sexual offence cycle that identifies their pre-offence thoughts, feelings, and behaviours. At each step of the cycle, the offender generates options or alternative behaviours that interrupt the offence cycle. RP is not considered a cure but it helps the sexual offender to manage the urge to offend sexually. RP is way of teaching sexual offenders to think and look ahead in order to prevent committing another sexual offence. In order for RP to be successful, the sexual offender must be motivated to stop offending.

The following are some relevant terms (used in Figure 12.3) associated with relapse prevention:

- *Offence cycle:* The sequences of thoughts, feelings, and behaviours that led to the sexual offence.
- *Lapse:* Any occurrence of fantasizing about sexual offending or engaging in behaviours in the offence cycle.
- *Relapse:* Occurrence of a sexual offence.
- *High-risk situations:* Any situation that increases the likelihood of a lapse or relapse.

- *Apparently irrelevant decisions:* Conscious or unconscious decisions made by offenders that put them in high-risk situations.
- *Coping strategy:* Development of avoidance strategies to avoid high-risk situations and escape plans if the high-risk situation cannot be avoided.
- *Abstinence violation effect:* Refers to how the offender reacts to a lapse. Both cognitive reactions (e.g., lack of will power) and emotional states (e.g., feeling guilty) are considered. If the offender views the lapse as an irreversible failure, this can promote a relapse. Alternatively, if the lapse is seen as a reasonable mistake in a learning process, the offender can become more confident in his ability to avoid or handle future lapses.

Figure 12.3 presents the sequences of events that may lead to a relapse in a child molester.

FIGURE 12.3

SEQUENCE OF EVENTS LEADING TO RELAPSE IN A CHILD MOLESTER

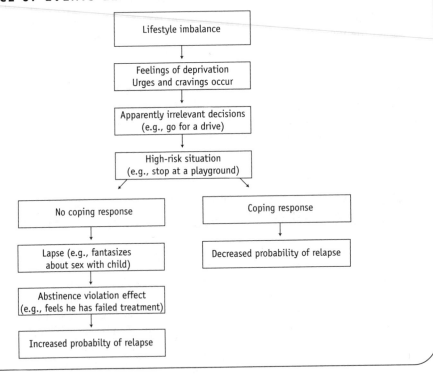

Effectiveness of Psychological Treatment of Sexual Offenders

If we are going to treat sexual offenders, it is important to know whether the treatment works. There is a lack of consensus about whether sex offender treatment is effective. Some researchers argue that treatment does not work (Quinsey et al., 1993), whereas others are more optimistic (Marshall, Eccles, & Barbaree, 1991).

There are numerous problems facing researchers wanting to evaluate the effectiveness of treatment programs. The main problem is that it is difficult to do the ideal controlled study. The optimal design would randomly assign motivated sexual offenders (i.e., offenders all wanting treatment) to either treatment or no treatment. Then both treated and untreated sexual offenders would be released at the same time and followed up for several years and rates of reoffending would be measured. Most treatment outcome studies have not used this design (see Marques, 1999, for one of the few studies to use random assignment). It is unlikely that many sexual offenders would agree to participate in this ideal study since untreated sexual offenders are held in custody longer than treated offenders. Another challenge for researchers has been the relatively low base rates of sexual recidivism, even in untreated offenders (Barbaree, 1997). On average, only 15% of sex offenders are detected committing a new sexual offence after five years and 20% after ten years (Hanson & Bussière, 1998; Hanson & Thornton, 2000). Thus, in order for researchers to detect any differences between treatment groups, they need to wait many years. Some researchers have begun to use unofficial data, such as child protection agency files, or self-reports to detect re-offending (see Marshall & Barbaree, 1988).

Four meta-analyses of sexual offender treatment programs have been published (Alexander, 1999; Gallagher et al., 1999; Hall, 1995; Hanson et al., 2002). Hanson et al. (2002) examined 42 studies with a total of 5078 treated sex offenders and 4376 untreated sex offenders. Averaged across the different types of treatment, the sexual recidivism rate was 12.3% for the treated sex offenders and 16.8% for the untreated sexual offenders. The following results were found:

- Sexual offenders who refused treatment or who dropped out of treatment had higher sexual recidivism rates compared to those who completed the treatment.
- Treatment effects are equally effective for adolescent and adult sex offenders.
- Both institutional treatment and community treatment are associated with reductions in sexual recidivism.
- Current treatments (cognitive-behavioural or systematic) were associated with stronger treatment effects than older treatment programs (behavioural or psychotherapy).

Hanson et al. (2002) conclude that "the treatments that appeared most effective were recent programs providing some form of cognitive-behavioral treatment, and, for adolescent sex offenders, systemic treatment aimed at a range of current life problems (e.g., family, school, peers)" (p. 187). Not all studies have reported positive effects of sexual offender treatment. For example, Hanson, Broom, and Stephenson (2004) compared the sexual recidivism rates of 403 treated sexual offenders with 321 untreated sexual offenders. In a 12-year follow-up, the rates of sexual reoffending were almost identical (21.1% for treated group and 21.8% for the untreated group).

THE PSYCHOPATH

Psychopaths have been called intra-species predators (Hare, 1993). They seek vulnerable victims to use for their own benefit. Sometimes they get what they want by charming their victims, while other times they use violence and intimidation to achieve their goals. Lacking in conscience and feelings for others, they satisfy their own selfish needs by preying on others. Psychopathy is defined as a personality disorder that has a collection of interpersonal, affective, and behavioural characteristics. Psychopaths are dominant, selfish, manipulative individuals who engage in impulsive and antisocial acts and who feel no remorse or shame for behaviour that often has a negative impact on others.

Descriptions of psychopathy exist in most cultures. Murphy (1976) found that the Inuit in Alaska use the term *kulangeta* to described an individual who "repeatedly lies and cheats and steals things and does not go hunting and, when the other men are out of the village, takes sexual advantage of many women—someone who does not pay attention to reprimands and who is always being brought to the elders for punishment" (p. 1026).

Assessment of Psychopathy

Hervey Cleckley (1976), a psychiatrist in Georgia, provided one of the most comprehensive clinical descriptions of the psychopath in his book *The Mask of Sanity*. The characteristics considered by Cleckley to be typical of the psychopath included superficial charm and good intelligence, unreliability and untruthfulness, lack of remorse or shame, inadequately motivated antisocial behaviour, failure to learn from experience, pathologic egocentricity, general poverty in affective relations, and a failure to follow any life plan.

Currently, the most popular method of assessing psychopathy in adults is the Hare Psychopathy Checklist-Revised (PCL-R; Hare, 1991, 2003). This assessment instrument was developed by Robert Hare at the University of British Columbia and is now being used around the world. The development of PCL-R was strongly influenced by the work of Hervey Cleckley. The PCL-R is a 20-item rating scale that uses a semi-structured interview and a review of file information to assess interpersonal (e.g., grandiosity, manipulativeness), affective (lack of remorse, shallow emotions), and behavioural (e.g., impulsivity, antisocial acts) features of psychopathy. A sample of items on the Hare PCL-R are listed in Table 12.2. Each item is scored on a three-point scale: 2 indicates that the item definitely applies; 1 that it applies to some extent; and 0 indicates that the symptom definitely does not apply to the individual. The items are summed to obtain a total score ranging from 0 to 40. Researchers have often subdi-

TABLE 12.2 SAMPLE ITEMS IN THE HARE PSYCHOPATHY CHECKLIST-REVISED

1. Glibness/superficial charm
5. Conning/manipulation
6. Lack of remorse or guilt

8. Callous/lack of empathy
14. Impulsivity
20. Criminal versatility

Source: Hare, 1991, 2003.
Copyright © 1990, 1991, Robert D. Hare, Ph.D. and Multi-Health Systems Inc. All rights reserved.
Reproduced with permission.

vided those administered the PCL-R into three groups: a high-PCL-R group (often called psychopaths) defined by a score of 30 or greater; a middle-scoring group (mixed group), with scores between about 20 and 30; and a low-scoring group (often called nonpsychopaths), with scores of below 20.

Initial factor analyses of the PCL-R indicated that it consisted of two correlated factors (Hare et al., 1990). Factor 1 reflects the combination of interpersonal and affective traits, whereas factor 2 is a combination of unstable and socially deviant traits. Researchers examined the differential correlates of these two factors and have found that factor 1 is more strongly related to predatory violence, emotional processing deficits, and poor treatment response (Hare et al., 2000; Patrick, Bradley, & Lang, 1993; Seto & Barbaree, 1999; Woodworth & Porter, 2002), whereas factor 2 is strongly related to reoffending, substance abuse, lack of education, and poor family background (Hare, 2003; Hemphill, Hare, & Wong, 1998; Porter et al., 2001; Rutherford et al., 1997). Some researchers have argued for a three-factor model of psychopathy (Cooke & Michie, 2001). These three factors are (1) arrogant and deceitful interpersonal style, (2) deficient affective experience, and (3) impulsive and irresponsible behavioural style. This factor structure splits the original factor 1 into two factors and removes some of the antisocial items from factor 2. The most recent factor structure of the PCL-R includes these three factors plus a fourth factor titled "Antisocial" that includes the antisocial items (Hare, 2003).

There has been a considerable amount of research supporting the use of the PCL-R in a range of samples, including male and female offenders, forensic psychiatric patients, sexual offenders, and substance abusers (Hare, 2003). Dr. Hare has been studying psychopaths for more than 35 years and is profiled in Box 12.5 on the next page.

Psychopathy and Antisocial Personality Disorder

Antisocial personality disorder (APD; American Psychiatric Association, 1994) refers to a personality disorder in which there is evidence for conduct disorder before age 15 and a chronic pattern of disregarding the rights of others since age 15. After age 15, a

BOX 12.5 CANADIAN RESEARCHER PROFILE: DR. ROBERT HARE

Dr. Robert Hare is one of the world's leading authorities on psychopathy. Currently, he is a professor (emeritus) in the Department of Psychology at the University of British Columbia and honorary professor of psychology at Cardiff University in Wales. Dr. Hare has a B.A. and M.A. from the University of Alberta and a Ph.D. from the University of Western Ontario.

Dr. Hare's more-than-35-year career studying psychopathy began when he encountered a manipulative inmate while working as a prison psychologist between his M.A. and Ph.D. studies. A book by Hervey Cleckley called *The Mask of Sanity* played a pivotal role in his thinking about the clinical nature of psychopathy. Dr. Hare's early research focused on the use of theories, concepts, and procedures from learning, motivation, and psychophysiology in the laboratory study of psychopathy, with emphasis on information-processing and emotional correlates. However, a recurrent issue was the lack of a reliable, valid, and generally acceptable method for assessing the disorder. In the late 1970s, he and his students and colleagues began development of what was to become the Hare Psychopathy Checklist-Revised (PCL-R). The PCL-R is recognized worldwide as the leading instrument for the assessment of the disorder, both for scientific research and for practical applications in mental health and criminal justice.

Dr. Hare consistently acknowledges and praises the important contributions of his students to the theory and research on psychopathy, and he is pleased that many of his students have established themselves as major figures in the field. He describes the collaborative efforts with his former students as invigorating and fruitful, with major advances being made in the assessment of psychopathy, its neurobiological nature, and its implications for the mental health and criminal justice systems. Currently, he is involved in a number of international research projects on assessment and treatment issues, risk for recidivism and violence, and functional neuroimaging. Although Dr. Hare has most often studied psychopaths in prison, he has recently begun to study them in a very different sphere—the corporate world.

He lectures widely about psychopathy, and consults with law enforcement, including the FBI, the RCMP, and Her Majesty's Prison Service. He has been recognized worldwide for his research on psychopathy, receiving the Silver Medal of the Queen Sophia Center in Spain, the Canadian Psychological Association Award for Distinguished Applications to the field of Psychology, the Isaac Ray Award from the American Psychiatric Association, the American Academy of Psychiatry and Law for Outstanding Contributions to Forensic Psychiatry and Psychiatric Jurisprudence, and the B. Jaye Anno Award for Excellence in Communication from the National Commission on Correctional Health Care.

Dr. Hare believes future forensic psychology researchers and clinicians should ensure that they are familiar with the important advances being made in cognitive/affective neuroscience and their implications for forensic psychology. The courses he most enjoyed teaching at the undergraduate level were "Brain and Behaviour" (third year) and "Forensic Psychology" (fourth year).

Dr. Hare enjoys listening to jazz and blues and is an avid sailor. He credits his wife, Averil, whom he met in the back row of a course in abnormal psychology at the University of Alberta, with much of his success. In spite of a demanding professional career of her own, she found the time and energy to actively support and encourage his work. To this day, she remains his best friend and closest confidant. Their only child, Cheryl, recently died after a long battle with multiple sclerosis and leukemia. Her courage and dignity in the face of adversity had a profound influence on their appreciation of the power of the human spirit.

person diagnosed with APD would need to display three or more of the following symptoms

- repeatedly engaging in criminal acts
- deceitfulness
- impulsivity
- irritability
- reckless behaviours
- irresponsibility
- lack of remorse

Although psychopathy and APD share some features, APD places more emphasis on antisocial behaviours than does the PCL-R. The prevalence of APD is very high in prisons, with up to 80% of adult offenders being diagnosed with this disorder (Motiuk & Porporino, 1991; Hare, Forth, & Strachan, 1992). Using a cut-off of 30 on the PCL-R, 10% to 25% of adult offenders can be classified as psychopaths (Hare, 2003). An asymmetrical relation exists between these two disorders: nearly all psychopathic offenders meet the diagnostic criteria for APD, but most offenders with APD are not psychopaths. APD symptoms are most strongly related to the behavioural features of psychopathy and not to the interpersonal or affective features. Figure 12.4 on page 390 illustrates the overlap between psychopathy and APD.

Psychopathy and Violence

The characteristics that define psychopathy are compatible with a criminal lifestyle and a lack of concern for societal norms. Characteristics that ordinarily help to inhibit aggression and violence, such as empathy, close emotional bonds, and internal inhibitions, are lacking or relatively ineffective in psychopaths. Psychopathy is significant because of its association with criminal behaviour in general and violence in particular. Although psychopaths make up a relatively small proportion of the population, their involvement in serious repetitive crime and violence is out of proportion to their

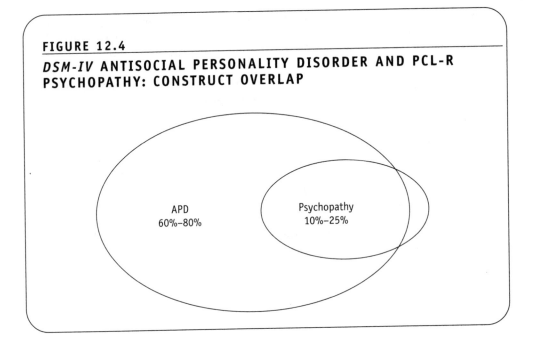

FIGURE 12.4

DSM-IV ANTISOCIAL PERSONALITY DISORDER AND PCL-R PSYCHOPATHY: CONSTRUCT OVERLAP

numbers. As stated by Hart (1998), "the two are so intimately connected that a full understanding of violence is impossible without consideration of the role played by psychopathy" (p. 367). See Box 12. 6 for a description of a psychopath.

Psychopaths are high-density, versatile offenders. The crimes of psychopaths run the gamut from minor theft and fraud to cold-blooded murder. Compared to nonpsychopathic offenders, they start their criminal career at a younger age and persist longer, engage in more violent offences, commit a greater variety of violent offences, engage in more violence within institutions, and, as we saw in Chapter 11, are more likely to be violent after release (Hare, 2003). For example, Hemphill, Templeton, Wong, and Hare (1998) reported that in a sample of 274 Canadian offenders, the mean age of first conviction for psychopaths was 18.6 years and for nonpsychopaths it was 24.3 years.

The nature of psychopaths' violence also differs from others: "Psychopathic violence is more likely to be predatory in nature, motivated by readily identifiable goals, and carried out in a callous, calculated manner without the emotional context that usually characterizes the violence of other offenders" (Hare, 2003, p. 136). Several studies have found that offenders who engage in instrumental violence score significantly higher on measures of psychopathy than do offenders engaging in reactive violence (Cornell et al., 1996; Serin, 1991). One study by Williamson, Hare, and Wong (1987) found that when nonpsychopaths commit violence, they are likely to target people they know and their violent behaviour is likely to occur in the context of strong emotional arousal. In contrast, psychopaths are more likely to target strangers and to be motivated by revenge or material gain.

BOX 12.6 CLIFFORD OLSON: A PREDATORY PSYCHOPATH

On August 22, 1997, a jury in Surrey, B.C., took just 15 minutes to reject Clifford Olson's bid for early parole. Olson is serving a life sentence for the murders of 11 children in 1980 and 1981. Clifford Olson is notorious, not only for being one of Canada's most prolific serial killers, but also for what he calls his "cash for corpses" deal he made with the police. Olson negotiated a payment of $10 000 for each body he uncovered for the RCMP. The money did not go to Olson but was put into trust for Olson's wife. In total, $100 000 was paid to this trust fund.

According to section 745 of the Canadian Criminal Code, first-degree and second-degree murderers can apply for a judicial hearing to request an earlier parole eligibility date after serving 15 years. This provision has been called the "faint hope clause" and was introduced in 1976, when the death penalty was abolished and replaced by mandatory life sentences for first-degree and second-degree murder. The parole ineligibility period for first-degree murder was 25 years; for second-degree murder it was 10 years, although the judge has the power to increase this period to up to 25 years. The underlying motivation for this clause was to provide murderers with an incentive to behave in prison, making prisons safer for correctional officers, and to motivate murderers to participate in rehabilitation.

Dr. Stanley Semrau, a forensic psychiatrist, was hired by the Crown prosecution to evaluate Clifford Olson for this judicial review hearing. Dr. Semrau assessed Clifford Olson on the Hare Psychopathy Checklist-Revised and gave him a score of 38 out of 40. At the judicial review hearing he stated, "It's certainly the highest score I have ever given anyone." Dr. Semrau also concluded that Olson was "completely untreatable" and was more dangerous now then he was when arrested in 1981, since he currently sees himself as "the ultimate serial killer."

In Dr. Semrau and Judy Gale's book *Murderous Minds on Trial*, they devote a chapter to describing the evaluation Dr. Semrau conducted on Clifford Olson. In this chapter, he states, "I saw almost nothing that wasn't a perfect fit with the psychopath's cold, guilt-free use of others for his own ends, and chronically antisocial and deviant lifestyle."

Partly in response to Clifford Olson's use of the "faint hope clause," changes were made to section 745 of the Criminal Code. On January 1, 1997, these changes came into force. Multiple (including serial) murderers are now ineligible for a section 745 review. Clifford Olson currently remains incarcerated in the maximum-security Saskatchewan Federal Institution. He is in protective custody in order to keep him away from other offenders and to keep other offenders and staff away from him. Clifford Olson is allowed out of his cell for one hour a day to participate in solitary exercise, to work alone as a cleaner, or for meetings.

Psychopaths' use of instrumental motives extends to homicide. Woodworth and Porter (2002) investigated the association between psychopathy and the nature of homicides committed by 135 Canadian offenders. Using PCL-R scores to divide the offenders into the three groups described above—nonpsychopaths (PCL-R scores of less than 20), medium scorers (PCL-R scores between 20 and 30), and psychopaths

(PCL-R scores of 30 or greater)—the percentage of homicides that were primarily instrumental (planned and motivated by an external goal) were 28%, 67%, and 93%, respectively. The authors concluded that psychopaths engage in "cold-blooded" homicides much more often than nonpsychopaths.

Not all psychopaths are violent, nor do they all end up in prison. Hare (1998) has estimated that about 1% of the general population are psychopaths. Paul Babiak (2000), an organizational psychologist, consulted with six companies undergoing dramatic organizational change, such as merging and downsizing. In each of these companies, Babiak found employees with many psychopathic features to be at the root of some of the company problems. These employees were skilled at getting information on other employees, spreading unwarranted vicious rumours about others, and causing dissension among employees. What they were not doing was pulling their own weight on the job. They were particularly good at manipulating the key players in the organization (employees who can provide them with information or upper management) and blaming others for their failures (see Babiak (1995) for a case study of the industrial psychopath).

Psychopathy and Sexual Violence

Psychopathy and sexual violence have been the focus of much research. As described above, psychopathy is associated with violent offences but is only weakly associated with sexual offences. For example, Brown and Forth (1997) reported that in a sample of 60 rapists, their PCL-R score was associated with their number of prior offences but not the number of prior sexual offences. In a larger sample of offenders, Porter et al. (2000) found that psychopaths engaged in significantly more violent offences than nonpsychopaths (7.3 versus 3.0, respectively) but engaged in *fewer* sexual offences (2.9 versus 5.9, respectively). One potential explanation for this finding is the high rate of sexual offending found in child molesters who tend not to be psychopaths.

In general, offenders who commit sexual homicides are the most psychopathic, followed by mixed sexual offenders (those who sexually assault both children and adults), followed by rapists, with the lowest psychopathy scores found among child molesters (Brown & Forth, 1997; Firestone et al., 1998; Porter et al., 2000; Quinsey, Rice, & Harris, 1995).

Other studies have evaluated the motivations of psychopaths when committing sexual crimes. Brown and Forth (1997) examined specific motivations for psychopathic and nonpsychopathic rapists. The Massachusetts Treatment Center Rapist Typology (MTC: R3; Knight & Prentky, 1990) identifies different types of rapists based on motivation and level of social competence. Brown and Forth reported that 81% of psychopathic rapists were opportunistic or vindictive, compared with 56% of the nonpsychopathic rapists. Nonpsychopaths were more likely to report feelings of anxiety or alienation in the 24-hour period leading up to the rape, whereas psychopaths reported positive emotions. Porter, Woodworth, Earle, Drugge, and Boer (2003) investigated the relation between psychopathy and severity of violence in a sample of 38 sexual homicide offenders. Level of sadistic violence (evidence for overkill and that the offender obtained enjoyment from hurting the victim) was related to the PCL-R total scores and with the interpersonal and affective features of psychopathy.

Psychopathy and Treatment

Are psychopathic adults responsive to treatment? Most clinicians and researchers are pessimistic, although some (e.g., Salekin, 2002) are more optimistic. As Hare (1998) states, "Unlike most other offenders, they suffer little personal distress, see little wrong with their attitudes and behavior, and seek treatment only when it is in their best interests to do so (such as when seeking probation or parole)" (p. 202).

The best-known study of treatment outcome in psychopaths was a retrospective study by Rice, Harris, and Cormier (1992). These researchers investigated the effects of an intensive therapeutic treatment program on violent psychopathic and non-psychopathic forensic psychiatric patients. Using a matched group design, forensic patients who spent two years in the treatment program (treated group) were paired with forensic patients who were assessed but not admitted to the program (untreated group). Using file information, all patients were scored on the PCL-R using file information and were divided into psychopaths (scores of 25 or greater) and non-psychopaths (scores of less than 25). Patients were followed for an average of 10 years after release. The violent recidivism rate was 39% for untreated nonpsychopaths, 22% for treated nonpsychopaths, 55% for untreated psychopaths, and 77% for treated psychopaths. Treatment was associated with a *reduction* in violent recidivism among nonpsychopaths, but an *increase* in violent recidivism among psychopaths. Some clinicians have concluded from the above study that we should not bother to treat psychopaths, since treatment will only make them worse: "This was the wrong program for serious psychopathic offenders" (Quinsey et al., 1998, p. 88).

Caution is required in interpreting the results of studies such as Rice, Harris, and Cormier (1992). Although at first glance such research implies that psychopaths are untreatable, an alternative but perhaps equally plausible account is that the treatments for psychopaths that have been tried so far have not worked (Hare et al., 2000; Richards, Casey, & Lucente, 2003; Seto & Barbaree, 1999). Reasons for why a treatment may not work include use of an inappropriate treatment and problems in implementing the treatment, such as inadequate training of those administering the treatment or lack of support from management.

Psychopathy in Youth

Research is increasingly focused on identifying the emergence of psychopathic traits in youth. The assumption is that psychopathy does not suddenly appear in adulthood but instead gradually develops from various environmental and biological antecedents. In line with this viewpoint, several measures have been recently developed to identify psychopathic traits early in development. Two assessment instruments have been adapted from the PCL-R: one for use with children and the other for adolescents. The Antisocial Process Screening Device (APSD; Frick & Hare, 2001) is designed for assessing the precursors of psychopathic traits in children. The child is assigned a rating on various questions by parents or teachers. A self-report version of this scale also has been developed for use with adolescents. Frick et al. (2000) found that the APSD has a three-dimensional structure consisting of a callous-unemotional factor, an impulsivity factor, and a narcissism factor. The Psychopathy Checklist: Youth Version (PCL:YV; Forth, Kosson, & Hare, 2003) is a rating scale designed to measure psychopathic traits and behaviours in male and female adolescents aged 12 to 18 years.

Reservations have been raised concerning the appropriateness of applying the construct of psychopathy to children and adolescents (Edens et al., 2001; Seagrave & Grisso, 2002; Zinger & Forth, 1998). One concern has been the use of the label "psychopath," a label that has many negative connotations for the public and for mental health and criminal justice professionals. As stated by Murrie, Cornell, Kaplan, McConville, & Levy-Elkon (2004), "the use of the label 'psychopath' has ominous connotations that may adversely influence treatment decisions, social service plans, and juvenile justice determinations" (p. 64).

Psychopathy in adults is associated with violence, is assumed to be stable trait, and is resistant to intervention attempts. Whether psychopathic traits in youth are stable remains to be studied. For example, would a child who scored high on the APSD also score high on the PCL:YV as an adolescent? If followed into adulthood, would he or she score high on the PCL-R? Such a longitudinal study has not yet been conducted, although a recent study of the APSD has indicated fairly high stability across a four-year period (Frick et al., 2003). Another concern that has been raised is whether "scores on measures of psychopathy arguably may be inflated by general characteristics of adolescence" (Edens et al. 2001, p. 59). Arguing against this last point are the few studies that have measured psychopathic traits in community youth that have found the scores on psychopathy measures to be very low (Forth et al., 2003; Skilling, Quinsey, & Craig, 2001).

Research has provided some support for extending the construct of psychopathy to youth. For example, boys who score high on the callous/unemotional dimension of the APSD have more police contacts, more conduct problems, and are more likely to have a parent with APD than are children who score low on this dimension. Research using the PCL:YV has found that adolescents with many psychopathic traits, like their adult counterparts, become involved in criminal behaviours at an earlier age, engage in more violence in institutions and in the community, and are at a higher risk of re-offending once released compared with other adolescents (Corrado et al., 2004; Forth et al., 2003; Kosson et al., 2002; Murrie et al., 2004). Research has also looked at the association between psychopathic traits and other symptoms in youth. For example, Campbell, Porter, and Santor (2004) found that psychopathic traits were related to delinquency and aggression but not to anxiety or depression symptoms in a sample of male and female adolescent offenders.

One aspect of psychopathy in youth that may differ from its adult counterpart is that youth with psychopathic traits may be more responsive to interventions (Salekin, Rogers, & Machin, 2001). In contrast, however, O'Neill, Lidz, and Heilbrun (2003) examined treatment outcome in a sample of 64 adolescent substance abusers and found that youth scoring high on the PCL:YV showed poor program attendance, poor quality of participation, and less clinical improvement, and were more likely to re-offend after completing the program.

Summary

1. Reactive homicide is defined as impulsive, unplanned, immediate, driven by negative emotions, and occurring in response to some perceived provocation. Instrumental homicide is defined as proactive rather than reactive and is a premediated, calculated behaviour, motivated by some goal.

2. Abused women remain in or return to an abusive relationship for a number of reasons. Environmental, socialization, and psychological barriers exist that make it difficult for abused women to leave an abusive relationship.

3. Social learning theory has been used to explain domestic violence. There are three main components to social learning theory: origins of aggression; instigators of aggression; and regulators of aggression. One way people acquire new behaviours is via observational learning. Instigators are events in the environment that act as stimuli for the behaviour, and behaviour is regulated by its consequences. Behaviours that are rewarded increase in frequency, and behaviours that are punished decrease in frequency.

4. Rapists are offenders who sexually assault adults, and child molesters are offenders who sexually assault children. Typologies of both rapists and child molesters have been proposed that focus on the motives for sexual abuse. Rapists have been classified into the following five primary types based on research by Knight and Prentky: opportunistic, pervasively angry, sexual, sadistic, and vindictive. Groth proposes a different rapist typology consisting of the following three types: angry, power, and sadistic. Groth proposes that child molesters be classified into two main types: regressed and fixated.

5. Treatment for sexual offenders involves recognizing denial, minimizations, and cognitive distortions; gaining victim empathy; modifying deviant sexual interest, enhancing social skills, dealing with substance abuse problems, and developing relapse-prevention plans. Meta-analyses of treatment programs have found that sexual offenders who complete a cognitive-behavioural treatment have lower rates of sexual recidivism than do dropouts or treatment refusers.

6. Psychopathy is a personality disorder defined by a cluster of interpersonal, affective, and behavioural features. Psychopaths begin their criminal career earlier, persist longer, and are more violent and versatile than other offenders. Most of the murders committed by psychopaths are instrumental.

7. Research is increasingly focused on identifying the emergence of psychopathic traits in youth, and assessment instruments have been developed to measure psychopathic traits in children and adolescents with some success. Concerns have been raised about the potential problems with labelling youth as psychopaths. These concerns have focused on (1) the issue of labelling a youth as a psychopath, (2) the stability of psychopathic traits from late childhood to early adulthood, and (3) the possibility that characteristics of psychopathy are common features of normally developing youth.

KEY CONCEPTS

anger rapist	376	infanticide	353	power rapist	376
antisocial personality		intimate partner violence	361	psychopaths	386
disorder	387	instigators	364	rape trauma syndrome	373
child molester	374	intra-familial child		rapist	374
domestic violence	361	molesters	374	reactive (or affective)	
dysphoric/borderline		instrumental (predatory)		aggression	360
batterer	367	aggression	360	regressed child	
exhibitionists	374	mandatory charging		molester	377
extra-familial child		policies	368	regulators	364
molesters	374	observational learning	364	relapse prevention	383
family-only batterer	367	patriarchy	363	sadistic rapist	376
femicide	359	pedophile	374	social learning theory	364
fixated child molester	377	penile phallometry	382	voyeurs	374
generally violent/		post-traumatic stress			
antisocial batterer	368	disorder	374		

DISCUSSION QUESTIONS

1. Homicide offenders have been classified into instrumental and reactive types. What are the treatment implications for these two types of murderers?

2. What are the barriers to some battered women leaving an abusive relationship? What could be done at both an individual and a societal level to help battered women?

3. Most police forces in North America have mandatory charging policies for domestic assault cases. What are the costs and benefits associated with these policies?

4. Correctional Service Canada has proposed a new treatment program for sexual offenders. You have been hired to develop an evaluation of the program to see whether it is effective. Describe how you plan to evaluate this program.

5. Several typologies have been proposed for child molesters and rapists. What are the similarities and differences?

6. Psychopaths have been called intra-species predators. How strong is the link between psychopathy and violence?

7. The term psychopathy has many negative connotations. What are the potential problems with using this label to identify youth?

ADDITIONAL INFORMATION

Readings

Dutton, D. (1995). *The domestic assault of women.* Vancouver: UBC Press.

Hare, R.D. (1993). *Without conscience: The disturbing world of psychopaths among us.* New York: Guilford Press.

Quinn, J.F., Forsyth, C.J., & Mullen-Quinn, C. (2004). Societal reaction to sex offenders: A review of the origins and results of the myths surrounding their crimes and treatment amenability. *Deviant Behavior, 25,* 215–232.

Web Sites

The National Clearinghouse on Family Violence (NCFV)
www.hc-sc.gc.ca/hppb/familyviolence/index.html

Dr. Robert Hare's Homepage
www.hare.org

Statistics Canada
www.statcan.ca

CHAPTER 13

Assessment and Treatment of Special Populations

LEARNING OBJECTIVES

■ Describe the history of youthful offender legislation.

■ Identify the psychiatric diagnoses and their trajectories relevant to youthful offenders.

■ List the risk and protective factors associated with externalizing disorders in youth.

■ List the factors that differentiate male and female adult offenders.

■ Describe the components associated with battered women syndrome.

■ Describe why Aboriginals are overrepresented in the criminal justice system.

■ Describe what an Aboriginal healing lodge is and explain why such lodges are used.

As a kid, Allison Kelly was no angel. She got into fights at school and in her neighbourhood on a daily basis. She would pick fights not only with children her own age and older, but even with adults. Her teacher also reported that on several occasions, Allison snuck into the school during recess and rummaged through the other children's backpacks, taking toys or other belongings she wanted. It was not uncommon for Allison to throw a temper tantrum when she did not get her way. She often refused to follow rules and would argue until the adults gave in to her demands.

When both the school and Allison's mother, failed to get Allison to change her behaviour, her mother brought her to a psychologist for an assessment. Allison refused to cooperate with the psychologist, throwing a stuffed bear at her and telling her that she could assess it instead. Based on the psychologist's observations, parent interviews, and teacher ratings, Allison was diagnosed with oppositional defiant disorder, a diagnosis that puts Allison at an increased risk for interaction with the criminal justice system.

YOUTHFUL OFFENDERS

Youth coming into contact with the criminal justice system pose several challenges to the adult-based system. Legislation has changed over the years in an attempt to address the special needs of youth. Moreover, it is critical to consider the developmental paths to youthful offending in order to prevent and rehabilitate. A number of treatment options have been developed for youthful offenders.

Historical Overview

Youth who committed criminal acts in Canada during the seventeenth and eighteenth centuries were treated as adult offenders. The criminal justice system made no accommodations or considerations for how youth were charged, sentenced, or incarcerated. They were kept in the same facilities as adults while awaiting their trials, received the same penalties as adults, and served their sentences with adults. Even in cases involving the death penalty, youth were dealt with in a similar manner as adults.

Canada enacted the Juvenile Delinquents Act (JDA) in 1908 partly in response to the justice system's past disregard for the special population of youthful offenders. The JDA applied to children and youth between the ages of 7 and 16 years (18 years in some jurisdictions). Terminology was used to reflect a difference between youth and adults. For example, youth were called "delinquents" rather than "offenders" and were considered to commit acts of delinquency such as truancy rather than criminal offences. A separate court system for youth was established and it was suggested that court proceedings be as informal as possible in that delinquents were seen as misguided children in need of guidance and support. When possible, parents were encouraged to be part of the judicial process. In serious cases, the JDA made it possible for delinquents to be transferred to adult court. Punishments for delinquents were to be consistent with how a parent would discipline a child. For example, delinquents could be sentenced to an industrial school where they learned skills or a trade for future employment. Other dispositions for delinquents included adjournment without penalty, fines, probation, and foster care. Table 13.1 on the next page highlights the key changes to the Canadian criminal justice system under the JDA.

Many saw the JDA as a positive step toward youth justice. However, the JDA was not without criticism. For example, the services to be provided to delinquents as outlined in the JDA were not always available. Also, given the informality of youth court,

TABLE 13.1 THE JUVENILE DELINQUENTS ACT'S KEY CHANGES TO CANADIAN CRIMINAL JUSTICE

1. A separate court system for youth was established.
2. A minimum age (seven years old) was set for which a child could be charged with a criminal offence.
3. Judges had sentencing discretion and options increased (e.g., foster care, fines, and institutionalization).
4. Parents were encouraged to be part of the judicial process.

some youth were denied their rights, such as the right to counsel and the right to appeal, and judges could impose open-ended sentences. Furthermore, the broad definition of delinquency included acts that were not illegal for adults.

The JDA was in effect until 1984, when it was replaced with the Young Offenders Act (YOA). The YOA represented a shift in how youth who broke the law were perceived. Youth were to be held responsible for their actions. However, the YOA acknowledged that youth were different from adults, having a different level of cognitive development, for example. The differences between youths and adults were to be recognized through the level of accountability and the consequences of the behaviour committed. The YOA also recognized the need to protect the public from young offenders. Lastly, the YOA recognized that youths should be afforded all of the rights stated in the Canadian Charter of Rights and Freedoms (R.S.C., 1985, c. Y-1, s. 3).

Changes in the YOA included the age of criminal responsibility. Under the YOA, youth had to be at least 12 years old (and up to 18 years) to be processed through the justice system. Children under 12 would be dealt with through child and family services. Some of the changes brought forward with the JDA remained with the YOA. For example, youth courts continued under the YOA. As with the JDA, for serious indictable offences such as murder, youth could be transferred to adult courts, provided they were at least 14 years of age (R.S.C, 1985, c. Y-1, s. 16).

The YOA allowed for youth cases to be diverted. **Diversion** is a decision not to prosecute the young offender but rather have him or her undergo an educational or community service program. However, for diversion to be possible, the young offender would have to plead guilty (R.S.C, 1985, c. Y-1, s. 4). Other dispositions available for young offenders included absolute discharge (i.e., the young offender received no sentence other than a guilty verdict), fine, compensation for loss or damaged property, restitution to the victim, prohibition order (i.e., no weapons), community service, probation, and custody. Two types of custody are available: open (placing the youth in a community residential facility, group home, childcare facility, or wilderness camp) or secure (incarcerating the youth in a prison facility; R.S.C, 1985, c. Y-1, s. 20).

There were a number of amendments made to the YOA. For example, Bill C-106 section 16 (1986) required the youth court to consider whether the Crown or defence would like to make an application to transfer the case to adult court. This amendment was introduced to address the problem of defendants making guilty pleas to avoid transfers. Bill C-37 changed section 16 once again in 1995. With this amendment, 16- and 17-year-olds changed with murder, manslaughter, or aggravated sexual assault would go to adult court. On application, these cases could stay in youth court, if the youth court felt the objectives of rehabilitation and public protection could be reconciled. Also under Bill C-37, sentences for youth changed. For first-degree murder, a ten-year maximum, with a six-year maximum to be served incarcerated, was available. For second-degree murder, a seven-year maximum, with a four-year maximum to be served incarcerated, was available. Table 13.2 highlights the key changes to the Canadian criminal justice system under the YOA.

Overall, the YOA attempted to make youth more accountable for their behaviour while supporting rehabilitation through treatment programs and providing alternatives to incarceration for less serious crimes. One of the major criticisms of the YOA was that serious, violent offences carried relatively short ("light") sentences. Other criticisms included disagreement over raising the minimum age of responsibility from age seven to twelve. Also, the YOA allowed for discrepancies in the factors leading to transfer to adult court that suggested an arbitrariness in how cases were handled.

On April 1, 2003, the Youth Criminal Justice Act (YCJA) replaced the YOA. The three main objectives of the YCJA are to

1. Prevent youth crime

2. Provide meaningful consequences and encourage responsibility of behaviour

3. Improve rehabilitation and reintegration of youth into the community

With the YCJA, there is a movement to keep young offenders out of the court and out of custody. There is an onus on police to consider community outlets and less serious alternatives for youth before bringing them to the attention of youth court (Youth Criminal Justice Act, 2002, s. 7). These alternatives are called **extrajudicial**

TABLE 13.2 THE YOUNG OFFENDERS ACT'S KEY CHANGES TO CANADIAN CRIMINAL JUSTICE

1. Youth are to be held accountable for their actions, however, not to the full extent that adults are.

2. The public has the right to be protected from young offenders.

3. Young offenders have legal rights and freedoms including those described in the Canadian Charter of Rights and Freedoms.

4. Children have to be at least 12 years of age to be charged with a criminal offence.

measures and include giving a warning or making a referral for treatment (with the consent of the youth; Youth Criminal Justice Act, 2002, s. 10).

Sentencing options have also increased under the YCJA. Judges are able to provide a reprimand (i.e., lecture or warning to the youth), an intensive support and supervision order, an attendance order (i.e., youth must attend a specific program), a deferred custody and supervision order (i.e., youth can serve sentence in community as long as imposed conditions are met), and an intensive rehabilitative custody and supervision order (i.e., youth in custody receive intensive services and supervision) (Youth Criminal Justice Act, 2002, s. 42).

In terms of transferring youth to adult court, the YCJA has made a number of changes from the process outlined in the YOA. Under the YCJA, the transfer process is eliminated. Rather, youth court determines whether the youthful defendant is guilty, and if so, the judge can impose an adult sentence with youth as young as 14 years old (can

A youth vandalizes a wall in the community.

be set at 15 or 16 years). An adult sentence cannot be applied unless the Crown notifies the youth court that it will be seeking an adult sentence (Youth Criminal Justice Act, 2002, s. 61). A key issue in determining sentencing is that the sentence must be proportionate to the seriousness of the offence (Youth Criminal Justice Act, 2002, s. 38(2)(c)).

The YCJA has made a serious attempt at improving the interests of victims. Under the YCJA, victims are to be informed of the court proceedings and given an opportunity to participate. Victims also have the right to access youth court records. Moreover, victims can participate in community-based dispositions (Youth Criminal Justice Act, 2002, s. 3). Table 13.3 highlights the key changes to the Canadian criminal justice system under the YCJA.

TABLE 13.3 THE YOUTH CRIMINAL JUSTICE ACT'S KEY CHANGES TO THE CANADIAN CRIMINAL JUSTICE SYSTEM

1. Less serious and less violent offences should be kept out of the formal court process.
2. The number of extrajudicial measures are increased.
3. There is greater focus on prevention and reintegration into the community.
4. Transfers to adult court are removed; instead, youth court judges can impose adult sentences.
5. The interests and needs of victims are recognized.

Youth Crime Rates

Generally, the total number of crimes committed by youth has been decreasing for the past few years. Unfortunately, the rate for committing more serious offences tends to be increasing. See Table 13.4 for a distribution of youthful cases by major crime category. See Box 13.1 on the next page for a case illustration of a serious youthful offence.

Regarding sentencing in youth court, probation is the most frequent sentence imposed. About 90% of youth under supervision by the criminal justice system in 2001 were on probation. Sentences of secure custody occurred in about 14% of the cases in 2002, more often than ten years before. However, the length of these sentences was shorter and Canada's youth incarceration reached its lowest point in seven years in 2001. Young offenders convicted of a violent crime were more likely to be sentenced to secure custody than were youth who commit other types of crime. A similar proportion of youthful offenders are sentenced to open custody as to secure custody (Statistics Canada, 2003, 2004).

Assessment of Youthful Offenders

Often there are two levels of consent a clinician will obtain before commencing the assessment of a child or adolescent. Because children and adolescents are not legally capable of providing consent, consent will be sought from parents or guardians. Following parental consent, assent or agreement to conduct the assessment will be sought from the child or adolescent. Although court-ordered assessments do not necessarily require consent or assent, clinicians often will seek consent/assent before commencing the assessment.

TABLE 13.4 CANADIAN YOUTHFUL CASES BY MAJOR CRIME CATEGORY

Crime Category	2000	2001	2002
Total cases	87 617	85 640	84 592
Violent crimes	22 674	22 510	22 462
Property crimes	34 694	33 086	32 465
Administration of justice offences	7 917	7 698	7 790
Other Criminal Code offences	4 506	4 525	4 267
Drug-related offences	5 767	6 058	5 907
Young Offender Act offences	10 766	10 414	10 325
Other federal statue offences	127	138	151

Source: Adapted from Statistics Canada, 2003, 2004.

BOX 13.1 DO YOUTHFUL OFFENDERS GET AWAY WITH MURDER?

One evening while lying in bed in a cottage in Gatineau, Quebec, Bob Dagenais heard someone drive up, so he got out of bed to check. He realized there were two males coming into his house, so he called 911. Before he could speak to the operator, he was shot. By now, his wife Bonnie was up and saw her husband fall to the ground. She was then shot dead also. Police arrived within an hour and found 27-year-old René Michaud and a 15-year-old sleeping, along with two shotguns, in a truck nearby. The pair were charged with the first- and second-degree murder of Bonnie and Bob Dagenais.

During Michaud's trial, he testified that he killed Bob Dagenais, but that it was an accident. The youth admitted to killing Bonnie Dagenais but said Michaud had told him to do it. The youth stated that Michaud talked about the possibility of killing someone as they started a break-in spree at cottages. The youth admitted that he wanted to live that experience. A jury verdict found Michaud guilty on the charges. Such a verdict receives an automatic 25 years to life in prison.

Although an argument was made for the youth to be transferred to adult court, it was not successful. The youth, whose name is protected by law, is scheduled to be tried sometime in 2004 in youth court. If convicted on the same charges as Michaud, the youth would only receive a maximum of six years at a youth detention centre, because the youth will be tried under the old Young Offenders Act.

Sources: CBC News, 2003 (October 23); CBC News, 2003 (November 13); CBC News Ottawa, 2002.

Broadly, children's emotional and behavioural difficulties can be categorized as **internalizing** or **externalizing problems** (Rutter, 1990). Internalizing problems are emotional difficulties such as anxiety, depression, and obsessions. Externalizing problems are behavioural difficulties such as delinquency, fighting, bullying, lying, and destructive behaviour. Externalizing problems have been considered more difficult to treat and more likely to have long-term persistence (Ebata, Peterson, & Conger, 1990; Robins, 1986). Externalizing disorders have been known to be quite stable, though symptoms often peak in teenage years and decrease in the late twenties (Rutter, 1995). Males are more likely to have externalizing difficulties than females, with a ratio of about 10:1 (Barkley, 1997; Rutter, 1990).

To assess externalizing problems, multiple informants are necessary to obtain an accurate assessment because the child or youth may not be aware of his or her behaviour or the influence it has on others (McMahon, 1994). Parents, teachers, and peers may be interviewed or asked to rate the child or adolescent. Also, it is important that behaviour be viewed within a developmental context. For example, rebelling against rules set by parents may be normative for adolescents but worrisome if younger children are oppositional and continually refuse to comply with parents' requests. The duration, severity, and frequency of troublesome behaviours should be measured.

There are three childhood psychiatric diagnoses that occur with some frequency in youthful offenders—**attention-deficit hyperactivity disorder** (ADHD), **oppositional** defiant disorder (ODD), and **conduct disorder** (CD). ADHD is described as an inattention and restlessness (APA, 1994). Table 13.5 provides a list of features associated with ADHD. To qualify for an ADHD diagnosis, a number of symptoms must be present, occur in two or more settings, and persist for at least six months. When making an ADHD diagnosis, it is important to consider the age of the child. In young children, many of the symptoms of ADHD are part of normal development and behaviour. Many children with ADHD also receive diagnoses of ODD or CD (Barkley, 1991).

TABLE 13.5 FEATURES OF ATTENTION-DEFICIT HYPERACTIVITY DISORDER*

Inattention Features

1. Does not pay attention to details or makes careless errors
2. Cannot keep attention on tasks or play
3. Does not appear to listen when spoken to
4. Fails to follow instructions or finish tasks
5. Has difficulty in organization
6. Does not engage in tasks requiring sustained attention
7. Loses items
8. Is easily distracted by irrelevant stimuli
9. Forgetful

Hyperactivity Features

1. Fidgets or squirms
2. Leaves seat
3. Runs or climbs at inappropriate times and settings
4. Has difficulty in engaging in tasks quietly
5. Often appears "on the go"
6. Talks excessively

Impulsivity Features

1. Blurts out responses
2. Has difficulty waiting
3. Interrupts or intrudes

Source: Adapted from APA, 1994.

*Some symptoms appear before age seven, impairment is in two or more settings (e.g., school and home), and there is significant impaired functioning.

ODD is described as a "pattern of negativistic, hostile, and defiant behaviour" (APA, 1994, p. 93). Table 13.6 provides a list of features associated with ODD. Approximately 40% of children with ODD develop CD (Loeber et al., 1993). If a child with ODD qualifies for a CD diagnosis, an ODD diagnosis is not used. Table 13.7 provides a list of features associated with CD. Approximately 50% of children meeting criteria for CD go on to receive diagnoses of antisocial personality disorder in adulthood (APA, 1994; Loeber & Farrington, 2000). Thus, CD often is the precursor to antisocial personality disorder.

Rates of Behaviour Disorders in Youth

It has been estimated that approximately 5% to 15% of children display severe behavioural problems (Rutter, 1990). This estimate may, however, be too low. Notably, in the Ontario Child Health Study in 1987, approximately 18% of children between the ages of 4 and 16 years were found to experience conduct disorder, hyperactivity, emotional disturbance, or a combination of these (Offord et al., 1987). Researchers have found that behavioural disorders commonly co-occur. For example, 20% to 50% of children with ADHD also have symptoms consistent with CD or ODD (Offord, Lipman, & Duku, 2001).

Trajectories of Youthful Offenders

When examining the aggressive histories of youthful offenders, two categories emerge. Young offenders may be categorized as those who started with social transgressions and behavioural problems in very early childhood (child-onset, life-course persistent) or those whose problem behaviours emerged in the teen years (adolescent-onset, adolescent limited; Moffitt, 1993). Thus, two developmental pathways to youthful antisocial behaviour have been suggested—childhood onset versus adolescent onset.

Age of onset is a critical factor in the trajectory to adult offending. A number of researchers have found that early onset of antisocial behaviour is related to more serious

---

TABLE 13.6 FEATURES OF OPPOSITIONAL DEFIANT DISORDER*

1. Loses temper	4. Deliberately annoys others
2. Argues with adults	5. Is angry and resentful
3. Refuses to follow adults' requests or rules	6. Is vindictive

Source: Adapted from APA, 1994.
*Significant impaired functioning.

TABLE 13.7 FEATURES OF CONDUCT DISORDER*

Aggression

1. Bullies, threatens, or intimidates

2. Initiates physical fights

3. Uses a weapon

4. Is physically cruel to people

5. Is physically cruel to animals

6. Has stolen while confronting a victim

7. Has forced sexual activity

Property Destruction

1. Sets fires

2. Destroys property of others

Deceit or Theft

1. Has broken into someone's property

2. Lies for gain

3. Has stolen without confronting a victim

Serious Violations

1. Stays out at night, regardless of rules (before age 13)

2. Runs away

3. Is truant before 13 years old

Source: Adapted from APA, 1994.
*Significant impaired functioning.

and persistent antisocial behaviour later in life (Fergusson & Woodward, 2000; Loeber & Farrington, 2000). Those with a childhood onset also may have a number of other difficulties, such as ADHD, learning disabilities, and academic difficulties (Hinshaw, Lahey, & Hart, 1993). The childhood-onset trajectory is a less frequent occurrence than adolescent onset, with about 3% to 5% of the general population showing a childhood-onset trajectory (Moffitt, 1993). It is important to remember, however, that most young children with behavioural difficulties do not go on to become adult offenders.

The adolescent-onset pattern occurs in about 70% of the general population (Moffitt, 1993). Many young people engage in social transgressions during their adolescence, but adolescents who only engage in few antisocial acts do not qualify for a CD diagnosis. Although it is more common for adolescent-onset youth to desist their antisocial behaviour in their early adulthood than for those with a childhood onset, some of these adolescent-onset youth continue to engage in antisocial acts in adulthood (Moffitt et al., 2002).

Dr. Richard Tremblay has conducted numerous studies examining the developmental paths of conduct-disordered youth (see Box 13.2 to learn more about Dr. Tremblay and his research). In a recent study by Brame, Nagin, and Tremblay (2001), a group of boys from Montreal were followed from the time they entered kindergarten through to their late teen years. The researchers found that participants' overall level of aggression decreased at they got older regardless of how high it was when the participants were youngsters. It was notable, however, that for a small proportion of youngsters with high levels of aggression, these high levels continued into their teen years. A much larger proportion of youngsters with high levels of aggression reported little to no aggression in their teen years. Thus, for a small group of youngsters with high levels of aggression, these levels will continue into later years.

Theories to Explain Antisocial Behaviour

BIOLOGICAL THEORIES To explain why some youth engage in antisocial acts, researchers have examined the relation between frontal lobe functioning and antisocial behaviour. The frontal lobe is responsible for the planning and inhibiting of behaviour. Moffit and Henry (1989) have found that conduct-disordered youth have less frontal lobe inhibition of behaviour. Thus, the likelihood that these youth will act impulsively is increased, making it more likely that they will make poor behavioural choices.

Physiologically, conduct-disordered youth have been found to have slower heart rates than youth who do not engage in antisocial behaviour (Wadsworth, 1976). Genetic studies have found a relation between paternal antisocial behaviour and child offspring antisocial behaviour (Frick et al., 1992). Moreover, adoption and twin studies also find a biological link to youthful offending. That is, children who have an antisocial biological father are more likely to engage in antisocial behaviour, even when raised apart from the biological father (Cadoret & Cain, 1980; Jarey & Stewart, 1985). Overall, the research explaining the relation among biology, physiology, genetics, and behaviour is preliminary at this point.

COGNITIVE THEORIES Kenneth Dodge and his colleagues proposed a model of conduct-disordered behaviour that focuses on the thought processes that occur in social interactions (Crick & Doge, 1994; Dodge, 2000). Thought processes start when individuals pay attention to and interpret social and emotional cues in their environment. The following step in the model is to consider alternative responses to the cues. Finally, a response is chosen and performed. Conduct-disordered youth demonstrate

BOX 13.2 CANADIAN RESEARCHER PROFILE: DR. RICHARD TREMBLAY

After Dr. Richard Tremblay completed his master's degree at the University of Montreal, he started working with offenders who had mental illnesses. It was at this time that he first started wondering what causes people to have such incredible problems. Dr. Tremblay describes wanting to know "how nice kindergarten children become juvenile delinquents and violent offenders." While at the University of London, England, doing his Ph.D., Dr. Tremblay decided to start answering some of the developmental questions he had wondered about. For his doctoral dissertation, he examined how juvenile delinquents changed over the course of the treatment they were receiving for their problems. Dr. Tremblay has stayed on this research path for more than 30 years now.

Dr. Tremblay uses longitudinal-experimental methodology (collecting data on participants at different points in time over their life span) to understand developmental paths and the factors that affect them. He has noted that it is important to study participants over long periods so that their changes can be identified, along with the factors that lead to the changes. An interesting trend in Dr. Tremblay's research is that the age of his participants is getting younger. When Dr. Tremblay first embarked

on his research, his participants were adolescents. Over the years, he has realized the need to look at younger and younger children, especially if the ultimate goal is to prevent deviant outcomes from ever occurring.

Over the next ten years, Dr. Tremblay plans to examine different preventative interventions with pregnant women at high risk of having chronically aggressive children. He will be taking into account genetic factors and changing parents' behaviour. With the use of scans, he will examine how these factors affect the brain development of the fetuses and the long-term development of their behaviour. Dr. Tremblay believes the future of the field will be to study gene–environment interactions to understand deviant development.

Dr. Tremblay holds a prestigious position as a Canada Research Chair in Child Development at the University of Montreal. In this position, he is dedicated to conducting research and training future researchers in the area. He believes that graduate students should have the experience of working on concrete problems and should become involved in research projects that are going on internationally. Dr. Tremblay's view on undergraduate training is to have students come in contact with leaders in the field via books, video, conferences, and invited speakers to their universities. He believes that in order for the field to advance, it is important that future researchers—students—identify what we do not yet know.

Dr. Tremblay's research is funded by numerous government agencies. His advances in the field of child development have been recognized by many awards and honours. Most recently, Dr. Tremblay was identified as one of Canada's top five medical scientists by *Time Magazine* in 2003.

cognitive deficits and distortions (Fontaine, Burks, & Dodge, 2002). These youth often attend to fewer cues and misattribute hostile intent to ambiguous situations. Moreover, conduct-disordered youth demonstrate limited problem-solving skills, producing few solutions to problems, and these solutions are usually aggressive in nature. Cognitive deficits are likely to be present in early childhood and may contribute to child-onset conduct disorder (Coy et al., 2001).

Dodge and his colleagues also have distinguished between two types of aggressive behaviour—reactive aggression and proactive aggression (Dodge, 1991; Schwartz et al., 1998). Reactive aggression is described as an emotionally aggressive response to a perceived threat or frustration. In contrast, proactive aggression is aggression directed at achieving a goal or receiving positive reinforcers. Referring to Dodge's model, deficiencies in the process occur at different points for reactive and proactive aggression. Reactively aggressive youth are likely to demonstrate deficiencies early in the cognitive process, such as focusing on only a few social cues and misattributing hostile intent to ambiguous situations. In contrast, proactive aggressive youth are likely to have deficiencies in generating alternative responses and often choose an aggressive response. Furthermore, reactive and proactive aggressors tend to have different trajectories. Reactive aggressors tend to have an earlier onset of problems than proactive aggressors (Dodge et al., 1997).

SOCIAL THEORIES Bandura's (1965) **social learning theory** suggests that children learn their behaviour from observing others. Children are more likely to imitate behaviour that receives positive reinforcement than behaviour that receives negative reinforcement or punishment. As children are developing, numerous models are available to imitate, including parents, siblings, peers, and media figures. Studies have found that children who are highly aggressive and engage in antisocial behaviour often have witnessed parents, siblings, or grandparents engage in aggression and antisocial behaviour (Farrington, 1995; Waschbusch, 2002). This is a pattern of intergenerational aggression, in which one aggressive generation produces the next generation that also is aggressive (Glueck & Glueck, 1968; Huesmann et al., 1984).

Watching extremely violent television and movies in which actors are rewarded for their aggression also increases children's likelihood of acting aggressively (Bushman & Anderson, 2001). In addition, playing aggressive video games presents a forum for youth to be reinforced for their aggression and, in turn, may increase their likelihood of acting aggressively in real life (Anderson & Dill, 2000).

Risk Factors

There are a number of individual and social factors, known as **risk factors**, that place children at increased risk for developmental psychopathology, such as emotional and behavioural problems (Coie et al., 1992; Fitzpatrick, 1997; Jessor, Turbin, & Costa, 1998; Rutter, 1988, 1990; Wasserman & Saracini, 2001; Werner & Smith, 1992). It is important to remember that it is not just one risk factor but rather multiple risk factors that can lead to negative child outcomes (Rutter, 1979).

INDIVIDUAL RISK FACTORS A variety of genetic or biological factors have been linked to behavioural problems. Even before a child is born, there are factors that can operate to increase the likelihood for later behavioural difficulties. For example, a parent's own history of ADHD or behavioural difficulties are known risk factors for their offspring, especially sons (Cohen et al., 2002, National Crime Prevention Council, 1995, 1997).

A pregnant woman's use of drugs and alcohol can place the fetus at risk for later behavioural problems (Cohen et al., 2002). Once the child is born, diet and exposure to high levels of lead are risk factors for externalizing disorders (Cohen et al., 2002, National Crime Prevention Council, 1995, 1997).

A child's temperament also can be a risk factor. For example, children who are difficult to soothe or have a negative disposition can be at risk for later behavioural difficulties (Farrington, 1995). It also has been found that children who are impulsive are at risk for behavioural problems (Farrington, 1995).

FAMILIAL RISK FACTORS Parents play a critical role in the development of their children. Parents who are neglectful (Shaw et al., 1994) or children who do not attach securely to their parents are at risk for later behavioural problems (Fagot & Kavanagh, 1990). Divorce and familial conflict are risk factors for children (Amato & Keith, 1991; Cummings, Davies, & Campbell, 2000). Parenting style also can be problematic. For example, parents who are inconsistent, overly strict, and apply harsh discipline pose risk to the child (Dekovic, 1999). In addition, not properly supervising a child presents a risk factor to the child for later behavioural problems (Dekovic, 1999; Farrington, 1995; Hoge, Andrews, & Leschied, 1996; National Crime Prevention Council, 1995, 1997; Patterson, Reid, & Dishion, 1998; Rutter, 1990).

It has been suggested that parents who drink heavily are less likely to respond appropriately to their children's behaviour, thus, increasing the likelihood of future negative behaviour (Lahey, Waldman, & McBurnett, 1999). Also, heavy drinking has been implicated in inept monitoring of children and less parental involvement, both being familial risk factors (Lahey et al., 1999).

Consequences of child abuse may be psychological, physical, behavioural, academic, sexual, interpersonal, self-perceptual, or spiritual (Health Canada, 2003). Boys, in particular, may respond to abuse by acting aggressively and later engaging in spousal abuse (Fergusson & Lynskey, 1997; Health Canada, 2003; Loos & Alexander, 1997). Cohen et al. (2002) found that physical abuse experienced during adolescence increases the risk for developing lifetime mental health difficulties and behaviour problems.

Numerous other family variables have been reported as risk factors, including low socioeconomic status, large family size, and parental mental health problems (Frick, 1994; Patterson, Reid, & Dishion, 1998; Waschbusch, 2002).

SCHOOL AND SOCIAL RISK FACTORS Having trouble reading and having a lower intelligence are both risk factors for antisocial behaviour (Elkins et al., 1997;

Rutter, 1990). The school environment also provides an opportunity for peer influences on behaviour. Young children who play with aggressive peers at an early age are at risk for externalizing behaviour (Fergusson & Horwood, 1998; Laird et al., 2001). Children with early CD symptoms who do not end up with CD, tend to associate with less delinquent peers compared with children who later qualify for a CD diagnosis (Fergusson & Horwood, 1996).

Social disapproval and being rejected are likely to occur with aggressive children and adolescents (Coie, Belding, & Underwood, 1988; Ebata et al., 1990; Rutter, 1990), and these rejected, aggressive children are at risk for behavioural problems (Parker & Asher, 1987; Rudolph & Asher, 2000).

Protective Factors

Although children may experience a similar environment and adversity, children's responses and outcomes vary, with some children prevailing and prospering, and others having a number of difficulties and negative outcomes. The child who has multiple risk factors but who can overcome them and prevail has been termed **resilient**. Resilience has been described as the ability to overcome stress and adversity (Winfield, 1994).

It has been suggested that resilient children may have **protective factors** that allow them to persevere in the face of adversity. The notion of protection and protective factors was introduced in the early 1980s (Garmezy, 1985). Garmezy (1991) identified a number of areas in which protectiveness can be present: genetic variables, personality dispositions, supportive family environments, and community supports. There is some debate over the definition of protective factors and how protective factors work. Many agree, however, that protective factors help improve or sustain some part of an individual's life (Leadbeater et al., 1999). Rutter (1990) identifies four ways that protective factors are effective:

1. Protective factors reduce negative outcomes by changing the risk level of the child's exposure to a risk factor.
2. They change the negative chain reaction following exposure to risk.
3. They help develop and maintain self-esteem and self-efficacy.
4. They avail opportunities to children they would not otherwise have.

Protective factors can be grouped intro three categories: individual, familial, and social/external factors (Grossman et al., 1992).

INDIVIDUAL PROTECTIVE FACTORS Protective factors that reside within the individual, known as resilient temperaments (Hoge, 1999), include exceptional social skills, child competencies, confident perceptions, values, attitudes, and beliefs within the child (Vance, 2001).

Work from twin studies has suggested that social support may have a heritable component, which is influenced by personality. For example, likeable children may respond to good role models in a positive manner, thus promoting a positive and continuing relationship.

FAMILIAL FACTORS Protective familial factors are those positive aspects of the child's parents and home environment. For example, by having a supportive relationship with a child, the child may display less negative behaviour. Thus, a good parent–child relationship is a protective factor for the child who is growing up in an underprivileged community.

SOCIAL/EXTERNAL PROTECTIVE FACTORS Peer groups can have a strong effect on child outcomes (Vance, 2001). Associating with deviant peers is a risk factor for antisocial behaviour. The converse is a protective factor. That is, associating with prosocial children is a protective factor against antisocial behaviour (Fergusson & Horwood, 1996).

Just as there are risk factors leading to increased negative outcomes, so too are there protective factors that may reduce negative outcomes in the presence of risk factors (Grossman et al., 1992; Masten et al., 1990). Protective factors may counteract risk (Loeber & Farrington, 1998; Rutter, 1988). Further research is necessary to understand the role protective factors play in positive outcomes.

Treatment

Conduct-disordered youth are a very challenging population to treat. Often treatment studies show negligible effects at reducing future antisocial behaviour. Below are descriptions of common approaches to the treatment of CD. See Box 13.3 on the next page for a discussion on boot camps as an alternative facility for youthful offenders.

PARENT TRAINING Given parenting style may pose a risk to children, it should not be surprising to find that often parents of conduct-disordered youth are provided with parent training. Parents are taught how to change their parent–child interactions such that the child's prosocial behaviour is emphasized and antisocial behaviour is de-emphasized (Kazdin, 1997). Parents are given strategies on how to reinforce positive behaviour. For example, parents may be told to put children on a reinforcement schedule. For every prosocial behaviour the child displays, a point is awarded. Once the child accumulates a certain number of points, the child can trade the points for a privilege or monetary reward. Parents are instructed on alternatives to corporal punishment such as imposing a "time-out," in which the child cannot interact with anyone for a set time period. Overall, parent-training programs are more effective at reducing conduct-disordered behaviour in younger children than with conduct-disordered adolescents (Kazdin, 1993).

COGNITIVE AND SOCIAL-SKILLS TRAINING Cognitive and social-skills training focuses on the child's thought processes and interpersonal skills. Deficiencies and distortions in how children perceive and think about interpersonal interactions are challenged (Lochman, Whidby, & FitzGerald, 2000). Children are given concrete

BOX 13.3 BOOT CAMPS FOR YOUTHFUL OFFENDERS

As an alternative to traditional custodial facilities such as detention centres and prisons, boot camps use a military-style environment to rehabilitate youthful offenders. The day typically starts at 6:00 A.M. and includes literacy training, life skills, physical fitness, personal-hygiene classes, substance-abuse counselling, and job training (Hendley, 2000). The day ends around 10:00 P.M. The youthful offenders wear military-style uniforms and learn marching steps.

Located near Barrie, Ontario, Project Turnaround in 1997 was the first Canadian boot camp to open. Modelled after boot camps in the United States, Project Turnaround was directed at 16- and 17-year-old offenders. The facility provided room for 32 inmates, with 54 staff supervising. But does Project Turnaround work at reducing the likelihood of reoffending?

In an evaluation of Project Turnaround, it was reported that approximately 33% of young offenders reoffend after completing their stay there (Agrell, 2003). In contrast, approximately 50% of youthful offenders in traditional custodial facilities will reoffend after being released. These rates were not statistically significant, and Ontario's premier, Dalton McGuinty, decided to close Project Turnaround in 2004.

Interestingly, young offenders attending boot camps have a more positive perception of the facilities than young offenders attending traditional custodial facilities. In a survey by Styve, MacKenzie, Gover, and Mitchell (2000), young offenders having gone through a boot camp (in the United States) perceived it as a more controlled, active, and structured environment with less potential for harm by other residents, compared with young offenders in more traditional correctional facilities. Boot camps also were perceived as providing more therapeutic and transitional programming than did traditional facilities. Although these perceptions may be positive, they do not seem to significantly influence recidivism rates.

Sources: Agrell, 2003; Hendley, 2000; Styve et al., 2000.

---

strategies to resolve interpersonal difficulties. Children practise these strategies in the treatment session. Often they will be taught to "self-talk"—that is, to make statements to themselves that help focus on nonaggressive solutions to problems. Role-playing and modelling of prosocial behaviour and positive interactions also occur in the treatment sessions. Children are requested to keep a log of their behaviour at home and school to monitor their progress (Kazdin, 1997). Cognitive and social-skills training programs often demonstrate a change in behaviour but for short periods.

MULTISYSTEMIC THERAPY Multisystemic therapy (MST) is a treatment approach that considers the child in the various contexts or systems he or she exists— family, peers, school, neighbourhood, and community (Henggeler & Borduin, 1990; Henggeler, Melton, & Smith, 1992; Henggeler et al., 1986; Henggeler, Schoenwald, & Pickrel, 1995; Henggeler et al., 1998). At the start of MST, conduct-disordered youth are assessed to determine their specific needs. Assessments include considering youth within their family context and their external influences of peers, school, neighbour-hood, and community. Based on this assessment, adolescents and their families are provided service. Areas that may be targeted in treatment include family communication, parent management, and cognitive-behavioural issues. Each youth is given a case manager who is accessible 24 hours a day, seven days a week, to deal with crises and coordinate services and treatment.

MST has been implemented in various parts of Canada and the United States. To evaluate MST's effectiveness, a four-year randomized study was conducted across four Ontario communities: London, Mississauga, Simcoe County, and Ottawa (National Crime Prevention Council, 2001). Approximately 200 families received MST from 1997 to 2001. During the same time period, another 200 families were asked to access the services that were available through their local youth justice and social service organizations. These services included probation and specialized programs.

All families participating in this study underwent psychological testing at the start of the study and then once again at the end. The psychological testing included measures to assess family functioning, caregiver depression, the youths' social skills, pro-criminal attitudes, and behaviour problems. In addition, the youth were followed for four years following the end of treatment (until 2004). Results from the data that are currently available show no treatment effect for MST. That is, MST has not been found to be more effective than the usual services available in Ontario. It is important to note, however, that MST may have benefited youths and their families on factors that were not measured. Moreover, some studies evaluating MST in the United States have found it more effective than incarceration, individual counselling, and probation (Henggeler et al., 1986, 1992, 1995). Targeted treatment that meets the needs of young people and their families appears to be critical to effective treatment.

FEMALE OFFENDERS

Female offenders might be described as the "forgotten minority." As you have seen in other chapters, a substantial amount of research has focused on male offenders. Why has there been so little research on female offenders? One reason is that few females commit crime; men simply engage in much more offending than women do. This gender bias in offending has been true across time periods, across different cultures, and across the age span (Wilson & Herrnstein, 1985). Since there are so few female offenders, the attitude of some researchers has been "Why bother to study them?" Also, there was an implicit assumption that research conducted with men could be applied to women. If the causes and explanations of female and male criminality were similar, then assessment procedures and treatment programs developed on male offenders could be applied directly to females. However, if there are important differences between female and male criminality, then it may be inappropriate to apply assessments and treatment developed on male offenders to females. Only recently have separate classification and assessment instruments been developed for female offenders. This section will focus on what we know and need to know about female offenders.

Historical Overview

Historically, much of the controversy in Canada surrounding female offenders has revolved around the issue of placement. The first federal prison for women in Canada was opened in 1934 in Kingston, Ontario. It was called, not too surprisingly, the Prison for Women. Prior to this time, federal women offenders were housed in separate wings of male institutions. With the opening of the Prison for Women, federal female offenders from across Canada were sent to Kingston to serve their sentences. This resulted in many women being separated not only by walls and bars from their family, friends, and communities, but also being geographically isolated from them. Within four years of opening, the Archambault Commission recommended the Prison for Women be closed. Numerous subsequent Royal Commissions and a 1981 Canadian Human Rights Commission all identified weaknesses in the variety and quality of vocational, educational, and intervention programs available to women.

In 1990, upon the recommendation of the report *Creating Choices: Report of the Task Force on Federally Sentenced Women*, the Solicitor General of Canada announced that the Prison for Women would be closed and be replaced by five regional facilities, including a healing lodge. Between 1995 and 1997 these new community-style regional facilities were opened, and on May 8, 2000, the last inmate left the Prison for Women, and on July 6, 2000, the Prison for Women was officially closed.

The opening of these regional facilities was a mixed success. Although they provided more appropriate venues for dealing with female offenders, they were initially subject to several problems, chiefly the management of the more violent women offenders. Women who had been held in maximum security at the Prison for Women were moved to less secure regional facilities. For example, within the first year at the Edmonton Institution for Women, there were several assaults on staff, an inmate murder, and seven escapes. Since the new regional facilities did not have the capability to manage maximum-security women, in 1996 Correctional Service of Canada transferred them to units in more secure men's institutions. In 2003 and 2004, additional secure units were built at each of the regional facilities to permit the return of women requiring maximum-security management.

Rates

Women represent about 9% of all offenders receiving a provincial sentence and about 4% of the federal offender population (Statistics Canada, 2003). With respect to federal offenders, these percentages translate to about 370 women, compared with about 12 000 men, serving a federal sentence. Gender differences are somewhat less for adolescent offenders, with 23% of the youth charged being females.

Prison sentences for men tend to be longer than for women. For example, in 2002, 53% of men and 70% of women were given a sentence of one month or less (Solicitor General, 2003). In Ontario, 32% of women incarcerated in provincial facilities have been charged with property offences, 22% with drug offences, and 19% with violent offences (Shaw, 1994). Most offenders (70% in 2003) who are serving a sentence of two years or more have been incarcerated for a violent offence. As Table 13.8 shows, about one in five federal offenders are incarcerated for committing murder. More men are serving federal sentences for violent offences, whereas women are more likely to be incarcerated for serious drug offences.

There are also dramatic differences in the costs of keeping male and female federal offenders in penitentiaries. In 2001–2002, the average annual cost of keeping a female offender incarcerated in a federal institution was $155 589, compared with an average of $79 538 for male offenders. The higher costs associated with keeping females incarcerated are due to their low numbers.

There is an overrepresentation of Aboriginals in the criminal justice system. About 3% of the Canadian population is Aboriginal, but 33% of female and 17% of male admissions to provincial facilities are Aboriginals. The same pattern emerges for federal facilities. Aboriginal women represent 29% of all incarcerated women, while Aboriginal men represent 18% of incarcerated men. In addition, Aboriginal women offenders (78%) are more likely to be serving a federal sentence for a violent offence (murder and schedule I offences) than non-Aboriginal women offenders (48%). The high number of Aboriginal women offenders was the motivation behind the development of the Okimaw Ohci Healing Lodge for women offenders.

Theories of Female Criminality

Early theories focused on a biological or physiological basis for female criminality. For example, Cesare Lombroso, an Italian physician, believed that the biological constitution of women was incompatible (being more maternal in nature) with crime, and that in order for a woman to commit a crime, she was assumed to have a biological abnormality (Lombroso & Ferrero, 1895).

TABLE 13.8 TYPES OF OFFENCES COMMITTED BY FEDERAL OFFENDERS

Type of Offence	Women	Men	Total
First- and second-degree murder	16%	18%	18%
Schedule I* offences	39%	53%	52%
Schedule II** offences	32%	14%	15%
Nonviolent offences	13%	15%	15%

Source: Adapted from Solicitor General, 2003.

*Schedule I offences: manslaughter, assault, armed robbery, and sexual offences.

**Schedule II offences: importing and trafficking narcotics.

In the 1970s crime rates increased in both the United States and Canada (Wilson & Herrnstein, 1985). For men this increase was partly attributed to an increased population of men in the age group of highest criminal activity. However, for women an alternative explanation was proposed. Adler (1975) attributed the increase in female crime to the women's liberation movement. Adler proposed that as women began to emerge from the narrow role of housewife into previously male-dominated areas, they also emulated male criminal behaviours. Adler called this new crime wave by women the "shady aspect of liberation" (p. 16). Research has failed to support Adler's theory (Campbell, Mackenzie, & Robinson, 1987; Trice & Lamb, 1996). In contrast to Adler's predictions, most female offenders actually endorse more sex-role stereotypes than nonoffenders do.

More recently, sociological theories of criminal behaviour, such as differential association, strain, and social control theories, have been tested to see if they can adequately explain female criminality (see Chapter 1 for a discussion of these theories). Alarid, Burton, and Cullen (2000) found support for both differential association and social control theories to account for the self-reported criminal behaviour in incarcerated female offenders. Katz (2000) used strain theory to illustrate how stressful events in the family and in the neighbourhood (e.g., early childhood victimization, adult racial discrimination, sexual discrimination, and having been a victim of domestic violence) all contributed to explaining women's involvement in criminal behaviour.

What Do We Know about Female Offenders?

Available research on female offenders is sparse, with much focused on examining a limited range of variables (e.g., sex-role stereotypes) or unrepresentative subgroups of offenders (e.g., battered women who kill or prostitutes). Women in prison come from similar backgrounds to those of men in prison. Like male offenders, female offenders tend to be, on average, in their early 30s, with Grade 9 education or lower, and on social assistance or in low-paying jobs at admission. Nonetheless, male and female offenders differ in several ways. About two-thirds of women offenders are mothers, with most being the sole supporters of their children. Compared with male offenders, female offenders are more likely to be victims of physical and sexual abuse, to engage in suicidal and self-injurious behaviours, to have less extensive criminal histories, and to have elevated rates of mental disorders.

In 1989, Correctional Service Canada conducted a mental health survey of 77 federal female offenders at the Prison for Women. Only 5% of the sample showed no evidence of a disorder, whereas almost 50% showed evidence of multiple disorders. Table 13.9 presents lifetime prevalence rates of *DSM-III* disorders in a sample of 1928 adult females in the community (Bland, Orn, & Newman, 1988), a sample of 77 federal female offenders (Correctional Service Canada, 1989), and a sample of 2185 federal male offenders (Motiuk & Porporino, 1991). All studies used the Diagnostic Interview Schedule to assess the mental disorder (exclusion criteria ignored). Female offenders had substantially higher rates of mental disorder than women in the general population and slightly higher rates as compared to federal male offenders. In both male and female offenders, common disorders included antisocial personality disorder, alcohol abuse, and drug abuse. The high rates of mental disorder in female offenders have also been reported in more recent research (Teplin, Abram, & McClelland, 1996; Warren et al., 2002). The most common mental disorders in women offenders include substance abuse, post-traumatic stress disorder, and major depression. There are also high levels of personality disorders in women offenders, notably antisocial personality and borderline personality disorder (Hurley & Dunne, 1991; Jordan et al., 1996).

Victimization Rates

The past decade has brought growing awareness of the high rates of sexual and physical victimization reported by women offenders. The prevalence of child abuse is difficult to obtain due to the different methodologies used. An Ontario survey of 3648 women from the community found that 12% of women report childhood sexual abuse and 21% report being physically abused (MacMillan et al., 2001). Substantially higher rates have been found with incarcerated samples. For example, about 50% of incarcerated federal women offenders report childhood sexual abuse and about 70% experienced childhood physical abuse (Shaw, 1994). Even higher rates have been reported for Aboriginal women offenders (60% report sexual abuse and 90% report physical abuse).

TABLE 13.9 LIFETIME PREVALENCE OF MENTAL DISORDERS IN CANADIAN GENERAL AND OFFENDER POPULATIONS

Disorder	Bland et al. (1988) Community Women (%)	CSC (1989) Women Offenders (%)	Motiuk and Porporino (1991) Male Offenders (%)
Schizophrenia	0.6	13.0	4.9
Post-traumatic stress disorder	—	29.9	—
Obsessive compulsive disorder	3.1	14.3	—
Bipolar disorder	—	7.8	3.6
Depression	11.4	49.4	21.4
Alcohol abuse	6.7	62.3	70.1
Drug abuse	3.2	57.1	53.7
Phobia	11.7	62.3	28.3
Generalized anxiety disorder	—	55.8	46.7
Panic disorder	1.7	13.0	3.7
Antisocial personality disorder	0.8	59.7	75.4

Browne, Miller, and Maguin (1999) examined the relation between earlier and later victimization in 150 incarcerated women. The authors found that 70% of the women reported experiencing severe physical abuse as a child or adolescent, and 59% were sexually abused. Eighty percent of women who reported experiencing severe physical abuse prior to age 18 also reported experiencing severe domestic violence; 40% of women who reported being sexually abused before age 18 reported being sexually assaulted by someone other than a spouse or dating partner in adulthood. This study illustrates the high degree of continuity between childhood victimization and adult victimization.

Haney and Kristianson (1997) describe how this high rate of childhood abuse among incarcerated offenders has implications for the mental health of women during incarceration. These authors have linked Finkelhor and Browne's (1985) traumatizing processes underlying child abuse, such as traumatic sexualization and powerlessness, to experiences of women in prison. The high rates of self-inflicted injuries, suicide, substance use, and violence of incarcerated women may be how these women cope with being exposed to situations that parallel their childhood abusive experiences. As stated by Haney and Kristianson (1997), "women might be less likely to re-offend if society also freed them of their revictimization during their incarceration" (p. 42).

Risk Factors

Although gender-specific risk factors may exist, the research to date has found more similarities than differences in both adolescents and adults (Blanchette, 2001; Simourd & Andrews, 1994). Blanchette (2001) provides a review of static and dynamic risk factors in female offenders. She concludes that many of the static risk factors associated with recidivism in men, such as criminal history and age, are also predictors with women. Similar dynamic risk factors for women and men include substance abuse, antisocial attitudes, and antisocial associates. Evidence also suggests that women have further risk factors, such as a history of self-injury or attempted suicide and self-esteem problems. Female offenders reoffend at a lower rate than do male offenders. In 2003, the percentage of successful full paroles and statutory releases for women was higher than for men (81% and 72% full parole, and 61% and 58% for statutory release). (Solicitor General, 2003). Overall, additional research is needed to understand the static and dynamic risk factors for recidivism in women offenders.

How well do the risk assessment instruments described in Chapter 11 predict reoffending in female offenders? The results have varied depending on the measures. The General Statistical Information on Recidivism (GSIR) scale provides an estimate of the probability that an offender will reoffend within a three-year follow-up period. Bonta, Pang, and Wallace-Capretta (1995) investigated the predictive validity of the GSIR in a sample of 81 female offenders. When compared with male offenders, female offenders tend to score lower on the GSIR, reflecting lower levels of risk. Although the GSIR was correlated with reoffending, there was no linear increase in recidivism rates found across the different levels of risk categories. Although the GSIR is used routinely with male offenders, Correctional Service of Canada does not use the GSIR with female offenders.

Another scale used to assess the risk of recidivism is the Level of Service Inventory-Revised (LSI-R). Similar to the GSIR, the LSI-R also tends to assess provincial female offenders at a lower risk than male provincial offenders (Coulson et al., 1996). Coulson and colleagues followed 526 provincial female offenders for three years. LSI-R total scores were positively related to general recidivism, parole failure, and halfway-house failure, indicating that the LSI-R is useful for predicting female reoffending.

The Hare Psychopathy Checklist-Revised (PCL-R; Hare, 2003) is a scale for the assessment of psychopathy. Although not originally designed as a risk-assessment measure, the PCL-R is a robust predictor of violent recidivism in diverse samples, including correctional offenders, young offenders, sexual offenders, and offenders with mental disorders. Several studies have examined psychopathy in female offenders, all reporting a lower prevalence in women than in men (Salekin, Rogers, & Sewell, 1997; Vitale et al., 2002; Warren et al., 2003). There is some evidence that the predictive validity of the PCL-R may extend to female offenders. Salekin, Rogers, Ustad, and Sewell (1998) followed 78 female inmates in a state jail in Texas for 14 months. PCL-R total scores were only weakly associated with general recidivism during this period. Stronger findings have been reported by Loucks and Zamble (2000), who followed 81 federal female offenders for about three years. The PCL-R was moderately correlated with new charges or major violations while on release ($r = 0.45$). In a large sample of 239 female offenders released from a maximum-security treatment institution, Richards, Casey, and Lucente (2003) reported that 60% of the offenders with high PCL-R scores were re-incarcerated, compared with 30% of those with low scores.

Finally, HCR-20 scores for male and female mentally disordered patients in Sweden were compared by Strand and Belfrage (2001). There were no gender differences in the HCR-20 total or on the Historical, Clinical and Risk Management subscales. Whether or not the HCR-20 has predictive validity with females has yet to be established.

The above research indicates that some risk assessment instruments developed and validated with male offenders may also be used with women. However, it is not appropriate to assume that this will always be the case, and a considerable amount of research still needs to be conducted.

Battered Women Who Kill

Each year in Canada about 15 men are killed by their partner. Most of these homicides are committed by women who kill their abusive partner. A question people often ask is, "If a woman is in an abusive relationship, why doesn't she just leave?" Woman in abusive relationships do often leave, although some return and some even stay in abusive relationships (see Chapter 12). An additional question is, "Why do some woman kill their abusive husbands while most do not?"

If a battered woman picks up a gun, shoots, and kills her husband while he lies sleeping on the couch, her defence lawyer will likely argue that his client's actions should be considered as **self-defence**. Self-defence is premised on the principle that if you are attacked you should be able to take reasonable actions to defend yourself. However, according to section 34(1) and (2) of the Canadian Criminal Code, a plea of self-defence requires that at the time of the murder the person should have a reasonable apprehension of death or serious bodily injury and that equal force or the least amount of force be used to repel the threat. The two key components include justified use of lethal force and a reasonable perception of danger. Gellespie (1989) has described the problems when battered woman who kill attempt to advance a self-defence plea. First, triers of fact (e.g., judges and juries) hold misconceptions about battered woman, and second, triers of fact must be convinced of the "reasonableness" of these lethal actions. Box 13.4 describes the case of Jane (Stafford) Hurshman-Corkum, a woman who killed her abusive husband.

The term "**battered woman syndrome**" (BWS) was coined by Lenore Walker (1984) to describe a woman's reactions to prolonged physical and psychological abuse inflicted by her spouse. BWS is now being used in trials that involve battered women who kill their abusers. The two key components of BWS that are often presented by court experts include **learned helplessness** and the **cycle-of-violence theory**.

Walker applied Martin Seligman's (1975) theory and research on animals to battered women. The animals in Seligman's experiments were placed in one of two conditions. In one condition, a dog was placed on one side of a cage that contained a small barrier down the middle of the cage. A tone would sound followed by a shock being administered to the dog through the floor of the cage where the dog stood. The dog would immediately run around at first but after a few trials would jump over the barrier to the "safe" side of the cage. In the other condition, a dog was put in the cage but there was no place to escape. These dogs would start responding to the tone but end up lying down and behaving "helpless." Walker linked these dogs' behaviours to battered woman who are exposed to repeated and often unpredictable attacks. These women often report feeling helpless, having no options, and focusing on survival rather than leaving (Walker, 1993).

The other component that has been proposed to contribute to the development of BWS is the cycle-of-violence theory. According to this theory, there are three phases. During phase one (tension-building phase), there is increasing tension, with minor verbal or physical abuse. The woman often attempts to appease the batterer by changing her behaviour. Phase two (acute battering act phase) involves the actual physical or sexual assault. Following this violence, the man apologizes for his behaviour, is attentive to the woman's needs, and promises to change (contrition phase). This cycle repeats itself often, with the acute violent act becoming more and more severe and the contrition phase becoming shorter and sometimes disappearing. These components were developed by conducting extensive interviews with 435 battered women (Walker, 1984).

BOX 13.4 THE BREAKING POINT: WHEN BATTERED WOMEN KILL

On March 11, 1982, Jane Hurshman-Corkum took a shotgun, put it to the head of her husband, Billy Stafford, as he sat passed out in his truck outside their home, and pulled the trigger. Billy was killed by a single shot to his head. For five years, Jane had experienced regular beatings by her husband. Some of these beatings were so severe that she was beaten to the point of unconsciousness. Billy had shot at her, held a knife to her throat, raped her, and forced her to engage in bizarre sexual acts. Billy also directed his violence toward his son, Darren. He viciously teased his son (e.g., withholding his Christmas toys from him), physically abused his son, and at times forced his son to eat his own vomit.

Billy Stafford was known and feared in the Bangs Falls area of Nova Scotia. He had a violent temper, was unpredictable, and would physically attack others.

Why didn't Jane Hurshman-Corkum simply leave Billy Stafford? Billy's two previous partners left after being abused by him (one fled to Alberta, the other to Ontario). Jane described feeling totally trapped with nowhere and no one to turn to. Billy had threatened to track her down and kill her, her sons, and her family if she ever tried to leave him.

The breaking point occurred on March 11, 1982. Earlier in the day, Billy had said that he planned to set fire to his neighbour's trailer and that he would "deal" with Jane's 16-year-old son Allen who was temporarily living with them. Jane finally decided that she had had enough and killed Billy.

Jane Hurshman-Corkum was arrested and charged with first-degree murder. At her first trial, her lawyer argued that she had acted in self-defence. The jury agreed and she was found not guilty. The courtroom applauded when the verdict was announced. The Crown appealed and 15 months later, on the advice of her lawyer, Jane pled guilty to the charge of manslaughter. She was sentenced to six months in jail and two years probation.

After her release from jail, Jane became a vocal advocate for battered women. She lobbied for the establishment of transition houses for battered women, and she became a symbol of hope and resistance in the fight against domestic violence.

Jane Hurshman-Corkum never got over the trauma of the abuse. She was often depressed and was embarrassed by her kleptomania (uncontrollable urges to steal that led to several shoplifting convictions). On February 22, 1992, she was found dead in her car in Halifax. The autopsy report ruled that Jane died from a point-blank bullet wound to her chest that was consistent with suicide.

Source: Vallée, 1998.

Almost as soon as BWS was described by Walker (1984), concerns were raised that it framed battered woman's behaviour as mental illness (Browne, 1987; Faigman & Wright, 1997; Schneider, 1986). There were also concerns about both the cycle-of-violence theory and learned helplessness components of BWS. Not all batterers display the phases described by the cycle of violence. Only 67% of battered woman in Walker's (1984) study reported experiencing the tension-building phase, and 58% experiences the contrition phase. In addition, many battered woman are not passive, submissive, or helpless (Bowker, 1993; Blackman, 1990; Fisher, Vidmar, & Ellis, 1993; McMahon,

1999). If a battered woman who kills her violent batterer does not fit the BWS profile, triers of fact might question her claim of self-defence (Terrance & Matheson, 2003). Jury decision-making research was covered in Chapter 8.

Recent jury simulation studies have found that expert testimony about BWS is associated with more lenient verdicts regardless of whether the woman is described as passive or active (Schuller & Hastings, 1996; Schuller & Rzepa, 2002). However, Schuller and Rzepa (2002) found that participants simulating jury members considered women portrayed as active (i.e., a battered woman who verbally and physically defended herself against her abusive husband) as less sympathetic, were less likely to believe the woman's report of threat, and thought that she had more options, compared with women portrayed as passive (i.e., a battered woman who attempted to appease her abusive husband).

COURT DECISIONS Although battered woman who kill have attempted to use the self-defence plea, usually they are not successful. For example, Ewing (1987) reported on the court decisions for 100 battered women who committed murder (three were found not guilty by reason of insanity, three had charges dropped, and nine pled guilty). Of the 85 who attempted to use the self-defence plea, 63 were convicted of some form of criminal homicide and 22 were acquitted (a conviction rate of 74%). For those convicted there was enormous variability in the sentences given, ranging from four years probation to life in prison. With respect to expert testimony, in 44 of the 85 cases an attempt was made to introduce expert testimony by the defence and in 26 cases it was deemed admissible (in 17 of these 26 cases the woman was convicted). It is likely that the use and admissibility of expert testimony relating to battered women has increased since this study. Whether or not an increasing reliance on expert testimony results in a greater number of acquittals is unknown.

CHARACTERISTICS OF WOMEN WHO KILL THEIR ABUSERS Several studies have sought to understand why some battered women kill their abusers while the majority do not. Browne (1987) interviewed 42 women who were charged with murder or attempted murder of their abusive spouse. A nonhomicide comparison sample of 205 abused women who had been physically abused at least twice and who were either still with their abusive partner or had left the relationship within one year were also interviewed. Much of the data was based on self-report, although all available police and hospital records, and any collateral information (family member reports), were reviewed.

Few differences were found between the women in the homicide group and the comparison group. The homicide group was slightly older than the comparison group (36 years versus 31 years) but there were no group differences in education level or employment history. Women in both the homicide and the nonhomicide comparison group had either witnessed parental violence or had been physically abused as a child (71% versus 65%) and about half had been sexually abused (57% versus 54%). Table 13.10 presents the seven variables in which the homicide and nonhomicide comparison groups were different. Group differences were primarily in the behaviours of the men: men in the homicide group were more likely to abuse drugs and alcohol, engaged in more frequent injurious behaviour, were more likely to commit sexual assault, were more likely to threaten to kill someone, and more of them abused their children. Women in the homicide group were more likely to think of committing suicide than were women in the nonhomicide comparison group. Many of the women in the homicide group had experienced many years of abuse prior to the homicide. What was the turning point for these women? Most women reported that there was a change in the pattern or severity of violence. For example, "He had never threatened the baby before" or "It was one thing when he was beating me, but when he hurt my daughter ..." (Browne, 1987, pp. 129–130).

Other researchers have also studied battered women who kill. Campbell (1986) reported that females convicted of spousal homicide were more likely than males convicted for spousal homicide to be responding to violence than to be initiating violence. Roberts (1996) compared 105 battered women who killed their abusive partners with a group of 105 battered women who did not kill their abusive partner. The battered women who killed were more likely (1) to have dropped out of high school, (2) to have a history of childhood sexual abuse, (3) to have a poor employment history, (4) to have cohabited with the partner, (5) to have attempted suicide, (6) to have a history of drug problems, and (7) to have access to a gun.

Hamilton and Sutterfield (1997) examined help-seeking behaviours (contacting family, friends, mental health professionals, and police) in 20 women incarcerated for killing their abusive partner and 29 women who had received services from a shelter for battered women. Help-seeking behaviours did not differ between the two groups. However, police response did differ. Police had been called by 60% of the incarcerated

TABLE 13.10 DIFFERENCES BETWEEN HOMICIDE GROUP AND NONHOMICIDE COMPARISON GROUP

Measure	Homicide Group	Nonhomicide Group
Made threats to kill others	83%	57%
Violent acts/once per week	40%	13%
Severity of physical violence escalated	80%	58%
Violence toward children	71%	51%
Daily substance use	79%	40%
Often raped partner	40%	13%
Suicide thoughts by women	48%	31%

Source: Adapted from Browne, 1987.

women and 65% of the women in shelters. Arrest of the their partners was the most common police intervention for the shelter group (31%), whereas only 5% of the incarcerated women reported their partners were arrested. Effective police intervention is crucial in domestic assault cases. If a battered woman calls the police for help and none is forthcoming, this will likely reinforce her belief that there is no escape from the violence. As Hamilton and Sutterfeld (1997) explain, "Failure of the community to respond to domestic violence can and does result in homicides, of victim and of abuser" (p. 54).

Although the studies described in this section focused on women who kill their abusers, it is important to remember that these cases are the exception, not the rule. In a lethal altercation between partners, it is more typically the woman who loses her life. Each year in Canada and the United States, about two-thirds of homicides between partners were of husbands killing wives, while one-third were wives killing husbands. For example, in Canada in 2003, 15 women killed their husbands, whereas 60 men killed their wives.

Treatment

A considerable amount of research has examined the effectiveness of intervention programs with male adolescent and adult offenders (e.g., Andrews et al., 1990; Izzo & Ross, 1990). However, much less is known about what works with female offenders. As concluded by Koons and her colleagues, "Woman offenders have experienced a long history of indifference and neglect in the development and implementation of correctional programs" (Koons et al., 1997, p. 517).

Koons and her colleagues (1997) conducted a survey of U.S. correctional and program administrators, asking them to identify promising treatment programs for female offenders. The programs that targeted substance-abuse education (55%), substance-abuse treatment (47%), parenting (44%) and life skills (42%), relationships (37%), and basic education (24%) were mentioned most often. Koons and her colleagues conducted focus groups with 104 program participants from promising programs (i.e., program addressed specific need and there was empirical evidence of effectiveness). Program participants felt that the most important factor relating to success was having qualified, dedicated, and caring staff, and a program that focused on skills acquisition.

Meta-analytic studies with male offenders (e.g., Andrews & Bonta, 1998; Andrews et al., 1990) have found that effective treatment programs are those that follow the principles of effective correctional treatment (i.e., risk, need, and responsivity principles; see Chapter 13 for a description of these principles). Dowden and Andrews (1999) conducted a meta-analysis of 26 studies to examine if these principles would also be associated with effective treatment for female adolescent and adult offenders. Stronger treatment effects were found for programs that targeted high-risk as compared to low-risk offenders (risk principle), that provided treatment of criminogenic needs as compared with noncriminogenic needs (need principle), and that used cognitive-behavioural interventions as compared to nonbehavioural interventions (responsivity principle). Promising targets include family (supervision and affection), antisocial associates, and antisocial cognitions. Less promising targets were substance abuse and school/work interventions.

Dowden and Andrews did not analyze their data separately for adolescent and adult females (the majority of the studies included adolescent offenders) and only five studies were from the 1990s. Some of their findings are intriguing, such as the limited impact of substance-abuse treatment. Such findings may have several interpretations. Perhaps substance-abuse treatment programs actually do have less impact than other treatment targets. Alternatively, some aspects of behaviour, such as substance abuse, may be inherently more difficult to treat. Finally, the implementation of treatments may be responsible for the relative success of a treatment target compared to another target. For example, more recent substance-abuse treatment programs might be more successful than earlier programs.

NEW DIRECTIONS IN TREATMENT: DIALECTICAL BEHAVIOUR THERAPY

High rates of borderline personality disorder are observed in female offenders (Jordan et al., 1996). **Dialectical behaviour therapy** (DBT) was originally developed by Linehan (1993) to treat patients with borderline personality disorder in the community. DBT is designed to obtain a balance between acceptance of one's current capabilities and the development of new coping skills. Personal and situational factors that reinforce maladaptive behaviours are identified and skills are developed to address problems with self-regulation (including emotions, cognitions, and relationships).

Promising outcome results have been obtained for inpatients, suicidal patients, and drug-dependent patients (Bohus et al., 2000; Linehan et al., 1999). Correctional Service Canada has adapted DBT (see McDonagh, Taylor, & Blanchette, 2002) to address correctional-specific targets, to use in different environments (prison versus inpatient or outpatient hospital), and to meet the needs of different samples of offenders (maximum-security offenders versus general offenders). In 2001, Correctional Service Canada implemented the adapted version of DBT in four of the regional women's institutions. Although a comprehensive evaluation of the program will be conducted as part of the implementation, no information is yet available about its success.

ABORIGINAL OFFENDERS

Historical Overview

The disproportionate involvement of Aboriginals in the criminal justice system has been recognized in Canada for a long time (LaPrairie, 1996). Indeed, since at least the early 1970s, Aboriginal people have been a concern to various Canadian criminal justice agencies (Aboriginal Task Force, 1989). Slowly, researchers, practitioners, and policymakers have begun to recognize the unique circumstances surrounding Aboriginal offenders, resulting in numerous initiatives to reduce the number of

Aboriginal people who come into contact with the law. In 1985, for example, Correctional Service Canada (CSC) started to introduce policies stressing the importance of Aboriginal culture. CSC began examining the process Aboriginal offenders go through once they enter the criminal justice system and started to work toward developing correctional programs that would better meet their needs. By 1993, the Corrections and Conditional Release Act stated explicitly that CSC must provide a range of Aboriginal-specific correctional programs (Corrections and Conditional Release Act, 1992, s. 80). In addition, provisions were put in place to transfer Aboriginal offenders to the Aboriginal community, where they could have access to services and programs that reflect their culture (Corrections and Conditional Release Act, 1992, s. 81).

The federal government has also made attempts to deal with the overrepresentation of Aboriginal offenders in the criminal justice system. For example, in 1996, Parliament passed Bill C-41, which discussed the principles and purposes of sentencing and introduced new sentencing options, such as the conditional sentence. In section 718.2 of Bill C-41, which deals with the use of incarceration, the government included the qualification "all available sanctions other than imprisonment should be considered for all offenders, *with particular attention to the circumstances of Aboriginal offenders*" (italics added; R.S.C., 1985, s. 718.2(e)). As discussed by Roberts and Melchers (2003), that section of Bill C-41 has been interpreted by the Supreme Court of Canada in *R. v. Gladue* (1999) as an attempt to "ameliorate the serious problem of over-representation of aboriginal people in prisons" (para. 93). Furthermore, the Supreme Court concluded that "the jail term for an Aboriginal offender may in some circumstances be less than the term imposed on a non-Aboriginal offender for the same offence" (para. 93). One significant result of this ruling has been the development of a court in Canada that focuses solely on processing Aboriginal offenders. This court is known as the Gladue Court (see Box 13.5).

Rates

Despite attempts to reduce Aboriginal involvement with the law, Aboriginal offenders are still greatly overrepresented in the Canadian criminal justice system. According to the most recent statistics, although Aboriginal people make up about 3% of the general population in Canada, Aboriginal offenders make up approximately 17% of federal prison inmates (Hendrick & Farmer, 2002). Furthermore, Aboriginal offenders currently represent approximately 12% of all offenders who are serving their sentence in the community (Trevethan, Moore, & Rastin, 2002b). As illustrated in Figure 13.1, this overrepresentation occurs across all regions of Canada, though it is more pronounced in certain regions. For example, in the Atlantic region, Aboriginals make up about 1% of the general population, 7% of the federal prison population, and 4% of the population of offenders serving time in the community. In contrast, Aboriginals make up about 6% of the general population in the Prairie provinces, but represent a staggering 40% of the federal prison population in that region, and about 31% of the population of offenders on conditional release.

BOX 13.5 THE GLADUE COURT

On April 23, 1999, the Supreme Court of Canada released its decision in *R. v. Gladue*, stating that section 718.2 of the Criminal Code should change the way judges approach the sentencing process. The Court stressed that prison terms were being relied on too often in Canada as a way of dealing with criminal behaviour, especially when it came to Aboriginal offenders. Following this ruling, Canadian judges expressed concern over how the Gladue decision should be applied. Judges had concerns about whether the courts had the time or expertise to deal with the special circumstances of Aboriginal offenders. In response to these concerns, it was proposed that a special court be devel-

oped, the Gladue Court, as a way of addressing the special circumstances of Aboriginal offenders.

The Gladue Court, located in Toronto, is now available to all Aboriginal people whose cases would normally have gone through the Old City Hall Courts located in Toronto. Currently, the Gladue Court performs the same activities as the Old City Hall Court: it accepts guilty pleas, sentences offenders, and does bail hearings. The difference is that the people working in the Gladue Court have an in-depth understanding of the range of programs and services available to Aboriginal offenders in Toronto.

Source: Aboriginal Legal Services of Toronto, 2001.

FIGURE 13.1

PROPORTION OF ABORIGINAL OFFENDERS SERVING TIME IN FEDERAL PRISONS AND IN THE COMMUNITY

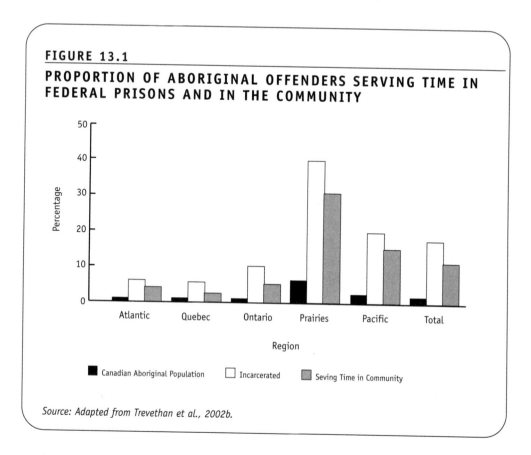

Source: Adapted from Trevethan et al., 2002b.

Aboriginal and non-Aboriginal offenders are also known to differ in terms of the crimes for which they get incarcerated. For example, research has consistently shown that Aboriginal offenders are more likely to be incarcerated for crimes against the person than non-Aboriginal offenders are (Trevethan et al., 2002b). As illustrated in Table 13.11, larger proportions of Aboriginal offenders than non-Aboriginal offenders are currently incarcerated for homicide, attempted murder, assault, and sexual assault. Non-Aboriginal offenders, however, are more often incarcerated for drug-related offences, robbery, and property-related offences.

OTHER ASPECTS OF OVERREPRESENTATION It is important to stress, so as to not minimize the problem, that Aboriginal overrepresentation goes far beyond just overrepresentation in prison and community offender populations. The problem is much more pervasive than that. For example, compared with non-Aboriginal offenders, Aboriginal offenders are also known to have more extensive contact with the criminal justice system prior to their current incarceration period, their chances of reoffending are consistently rated as much higher, and the perceived likelihood of their successful reintegration into society is much lower (Trevethan et al., 2002b).

POSSIBLE EXPLANATIONS FOR ABORIGINAL OVERREPRESENTATION
How do we explain this overrepresentation of Aboriginal offenders in the Canadian criminal justice system? According to LaPrairie (1996), four possible, overlapping explanations have been provided:

1. Higher Aboriginal offending rates
2. The commission, by Aboriginal offenders, of offences that are more likely to result in prison sentences

TABLE 13.11 OFFENCES LEADING TO FEDERAL INCARCERATION: ABORIGINAL AND NON-ABORIGINAL OFFENDERS

Offence	Aboriginal	Non-Aboriginal
Homicide or attempted murder	29%	27%
Robbery	22%	25%
Sexual assault	17%	14%
Assault	15%	9%
Property offence	8%	10%
Drug offence	3%	8%
Impaired driving	1%	<1%

Source: Adapted from Trevethan et al., 2002b.

3. Criminal justice policies and practices that have a differential impact on Aboriginal offenders due to their socioeconomic conditions

4. Differential processing through the criminal justice system as a result of culture conflict and racial discrimination

Little research has examined any of these potential causes. Currently, the primary contributing factors appear to be a higher Aboriginal offending rate and the fact that Aboriginal offenders tend to commit crimes that are more likely to result in prison sentences (i.e., crimes against the person) (LaPrairie, 1996). This is not to say, however, that the other two factors play no role at all. For example, as LaPrairie (1996) suggests, criminal justice policies and practices can have a differential impact on socially and economically disadvantaged Aboriginal offenders. Consider an Aboriginal offender who has committed a crime and receives a hefty fine. Due to his economic situation he cannot pay the fine and, as a result, gets sent to prison. This situation no doubt contributes to Aboriginal overrepresentation, since more Aboriginal than non-Aboriginal offenders are known to be serving time for fine defaults, but the first two factors listed above appear to be more important.

Risk Factors

As forensic psychologists, our goal must be to understand "why Aboriginal offenders are so disproportionately involved in and vulnerable to the policies and practices of the criminal justice system" (LaPrairie, 1996, p. 64). A significant part of this endeavour will likely involve an understanding of the various risk factors that Aboriginal offenders possess. Based on existing research, it is clear that Aboriginal offenders generally represent a particularly high-risk group with respect to both their childhood and adult backgrounds.

CHILDHOOD RISK FACTORS When surveyed, a large number of Aboriginal offenders report serious traumas in their childhood that could have potentially contributed to their later involvement with the criminal justice system. For example, Johnston (2000) reports the results from two studies he conducted with Aboriginal offenders in Canadian federal institutions. As shown in Table 13.12 on the next page, both studies indicate similar traumatic experiences, ranging from learning problems to physical abuse, occurring in a significant portion of each sample. Another recent study has confirmed that early childhood instability is prevalent among Aboriginal offenders and perhaps more so than in non-Aboriginal offenders. Trevethan, Moore, Auger, MacDonald, and Sinclair (2002c) interviewed 175 Aboriginal and 148 non-Aboriginal offenders in Canadian federal institutions and found that a significantly higher proportion of Aboriginal offenders rated their childhood as unstable (36% versus 26%) and were involved in the child welfare system (63% versus 36%). Compared with non-Aboriginal offenders, Aboriginal offenders in Trevethan et al.'s (2002c) study also reported significantly higher rates of family violence in their

TABLE 13.12 CHILDHOOD BACKGROUND INFORMATION FROM JOHNSTON'S STUDIES

Background Factor	1994 Sample	1997 Sample
Alcohol abuse	84.4%	57.9%
Behavioural problems	65.6%	57.1%
Drug abuse	50%	60.4%
Physical abuse	50%	45.2%
Parental absence	35.9%	41.4%
Poverty	35.9%	35.3%
Learning problems	15.6%	36.9%

Source: Adapted from Johnston, 2000.

household, higher rates of substance use by family members, poorer economic conditions while growing up, and more family members involved in criminal activity.

ADULT RISK FACTORS In adulthood, Aboriginal offenders also appear to exhibit a range of risk factors. Many of these risk factors appear to be the same ones that non-Aboriginal offenders exhibit. For example, Bonta, LaPrairie, and Wallace-Capretta (1997) set out to determine whether a risk assessment tool developed on non-Aboriginal offenders, the Manitoba Risk-Needs Scale, could be used successfully with Aboriginal offender populations. They collected data from 390 Aboriginal and 513 non-Aboriginal offenders and found that scores on the assessment scale were significantly related to recidivism for both their non-Aboriginal and Aboriginal sample. In addition, they found that almost all of the scale items that predicted risk in the non-Aboriginal sample also predicted risk in the Aboriginal sample. Included among these factors were a history of substance abuse, prior criminal convictions, antisocial attitudes, and association with antisocial peers.

These findings suggest that predictors of recidivism may, to some extent at least, be independent of culture, as some researchers have argued (e.g., Andrews & Bonta, 2003). This is not to say that Aboriginal-specific factors are unimportant, however. Recent research suggests that there are a number of factors specific to Aboriginal offenders that may assist in predicting whether an offender will reoffend. For example, in a study by Sioui and Thibault (2002), participation in cultural and spiritual activities while incarcerated, and involvement in Aboriginal-specific education and employment programs, were both related to decreases in recidivism for Aboriginal offenders.

RECIDIVISM Regardless of whether Aboriginal and non-Aboriginal offenders exhibit the same risk factors, it now seems to be generally accepted that Aboriginal offenders reoffend at a significantly higher rate than non-Aboriginal offenders, at least at the federal level. For example, Sioui and Thibault (2002) examined the recidivism rates (i.e., technical violations or new offences) of 30 041 male offenders who were released on day parole, full parole, or statutory release from federal penitentiaries in Canada. Eighty-four percent of these offenders were non-Aboriginal and the remaining 16% were Aboriginal. Consistent with other studies, Sioui and Thibault found that a larger proportion of Aboriginal than non-Aboriginal offenders were re-admitted to a federal institution, regardless of the type of release. More specifically, 18% of Aboriginal offenders were re-admitted in the first six months after release, compared with 11% of non-Aboriginal offenders. What is not yet clear is whether these findings hold for offenders serving time in provincial prisons. For example, Bonta (1989) found only nonsignificant differences in the re-incarceration rates for Aboriginal and non-Aboriginal offenders when he examined offenders released from provincial institutions (incarceration rates of 43.8% and 42.3%, respectively, one year after release). The reasons for these differences between federal and provincial offenders are not yet understood and require further research.

Treatment

Although Aboriginal and non-Aboriginal offenders often exhibit similar sorts of treatment needs while incarcerated, the level of need is not the same (La Prairie, 1996). Studies have consistently shown that larger proportions of Aboriginal offenders are rated as being high need. For example, Trevethan and her colleagues (2002b) recently conducted a study where they compared the treatment needs of Aboriginal and non-Aboriginal offenders in federal custody. They found that Aboriginal offenders were rated as having higher treatment needs in the following areas: personal/emotional issues, substance abuse, employment, marital/family issues, and social interactions/peer associations (see Figure 13.2 on the next page). In contrast, the only domain in which non-Aboriginal offenders were rating as having higher treatment needs was with their attitudes.

ABORIGINAL CORRECTIONAL PROGRAMS It is often assumed that loss of culture is at the heart of the Aboriginal overrepresentation problem. This has led to the belief that re-establishing culture is at least part of the solution, thus prompting correctional agencies to develop and implement a range of programs tailored to Aboriginal offenders in provincial and federal custody, as well as in the community. The correctional programs that are now being offered to Aboriginal offenders through CSC include traditional spiritual practices, substance abuse treatment, Aboriginal literacy classes, Aboriginal cultural skills, sweat lodge ceremonies, and family violence programs (LaPrairie, 1996). In the next section we will discuss one particular program that is receiving a lot of attention from researchers and practitioners—**Aboriginal healing lodges.**

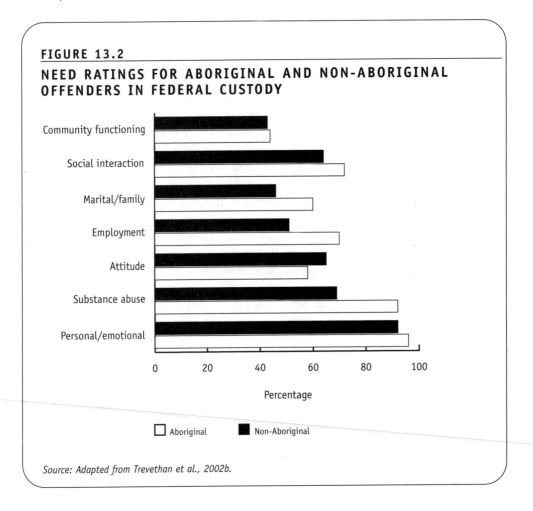

FIGURE 13.2

NEED RATINGS FOR ABORIGINAL AND NON-ABORIGINAL OFFENDERS IN FEDERAL CUSTODY

Source: Adapted from Trevethan et al., 2002b.

HEALING LODGES FOR ABORIGINAL OFFENDERS Section 81 of the Corrections and Conditional Release Act allows for the Aboriginal community to take responsibility for overseeing Aboriginal offenders under certain conditions (e.g., the offender must agree to the arrangement). This enables the Aboriginal community to provide correctional services to Aboriginal offenders in a manner that respects the culture of Aboriginal people. These services are often provided in Aboriginal healing lodges, which were initially introduced by CSC about ten years ago. According to CSC (2004, p. 1), healing lodges

> offer services and programs that reflect Aboriginal culture in a space that incorporates Aboriginal peoples' tradition and beliefs. In the healing lodge, the needs of Aboriginal offenders serving federal sentences are addressed through Aboriginal teachings and ceremonies, contact with Elders and children, and interaction with nature. A holistic philosophy governs the approach, whereby individualized programming is delivered within a context of community interaction, with a focus on preparing for release. In the healing lodges, an

emphasis is placed on spiritual leadership and on the value of the life experience of staff members, who act as role models.

Currently, there are nine Aboriginal healing lodges across Canada. These healing lodges differ in many ways but they all focus on providing correctional services that respect the Aboriginal culture (Crutcher & Trevethan, 2002). Some of the lodges are managed directly by CSC, whereas Aboriginal agencies or communities manage others. Only one of the lodges is for female offenders (see Box 13.6). Some healing lodges offer correctional programs in structures that resemble correctional facilities, while others offer their programs in structures that are more traditional in nature (Crutcher & Trevethan, 2002; see the photograph of the Okimaw Ohci spiritual lodge in Box 13.6).

BOX 13.6 THE OKIMAW OHCI HEALING LODGE

The spiritual lodge at the Okimaw Ohci Healing Lodge for women offenders.

Opened in November 1995, the CSC-run Okimaw Ohci Healing Lodge is the only North American correctional facility designed specifically for female Aboriginal offenders. Okimaw Ohci is Cree for Thunder Hills, the location in Maple Creek, Saskatchewan, where the healing lodge is located. The healing lodge consists of 28 shared accommodation beds, two segregation cells, and a spiritual lodge built in the form of a teepee. Okimaw Ohci provides a range of programs for its residents. Like other correctional facilities in Canada, some of these programs consist of conventional anger-management classes and substance-abuse programs. Other programs focus more directly on promoting healing through cultural means, such as sweetgrass ceremonies.

One particularly important aspect of the healing lodge is its mother–child program, which consists of several toddlers living full-time with their mothers at the lodge. This reflects the belief within the Aboriginal community that children can play a central role in the healing process of adults. Nature also plays a role in the rehabilitation process at Okimaw Ohci and a variety of wildlife, including beavers, moose, and deer, are regularly seen by the residents. Okimaw Ohci will accommodate federally sentenced female Aboriginal and non-Aboriginal offenders for all or part of their sentence (though the large majority of offenders have been Aboriginal). By December 2003, the Lodge had accepted more than 170 offender transfers. The number of residents who have been re-admitted (for committing a new offence) after release from Okimaw Ohci is relatively low (approximately 12%).

Sources: Warick, 1997; Trevethan et al., 2002a.

Little research is available on the effectiveness of Aboriginal healing lodges. The research that does exist can be divided into three categories: research that has examined recidivism in Aboriginal offenders once they leave the healing lodge, indirect research that has examined the impact of culture-specific interventions more generally, and survey research that has focused on the views of offenders who have served time in healing lodges. To some extent, the research findings that emerge from these studies are contradictory.

For example, direct research indicates that, of the 426 healing lodge residents that have so far been released, 166 of them have been re-admitted to a federal facility (Trevethan et al., 2002a). According to Trevethan and her colleagues, half of these re-admissions were for technical violations (e.g., failing to appear at the probation office at a scheduled time) and half were for the commission of a new offence. The recidivism rate for new offences was approximately 19%, which is significantly higher than the 13% recidivism rate for new offences for Aboriginal offenders released from minimum-security facilities. It must be noted, however, that significant differences exist in the recidivism rates across healing lodges (with some rates being about 13%) and that, at intake, residents of healing lodges are assessed as higher risk to reoffend than Aboriginal offenders in minimum-security facilities (Trevethan et al., 2002a).

These findings are unexpected given the results of research from the other two categories. For example, a number of studies have found that culturally appropriate programs for Aboriginal offenders contribute to program completion and decreases in recidivism. For instance, Ellerby and MacPherson (2001) found that traditional Aboriginal healing methods are more effective than non-Aboriginal approaches for treating Aboriginal sex offenders. Furthermore, Sioui and Thibault (2001) found that elder involvement and participation in cultural and spiritual activities was associated with a decrease in recidivism in Aboriginal offenders. Moreover, some research has suggested that program delivery by Aboriginal staff is also important. Johnston (1997), for example, found that Aboriginal offenders were more comfortable dealing with Aboriginal staff and viewed them as more trustworthy than non-Aboriginal staff.

Surveys of offenders serving their time in healing lodges also indicate that healing lodges are viewed in a positive light and should result in lower recidivism rates compared with conventional correctional programs. For example, Pfeifer and Hart-Mitchell (2001), who examined provincial offenders at Wahpeton Healing Lodge in Saskatchewan, found that many offenders were more comfortable participating in cultural activities at the lodge because the staff were more attentive and nonjudgmental than institutional staff. In addition, the offenders generally felt that the culture-specific programming would enable them to trust people, stay out of trouble, and deal more positively with their problems. Likewise, in their interviews with healing lodge residents, Crutcher and Trevethan (2002) found that 80% of offenders were very satisfied with their experience at the healing lodge. They felt that the healing lodge helped them better understand themselves, and they felt less angry and more in control of their behaviour.

Is an End to Aboriginal Overrepresentation in Sight?

No simple answer exists to this question, just as no simple answer exists as to why Aboriginal overrepresentation occurs in the first place. To be sure, various objectives are being pursued to bring the problem of Aboriginal overrepresentation to an end. For example, policies and procedures that have been put in place by both government and criminal justice agencies appear to be having a limited effect on the rate of overrepresentation in recent years (Roberts & Melchers, 2003). Unfortunately, other factors are clearly working against these attempts. The two factors discussed most often are the increase in the Aboriginal youth population and the growing concentration of Aboriginal people in urban areas, especially in the Western provinces (Boe, 2000).

Compared with the general Canadian population, the Aboriginal population in Canada today is much younger and, as a consequence, "there are proportionally many more Aboriginal people in the *high-risk* youth age groups" (italics added, Boe, 2002, p. 13). For example, according to Boe (2000), the average age of the Aboriginal population was 25.5 years in 1996, compared with an approximate average age in the general Canadian population of 35 years. Furthermore, children under 15 years of age accounted for about 35% of the Aboriginal population in 1996, compared with 20% of the general population. Given the higher birth rate that exists in the Canadian Aboriginal community, this problem can only increase. Indeed, as Boe (2000) reports, in 1996 there were approximately 144 000 Aboriginal people in Canada between the ages of 15 and 24. Based on Statistics Canada projections, this number is likely to increase to 181 000 by 2006.

If current trends continue, chances are that these young individuals will also primarily reside in urban areas. For example, in 1951, approximately 27% of Aboriginal people lived in urban areas. By 1996, this percentage rose to a staggering 63% (LaPrairie, 2002). The relocation of Aboriginal people into large urban areas is expected to increase the chances of Aboriginal overrepresentation in the criminal justice system because Aboriginal groups living in urban areas are more likely to become involved with the criminal justice system (LaPrairie, 1992, 2002). The reason for this appears to be that many of the Aboriginal people leaving reserves lack the education and skills needed to make it in large urban areas, and some suffer from substance abuse problems that contribute to their involvement in crime (LaPrairie, 1996).

What these findings indicate is that criminal justice interventions may help manage Aboriginal overrepresentation in the short term, but large-scale social issues need to be addressed if we ever hope to eliminate the problem totally.

SUMMARY

1. The Juvenile Delinquents Act (JDA) in 1908 was the first piece of legislation in Canada to address youthful offenders. In 1984, the Young Offender's Act (YOA) replaced the JDA with several notable changes to youth justice. Although the YOA underwent several amendments, it was finally replaced in 2003 with the Youth Criminal Justice Act.

2. There are three common disorders diagnosed in youthful offenders; attention-deficit hyperactivity disorder, oppositional defiant disorder, and conduct disorder. Young children diagnosed with conduct disorder are at greatest risk for youthful and adult criminal offending.

3. Risk factors increase the likelihood of behavioural (and emotional) disorders in children and youth. These include individual factors such as difficult tempera-ment, familial factors such as poor parental supervision, school factors such as reading difficulties, and social factors such as delinquent peers. Protective factors provide a buffer against the risk factors a child may experience. Protective factors include individual factors such as adaptive coping mechanisms, familial factors such as a warm and caring parent–child relationship, and social factors such as positive role models.

4. Women engage in much lower rates of offending than do men. Although gender-specific risk factors may exist, the research to date has found more similarities than differences in both adolescents and adults. Compared with male offenders, female offenders are more likely to be victims of physical and sexual abuse, to engage in suicidal and self-injurious behaviours, to have less extensive criminal histories, and to have elevated rates of mental disorders.

5. Battered woman syndrome (BWS) is now being used in trials that involve bat-tered women who kill their batterers. The two key components of BWS often pre-sented by court experts are learned helplessness and the cycle-of-violence theory.

6. There are four common explanations for Aboriginal overrepresentation. These include (1) a higher Aboriginal offending rate, (2) the commission by Aboriginal offenders of crimes that are more likely to result in prison sentences, (3) criminal justice practices that have a differential impact on Aboriginal offenders due to their socioeconomic situation, and (4) differential processing through the crimi-nal justice system as a result of discrimination. Although all factors probably contribute to Aboriginal overrepresentation, the two primary factors appear to be higher offending rates and the commission of offences that are more likely to result in prison sentences.

7. To deal with the issue of Aboriginal overrepresentation in the criminal justice sys-tem, Aboriginal-specific correctional programs have been developed. One of these programs involves transferring offenders out of prisons and into Aboriginal heal-

ing lodges. These lodges provide conventional correctional programs, such as substance abuse counselling, but they also have an Aboriginal focus, stressing Aboriginal teachings and ceremonies, contact with elders and children, and interaction with nature. Research that has examined the effectiveness of these healing lodges, in terms of offender rehabilitation, is mixed.

KEY CONCEPTS

Aboriginal healing lodge 433	dialectical behaviour	oppositional defiant
attention deficit	therapy 427	disorder 405
hyperactivity disorder 404	diversion 400	protective factors 412
battered woman	extrajudicial 401	resilient 412
syndrome 422	externalizing problems 404	risk factors 410
conduct disorder 405	internalizing problems 404	self-defence 422
cycle-of-violence	learned helplessness 422	social learning theory 410
theory 422	multisystemic therapy 414	

DISCUSSION QUESTIONS

1. Fifteen-year-old Andrew Smith was appearing before youth court justice Judge Brown for the third time in two years. Andrew's most current offences were robbery and possession of a handgun. Given the objectives of the Youth Criminal Justice Act, discuss sentencing options available to Judge Brown. Consider what option is most appropriate in this case. Why?

2. In your opinion, what factors should the courts consider when determining whether a young offender should be given an adult sentence?

3. Various unconventional treatment approaches have been proposed as a way of dealing with young offenders. We discussed boot camps in this chapter. Other approaches include taking young offenders to prison to witness first-hand the prison environment or taking young offenders to the morgue. Do you think these sorts of approaches will successfully rehabilitate young offenders? Why or why not?

4. Under what circumstances should expert testimony concerning battered woman syndrome be admissible in court? Do you think changes are needed to the self-defence plea?

5. There is controversy over whether gender-specific risk factors exist. Develop a study to address this issue.

6. As you saw in this chapter, a number of provisions are now in place to ensure that the special circumstances of Aboriginal offenders are considered when they come

into contact with the criminal justice system. For example, some Aboriginal offenders can now be transferred to Aboriginal communities in which they can reside in healing lodges. Do you think non-Aboriginal offenders should be given these same options? For example, should non-Aboriginal offenders be able to serve their sentence in an Aboriginal healing lodge instead of a regular minimum-security facility? Why or why not?

7. The government of Canada has just proposed a new policy it believes will reduce the problem of Aboriginal overrepresentation in the criminal justice system by the year 2010. Develop a study that will allow the government to determine whether the policy is working.

ADDITIONAL INFORMATION

Readings

Hoge, R.D., & Andrews, D.A. (1996). *Assessing the youthful offender: Issues and techniques.* New York: Plenum.

Vallée, B. (1998). *Life and death with Billy.* Toronto: Random House.

LaPrairie, C. (1996). *Examining Aboriginal corrections.* Ottawa: Solicitor General of Canada, Corrections Branch.

Web Sites

The Institute for the Study of Antisocial Behaviour in Youth
www.iay.org

The Canadian Associations of the Elizabeth Fry Societies
www.elizabethfry.ca

The Aboriginal Initiative Program at Correctional Service Canada
www.csc-scc.gc.ca/text/prgrm/correctional/abissues/who_e.shtml

GLOSSARY

Aboriginal healing lodge A facility in which Aboriginal offenders can be exposed to correctional services in an environment that incorporates Aboriginal traditions and beliefs

Absolute discharge The defendant is released into the community without restrictions to his or her behaviour

Absolute judgment Witness compares each lineup member to his or her memory of the culprit to decide whether the lineup member is the culprit

Access Noncustodial parents' right to see their children

Actuarial prediction Decisions are based on risk factors that are selected and combined based on their empirical or statistical association with a specific outcome

Actus reus A wrongful deed

Adaptive coping skills Skills that allow people to deal more effectively with stressful events

Adjournment Delaying the trial to some time in the future

Alternate forms reliability Coefficient of association between two forms of the same measure

Anatomically detailed dolls A doll, sometimes like a rag doll, that is consistent with the male or female anatomy

Anger rapist A rapist, as defined by Groth, who uses more force than necessary to obtain compliance from the victim and who engages in a variety of sexual acts to degrade the victim

Anterograde amnesia Memory deficits consisting of an impaired ability to establish new memories

Antisocial personality disorder (APD) A personality disorder characterized by a history of behaviour in which the rights of others are violated

Assent Agreeableness to participate

Assessment centre A facility in which the behaviour of police applicants can be observed in a number of situations by multiple observers

Attention deficit hyperactivity disorder (ADHD) A disorder in a youth characterized by a persistent pattern of inattention and hyperactivity or impulsivity

Automatism Unconscious, involuntary behaviour such that the person committing the act is not aware of what he or she is doing

Base rate Represents the percentage of people within a given population who engage in a specific behaviour or have a mental disorder

Baseline Normal pattern of responding

Battered woman syndrome (BWS) A collection of symptoms and behaviours believed to be common to women who have experienced chronic and severe intimate abuse

Biased lineup A lineup that "suggests" who the police suspect and thereby who the witness should identify

Black sheep effect When evidence is strong, similarity between defendant and jury leads to punitiveness

Broad based approach Approach to scientific jury selection that starts with the presumption that there are certain traits or attitudes that people have that make them more likely to be pro-prosecution versus pro-defence

Capping Notion introduced through Bill C-30 where there is a maximum period of time a person with a mental illness could be affected by their disposition

Case-specific approach Approach to scientific jury selection that starts with the issues and facts of the case. A specific questionnaire then is developed assessing a number of characteristics that may influence the verdict

Challenge for cause An option to reject biased jurors

441

Change of venue Moving a trial to a community other than the one in which the crime occurred

Child molester Someone who has actually sexually molested a child. See also pedophile

Classic trait model A model of personality that assumes the primary determinants of behaviour are stable, internal traits

Clinical forensic psychologists Psychologists who are broadly concerned with the assessment and treatment of mental health issues as they pertain to the law or legal system

Clinical risk factors Types and symptoms of mental disorders (e.g., substance abuse)

Coerced-compliant false confessions A confession that results from a desire to escape a coercive interrogation environment or gain a benefit promised by the police

Coerced-internalized false confessions A confession that results from suggestive interrogation techniques, whereby the confessor actually comes to believe he or she committed the crime

Cognitive ability tests Procedure for measuring verbal, mathematical, memory, and reasoning abilities

Cognitive interview Interview procedure for use with eyewitnesses based on principles of memory storage and retrieval

Cohort effects The effect of belonging to a given generation that may be responsible for differences on the dependent variable

Community service A sentence that involves the offender performing a duty in the community, often as a way of paying off a fine

Community treatment order Sentence that allows the mentally ill offender to live in the community, with the stipulation that the person will agree to treatment or detention in the event his or her condition deteriorates

Competency inquiry Questions posed to child witnesses under 14 to determine whether they are able to communicate the evidence and understand the difference between the truth and a lie, and in the circumstances of testifying, feel compelled to tell the truth

Compliance A tendency to go along with demands made by people perceived to be in authority, even though the person may not agree with them

Conditional discharge A defendant is released; however, release carries certain conditions (e.g., not to possess firearms) that the defendant must meet. Failure to meet the conditions imposed with a conditional discharge may result in the defendant being incarcerated or sent to a psychiatric facility

Conditional sentence A sentence served in the community

Conduct disorder (CD) A disorder characterized by a persistent pattern of behaviour in which a youth violates the rights of others or age-appropriate societal norms or rules

Confabulation Making things up

Confederate Someone who is hired by the researcher and is informed to act in a certain way to produce an experimental condition

Confound When a variable co-varies with the independent variable that the researcher is unaware of

Contextual risk factor Risk factors that refer to aspects of the current environment (e.g., access to victims or weapons). Sometimes called situational risk factors

Control Question Test Type of polygraph test that includes irrelevant questions that are unrelated to the crime, relevant questions concerning the crime being investigated, and control questions concerning the person's honesty and past history prior to the event being investigated

Convergent validity The degree that different measures that are intended to measure the same construct produce similar results

Correlation coefficient The statistic used to describe the relationship between variables and is a number that can vary from −1.00 to +1.00

Countermeasures   As applied to polygraph research, techniques used to try to conceal guilt

Criminal profiling   An investigative technique for identifying the major personality and behavioural characteristics of an individual based upon an analysis of the crimes he or she has committed

Criterion-based content analysis (CBCA)   Criteria used to distinguish truthful from false statements made by children

Cronbach's alpha   Coefficient that results by correlating the response for each item with each other item from a measure

Cross-race effect   The phenomenon of witnesses remembering own-race faces with greater accuracy than faces from other races. Also known as the other-race effect

Cue-utilization hypothesis   Proposed by Easterbrook (1959) to explain why a witness may focus on the weapon rather than other details. The hypothesis suggests that when emotional arousal increases, attentional capacity decreases

Culprit   The guilty person who committed the crime

Cycle of violence theory   The theory that within intimate violence there is a tension-building phase, an acute battering act phase, and a contrition phase

Dangerous offender   A label attached to offenders who are proven to constitute a significant danger to others

***Daubert* criteria**   A standard for accepting expert testimony, which states that scientific evidence is valid if the research upon which it is based has been peer reviewed, is testable, has a recognized rate of error, and adheres to professional standards

Day parole   A form of parole that allows the offender to enter the community for up to one day (e.g., for the purpose of attending correctional programs)

Deception detection   Detecting when someone is being deceptive

Deductive criminal profiling   Profiling the background characteristics of an unknown offender based on evidence left at the crime scenes by that particular offender

Defensiveness   Conscious denial or extreme minimization of physical or psychological symptoms

Deliberation   When jury members discuss the evidence privately among themselves to reach a verdict that is then provided to the court

Demand characteristics   Any factors (including experimenter bias) present in the study, other than the independent variables, that suggest to the participant how to respond

Dependent variables   Variables that are measured

Dialectical behaviour therapy (DBT)   Therapy designed to treat borderline personality disordered patients

Direct question recall   Witnesses are asked a series of specific questions about the crime or the culprit

Dispositional risk factor   Risk factors that reflect the individual's traits, tendencies, or styles (e.g., negative attitudes)

Disputed confessions   A confession that is later disputed at trial

Distractors   Lineup members who are known to be innocent for the crime in question. Also known as foils

Divergent validity   The degree to which measures purported to assess different constructs do not agree with each other

Diversion   A decision not to prosecute a young offender but rather have him or her undergo an educational or community-service program. Also an option for the courts dealing with offenders with mental illnesses who are facing minor charges. The court can divert the offender directly into a treatment program rather than have him or her go through the court process

Domestic violence   Any violence occurring between family members

Dynamic risk factor Risk factors that fluctuate over time and are amenable to changing

Dysphoric/borderline batterer A male spousal batterer who exhibits some violence outside the family, is depressed and has borderline personality traits, and has problems with jealousy

Effect size A measure of the strength of the relationship between the independent and dependent variable

Elimination lineup Lineup procedure for children that first asks them to pick out the person who looks most like the culprit from the photos displaced. Next, children are asked if the most similar person selected is in fact the culprit

Emotional maltreatment Acts or omissions by caregivers that cause or could cause serious behavioural, cognitive, emotional, or mental disorders

Enhanced cognitive interview Interview procedure that includes various principles of social dynamics in addition to the memory retrieval principles used in the original cognitive interview

Estimator variables Variables that are present at the time of the crime and that cannot be changed

Event-related brain potentials (ERP) Brain activity measured by placing electrodes on the scalp and electrical patterns related to presentation of a stimulus are recorded

Exhibitionist Someone who obtains sexual gratification by exposing genitals to strangers

Experimental forensic psychologists Psychologists who are broadly concerned with the study of human behaviour as it relates to the law or legal system

Experimenter bias The subtle cues that are displayed by the researcher suggesting how a participant should respond

Expert witness A witness who provides the court with information (often an opinion on a particular matter) that assists the court in understanding an issue of relevance to a case

External validity The degree to which we can generalize our results to different populations, settings, and conditions

Externalizing problems Behavioural difficulties such as delinquency, fighting, bullying, lying, or destructive behaviour experienced by a youth

Extra-familial child molester Someone who sexually abuses children not related to the abuser

Extrajudicial Term applied to measures taken to keep young offenders out of court and out of custody (e.g., giving a warning or making a referral for treatment)

Extroversion A personality trait that some researchers believe is the result of cortical underarousal

Fabricating Making false claims

Factitious disorder A disorder in which the person's physical and psychological symptoms are intentionally produced and are adopted to assume the role of a sick person

Fair lineup A lineup where the suspect does not stand out from the other lineup members

False confession A confession that is either intentionally fabricated or is not based on actual knowledge of the facts that form its content

False memory syndrome Term to describe clients' false beliefs that they were sexually abused as children, having no memories of this abuse until they enter therapy to deal with some other psychological problem such as depression or substance abuse

False negative An incorrect prediction that occurs when a person is predicted not to engage in some type of behaviour (e.g., violent acts) but does

False positive An incorrect prediction that occurs when a person is predicted to engage in some type of behaviour (e.g., violent acts) but does not

Family-only batterer A male spousal batterer who is typically not violent outside the home, does not show much psychopathology, and does not posses negative attitudes supportive of violence

Femicide   Killing of women

Fine   A sentence where the offender has to make a monetary payment to the courts

Fixated child molester   A child molester, as defined by Groth, who has a long-standing, exclusive sexual orientation preference for children

Foils   Lineup members who are known to be innocent for the crime in question. Also known as distractors

Forensic psychiatry   A field of medicine that deals with all aspects of human behaviour as it relates to the law or legal system

Forensic psychology   A field of psychology that deals with all aspects of human behaviour as it relates to the law or legal system

Free narrative   Witnesses are asked to either write or orally state all they remember about the event without the officer (or experimenter) asking questions. Also known as open-ended recall

Full parole   A form of parole that allows the offender to serve the remainder of his or her sentence under supervision in the community

Fundamental principle of sentencing   Belief that sentences should be proportionate to the gravity of the offence and the degree of responsibility of the offender

General acceptance test   A standard for accepting expert testimony, which states that expert testimony will be admissible in court if the basis of the testimony is generally accepted within the relevant scientific community

General deterrence   Sentencing in order to reduce the probability that members of the general public will offend in the future

Generally violent/antisocial batterer   A male spousal batterer who is violent outside the home, engages in other criminal acts, has drug and alcohol problems, has impulse-control problems, and possesses violence-supportive beliefs

Geographic profiling systems   Computer systems that use mathematical models of offender spatial behaviour to make predictions about where unknown serial offenders are likely to reside

Geographic profiling   An investigative technique that uses crime scene locations to predict the most likely area where an offender resides

Ground truth   As applied to polygraph research, the knowledge of whether the person is actually guilty or innocent

Gudjonsson Compliance Scale   A scale developed by Gisli Gudjonsson that is used to measure a person's level of compliance

Gudjonsson Suggestibility Scale   A scale developed by Gisli Gudjonsson that is used to measure a person's level of suggestibility

Guilty Knowledge Test   Type of polygraph test designed to determine if the person knows details about a crime

Hearsay   A second party reports what another said

Heuristics   Shortcuts people use to help make decisions

Historical risk factor   Risk factor that refers to events that have been experienced in the past (e.g., age at first arrest). Also known as static risk factor

Hung jury   A jury that cannot reach a unanimous verdict

Hypnotically refreshed memory   Where a hypnotized person is able to produce a greater number of details than a person who has not been hypnotized

Hypothesis   A testable explanation for a phenomenon

Idiographic   An attempt to understand something by examining the specific details of individual cases

Illusory correlation   Belief that a correlation exists between two events that in reality are either not correlated or correlated to a much lesser degree

Impartiality   A characteristic of jurors who are unbiased

Imprisonment   A sentence served in prison

In need of protection   A term used to describe a child's need to be separated from his or his caregiver due to maltreatment

Incidence   Number of new cases in a specific population occurring in a given time period, usually a year

Independent variables   Variables that are manipulated or selected to be examined

Inductive criminal profiling   Profiling the background characteristics of an unknown offender based on what we know about other solved cases

Infanticide   Although the term literally means killing of an infant, it has been used more specifically to refer to a woman killing her newly born child due to a mental disorder arising from the effects of childbirth

Informed consent   An explicitly expressed willingness to participate in a research project based on clear understanding of the nature of the research, of the consequences of participating (or not participating), and of all factors that might be expected to influence willingness to participate

Insanity   Impairment of mental or emotional functioning that affects perceptions, beliefs, and motivations at the time of the offence

Instigators   In social learning theory, these are events in the environment that act as a stimulus for acquired behaviours

Instrumental aggression   Violence that is premeditated, calculated behaviour, motivated by some goal. Also known as predatory violence

Internal validity   The degree to which differences in the dependent variable can be attributed to the effect of the independent variable rather than some other ambiguous variable

Internalization   Accepting that something suggested to you is true

Internalizing problems   Emotional difficulties such as anxiety, depression, and obsessions experienced by a youth

Inter-rater reliability   The degree to which different raters give similar ratings to each report

Intimate partner violence   Any violence occurring between intimate partners who are living together or separated. Also known as spousal violence

Intra-familial child molesters   People who sexually abuse their own biological children or children for whom they assume a parental role, such as a stepfather or live-in boyfriend. Also known as incest offenders

Investigator bias   Bias that can result when police officers enter an interrogation setting already believing that the suspect is guilty

Inwald Personality Inventory   An assessment instrument used to identify police applicants who are suitable for police work by measuring their personality attributes and behaviour patterns

Job analysis   A procedure for identifying the knowledge, skills, and abilities that make up a good police officer

Jury Act   Provincial and territorial legislation that outlines the eligibility criteria for jury service and how prospective jurors must be selected

Jury nullification   Occurs when a jury ignores the law and the evidence, rendering a verdict based on some other criteria

Jury summons   A court order that states a time and place to go for jury duty

Known-groups design   As applied to malingering research, involves comparing genuine patients and malingers attempting to fake the disorder the patients have

Learned helplessness   A learned passive and withdrawing response to events in which the person perceives he or she has little control

Learning theories   Theories that attempt to explain criminal conduct by focusing on principles of conditioning (e.g., being rewarded for criminal behaviour)

Leniency bias   When jurors move toward greater leniency during deliberations

Levels   Variations of a particular independent variable

Lineup   A set of people presented to the witness who must state whether the culprit is present and, if so, which one

Linkage blindness   An inability on the part of the police to link geographically dispersed serial crimes committed by the same offender because of a lack of information sharing among police agencies

Long-term offender   A label attached to offenders who are proven to be a high risk for reoffending

Malingering   Intentionally faking psychological or physical symptoms for some type of external gain

Mandatory charging policies   Policies that give police the authority to lay charges against a suspect where there is reasonable and probable grounds to believe a domestic assault has occurred

Maximization techniques   Scare tactics used by police interrogators that are designed to intimidate a suspect believed to be guilty

Memory impairment hypothesis
Explanation for the misinformation effect where the original memory is replaced with the new, incorrect, information

Mens rea   Criminal intent

Minimization techniques   Soft sell tactics used by police interrogators that are designed to lull the suspect into a false sense of security

Minnesota Multiphasic Personality Inventory
An assessment instrument for identifying people with psychopathological problems

Misinformation acceptance hypothesis
Explanation for the misinformation effect where the incorrect information is provided because the witness guesses what the officer or experimenter wants the response to be

Misinformation effect   Phenomenon where a witness who is presented with inaccurate information after an event will incorporate that "misinformation" in a subsequent recall task. Also known as post-event information effect

***Mohan* criteria**   A standard for accepting expert testimony, which states that expert testimony will be admissible in court if the testimony is relevant, necessary for assisting the trier of fact, does not violate any exclusionary rules, and is provided by a qualified expert

Multisystemic therapy (MST)   A treatment approach that considers the youth in the various contexts or systems he or she exists—family, peers, school, neighbourhood, and community

Munchausen syndrome   A rare factitious disorder in which a person intentionally produces a physical complaint and constantly seeks physician consultations, hospitalizations, and even surgery to treat the nonexistent illness

Narrative elaboration   An interview procedure whereby children learn to organize their story into relevant categories—participants, settings, actions, conversation/affective states, and consequences

National Parole Board   The organization in Canada responsible for making parole decisions

Need principle   Principle that correctional interventions should target known criminogenic needs (i.e., factors that relate to reoffending)

Neglect/failure to provide   When a child's caregivers do not provide the requisite attention to the child's emotional, psychological, or physical development

Neuroticism   A personality trait that some researchers believe is the result of an overreactive autonomic nervous system

Nomothetic   An attempt to understand something by uncovering broad patterns and general trends

Norm   Average performance

Observational learning   Learning behaviours by watching others perform these behaviours

Observer drift   Occurs when an observer changes how he or she is coding behaviours over time due to fatigue or boredom

Occupational stressors   In policing, stressors relating to the job itself

Open-ended recall   Witnesses are asked to either write or orally state all they remember about the event without the officer (or experimenter) asking questions. Also known as a free narrative

Operational definition   Definition of a concept in terms of the operations used to produce and measure it

Oppositional defiant disorder (ODD)   A disorder in a youth characterized by a persistent pattern of negativistic, hostile, and defiant behaviours

Organizational stressors   In policing, stressors relating to organizational issues

Organized-disorganized model   A profiling model used by the FBI that assumes that the crime scenes and backgrounds of serial offenders can be categorized as organized or disorganized

Other-race effect   Phenomenon of witnesses remembering own-race faces with greater accuracy than faces from other races. Also known as the cross-race effect

Parallel parenting   System that divides decision-making power between parents

Parole   The release of offenders from prison into the community before their sentence term is complete

Patriarchy   Broad set of cultural beliefs and values that support the male dominance of women

Pedophile   Person whose primary sexual orientation is towards children. See also child molester

Penile phallometry   A measurement device placed around the penis to measure changes in sexual arousal

Person characteristics   Characteristics that are part of the individual

Personality theories   Theories that attempt to explain criminal conduct by focusing on the personality makeup of offenders

Physical abuse   The deliberate application of force to any part of a child's body that results in or may result in a nonaccidental injury

Polarization   When individuals tend to become more extreme in their initial position following a group discussion

Police discretion   A policing task that involves discriminating between circumstances that require absolute adherence to the law and circumstances where a degree of latitude is justified

Police interrogation   A process whereby the police interview a suspect for the purpose of gathering evidence and obtaining a confession

Police selection procedures   A set of procedures used by the police to either screen out undesirable candidates or select in desirable candidates

Polygraph disclosure tests   Polygraph tests that are used to uncover information about an offender's past behaviour

Polygraph   A device for recording an individual's autonomic nervous system responses

Post-event information effect   Phenomenon where a witness who is presented with inaccurate information after an event will incorporate that "misinformation" in a subsequent recall task. Also known as the misinformation effect

Post-traumatic stress disorder   Anxiety disorder that can develop in response to exposure to an extremely traumatic event. Symptoms include frequent, distressing, and intrusive memories of the event, avoiding stimuli associated with the traumatic event, and persistent anxiety or increased arousal symptoms

Power rapist   A rapist, as defined by Groth, who seeks to establish dominance and control over the victim

Prevalence   In the study of child abuse, the proportion of a population at a specific point in time that was maltreated during childhood

Prima facie case   Case in which the Crown prosecutor must prove there is sufficient evidence to bring the case to trial

Privacy   The notion of an individual's right to decide how information about him or her is communicated to others, if at all

Probation   The defendant is released into the community with certain restrictions on his or her behaviour

Protective factors   Factors that mitigate or reduce the likelihood of a negative outcome (e.g., aggression, psychopathology)

Psychoanalytic theories   Theories that attempt to explain criminal conduct by focusing on dynamic internal forces within people and the importance of early childhood events and experiences

Psychology and the law   The use of psychology to examine the operation of the legal system

Psychology in the law   The use of psychology in the legal system as that system operates

Psychology of the law   The use of psychology to examine the law itself

Psychopath   An individual who is defined by a collection of interpersonal, affective, and behavioural characteristics including manipulation, lack of remorse or empathy, impulsivity, and antisocial behaviours

Racial profiling   Police-initiated action that relies on the race or ethnicity of an individual, rather than that individual's criminal behaviour

Random assignment   Experimental condition in which each participant starts off with an equal chance of being assigned to any one of the groups or conditions. Also known as randomization

Random error   Temporary chance fluctuations

Rape trauma syndrome   A group of symptoms or behaviours that are frequent aftereffects of having been raped

Rapist   People who sexually assault victims more than 16 years of age

Reactive aggression   Violence that is impulsive, unplanned, immediate, driven by negative emotions, and occurring in response to some perceived provocation. Also known as affective violence

Reactivity   The notion where an individual changes his or her behaviour when he or she is aware of being observed

Recall memory   Reporting details of a previously witnessed event or person

Recognition memory   Determining whether a previously seen item or person is the same as what is currently being viewed

Regressed child molester   A child molester, as defined by Groth, whose primary sexual orientation is for adults, but whose sexual interests revert to children after a stressful event or due to feelings of inadequacy

Regulators   In social learning theory, these are consequences of behaviours

Reid model   A nine-step model of interrogation used frequently in North America to extract confessions from suspects

Relapse prevention   A method of treatment designed to prevent the occurrence of an undesired behaviour (e.g., sexual assault)

Relative judgment   Witness compares lineup members to each other and the person that looks most like the culprit is identified

Relevant/Irrelevant Test   Type of polygraph test that includes relevant questions concerning the crime being investigated and irrelevant questions that are unrelated to the crime

Reliable   A measure that provides a consistent or similar result each time you use the measure

Reparations   A sentence where the offender has to make a monetary payment to the victim or the community

Representativeness   A jury composition that represents the community where the crime occurred

Resilient   Characteristic of a child who has multiple risk factors but who does not develop problem behaviours or negative symptoms

Resolution conference   Involves an offender and his or her family coming together with the victim and the police in an attempt to solve a problem

Responsivity principle   Principle that correctional interventions should match the general learning style of offenders

Restitution   See **reparations**

Retracted confessions   A confession that the confessor later declares to be false

Retrograde amnesia   Memory deficits consisting of an inability to recall specific, highly salient incidents from the past

Review boards   Legal bodies mandated to oversee the care and disposition of defendants found unfit and/or not criminally responsible on account of a mental disorder

Risk factor   A measurable feature of an individual that predicts the behaviour of interest (e.g. violence or psychopathology)

Risk principle   Principle that correctional interventions should target offenders who are at high risk to reoffend

Sadistic rapist   A rapist, as defined by Groth, who obtains sexual gratification by hurting the victim

Scientific jury selection   Rejecting prospective jurors who would be unsympathetic to one's case and accepting those who would be sympathetic based on predetermined characteristics

Selection interview   In recruiting police officers, an interview used by the police to determine the extent to which an applicant possesses the knowledge, skills, and abilities deemed important for the job

Self-defence   The principle that if you are attacked you should be able to take reasonable actions to defend yourself

Sentencing disparity   Variations in sentencing severity for similar crimes committed under similar circumstances

Sentencing guidelines   Guidelines that are intended to reduce the degree of discretion that judges have when handing down sentences

Sequential lineup   Alternative lineup procedure where the lineup members are presented serially to the witness and the witness must make a decision as to whether the lineup member is the culprit before seeing another member. Also a witness cannot ask to see previously seen photos and the witness is unaware of the number of photos to be shown

Sexual abuse   When an adult or youth uses a child for sexual purposes

Shift   The extent to which people who are completing the Gudjonsson Suggestibility Scale alter their answers when put under pressure by the interviewer

Showup   Identification procedure that shows one person to the witness; the suspect

Simulation design   As applied to malingering research, people are told to pretend they have specific symptoms or disorder

Simultaneous lineup   The most common lineup procedure that presents all lineup members at one time to the witness

Situational test   A simulation of a real-world policing task

Social learning theory   A theory of human behaviour based on learning from watching others in the social environment and reinforcement contingencies

Socially desirable responding   When a participant provides responses that make him or her look good rather than providing truthful responses

Somatoform disorders   A disorder in which physical symptoms suggest a physical illness but have no known underlying physiological cause and the symptoms are not intentionally produced

Source misattribution hypothesis
Explanation for the misinformation effect—

where the witness has two memories, the original and the misinformation; however, the witness cannot remember where each memory originated or the source of each

Specific deterrence   Sentencing in order to reduce the probability that an offender will reoffend in the future

Split-half reliability   Coefficient between two halves of the same measure

Standardization   Ensuring that the measure is administered the same way every time

Statement Validity Analysis (SVA)   A comprehensive protocol to distinguish truthful or false statements made by children containing three parts—a structured interview of the child witness, a systematic analysis of the verbal content of the child's statements (criteria-based content analysis), and the application of the statement validity checklist

Static risk factor   Risk factor that does not fluctuate over time and is not changed by treatment (e.g., age at first arrest). Also known as historical risk factor

Statutory release   The release of offenders from prison after they have served two-thirds of their sentence

Step-wise interview   Interview protocol with a series of "steps" designed to start the interview with the least leading and directive type of questioning then proceeding to more specific forms of questioning, as necessary

Structured professional judgment   Decisions are guided by a predetermined list of risk factors that have been selected from the research and professional literature. Judgment of risk level is based on the evaluator's professional judgment

Suggestibility   A tendency to accept information communicated during questioning

Suspect   A person the police "suspect" committed the crime, who may be guilty or innocent for the crime in question

System variables   Variables that can be manipulated to increase (or decrease) eyewitness accuracy

Systematic disparity   Consistent disagreement among judges about sentencing decisions due to factors such as how lenient judges think sentences should be

Target-absent lineup   A lineup that does not contain the culprit but contains innocent suspects

Target-present lineup   A lineup that contains the culprit

Temporary absence   A form of parole that allows the offender to enter the community on a temporary basis (e.g., for the purpose of attending correctional programs)

Test-retest coefficient   The coefficient that results between two test administrations of the same measure

Theory of maternal deprivation   Theory that early separation from one's mother plays a role in the development of antisocial behaviour

True negative   A correct prediction that occurs when a person who is predicted not to engage in some type of behaviour (e.g., violent act) does not

True positive   A correct prediction that occurs when a person who is predicted to engage in some type of behaviour (e.g., violent act) does so

Truth-bias   The tendency of people to judge more messages as truthful than deceptive

Unfit to stand trial   Refers to an inability to conduct a defence at any stage of the proceedings on account of a person's mental disorder

Unstructured clinical judgment   Decisions characterized by a substantial amount of professional discretion and lack of guidelines

Unsystematic disparity   Inconsistent disagreement among judges about sentencing decisions due to factors such as the judge's mood

Unwarranted sentencing disparity
Variations in sentencing severity for similar crimes committed under similar circumstances that result from reliance by the judge on legally irrelevant factors

Use-of-force continuum   A model that is supposed to guide police officer decision making in use-of-force situations by providing the officer with some guidance as to what level of force is appropriate given the suspect's behaviour and other environmental conditions

Valid   A measure that measures what it was set out to measure

VICLAS   The Violent Crime Linkage Analysis System, which was developed by the RCMP to collect and analyze information on serious crimes from across Canada

Voir dire   The question period when jurors are selected to serve on the jury

Voluntary false confessions   A false confession that is provided without any elicitation from the police

Voyeurs   People who obtain sexual gratification by observing unsuspecting people, usually strangers, who are either naked, in the process of undressing, or engaging in sexual activity

Walk-by   Identification procedure that occurs in a naturalistic environment. The police take the witness to a public location where the suspect is likely to be. Once the suspect is in view, the witness is asked whether he or she sees the culprit

Weapon focus   Term used to describe the phenomenon of a witness's attention being focused on the culprit's weapon rather than on the culprit

White lies   Untruthful statements told with no malicious intent

Yield   The extent to which people who are completing the Gudjonsson Suggestibility Scale give in to leading questions

REFERENCES

Abdollahi, M.K. (2002). Understanding police stress research. *Journal of Forensic Psychology Practice, 2,* 1–24.

Abel, G.G., Becker, J.V., Mittelman, M., & Cunningham-Rathner, J. (1987). Self-reported sex crimes of nonincarcerated paraphiliacs. *Journal of Interpersonal Violence, 2,* 3–25.

Aboriginal Legal Services of Toronto. (2001). Retrieved June 10, 2004, from http://www.aboriginallegal.ca/docs/apc_factsheet.htm

Aboriginal Task Force. (1989). *Task Force on Aboriginal Peoples in Federal Corrections: Final Report.* Ottawa, ON: Solicitor General of Canada.

Ackerman, M.J. (1999). *Forensic psychological assessment.* New York, NY: John Wiley & Sons.

Adams, K. (1999). *What we know about police use of force.* Washington, DC: U.S. Department of Justice.

Adams-Tucker, C. (1982). Proximate effects of sexual abuse in childhood: A report on 28 children. *American Journal of Psychiatry, 139,* 1252–1256.

Adler, F. (1975). *Sisters in crime: The rise of the new female criminal.* New York, NY: McGraw-Hill.

Affonso, D.D., & Domino, G. (1984). Postpartum depression: A review. *Birth: Issues in Perinatal Care and Education, 11,* 231–235.

Agosti, V. (1995). The efficacy of treatments in reducing alcohol consumption: A meta-analysis. *International Journal of the Addictions, 30,* 1067–1077.

Agrell, S. (2003, November 17). Liberals may shut youth boot camp. *National Post.* Retrieved June 1, 2004, from http://www.nationalpost.com/components/printstory/printstory.asp?id=2520BBE9-64CE

Ainsworth, P.B. (1993). *Psychological testing and police applicant selection: Difficulties and dilemmas.* Paper presented to the European Conference on Law and Psychology, Oxford, UK.

Aitken, C.C.G., Connolly, T., Gammerman, A., Zhang, G., Bailey, D., Gordon, R., & Oldfield, R. (1996). Statistical modelling in specific case analysis. *Science & Justice, 36,* 245–256.

Alarid, L.F., Burton, V S. Jr., & Cullen, F.T. (2000). Gender and crime among felony offenders: Assessing the generality of social control and differential association theories. *Journal of Research in Crime and Delinquency, 37,* 171–199.

Alexander, D.A., Innes, G., Irving, B.L., Sinclair, S.D., & Walker, L.G. (1991). *Health, stress and policing: A study in Grampian policing.* London, UK: The Police Foundation.

Alexander, M.A. (1999). Sexual offender treatment efficacy revisited. *Sexual Abuse: Journal of Research and Treatment, 11,* 101–116.

Alison, L.J., Bennell, C., Mokros, A., & Ormerod, D. (2002). The personality paradox in offender profiling: A theoretical review of the processes involved in deriving background characteristics from crime scene actions. *Psychology, Public Policy, and Law, 8,* 115–135.

Alison, L.J., Smith, M., & Morgan, K. (2003). Interpreting the accuracy of offender profiles. *Psychology, Crime and Law, 9,* 185–195.

Alison, L.J., Smith, M., Eastman, O., & Rainbow, L. (2003). Toulmin's philosophy of argument and its relevance to offender profiling. *Psychology, Crime and Law, 9,* 173–183.

Allen, J.J. & Iacono, W.G. (1997). A comparison of methods for the analysis of event-related potentials in deception detection. *Psychophysiology, 34,* 234–240.

Allen, J.J., Iacono, W.G., & Danielson, K.D. (1992). The identification of concealed memories using the event-related potential and implicit behavioral measures: A methodology for prediction in the face of individual differences. *Psychophysiology, 29,* 504–522.

Allen, J.J.B. (2002). The role of psychophysiology in clinical assessment: ERPs in the evaluation of memory. *Psychophysiology, 39,* 261–280.

Alpert, G.P., & Dunham, R. (1999). *The force factor: Measuring and assessing police use of force and suspect resistance.* Washington, DC: U.S. Department of Justice.

Amato, P.R. (2000). The consequences of divorce for adults and children. *Journal of Marriage and the Family, 62,* 1269–1287.

Amato, P.R., & Keith, B. (1991). Parental divorce and the well being of children: A meta-analysis. *Psychological Bulletin, 110,* 26–46.

American Board of Forensic Psychology & American Psychology-Law Society. (1995). *Petition for the recognition of a specialty in professional psychology* [Online]. Retrieved June 1, 2004, from http://www.unl.edu/ap-ls/petition.PDF

American Psychiatric Association (1994). *Diagnostic and statistical manual of mental disorders* (4th ed.). Washington, DC: American Psychiatric Association.

American Psychological Association. (2004). Retrieved June 8, 2004, from http://www.apa.org/psyclaw/jenkins.html

Ammerman, R.T., Cassisi, J.E., Hersen M., & Van Hasselt, V.B. (1986). Consequences of physical abuse and neglect in children. *Clinical Psychology Review, 6,* 291–310.

Anderson, C.A., & Dill, F.E. (2000). Video games and aggressive thoughts, feelings, and behavior in the laboratory and in life. *Journal of Personality and Social Psychology, 78,* 772–790.

Anderson, D.E., Ansfield, M., & DePaulo, B.M. (1999). Love's best habit: Deception in the context of relationships. In P. Philippot, R. S. Feldman & E. J. Coats (Eds.), *The social context of nonverbal behavior* (pp. 372–409). New York, NY: Cambridge University Press.

Anderson, M., Gillig, P.M., Sitaker, M., McCloskey, K., Malloy, K., & Grigsby, N. (2003). "Why doesn't she just leave?": A descriptive study of victim reported impediments to her safety. *Journal of Family Violence, 18,* 151–155.

Andrews, D. (2001). Principles of effective correctional programs. In L. Motiuk and R. Serin (Eds.), *Compendium 2000 on effective correctional programming* (pp. 9–17). Ottawa: Correctional Service Canada.

Andrews, D., Dowden, C., & Gendreau, P. (1999). *Clinically relevant and psychologically informed approaches to reduced reoffending: A meta-analytic study of human service, risk, need, responsivity, and other concerns in justice contexts.* Unpublished manuscript, Carleton University.

Andrews, D., Robblee, M., & Saunders, R. (1984). *The sentencing factors inventory.* Toronto: Ontario Ministry of Correctional Services.

Andrews, D.A., & Bonta, J. (1998). *The psychology of criminal conduct* (2nd ed.). Cincinnati, OH: Anderson Publishing Co.

Andrews, D.A., & Bonta, J. (2001). *The psychology of criminal conduct* (3rd ed.). Cincinnati: Anderson Publishing.

Andrews, D.A. & Bonta, J. (2003). *The psychology of criminal conduct* (4th ed.). Cincinnati, OH: Anderson Publishing.

Andrews, D.A., & Bonta, J.L. (1995). *The Level of Service Inventory-Revised.* Toronto, ON: Multi-Health Systems.

Andrews, D.A., Zinger, I., Hoge, R.D., Bonta, J., Gendreau, P., & Cullen, F.T. (1990). Does correctional treatment work? A clinically relevant and psychologically informed meta-analysis. *Criminology, 28,* 369–404.

Anshel, M.H. (2000). A conceptual model and implications for coping with stressful events in police work. *Criminal Justice and Behavior, 27,* 375–400.

Anson, R.H., & Bloom, M.E. (1988). Police stress in an occupational context. *Journal of Police Science and Administration, 16,* 229–235.

Antonowicz, D., & Ross, R. (1994). Essential components of successful rehabilitation programs for offenders. *International Journal of Offender Therapy and Comparative Criminology, 38,* 97–104.

Archer, J. (2002). Sex differences in physically aggressive acts between heterosexual partners: A meta-analytic review. *Aggression and Violent Behavior, 7,* 313–351.

Arditti, J.A. (1999). Rethinking relationships between divorced mothers and their children: Capitalizing on family strengths. *Family Relations, 48,* 109–119.

Ascione, F.R. (1998). Battered women's reports of their partners' and their children's cruelty to animals. *Journal of Emotional Abuse, 1,* 119–133.

Ash, P., Slora, K.B., & Britton, C.F. (1990). Police agency officer selection practices. *Journal of Police Science and Administration, 17,* 258–269.

Atkinson, J.L. (1996). Female sex offenders: A literature review. *Forum on Corrections Research, 8,* 39–43.

Babcock, J.C., Green, C.E., & Robie, C. (2004). Does batterers' treatment work? A meta-analytic review of domestic violence treatment. *Clinical Psychology Review, 23,* 1023–1053.

Babiak, P. (1995). When psychopaths go to work: A case study of an industrial psychopath. *Applied Psychology: An International Review, 44,* 171–188.

Babiak, P. (2000). Psychopathic manipulation at work. In C.B. Gacono (Ed.), *Clinical and forensic assessment of psychopathy: A practitioner's guide* (pp. 287–311). Mahwah, NJ: Lawrence Erlbaum Associates, Publishers.

Baeber, R.J., Marston, A., Michelli, J., & Mills, M.J. (1985). A brief test for measuring malingering in schizophrenic individuals. *American Journal of Psychiatry, 142,* 1478–1481.

Baer, R.A., Wetter, M.W., & Berry, D.T.T. (1995). Sensitivity of MMP-2 validity scales to underreporting of symptoms. *Psychological Assessment, 7,* 419–423.

Bagby, R.M., Nicholson, R.A., Bacchiochi, J.R., Ryder, A.B., & Bury, A.S. (2002). The predictive capacity of MMPI-2 and PAI validity scales and indexes of coached and uncoached feigning. *Journal of Personality Assessment, 78,* 69–86.

Bala, N. (1999a). Child witnesses in the Canadian criminal courts. *Psychology, Public Policy, and Law, 5,* 323–354.

Bala, N. (1999b). *The best interests of the child in the post-modern era: A central but paradoxical concept.* Paper presented at the Law Society of Upper Canada Special lectures 2000: Family Law. Toronto, Ontario

Bala, N., Lindsay, R.C.L., Lee, K., & Talwar, V. (September, 2002). *The legal competence of child witnesses: Assessing present practices and the need for law reform.* Presentation at the Faculty of Law, Queen's University, Kingston, Ontario, Canada. Retrieved June 24, 2004, from http://qsilver.queensu.ca/law/witness/childcompsept20001_files

Ball, E.M., Young, D., Dotson, L.A., & Brothers, L.T. (1994). Factors associated with dangerous behavior in forensic inpatients: Results from a pilot study. *Bulletin of the American Academy of Psychiatry and the Law, 22,* 605–620.

Bandura, A. (1965). Influence of models' reinforcement contingencies on the acquisition of imitative responses. *Journal of Personality and Social Psychology, 1,* 589–595.

Bandura, A. (1973). *Aggression: A social learning analysis.* Englewood Cliffs, NJ: Prentice-Hall.

Bandura, A. (1977). *Social learning theory.* New York: Prentice-Hall.

Banning, A. (1989). Mother–son incest: Confronting a prejudice. *Child Abuse and Neglect, 13,* 563–570.

Barbaree, H. (1997). Evaluating treatment efficacy with sexual offenders: The insensitivity of recidivism studies to treatment effects. *Journal of Research and Treatment, 9,* 111–128.

Barbaree, H.E. (1991). Denial and minimization among sex offenders: Assessment and treatment outcome. *Forum on Corrections Research, 3,* 300–333.

Barbaree, H.E., Seto, M.C., Langton, C.M., & Peacock, E.J. (2001). Evaluating the predictive accuracy of six risk assessment instruments for adult sex offenders. *Criminal Justice and Behavior, 28,* 490–521.

Barbaree, H.E., Seto, M.C., Serin, R., Amos, N., & Preston, D. (1994). Comparisons between sexual and nonsexual rapist subtypes: Sexual arousal to rape, offense precursors, and offense characteristics. *Criminal Justice and Behavior, 21,* 95–114.

Barkley, R.A. (1991). Attention deficit hyperactivity disorder. *Psychiatric Annals, 21,* 725–733

Barkley, R.A. (1997). Attention-deficit/hyperactivity disorder. In E.J. Mash & L.G. Terdal (Eds.), *Assessment of childhood disorders* (pp. 71–129). New York: Guilford Press.

Baron, R.A., & Bryne, D. (1991). *Social psychology: Understanding human interaction* (6th ed.). Toronto: Allyn & Bacon.

Bartol, C.R., & Bartol, A.M. (1987). History of forensic psychology. In I.B. Weiner & A. Hess (Ed.), *Handbook of forensic psychology* (pp. 3–21). New York: Wiley.

Bartol, C.R., & Bartol, A.M. (1994). *Psychology and law* (2nd ed.). Pacific Grove, California: Brooks/Cole Publishing Company.

Bartol, C.R., & Bartol, A.M. (2004). *Introduction to forensic psychology.* London: Sage Publications.

Beck, K.A., & Ogloff, J.R.P. (1995). Child abuse reporting in British Columbia: Psychologists' knowledge of and compliance with the reporting law. *Professional Psychology: Research and Practice, 26,* 245–251.

Beck, N.C., Menditto, A.A., Baldwin, L., Angelone, E., & Maddox, M. (1991). Reduced frequency of aggressive behavior in forensic patients in a social learning program. *Hospital and Community Psychiatry, 42,* 750–752.

Behrman, B.W., & Davey, S.L. (2001). Eyewitness identification in actual criminal cases: An archival analysis. *Law and Human Behavior, 25,* 475–491.

Bekerian, D.A., & Dennett, J.L. (1993). The cognitive interview technique: Reviving the issues. *Applied Cognitive Psychology, 7,* 275–298.

Benaquisto, L. (2000). Inattention to sanctions in criminal conduct. In R. Silverman, T. Teevan, & V. Sacco (Eds.), *Crime in Canadian society* (pp. 203–215). Toronto: Harcourt Brace and Co.

Benjamin, L.T., & Crouse, E.M. (2002). The American Psychological Association's response to *Brown v. Board of Education:* The case of Kenneth B. Clark. *American Psychologist, 57,* 38–50.

Bennell, C., & Canter, D.V. (2002). Linking commercial burglaries by modus operandi: Tests using regression and ROC analysis. *Science & Justice, 42,* 153–164.

Ben-Porath, Y.S. (1994). The ethical dilemma of coached malingering research. *Psychological Assessment, 6,* 14–15.

Ben-Shakhar, G., & Elaad, E. (2003). The validity of psychophysiological detection of information with the guilty knowledge test: A meta-analytic review. *Journal of Applied Psychology, 88,* 131–151.

Ben-Shakhar, G., & Furedy, J. J. (1990). *Theories and applications in the detection of deception: Psychophysiological and cultural perspectives.* New York: Springer-Verlag.

Birch, D.E. (1992). Duty to protect: Update and Canadian perspective. *Canadian Psychology, 33,* 94–101.

Birkenmayer, A., & Roberts, J.V. (1997). Sentencing in adult provincial courts. *Juristat, 17,* 1–15.

Bittner, E. (1967). Police discretion in emergency apprehension of mentally ill persons. *Social Problems, 14,* 278–292.

Blackman, J. (1990). Emerging images of severely battered women and the criminal justice system. *Behavioral Sciences and the Law, 8,* 121–130.

Blanchette, K. (2001). *Classifying female offenders for effective intervention: Application of the case-based principles of risk and need.* Unpublished Comprehensive Paper, Carleton University, Ottawa, ON.

Bland, R., Orn, H., & Newman, S. (1988). Lifetime prevalence of psychiatric disorders in Edmonton. *Acta Psychiatrica Scandinavica, 77,* 24–32.

Bland, R.C., Newman, S.C., Dyck, R.J., & Orn, H. (1990). Prevalence of psychiatric disorders and suicide attempts in a prison population. *Canadian Journal of Psychiatry, 35,* 407–413.

Bland, R.C., & Orn, H. (1986). Family violence and psychiatric disorder. *Canadian Journal of Psychiatry, 31,* 129–137.

Blatchford, C. (2002, April 19). Dooley parents convicted of murder. *National Post.* Retrieved May 14, 2004, from http://ww.canada.com/national/features/dooleytrial/index.html

Boaz, T.L., Perry, N.W., Raney, G., Fieschler, I.S., & Shuman, D. (1991). Detection of guilty knowledge with event related potentials. *Journal of Applied Psychology, 76,* 788–795.

Boe, R. (2000). Aboriginal inmates: Demographic trends and projections. *Forum on Corrections Research, 12,* 7–9.

Boe, R. (2002). Future demographic trends may help Canada's Aboriginal youth. *Forum on Corrections, 14,* 13–16.

Bohner, G., Siebler, F., Sturm, S., Effler, D., Litters, M., Reinhard, M., & Rutz, S. (1998). Rape myth acceptance and accessibility of the gender category. *Group Processes and Intergroup Relations, 1,* 67–79.

Bohus, M., Haaf, B., Stiglmayr, C., Pohl, U., Boehme, R., & Linehan, M.M. (2000). Evaluation of behavioral therapy for borderline personality disorder: A prospective study. *Behavior Research & Therapy, 38,* 875–887.

Bok, S. (1978). *Lying: Moral choice in public and private life.* London: Quartet Books.

Bonazzoli, M.J. (1998). Jury selection and bias: Debunking invidious stereotypes through science. *Quinnipiac Law Review, 18,* 247–305.

Bonnie, R.J., & Grisso, T. (2000). Adjudicative competence and youthful offenders. In T. Grisso & R.G. Schwartz (Eds.), *Youth on trial: A developmental perspective on juvenile justice* (pp. 73–103). Chicago: University of Chicago Press.

Bonta, J. (1989). Native inmates: Institutional response, risk, and needs. *Canadian Journal of Criminology, 31,* 49–62.

Bonta, J. (2002). Offender risk assessment: Guidelines for selection and use. *Criminal Justice and Behavior, 29,* 355–379.

Bonta, J., LaPrairie, C., & Wallace-Capretta, S. (1997). Risk prediction and re-offending: Aboriginal and non-aboriginal offenders. *Canadian Journal of Criminology, 39,* 127–144.

Bonta, J., Pang, B., & Wallace-Capretta, S. (1995). Predictors of recidivism among incarcerated female offenders. *Prison Journal, 75,* 277–294.

Bonta, J., Zinger, I., Harris, A., & Carriere, D. (1998). The dangerous offender provisions: Are they targeting the right offenders? *Canadian Journal of Criminology, 40,* 377–400.

Bonta, J.L. (1996). Risk-needs assessment and treatment. In A.T. Harland (Ed.), *Choosing correctional options that work: Defining the demand and evaluating the supply* (pp. 18–32). Thousand Oaks, CA: Sage.

Bonta, J.L., Harman, W.G., Hann, R.G., & Cormier, R.B. (1996). The prediction of recidivism among federally sentenced offenders: A re-validation of the SIR scale. *Canadian Journal of Criminology, 38,* 61–79.

Bonta, J.L., Law, M., & Hanson, R.K. (1998). The prediction of criminal and violent recidivism among mentally disordered offenders: A meta-analysis. *Psychological Bulletin, 123,* 123–142.

Boothby, J. & Clements, C.B. (2000). A national survey of correctional psychologists. *Criminal Justice and Behavior, 27,* 715–731.

Borum, R. (1996). Improving the clinical practice of violence risk assessment: Technology, guidelines and training. *American Psychologist, 51,* 945–956.

Borum, R., Otto, R., & Golding, S. (1993). Improving clinical judgment and decision making in forensic evaluation. *Journal of Psychiatry and Law, 21,* 35–76.

Bowker, L. (1993). A battered woman's problems are social, not psychological. In R. Gelles & D. Loseke (Eds.), *Current controversies on family violence* (pp. 154–165). Newbury Park, CA: Sage.

Bowlby, J. (1944). Forty-four juvenile thieves. *International Journal of Psychoanalysis, 25,* 1–57.

Boyd, C. (2003, July 17). Girl's abduction exposes extent of Internet luring. *The Globe and Mail.* Retrieved April 30, 2004, from http://www.globeandmail.com

Bradfield, A.L., Wells, G.L., & Olson, E.A. (2002). The damaging effect of confirming feedback on the relation between eyewitness certainty and identification accuracy. *Journal of Applied Psychology, 87,* 112–120.

Bradford, J.M., & Pawlak, A. (1993). Effects of cyproterone acetate on sexual arousal patterns of pedophiles. *Archives of Sexual Behavior, 22,* 629–641.

Brame, B., Nagin, D.S., & Tremblay, R.E. (2001). Developmental trajectories of physical aggression from school entry to late adolescence. *Journal of Child Psychology and Psychiatry, 42,* 503–512.

Breslin, N.A. (1992). Treatment of schizophrenia: Current practice and future promise. *Hospital and Community Psychiatry, 43,* 877–885.

Brewer, N., Potter, R., Fisher, R.P., Bond, N., & Luszcz (1999). Beliefs and data on the relationship between consistency and accuracy of eyewitness testimony. *Applied Cognitive Psychology, 13,* 297–313.

Brewster, A.L., Nelson, J.P., & Hymel, K.P. (1998). Victim, perpetrator, family, and incident characteristics of 32 infant maltreatment deaths in the United States Air Force. *Child Abuse and Neglect, 22,* 91–101.

Brigham, J.C. (1999). What is forensic psychology, anyway? *Law and Human Behavior, 23,* 273–298.

British Columbia Ministry of Attorney General. (2000). *Policy on the criminal justice system response to violence against women and children: Violence against women in relationships policy.* Victoria, BC: British Columbia Ministry of Attorney General.

Brodsky, S. (1991). *Testifying in court: Guidelines and maxims for the expert witness.* Washington, DC: American Psychological Association.

Brooks, N. (1983). *Police guidelines: Pretrial identification procedures.* Ottawa: Law Reform Commission

Brown, D., Scheflin, A.W., & Hammond, D.C. (1998). *Memory, trauma treatment, and the law.* New York: Norton

Brown, J.M., & Campbell, E.A. (1994). *Stress and policing: Sources and strategies.* New York. John Wiley and Sons.

Brown, S.L., & Forth, A.E. (1997). Psychopathy and sexual assault: Static risk factors, emotional precursors, and rapist subtypes. *Journal of Consulting and Clinical Psychology, 65,* 848–857.

Browne, A. (1987). *When battered women kill.* New York, NY: Free Press.

Browne, A., & Finkelhor, D. (1986). Impact of child sexual abuse: A review of the research. *Psychological Bulletin, 99,* 66–77.

Browne, A., Miller, B., & Maguin, E. (1999). Prevalence and severity of lifetime physical and sexual victimization among incarcerated women. *International Journal and Psychiatry, 22,* 301–322.

Bull, R., & Clifford, B.R. (1984). Earwitness voice recognition accuracy. In G. Wells, & E. Loftus (Eds.), *Eyewitness testimony, psychological perspectives* (pp. 92–123). Cambridge: Cambridge University Press.

Bumby, K.M. & Hansen, D. J. (1997). Intimacy deficits, fear of intimacy, and loneliness among sexual offenders. *Criminal Justice and Behavior, 24*, 315–331.

Burgess, A.W., & Holmstrom, L.L. (1974). Rape trauma syndrome. *American Journal of Psychiatry, 131*, 981–986.

Burke, R.J. (1993). Work-family stress, conflict, coping, and burnout in police officers. *Stress Medicine, 9*, 171–180.

Burt, M.R. (1980). Cultural myths and supports for rape. *Journal of Personality and Social Psychology, 38*, 217–230.

Bushman, B.J., & Anderson, C.A. (2001). Media violence and the American public: Scientific facts versus media misinformation. *American Psychologist, 56*, 477–489.

Butcher, J.N., Dahlstrom, W.G., Graham, J.R., Tellegen, A., & Kaemmer, B. (1989). *MMPI-2: Manual for administration and scoring*. Minneapolis: University of Minnesota Press.

Cadoret, R.J., & Cain, C. (1980). Sex differences in predictors of antisocial behavior in adoptees. *Archives of General Psychiatry, 37*, 1171–1175.

Campbell, C. (1976). Portrait of a mass killer. *Psychology Today, 9*, 110–119.

Campbell, C., Mackenzie, D., & Robinson, J. (1987). Female offenders: Criminal behaviour and gender-role identity. *Psychological Reports, 60*, 867–873.

Campbell, D. (2004, April 24). Sportscaster's killer wants release from custody. *The Ottawa Citizen*, Section E, p.1, and 2.

Campbell, J. C. (1986). Nursing assessment for risk of homicide with battering women. *Advances in Nursing Science, 8*, 36–51.

Campbell, J.C., Webster, D., & Koziol-McLain, J. (2003). Risk factors for femicide in abusive relationships: Results from a multisite case control study. *American Journal of Public Health, 93*, 1089–1097.

Campbell, M.A., Porter, S., & Santor, D. (2004). Psychopathic traits in adolescent offenders: An evaluation of criminal history, clinical, and psychosocial corre-

lates. *Behavioral Sciences and the Law, 22*, 23–47.

Canadian Association of Chiefs of Police. (2000). *The national use of force framework*. Retrieved June 4, 2004, from http://www.cacp.ca/english/committees/download.asp?id=169

Canadian Centre for Justice Statistics. (1997, February). Sentencing in adult provincial courts—A study of nine Canadian jurisdictions. *Juristat, 17*.

Canter, D.V., Alison, L.J., Wentink, N., & Alison, E. (2004). The organized/disorganized typology of serial murder: Myth or model? *Psychology, Public Policy, and Law, 10*, 293–320.

Canter, D.V., Coffey, T., Huntley, M., & Missen, C. (2000). Predicting serial killers' home base using a decision support system. *Journal of Quantitative Criminology, 16*, 457–478.

Caprara, G.V., Barbaranelli, C., & Pastorelli, C. (2001). Facing guilt: Role of negative affectivity, need for reparation, and fear of punishment in leading to prosocial behaviour and aggression. *European Journal of Personality, 15*, 219–237.

Cattell, J.M. (1895). Measurements of the accuracy of recollection. *Science, 2*, 761–766.

CBC News Ottawa. (2002, November 26). First degree murder charges laid in Dagenais case. *CBC News Ottawa*. Retrieved June 1, 2004, from http://ottawa.cbc.ca/newsinreview/nov/nov26.html

CBC News. (2003, November 13). *Michaud guilty on both counts. CBC Online News*. Retrieved June 1, 2004, from http://ottawa.cbc.ca/features/2003/nov13_2.html

CBC News. (2003, October 23). Shoot her again, teen says co-accused ordered. *CBC News*. Retrieved June 1, 2004, from http://www.cbc.ca/stories.2003/10/23/dagenais_trial 031023

Ceci, S.J., & Bruck, M. (1993). The suggestibility of the child witness: A historical review and synthesis. *Psychological Bulletin, 113*, 403–439.

Cervone, D., & Shoda, Y. (Eds.) (1999). *The coherence of personality: Social-cognitive bases of consistency, variability and organization.* New York: Guilford Press.

Chadee, D. (1996). Race, trial evidence and jury decision making. *Caribbean Journal of Criminology and Social Psychology, 1*, 59–86.

Chaiken, J. M, & Chaiken, M.R. (1983). Crime rates and the active offender. In J.Q. Wilson (Ed.). *Crime and public policy* (pp. 203–229). New Brunswick, OH: Transaction Books.

Chapman, L.J., & Chapman, J.P. (1967). Genesis of popular but erroneous psychodiagnostic observations. *Journal of Abnormal Psychology, 74*, 193–204.

Cheung, P.T.K. (1986). Maternal filicide in Hong Kong. *Medicine, Science, and Law, 26*, 185–192.

Chiroro, P., & Valentine, T. (1995). An investigation of the contact hypothesis of the own-race bias in face recognition. *Quarterly Journal of Experimental Psychology, 48*, 879–894.

Cirincione, C., Steadman, H.J., Clark-Robbins, P.C., & Monahan, J. (1992). Schizophrenia as a contingent risk factor for criminal violence. *International Journal of Law and Psychiatry, 15*, 347–358.

City of Vancouver Police Department (2003). Retrieved June 1, 2004, from http://www.city.vancouver.bc.ca/police/recruiting/jobpre.htm

Clancy, K., Bartolomeo, J., Richardson, D., & Wellford, C. (1981). Sentence decision-making: The logic of sentence decisions and the extent and sources of sentence disparity. *Journal of Criminal Law and Criminology, 72*, 524–554.

Cleckley, H.R. (1976). *The mask of sanity* (5th ed.). St. Louis, MO: Mosby.

Clifford, B.R. (1980). Voice identification by human listeners: On earwitness reliability. *Law and Human Behavior, 4*, 373–394.

Cochrane, R. E., Tett, R. P., & Vandecreek, L. (2003). Psychological testing and the selection of police officers: A national survey. *Criminal Justice and Behavior, 30*, 511–537.

Cocozza, J.J., Melick, M.E., & Steadman, H.J. (1978). Trends in violent crime among ex-mental patients. *Criminology: An Interdisciplinary Journal, 16*, 317–334.

Cocozza, J.J., & Steadman, H.J. (1978). Prediction in psychiatry: An example of misplaced confidence in experts. *Social Problems, 25*, 265–276.

Cohen, A.J., Adler, N., Kaplan, S.J., Pelcovitz, D., & Mandel, F.G. (2002). Interactional effects of marital status and physical abuse on adolescent psychopathology. *Child Abuse and Neglect, 26*, 277–288.

Coie, J.D., Belding, M., & Underwood, M. (1988). Aggression and peer rejection in childhood. In B.B. Lahey & A.E. Kazdin (Eds.), *Advances in clinical child psychology*, Vol. II (pp. 125–158). New York: Plenum.

Coie, J.D., Lochman, J.E., Terry, R., & Hyman, C. (1992). Predicting early adolescent disorder from childhood aggression and peer rejection. *Journal of Consulting and Clinical Psychology, 60*, 783–792.

Cole, W.G., & Loftus, E.F. (1979). Incorporating new information into memory. *American Journal of Psychology, 92*, 413–425.

Collins, P.I., Johnson, G.F., Choy, A., Davidson, K.T., & Mackay, R.E. (1998). Advances in violent crime analysis and law enforcement: The Canadian violent crime linkage analysis system. *Journal of Government Information, 25*, 277–284.

Conaway, L.P., & Hansen, D.J. (1989). Social behavior of physically abused and neglected children: A critical review. *Clinical Psychology Review, 9*, 627–652.

Cook, S., & Wilding, J. (1997). Earwitness testimony 2: Voices, faces, and context. *Applied Cognitive Psychology, 11*, 527–541.

Cooke, D.J., & Michie, C. (2001). Refining the construct of psychopathy: Towards a hierarchical model. *Psychological Assessment, 13*, 171–188.

Cooper, J., Bennett, E.A., & Sukel, H.L. (1996). Complex scientific testimony: How do jurors make decisions? *Law and Human Behavior, 20*, 379–394.

Copson, G. (1995). *Coals to Newcastle? Part 1: A study of offender profiling.* London, UK: Home Office.

Corder, B.F., Ball, B.C., Haizlip, T.M., Rollins, R., & Beaumont, R. (1976). Adolescent parricide: A comparison with other adolescent murder. *American Journal of Psychiatry, 133,* 957–961.

Cornell, D.G., & Hawk, G.L. (1989). Clinical presentation of malingerers diagnosed by experienced forensic psychologists. *Law and Human Behavior, 13,* 374–383.

Cornell, D.G., Benedek, E.P., & Benedek, D.M. (1987). Characteristics of adolescents charged with homicide: Review of 72 cases. *Behavioral Sciences and the Law, 5,* 11–23.

Cornell, D.G., Warren, J., Hawk, G., Stafford, E., Oram, G., & Pine, D. (1996). Psychopathy in instrumental and reactive violent offenders. *Journal of Consulting and Clinical Psychology, 64,* 783–790.

Corrado, R.R., Vincent, G.M., Hart, S.D., & Cohen, I.M. (2004). Predictive validity of the Psychopathy Checklist: Youth Version for general and violent recidivism. *Behavioral Sciences and the Law, 22,* 5–22.

Correctional Service Canada. (1989). *Mental health survey of federally sentenced female offenders at Prison for Women.* Unpublished raw data.

Correctional Service Canada. (2004). *Healing Lodges for Aboriginal Federal Offenders.* Ottawa, ON: Correctional Service Canada.

Cottle, C.C., Lee, R.J., & Heilbrun, K. (2001). The prediction of criminal recidivism in juveniles: A meta-analysis. *Criminal Justice and Behavior, 28,* 367–394.

Coulson, G., Ilacqua, G., Nutbrown, V., Giulekas, D., & Cudjoe, F. (1996). Predictive utility of the LSI for incarcerated female offenders. *Criminal Justice and Behavior, 23,* 427–439.

Coy, E., Speltz, M.L., DeKlyen, M., & Jones, K. (2001). Social-cognitive processes in preschool boys with and without oppositional defiant disorder. *Journal of Abnormal Child Psychology, 29,* 107–119.

Crawford, M., & Gartner, R. (1992). *Women killing: Intimate femicide in Ontario, 1974–1990.* Women's Directorate, Ministry of Social Services, Toronto, Ontario.

Crick, N.R., & Dodge, K.A. (1994). A review and reformulation of social information-processing mechanisms in children's social adjustment. *Psychological Bulletin, 115,* 74–101.

Cronbach, L.J. (1951). Coefficient alpha and the internal structure of tests. *Psychometrika, 16,* 297–334.

Cross, J.F., Cross, J., & Daly, J. (1971). Sex, race, age, and beauty as factors in recognition of faces. *Perception and Psychophysics, 10,* 393–396.

Cross, T.P., & Saxe, L. (2001). Polygraph testing and sexual abuse: The lure of the magic lasso. *Child Maltreatment: Journal of the American Professional Society of the Abuse of Children, 6,* 195–206.

Crutcher, N., & Trevethan, S. (2002). An examination of healing lodges for federal offenders in Canada. *Forum on Corrections Research, 14,* 52–54.

Cullen, F., & Gendreau, P. (2000). Assessing correctional rehabilitation: Policy, practice, and prospects. In J. Horney (Ed.), *NIJ Criminal justice 2000: Changes in decision-making and discretion in the criminal justice system* (pp. 109–175). Washington, DC: U.S. National Institute of Justice.

Cummings, E.M., Davies, P.T., & Campbell, S.B. (2000). *Developmental psychopathology and family process: Theory, research, and clinical implications.* New York: The Guilford Press.

Cutler, B.L., & Penrod, S.D. (1989a). Forensically relevant moderators of the relationship between eyewitness identification accuracy and confidence. *Journal of Applied Psychology, 74,* 650–652.

Cutler, B.L., & Penrod, S.D. (1989b). Moderators of the confidence-accuracy relation in face recognition: The role of information processing and base rates. *Applied Cognitive Psychology, 3,* 95–107.

Cutler, B.L., Fisher, R.P., & Chicvara, C.L. (1989). Eyewitness identification from live versus videotaped lineups. *Forensic Reports, 2,* 93–106.

Daly, M., & Wilson, M. (1988). Evolutionary social psychology and family homicide. *Science, 242,* 519–524.

Daly, M., & Wilson, M.I. (1982). Homicide and kinship. *American Anthropologist, 84,* 372–378.

Daly, M., & Wilson, M.I. (1996). Violence against stepchildren. *Current Directions in Psychological Science, 5,* 77–81.

Darby, P.J., Allan, W.D., Kashani, J.H., Hartke, K.L., & Reid, J.C. (1998). Analysis of 112 juveniles who committed homicide: Characteristics and a closer look at family abuse. *Journal of Family Violence, 13,* 365–375.

Davies, G., Tarrant, A., & Flin, R. (1989). Close encounters of the witness kind: Children's memory for a simulated health inspection. *British Journal of Psychology, 80,* 415–429.

Davies, G.M., Stevenson-Robb, Y., & Flin, R. (1988). Telling tales out of school: Children's memory for an unexpected event. In M. Gruneberg, P. Morris, & R. Sykes (Eds.), *Practical aspects of memory* (pp. 122–127). Chichester: Wiley.

Davis, G.E., & Leitenberg, H. (1987). Adolescent sex offenders. *Psychological Bulletin, 101,* 417–427.

Decaire, M.W. (2004). Retrieved June 1, 2004, from http://flash.lakeheadu.ca/~pals/forensics/special.htm

Deitz, S.R., Blackwell, K.T., Daley, P.C., & Bentley, B.J. (1982). Measurement of empathy toward rape victims and rapists. *Journal of Personality and Social Psychology, 43,* 372–384.

DeKeseredy, W.S., & Kelley, K. (1993). The incidence and prevalence of woman abuse in Canadian university and college dating relationships. *The Canadian Journal of Sociology, 18,* 57–159.

Dekovic, M. (1999). Risk and protective factors in the development of problem behavior during adolescence. *Journal of Youth and Adolescence, 28,* 667–685.

DeLoache, J.S., & Marzolf, D.P. (1995). The use of dolls to interview young children: Issues of symbolic representation. *Journal of Experimental Child Psychology, 60,* 155–173.

Demo, D.H., & Acock, A.C. (1988). The impact of divorce on children. *Journal of Marriage and the Family, 50,* 619–648.

Department of Justice. (2002). Bureau of Justice Statistics. Retrieved May 10, 2004, from http://www.ojp.usdoj.gov/bjs/glance/tables/hmrttab.htm

Department of Justice Canada. (2003). *A strategy for the renewal of youth justice.* http://canada.justice.gc.ca/en/ps/yj/yoas3.html

DePaulo, B.M., Charlton, L., Cooper, H., Lindsay, J.J., & Muhlenbruck, L. (1997). The accuracy-confidence correlation in the detection of deception. *Personality and Social Psychology Review, 1,* 346–357.

DePaulo, B.M., Kashy, D.A., Kirkendol, S.E., Wyer, M.M., & Epstein, J.A. (1996). Lying in everyday life. *Journal of Personality and Social Psychology, 70,* 979–995.

DePaulo, B.M., & Kirkendol, S.E. (1989). The motivational impairment effect in the communication of deception. In Y.C. Yuille (Ed.), *Credibility assessment* (pp. 51–70). Dordrecht: Kluwer.

DePaulo, B.M., Lassiter, G.D., & Stone, J.I. (1982). Attentional determinants of success at detecting deception and truth. *Personality and Social Psychology Bulletin, 8,* 273–279.

DePaulo, B.M., LeMay, C.S., & Epstein, J.A. (1991). Effects of importance of success and expectations for success on effectiveness at deceiving. *Personality and Social Psychology Bulletin, 17,* 14–24.

DePaulo, B.M., Lindsay, J.J., Malone, B.E., Muhlenbruck, L., Charlton, K., & Cooper, H. (2003). Cues to deception. *Psychological Bulletin, 129,* 74–118.

DePaulo, B.M., & Pfeifer, R.L. (1996). On-the-job experience and skill at detecting deception. *Journal of Applied Social Psychology, 16,* 249–267.

Dernevik, M., Grann, M., & Johansson, S. (2002). Violent behaviour in forensic psychiatric patients: Risk assessment and different risk-management levels using the HCR-20. *Psychology, Crime and Law, 8,* 93–111.

Devine, D.J., Clayton, L.D., Dunford, B.B., Seying, R., & Pryce, J. (2001). Jury decision making: 45 years of empirical research on deliberating groups. *Psychology, Public Policy, and Law, 7,* 622–727.

Devlin, Honourable Lord Patrick (chair). (1976). *Report to the secretary of state for the Home Department of the departmental committee on evidence of identification in criminal cases.* London: Her Majesty's Stationery Office.

Diamond, S.S., & Zeisel, H. (1975). Sentencing councils: A study of sentencing disparity and its reduction. *University of Chicago Law Review, 43,* 109–149.

Dobash, R., & Dobash, R.E. (1979). Violence against women. New York: Free Press.

Dobson, V. & Sales, B.D. (2000). The science of infanticide and mental illness. *Psychology, Public Policy, and Law, 6,* 1098–1112.

Dodge, K.A. (1991). The structure and function of reactive and proactive aggression. In D. Pepler & K. Rubin (Eds.), *The development and treatment of childhood aggression* (pp. 201–218). Hillsdale, NJ: Earlbaum.

Dodge, K.A. (2000). Conduct disorder. In A.J. Sameroff, M. Lewis, & S.M. Miller (Eds.), *Handbook of developmental psychopathology* (2nd ed., pp. 447–463). New York, NY: Kluwer Academic/Plenum Publishers.

Dodge, K.A., Lochman, J.E., Harnish, J.D., Bates, J.E., & Pettit, G.S. (1997). Reactive and proactive aggression in school children and psychiatrically impaired chronically assaultive youth. *Journal of Abnormal Psychology, 106,* 37–51.

Doehring, D.G., & Ross, R.W. (1972). Voice recognition by matching the sample. *Journal of Psycholinguistic Research, 1,* 233–242.

Doerner, W.G. (1997). The utility of the oral interview board in selecting police academy admissions. *Policing: An International Journal of Police Strategies & Management, 20,* 777–785.

Doob, A.N. (1985). The many realities of crime. In A.N. Doob & E.L. Greenspan (Eds.), *Perspectives in criminal law* (pp. 103–122). Aurora: Canada Law Book.

Doob, A.N., & Roberts, J.A. (1988). Public punitiveness and knowledge of the facts: Some Canadian surveys. In N. Walker and M. Hough (Eds.), *Public attitudes to sentencing: Surveys from five countries* (pp. 111–133). Aldershot: Gower.

Douglas, J.E., Burgess, A.W., Burgess, A.G., & Ressler, R.K. (1992). *Crime classification Manual.* New York, NY: Lexington Books.

Douglas, J.E., & Burgess, A.W. (1986). Criminal profiling: A viable investigative tool against violent crime. *FBI Law Enforcement Bulletin, 12,* 9–13.

Douglas, J.E., & Olshaker, M. (1995). *Mindhunter: Inside the FBI's elite serial crime unit.* New York: Charles Scribner's.

Douglas, J.E., Ressler, R.K., Burgess, A.W., & Hartman, C.R. (1986). Criminal profiling from crime scene analysis. *Behavioral Sciences and the Law, 4,* 401–421.

Douglas, K.S., & Webster, C.D. (1999). Predicting violence in mentally and personality disordered individuals. In R. Roesch, S.D. Hart, & J.P. Ogloff (Eds.), *Psychology and the law: The state of the discipline* (pp. 175–239). New York: Kluwer Academic/Plenum.

Dowden, C., & Andrews, D. A. (1999). What works for female offenders: A meta-analytic review. *Crime & Delinquency, 45,* 438–452.

Dowden, C., & Brown, S.L. (2002). The role of substance abuse factors in predicting recidivism: A meta-analysis. *Psychology, Crime, and Law, 8,* 243–264.

Dutton, D.G. (1995). *The domestic assault of women: Psychological and criminal justice perspectives.* Vancouver, BC: University of British Columbia Press.

Dutton, D.G., & Kerry, G. (1999). Modus operandi and personality disorder in incarcerated spousal killers. *International Journal of Law and Psychiatry, 22,* 287–299.

Easterbrook, J.A. (1959). The effect of emotion on cue utilization and the organization of behavior. *Psychological Review, 66,* 183–201.

Ebata, A.T., Peterson, A.C., & Conger, J.J. (1990). The development of psychopathology in adolescence. In J. Rolf, A.S. Masten, D. Cicchetti, K. Nuechterlein, & S. Weintraub (Eds.), *Risk and protective factors in the development of psychopathology* (pp. 308–333). Cambridge, MA: Cambridge University Press.

Ebbesen, E.G., & Konecni, V.J. (1997). Eyewitness memory research: Probative versus prejudicial value. *Expert Evidence, 5,* 2–28.

Edens, J.F., Skeem, J.L., Cruise, K.R., & Cauffman, E. (2001). Assessment of "Juvenille Psychopathy" and its association with violence: A critical review. *Behavioral Sciences and the Law, 19,* 53–80.

Edwards, G., & Mazzuca, J. (1998). Sixty-one percent support death penalty for murder. *The Gallup Poll, 58,* 68.

Egeth, H.E. (1993). What do we not know about eyewitness identification. *American Psychologist, 48,* 577–580.

Egger, S.A. (2002). *The serial killers among us: An examination of serial murder and its investigation* (2nd ed.). New Jersey: Prentice Hall.

Eisendrath, S.J. (1996). Current overview of physical factitious disorders. In M.D. Feldman & S.J. Eisendrath (Eds.), *The spectrum of factitious disorders* (pp. 21–36). Washington DC: American Psychiatric Association.

Ekman, P. (1992). *Telling lies: Clues to deceit in the marketplace, politics, and marriage.* New York: W. W. Norton.

Ekman, P., & Friesen, W.V. (1974). Detecting deception from the body or face. *Journal of Personality and Social Psychology, 29,* 288–298.

Ekman, P., & O'Sullivan, M. (1991). Who can catch a liar? *American Psychologist, 46,* 913–920.

Ekman, P., & O'Sullivan, M., & Frank, M. G. (1999). A few can catch a liar. *Psychological Science, 10,* 263–266.

Elaad, E. (1990). Detection of guilty knowledge in real-life criminal applications. *Journal of Applied Psychology, 75,* 521–529.

Elaad, E., Ginton, A., & Jungman, N. (1992). Detection measures in real-life criminal guilty knowledge tests. *Journal of Applied Psychology, 77,* 757–767.

Elbogen, E.B. (2002). The process of violence risk assessment: A review of descriptive research. *Aggression and Violent Behavior, 7,* 591–604.

Elbogen, E.B., Williams, A.L., Kim, D., Tomkins, A.J., & Scalora, M.J. (2001). Gender and perceptions of dangerousness in civil psychiatric patients. *Legal and Criminological Psychology, 6,* 215–228.

Elkins, I.J., Iacono, W.G., Doyle, A.E., & McGue, M. (1997). Characteristics associated with the persistence of antisocial behavior: Results from recent longitudinal research. *Aggression and Violent Behavior, 2,* 102–124.

Ellerby, L.A., & MacPherson, M. (2001). *Exploring the profile of Aboriginal sex offenders: Contrasting Aboriginal and non-Aboriginal sexual offenders to determine unique client characteristics and potential implications for sex offender assessment and treatment strategies.* Research Report No. R-122. Ottawa, ON: Correctional Service Canada.

Elliott, D. (1994). Serious violent offenders: Onset, development course, and termination. The American Society of Criminology 1993 presidential address. *Criminology, 32,* 1–21.

Ellis, D. (1989). Male abuse of a married or cohabiting female partner: The application of sociological theory to research findings. *Violence and Victims, 4,* 235–255.

Ellis, H.D., Shepherd, J.W., & Davies, G.M. (1980). The deterioration of verbal descriptions of faces over different delay intervals. *Journal of Police Science and Administration, 8,* 101–106.

Ellsworth, P.C., & Mauro, R. (1998). Psychology and law. In D.T. Gilbert, S.T. Fiske, & G. Lindzey. *The handbook of social psychology* (pp. 684–732). New York: Aronson.

Ellsworth, P.C., & Reifman, A. (2000). Juror comprehension and public policy: Perceived problems and proposed solutions. *Psychology, Public Policy, and Law, 6,* 788–821.

Ennis, B. J., & Litwack, T.R. (1974). Psychiatry and the presumption of expertise: Flipping coins in the courtroom. *California Law Review, 62,* 693–752.

Ewing, C. (1987). *Battered women who kill: Psychological self-defence as legal justification.* Lexington, MA: Lexington Books.

Ewing, C.P., & Aubrey, M. (1987). Battered woman and public opinion: Some realities about the myths. *Journal of Family Violence, 2,* 257–264.

Ex-Marine jailed for abduction. (2004, April 2). *This Is London.* Retrieved April 30, 2004, from http://www.Thisislondon.com

Ex-Marine: No sex with girl. (2003, July 17). *CBS News.* Retrieved April 30, 2004, from http://www.cbsnews.com

Fabricatore, J.M. (1979). Pre-entry assessment and training: Performance evaluation of police officers. In C.D. Speilberger (Ed.), *Police selection and evaluation: Issues and techniques* (pp. 77–86). New York: Praeger Publishers.

Fagot, B.I., & Kavanagh, K. (1990). The prediction of antisocial behavior from avoidant attachment classifications. *Child Development, 61,* 864–873.

Faigman, D.L., & Wright, A.J. (1997). The battered woman syndrome in the age of science. *Arizona Law Review, 39,* 67–115.

Falkenberg, S., Gaines, L.K,. & Cordner, G. (1991). An examination of the constructs underlying police performance appraisals. *Journal of Criminal Justice, 19,* 151–160.

Faller, K.C. (1987). Women who sexually abuse children. *Violence and Victims, 2,* 263–276.

Fang, F., Liu, Y., & Shen, Z. (2003). Lie detection with contingent negative variation. *International Journal of Psychophysiology, 50,* 247–255.

Farkas, G.M., DeLeon, P.H., & Newman, R. (1997). Sanity examiner certification: An evolving national agenda. *Professional Psychology: Research and Practice, 28,* 73–76.

Farrington, D.P. (1989). Early predictors of adolescent aggression and adult violence. *Violence and Victims, 4,* 79–100.

Farrington, D.P. (1991). Psychological contributions to the explanation of offending. *Issues in Criminological and Legal Psychology, 1,* 7–19.

Farrington, D.P. (1995). The development of offending and antisocial behavior from childhood: Key findings from the Cambridge Study in Delinquent Development. *Journal of Child Psychology and Psychiatry, 36,* 929–964.

Farwell, L.A., & Donchin, E. (1991). The truth will out: Interrogative polygraphy ("lie detection") with event related brain potentials. *Psychophysiology, 28,* 531–547.

Faver, C.A., & Strand, E.B. (2003). To leave or to stay? Battered women's concern for vulnerable pets. *Journal of interpersonal violence, 18,* 1367–1377.

Federoff, J. P., & Federoff, I. C. (1992). Buspirone and paraphilic sexual behavior. *Journal of Offender Rehabilitation, 18,* 89–108.

Feinman, S., & Entwisle, D.R. (1976). Children's ability to recognize other children's faces. *Child Development, 47,* 506–510.

Feldman, D. (1969). Psychoanalysis and crime. In D.R. Cressey & D.A. Ward (Eds.), *Delinquency, crime, and social process* (pp. 433–442). New York: Harper and Row.

Feldman, M.P. (1977). *Criminal behaviour: A psychological analysis.* Chichester: Wiley.

Felner, R.D., & Terre, L. (1987). Child custody dispositions and children's adaptation following divorce. In L.A. Weithorn (Ed.),

Psychology and child custody determinations: Knowledge, roles, and expertise (pp. 106–153). Lincoln: University of Nebraska Press.

Fergusson, D.M., & Horwood, L.J. (1996). The role of adolescent peer affiliations in the continuity between childhood behavioral adjustment and juvenile offending. *Journal of Abnormal Child Psychology, 24,* 205–221.

Fergusson, D.M., & Horwood, L.J. (1998). Early conduct problems and later life opportunities. *Journal of Child Psychology and Psychiatry, 39,* 1097–1108.

Fergusson, D.M., & Lynskey, M.T. (1997). Early reading difficulties and later conduct problems. *Journal of Child Psychology and Psychiatry, 38,* 899–907.

Fergusson, D.M., & Woodward, L.J. (2000). Educational, psychological, and sexual outcomes of girls with conduct problems in early adolescence. *Journal of Child Psychology and Psychiatry, 41,* 779–792.

Fiedler, K., & Walka, I. (1993). Training lie detectors to use nonverbal cues instead of global heuristics. *Human Communication Research, 20,* 199–223.

Finkel, N.J., Burke, J.E., & Chavez, L.J. (2000). Commonsense judgments of infanticide: Murder, manslaughter, madness, or miscellaneous? *Psychology, Public Policy, and Law, 6,* 1113–1137.

Finkelhor, D. (1984). *Child sexual abuse: New theory and research.* New York: Free Press.

Finkelhor, D., & Browne, A. (1985). The traumatic impact of child sexual abuse: A conceptualization. *American Journal of Orthopsychiatry, 55,* 530–541.

Finkelhor, D., & Dziuba-Leatherman, J. (1994). Children as victims of violence: A national survey. *Pediatrics, 94,* 413–420.

Finkelhor, D., Hotaling, G.T., Lewis, I.A., & Smith, C. (1989). Sexual abuse and its relationship to later sexual satisfaction, marital status, religion, and attitudes. *Journal of Interpersonal Violence, 4,* 379–399.

Finn, P., & Tomz, J.E. (1996). *Developing a law enforcement stress program for officers and their families.* Washington, DC: U.S. Department of Justice.

Firestone, P., Bradford, J.M., Greenberg, D.M., & Larose, M.R. (1998). Homicidal sex offenders: Psychological, phallometric, and diagnostic features. *Journal of the American Academy of Psychiatry and the Law, 26,* 537–552.

Fisher, K., Vidmar, N., & Ellis, R. (1993). The culture of battering and role of mediation in domestic violence cases. *SMU Law Review, 46,* 2117–2173.

Fisher, R.P. (1995) Interviewing victims and witnesses of crime. *Psychology, Public Police, and Law, 1,* 732–764.

Fisher, R.P., & Geiselman, R.E. (1992). *Memory-enhancing techniques for investigative interviewing.* Springfield: Charles C. Thomas.

Fisher, R.P., Geiselman, R.E., & Raymond, D.S. (1987). Critical analysis of police interviewing techniques. *Journal of Police Science and Administration, 15,* 177–185.

Fitzgerald, M. (1999). *Searches in London.* London, UK: Home Office.

Fitzpatrick, K.M. (1997). Fighting among America's youth: A risk and protective factors approach. *Journal of Health and Social Behavior, 38,* 131–148.

Flynn, C.P. (2000). Woman's best friend: Pet abuse and the role of companion animals in the lives of battered women. *Violence against women, 6,* 162–177.

Foa, E.B., & Rothbaum, B.O. (1998). *Treating the trauma of rape: Cognitive-behavioral therapy for PTSD.* New York: Guilford.

Fontaine, R.G., Burks, V.S., & Dodge, K.A. (2002). Response decision processes and externalizing behavior problems in adolescents. *Development and Psychopathology, 14,* 107–122.

Forcese, D. (1999). *Policing Canadian society.* Scarborough, ON: Prentice Hall.

Forrest, J.A., & Feldman, R.S. (2000). Detecting deception and judge's involvement: Lower task involvement leads to better lie detection. *Personality and Social Psychology Bulletin, 26,* 118–125.

Forth, A.E., Hart, S.D., & Hare, R.D. (1990). Assessment of psychopathy in male young offenders. *Psychological Assessment: A Journal of Consulting and Clinical Psychology, 2,* 342–344.

Forth, A.E., Kosson, D.S., & Hare, R.D. (2003). *The Psychopathy Checklist: Youth Version manual.* Toronto, ON: Multi-Health Systems.

Frank, M.G., & Ekman, P. (1997). The ability to detect deceit generalizes across different types of high-stake lies. *Journal of Personality and Social Psychology, 72,* 1429–1439.

Franke, W.D., Collins, S.A., & Hinz, P.N. (1998). Cardiovascular disease morbidity in an Iowa law enforcement cohort, compared with the general population. *Journal of Occupational and Environmental Medicine, 40,* 441–444.

Frederick, R.I., Carter, M., & Powel, J. (1995). Adapting symptom validity testing to evaluate suspicious complaints of amnesia in medicolegal evaluations. *Bulletin of the American Academy of Psychiatry and Law, 23,* 231–237.

Frederick, R.I., Crosby, R.D., & Wynkoop, T.F. (2000). Performance curve classification of invalid responding on the Validity Indicator Profile. *Archives of Clinical Neuropsychology, 15,* 281–300.

Freud, S. (1906/1959). Psycho-analysis and the establishment of the facts in legal proceedings. In J. Stachey (Ed.), *The standard edition of the complete psychological works of Sigmund Freud* (Volume 9) (pp. 103–114). London: Hogarth.

Frick, P.J. (1994). Family dysfunction and the disruptive disorders: A review of recent empirical findings. In T.H. Ollendick & Prinz, R.J. (Eds.), *Advances in clinical child psychology.* (Vol. 16) New York: Plenum Press.

Frick, P.J., Bodin, S.D., & Barry, C.T. (2000). Psychopathic traits and conduct problems in community and clinic-referred samples of children: Further development of the Psychopathy Screening Device. *Psychological Assessment, 12,* 382–393.

Frick, P.J., & Hare, R.D. (2001). *Antisocial Process Screening Device.* Toronto, ON: Multi-Health Systems.

Frick, P.J., Kimonis, E.R., Dandreaux, D.M., & Farell, J.M. (2003). The 4 year stability of psychopathic traits in non-referred youth. *Behavioral Sciences and the Law, 21,* 713–736.

Frick, P.J., Lahey, B.B., Loeber, R., Stouthamer, M., Christ, M.A.G., & Hanson, K. (1992). Familial risk factors to oppositional defiant disorder and conduct disorder: parental psychopathology and maternal parenting. *Journal of Consulting and Clinical Psychology, 60,* 49–55.

Friedrich, W.N., & Luecke, W.J. (1988). Young school-age sexually aggressive children. *Professional Psychology: Research and Practice, 19,* 155–164.

Fritz, G., Stoll, K., & Wagner, N. (1981). A comparison of males and females who were sexually molested as children. *Journal of Sex and Marital Therapy, 7,* 54–58.

Fukuda, K. (2001). Eye blinks: New indices for the detection of deception. *International Journal of Psychophysiology, 40,* 239–245.

Furedy, J.J. (1996). The North American Polygraph and psychophysiology: Disinterested, uninterested, and interested perspectives. *International Journal of Psychophysiology, 21,* 97–105.

Fyfe, J.J. (1979). Administrative interventions on police shooting discretion: An empirical examination. *Journal of Criminal Justice, 7,* 309–324.

Fyfe, J.J. (1981). Who shoots? A look at officer race and police shooting. *Journal of Police Science and Administration, 9,* 367–382.

Gabor, T., & Crutcher, N. (2002). *Mandatory minimum penalties: Their effect on crime, sentencing disparities, and justice system expenditures.* Ottawa: Department of Justice Canada.

Gallagher, C.A., Wilson, D.B., Hirschfield, P., Coggeshall, M.B., & MacKenzie, D.L. (1999). A quantitative review of the effects of sex offender treatment of sexual reoffending. *Corrections Management Quarterly, 3,* 19–29.

Gallup Poll. (1999). *Racial profiling is seen as wide-spread, particularly among young black men.* Princeton, NJ: Gallup Poll Organization.

Ganis, G., Kosslyn, S.M., Stose, S., Thompson, W.L., & Yurgelun-Todd, D.A. (2003). Neural correlates of different types of deception: An fMRI investigation. *Cerebral Cortex, 13,* 830–836.

Garber, C.M. (1947). Eskimo infanticide. *Scientific Monthly, 64,* 98–102.

Garmezy, N. (1985). Stress-resistant children: The search for protective factors. In J.E. Stevenson (Ed.), *Recent research in developmental psychopathology* (pp. 213–233). New York, NY: Pergamon.

Garmezy, N. (1991). Resilience in children's adaptation to negative life events and stressed environments. *Pediatric Annuals, 20,* 460–466.

Gaudet, F.J. (1938). Individual differences in the sentencing tendencies of judges. *Archives of Psychology, 230,* 1–57.

Geberth, V.J. (1990). *Practical homicide investigation: Tactics, procedures, and forensic techniques* (2nd ed.). New York: Elsevier.

Geiselman, R.E., Fisher, R.P., Firstenberg, I., Hutton, L.A., Sullivan, S., Avetissian, I., & Prosk, A. (1984). Enhancement of eyewitness memory: An empirical evaluation of the cognitive interview. *Journal of Police Science and Administration, 12,* 74–80.

Geiselman, R.E., Fisher, R.P., MacKinnon, D.P., & Holland, H.L. (1985). Eyewitness memory enhancement in the police interview: Cognitive retrieval mnemonics versus hypnosis. *Journal of Applied Psychology, 70,* 401–412.

Geiselman, R.E., Fisher, R.P., MacKinnon, D.P., & Holland, H.L. (1986). Enhancement of eyewitness memory with the cognitive interview. *American Journal of Psychology, 99,* 385–401.

Geller, W., & Scott, M.S. (1992). *Deadly force: What we know.* Washington, DC: Police Executive Forum.

Gellespie, C. (1989). *Justifiable homicide.* Columbus, OH: Ohio State University Press.

Gendreau, P., Goggin, C., & Smith, P. (2002). Is the PCL-R really the "unparalleled" measure of offender risk? A lesson in knowledge cumulation. *Criminal Justice and Behavior, 29,* 397–426.

Gendreau, P., Goggin, C., Cullen, F., & Andrews, D. (2001). The effects of community sanctions and incarceration of recidivism. In L. Motiuk and R. Serin (Eds.), *Compendium 2000 on effective correctional programming* (pp. 18–21). Ottawa: Correctional Service Canada.

Gendreau, P., Little, T., & Goggin, C. (1996). A meta-analysis of the predictors of adult offender recidivism: What works! *Criminology, 34,* 575–607.

Gentleman, J.F., & Park, E. (1997). Divorce in the 1990s. *Health Reports, 9,* 53–58.

Ginton, A., Daie, N., Elaad, E., & Ben-Shakhar, G. (1982). A method for evaluating the use of the polygraph in a real-life situation. *Journal of Applied Psychology, 67,* 131–137.

Glover, A.J.J., Nicholson, D.E., & Hemmati, T. (2002). A comparison of predictors of general and violent recidivism among high-risk federal offenders. *Criminal Justice and Behavior, 29,* 235–249.

Glueck, S., & Glueck, E.T. (1968). *Delinquents and nondelinquents in perspective.* Cambridge, MA: Harvard University Press.

Golden, O. (2000). The federal response to child abuse and neglect. *American Psychologist, 55,* 1050–1053.

Golding, S.L. (1993). *Training manual: Interdisciplinary fitness interview revised.* Department of Psychology, University of Utah.

Golding, S.L., Roesch, R., & Schreiber, J. (1984). Assessment and conceptualization of competency to stand trial. Preliminary data on the interdisciplinary fitness interview. *Law and Human Behavior, 8,* 321–334.

Goldstein, A.G. (1979). Race-related variation of facial features: Anthropometric data I. *Bulletin of the Psychonomic Society, 13,* 187–190.

Gondolf, E.W. (1985). *Men who batter: An integrated approach for stopping wife abuse.* Holmes Beach, CA: Learning Publications.

Gondolf, E.W. (1988). Who are these guys? Towards a behavioral typology of batterers. *Violence and Victims, 3,* 187–202.

Gonzalez, R., Ellsworth, P., & Pembroke, M. (1993). Response biases in lineups and showups. *Journal of Personality and Social Psychology, 64,* 525–537.

Goodman, G.S., Pyle-Taub, E.P., Jones, D.P.H., England, P., Port, L.K., Rudy, L., & Prado, L. (1992). Testifying in court: The effects on child sexual assault victims. *Monographs of the Society for Research in Child Development, 57 (Serial No. 229),* 1–163.

Goodman, G.S., Quas, J.A., Batterman-Faunce, J.M., Riddlesberger, M., & Kuhn, J. (1997). Children's reactions to and memory for a stressful event: Influences of age, anatomical dolls, knowledge, and parental attachment. *Applied Developmental Science, 1,* 54–75.

Gorey, K., & Leslie, D. (1997). The prevalence of child sexual abuse: Integrative review adjustment for potential response and measurement bias. *Child Abuse and Neglect, 21,* 391–398.

Gough, H.G. (1950). The F minus K dissimulation index for the MMPI. *Journal of Consulting Psychology, 14,* 408–413.

Gowan, M.A., & Gatewood, R.D. (1995). Personnel selection. In N. Brewer & C. Wilson (Eds.), *Psychology and policing* (pp. 177–204). Hillsdale, NJ: Lawrence Erlbaum Associates.

Graham, J.R. (1999). *MMPI-2: Assessing personality and psychopathology* (3rd ed.). New York: Oxford University Press.

Granger, C. (1996). *The criminal jury trial in Canada.* Toronto, ON: Carswell.

Grann, M., Belfrage, H., & Tengström, A. (2000). Actuarial assessment of risk for violence: Predictive validity of the VRAG and the historical part of the HCR-20. *Criminal Justice and Behavior, 27,* 97–114.

Grann, M., & Wedin, I. (2002). Risk factors for recidivism among spousal assault and spousal homicide offenders. *Psychology, Crime and Law, 8,* 5–23.

Greco, C.M., & Cornell, D.G. (1992). Rorschach object relations of adolescents who committed homicide. *Journal of Personality Assessment, 59,* 574–583.

Greene, E., Raitz, A., & Lindblad, H. (1989). Jurors' knowledge of battered women. *Journal of Family Violence, 4,* 105–125.

Gretton, H., McBride, M., Hare, R.D., O'Shaughnessy, R., & Kumka, G. (2001). Psychopathy and recidivism in adolescent sex offenders. *Criminal Justice and Behavior, 28,* 427–449.

Grisso, T. (1993). The differences between forensic psychiatry and forensic psychology. *Bulletin of the American Academy of Psychiatry and the Law, 21,* 133–145.

Grisso, T. (1998). *Forensic evaluation of juveniles.* Sarasota, FL: Professional Resource Press.

Grossman, F.K., Beinashowitz, J., Anderson, L., Sakurai, M., Finnin, L., & Flaherty, M. (1992). Risk and resilience in young adolescents. *Journal of Youth and Adolescence, 21,* 529–550.

Groth, A.N. (1979). *Men who rape: The psychology of the offender.* New York: Plenum.

Groth, A.N., Hobson, W.F., & Gary, T.S. (1982). The child molester: Clinical observations. *Journal of Social Work and Human Sexuality, 1,* 129–144.

Grove, W., & Meehl, P (1996). Comparative efficiency of informal (subjective, impressionistic) and formal (mechanical, algorithmic) prediction procedures: The clinical-statistical controversy. *Psychology, Public Policy and Law, 2,* 293–323.

Grove, W.M., Zald, D.H., Lebow, B.S., Snitz, B.F., & Nelson, C. (2000). Clinical versus mechanical prediction: A meta-analysis. *Psychological Assessment, 12,* 19–30.

Gudjonsson, G.H. (1984). A new scale of interrogative suggestibility. *Personality and Individual Differences, 5,* 303–314.

Gudjonsson, G.H. (1989). Compliance in an interrogation context: A new scale. *Personality and Individual Differences, 10,* 535–540.

Gudjonsson, G.H. (1992a). *The psychology of interrogations, confessions, and testimony.* Chichester, UK: John Wiley & Sons.

Gudjonsson, G.H. (1992b). Interrogation and false confessions: Vulnerability factors. *British Journal of Hospital Medicine, 47,* 597–599.

Gudjonsson, G.H., & MacKeith, J.A.C. (1988). Retracted confessions: Legal, psychological and psychiatric aspects. *Medicine, Science, and the Law, 28,* 187–194.

Gureje, O., Simon, G.E., Ustun, T. B., & Goldberg, D.P. (1997). Somatization in cross-cultural perspective: A world health organization study in primary care. *American Journal of Psychiatry, 154,* 989–995.

Gylys, J.A., & McNamara, J.R. (1996). Acceptance of rape myths among prosecuting attorneys. *Psychological Reports, 79,* 15–18.

Haggard, U., Gumpert, C.H., & Grann, M. (2001). Against all odds: A qualitative follow-up study of high-risk violent offenders who were not reconvicted. *Journal of Interpersonal Violence, 16,* 1048–1065.

Hall, G.C. (1995). Sexual offender recidivism revisited: A meta-analysis of recent treatment studies. *Journal of Consulting and Clinical Psychology, 63,* 802–809.

Hamilton, G. & Sutterfield, T. (1997). Comparison of women who have and have not murdered their abusive partners. *Women & Therapy, 20,* 45–55.

Hanes, A. (2004, April 28). Charge dropped for father who forgot child in car for 8 hours. *National Post.* Retrieved May 5, 2004, from http://www.canada.com

Haney, C. (1980). Psychology and legal change: On the limits of a factual jurisprudence. *Law and Human Behavior, 17,* 371–398.

Haney, J., & Kristianson, C. M. (1997). An analysis of the impact of prison on women survivors of childhood sexual abuse. *Women & Therapy, 20,* 29–44.

Hankins, G.C., Barnard, G.W., & Robbins, L. (1993). The validity of the M Test in residential forensic facility. *Bulletin of the American Academy of Psychiatry and Law, 21,* 111–121.

Hans, V.P., & Doob, A.N. (1976). Section 12 of the Canada Evidence Act and the deliberation of simulated juries. *Criminal Law Quarterly, 18,* 235–253.

Hanson, R.K. (1990). The psychological impact of sexual assault on women and children: A review. *Annuals of Sex Research, 3,* 187–232.

Hanson, R.K. (1997). Invoking sympathy-assessment and treatment of empathy deficits among sexual offenders. In B.K. Schwartz & H.R. Cellini (Eds.), *The sex offender: New insights, treatment innovations and legal developments* (pp.1.1–1.12). Kingston, NJ: Civic Research Institute.

Hanson, R.K., Broom, I., & Stephenson, M. (2004). Evaluating community sex offender treatment programs: A 12-year follow-up of 724 offenders. *Canadian Journal of Behavioural Sciences, 36,* 85–94.

Hanson, R.K., & Bussière, M.T. (1998). Predicting relapse: A meta-analysis of sexual offender recidivism studies. *Journal of Consulting and Clinical Psychology, 66,* 348–362.

Hanson, R.K., Gordon, A., Harris, A.J.R., Marques, J.K., Murphy, W., Quinsey, V.L., & Seto, M.C. (2002). First report of the collaborative outcome data project on the effectiveness of psychological treatment for sex offenders. *Sexual Abuse: A Journal of Research and Treatment, 14,* 169–194.

Hanson, R.K., & Harris, A.J. (2000). Where should we intervene? Dynamic predictors of sexual offense recidivism. *Criminal Justice and Behavior, 27,* 6–35.

Hanson, R.K., & Scott, H. (1995). Assessing perspective-taking among sexual offenders, nonsexual criminals, and offenders. *Sexual Abuse: Journal of Research and Treatment, 7,* 259–277.

Hanson, R.K., & Thornton, D. (1999). *Static-99: Improving actuarial risk assessment for sexual offenders*. Ottawa, Ontario, Canada: Department of Solicitor General.

Hanson, R.K., & Thornton, D. (2000). Improving risk assessments for sex offenders: A comparison of three actuarial scales. *Law and Human Behavior, 24,* 119–136.

Hanson, T.L. (1999). Does parental conflict explain why divorce is negatively associated with child welfare. *Social Forces, 77,* 1283–1316.

Hare, R.D. (1991). *The Hare Psychopathy Checklist-Revised.* Multi-Health systems: Toronto, ON.

Hare, R.D. (1993). *Without Conscience: The disturbing world of the psychopaths among us.* New York: Pocket Books.

Hare, R.D. (1998). The Hare PCL-R: Some issues concerning its use and misuse. *Legal and Criminological Psychology, 3,* 99–119.

Hare, R.D. (2003). *The Hare Psychopathy Checklist-Revised.* (2nd ed.). Toronto, ON: Multi-Health Systems.

Hare, R.D., Clark, D., Grant, M., & Thornton, D. (2000). Psychopathy and the predictive validity of the PCL-R: An international perspective. *Behavioral Sciences and the Law, 18,* 623–645.

Hare, R.D., Forth, A.E., & Strachan, K.E. (1992). Psychopathy and crime across the life span. In R.D. Peters & R.J. McMahon (Eds.), *Aggression and violence throughout the life span* (pp. 285–300). Thousand Oaks, CA: Sage Publications Inc.

Hare, R.D., Harpur, T.J., Hakstian, A.R., Forth, A.E., Hart, S.D., & Newman, J.P. (1990). The Revised Psychopathy Checklist: Reliability and factor structure. *Psychological Assessment: A Journal of Consulting and Clinical Psychology, 2,* 338–341.

Hargrave, G.E., & Hiatt, D. (1987). Law enforcement selection with the interview, MMPI, and CPI: A study of reliability and validity. *Journal of Police Science and Administration, 15,* 110–117.

Harris, D. (1999a). *Driving while black: Racial profiling on our nation's highways.* Washington, DC: American Civil Liberties Union.

Harris, D. (1999b). The stories, the statistics, and the law: Why "driving while black" matters. *Minnesota Law Review, 84,* 265–326.

Harris, R.D., Rice, M.E., & Cormier, C.A. (2002). Prospective replication of the Violence Risk Appraisal Guide in predicting violent recidivism among forensic patients. *Law and Human Behavior, 26,* 377–394.

Harris, G.T., Rice, M.E., & Quinsey, V.L. (1993). Violent recidivism of mentally disordered offenders: The development of a statistical prediction instrument. *Criminal Justice and Behavior, 20,* 315–335.

Harris, G.T., Rice, M.E., Quinsey, V.L., Lalumiere, M.L., Boer, D., & Lang, C. (2003). A multisite comparison of actuarial risk instruments for sex offenders. *Psychological Assessment, 15,* 413–425.

Harrison, L.A., & Esqueda, C.W. (1999). Myths and stereotypes of actors involved in domestic violence: Implications for domestic violence culpability attributions. *Aggression and Violent Behavior, 4,* 129–138.

Harrison, S. (1993). *Diary of Jack the Ripper: The discovery, the investigation, the debate.* New York: Hyperion.

Hart, S.D. (1998). The role of psychopathy in assessing risk for violence: Conceptual and methodological issues. *Legal and Criminological Psychology, 3,* 121–137.

Hart, S.D., Cox, D.N., & Hare, R.D. (1995). *Manual for the Psychopathy Checklist: Screening Version (PCL: SV).* Toronto, ON: Multi-Health Systems.

Hart, S.D., Kropp, P.R., & Hare, R.D. (1988). Performance of male psychopaths following conditional release from prison. *Journal of Consulting and Clinical Psychology, 56,* 227–232.

Hastie, R. (Ed.). (1993). *Inside the juror: The psychology of juror decision making.* New York: Cambridge University Press.

Hastie, R., Penrod, S.D., & Pennington, N. (1983). *Inside the jury.* Cambridge, MA: Harvard University Press.

Hathaway, S.R., & McKinley, J.C. (1942). *The Minnesota Multiphasic Personality Inventory Manual.* New York: Psychological Corporation.

Hazelwood, R.R., & Douglas, J.E. (1980). The lust murderer. *FBI Law Enforcement Bulletin, 50,* 18–22.

Health Canada. (2003). *The consequences of child maltreatment: A reference guide for health practitioners.* Report prepared by Jeff Latimer. Ottawa, ON: Health Canada.

Heilbrun, K. (1997). Prediction versus management models relevant to risk assessment: The importance of legal decision-making context. *Law and Human Behavior, 21,* 347–359.

Hemphill, J. F., Hare, R.D., & Wong, S. (1998). Psychopathy and recidivism: A review. *Legal and Criminological Psychology, 3,* 139–170.

Hemphill, J. F., Templeman, R., Wong, S., & Hare, R.D. (1998). Psychopathy and crime: Recidivism and criminal careers. In D.J. Cooke, A.E. Forth, & R.D. Hare (Eds.) *Psychopathy: Theory, Research and implications for society* (pp. 375–398). Boston: Kluwer.

Hendley, N. (2000, January, 20). The shine is off boot camps. *Eye Weekly.* Retrieved June 1, 2004, from http://www.eye.net/eye/issue/issue_01.20.00/news/bootcamp.html

Hendrick, D., & Farmer, L. (2002). Adult correctional services in Canada, 2000/01. *Juristat, 22(10).*

Henggeler, S.W., & Borduin, C.M. (1990). *Family therapy and beyond: A multisystemic approach to treating the behavior problems of children and adolescents.* Pacific Grove, CA: Brooks/Cole.

Henggeler, S.W., Melton, G.B., & Smith, L.A. (1992). Family preservation using multisystemic therapy: An effective alternative to incarcerating serious juvenile offenders. *Journal of Consulting and Clinical Psychology, 60,* 953–961.

Henggeler, S.W., Rodick, J.D., Borduin, C.M., Hanson, C.L., Watson, S.M., & Urey, J.R. (1986). Multisystemic treatment of juvenile offenders: Effects on adolescent behavior and family interaction. *Developmental Psychology, 22,* 132–141.

Henggeler, S.W., Schoenwald, S.K. Borduin, C.M., Rowland, M.D., & Cunningham, P.B. (1998). *Multisystemic treatment of antisocial behavior in children and adolescents.* New York, NY: Guilford Press.

Henggeler, S.W., Schoenwald, S.K., & Pickrel, S.A.G. (1995). Multisystemic therapy: Bridging the gap between university and community-based treatment. *Journal of Consulting and Clinical Psychology, 63,* 709–717.

Hess, A.K. (1987). Dimensions of forensic psychology. In I.B. Weiner & A.K. Hess (Eds.), *The handbook of forensic psychology* (1st ed.) (pp. 22–49). New York: John Wiley and Sons.

Hess, A.K. (1999). Defining forensic psychology. In A.K. Hess & I.B. Weiner (Eds.), *The handbook of forensic psychology* (2nd ed.) (pp. 24–47). New York: John Wiley and Sons.

Heuer, L., & Penrod, S. (1989). Instructing jurors: A field experiment with written and preliminary instructions. *Law and Human Behavior, 13,* 409–430.

Heuer, L., & Penrod, S. (1994). Juror note taking and question asking during trials: A national field experiment. *Law and Human Behavior, 18,* 121–150.

Hilgard, E.R. (1965). *Hypnotic susceptibility.* New York: Harcourt Brace Javanovich.

Hillbrand, M. (1995). Aggression against self and aggression against others in violent psychiatric patients. *Journal of Consulting and Clinical Psychology, 63,* 668–671.

Hilton, N.Z., & Simmons, J.L. (2001). The influence of actuarial risk assessment in clinical judgments and tribunal decisions about mentally disordered offenders in maximum security. *Law and Human Behavior, 25,* 393–408.

Hinshaw, S.P., Lahey, B.B., & Hart, E.L. (1993). Issues of taxonomy and comorbidity in the development of conduct disorder. *Development and Psychopathology, 5,* 31–49.

Hirschel, D., & Buzawa, E. (2002). Understanding the context of dual arrest with directions for future research. *Violence Against Women, 8,* 1449–1473.

Hirschel, D.J., Hutchison, I.W., & Dean, C.W. (1992). The failure of arrest to deter spouse abuse. *Journal of Research in Crime and Delinquency, 29,* 7–33.

Hirschi, T. (1969). *Causes of delinquency.* Los Angeles, CA: University of California Press.

Hirsh, H.R., Northrop, L.C., & Schmidt, F.L. (1986). Validity generalization for law enforcement occupations. *Personnel Psychology, 39,* 399–420.

Ho, T. (1999). Assessment of police officer applicants and testing instruments. *Journal of Offender Rehabilitation, 29,* 1–23.

Hodgins, S. (1992). Mental disorder, intellectual deficiency and crime: Evidence from a birth cohort. *Archives of General Psychiatry, 49,* 476–483.

Hodgins, S. (Ed.) (1993). The criminality of mentally disordered person. In S. Hodgins (Ed.), *Mental disorder and crime* (pp. 3–21). Newbury Park, CA: Sage

Hogarth, J. (1971). *Sentencing as a human process.* Toronto: University of Toronto Press.

Hoge, R.D. (1999). *Assessing adolescents in educational, counselling, and other settings.* Mahwah, New Jersey: Lawrence Erlbaum Associates.

Hoge, R.D., Andrews, D.A., & Lescheid, A.W. (1996). An investigation of risk and protective factors in a sample of youthful offenders. *Journal of Child Psychology and Psychiatry and Allied Disciplines, 37,* 419–424.

Hoge, S., Poythress, N., Bonnie, R., Monahan, J., Eisenberg, M., & Feucht-Haviar, T. (1997). The MacArthur Adjudication Competence Study: Diagnosis, psychopathology, and adjudicative competence-related abilities. *Behavioral Sciences and the Law, 15,* 329–345.

Hoge, S.K., Bonnie, R.J., Poythress, N., & Monahan, J. (1992). Attorney–client decision-making in criminal cases: Client competence and participation as perceived by their attorneys. *Behavioral Sciences and the Law, 10,* 385–394.

Hogue, T.E., & Peebles, J. (1997). The influence of remorse, intent, and attitudes toward sex offenders on judgments of a rapist. *Psychology, Crime, and Law, 3,* 249–259.

Hollin, C. (1989). *Psychology and crime: An introduction to criminological psychology.* New York: Routledge.

Holmes, R.M., & Holmes, S.T. (2002). *Profiling violent crimes: An investigative tool* (3rd ed.). Thousand Oaks, CA: Sage.

Holtzworth-Munroe, A., & Stuart, G.L. (1994). Typologies of male batterers: Three subtypes and the differences among them. *Psychological Bulletin, 116,* 476–497.

Homant, R.J., & Kennedy, D.B. (1998). Psychological aspects of crime scene profiling: Validity research. *Criminal Justice and Behavior, 25,* 319–343.

Home Office (1998). *Statistics on race and the criminal justice system.* London: Home Office.

Honts, C.R., & Raskin, D.C. (1988). A field study of the validity of the directed lie control question. *Journal of Police Science and Administration, 16,* 56–61.

Honts, C.R., Raskin, D.C., & Kircher, J.C. (1994). Mental and physical countermeasures reduce the accuracy of polygraph tests. *Journal of Applied Social Psychology, 79,* 252–259.

Hops, H., Davis, B., & Longoria, N. (1995). Methodological issues in direct observation: Illustrations with the Living in Familial Environments (LIFE) coding system. *Journal of Clinical Child Psychology, 55,* 341–346.

Horowitz, I.A., & ForsterLee, L. (2001). The effects of note-taking and trial transcript access on mock jury decisions in a complex civil trial. *Law and Human Behavior, 25,* 373–391.

Horowitz, I.A., & Seguin, D.G. (1986). The effects of bifurcation and death qualification on assignment of penalty in capital crimes. *Journal of Applied Social Psychology, 16,* 165–185.

Howitt, D. (2002). *Forensic and criminal psychology.* London, UK: Pearson Education.

Huesmann, L.R., Eron, L.D., Lefkowitz, M.M., & Walder, L.O. (1984). Stability of aggression over time and generations. *Developmental Psychology, 20,* 1120–1134.

Huff, C.R., Rattner, A., & Sagarin, E. (1996). *Convicted but innocent: Wrongful conviction and public policy.* Thousand Oaks, CA: Sage.

Humm, D.G., & Humm, K.A. (1950). Humm-Wadsworth temperament scale appraisals compared with criteria of job success in the Los Angeles Police Department. *The Journal of Psychology, 30,* 63–57.

Hung, K., & Bowles, S. (1995). Public perceptions of crime. *Juristat, 15.*

Hurley, W., & Dunne, M. (1991). Psychological distress and psychiatric morbidity in women prisoners. *Australia and New Zealand Journal of Psychiatry, 25,* 461–470.

Iacono, W.G., Cerri, A.M., Patrick, C.J., & Fleming, J.A.E. (1992). Use of antianxiety drugs as countermeasures in the detection of guilty knowledge. *Journal of Applied Psychology, 77,* 60–64.

Iacono, W.G., & Lykken, D.T. (1997). The validity of the lie detector: Two surveys of scientific opinion. *Journal of Applied Psychology, 82,* 426–433.

Iacono, W.G., & Patrick, C. J. (1988). Polygraphy techniques. In R. Rogers (Ed.), *Clinical assessment of malingering and deception* (2nd ed., pp. 252–281). New York: Guilford Press.

Iacono, W.G., & Patrick, C.J. (1999). Polygraph ("Lie Detector") testing: The state of the art. In A.K. Hess & I.B. Weiner (Eds.), *The handbook of forensic psychology* (2nd ed., pp. 440–473). New York: Wiley.

Iacono, W.G., & Patrick, C.J. (in press). Polygraph ("Lie Detector") testing: Current status and emerging trends. In A. K. Hess & I. B. Weiner (Eds.), *The handbook of forensic psychology* (3rd ed.).

Ilacqua, G.E., Coulson, G.E., Lombardo, D., & Nutbrown, V. (1999). Predictive validity of the Young Offender Level of Service Inventory for criminal recidivism of male and female young offenders. *Psychological Reports, 84,* 1214–1218.

Inbau, F.E., Reid, J.E., Buckley, J.P., & Jayne, B.C. (2001). *Criminal interrogation and confessions* (4th ed.). Gaithersberg, MD: Aspen.

Inciardi, J.A. (1986). Getting busted for drugs. In G. Beschner & A.S. Friedman (Eds.). *Teen drug use* (pp. 63–83). Lexington, MA: Lexington Books.

Inwald, R.E. (1992). *Inwald personality inventory technical manual* (revised ed.). Kew Gardens, NY: Hilson Research.

Izzett, R.R., & Leginski, W. (1974). Group discussion and the influence of defendant characteristics in a simulated jury setting. *The Journal of Social Psychology, 93,* 271–279.

Izzo, R. L., & Ross, R. R. (1990). Meta-analysis of rehabilitation programs for juvenile delinquents. *Criminal Justice and Behavior, 17,* 134–142.

Jacobs, P.A., Brunton, M., Melville, M.M., Brittain, M.M., & McClemonts, W.F. (1965). Aggressive behaviour, mental subnormality, and the XYY male. *Nature, 208,* 351–352.

Jaffe, P., Hastings, E., Reitzel, D., & Austin, G. (1993). The impact of police laying charges. In Z. Hilton (Ed.) *Legal responses to wife assault: Current trends and evaluation* (pp. 62–95). Newbury Park, CA: Sage.

Janoff-Bulman, R. (1979). Characterological versus behavioral self-blame: Inquiries into depression and rape. *Journal of Personality and Social Psychology, 37,* 1798–1809.

Jarey, M.L., & Stewart, M.A. (1985). Psychiatric disorder in the parents of adopted children with aggressive conduct disorder. *Neuropsychobiology, 13,* 7–11.

Jessor, R., Turbin, M.S., & Costa, F. (1998). Risk and protection in successful outcomes among disadvantaged adolescents. *Applied Developmental Science, 2,* 194–208.

John Howard Society. (1999). *Sentencing in Canada.* Toronto: John Howard Society.

John Howard Society. (2001). Retrieved May 10, 2004, from http://www.johnhoward.on.ca/Library/death/mar01.pdf

Johnson, H. (1996). *Dangerous domains: Violence against women in Canada.* Toronto: Nelson.

Johnson, H., & Sacco, V.F. (1995). Researching violence against women: Statistics Canada's national survey. *Canadian Journal of Criminology, 37,* 281–304.

Johnson, R., Jr., Barnhardt, J., & Zhu, J. (2004). The contribution of executive processes to deceptive responding. *Neuropsychologia, 42,* 878–901.

Johnston, J. C. (1997). *Aboriginal offender survey: Case files and interview sample.* Research Report No. R-61. Ottawa, ON: Correctional Service Canada.

Johnston, J.C. (2000). Aboriginal federal offender surveys: A synopsis. *Forum on Corrections Research,12,* 25–27.

Jones, A.B., & Llewellyn, J. (1917). *Malingering.* London: Heinemann.

Jones, W.D. (1997). *Murder of justice: New Jersey's greatest shame.* New York: Vantage Press.

Jordan, B.K., Schlenger, W.E., Fairbank, J.A., & Caddell, J.M. (1996). Prevalence of psychiatric disorders among incarcerated women II. Convicted felons entering prison. *Archives of General Psychiatry, 53,* 513–519.

Junginger, J. (1990). Predicting compliance with command hallucinations. *American Journal of Psychiatry, 147,* 245–247.

Justice Canada. (2002). *Statistical survey of provincial and territorial Review Boards* (as cited in Special study on mentally disordered accused and the criminal justice system). Canadian Centre for Justice Statistics. Prepared by Shirley Steller. Statistics Canada, Catalogue no. 85-559, Ministry of Industry, 2003.

Kagehiro, D.K. (1990). Defining the standard of proof injury instructions. *Psychological Science, 1,* 194–200.

Kahneman, D., & Tversky, A. (1982). Variants of uncertainty. *Cognition, 11,* 143–157.

Kalmuss, D.S.(1984). The intergenerational transmission of marital aggression. *Journal of Marriage and the Family, 46,* 11–19.

Kalvern, H., & Zeisel, H. (1966). *The American jury.* Boston: Little, Brown.

Kanas, N. & Barr, M.A. (1984). Self-control of psychotic productions in schizophrenics [Letter to the editor]. *Archives of General Psychiatry, 41,* 919–920.

Kassin, S.M. (1997). The psychology of confession evidence. *American Psychologist, 52,* 221–233.

Kassin, S.M. (1998). Eyewitness identification procedures: The fifth rule. *Law and Human Behavior, 22,* 649–653.

Kassin, S.M., Ellsworth, P., & Smith, V.L. (1989). The "general acceptance" of psychological research on eyewitness testimony. *American Psychologist, 49,* 878–893.

Kassin, S.M., Goldstein, C.C., & Savitsky, K. (2003). Behavioral confirmation in the interrogation room: On the dangers of presuming guilt. *Law and Human Behavior, 27,* 187–203.

Kassin, S.M., & Kiechel, K.L. (1996). The social psychology of false confessions: Compliance, internalization, and confabulation. *Psychological Science, 7,* 125–128.

Kassin, S.M., & McNall, K. (1991). Police interrogations and confessions. *Law and Human Behavior, 15,* 233–251.

Kassin, S.M., & Sommers, S.R. (1997). Inadmissible testimony, instructions to disregard, and the jury: Substantive versus procedural considerations. *Personality and Social Psychology Bulletin, 23,* 1046–1054.

Kassin, S.M., & Sukel, H. (1997). Coerced confessions and the jury: An experimental test of the "harmless error" rule. *Law and Human Behavior, 21,* 27–46.

Kassin, S.M., Tubb, V., Hosch, H.M., & Memon, A. (2001). On the "general acceptance" of eyewitness testimony research. *American Psychologist, 56,* 405–416.

Kassin, S.M., & Wrightsman, L.S. (1985). Confession evidence. In S.M. Kassin & L.S. Wrightsman (Eds.), *The psychology of evidence and trial procedures* (pp. 67–94). London, UK, Sage.

Katz, R.S. (2000). Explaining girls' and women's crime and desistance in the context of their victimization experiences: A developmental test of revised strain theory and the life course perspective. *Violence Against Women, 6,* 633–660.

Kaufman, J., & Zigler, E. (1987). Do abused children become abusive parents? *American Journal of Orthopsychiatry, 57,* 186–192.

Kazdin, A.E. (1993). Treatment of conduct disorder: Progress and directions in psychotherapy research. *Development and Psychopathology, 5,* 277–310.

Kazdin, A.E. (1997). Practitioner review: Psychosocial treatments for conduct disorder in children. *Journal of Child Psychology and Psychiatry and Allied Disciplines, 38,* 161–178.

Kebbell, M.R., & Wagstaff, G.F. (1998). Hypnotic interviewing: The best way to interview eyewitnesses. *Behavioural Sciences and the Law, 16,* 115–129.

Kemp, R., Towell, N., & Pike, G. (1997). When seeing should not be believing: Photographs, credit cards, and Fraud. *Applied Cognitive Psychology, 11,* 211–222.

Kendall-Tackett, K.A., Williams, L.M., & Finkelhor, D. (1993). Impact of sexual abuse in children: A review and synthesis of recent empirical studies. *Psychological Bulletin, 113,* 164–180.

Kendell, R.E., Chalmers, J.C., & Platz, C.L. (1987). Epidemiology of puerperal psychoses. *British Journal of Psychiatry, 150,* 662–673.

Kershner, R. (1996). Adolescent attitudes about rape. *Adolescence, 31,* 29–33.

Kilpatrick, D.G., Saunders, B.E., Veronen, L.J., Best, C.L., & Von, J.M. (1987). Criminal victimization: Lifetime prevalence, reporting to police, and psychological impact. *Crime and Delinquency, 33,* 479–489.

Kind, S.S. (1987). Navigational ideas and the Yorkshire ripper investigation. *Journal of Navigation, 40,* 385–393.

Kingsbury, S.J., Lambert, M.T., & Hendrickse, W. (1997). A two-factor model of aggression. *Psychiatry: Interpersonal and Biological Processes, 60,* 224–232.

Klassen, D., & O'Connor, W.A. (1989). Assessing the risk of violence in released mental patients: A cross-validation study. *Psychological Assessment, 1,* 75–81.

Klassen, D., & O'Connor, W.A. (1994). Demographic and case history variables in risk assessment. In J. Monahan & H.J. Steadman (Eds.). *Violence and mental disorder: Developments in risk assessment* (pp. 229–257). Chicago, IL: University of Chicago Press.

Kleinman, L., & Gordon, M. (1986). An examination of the relationship between police training and academy performance. *Journal of Police Science and Administration, 14,* 293–299.

Kleinmuntz, B., & Szucko, J.J. (1984). Lie detection in ancient and modern times: A call for contemporary scientific study. *American Psychologist, 39,* 766–776.

Knight, R.A. (1999). Validation of a typology for rapists. *Journal of Interpersonal Violence, 14,* 303–330.

Knight, R.A., & Prentky, R.A. (1990). Classifying sexual offenders: The development and corroboration of taxonomic models. In W.L. Marshall & D.R. Laws (Eds.). *Handbook of sexual assault: Issues, theories, and treatment of the offender* (pp. 23–52). New York, NY: Plenum Press.

Knight, R.A., Prentky, R.A., & Cerce, D.D. (1994). The development, reliability, and validity of an inventory for the multidimensional assessment of sex and aggression. *Criminal Justice and Behavior, 21,* 72–94.

Kocsis, R.N. Irwin, H.J., Hayes, A.F., & Nunn, R. (2000). Expertise in psychological profiling: A comparative assessment. *Journal of Interpersonal Violence, 15,* 311–331.

Köhnken, G. (1987). Training police officers to detect deceptive eyewitness statements. Does it work? *Social Behavior, 2,* 1–17.

Köhnken, G. (1995). Interviewing adults. In R. Bull and D. Carson (Eds.), *Handbook of psychology in legal contexts* (pp. 215–233). Toronto: Wiley.

Konecni, V.J., & Ebbesen, E.B. (1984). The mythology of legal decision making. *International Journal of Law and Psychiatry, 7,* 5–18.

Koocher, G.P., Goodman, G.S., White, C.S., Friedrich, W.N., Sivan, A.B., & Reynolds, C.R. (1995). Psychological science and the use of anatomically detailed dolls in child sexual-abuse assessments. *Psychological Bulletin, 118,* 199–222.

Koons, B.A., Burrow, J.D., Morash, M., & Bynum, T. (1997). Expert and offender perceptions of program elements linked to successful outcomes for incarcerated women. *Crime & Delinquency, 43,* 512–532.

Koss, M.P. (1993). Detecting the scope of rape: A review of the prevalence research methods. *Journal of Interpersonal Violence, 8,* 198–222.

Kosson, D.S., Cyterski, T.D., Steuerwald, B.L., Neumann, C.S., & Walker-Matthews, S. (2002). Reliability and validity of the Psychopathy Checklist: Youth Version (PCL:YV) in nonincarcerated adolescents males. *Psychological Assessment, 14,* 97–109.

Kramer, G.P., Kerr, N.L., & Carroll, J.S. (1990). Pretrial publicity, judicial remedies, and jury bias. *Law and Human Behavior, 14,* 409–438.

Kramer, J.H., & Lubitz, R.L. (1985). Pennsylvania's sentencing reform: The impact of commission established guidelines. *Crime and Delinquency, 31,* 481–500.

Krantz, S.E. (1988). The impact of divorce on children. In S.M. Dornbusch & M.H. Strober (Eds.), *Feminism, children, and the new families* (pp. 249–273). New York: Guilford Press.

Krauss, D.A., Sales, B.D., Becker, J.V., & Figueredo, A.J. (2000). Beyond prediction to explanation in risk assessment research: A comparison of two explanatory theories of criminality and recidivism. *International Journal of Law and Psychiatry, 23,* 91–112.

Kraut, R.E. (1980). Humans as lie detectors: Some second thoughts. *Journal of Communication, 30,* 209–216.

Kroes, W.H., Margolis, B.L., & Hurrell, J.J. (1974). Job stress in policemen. *Journal of Police Science and Administration, 2,* 145–155.

Kroner, D.G., & Mills, J.F. (2001). The accuracy of five risk appraisal instruments in predicting institutional misconduct and new convictions. *Criminal Justice and Behavior, 28,* 471–489.

Kropp, P.R., & Hart, S.D. (2000). The Spousal Assault Risk Assessment (SARA) Guide: Reliability and validity in adult male offenders. *Law and Human Behavior, 24,* 101–118.

Kropp, P.R., Hart, S., Webster, C., & Eaves, D. (1999). *Manual for the Spousal Assault Risk Assessment Guide* (3rd ed). Toronto: Multi-Health Systems.

Kurdek, L.A. (1981). An integrative perspective on children's divorce adjustment. *American Psychologist, 26,* 856–866.

Laboratory of Community Psychiatry, Harvard Medical School. (1973). *Competency to stand trial and mental fitness* (DHEW Pub. No. ADM-77-103). Rockville, MD: Department of Health, Education, and Welfare.

Lahey, B.B., Waldman, I.D., & McBurnett, K. (1999). The development of antisocial behavior: An integrative causal model. *Journal of Child Psychology and Psychiatry, 40,* 669–682.

Laird, R.D., Jordan, K.Y., Dodge, K.A., Petit, G.S., & Bates, J.E. (2001). Peer rejection in childhood, involvement with antisocial peers in early adolescence and the development of externalizing behavior problems. *Development and Psychopathology, 13,* 337–354.

Lamb, M.E., Hershkowitz, I., Sternber, K.J., Boat, B., & Everson, M.D. (1996). Investigative interviews of alleged sexual abuse victims with and without anatomical dolls. *Child Abuse and Neglect, 12,* 1251–1259.

Lamberth, J. (August 16, 1999). Driving while black: A statistician proves that prejudice still rules the road. *Washington Post.*

Lamphear, V.S. (1985). The impact of maltreatment on children's psychosocial adjustment: A review of the research. *Child Abuse and Neglect, 9,* 251–263.

Langevin, R. (1979). The effect of assertiveness training, Provera and sex of therapist in the treatment of genital exhibitionism. *Journal of Behavior Therapy and Experimental Psychiatry, 10,* 275–282.

Langevin, R., Handy, L., Paitich, D., & Russon, A. (1985). A new version of the Clarke Sex History Questionnaire for Males. In R. Langevin (Ed.), *Erotic preference, gender identity, and aggression in men: New research studies* (pp. 287–306). Hillsdale, NJ: Erlbaum.

Langleben, D.D., Schroeder, L., Maldjian, J.A., Gur, R.C., McDonald, S., Ragland, J.D., O'Brien, C.P., & Childress, A.R. (2002). Brain activity during simulated deception: An event-related functional magnetic resonance study. *Neuroimage, 15,* 727–732.

LaPrairie, C. (1989). *The role of sentencing in the over-representation of aboriginal people in correctional institutions.* Ottawa: Department of Justice Canada.

LaPrairie, C. (1992). Aboriginal crime and justice: Explaining the present, exploring the future. *Canadian Journal of Criminology, 34,* 281–298.

LaPrairie, C. (1996). *Examining Aboriginal corrections.* Ottawa, ON: Solicitor General of Canada, Corrections Branch.

LaPrairie, C. (2002). Aboriginal over-representation in the criminal justice system: A tale of nine cities. *Canadian Journal of Criminology, 44,* 181–208.

Larson, J.A. (1921). Modification of the Marston deception test. *Journal of the American Institute of Criminal Law and Criminology, 12,* 391–399.

Laub, J.H., Nagin, D.S., & Sampson, R.J. (1998). Trajectories of change in criminal offending: Good marriages and the desistance process. *American Sociological Review, 63,* 225–238.

Law Reform Commission of Canada (1976). *Mental Disorder in the Criminal Process.*

Lea, S., Auburn, T., & Kibblewhite, K. (1999). Working with sex offenders: The perceptions and experiences of professionals and paraprofessionals. *International Journal of Offender Therapy and Comparative Criminology, 43,* 103–119.

Leadbeater, B.J., Kuperminc, G.P., Blatt, S.J., & Hertzog, C. (1999). A multivariate model of gender differences in adolescents' internalizing and externalizing problems. *Developmental Psychology, 35,* 1268–1282.

Leblanc, M. (1993). Late adolescent deceleration of criminal activity and development of self- and social control. *Studies on Crime and Crime Prevention, 2,* 51–68.

Lees-Haley, P.R. (1997). MMPI-2 base rates for 492 personal injury plaintiffs: Implications and challenges for forensic assessment. *Journal of Clinical Psychology, 53,* 745–755.

Leippe, M.R. (1995). The case for expert testimony about eyewitness memory. *Psychology, Public Policy, and Law, 1,* 909–959.

Leichtman, M.D., & Ceci, S.J. (1995). The effects of stereotypes and suggestions on preschoolers' reports. *Developmental Psychology, 31,* 568–578.

Leo, R.A. (1992). From coercion to deception: The changing nature of police interrogation in America. *Crime, Law and Social Change, 18,* 35–39.

Leo, R.A., & Ofshe, R.J. (1998). The consequences of false confessions: Deprivations of liberty and miscarriages of justice in the age of psychological interrogation. *The Journal of Criminal Law and Criminology, 88,* 429–496.

Lidz, C.W., Mulvey, E.P., & Gardner, W. (1993). The accuracy of predictions of violence to others. *Journal of the American Medical Association, 269,* 1007–1011.

Lieberman, J.D., & Sales, B.D. (1997). What social science teaches us about the jury instruction process. *Psychology, Public Policy, and Law, 3,* 589–644.

Lightfoot, L.O., & Barbaree, H.E. (1993). The relationship between substance use and abuse and sexual offending in adolescents. In H.E. Barbaree & W.L. Marshall (Eds.), *Juvenile sex offender* (pp. 203–224). New York, NY: Guilford Press.

Lindberg, M., Chapman, M.T., Samsock, D., Thomas, S.W., & Lindberg, A. (2003). Comparisons of three different investigative interview techniques with young children. *The Journal of Genetic Psychology, 164,* 5–28.

Lindsay, D.S. (1994). Memory source monitoring and eyewitness testimony. In D.F. Ross, J.D. Read, & M.P. Toglia (Eds.), *Adult eyewitness testimony: Current trends and development* (pp. 27–55). New York: Cambridge University Press.

Lindsay, D.S., & Read, J.D. (1995). "Memory work" and recovered memories of childhood sexual abuse: Scientific evidence and public, professional, and personal issues. *Psychology, Public Policy, and Law, 1,* 846–909.

Lindsay, P.S. (1977). Fitness to stand trial in Canada: An overview in light of the recommendations of the law reform commission of Canada. *Criminal Law Quarterly, 19,* 303–348.

Lindsay, R.C.L., Lea, J.A., & Fulford, J.A. (1991). Sequential lineup presentation: Technique matters. *Journal of Applied Psychology, 76,* 741–745.

Lindsay, R.C.L., Martin, R., & Webber, L. (1994). Default values in eyewitness descriptions: A problem for the match-to-description lineup foil selection strategy. *Law and Human Behavior, 18,* 527–541.

Lindsay, R.C.L., Wallbridge, H., & Drennan, D. (1987). Do clothes make the man? An exploration of the effect of lineup attire on eyewitness identification accuracy.

Canadian Journal of Behavioural Science, 19, 463–478.

Lindsay, R.C.L., & Wells, G.L. (1985). Improving eyewitness identification from lineups: Simultaneous versus sequential lineup presentations. *Journal of Applied Psychology, 70,* 556–564.

Linehan, M.M. (1993). *Cognitive-behavioral treatment of borderline personality disorder.* New York, NY: Guildford Press.

Linehan, M.M., Schmidt, H., Dimeff, L.A., Craft, J.C., Kanter, J., & Comtois, K.A. (1999). Dialectical behavior therapy for patients with borderline personality disorder and drug-dependence. *American Journal of Addictions, 8,* 279–292.

Link, B.G., Andrews, H.A., & Cullen, F.T. (1992). The violent and illegal behavior of mental patients reconsidered. *American Sociological Review, 57,* 275–292.

Link, B.G., & Steuve, A. (1994). Psychotic symptoms and the violent/illegal behavior of mental patients compared to community controls. In J. Monahan & H. J. Steadman (Eds.), *Violence and mental disorder: Developments in risk assessment* (137–159). Chicago: University of Chicago Press.

Lipsey, M.W. (1992). Juvenile delinquency treatment: A meta-analytic inquiry into the variablilty of effects. In T.D. Cook, H. Cooper, D.S. Corday, H. Hartmann, L.V. Hedges, R.J. Light, T.A. Louis, & F. Mosteller (Eds.), *Meta-analysis for explanation* (pp. 83–127). New York: Sage.

Lipsey, M.W., & Derzon, J.H. (1998). Predictors of violent or serious delinquency in adolescence and early adulthood: A synthesis of longitudinal research. In R. Loeber & D.P. Farrington (Eds.). *Serious and violent juvenile offenders: Risk factors and successful interventions* (pp. 86–105). Thousand Oaks, CA: Sage Publications.

Lipsitt, P.D., Lelos, D., & McGarry, L. (1971). Competency to stand trial: A screening instrument. *American Journal of Psychiatry, 128,* 104–109.

Lisak, D., & Roth, S. (1988). Motivational factors in nonincarcerated sexually aggressive men. *Journal of Personality and Social Psychology, 55,* 795–802.

Litman, L.C. (2004). Retrieved May 10, 2004, from http://www.cpa.ca/ PharmPsych/Litman2.pdf

Lochman, J.E., Whidby, J.M., & FitzGerald, D.P. (2000). Cognitive-behavioral assessment and treatment with aggressive children. In P.C. Kendall (Ed.), *Child and adolescent therapy: Cognitive-behavioral procedures* (2nd ed.). New York, NY: Guilford.

Loeber, R., & Farrington, D.P. (Eds.). (1998). *Serious and violent juvenile offenders.* Thousand Oaks, CA: Sage Publications.

Loeber, R., & Farrington, D.P. (2000). Young children who commit crime: Epidemiology, developmental origins, risk factors, early interventions, and policy implications. *Development and Psychopathology, 12,* 737–762.

Loeber, R., Keenan, K., Lahey, B.B., Green, S.M., & Thomas, C. (1993). Evidence for developmentally based diagnoses of Oppositional Defiant Disorder and Conduct Disorder. *Journal of Abnormal Psychology, 100,* 379–390.

Loftus, E., & Palmer, J.C. (1974). Reconstructions of automobile destruction: An example of the interaction between language and memory. *Journal of Verbal Learning and Verbal Behavior, 12,* 585–589.

Loftus, E.F. (1975). Leading questions and the eyewitness report. *Cognitive Psychology, 7,* 560–572.

Loftus, E.F. (1979a). Reactions to blatantly contradictory information. *Memory and Cognition, 7,* 368–374.

Loftus, E.F. (1979b). The malleability of human memory. *American Scientist, 67,* 312–320.

Loftus, E.F. (1983). Silence is not golden. *American Psychologist, 38,* 564–572.

Loftus, E.F., Altman, D., & Geballe, R. (1975). Effects of questioning upon a witness' later recollections. *Journal of Police Science and Administration, 3,* 162–165.

Loftus, E.G., Miller, D.G., & Burns, H.J. (1978). Semantic integration of verbal information into a visual memory. *Journal of Experimental Psychology. Human Learning and Memory, 4,* 19–31.

Lombroso, C., & Ferrero, W. (1895). *The female offender.* Fisher Unwin, London.

London Family Court Clinic (1993). *Three years after the verdict: A longitudinal study of the social and psychological adjustment of child witnesses referred to the child witness project* (FVDS #4887-06-91-026). London, ON: London Family Court Clinic Inc.

Lonsway, K.A., & Fitzgerald, L.F. (1994). Rape myths: In review. *Psychology of Women Quarterly, 18,* 133–164.

Loo, R. (1994). Burnout among Canadian police managers. *The International Journal of Organizational Analysis, 2,* 406–417.

Loo, R. (2003). A meta-analysis of police suicide rates: Findings and issues. *Suicide and Life-Threatening Behavior, 33,* 313–335.

Loos, M.E., & Alexander, P.C. (1997). Differential effects associated with self-reported histories of abuse and neglect in a college sample. *Journal of Interpersonal Violence, 12,* 340–360.

Loucks, A.D., & Zamble, E. (2000). Predictors of criminal behavior and prison misconduct in serious female offenders. *Empirical and Applied Criminal Justice Review, 1,* 1–47.

Louis de la Parte Florida Mental Health Institute, The Department of Mental Health Law and Policy. (2002). Retrieved June 20, 2004, from http://www.fmhi.usf.edu/mhlp/ Research.htm

Lowry, P.E. (1996). A survey of the assessment center process in the public sector. *Public Personnel Management, 25,* 307–321.

Luo, B., Cheu, J.W., & Siegel, A. (1998). Cholecystokinin B receptors in the peri-aqueductal gray potentiate defensive rage behavior elicited from the medial hypothalamus of the cat. *Brain Research, 796,* 27–37.

Luus, C.A.E., & Wells, G.L. (1991). Eyewitness identification and the selection of distractors for lineups. *Law and Human Behavior, 15,* 43–57.

Luus, C.A.E., & Wells, G.L. (1994). The malleability of eyewitness confidence: Cowitness and perseverance effects. *Journal of Applied Psychology, 79,* 714–723.

Lykken, D.T. (1960). The validity of the guilty knowledge technique: The effects of faking. *Journal of Applied Psychology, 44,* 258–262.

Lykken, D.T. (1998). *A tremor in the blood. Uses and abuses of the lie detector.* New York: Plenum.

Maccoby, E.E., & Mnookin, R.H. (1992). *Dividing the child: Social and legal dilemmas of custody.* Cambridge: Harvard University Press.

MacCoun, R.J., & Kerr, N.L. (1988). Asymmetric influence in mock deliberation: Jurors' bias for leniency. *Journal of Personality and Social Psychology, 54,* 21–33.

MacDonald, J.M., Manz, P.W., Alpert, G.P., & Dunham, R.G. (2003). Police use of force: Examining the relationship between calls for service and the balance of police force and suspect resistance. *Journal of Criminal Justice, 31,* 119–127.

MacMillan, H.L. (2000). Child maltreatment: What we know in the year 2000. *Canadian Journal of Psychiatry, 45,* 702–709.

MacMillan, H.L., Fleming, J.E., Streiner, D.L., Lin, E., Boyle, M.H., Jamieson, E., Duku, E.K., Walsh, C.A., Wong, M.Y.Y., & Beardslee, W.R. (2001). Childhood abuse and lifetime psychopathology in a community sample. *American Journal of Psychiatry, 158,* 1878–1883.

Magdol, L., Moffitt, T.E., & Caspi, A. (1997). Gender differences in partner violence in a birth cohort of 21-year-olds: Bridging the gap between clinical and epidemiological approaches. *Journal of Consulting and Clinical Psychology, 65,* 68–78.

Malinosky-Rummell, R., & Hansen, D.J. (1993). Long-term consequences of childhood physical abuse. *Psychological Bulletin, 114,* 68–79.

Malpass, R.S., & Devine, P.G. (1981). Eyewitness identification: Lineup instructions and the absence of the offender. *Journal of Applied Psychology, 66,* 482–489.

Mann, S., Vrij, A., & Bull, R. (2004). Detecting true lies: Police officers' ability to detect suspects' lies. *Journal of Applied Psychology, 89,* 137–149.

Mark, V.H., & Ervin, F.R. (1970). *Violence and the brain.* New York: Harper and Row.

Marlatt, G.A., & Gordon, J.R. (Eds.) (1985). *Relapse prevention: Maintenance strategies in the treatment of addictive behaviors.* New York: Guilford.

Marques, J.K. (1999). How to answer the questions "Does sexual offender treatment work?" *Journal of Interpersonal Violence, 14,* 437–451.

Marshall, W.L. (1999). Current status of North American assessment and treatment programs for sexual offenders. *Journal of Interpersonal Violence, 14,* 221–239.

Marshall, W.L., Anderson, D., & Champagne, F. (1997). Self-esteem and its relationship to sexual offending. *Psychology, Crime and Law, 3,* 161–186.

Marshall, W.L., & Barbaree, H.E. (1988). An outpatient treatment program for child molesters. *Annals of the New York Academy of Sciences, 528,* 205–214.

Marshall, W.L., & Barbaree, H.E. (1990). An integrated theory of the etiology of sexual offending. In W.L. Marshall & D.R. Laws, *Handbook of sexual assault: Issues, theories, and treatment of the offender* (pp. 257–275). New York, NY: Plenum Press.

Marshall, W.L., Barbaree, H.E., & Fernandez, Y.M. (1995). Some aspects of social competence in sexual offenders. *Sexual Abuse: Journal of Research and Treatment, 7,* 113–127.

Marshall, W.L., Eccles, A., & Barbaree, H.E. (1991). The treatment of exhibitionists: A focus on sexual deviance versus cognitive and relationship features. *Behavior Research and Therapy, 29,* 129–135.

Marshall, W.L., & Fernandez, Y.M. (2003). Sexual preferences are they useful in the assessment and treatment of sexual offenders? *Aggression and Violent Behavior, 8,* 131–143.

Martinson, R. (1974). What works? Questions and answers about prison reform. *The Public Interest, 35,* 22–54.

Masten, A.S., Best, K.M., & Garmezy, N. (1990). Resilience and development: Contributions from the study of children who overcome adversity. *Development and Psychopathology, 2,* 425–444.

McCloskey, M., & Egeth, H. (1983). Eyewitness identification: What can a psychologist tell a jury? *American Psychologist, 38,* 550–563.

McCloskey, M., & Zaragoza, M. (1985). Misleading post event information and memory for events: Arguments and evidence against memory impairment hypothesis. *Journal of Experimental Psychology: General, 114,* 1–16.

McCormick, C.T. (1972). *Handbook of the law of evidence* (2nd ed.). St. Paul, MN: West.

McCraty, R., Tomasino, D., Atkinson, M., & Sundram, J. (1999). *Impact of the HeartMath self-management skills program on physiological and psychological stress in police officers.* Boulder Creek, CA: HeartMath Research Center, Institute of HeartMath.

McDonagh, D., Taylor, K., & Blanchette, K. (2002). Correctional adaptation of dialectical behaviour therapy (DBT) for federally sentenced women. *Forum on Corrections, 14,* 36–39.

McFatter, R.M. (1986). Sentencing disparity. *Journal of Applied Social Psychology, 16,* 150–164.

McGurk, B.J., & McDougall, C. (1981). A new approach to Eysenck's theory of criminality. *Personality and Individual Differences, 2,* 338–340.

McKenna, P.F. (2002). *Police powers I.* Toronto, ON: Prentice Hall.

McMahon, M. (1999). Battered women and bad science: The limited validity and utility of battered women syndrome. *Psychiatry, Psychology, and Law, 6,* 23–49.

McMahon, R.J. (1994). Diagnosis, assessment, and treatment of externalizing problems in children: The role of longitudinal data. *Journal of Consulting and Clinical Psychology, 62,* 901–917.

McNiel, D.E., & Binder, R.L. (1994). The relationship between acute psychiatric symptoms, diagnosis, and short-term risk of violence. *Hospital and Community Psychiatry, 45,* 133–137.

McNiel, D.E., Sandberg, D.A., & Binder, R.L. (1998). The relationship between confidence and accuracy in clinical assessment of psychiatric patients' potential for violence. *Law and Human Behavior, 22,* 655–669.

Meadow, R. (1977). Munchausen syndrome by proxy: The hinterland of child abuse. *Lancet, 2,* 343–345.

Meehl, P.E. (1954). *Clinical vs. statistical prediction.* Minneapolis: University of Minnesota Press.

Meissner, C.A., & Brigham, J.C. (2001). Thirty years of investigating the own-race bias in memory for faces: A meta-analytic review. *Psychology, Public Policy, and Law, 7,* 1–35.

Meissner, C.A., & Russano, M.B. (2003). The psychology of interrogations and false confessions: Research and recommendations. *The Canadian Journal of Police and Security Services: Practice, Policy and Management, 1,* 53–64.

Meissner, D. (2000, March 5). Reena Virk murder trial set to begin this week. *The Canadian Press.* Retrieved May 12, 2004, from http://acmi.canoe.ca/CNEWSLaw0003/13_virk6.html

Meloy, J.R. (1997). Predatory violence during mass murder. *Journal of Forensic Sciences, 42,* 326–329.

Melton, G., Petrila, J., Poythress, N.G., & Slobogin, C. (1997). Competency to stand trial. In *Psychological evaluations for the court: A handbook for mental health professionals and lawyers* (2nd ed., pp. 119–155). New York: Guilford Press.

Melton, G.B., Petrila, J., Poythress, N.G., & Slobogin, C. (1987). *Psychological evaluations for the courts.* New York: Guilford.

Melton, H.C. (1999). Police response to domestic violence. *Journal of Offender Rehabilitation, 29,* 1–21.

Memon, A., & Bull, R. (1991). The cognitive interview: Its origins, empirical support, evaluation and practical implications. *Journal of Community and Applied Social Psychology, 1,* 291–307.

Memon, A., & Gabbert, G. (2003). Improving the identification accuracy of senior witnesses: Do prelineup questions and sequential testing help? *Journal of Applied Psychology, 88,* 341–347.

Memon, A., & Shuman, D.W. (1998). Juror perception of experts in civil disputes: The role of race and gender. *Law and Psychology Review, 22,* 179–197.

Menard, S., & Huizinga, D. (1989). Age, period, and cohort size effects on self-reported alcohol, marijuana, and polydrug use: Results from the National Youth Survey. *Social Science Research, 18,* 174–194.

Mental Health, Law, and Policy Institute, Department of Psychology, Simon Fraser University. (2004). Retrieved May 10, 2004, from http://www2.sfu.ca/mhlpi/

Merton R.K. (1938). Social structure and anomie. *American Sociological Review, 3,* 672–682.

Messman-Moore, T.L., & Long, P.J. (2003). The role of childhood sexual abuse sequelae in the sexual revictimization of women: An empirical review and theoretical reformulation. *Clinical Psychology Review, 23,* 537–571.

Miethe, T.D., & Drass, K.A. (1999). Exploring the social context of instrumental and expressive homicides: An application of qualitative comparative analysis. *Journal of Quantitative Criminology, 15,* 1–21.

Millis, J.B., & Kornblith, P.R. (1992). Fragile beginnings: Identification and treatment of postpartum disorders. *Health and Social Work, 17,* 192–199.

Millon, C.M. (1987). Concordance among Borderline personality disorder measures and the predictivity of their clinical attributes. *Dissertation Abstracts International, 47,* 50–61.

Mischel, W. (1968). *Personality and assessment.* New York: Lawrence Erlbaum.

Mitchell, K.J., Finkelhor, D., & Wolak, J. (2001). Risk factors for and impact of online sexual solicitation of youth. *Journal of the American Medical Association, 285,* 3011–3014.

Mitchell, K.J., Livosky, M., & Mather, M. (1998). The weapon focus effect revisited: The role of novelty. *Legal and Criminological Psychology, 3,* 287–303.

Mitchell, M., & Jolley, J. (1988). *Research design explained.* New York: Holt, Rinehart, and Winston, Inc.

Moffitt, T.E. (1993). Adolescence-limited and life-course persistent antisocial behaviour: A developmental taxonomy. *Psychological Review, 100,* 674–701.

Moffitt, T.E., Caspi, A., Harrington, H., & Milne, B.J. (2002). Males on the life-course persistent and adolescence limited antisocial pathways: Follow-up at age 26 years. *Development and Psychopathology, 14,* 179–207.

Moffitt, T.E., & Henry, B. (1989). Neurological assessment of executive functions in self-reported delinquents. *Developmental and Psychopathology, 1,* 105–118.

Monahan, J. (1981). *Predicting violent behavior: An assessment of clinical techniques.* Beverly Hills, CA: Sage.

Monahan, J., & Steadman, H. J. (1994). *Violence and mental disorder: Developments in risk assessment.* Chicago: University of Chicago Press.

Monahan, J., Steadman, H.J., Appelbaum, P.S., Robbins, P.C., Mulvey, E.P., Silver, E., et al. (2000). Developing a clinically useful actuarial tool for assessing violence risk. *British Journal of Psychiatry, 176,* 312–319.

Moran, R. (1985). The modern foundation for the insanity defense: The cases of James Hadfield (1800) and Daniel M'Naughten

(1843). *Annals of the American Academy of Political and Social Science, 477,* 31–42.

Morgan, P. (1975). *Child care: Sense and fable.* London: Temple Smith.

Mossman, D. (1994). Assessing predictions of violence: Being accurate about accuracy. *Journal of Consulting and Clinical Psychology, 62,* 783–792.

Motiuk, L.L., & Porporino, F.J. (1991). *The prevalence, nature, and severity of mental health problems among federal male inmates in Canadian penitentiaries* (Research Report No. 24). Ottawa: Correctional Service of Canada.

Motiuk, L.L., & Sevin, R.C. (2001). *Compendium 2000 on effective correctional programming.* Ottawa: Correctional Service of Canada.

Munsterberg, H. (1908). *On the witness stand.* Garden City, New York: Doubleday.

Murphy, J.M. (1976). Psychiatric labelling in cross-cultural perspective: Similar kinds of behaviour appear to be labelled abnormal in diverse cultures. *Science, 191,* 1019–1028.

Murrie, D.C., Cornell, D.G., Kaplan, S., McConville, D., & Levy-Elkon, A. (2004). Psychopathy scores and violence among juvenile offenders: A multi-measure study. *Behavioral Sciences and the Law, 22,* 49–67.

Myers, B., Rosol, A., & Boelter, E. (2003). Polygraph evidence and juror judgments: The effects of corroborating evidence. *Journal of Applied Psychology, 35,* 948–962.

Myers, W.C., Scott, K., Burgess, A.W., & Burgess, A.G. (1995). Psychopathology, biopsychosocial factors, crime characteristics, and classification of 25 homicidal youths. *Journal of the American Academy of Child and Adolescent Psychiatry, 34,* 1483–1489.

Narby, D.J., Cutler, B.L., & Moran, G. (1993). A meta-analysis of the association between authoritarianism and jurors' perceptions of defendant culpability. *Journal of Applied Psychology, 78,* 34–42.

National Crime Prevention Council. (1995). *Risk or threat to children.* Ottawa, ON: National Crime Prevention Council.

National Crime Prevention Council. (1997). *Preventing crime by investing in families and communities: Promoting positive outcomes in youth twelve- to eighteen-years-old.* Ottawa, ON: National Crime Prevention Council.

National Crime Prevention Council (2001). *Randomized field trial of multisystemic therapy in Ontario: Final results of a four-year study.* Ottawa, ON: National Crime Prevention Council.

National Parole Board (2002a). *Offenders serving a life sentence for murder: A statistical overview.* Ottawa: National Parole Board.

National Parole Board (2002b). *National parole board policy manual.* Ottawa: National Parole Board.

National Parole Board. (2003a). Retrieved June 10, 2004, from http://www.npb-cnlc.gc.ca/about/part1_e.htm

National Parole Board. (2003b). Retrieval May 25, 2004, from http://www.npb-cnlc.gc.ca/whatsn/myths053001_e.htm

National Parole Board (2004). *2003–2004 performance monitoring report.* Ottawa: National Parole Board.

National Research Council (2003). *The polygraph and lie detection.* Washington, DC: National Academies Press.

Navon, D. (1990). How critical is the accuracy of eyewitness memory? Another look at the issue of lineup diagnosticity. *Journal of Applied Psychology, 75,* 506–510.

Nazroo, J. (1995). Uncovering gender differences in the use of marital violence: The effect of methodology. *Sociology, 29,* 475–494.

Newhill, C.E., Mulvey, E.P., & Lidz, C.W. (1995). Characteristics of violence in the community by female patients seen in a psychiatric emergency service. *Psychiatric Services, 46,* 785–789.

Ng, W., & Lindsay, R.C.L. (1994). Cross-race facial recognition: Failure of the contact hypothesis. *Journal of Cross-Cultural Psychology, 25,* 217–232.

Nicholson, R.A., & Kugler, K. (1991). Competent and incompetent criminal defendants: A quantitative review of comparative research. *Psychological Bulletin, 109,* 355–370.

Niedermeier, K.E., Horowitz, I.A., & Kerr, N.L. (1999). Informing jurors of their nullification power: A route to a just verdict or judicial chaos? *Law and Human Behavior, 23,* 331–351.

Nietzel, M.T. (1979). *Crime and its modification: A social learning perspective.* Oxford: Pergamon.

Nisbett, R.E., & Wilson, T.D. (1977). Telling more than we can know: Verbal reports on mental processes. *Psychological Review, 84,* 231–259.

Note. (1953). Voluntary false confessions: A neglected area in criminal investigation. *Indiana Law Review, 28,* 374–392.

Nuffield, J. (1982). *Parole decision-making in Canada.* Ottawa: Solicitor General of Canada.

O'Hara, M.W. (1995). Childbearing. In M.W. O'Hara, R.C. Reiter, S.R. Johnson, A. Milburn, & J. Engeldinger (Eds.). *Psychological aspects of women's reproductive health* (pp. 26–48). New York, NY: Springer Publishing Co.

O'Leary, K.D., Barling, J., & Arias, I. (1989). Prevalence and stability of physical aggression between spouses: A longitudinal analysis. *Journal of Consulting and Clinical Psychology, 57,* 263–268.

O'Neill, M.L., Lidz, V., & Heilbrun, K. (2003). Adolescents with psychopathic characteristics in a substance abusing cohort: Treatment process and outcomes. *Law and Human Behavior, 27,* 299–313.

Odgers, C.L., & Moretti, M.M. (2002). Aggressive and antisocial girls: Research update and challenges. *International Journal of Forensic Mental Health, 1,* 103–119.

Office of Juvenile Studies and Delinquency Prevention. (1992). *Juvenile justice bulletin: OJJDP update on statistics.* Washington,

DC: Office of Juvenile Studies and Delinquency Prevention.

Offord, D.R., Boyle, M.H., Szatmari, P., Rae Grant, J.L., Links, P.S., Cadman, D.T., Byles, J.A., Crawford, J.W., Blum, H.M., Byrne, C., Thomas, H., & Woodward, C.A. (1987). Ontario Child Health Study: II Six month prevalence of disorder and rates of service utilization. *Archives of General Psychiatry, 44,* 832–836.

Offord, D.R., Lipman, E.L., & Duku, E.K. (2001). Epidemiology of problem behaviour up to age 12 years. In R. Loeber & D.P. Farrington (Eds.), *Child delinquents* (pp. 95–134). Thousand Oaks, CA: Sage Publications.

Ofshe, R.J. (1989). Coerced confessions: The logic of seemingly irrational action. *Journal of Cultic Studies, 6,* 1–15.

Ofshe, R.J., & Leo, R.A. (1997). The social psychology of police interrogation: The theory and classification of true and false confessions. *Studies in Law, Politics, and Society, 16,* 189–251.

Ofshe, R.J., & Watters, E. (1994). *Making monsters: False memories, psychotherapy, and sexual hysteria.* New York: Charles Scribner's.

Ogloff, J.R.P. (Ed.). (2002). *Taking psychology and law into the 21st century.* New York: Kluwer Academic.

Ogloff, J.R.P., & Cronshaw, S.F. (2001). Expert psychological testimony: Assisting or misleading the trier of fact. *Canadian Psychology, 42,* 87–91.

Ogloff, J.R.P., Schweighofer, A., Turnbull, S., & Whittemore, K. (1992). Empirical research and the insanity defense: How much do we really know? In J.R.P. Ogloff (Ed.), *Psychology and law: The broadening of the discipline* (pp. 171–210). Durham, NC: Carolina Academic Press.

Ogloff, J.R.P., & Vidmar, N. (1994). The effect of pretrial publicity on jurors: A study to compare the relative effects of television and print media in a child sex abuse case. *Law and Human Behavior, 18,* 507–525.

Ogloff, J.R.P., Wallace, D.H., & Otto, R.K. (1991). Competencies in the criminal process. In D. K. Kagehiro & W.S. Laufer (Eds.), *Handbook of psychology and law* (pp. 343–360). New York, NY: Springer Verlag.

Olczak, P.V., Kaplan, M.F., & Penrod, S. (1991). Attorneys' lay psychology and its effectiveness in selecting jurors: Three empirical studies. *Journal of Social Behavior and Personality, 6,* 431–452.

Olio, K.A., & Cornell, W.F. (1998). The façade of scientific documentation: A case study of Richard Ofshe's analysis of the Paul Ingram case. *Psychology, Public Policy, and Law, 4,* 1182–1197.

Orchard, T.L., & Yarmey, A.D. (1995). The effects of whispers, voice-sample duration, and voice distinctiveness on criminal speaker identification. *Applied Cognitive Psychology, 9,* 249–260.

Otto, R., & Heilbrun, K. (2002). The practice of forensic psychology: A look toward the future in light of the past. *American Psychologist, 57,* 5–19.

Ouimet, M., & Leblanc, M. (1993). Life events and continuation of criminal activities during adolescence and young adulthood. *Revenue Internationale de Criminologie et de Police Technique, 46,* 321–344.

Paglia, A., & Schuller, R.A. (1998). Jurors' use of hearsay evidence: The effects of type and timing of instructions. *Law and Human Behavior, 22,* 501–518.

Paik, H., & Comstock, G. (1994). The effects of television violence on antisocial behavior: A meta-analysis. *Communication Research, 21,* 516–546.

Palys, T.S., & Divorski, S. (1986). Explaining sentencing disparity. *Canadian Journal of Criminology, 28,* 347–362.

Pankratz, L. (1988). Malingering on intellectual and neuropsychological measures. In R. Rogers (Ed.), *Clinical assessment of malingering and deception* (1st ed., pp. 168–192). New York: Guilford Press.

Paolucci, E., Genuis, M., & Violato, C. (2001). A meta-analysis of the published research on the effects of child sexual abuse. *Journal of Psychology, 135,* 17–36.

Parker, A.D., & Brown, J. (2000). Detection of deception: Statement Validity Analysis as a means of determining truthfulness or falsity of rape allegations. *Legal and Criminological Psychology, 5,* 237–259.

Parker, J.G., & Asher, S.R. (1987). Peer relations and later personal adjustment: Are low accepted children at risk? *Psychological Bulletin, 102,* 357–389.

Parliament, L., & Yarmey, A. D. (2002). Deception in eyewitness identification. *Criminal Justice and Behavior, 29,* 734–746.

Parwatikar, S.D., Holcomb, W.R., & Menninger, K.A., II. (1985). The detection of malingered amnesia in accused murders. *Bulletin of American Academy of Psychiatry and Law, 13,* 97–103.

Patrick, C.J., Bradley, M.M., & Lang, P.J. (1993). Emotion in the criminal psychopath: Startle reflex modulation. *Journal of Abnormal Psychology, 102,* 82–92.

Patrick, C.J., & Iacono, W.G. (1989). Psychopathy, threat, and polygraph test accuracy. *Journal of Applied Psychology, 74,* 347–355.

Patrick, C.J., & Iacono, W.G. (1991). Validity of the control question polygraph test: The problem of sampling bias. *Journal of Applied Social Psychology, 76,* 229–238.

Patterson, G.R., Reid, J.B., & Dishion, T.J. (1998). *Antisocial boys.* Eugene, OR: Castalia.

Paul, G.L., & Lentz, R.J. (1977).*Psychosocial treatment of chronic mental patients: Milieu versus social learning programs.* Cambridge, MA: Harvard University Press.

Pavlidis, I., Eberhardt, N.L., & Levine, J.A. (2002). Seeing though the face of deception. *Nature, 415,* 35.

Pearson, F.S., Lipton, D.S., & Cleland, C.M. (November 20, 1996). *Some preliminary findings from the CDATE project.* Paper presented at the Annual Meeting of the American Society of Criminology, Chicago.

Pence, E., & Paymar, M. (1993). *Education groups for men who batter: The Duluth model*. New York, NY: Springer Publishing Co.

Pennington, N., & Hastie, R. (1986). Evidence evaluation in complex decision making. *Journal of Personality and Social Psychology, 51,* 242–258.

Pennington, N., & Hastie, R. (1988). Explanation-based decision making: Effects of memory structure on judgement. *Journal of Experimental Psychology: Learning, Memory, and Cognition, 14,* 521-533.

Penrod, S.D., & Cutler, B. (1995). Witness confidence and witness accuracy: Assessing their forensic relation. *Psychology, Public Policy, and Law, 1,* 817–845.

Penrod, S.D., & Heuer, L. (1997). Tweaking commonsense: Assessing aids to jury decision making. *Psychology, Public Policy, and Law, 3,* 259–284.

Perez, D.A., Hosch, H.M., Ponder, B., & Trejo, G.C. (1993). Ethnicity of defendants and jurors as influences on jury decisions. *Journal of Applied Social Psychology, 23,* 1249–1262.

Peters, M. (2001). Forensic psychological testimony: Is the courtroom door now locked and barred? *Canadian Psychology, 42,* 101–108.

Peterson, C., & Biggs, M. (1997). Interviewing children about trauma: Problems with "specific" questions. *Journal of Traumatic Stress, 10,* 279–290.

Peterson, C., & Grant, M. (2001). Forced-choice: Are forensic interviewers asking the right questions? *Canadian Journal of Behavioural Science, 2001,* 112–127.

Pfeifer, J., & Hart-Mitchell, R. (2001). Evaluating the effect of healing lodge residency on adult offenders. Canadian Institute for Peace, Justice and Security, University of Regina.

Picard, A., (2003, July 22). Grieving mother's farewell: "Adieu, my little flower." *Globe and Mail*. Retrieved April 30, 2004, from http://www.globeandmail.com.

Pickel, K.L. (1998). Unusualness and threat as possible causes of weapon focus. *Memory, 6,* 277–295.

Pickel, K.L. (1999). The influence of context on the "weapon focus" effect. *Law and Human Behavior, 23,* 299–311.

Pinizzotto, A.J., & Finkel, N.J. (1990). Criminal personality profiling: An outcome and process study. *Law and Human Behavior, 14,* 215–233.

Pithers, W.D., Martin, G.R., & Cumming, G.F. (1989). Vermont Treatment Program for Sexual Aggressors. In R.D. Laws (Ed.), *Relapse prevention with sex offenders* (pp. 292–310). New York, NY: Guilford Press.

Polak, A., & Harris, P. L. (1999). Deception by young children following noncompliance. *Developmental Psychology, 35,* 561–568.

Pollock, P.H. (1999). When the killer suffers: Post-traumatic stress reactions following homicide. *Legal and Criminological Psychology, 4,* 185–202.

Pope, H.G., Jonas, J.M., & Jones, B. (1982). Factitious psychosis: Phenomenology, family history, and long-term outcome of nine patients. *American Journal of Psychiatry, 139,* 1480–1483.

Porporino, F. J., & Motiuk, L. L. (1995). The prison careers of mentally disordered offenders. *International Journal of Law and Psychiatry, 18,* 29–44.

Porter, S., & Birt, A.R. (2001). Is traumatic memory special? A comparison of traumatic memory characteristics with memory for other emotional life experiences. *Applied Cognitive Psychology, 15,* S101–S117.

Porter, S., Birt, A., & Boer, D.P. (2001). Investigation of the criminal and conditional release profiles of Canadian federal offenders as a function of psychopathy and age. *Law and Human Behavior, 25,* 647–661.

Porter, S., Campbell, M.A., Stapleton, J., & Birt, A.R. (2002). The influence of judge, target, and stimulus characteristics on the accuracy of detecting deceit. *Canadian Journal of Behavioural Science, 34,* 172–185.

Porter, S., Fairweather, D., Drugge, J., Herve, H., Birt, A., & Boer, D.P. (2000). Profiles of psychopathy in incarcerated sexual offenders. *Criminal Justice and Behavior, 27,* 216–233.

Porter, S., Woodworth, M., & Birt, A. (2000). Truth, lies, and videotape: An investigation of the ability of federal parole officers to detect deception. *Law and Human Behavior, 24,* 643–658.

Porter, S., Woodworth, M., Earle, J., Drugge, J., & Boer, D. (2003). Characteristics of sexual homicides committed by psychopathic and nonpsychopathic offenders. *Law and Human Behavior, 27,* 459–470.

Pozzulo, J.D., & Balfour, J. (2004). *The impact of change in appearance on children's eyewitness identification accuracy: Comparing simultaneous and elimination lineup procedures.* Manuscript submitted for publication.

Pozzulo, J.D., & Lawandi, A. (2004). *Comparing the simultaneous and elimination lineup procedures with adult eyewitnesses.* Manuscript in preparation.

Pozzulo, J.D., & Lindsay, R.C.L. (1998). Identification accuracy of children versus adults: A meta-analysis. *Law and Human Behavior, 22,* 549–570.

Pozzulo, J.D., & Lindsay, R.C.L. (1999). Elimination lineups: An improved identification procedure for child eyewitnesses. *Journal of Applied Psychology, 84,* 167–176.

Pozzulo, J.D., & Warren, K.L. (2003). Descriptions and identifications of strangers by youth and adult eyewitnesses. *Journal of Applied Psychology, 88,* 315–323.

Prentky, R.A., Knight, R.A., Lee, A.F.S., & Cerce, D.D. (1995). Predictive validity of lifestyle impulsivity for rapists. *Criminal Justice and Behavior, 22,* 106–128.

Pryke, S., Lindsay, R.C.L., Dysart, J.E., & Dupuis, P. (2004). Multiple independent identification decisions: A method of calibrating eyewitness identifications. *Journal of Applied Psychology, 89,* 73–84.

Pugh, G. (1985a). The California Psychological Inventory and police selection. *Journal of Police Science and Administration, 13,* 172–177.

Pugh, G. (1985b). Situation tests and police selection. *Journal of Police Science and Administration, 13,* 31–35.

Putnam, F.W. (2003). Ten-year research update review: Child sexual abuse. *Journal of the American Academy of Child Adolescent Psychiatry, 42,* 269–278.

Pynes, J., & Bernardin, H.J. (1992). Entry-level police selection: The assessment centre is an alternative. *Journal of Criminal Justice, 20,* 41–52.

Quinsey, V.L., & Ambtman, R. (1979). Variables affecting psychiatrists' and teachers' assessments of the dangerousness of mentally ill offenders. *Journal of Consulting and Clinical Psychology, 47,* 353–362.

Quinsey, V.L., Chaplin, T.C., & Upfold, D. (1984). Sexual arousal to nonsexual violence and sadomasochistic themes among rapists and non-sex-offenders. *Journal of Consulting and Clinical Psychology, 52,* 651–657.

Quinsey, V.L., & Earls, C.M. (1990). The modification of sexual preferences. In W.L. Marshall & D.R. Laws, *Handbook of sexual assault: Issues, theories, and treatment of the offender* (pp. 279–295). New York, NY: Plenum Press.

Quinsey, V.L., Harris, G.T., Rice, M.E., & Cormier, C. (1998). *Violent offenders: Appraising and managing risk.* Washington, DC: American Psychological Association.

Quinsey, V.L., Harris, G.T., Rice, M.E., & Lalumiere, M.L. (1993). Assessing the treatment efficacy in outcome studies of sex offenders. *Journal of Interpersonal Violence, 8,* 512–523.

Quinsey, V.L., Khanna, A., & Malcolm, P.B. (1998). A retrospective evaluation of the regional treatment centre sex offender treatment program. *Journal of Interpersonal Violence, 13,* 621–644.

Quinsey, V.L., & Maguire, A. (1983). Offenders remanded for a psychiatric examination: Perceived treatability and disposition.

International Journal of Law and Psychiatry, 6, 193–205.

Quinsey, V.L., Rice, M.E., & Harris, G.T. (1995). Actuarial prediction of sexual recidivism. *Journal of Interpersonal Violence, 10,* 85–105.

Ramirez, D., McDevitt, J., & Farrell, A. (2000). *A resource guide on racial profiling data collection systems: Promising practice and lessons learned.* Washington, DC: U.S. Department of Justice.

Raskin, D.C., & Hare, R.D. (1978). Psychopathy and detection of deception in a prison population. *Psychophysiology, 15,* 126–136.

Raskin, D.C., Honts, C.R., & Kircher, J.C. (1997). The scientific status of research on polygraph techniques: The case for polygraph tests. In D.L. Faigman, D. Kaye, M.J. Saks, & J. Sanders (Eds.), *Modern scientific evidence: The law and science of expert testimony* (pp. 565–582). St. Paul, MN: West.

Rasmussen, L.A., Burton, J.E., & Christopherson, B.J. (1992). Precursors to offending and the trauma outcome process in sexually reactive children. *Journal of Child Sexual Abuse, 1,* 33–48.

Ratner, P.A. (1998). Modeling acts of aggression and dominance as wife abuse and exploring their adverse health effects. *Journal of Marriage and the Family, 60,* 453–465.

Read, J.D. (1999). The recovered/false memory debate: Three steps forward, two steps back? *Expert Evidence, 7,* 1–24.

Rees, L.M., Tombaugh, T.N., Gansler, D.A., & Moczynski, N.P. (1998). Five validation experiments of the Test of Malingered Memory (TOMM). *Psychological Assessment, 10,* 10–20.

Reifman, A., Gusick, S.M., & Ellsworth, P.C. (1992). Real jurors' understanding of the law in real cases. *Law and Human Behavior, 16,* 539–554.

Reinhart, M.A. (1987). Sexually abused boys. *Child Abuse and Neglect, 11,* 229–235.

Reiser, M. (1982). *Police psychology: Collected papers.* Los Angeles, CA: LEHI.

Reiser, M. (1989). Investigative hypnosis. In D. Raskin (Ed.), *Psychological methods in criminal investigation and evidence* (pp. 151–190). New York: Springer.

Resick, P.A. (1993). The psychological impact of rape. *Journal of Interpersonal Violence, 8,* 223–255.

Resnick, P.J. (1969). Child murder by parents: A psychiatric review of filicide. *American Journal of Psychiatry, 126,* 325–334.

Resnick, P.J. (1970). Murder of the newborn: A psychiatric review of neonaticide. *American Journal of Psychiatry, 126,* 1414–1420.

Resnick, P.J. (1997). Malingered psychosis. In R. Rogers (Ed.), *Clinical assessment of malingering and deception* (2nd ed., pp. 47–67). New York: Guilford Press.

Ressler, R.K., Burgess, A.W., Douglas, J.E., Hartman, C.R., & D'Agostino, R.B. (1986). Sexual killers and their victims: Identifying patterns through crime scene analysis. *Journal of Interpersonal Violence, 1,* 288–308.

Reuter, R.P. (1995, July 25). Consider "9 days of deceit" prosecutors urge Smith jury. *Toronto Star,* p. A4.

Rice, M.E., & Harris, G.T. (1990). The predictors of insanity acquittal. *International Journal of Law and Psychiatry, 13,* 217–224.

Rice, M.E., & Harris, G.T. (1992). A comparison of criminal recidivism among schizophrenic and nonschizophrenic offenders. *International Journal of Law and Psychiatry, 15,* 397–406.

Rice, M.E., & Harris, G.T. (1997). Cross validation and extension of the Violence Risk Appraisal Guide with child molesters and rapists. *Law and Human Behavior, 21,* 231–241.

Rice, M.E., & Harris, G.T. (1997). The treatment of mentally disordered offenders. *Psychology, Public Policy, and Law, 3,* 126–183.

Rice, M.E., Harris, G.T., & Cormier, C.A. (1992). An evaluation of a maximum security therapeutic community for psychopaths and other mentally disordered offenders. *Law and Human Behaviour, 16,* 399–412.

Richards, H.J., Casey, J.O., & Lucente, S.W. (2003). Psychopathy and treatment response in response to incarcerated female substance abusers. *Criminal Justice and Behavior, 30,* 251–276.

Rind, B., Jaeger, M., & Strohmetz, D.B. (1995). Effect of crime seriousness on simulated jurors' use of inadmissible evidence. *Journal of Social Psychology, 135,* 417–424.

Risin, L.I., & Koss, M. P. (1987). The sexual abuse of boys: Prevalence and descriptive characteristics of childhood victimizations. *Journal of Interpersonal Violence, 2,* 309–323.

Roberts, A.R. (1996). Battered women who kill: A comparative study of incarcerated participants with a community sample of battered women. *Journal of Family Violence, 11,* 291–304.

Roberts, J.V. & Birkenmayer, A. (1997). Sentencing in adult provincial courts. *Juristat, 17.*

Roberts, J.V. (1991). Sentencing reform: The lessons of psychology. *Canadian Psychology, 32,* 466–477.

Roberts, J.V., & Melcher, R. (2003). The incarceration of Aboriginal offenders: Trends from 1978 to 2001. *Canadian Journal of Criminology and Criminal Justice, 45,* 211–242.

Robins, L.N. (1986). The consequences of conduct disorder in girls. In D. Olweus, J. Block, & M. Radke-Yarrow (Eds.), *Development of antisocial and prosocial behavior* (pp. 385–408). New York, NY: Academic Press.

Roebers, C.M., Bjorklund, D.F., Schneider, W., & Cassel, W.S. (2002). Differences and similarities in event recall and suggestibility between children and adults in Germany and the United States. *Experimental Psychology, 49,* 132–140.

Roesch, R., Eaves, D., Sollner, R., Normandin, M., & Glackman, W. (1981). Evaluating fitness to stand trial: A comparative analysis of fit and unfit defendants. *International Journal of Law and Psychiatry, 4,* 145, 157.

Roesch, R., Ogloff, J.R.P., Hart, S.D., Dempster, R.J., Zapf, P.A., & Whittemore, K.E. (1997). The impact of Canadian Criminal Code changes on remands and assessments of fitness to stand trial and criminal responsibility in British Columbia. *Canadian Journal of Psychiatry, 42,* 509–514.

Roesch, R., Zapf, P.A., Eaves, D., & Webster, C.D. (1998). *The Fitness Interview Test* (rev. ed.). (Available from Mental Health Law, and Policy Institute, Simon Fraser University, Burnaby British Columbia, Canada, V5A 1S6.)

Rogers, R. (1984). *Rogers Criminal Responsibility Assessment Scales.* Psychological Assessment Resources. Odessa, FL.

Rogers, R. (1986). *Conducting insanity evaluations.* New York: Van Nostrand Reinhold.

Rogers, R. (1988). Structured interviews and dissimulation. In R. Rogers (Ed.), *Clinical assessment of malingering and deception* (1st ed., pp. 250–268). New York: Guilford Press.

Rogers, R. (1990). Models of feigned mental illness. *Professional Psychology, 21,* 182–188.

Rogers, R. (1997). Structured interviews and dissimulation. In R. Rogers (Ed.), *Clinical assessment of malingering and deception* (2nd ed., pp. 301–327). New York: Guilford Press.

Rogers, R., Bagby, R.M., & Dickens, S.E. (1992). *Structured Interview of Reported Symptoms (SIRS) and professional manual.* Odessa, FL: Psychological Assessment Resources.

Rogers, R., & Ewing, C.P. (1992). The measurement of insanity: Debating the merits of the R-CRAS and its alternatives. *International Journal of Law and Psychiatry, 15,* 113–123.

Rogers, R., & Sewell, K.W. (1999). The R-CRAS and insanity evaluations: A reexamination of construct validity. *Behavioral Sciences and the Law, 17,* 181–194.

Rogers, R., Sewell, K.W., & Goldstein, A.M. (1994). Explanatory models of malingering: A prototypical analysis. *Law and Human Behavior, 18,* 543–552.

Rogers, R., Sewell, K.W., Martin, M.A., & Vitacco, J.J. (2003). Detection of feigned mental disorders: A meta-analysis of the MMPI-2 and malingering. *Assessment, 10,* 160–177.

Rogers, R., Ustad, K.L., & Salekin, R.T. (1998). Convergent validity of the Personality Assessment Inventory: A study of emergency referrals in a correctional setting. *Assessment, 5,* 3–12.

Rohman, L.W., Sales, B.D., & Lou, M. (1990). The best interests standard in child custody decisions. In D. Weisstub (Ed.), *Law and mental health: International perspectives* (Vol. 5, pp. 40–90). Elmsford, NJ: Pergamon.

Rosenberg, D.A. (1987). A web of deceit: A literature review of Munchausen syndrome by proxy. *Child Abuse & Neglect, 11,* 547–563.

Rosenfeld, B., & Harmon, R. (2002). Factors associated with violence in stalking and obsessional harassment cases. *Criminal Justice and Behavior, 29,* 671–691.

Rosenfeld, J.P., Angell, A., Johnson, M., & Qian, J. (1991). An ERP-based, control-question lie detector analog: Algorithms for discriminating effects within individuals' average waveforms. *Psychophysiology, 38,* 319–335.

Rosenfeld, J.P., Nasman, V.T., Whalen, R., Cantwell, B., & Mazzeri, L. (1987). Late vertex positivity in event-related potentials as a guilty knowledge indicator: A new method of lie detection. *Polygraph, 16,* 223–231.

Rosenfeld, J.P., Soskins, M., Bosh, G., & Ryan, A. (2004). Simple, effective countermeasures to P300-based tests of detection of concealed information. *Psychophysiology, 41,* 205–219.

Rosenfeld, J.P., Sweet, J.L., Chuang, J., Ellwanger, J., & Song, L. (1996). Detection of simulated malingering using forced choice recognition enhanced with event-related potential recording. *Neurophysiology, 120,* 163–179.

Rosenhan, D.J., Eisner, S.L., & Robinson, R.J. (1994). Notetaking can aid juror recall. *Law and Human Behavior, 18,* 53–61.

Rosenhan, D.L. (1973). On being sane in insane places. *Nature, 179,* 250–257.

Rossmo, D.K. (1995). Place, space and police investigations: Hunting serial violent criminals. In J.E. Eck & D. Weisburd (Eds.), *Crime and place* (pp. 217–235). Monsey, NY: Criminal Justice Press.

Rossmo, D.K. (2000). *Geographic profiling.* Boca Raton, FL: CRC Press.

Rothbaum, B.O., Foa, E.B., Riggs, D., Murdock, T., & Walsh, W. (1992). A prospective examination of post-traumatic stress disorder in rape victims. *Journal of Traumatic Stress, 5,* 455–475.

Royal Canadian Mounted Police. (2003). *Preparatory guide for RCMP regular member selection interview.* Retrieved March 1, 2004, from http://www.rcmp-grc.gc.ca/recruiting/rmsigp.pdf

Ruby, C.L., & Brigham, J.C. (1997). The usefulness of the criteria-based content analysis technique in distinguishing between truthful and fabricated allegations: A critical review. *Psychology, Public Policy, and Law, 3,* 705–727.

Rudolph, K.D., & Asher, S.R. (2000). Adaptation and maladaptation in the peer system: Developmental processes and outcomes. In A.J. Sameroff, M. Lewis, & S.M. Miller (Eds.), *Handbook of developmental psychopathology* (2nd ed., pp. 157–175). New York, NY: Kluwer Academic/Plenum Publishers.

Rutherford, M.J., Alterman, A.I., Cacciola, J.S., & McKay, J.R. (1997). Validity of the psychopathy checklist-revised in male methadone patients. *Drug and Alcohol Dependence, 44,* 143–149.

Rutter, M. (1979). Protective factors in children's responses to stress and disadvantage. In M.W. Kent & J.E. Rolf (Eds.), *Primary Prevention of Psychopathology, Vol. 3: Social Competence in Children* (pp. 49–74). New England: University Press of New England.

Rutter, M. (1988). *Studies of psychosocial risk: The power of longitudinal data.* Cambridge, MA: Cambridge University Press.

Rutter, M. (1990). Psychosocial resilience and protective mechanisms. In J. Rolf, A.S. Masten, D. Cicchetti, K. Nuechterlein, & S. Weintraub (Eds.), *Risk and protective factors in the development of psychopathology* (pp. 181–214). Cambridge, MA: Cambridge University Press.

Rutter, M. (Ed.). (1995). *Psychosocial disturbances in young people: Challenges for prevention.* Cambridge, MA: Press Syndicate of the University of Cambridge.

Ryan, G., Miyoshi, T.J., Metzner, J.L., Krugman, R.D., & Fryer, G.E. (1996). Trends in a national sample of sexually abusive youths. *Journal of the American Academy of Child and Adolescent Psychiatry, 35,* 17–25.

Saks, M.J., & Marti, M.W. (1997). A meta-analysis of the effects of jury size. *Law and Human Behavior, 21,* 451-466.

Salekin, R.T. (2002). Factor-analysis of the Millon Adolescent Clinical Inventory in a juvenile offender population: Implications for treatment. *Journal of Offender Rehabilitation, 34,* 15–29.

Salekin, R.T., Rogers, R., & Machin, D. (2001). Psychopathy in youth: Pursuing diagnostic clarity. *Journal of Youth and Adolescence, 30,* 173–195.

Salekin, R.T., Rogers, R:, & Sewell, K.W. (1996). A review and meta-analysis of the Psychopathy Checklist and Psychopathy Checklist-Revised: Predictive validity of dangerousness. *Clinical Psychology: Science and Practice, 3,* 203–215.

Salekin, R.T., Rogers, R., & Sewell, K.W. (1997). Construct validity of psychopathy in female offender sample: A multitrait-multimethod evaluation. *Journal of Abnormal Psychology, 106,* 576–585.

Salekin, R.T., Rogers, R., Ustad, K.L., & Sewell, K.W. (1998). Psychopathy and recidivism among female inmates. *Law and Human Behavior, 22,* 109–128.

Sanders, B.A. (2003). Maybe there's no such thing as a "good cop": Organizational challenges in selecting quality officers. *Policing: An International Journal of Police Strategies and Management, 26,* 313–328.

Sandys, M., & Dillehay, R.C. (1995). First ballot votes, predeliberation dispositions and final verdicts in jury trials. *Law and Human Behavior, 19,* 175–195.

Saslove, H., & Yarmey, A.D. (1980). Long-term auditory memory: Speaker identification. *Journal of Applied Psychology, 65,* 111–116.

Saunders, D.G. (2002). Are physical assaults by wives and girlfriends a major social problem? A review of the literature. *Violence Against Women, 8,* 1424–1448.

Saunders, J.W.S. (2001). Experts in court: A view from the bench. *Canadian Psychology, 42,* 109–118.

Saunders, P., & Thompson, J. (2002, Feb. 7). The missing women of Vancouver. *CBC News Online.* Retrieved July 23, 2003, from http://www.cbc.ca/news/features/bc_missing women.html

Saywitz, K., Goodman, G.S., Nicholas, E., & Moan, S. (1991). Children's memories of physical examinations involving genital touch: Implications for reports of child sexual abuse. *Journal of Consulting and Clinical Psychology, 59,* 682–691.

Saywitz, K.J., & Snyder, L. (1996). Narrative elaboration: Test of a new procedure for interviewing children. *Journal of Consulting and Clinical Psychology, 64,* 1347–1357.

Scheck, B. Neufeld, P., & Dwyer, J. (2000). *Actual innocence.* Garden City, NY: Doubleday.

Schneider, E.M. (1986). Describing and changing: Women's self-defence work and the problem of expert testimony on battering. *Women's Rights Law Reports, 9,* 195–222.

Schuller, R.A. (1992). The impact of battered woman syndrome evidence on jury decision processes. *Law and Human Behavior, 16,* 597–620.

Schuller, R.A. (1995). Expert evidence and hearsay: The influence of "secondhand" information on jurors' decisions. *Law and Human Behavior, 19,* 345–362.

Schuller, R.A., & Cripps, J. (1998). Expert evidence pertaining to battered women: The impact of gender and timing of testimony. *Law and Human Behavior, 22,* 17–31.

Schuller, R.A., & Hastings, P. (1996). Trials of battered women who kill: The impact of alternative forms of expert evidence. *Law and Human Behavior, 20,* 167–187.

Schuller, R.A., & Hastings, P.A. (2002). Complainant sexual history evidence: Its impact on mock jurors' decisions. *Psychology of Women Quarterly, 26,* 252–261.

Schuller, R.A., & Rzepa, S. (2002). Expert testimony pertaining to battered woman syndrome: Its impact on jurors' decisions. *Law and Human Behavior, 26,* 655–673.

Schuller, R.A., Smith, V.L., & Olson, J.M. (1994). Jurors' decisions in trials of battered women who kill: The role of prior beliefs and expert testimony. *Journal of Applied Social Psychology, 24,* 316–337.

Schwartz, D., Dodge, K.A., Coie, J.D., Hubbard, J.A., Cillessen, A.H.N., Lemerise, E.A., & Bateman, H. (1998). Social-cognitive and behavioral correlates of aggression and victimization in boys' play groups. *Journal of Abnormal Child Psychology, 26,* 431–440.

Scogin, F., Schumacher, J., Gardner, J., & Chaplin, W. (1995). Predictive validity of psychological testing in law enforcement settings. *Professional Psychology: Research and Practice, 26,* 68–71.

Seagrave, D., & Grisso, T. (2002). Adolescent development and the measurement of juvenile psychopathy. *Law and Human Behavior, 26,* 219–239.

Seligman, M.E. (1975). *Helplessness: On depression, development, and death.* San Francisco, CA: W.H. Freeman.

Serin, R.C. (1991). Psychopathy and violence in criminals. *Journal of Interpersonal Violence, 6,* 423–431.

Serin, R.C., & Amos, N.L. (1995). The role of psychopathy in the assessment of dangerousness. *International Journal of Law and Psychiatry, 18,* 231–238.

Seto, M.C., & Barbaree, H.E. (1999). Psychopathy, treatment behavior, and sex offender recidivism. *Journal of Interpersonal Violence, 14,* 1235–1248.

Seymour, T.L., Seifert, C.M., Shafto, M.G., & Mosmann, A.L. (2000). Using response time measures to assess "guilty knowledge." *Journal of Applied Psychology, 85,* 30–37.

Shaughnessy, J.J., Zechmeister, E.B., & Zechmeister, J.S. (2000). *Research methods in psychology* (5th ed.). Boston, MA: McGraw-Hill.

Shaw, D.S., Keenan, K., & Vondra, J.I. (1994). Developmental precursors of externalizing behaviour: Ages 1 to 3. *Developmental Psychology, 30,* 355–364.

Shaw, J.S., III (1996). Increases in eyewitness confidence resulting from postevent questioning. *Journal of Experimental Psychology: Applied, 12,* 126–146.

Shaw, J.S., III, & McClure, K.A. (1996). Repeated postevent questioning can lead to elevated levels of eyewitness confidence. *Law and Human Behavior, 20,* 629-654.

Shaw, M. (1994). Women in prison: A literature review. *Forum on Corrections Research, 6,* 13–18.

Sheehan, P.W., & Tilden, J. (1984). Real and simulated occurrences of memory distortion in hypnosis. *Journal of Abnormal Psychology, 93,* 47–57.

Sheehan, R., & Cordner, G.W. (1989). *Introduction to police administration* (2nd ed.). Cincinnati, OH: Anderson Publishing Co.

Sheldon, D.H., & Macleod, M.D. (1991). From normative to positive data: Expert psychological evidence re-examined. *Criminal Law Review,* 811.

Sheldon, W.H. (1949). *Varieties of delinquent youths: A psychology of constitutional differences.* New York: Harper & Row.

Shepherd, J.W. (1981). Social factors in face recognition. In G. Davies, H. Ellis, & J. Shepherd (Eds.), *Perceiving and remembering faces* (pp. 55–79). London: Academic Press.

Shepherd, J.W., Deregowski, J.B. (1981). Races and faces: A comparison of the responses of Africans and Europeans to faces of the same and different races. *British Journal of Social Psychology, 20,* 125–133.

Sheridan, M.S. (2003). The deceit continues: An updated literature review of Munchausen syndrome by proxy. *Child Abuse & Neglect, 27,* 431–451.

Sherman, L.W., & Berk, R.A. (1984). The specific deterrent effects of arrest for domestic assault. *American Sociological Review, 49,* 261–272.

Sherman, L.W., Schmidt, J.D., & Rogan, D.P. (1992). *Policing domestic violence: Experiments and dilemmas.* New York: Free Press.

Shover, N., & Thompson, C.Y. (1992). Age differential expectations, and crime desistance. *Criminology, 30,* 89–104.

Siegal, L., & Senna, J. (1994). *Juvenile delinquency: Theory, practice and law* (5th ed.). St. Paul, MN: West Publishing Company.

Simourd, D.J., & Malcolm, P.B. (1998). Reliability and validity of the Level of Service Inventory-Revised among federally incarcerated sex offenders. *Journal of Interpersonal Violence, 13,* 261–274.

Simourd, D.J., Hoge, R.D., Andrews, D.A., & Leschied, A.W. (1994). An empirically based typology of male young offenders. *Canadian Journal of Criminology, 36,* 447–461.

Simourd, L., & Andrews, D.A. (1994). Correlates of delinquency: A look at gender differences. *Forum on Corrections Research, 6,* 26–31.

Sioui, R., & Thibault, J. (2001). *Pertinence of cultural adaptation of Reintegration Potential Reassessment (RPR) scale to Aboriginal context.* Research Report No. R-109. Ottawa, ON: Correctional Service Canada.

Sioui, R., & Thibault, J. (2002). Examining reintegration potential for Aboriginal offenders. *Forum on Corrections Research, 14,* 49–51.

Sjöstedt, G., & Langström, N. (2001). Actuarial assessment of sex offender recidivism risk: A cross-validation of the RRASOR and the Static-99 in Sweden. *Law and Human Behavior, 25,* 629–645.

Skilling, T.A., Quinsey, V.L., & Craig, W.M. (2001). Evidence of a taxon underlying serious antisocial behavior in boys. *Criminal Justice and Behavior, 28,* 450–470.

Skinner, B.F. (1974). *About behaviorism.* London: Cape.

Slone, A.E., Brigham, J.C., & Meissner, C.A. (2000). Social and cognitive factors affecting the own-race bias in Whites. *Basic and Applied Social Psychology, 22,* 71–84.

Smith, C., & Thornberry, T.P. (1995). The relationship between childhood maltreatment and adolescent involvement in delinquency. *Criminology, 33,* 451–481.

Smith, D.A., Visher, C.A., & Davidson, L.A. (1984). Equity and discretionary justice: The influence of race on police arrest decisions. *Journal of Criminal Law and Criminology, 75,* 234–249.

Smith, G.P. (1997). Assessment of malingering with self-report measures. In R. Rogers (Ed.), *Clinical assessment of malingering and deception* (2nd ed., pp. 351–372). New York: Guilford Press.

Smith, G.P., & Borum, R. (1992). Detection of malingering in a forensic sample: A study of the M test. *Journal of Psychiatry and Law, 20,* 505–514.

Smith, M.D. (1990). Patriarchal ideology and wife beating: A test of a feminist hypothesis. *Violence and Victims, 5,* 257–273.

Smith, V.L. (1991). Impact of pretrial instruction on jurors' information processing and decision making. *Journal of Applied Psychology, 76,* 220–228.

Snook, B., Zito, M., Bennell, C., & Taylor, P.J. (in press). On the accuracy and complexity of geographic profiling strategies. *Journal of Quantitative Criminology.*

Söchting, I., Fairbrother, N., & Koch, W. J. (2004). Sexual assault of women: Prevention efforts and risk factors. *Violence Against Women, 10,* 73–93.

Solicitor General. (2003). *Corrections and conditional release statistical overview.* Ottawa, ON: Solicitor General of Canada.

Sonkin, D. J., Martin, D., & Walker, I. E. (1985). *The male batterer: A treatment approach.* New York: Springer.

Spanos, N.P., DuBreuil, S.C., & Gwynn, M.I. (1991–1992). The effects of expert testimony concerning rape on the verdicts and beliefs of mock jurors. *Imagination, Cognition, and Personality, 11*, 37–51.

Spanos, N.P., Myers, B., DuBreuil, S.C., & Pawlak, A.E. (1992–1993). The effects of polygraph and eyewitness testimony on the beliefs and decisions of mock jurors. *Imagination, Cognition, and Personality, 12*, 103–113.

Sparwood Youth Assistance Program. (2004). Retrieved June 1, 2004, from http://www.sparwood.bc.ca/syap-out.htm

Spiegel, D., & Spiegel, H. (1987). Forensic uses of hypnosis. In I.B. Weiner & A.K. Hess (Eds.), *Handbook of forensic psychology* (pp. 474–498). New York: Wiley.

Spielberger, C.D., Westberry, L.G., Grier, K.S., & Greenfield, G. (1981). *The police stress survey: Sources of stress in law enforcement.* Tampa, FL: Human Resources Institute.

Sporer, S.L. (1996). Psychological aspects of person descriptions. In S. Sporer, R. Malpass, G. Koehnken (Eds.), *Psychological issues in eyewitness identification* (pp. 53–86). Mahwah, New Jersey: Erlbaum.

Sporer, S.L., & Penrod, S.D., Read, D., & Cutler, B.L. (1995). Choosing confidence and accuracy: A meta-analysis of the confidence-accuracy relations in eyewitness identification studies. *Psychological Bulletin, 118*, 315–327.

Sprott, J.B., & Doob, A. (1997). Fear, victimization, and attitudes to sentencing, the courts, and the police. *Canadian Journal of Criminology, 39*, 275–291.

Stack, S. (1997). Homicide followed by suicide: An analysis of Chicago data. *Criminology, 35*, 435–453.

Stanton, J., & Simpson, A. (2002). Filicide: A review. *International Journal of Law and Psychiatry, 25*, 1–14.

Statistics Canada. (2000). Family Violence. *The Daily*, July 25, 2000. Retrieved June 10, 2004, from http://www.statcan.ca/Daily/English/00075/d000725b.htm

Statistics Canada. (2003). *The Daily*, October 1, 2003. Retrieved June 1, 2004, from http://www.statcan.ca/Daily/English/031001/d031001a.htm

Statistics Canada. (2003, June 20). Youth court statistics. *The Daily*. Retrieved June 10, 2004, from http://www.statcan.ca/Daily/English/030620/d030620d.htm

Statistics Canada. (2004, March 12). Youth court statistics. *The Daily*. Available at: http://www.statcan.ca/Daily/English/040312/d040312c.htm

Steadman, H.J. (2000). From dangerousness to risk assessment of community violence: Taking stock at the turn of the century. *Journal of the American Academy of Psychiatry and the Law, 28*, 265–271.

Steadman, H.J., & Cocozza, J. (1974). *Careers of the criminally insane.* Lexington, Mass: Lexington Books.

Steadman, H.J., McGreevy, M.A., Morrissey, J.P., Callahan, L.A., Robbins, P.C., & Cirincione, C. (1993). *Before and after Hinckley: Evaluating insanity defense reform.* New York: Guilford Press.

Steadman, H.J., Monahan, J., Appelbaum, P.S., Grisso, T., Mulvey, E.P., Roth, L.H., et al. (1994). Designing a new generation of risk assessment research. In J. Monahan & H. J. Steadman (Eds.), *Violence and mental disorder: Developments in risk assessment* (297–318). Chicago: University of Chicago Press.

Steadman, H.J., Mulvey, E.P., Monahan, J., Robbins, P.C., Appelbaum, P.S., Grisso, T., Roth, L.H., & Silver, E. (1998). Violence by people discharged from acute psychiatric inpatient facilities and by others in the same neighborhoods. *Archives of General Psychiatry, 55*, 393–401.

Steadman, H.J., Silver, E., Monahan, J., Appelbaum, P.S., Robbins, P.C., Mulvey, E.P., Grisso, T., Roth, L.H., & Banks, S. (2000). A classification tree approach to the development of actuarial violence risk assessment tools. *Law and Human Behavior, 24*, 83–100.

Steblay, N.M. & Bothwell, R.B. (1994). Evidence for hypnotically refreshed testimony: The view from the laboratory. *Law and Human Behavior, 18,* 635–651.

Steblay, N.M. (1992). A meta-analytic review of the weapon focus effect. *Law and Human Behavior, 16,* 413–424.

Steblay, N.M. (1997). Social influence in eyewitness recall: A meta-analytic review of lineup instruction effects. *Law and Human Behavior, 21,* 283–298.

Steblay, N.M., Besirevic, J., Fulero, S.M., & Jimenez-Lorente, B. (1999). The effects of pretrial publicity on juror verdicts: A meta-analytic review. *Law and Human Behavior, 23,* 219–235.

Steblay, N.M., Dysart, J., Fulero, S., & Lindsay, R.C.L. (2001). Eyewitness accuracy rates in sequential and simultaneous lineup presentations: A meta-analytic comparison. *Law and Human Behavior, 25,* 459–474.

Stein, K. (2001). *Public perceptions of crime and justice in Canada: A review of opinion polls.* Ottawa: Department of Justice Canada.

Stein, M., Koverola, C., Hanna, C., Torchia, M., & McClarry, B. (1997). Hippocampal volume in woman victimized by childhood sexual abuse. *Psychological Medicine, 27,* 951–959.

Stellar, M. (1989). Recent developments in statement analysis. In J.C. Yuille (Ed.), *Credibility assessment* (pp. 135-154). Dordrecht, the Netherlands: Kluwer.

Stern, W. (1910). Abstracts of lectures on the psychology of testimony and on the study of individuality. *American Journal of Psychology, 21,* 270–282.

Stevens, D.J. (1994). Predatory rapists and victim selection techniques. *Social Science Journal, 31,* 421–433.

Stewart, E. (2000). The comparative constitution of twinship: Strategies and paradoxes. *Twin Research, 3,* 142–147.

Storm, J., & Graham, J.R. (2000). Detection of coached general malingering on the MMPI-2. *Psychological Assessment, 12,* 158–165.

Strand, S., & Belfrage, H. (2001). Comparison of HCR-20 scores in violent mentally disordered men and women: Gender differences and similarities. *Psychology, Crime, & Law, 7,* 71–79.

Strand, S., Belfrage, H., Fransson, G., & Levander, S. (1999). Clinical and risk management factors in risk prediction of mentally disordered offenders—more important than historical data? A retrospective study of 40 mentally disordered offenders assessed with the HCR-20 violence risk assessment scheme. *Legal and Criminological Psychology, 4,* 67–76.

Straus, M.A. (1977). Wife beating: How common and why? *Victimology, 2,* 443–458.

Straus, M.A. (1979). Measuring family conflict and violence: The Conflict Tactics Scale. *Journal of Marriage and the Family, 41,* 75–88.

Straus, M.A. (1990). Measuring intrafamily conflict and violence: The Conflict Tactics (CTS) Scales. In M. Straus & R. Gelles (Eds.), *Physical violence in American families: Risk factors and adaptations to violence in 8,145 families* (pp. 29–47). New Brunswick, NJ: Transaction.

Straus, M.A., Gelles, R. J., & Steinmetz, S. (1980). *Behind closed doors: Violence in the American family.* Garden City, NY: Anchor/Doubleday.

Straus, M.A., Hamby, S.L., Boney-McCoy, S., & Sugarman, D.B. (1996). The revised Conflict Tactics Scales (CTS2): Development and preliminary psychometric data. *Journal of Family Issues, 17,* 283–316.

Styve, G.J., MacKenzie, D.L., Gover, A.R., & Mitchell, O. (2000). Perceived conditions of confinement: A national evaluation of juvenile boot camps and traditional facilities. *Law and Human Behavior, 24,* 297–308.

Sue, S., Smith, R.E., & Caldwell, C. (1973). Effects of inadmissible evidence on the decisions of simulated jurors: A moral dilemma. *Journal of Applied Social Psychology, 3,* 345–353.

Sundby, S.E. (1997). The jury as critic: An empirical look at how capital juries perceive expert and lay testimony. *Virginia Law Review, 83*, 1109–1188.

Sutherland, E.H. (1939). *Principles of criminology*. Philadelphia: J.B. Lippincott Company.

Swanson, J.W. (1994). Mental disorder, substance abuse, and community violence: An epidemiological approach. In J. Monahan & H. J. Steadman (Eds.), *Violence and mental disorder: Developments in risk assessment* (101–137). Chicago: University of Chicago Press.

Swanson, J.W., Borum, R., Swartz, M.S., & Monahan, J. (1996). Psychotic symptoms and disorders and the risk of violent behavior in the community. *Criminal Behavior and Mental Health, 6*, 317–338.

Swanson, J.W., Borum, R., Swartz, M.S., Hiday, V.A., Wagner, H.R., & Burns, B.J. (2001). Can involuntary outpatient commitment reduce arrests among persons with severe mental illness? *Criminal Justice and Behavior, 28*, 156–189.

Swanson, J.W., Holzer, C.E., Ganju, V.K., & Jono, R.T. (1990). Violence and psychiatric disorder in the community: Evidence from the epidemiologic catchment area surveys. *Hospital and Community Psychiatry, 41*, 761–770.

Sykes, J.B. (Ed.). (1982). *The Concise Oxford Dictionary* (7th ed.). Oxford: Oxford University Press.

Szymanski, L.A., Devlin, A.S., Chrisler, J.C., & Vyse, S.A. (1993). Gender role and attitudes toward rape in male and female college students. *Sex Roles, 29*, 37–57.

Talwar, V., & Lee, K. (2002). Emergence of white-lie telling in children between 3 and 7 years of age. *Merrill-Palmer Quarterly, 48*, 160–181.

Tanford, J.A. (1992). The law and psychology of jury instructions. In J.R.P. Ogloff (Ed.), *Law and psychology: The broadening of the discipline* (pp. 305–329). Durham, NC: Carolina Academic Press.

Taylor, S.P., & Sears, J.D. (1988). The effects of alcohol and persuasive social pressure on human physical aggression. *Aggressive Behavior, 14*, 237–243.

Technical Working Group for Eyewitness Evidence. (1999). *Eyewitness evidence: A guide for law enforcement.* Washington, DC: United States Department of Justice, Office of Justice Programs. NCJ 178240. Available at: www.ojp.usdoj.gov.

Temrin, H., Buchmayer, S., & Enquist, M. (2000). Step-parents and infanticide New data contradict evolutionary predictions. *Proceedings of the Royal Society of London, Series B: Biological Sciences, 267*, 943–945.

Teplin, L.A. (1984). Criminalizing mental disorder: The comparative arrest rate of the mentally ill. *American Psychologist, 39*, 784–803.

Teplin, L.A. (1986). *Keeping the peace: The parameters of police discretion in relation to the mentally disordered.* Washington, DC: U.S. Department of Justice.

Teplin, L.A. (2000). *Keeping the peace: Police discretion and mentally ill persons. National Institute of Justice Journal*, July, 8–15.

Teplin, L.A. Abram, K.M., & McClelland, G.M. (1994). Does psychiatric disorder predict violent crime among released jail detainees? *American Psychologist, 49*, 335–342.

Teplin, L.A., Abram, K.M., & McClelland, G.M. (1996). Prevalence of psychiatric disorders among incarcerated women I. Pretrial jail detainees. *Archives of General Psychiatry, 53*, 505–512.

Terman, L.M. (1917). A trial of mental and pedagogical tests in a civil service examination for policemen and firemen. *Journal of Applied Psychology, 1*, 17–29.

Terrance, C. & Matheson, K. (2003). Undermining reasonableness: Expert testimony in a case involving a battered woman who kills. *Psychology of Women Quarterly, 27*, 37–45.

Test, M.A., (1992). Training in community living. In R.P Liberman (Ed.), *Handbook of psychiatric rehabilitation* (pp. 153-170). New York: Macmillan.

The Guardian. (October 28, 1988). Police set up unit for stress crisis.

Thompson, J.S., Stuart, G.L., & Holden, C.E. (1992). Command hallucinations and legal insanity. *Forensic Reports, 5,* 29–43.

Tibbets, J. (2003, July 21). Divorce courts shift to parallel parenting. *The Ottawa Citizen,* (p. A5).

Tjaden, P., & Thoennes, N. (1998). *Stalking in America: Findings from the National Violence Against Women Survey.* Washington, DC: American Psychological Association.

Tjaden, P.G., & Thoennes, N. (2001). Coworker violence and gender: Findings from the National Violence Against Women Survey. *American Journal of Preventive Medicine, 20,* 85–89.

Tolan, P., & Thomas, P. (1995). The implications of age of onset for delinquency risk: II. Longitudinal data. *Journal of Abnormal Child Psychology, 23,* 157–181.

Tolman, R.M., & Weisz, A. (1995). Coordinated community intervention for domestic violence: The effects of arrest and prosecution on recidivism of woman abuse perpetrators. *Crime and Delinquency, 41,* 481–495.

Tombaugh, T.N. (1996). *Test of Malingered Memory (TOMM).* Toronto: Multi-Health Systems.

Tombaugh, T.N. (2002). The Test of Memory Malingering (TOMM) in forensic psychology. *Journal of Forensic Neuropsychology, 2,* 69–96.

Trevethan, S., Crutcher, N., & Rastin, C.J. (2002a). *An examination of healing lodges for federal offenders in Canada. Research Report.* Ottawa, ON: Correctional Service Canada.

Trevethan, S., Moore, J., & Rastin, C.J. (2002b). A profile of Aboriginal offenders in federal facilities and serving time in the community. *Forum on Corrections Research, 14,* 17–19.

Trevethan, S., Moore, J., Auger, S., MacDonald, M. & Sinclair, J. (2002c). Childhood experiences affect Aboriginal offenders. *Forum on Corrections Research, 14,* 7–9.

Trice, A.D., & Lamb, M. (1996). Sex-role orientation among incarcerated women. *Psychological Reports, 79,* 92–94.

Trocme, N., MacLaurin, B., Fallon, B., Daciuk, J., Billingsley, D., Tourigny, M., Mayer, M., Wright, J., Barter, K., Burford, G., Hornick, J., Sullivan, R., & McKenzie, B. (2001). *Canadian incidence study of reported child abuse and neglect: Final report.* Ottawa, Ontario: Minister of Public Works and Government Services Canada

Turtle, J.W., Lindsay, R.C.L., & Wells, G.L. (2003). Best practice recommendations for eyewitness evidence procedures: New ideas for the oldest way to solve a case. *The Canadian Journal of Police and Security Services, 1,* 5–18.

Turvey, B. (2002). *Criminal profiling: An introduction to behavioral evidence analysis* (2nd ed.). San Diego, CA: Academic Press.

Tversky, A., & Kahneman, D. (1981). The framing of decisions and the psychology of choice. *Science, 211,* 453–458.

Tweed, R.G., & Dutton, D.G. (1998). A comparison of impulsive and instrumental subgroups of batters. *Violence and Victims, 13,* 217–230.

U.S. Bureau of Justice Statistics. (2001). *Contacts between police and the public: Findings from the 1999 national survey.* Washington, DC: U.S. Bureau of Statistics.

U.S. Department of Justice (2001). *Internet crimes against children.* Office for victims of Crime Bulletin. Washington, DC: Author.

Uggen, C. (1999). Ex-offenders and the conformist alternative: A job quality model of work and crime. *Social Problems, 46,* 127–151.

Ullman, S.E., & Knight, R.A. (1993). The efficacy of women's resistance strategies in rape situations. *Psychology of Women Quarterly, 17,* 23–38.

Ulrich, D., & Trumbo, D. (1965). The selection interview since 1949. *Psychological Bulletin, 63,* 100–116.

Vallée, B. (1998). *Life and death with Billy.* Toronto: Random House.

Valliant, P.M., Furac, C.J., & Antonowicz, D.H. (1994). Attitudes toward sex offenders by female undergraduate students enrolled in a psychology program. *Social Behavior and Personality, 22,* 105–110.

Van Koppen, P.J., & Lochun, S.K. (1997). Portraying perpetrators: The validity of offender descriptions by witnesses. *Law and Human Behavior, 21,* 661–685.

Vance, J.P. (2001). Neurobiological mechanisms of psychosocial resiliency. In J.M. Richman & M.W. Fraser (Eds.), *The context of youth violence: Resilience, risk, & protection* (pp. 43–81). Westport, CN: Praeger.

Varendonck, J. (1911). Les temoignages d'enfants dans un proces retentisaant. *Archives de Psycholgie, 11,* 129–171.

Viljoen, J.L., Roesch, R., Ogloff, J.R.P., & Zapf, P.A. (2003). The role of Canadian psychologists in conducting fitness and criminal responsibility evaluations. *Canadian Psychology, 44,* 369–381.

Violanti, J.M., & Aron, F. (1994). Ranking police stressors. *Psychological Reports, 75,* 824–826.

Violanti, J.M., Marshall, J.R., & Howe, B. (1985). Stress, coping and alcohol use: The police connection. *Journal of Police Science and Administration, 31,* 106–110.

Violanti, J.M., Vena, J.E., & Marshall, J.R. (1986). Disease risk and mortality among police officers: New evidence and contributing factors. *Journal of Police Science and Administration, 14,* 17–23.

Vitale, J.E., Smith, S.S., Brinkely, C.A., & Newman, J.P. (2002). The reliability and validity of the Psychopathy Checklist-Revised in a sample of female offenders. *Criminal Justice and Behavior, 29,* 202–231.

Vrij, A. (1994). The impact of information and setting on detection of deception by police detectives. *Journal of Nonverbal Behavior, 18,* 117–127.

Vrij, A. (1995). Behavioural correlates of deception in simulated police interview. *Journal of Psychology: Interdisciplinary and Applied, 129,* 15–29.

Vrij, A. (1998). Nonverbal communication and credibility. In A. Memon, A. Vrij, & R. Bull (Eds.), *Psychology and law: Truthfulness, accuracy, and credibility* (pp. 32–58). London: McGraw-Hill.

Vrij, A. (2000). *Detecting lies and deceits: The psychology of lying and the implications for professional practice.* Chichester, England: Wiley.

Vrij, A., Edward, K., Roberts, K.P., & Bull, R. (2000). Detecting deceit via analysis of verbal and nonverbal behaviour. *Journal of Nonverbal Behaviour, 24,* 239–263.

Vrij, A., & Mann, S. (2001). Who killed my relative? Police officers' ability to detect real-life high-stake lies. *Psychology, Crime, and Law, 7,* 119–132.

Vrij, A., & Semin, G.R. (1996). Lie experts' beliefs about nonverbal indicators of deception. *Journal of Nonverbal Behavior, 20,* 65–80.

Wadsworth, M.E.J. (1976). Delinquency, pulse rates, and early emotional deprivation. *British Journal of Criminology, 16,* 245–256.

Wagstaff, G.F., MacVeigh, J., Boston, R., Scott, L., Brunas-Wagstaff, J., & Cole, J. (2003). Can laboratory findings on eyewitness testimony be generalized to the real world? An archival analysis of the influence of violence, weapon presence, and age on eyewitness accuracy. *The Journal of Psychology, 137,* 17–28.

Wakefield, H., & Underwager, R. (1998). Coerced or nonvoluntary confessions. *Behavioral Sciences and the Law, 16,* 423–440.

Walker, L. (1979). *The battered woman.* New York: Harper Perennial.

Walker, L.E. (1984). *The battered woman syndrome.* New York, NY: Springer.

Walker, L.E. (1993). Battered woman as defendants. In N.Z. Hilton (Ed.), *Legal response to wife assault: Current trends and evaluation* (pp. 233–257). Thousand Oaks, CA: Sage.

Walker, S., & Katz, C.M. (2001). *The police in America* (4th ed.). New York: McGraw Hill, Inc.

Wallace, H.S. (1993). Mandatory minimums and the betrayal of sentencing reform: A legislative Dr. Jekyll and Mr. Hyde. *Federal Probation, 57*, 9.

Walma, M.W., & West. L. (2002). *Police powers and procedures.* Toronto, ON: Emond Montgomery Publications Limited.

Waltz, J., Babcock, J.C., Jacobson, N.S., & Gottman, J.M. (2000). Testing a typology of batterers. *Journal of Consulting and Clinical Psychology, 68*, 658–669.

Warick, J. (1997, November 29). Power in the spirit: Okimaw Ohci Healing Lodge. *The Saskatchewan Star Phoenix*, p. C1.

Warick, J. (2003 July, 5). Saskatchewan considers racially balanced juries. *The Ottawa Citizen*, p. A16.

Warren, J.L., Burnette, M., South, C.S., Chauhan, P., Bale, R., & Friend, R. (2002). Personality disorders and violence among female prison inmates. *Journal of the American Academy of Psychiatry and the Law, 30*, 502–509.

Warren, J.L., Burnette, M., South, C.S., Chauhan, P., Bale, R., Friend, R., & Van Patten, I. (2003). Psychopathy in women: Structural modelling and co-morbidity. *International Journal of Law and Psychiatry, 26*, 223–242.

Waschbusch, D.A. (2002). A meta-analytic examination of comorbid hyperactive-impulsive-attention problems and conduct problems. *Psychological Bulletin, 128*, 118–150.

Waschbusch, D.A., Porter, S., Carrey, N., Kazmi, S.O., Roach, K.A., & D'Amico, D.A. (2004). Investigation of the heterogeneity of disruptive behaviour in elementary-age children. *Canadian Journal of Behavioural Science, 36*, 97–112.

Wasserman, G.A., & Saracini, A.M. (2001). Family risk factors and interventions. In R. Loeber, & D.P. Farrington (Eds.), *Child delinquents: Development, intervention, and service needs* (pp. 165–190). Thousand Oaks, CA: Sage.

Webster, C.D., & Jackson, M.A. (Eds.). (1997) *Impulsivity: Theory, assessment, and treatment.* New York: Guilford.

Webster, C.D., Douglas, K., Eaves, D., & Hart, S. (1997). *HCR-20: Assessing risk for violence, Version 2.* Burnaby, British Columbia: Simon Fraser University and Forensic Psychiatric Services Commission of British Columbia.

Webster, C.D., Menzies, R.S., Butler, B.T., & Turner, R.E. (1982). Forensic psychiatric assessment in selected Canadian cities. *Canadian Journal of Psychiatry, 27*, 455–462.

Weinshenker, N.J., & Siegel, A. (2002). Bimodial classification of aggression: Affective defense and predatory attack. *Aggression and Violent Behavior, 7*, 237–250.

Wells, G.L. (1978). Applied eyewitness-testimony research: System variables and estimator variables. *Journal of Personality and Social Psychology, 12*, 1546–1557.

Wells, G.L. (1993). What do we know about eyewitness identification? *American Psychologist, 48*, 553–571.

Wells, G.L., & Bradfield, A.L. (1998). "Good, you identified the suspect": Feedback to eyewitnesses distorts their reports of the witnessing experience. *Journal of Applied Psychology, 83*, 366–376.

Wells, G.L., Leippe, M.R., & Ostrom, T.M. (1979). Guidelines for empirically assessing the fairness of a lineup. *Law and Human Behavior, 3*, 285–293.

Wells, G.L., Malpass, R.S., Lindsay, R.C.L., Turtle, J.W., & Fulero, S.M. (2000). From the lab to the police station: A successful application of eyewitness research. *American Psychologist, 55*, 581–598.

Wells, G.L., & Olson, E.A. (2003). Eyewitness testimony. *Annual Psychology Review, 54*, 277–295.

Wells, G.L., Rydell, S.M., & Seelau, E.P. (1993). On the selection of distractors for eyewitness lineups. *Journal of Applied Psychology, 78*, 835–844.

Wells, G.L., Small, M., Penrod, S., Malpass, R.S., Fulero, S.M., & Brimacombe, C.A.E. (1998). Eyewitness identification procedures: Recommendations for lineups and photospreads. *Law and Human Behavior, 22,* 603–647.

Wells, G.L., & Turtle, J.W. (1986). Eyewitness identification: The importance of lineup models. *Psychological Bulletin, 99,* 320–329.

Werner, E.E., & Smith, R.S. (1992). *Overcoming the odds: High-risk children from birth to adulthood.* Ithaca, NK: Cornell University Press.

Wetter, M.W., & Corrigan, S.K. (1995). Providing information to clients about psychological tests: A survey of attorneys' and law students' attitudes. *Professional Psychology: Research and Practice, 26,* 474–477.

Whipple, G.M. (1909). The observer as reporter: A survey of "the psychology of testimony." *Psychological Bulletin, 6,* 153–170.

Whipple, G.M. (1910). Recent literature on the psychology of testimony. *Psychological Bulletin, 7,* 365–368.

Whipple, G.M. (1911). The psychology of testimony. *Psychological Bulletin, 8,* 307–309.

Whipple, G.M. (1912). The psychology of testimony and report. *Psychological Bulletin, 9,* 264–269.

Whipple, G.M. (1913). Psychology of testimony and report. *Psychological Bulletin, 10,* 264–268.

White, M.D. (2001). Controlling police discretion to use deadly force: Re-examining the importance of administrative policy. *Crime and Delinquency, 47,* 131–151.

White, W.S. (1997). False confessions and the constitution: Safeguards against untrustworthy confessions. *Harvard Civil Rights-Civil Liberties Law Review, 32,* 105–131.

Widom, C., & Ames, M. (1994). Criminal consequences of childhood sexual victimization. *Child Abuse and Neglect, 18,* 303–318.

Widom, C.S. (1989a). Does violence beget violence? A critical examination of the literature. *Psychological Bulletin, 106,* 2–28.

Widom, C.S. (1989b). The cycle of violence. *Science, 244,* 160–166.

Wigmore, J.H. (1909). Professor Munsterberg and the psychology of testimony. *Illinois Law Review, 3,* 399–434.

Williamson, S., Hare, R.D., & Wong, S. (1987). Violence: Criminal psychopaths and their victims. *Canadian Journal of Behavioral Science, 19,* 454–462.

Wilson, J.Q., & Herrnstein, R. J. (1985). *Crime and human nature.* New York, NY: Simon and Schuster.

Wilson, M., & Daly, M. (1993). Spousal homicide risk and estrangement. *Violence and Victims, 8,* 3-16.

Wilson, M., Daly, M., & Daniele, A. (1995). Familicide: The killing of spouse and children. *Aggressive Behavior, 21,* 275–291.

Wilson, P., Lincoln, R., & Kocsis, R. (1997). Validity, utility and ethics of profiling for serial violent and sexual offenders. *Psychiatry, Psychology and Law, 4,* 1–12.

Winfield, L. (1994). *NCREL Monograph: Developing resilience in urban youth.* NCREL: Urban Education Monograph Series.

Woodsworth, M., & Porter, S. (1999). Historical foundations and current applications of criminal profiling in violent crime investigations. *Expert Evidence, 7,* 241–264.

Woodworth, M., & Porter, S. (2002). In cold blood: Characteristics of criminal homicides as a function of psychopathy. *Journal of Abnormal Psychology, 111,* 436–445.

Worling, J.R., & Curwen, T. (2000). Adolescent sexual offender recidivism: Success of specialized treatment and implications for risk prediction. *Child Abuse and Neglect, 24,* 965–982.

Wrightsman, L.S. (2001). *Forensic psychology.* Belmont, CA: Wadsworth.

Yarmey, A.D. (2001). Expert testimony: Does eyewitness memory research have probative value for the courts? *Canadian Psychology, 42,* 92–100.

Yarmey, A.D., Jacob, J., & Porter, A. (2002). Person recall in field settings. *Journal of Applied Social Psychology, 32,* 2354–2367.

Yarmey, A.D., & Jones, H.P.T. (1983). Is the psychology of eyewitness identification a matter of common sense? In S. Lloyd-Bostock & B.R. Clifford (Eds.), *Evaluating witness evidence* (pp. 13–40). Chichester, UK: John Wiley and Sons.

Yarmey, A.D., & Yarmey, M.J. (1997). Eyewitness recall and duration estimates in field settings. *Journal of Applied Social Psychology, 27,* 330–344.

Yarmey, A.D., Yarmey, M.J., & Yarmey, A.L. (1996). Accuracy of eyewitness identifications in showups and lineups. *Law and Human Behavior, 20,* 459–477.

Yllo, K., & Straus, M. (1990). Patriarchy and violence against wives: The impact of structural and normative factors. In M. Straus & R. Gelles (Eds.), *Physical violence in American families* (pp. 383–399). New Brunswick, NJ: Transaction.

Yuille, J.C., Hunter, R., Joffe, R., & Zaparniuk, J. (1993). Interviewing children in sexual abuse cases. In G. Goodman, B. Bottoms, (Eds.), *Child victims, child witnesses: Understanding and improving testimony* (pp. 95–115). New York, NY: Guilford Press.

Yurchesyn, K.A., Keith, A., & Renner, K.E. (1992). Contrasting perspectives on the nature of sexual assault provided by a service for sexual assault victims and by the law courts. *Canadian Journal of Behavioral Science, 24,* 71–85.

Zamble, E., & Quinsey, V.L. (1997). *The criminal recidivism process.* Cambridge: Cambridge University Press.

Zanis, D.A., Mulvaney, F., Coviello, D., Alterman, A.I., Savitz, B., & Thompson, W. (2003). The effectiveness of early parole to substance abuse treatment facilities on 24-month criminal recidivism. *Journal of Drug Issues, 33,* 223–236.

Zapf, P., & Roesch, R. (1998). Fitness to stand trial: Characteristics of remands since the 1992 criminal code amendments. *Canadian Journal of Psychiatry, 43,* 287–293.

Zill, N., Morrison, D.R., & Coiro, M.J. (1993). Long-term effects of parental divorce on parent-child relationships, adjustment, and achievement in young adulthood. *Journal of Family Psychology, 7,* 91–103.

Zinger, I., & Forth, A.E. (1998). Psychopathy and Canadian criminal proceedings: The potential for human rights abuses. *Canadian Journal of Criminology, 40,* 237–276.

Zingraff, M.T., Leiter, J., Johnsen, M.C., & Myers, K.A. (1994). The mediating effect of good school performance on the maltreatment delinquency relationship. *Journal of Research in Crime and Delinquency, 31,* 62–91.

Zoucha-Jensen, J.M., & Coyne, A. (1993). The effects of resistance strategies on rape. *American Journal of Public Health, 83,* 1633–1634.

CREDITS

Text Credits

p. 12, From Ceci, S.J. & Bruck, M. (1993). Suggestibility of the child witness: A historical review and synthesis. Psychological Bulletin, 113, 403–439. (p. 406) © 1993 by the American Psychological Association. Adapted with permission. **p. 57**, Excerpt from Recruiting Unit, Vancouver Police Department Web site: http://www.city.vancouver.bc.ca/police/recruiting/jobpre.htm. © 2004 Vancouver Police Department. Reprinted with permission. **p. 64**, Doerner, W.G. (1997). The utility of the oral interview board in selecting police academy admissions. Policing: An International Journal of Police Strategy and Management, 20, 777–785. Republished with permission of Emerald Group Publishing Limited http://www.emeraldinsight.com. **p. 67**, Adapted from Pynes, J. & Bernardin, H.J. (1992). Entry-level police selection: The assessment centre is an alternative. Journal of Criminal Justice, 20, 41–52, © 1992, with permission of Elsevier. **p. 71**, Teplin, L.A. (2000). Keeping the peace: Police discretion and mentally ill persons. National Institute of Justice Journal, July, 8–15. **p. 76**, Walma, M.W. & West. L. (2002). Police powers and procedures. Toronto, ON: Emond Montgomery Publications Limited. Reprinted with permission. **p. 77**, Canadian Association of Chiefs of Police. (2000). a) The National Use of Force Framework. www.cacp.ca/english/committees/download.asp?id=169. Reprinted with permission of CACP.; Canadian Association of Chiefs of Police. (2000). b) The National Use of Force Framework. www.cacp.ca/english/committees/download.asp?id=170. Reprinted with permission of CACP. **p. 79**, McCraty, R., Tomasino, D., Atkinson, M., & Sundram, J. (1999). Impact of the HeartMath self-management skills program on physiological and psychological stress in police officers. Boulder Creek, CA: HeartMath Research Center, Institute of HeartMath. © 1999 Institute of HeartMath. **p. 90**, Wakefield, H. & Underwager, R. (1998). Coerced or nonvoluntary confessions. Behavioral Sciences and the Law, 16, 423–440. (p. 428) © 1998 John Wiley & Sons Limited. Reproduced with permission. **p. 104**, Kassin, S.M. & Kiechel, K.L. (1996). The social psychology of false confessions: Compliance, internalization, and confabulation. Psychological Science, 7(3), 125–128. Reprinted with permission. **p. 115**, Kocsis, R.N. Irwin, H.J., Hayes, A.F. & Nunn, R. (2000). Expertise in psychological profiling: A comparative assessment. Journal of Interpersonal Violence, 13, 311–331. © 2000 by Sage Publications. Reprinted by permission of Sage Publications. **p. 137**, National Research Council (2003). The polygraph and its detection. Washington, DC: National Academies Press. Reprinted with permission. **p. 171**, Geiselman, Fisher, MacKinnon, and Holland (1986). Enhancement of eyewitness memory with the cognitive interview. American Journal of Psychology, 99, 385–401. From American Journal of Psycholoygy © 1986 by the Board of Trustees of the University of Illinois. Used with permission of the University of Illinois Press. **p. 172**, From Fisher, R.P., & Geiselman, R.E., Memory-enhancing techniques for investigative interviewing, 1992. Courtesy of Charles C. Thomas Publisher, Ltd., Springfield, Illinois. **p. 207**, Saywitz, K.J., & Snyder, L. (1996). Narrative Elaboration: Test of a new procedure for interviewing children. Journal of Consulting and Clinical Psychology, 64, 1347–1357 © 1996 by the American Psychological Association. Reprinted with permission. **p. 213**, Bala, N., Lindsay, R.C.L., Lee, K., & Talwar, V. (September, 2000). The legal competence of child witnesses: Assessing present practices and the need for law reform. Presentation at the Faculty of Law, Queen's University. Kingston, Ontario, Canada. Available at http://qsilver.queensu.ca/law/witness/childcompsept20001_files/frame.htm. Used with permission. **p. 222**, From MacMillan, H.L. (2000). Child maltreatment: What we know in the year 2000. Canadian Journal of Psychiatry, 45, p.704. Reprinted with permission of the Canadian Psychiatric Association. **p. 246**, Penrod, S.D., & Heuer, L. (1997). Tweaking commonsense: Assessing aids to jury decision making. Psychology, Public Policy, and Law, 3, 259–284 (p. 271 and 280). **p. 258**, Kluwer Academic Publishers, Law and Human Behavior, 22, 17–31, 1998, p.24, Expert evidence pertaining to battered women: The impact of gender and timing of testimony, Schuller, R.A., & Cripps, J. © 1998 American Psychology-Law Society/Division 41 of the American Psychological Association: with kind permission of Springer Science and Business Media. Reprinted with permission of the authors. **p. 264**, Adapted from the Statistics Canada publication "Special study on mentally disordered accused and the criminal justice system," Catalogue no. 85-559, Table A1, p.26, January 2003, available at: <www.statcan.ca/english/freepub/85-559-XIE/85-559-XIE00201.pdf>. **p. 266**, Ackerman, M.J. Forensic Psychological Assessment. © 1999 John Wiley & Sones. Reprinted with permission of John Wiley & Sons, Inc. **p. 277**, Adapted from the Statistics Canada publication "Special study on mentally disordered accused and the criminal justice system," Catalogue no. 85-559, Table A1, p.26, January 2003, available at: <www.statcan.ca/english/freepub/85-559-XIE/85-559-XIE00201.pdf>. **p. 279**, Adapted from the Statistics Canada publication "Special study on mentally disordered accused and the criminal justice system," Catalogue no. 85-559, Figure 3.2, p.15, January 2003, available at: <www.statcan.ca/english/freepub/85-559-XIE/85-559-XIE00201.pdf>. **p. 298**, Reprinted with permission from Journal of Applied Social Psychology, 1986, Vol. 15, No.2, pp. 150–164. © V.H. Winston & Son, Inc., 360 South Ocean Boulevard, Palm Beach, FL 33480. All rights reserved. **p. 299**, Reprinted with permission from

Photo Credits

CASE INDEX

NAME INDEX

SUBJECT INDEX